Artificial Intelligence Remote Sensing for Earth Observation

Artificial Intelligence Remote Sensing for Earth Observation

Guest Editors

Haokui Zhang
Jie Feng
Xizhe Xue
Chen Ding

MDPI

Basel • Beijing • Wuhan • Barcelona • Belgrade • Novi Sad • Cluj • Manchester

Guest Editors

Haokui Zhang
School of Cybersecurity
Northwestern Polytechnical University
Xi'an
China

Jie Feng
School of Artificial Intelligence
Xidian University
Xi'an
China

Xizhe Xue
Department of Aerospace and Geodesy
Technical University of Munich
Munich
Germany

Chen Ding
School of Computer science
Xi'an University of Posts & Telecommunications
Xi'an
China

Editorial Office
MDPI AG
Grosspeteranlage 5
4052 Basel, Switzerland

This is a reprint of the Special Issue, published open access by the journal *Remote Sensing* (ISSN 2072-4292), freely accessible at: https://www.mdpi.com/journal/remotesensing/special_issues/TL934Q45DN.

For citation purposes, cite each article independently as indicated on the article page online and as indicated below:

Lastname, A.A.; Lastname, B.B. Article Title. *Journal Name* **Year**, *Volume Number*, Page Range.

ISBN 978-3-7258-7016-5 (Hbk)
ISBN 978-3-7258-7017-2 (PDF)
https://doi.org/10.3390/books978-3-7258-7017-2

Contents

remote sensing

MDPI

Article

An Enhanced Shuffle Attention with Context Decoupling Head with Wise IoU Loss for SAR Ship Detection

Yunshan Tang [1,2], Yue Zhang [1,2], Jiarong Xiao [1], Yue Cao [1] and Zhongjun Yu [1,2,*]

[1] Aerospace Information Research Institute, Chinese Academy of Sciences, Beijing 100094, China
[2] School of Electronic, Electrical and Communication Engineering, University of Chinese Academy of Sciences, Beijing 100049, China
* Correspondence: yuzj@ucas.ac.cn

Abstract: Synthetic Aperture Radar (SAR) imagery is widely utilized in military and civilian applications. Recent deep learning advancements have led to improved ship detection algorithms, enhancing accuracy and speed over traditional Constant False-Alarm Rate (CFAR) methods. However, challenges remain with complex backgrounds and multi-scale ship targets amidst significant interference. This paper introduces a novel method that features a context-based decoupled head, leveraging positioning and semantic information, and incorporates shuffle attention to enhance feature map interpretation. Additionally, we propose a new loss function with a dynamic non-monotonic focus mechanism to tackle these issues. Experimental results on the HRSID and SAR-Ship-Dataset demonstrate that our approach significantly improves detection performance over the original YOLOv5 algorithm and other existing methods.

Keywords: ship detection; synthetic aperture radar (SAR); decoupled head; attention mechanism; YOLOv5

1. Introduction

Synthetic Aperture Radar (SAR) is a microwave sensor that is unaffected by external environmental factors such as clouds, fog, snow, and night situations. It is capable of continuously monitoring local terrain scenes, possessing strong penetration capabilities and high-resolution imaging characteristics, enabling accurate detection of obscured or camouflaged targets [1]. It finds widespread applications in civilian and military sectors including topographic mapping, disaster assessment, environmental monitoring, target reconnaissance, and target localization. Among these applications, marine target detection is a significant subdivision of SAR object detection, with ship target detection being a primary focus within marine target detection.

In traditional ship detection algorithms, CFAR [2,3] and other adaptive algorithms are widely utilized due to their capability of adaptively scanning images. The CFAR method analyzes input noise to establish thresholds, thereby identifying the presence of a target when the energy of the input signal surpasses these thresholds. To cater to the diverse requirements of various SAR image applications, multiple statistical models have been proposed, encompassing Gaussian, gamma, Weibull, log-normal, G0, and K distributions [4,5]. Moreover, enhancements and variations of CFAR algorithms continually emerge [6–8]. Nevertheless, these approaches often require the manual configuration of features, which is laborious, and exhibit limited transfer ability. While these methods excel in scenarios involving single-class ships and locally uniform background noise, their efficacy wanes in scenarios such as nearshore ship detection with intense interference, as well as multi-scale ship detection [9,10]. Additionally, they lack the capability to process targets end-to-end. Hence, there exists an imperative need for more sophisticated and robust algorithms to tackle these challenges.

After AlexNet [11] achieved significant acclaim in the 2012 ImageNet competition, convolutional neural networks (CNNs) have seen a resurgence in importance within the domain of image processing. Represented by R-CNN [12], CNN-based algorithms have been employed in object detection, pioneering the development of two-stage object detection. Subsequent advancements such as SPPNet [13], Fast R-CNN [14], and Faster R-CNN [15] have further refined two-stage detection algorithms, achieving real-time processing improvements in both accuracy and speed. The evolution of two-stage detection algorithms has led to the emergence of models such as Feature Pyramid Networks (FPNs) [16], Cascade R-CNN [17], Mask R-CNN [18], and Libra R-CNN [19], among others [20]. The two-stage algorithm first proposes a region proposal, then proceeds to classify it and refine the bounding box through the subsequent stage network. While more accurate than one-stage algorithms, it suffers from much slower processing speeds.

The two-stage algorithms still face bottlenecks in speed, and there is still a certain gap in real-time image object detection. Addressing such issues, the You Only Look Once (YOLO) [21] algorithm was proposed. As the pioneering work of single-stage detection algorithms, it no longer needs to generate region proposals and process them in two steps, but directly produces the output results for bounding boxes and class, achieving a nearly 10-fold speedup compared to the previous two-stage algorithms. Wei Liu proposed Single Shot MultiBox Detector (SSD) [22], which introduces the concept of multi-scale and multi-resolution detection. Subsequently, the YOLOv2 [23] and YOLOv3 [24] algorithms address the poor accuracy issue of single-stage algorithms by incorporating ideas such as multi-box detection, feature fusion, and multi-scale outputs into the network. While maintaining fast processing speeds, these enhancements lead to a significant increase in accuracy. Following RetinaNet [25], single-stage networks have surpassed the accuracy of the best two-stage object detection networks at the time. CornerNet [26] and CenterNet [27] further introduce the concepts of corner points and center points in deep learning. YOLOv4 [28] integrates numerous contemporary ideas such as Complement IoU (CIoU) [29], PANet [30], and Mix up data augmentation [31] to achieve both fast processing speeds and higher accuracy in object detection algorithms. YOLOX [32] introduces decoupled head into object detection, achieving better results on top of existing algorithms. This paper selects the YOLOv5 [33] framework as the baseline for experimentation.

While existing networks have achieved good results in optical images, there are still notable cases of false alarms and missed detections in SAR ship detection, particularly in scenarios with strong interference near shorelines and in situations involving multi-scale and small targets, as depicted in Figure 1. Therefore, there is an urgent need for algorithmic improvements tailored to SAR images.

Figure 1. Several typical examples of situations with small vessel targets and an inshore background.

With the introduction of the SAR Ship Detection Dataset (SSDD) [34] and the emergence of more SAR target detection datasets [35,36], a plethora of papers on SAR domain object detection have been proposed [37]. The earliest works typically employed classical networks such as Faster R-CNN [34], SSD [38], and YOLOv2 [39], without improvements specifically tailored to SAR ship target problems, resulting in a relatively mediocre performance.

Attention mechanisms, by weighting key feature maps and spatial regions of importance, are commonly employed for the deep mining of multi-scale and small object information, serving as a means to address targets in complex nearshore scenes effectively [40–50].

In earlier endeavors, the integration of the Squeeze and Excitation (SE) attention mechanism with Faster R-CNN has demonstrated excellent detection results on the early version of the SSDD dataset [40]. Zhao et al. [41] proposed utilizing the Convolutional Block Attention Module (CBAM) and Receptive Fields Block (RFB) to address detection and recognition challenges on top of YOLOv5. Wang et al. [42] introduced the sim attention mechanism and C3 channel shuffling to tackle multi-scale ship detection issues in complex scenarios. Li et al. [43] presented coordinate attention to enhance the performance of detecting small objects. Tang et al. [44] devised a Multiscale Receptive Field Convolution Block with Attention Mechanism (AMMRF) to leverage positional information in feature maps, accurately capturing regions crucial for detection in feature maps, as well as capturing relationships between feature map channels to better understand the ship–background dynamics. A study [45] proposed the United Attention Module (UAM) and Global Context-guided Feature Balanced Pyramid (GC-FBP) to enhance ship detection performance. Wu et al. [46] introduced a method based on the coordinate attention (CA) mechanism and Asymptotic Feature Fusion (AFF) to alleviate the problem of small object position loss and enhance the model's ability to detect multi-scale targets. Hu et al. [47] put forward a Balance Attention Network (BANet), employing both Local Attention Module (LAM) and Non-Local Attention Module (NLAM) to respectively capture the local information of ships, strengthen network robustness, and equilibrate local and non-local features. Ren [48] proposed incorporating the Channel and Position Enhancement Attention (CPEA) module to enhance the precision of target localization by utilizing positional data. DSF-Net [49] incorporated the Pixel-wise Shuffle Attention module (PWSA) to boost feature extraction capabilities and employed Non-Local Shuffle Attention (NLSA) to enhance the long-term dependency of features, thereby promoting information exchange. Cui et al. [50] proposed the addition of a Spatial Shuffle-Group Enhance (SSE) attention module to the CenterNet network to enhance its performance. Cai et al. [51] introduced FS-YOLO, which incorporates a Feature Enhancement Module (FEM) and a Spatial Channel Pooling Module (ESPPCSPC) on top of the original YOLO backbone, thereby improving network performance. Wang et al. [52] integrated the Global Context-Aware Subimage Selection (GCSS) module with the Local Context-Aware False Alarms Suppression (LCFS) module to enhance the network's adaptability to duplicated scenes. Cheng et al. [53] improved the YOLOX backbone by proposing the S2D network, which better integrates information from the neck component and enhances the network's performance in detecting small objects. Additionally, Zhang et al. [54] discovered the modulation effects of target motion on polarization and Doppler. Meanwhile, Gao et al. [55] employed the dualistic cascade convolutional method to enhance the performance of ship target detection.

Many papers have also focused on improving the loss function to enhance object detection performance. Zhang et al. [56] introduced the center loss to ensure an equitable allocation of loss contributions among different factors and reduce the sensitivity of object detection to changes in ground truth box shapes. YOLO-Lite [48] utilized a confidence loss function to improve the accuracy of ship object detection. DSF-Net [49] employed an R-tradeoff loss to improve small detects, accelerate training efficiency, and reduce false positive rates. Zhou [57] developed a loss function that employs a dual Euclidean distance approach, leveraging the corner coordinates of predicted and ground truth boxes, which accurately describes various overlapping scenarios. Zhang [58] used global average precision loss (GAP loss) to enable the model to quickly differentiate between positive and negative samples to enhance accuracy. The paper [59] utilized a KLD loss function to improve accuracy. Chen [60] used the SIoU loss to aid the training process of the network.

These loss functions enhance the detection capability for small objects to some degree, accelerate training convergence, and elevate accuracy. However, they do not consider the impediment caused by inferior instances to the learning ability of the object detection model, resulting in limited performance improvement.

Many articles have also explored the use of decoupled heads [43,47,61] to decouple the semantic information head and bounding box information head, preventing interference between different features and achieving better results. However, these simple decoupled heads only provide limited performance improvements as they do not consider the differences in semantic and bounding box information.

Therefore, in this paper, based on the YOLOv5 backbone, we propose the SAR Ship Context Decoupled Head (SSCDH), which is based on the characteristics of localization and semantic information. We use shuffle attention to enhance the focus on understanding complex backgrounds. Additionally, we introduce a new Wise IoU loss grounded in a dynamic non-monotonic focus framework and designed to utilize the degree of anomaly. The goal is to improve the accuracy of ship detection. Hence, the primary advancements of this paper include the following:

1. In order to enhance the effectiveness of the original decoupling head model, we design dedicated decoupling heads that align with the specific characteristics of positioning and semantic information.
2. To improve the model's capability in detecting objects of varying scales, we incorporate a shuffle attention module into the larger feature layers of the original model's neck.
3. To boost the accuracy of object detection, we utilize the Wise IoU loss function, which leverages attention-based bounding box regression loss and a dynamic non-monotonic focus mechanism.
4. To demonstrate the effectiveness of the proposed technique, we conduct extensive experiments using the HRSID dataset and the SAR-Ship-Dataset.

The first part of this paper served as an introduction, which presents the background, related works pertinent to this study, and the identified issues. The second part focuses on the methods, describing the network structure and the design approach for each module. The third part presents the experimental details and results. The fourth part discusses the effectiveness of our chosen head and attention mechanism. Finally, the fifth part concludes the entire paper.

2. Methods

This section introduces the method of the proposed SSCDH. The first part provides an overview of the architecture of the proposed model. The second part discusses the shuffle attention module utilized in our model, along with its principles of spatial and channel attention mechanisms. The third part introduces the decoupled heads based on contextual information from ships. Lastly, the fourth part describes the Wise IoU loss function employed.

2.1. Network Architecture

The network is based on YOLOv5 architecture [33]. The overall structure of the proposed method is shown in Figure 2. The input RGB image size is $H \times W \times 3$, where H represents the height of the image and W represents the width of the image. The input image passes through 1 large convolutional module and 2 convolutional and residual convolutional modules, resulting in a feature map of size $\frac{H}{8} \times \frac{W}{8} \times 256$ after 3 downsampling operations. Subsequently, another convolutional and residual module produces a feature map of size $\frac{H}{16} \times \frac{W}{16} \times 512$, followed by another similar module yielding a feature map of size $\frac{H}{32} \times \frac{W}{32} \times 1024$. These feature maps are then forwarded to the SPP bottleneck module and subsequently to the neck module, still retaining the dimensions $\frac{H}{32} \times \frac{W}{32} \times 1024$.

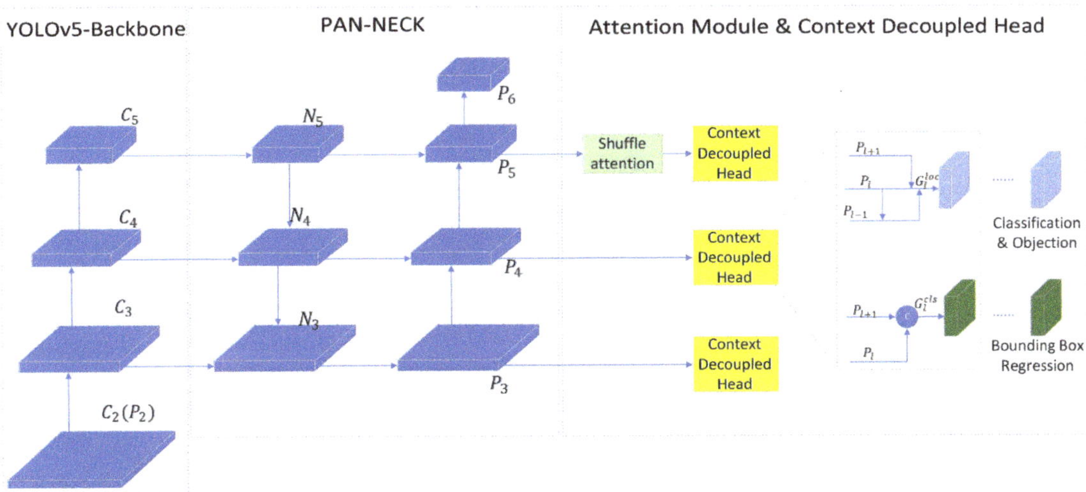

Figure 2. Overview of the proposed method's structure. We used the backbone of YOLOv5 and neck of PAN for the network, while the shuffle attention module and Context Decoupled Head added in this paper are in the Attention Module and Context Decoupled Head part of this figure.

The feature map of size $\frac{H}{32} \times \frac{W}{32} \times 1024$ is processed through a 512-channel 1×1 convolutional layer, resulting in a feature map of size $\frac{H}{32} \times \frac{W}{32} \times 512$. This is then upsampled twice and concatenated with another feature map. The feature map obtained after the first upsampling, $\frac{H}{16} \times \frac{W}{16} \times 512$, is concatenated with the feature map from the backbone, resulting in a feature map of size $\frac{H}{16} \times \frac{W}{16} \times 1024$. This is followed by another convolutional layer to obtain a feature map measuring $\frac{H}{16} \times \frac{W}{16} \times 512$, which is then upsampled to obtain a feature map of size $\frac{H}{8} \times \frac{W}{8} \times 512$. A 256-channel 1×1 convolution is applied to obtain the P_3 feature map of size $\frac{H}{8} \times \frac{W}{8} \times 256$.

Additionally, the feature map of size $\frac{H}{8} \times \frac{W}{8} \times 256$ undergoes downsampling using a 256-channel convolution with a kernel size of 3, padding of 1, and a stride of 2, resulting in a feature map of size $\frac{H}{16} \times \frac{W}{16} \times 256$. This is concatenated with the output of the second convolution, resulting in a feature map of size $\frac{H}{16} \times \frac{W}{16} \times 512$, which is then passed through a convolutional residual block to obtain the P_4 feature map measuring $\frac{H}{16} \times \frac{W}{16} \times 512$.

Similarly, the feature map of size $\frac{H}{16} \times \frac{W}{16} \times 512$ undergoes downsampling using a 512-channel convolution with a kernel size of 3, padding of 1, and a stride of 2, resulting in a feature map of size $\frac{H}{32} \times \frac{W}{32} \times 512$. This is concatenated with the output of the second convolution, resulting in a feature map measuring $\frac{H}{32} \times \frac{W}{32} \times 1024$. Another convolutional residual block is applied to obtain the feature map P_5 measuring $\frac{H}{32} \times \frac{W}{32} \times 1024$. A shuffle attention module is then applied to this feature map to enhance feature extraction.

Subsequently, the model undergoes another convolution operation with 1024 channels, a stride of 2, a kernel dimension of 3, along with a padding of 1. The generated feature map is then directed to the next C3 module, yielding the feature map P_6 of size $\frac{H}{64} \times \frac{W}{64} \times 1024$.

Finally, the SAR Ship Context Decoupled Head is utilized to fuse features from multiple hierarchical levels. The feature map measuring $\frac{H}{4} \times \frac{W}{4} \times 128$ obtained after the second downsampling is used as P_2, the feature map. Consequently, P_3' is derived by incorporating information from P_2, P_3, and P_4 feature maps. Similarly, P_4' incorporates information from P_3, P_4, and P_5 feature maps, and P_5' incorporates information from P_4, P_5, and P_6 feature maps. This process ultimately yields the final bounding box positions and confidence scores for target classification.

2.2. Shuffle Attention Module

The application of the SE [62] mechanism considers the crucial role of channel attention in target recognition and detection, which has found widespread application in object detection. CBAM [63] combines both channel attention and spatial attention mechanisms, resulting in a notable enhancement in the accuracy of computation. The shuffle attention (SA) module [64] also integrates channel attention and spatial attention mechanisms while incorporating the concept of group convolutional kernel channel rearrangement. This achieves superior results compared to other attention mechanisms. In this proposed method, we chose to integrate the shuffle attention component after 32× downsampling layers, aiming to elevate the understanding of the semantic and channel information for the final layer, thereby achieving more accurate detection capabilities for complex scenes, small targets, and multi-scale objects. Figure 3 illustrates the shuffle attention process framework.

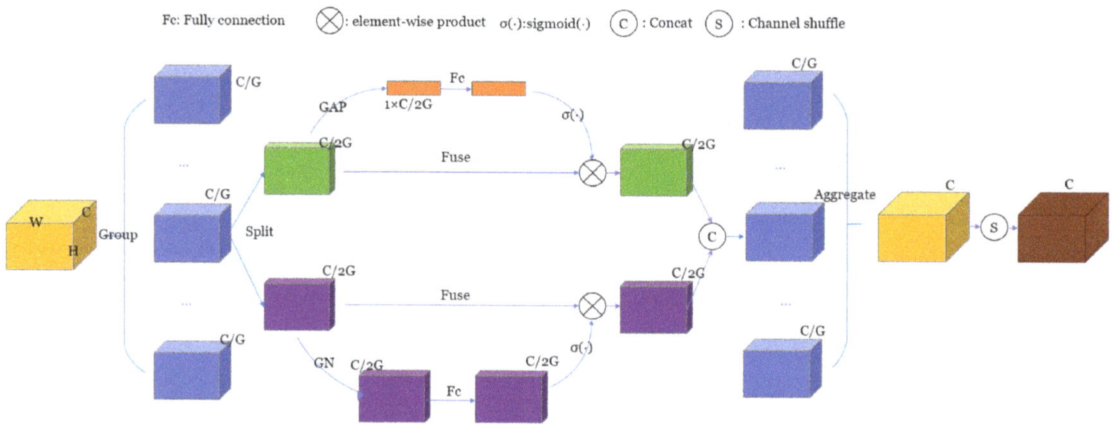

Figure 3. The structure of the shuffle attention process.

First, shuffle attention employs "channel partitioning" to concurrently process sub-features for each group. Next, in the channel attention pathway, global average pooling is utilized to compute statistics at the channel level. This is followed by the application of a pair of parameters to adjust the scaling and shifting of the channel vectors. For the spatial attention pathway, group normalization (GN) is utilized to derive statistics at the spatial level, resulting in a condensed feature representation similar to that of the channel pathway. Then, these two pathways are combined. Following this, all the derived sub-features are consolidated and, ultimately, the channel shuffle technique is applied to enhance the data exchange between the various sub-features.

Shuffle attention achieves the grouping of features, initially, by partitioning the feature maps of a given size $C \times H \times W$ into G groups. Here, C indicates the total number of channels, while H signifies the vertical dimension of the feature map, and W corresponds to its horizontal dimension. Specifically, shuffle attention divides the feature maps of $\boldsymbol{X}$ as G clusters, denoted as $\boldsymbol{X} = [\boldsymbol{X}_1, \ldots, \boldsymbol{X}_G]$, where each $\boldsymbol{X}_k$ is of the size $\frac{C}{G} \times H \times W$. Consequently, during training, every individual component map $\boldsymbol{X}_k$ progressively captures different interpretive insights.

Subsequently, an attention module is used to generate the corresponding significance weights for each component map. In detail, each attention unit processes the input feature map $\boldsymbol{X}_k$ by splitting it into two separate pathways, denoted as $\boldsymbol{X}_{k1}$ and $\boldsymbol{X}_{k2}$, each of size $\frac{C}{2G} \times H \times W$. One branch, $\boldsymbol{X}_{k1}$, is used to create channel attention maps using connections between channels to improve channel effectiveness. Meanwhile, the other branch, $\boldsymbol{X}_{k2}$, produces spatial attention maps using connections between spatial features to identify more useful spatial characteristics.

First, we extract channel-level statistical information from the input X_{k1} by utilizing global average pooling (GAP), embedding global information into s of size $\frac{C}{2G} \times 1 \times 1$. s can be obtained by performing spatial average pooling with dimensions $H \times W$, defined as

$$s = \text{GAP}(X_{k1}) = \frac{1}{H \times W} \sum_{i=1}^{H} \sum_{j=1}^{W} X_{k1}(i, j). \quad (1)$$

Next, employing a basic gating function combined with a Sigmoid activation, we construct a compact feature to precisely and adaptively select. The ultimate result of channel attention X'_{k1} can be derived as follows:

$$X'_{k1} = \sigma(F_c(s))X_{k1} = \sigma(W_1 s + b_1)X_{k1}, \quad (2)$$

where W_1 and b_1 are parameters of size $\frac{C}{2G} \times 1 \times 1$ and used for the fully connected and bias term s, $F_c(\cdot)$ represents the full collection operation, and $\sigma(\cdot)$ represents the Sigmoid activation function.

Simultaneously, we process data to obtain spatial-level statistical information, enhancing the representation through a Group Norm (GN) operation. The ultimate result of spatial attention can be derived as follows:

$$X'_{k2} = \sigma(W_2 \text{GN}(X_{k2}) + b_2)X_{k2}, \quad (3)$$

where W_2 and b_2 are parameters of size $\frac{C}{2G} \times 1 \times 1$.

Finally, we merge the passways of the channel and spatial attention to obtain the output of the same size as the input, $X'_k = [X'_{k1}, X'_{k2}]$, with dimensions $\frac{C}{G} \times H \times W$. Subsequently, all components are aggregated. Lastly, we employ a "channel shuffle" that enhances the flow of information between groups across channel dimensions. The final output of the SA module matches the size of the input X.

2.3. SAR Ship Context Decoupled Head

The preference inconsistency towards feature context between classification and localization is strong. Specifically, localization tends to emphasize boundary features for accurate bounding box regression, whereas object classification leans towards semantic context. Existing methods like YOLOX utilize decoupled heads to handle different feature contexts for various tasks. However, since these heads work with the same input features, there is an imbalance between classification and localization.

Based on the structure and principles of Task-Specific Context Decoupling (TSCODE) [65], we separately manage the encoding of features for categorization and positioning, known as context decoupling, to selectively employ more suitable semantic contexts for specific tasks. For the classification branch, rich semantic contextual features present in the image are typically required to infer object categories. Therefore, we use feature encoding that is broad but captures strong semantic details. For the localization branch, which requires precise boundary information, we offer high-resolution feature maps to better define object edges.

While classification in object detection is less detailed and focuses on identifying objects within a bounding box, using downsampled feature maps for classification does not significantly impact performance but does lower computational costs. On the other hand, object categories can be inferred from their surrounding environments; for instance, ship targets are likely to appear on the sea surface or docked at port edges. Employing broad insights derived from detailed semantic information improves classification performance.

Building on these findings, we developed Semantic Context Encoding (SCE) to enhance classification efficiency and accuracy. As illustrated in Figure 4, SCE uses two levels of feature maps, P_l and P_{l+1}, at each pyramid level l to produce a feature map with rich semantic information for classification.

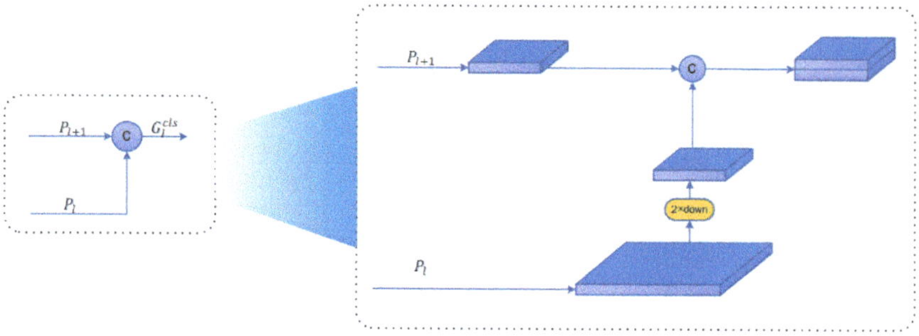

Figure 4. Semantic Context Encoding (SCE).

Initially, we downsample P_l by a factor of two and then concatenate it with P_{l+1}, to yield the final classification feature map, G_l^{cls}:

$$G_l^{cls} = \text{Concat}(\text{DConv}(P_l), P_{l+1}), \tag{4}$$

where Concat((•)) signifies a concatenation operation, and DConv(•) refers to a shared convolutional layer used for downsampling. It is noteworthy that the resolution of G_l^{cls} is half of P_l.

Subsequently, G_l^{cls} is passed through to $F_c(\cdot) = \{f_{cls}(\cdot), C(\cdot)\}$ to predict classification scores, where $f_{cls}(\cdot)$ represents the classification loss function and $C(\cdot)$ represents further classification and the Objection Operation. We employ $f_{cls}(\cdot)$, consisting of two convolutional layers with 512 channels. Given that G_l^{cls} is downsampled by a factor of 2 compared to P_l, at each position (x, y) in G_l^{cls}, the predicted classification scores of its four nearest neighbors in P_l are computed, denoted as $\tilde{C} \in R^{H_{l+1} \times W_{l+1} \times 4N}$, where N is the number of classes, and H_{l+1} and W_{l+1} represent the height and width of the feature map. Subsequently, $\tilde{C}$ is reshaped to $\tilde{C} \in R^{H_l \times W_l \times N}$ to recover the resolution

$$\tilde{C}[2x+i, 2y+j, c] = \tilde{C}[x, y, (2i+2j)c], \forall i, j \in \{0, 1\}. \tag{5}$$

This approach not only leverages the sparse key features from P_l but also incorporates the rich semantic information from higher levels on the pyramid as P_{l+1}.

Localization is more complex than classification, needing additional details for key-point prediction. Methods usually use a one-scale feature map P_l, though lower pyramid levels often have stronger responses to object contours, edges, and fine textures. Nevertheless, higher-level feature maps are crucial for localization as they facilitate the comprehensive observation of the entire object, thus giving more details to understand the complete shape of the object.

Based on these findings, we recommend Detail Preserving Encoding (DPE) for accurate localization. At each layer l of the pyramid, our DPE integrates feature maps from three layers: P_{l-1}, P_l, and P_{l+1}. P_{l-1} supplies detailed edge features, whereas P_{l+1} gives a broader object view.

Figure 5 shows the DPE structure. The feature map on P_l is first upsampled by a factor of 2 and then aggregated with P_{l-1}. Subsequently, it is downsampled to the resolution of P_l through a 3 × 3 convolutional layer with a stride of 2. Finally, P_{l+1} is upsampled and combined to produce the final classification feature map, G_l^{loc}. The computation process is as follows:

$$G_l^{loc} = P_l + \mu(P_{l+1}) + \text{DConv}(P_{l-1} + \mu(P_l)). \tag{6}$$

Here, $\mu(\bullet)$ signifies upsampling, while DConv(•) indicates a shared convolutional layer for downsampling. Specifically, we compute G_3^{loc} using C_2, P_3, and P_4. Subsequently, further bounding box predictions at the l-th pyramid level are performed through $F_r(\cdot) =$

$\{f_{los}(\cdot), R(\cdot)\}$, where $f_{los}(\cdot)$ represents the locational loss function and $R(\cdot)$ represents the further bounding box regression operation.

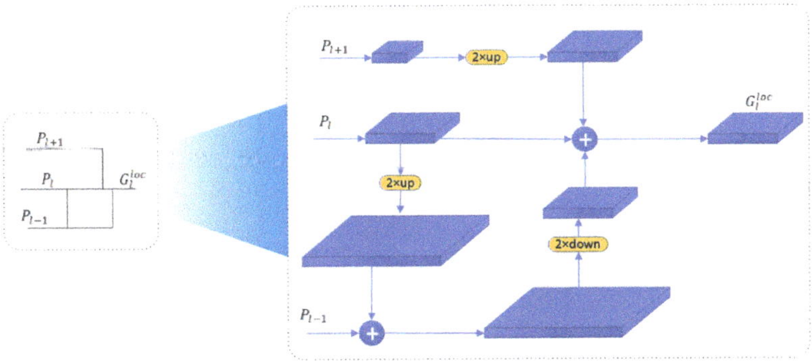

Figure 5. Detail Preserving Encoding (DPE).

2.4. Wise IoU Loss

In the field of object detection, Intersection over Union (IoU) evaluates the overlap between anchor boxes and target boxes. Compared to employing the norm as the bounding box loss function, IoU loss effectively mitigates interference from the proportional representation of bounding box sizes, which allows the model to efficiently balance learning for both large and small objects when IoU loss is utilized for bounding box regression. IoU loss is defined as

$$L_{IoU} = 1 - \text{IoU}. \tag{7}$$

However, when IoU is zero (i.e., $W_i = 0$ or $H_i = 0$), the gradient of the IoU loss $\frac{\partial L_{IoU}}{\partial W_i} = 0$, resulting in the disappearance of gradients during back-propagation and the failure to update the overlapping distance W_i.

To address this issue, existing research accounts for various geometric aspects of bounding boxes and incorporates a penalty term R_i. The existing bounding box regression (BBR) loss follows the paradigm

$$L_i = L_{IoU} + R_i. \tag{8}$$

The Generalized Intersection over Union (GIoU) loss function extends the standard IoU loss by incorporating a penalty term. Unlike traditional IoU, which only assesses the overlap between boxes, GIoU also evaluates the surrounding non-overlapping regions. However, when one box is fully enclosed within another, GIoU cannot differentiate its relative positional relationships.

To address the limitations of GIoU, Distance-IoU (DIoU) [29] adjusts the penalty term by maximizing the overlap area. This is achieved through minimizing the normalized distance between the center points of two bounding boxes. This modification aims to prevent divergence issues that can occur during the training process when using IoU loss and GIoU loss.

DIoU is defined as the relative spacing between the centers of two bounding boxes:

$$R_{DIoU} = \frac{\rho^2(b, b^{gt})}{c^2} \tag{9}$$

where b and b^{gt} are the centers of the predicted and ground truth bounding boxes, respectively. The term ρ represents the Euclidean distance between these centers, while c refers to the diagonal length of the minimal bounding rectangle that can enclose both the predicted and actual boxes.

This method effectively addresses the gradient vanishing issue encountered with L_{IoU} and incorporates a geometric aspect. By utilizing R_{IoU}, DIoU can make more intuitive selections when faced with anchor boxes that have identical L_{IoU} values.

Furthermore, considering the aspect ratio in addition to DIoU leads to the proposed CIoU:

$$R_{CIoU} = R_{DIoU} + \alpha v, \tag{10}$$

where

$$\alpha = \frac{v}{L_{IoU} + v} \tag{11}$$

and v describes the consistency of aspect ratios:

$$v = \frac{4}{\pi^2}(tan^{-1}\frac{w}{h} - tan^{-1}\frac{w_{gt}}{h_{gt}})^2. \tag{12}$$

Here, w and w_{gt} denote the widths of the prediction box and the ground truth box, while h and h_{gt} represent the heights of the prediction box and the ground truth box, respectively. Because the unavoidable presence of poor-quality instances in the dataset leads to increased penalties, especially when influenced by factors like geometry, distance, and aspect ratio, thus diminishing the model's generalization performance. In order to reduce the effects of geometry when anchor boxes align closely to target boxes, while intervening less during training to elevate the model's ability to generalize, we construct WIoU v1 [66] as

$$L_{WIoUv1} = R_{WIoU} L_{IoU}. \tag{13}$$

The IoU score $L_{IoU} \in [0,1]$ significantly diminishes the penalization for high-quality anchor boxes in R_{WIoU}, emphasizing the gap between center points when anchor boxes closely match with target boxes, where $R_{WIoU} \in [1,e)$ is the term amplifying L_{IoU} for regular quality anchor boxes.

$$R_{WIoU} = exp(\frac{(x - x_{gt})^2 + (y - y_{gt})^2}{W_g^2 + H_g^2}). \tag{14}$$

Here, W_g and H_g denote the size of the minimum bounding box, while the numerator represents the l_2 distance between the prediction box and ground truth. For the purpose of stopping R_{WIoU} from causing gradients hindering optimization, W_g and H_g are excluded from the computation framework and the computation is denoted by the superscript *. This effectively eliminates factors hindering convergence, thus avoiding the introduction of new metrics like the aspect ratio.

Inspired by focal loss, which concentrates model attention on challenging samples, improving classification performance, we introduce a monotonic focusing coefficient $L_{IoU}^{\gamma *}$ for L_{WIoUv1}:

$$L_{WIoUv2} = L_{IoU}^{\gamma *} L_{WIoUv1}, \gamma > 0. \tag{15}$$

The introduction of the focusing coefficient alters the gradient propagation of WIoU v2:

$$\frac{\partial L_{WIoUv2}}{\partial L_{IoU}} = L_{IoU}^{\gamma *} \frac{\partial L_{WIoUv1}}{\partial L_{IoU}}, \gamma > 0. \tag{16}$$

It is noteworthy that the gradient gain $r = L_{IoU}^{\gamma *} \in [0,1]$. During model training, as L_{IoU} decreases, the gradient gain also diminishes, resulting in diminished efficiency in the final training phases. Thus, we introduce the average of L_{IoU} as a normalization factor:

$$L_{WIoUv2} = (\frac{L_{IoU}^{\gamma *}}{\overline{L_{IoU}}})^{\gamma} L_{WIoUv1}. \tag{17}$$

Here, $\overline{L_{IoU}}$ denotes the exponentially weighted momentum-weighted moving average with parameter m. Dynamic adjusting of the normalization parameter maintains the gradient improvement $r = (\frac{L_{IoU}^{\gamma *}}{\overline{L_{IoU}}})^{\gamma}$ on a more elevated perspective overall, thus dealing with the challenge of reduced convergence speed in later training phases.

The abnormality of anchor boxes is distinguished by the proportion of L_{IoU} to $\overline{L_{IoU}}$:

$$\beta = \frac{L_{IoU}^{\gamma *}}{\overline{L_{IoU}}} \in [0, +\infty). \tag{18}$$

Lower abnormality implies a higher quality of anchor boxes. We assign smaller gradient improvement to them, focusing the regression on anchor boxes of normal quality. Additionally, assigning reduced gradient improvement to anchor boxes with higher abnormality effectively prevents large gradients from low-quality samples. We construct a non-monotonic focusing coefficient apply it to WIoU v1:

$$L_{WIoUv3} = rL_{WIoUv1}, r = \frac{\beta}{\delta \alpha^{\beta - \delta}}. \tag{19}$$

Here, when $\beta = \delta$, r = 1. When the abnormality of anchor boxes satisfies $\beta = C$, where C represents a constant, the reference box will obtain the maximum gradient benefit. Since $\overline{L_{IoU}}$ is variable, the standards for categorizing anchor box quality are, likewise, flexible, enabling WIoU v3 to adopt the most suitable gradient gain distribution method at each moment.

3. Experiment and Results

3.1. Experiment Setup

The experiment was carried out on PyTorch 1.13.1, CUDA 12.0, on a system equipped with an NVIDIA Quadro P5000 GPU and Windows 10. The model started with weights that were previously trained provided by ImageNet, and trained with the stochastic gradient descent algorithm for 400 epochs, with a starting learning rate of 0.01, momentum of 0.937, and weight decay of 0.0005. Additionally, a warm-up of weights was performed for the first 3 epochs, with a momentum of 0.8 during the warm-up phase. Furthermore, batch sizes of 64 and 16 were used for HRSID and SAR-Ship-Dataset, respectively. All remaining parameters were aligned with the initial YOLOv5 setup. The same settings were utilized in every experiment that involved alternative techniques to ensure a fair comparison. Table 1 presents the setup for the experiment.

Table 1. Table of experiment setup.

Experiment Details	
PyTorch Version	1.13.1
CUDA Version	12.0
GPU	NVIDIA Quadro P5000
Operating System	Windows 10
Batch Size (HRSID)	64
Batch Size (SAR-Ship-Dataset)	16

3.2. Dataset

3.2.1. HRSID

The HRSID dataset, annotated and publicly released by Wei et al. [35], comprises 5604 SAR image samples from Germany's TerraSAR-X, and TanDEM, the Sentinel-1 satellite of the European Space Agency that includes 16,951 annotated ship targets. Images are divided into patches of 800 × 800 pixels and have resolutions of 0.5 m, 1 m, and 3 m. They cover international maritime routes such as those in São Paulo, Barcelona, Chittagong, and Bangladesh. The dataset encompasses diverse ship environments, ranging from good to poor sea conditions, coastal scenes, and simple offshore scenes. Given the variety of complex scenes in the HRSID dataset, it is appropriate for evaluating SAR detection performance in challenging environments. The dataset creators partitioned HRSID, allocating 65% for training and 35% for validation. All experiments conducted in this paper on HRSID were trained and tested using this partitioning.

3.2.2. SAR-Ship-Dataset

To address the issue of network training relying on large amounts of data, Wang et al. [36] built a dataset named SAR-Ship-Dataset. The SAR-Ship-Dataset comprises 43,819 images and 59,535 ship targets, sourced from 108 Sentinel-1 images and 102 Gaofen-3 SAR images. The images are cropped into 256 × 256 patches, with resolutions of 3 m, 5 m, 8 m, and 10 m. The original authors did not provide an official partitioning of training and validation sets. We randomly partitioned and selected the experimental data based on a proportion of 4:1 for the training and testing sets.

3.2.3. Analysis of the Two Datasets

The SAR-Ship-Dataset has a large scale, containing 43,819 images, including a significant number of high-noise images, which enhances the robustness of models trained on this dataset for real-world applications. However, the slices of the SAR-Ship-Dataset are 256 × 256 pixels, which is relatively small. This limitation may pose some challenges to the generalization capability of the dataset during training. Because of the small slice size, various models generally achieve high AP50 results on this dataset. However, the smaller slice dimensions result in lower AP50-95 scores, which require higher accuracy.

In contrast, the slices of the HRSID dataset are 800 × 800 pixels, which allows for a more substantial inclusion of land information and accommodates a variety of ship target sizes at different scales, as well as a greater range of complex dense scenes and nearshore environments. This larger slice size is advantageous for distinguishing multi-scale ship targets in images and for effectively addressing nearshore conditions. Although the larger slice size results in slightly lower AP50 scores across different models, the AP50-95 scores of the models are relatively higher. However, it is worth noting that the HRSID dataset has a relatively limited number of images, with only 5604 available, which could somewhat influence the model's overall capabilities. Additionally, the increased clarity of the HRSID images might lead to some challenges in maintaining robustness in scenarios that involve significant noise.

3.3. *Evaluation Metrics*

To evaluate ship detection systems, we utilized metrics including precision (P), recall rate (R), F1 Score, and average precision (AP). The formulas for precision and recall are outlined below:

$$P = \frac{\text{TP}}{\text{TP} + \text{FP}}, \tag{20}$$

$$R = \frac{\text{TP}}{\text{TP} + \text{FN}}. \tag{21}$$

In these formulas, true positive (TP) refers to instances correctly identified as positive, while false positive (FP) indicates cases incorrectly classified as positive. False negative (FN) refers to ship targets missed due to misclassification as background. Precision indicates the likelihood of correct predictions, while recall measures the probability of successfully identifying true positive samples.

The F1 Score assesses the balance between precision and recall and is calculated using

$$\text{F1 Score} = 2 \times \frac{P \times R}{P + R}. \tag{22}$$

Because precision and recall are mutually influenced, a high precision often implies a low recall and vice versa. Their relationship is represented by the P-R curve. The formula for average precision (AP) is as follows:

$$\mathrm{AP} = \int_0^1 P(R)dR. \tag{23}$$

When the IoU threshold is defined as 0.5, we obtain the result for AP50. AP50-95 is the average of AP values computed across different instances as the IoU threshold varies between 0.5 and 0.95 in increments of 0.05.

3.4. Ablation Study

This part investigates the impact of various enhancements on object detection performance through an ablation study conducted on two datasets: HRSID and SAR-Ship-Dataset. Modifications to the baseline YOLOv5 model, including Wise IoU loss, shuffle attention, and Context Decoupled Head, individually and in combination, are evaluated.

Table 2 summarizes the performance improvements achieved by different enhancements on the HRSID dataset. The baseline model attains a precision of 91.4% and a recall of 86.5%, with AP50 and AP50-95 scores of 93.4% and 68.1%. Integrating Wise IoU loss slightly improves recall and AP50 by 1.0% and 0.4%, respectively, with AP50-95 increasing by 1.4%. Adding shuffle attention results in improved precision, recall, and AP50 by 0.8%, 0.8%, and 0.4%, while increasing AP50-95 to 69.3%. Combining both enhancements results in a further increase in precision to 92.8% and recall to 88.0%, with notable improvements in AP50 to 94.2% and AP50-95 to 70.5%. Incorporating the Context Decoupled Head yields notable improvements across all metrics, with precision, recall, AP50, and AP50-95 increasing by 0.9%, 1.8%, 0.7%, and 2.6%, respectively. Combining Wise IoU loss and shuffle attention with the Context Decoupled Head further enhances performance. The highest overall improvements are observed in the model incorporating all three enhancements, with AP50 increasing by 1.1% and AP50-95 by 4.0% compared to the baseline model.

Table 2. Detection results on HRSID.

Baseline	+Wise IoU Loss	+Shuffle Attention	+Context Decoupled Head	Precision (%)	Recall (%)	F1 Score (%)	AP50 (%)	AP50-95 (%)
✓				91.4	86.5	88.9	93.4	68.1
✓	✓			91.4	87.5	89.4	93.8 (+0.4)	69.5
✓		✓		92.2	87.3	89.7	93.8 (+0.4)	69.3
✓			✓	92.3	88.3	90.3	94.1 (+0.7)	70.7
✓	✓	✓		92.8	88.0	90.4	94.2 (+0.8)	70.5
✓	✓		✓	92.3	88.9	90.6	94.3 (+0.9)	71.3
✓		✓	✓	92.5	88.7	90.6	94.3 (+0.9)	71.1
✓	✓	✓	✓	92.4	89.4	91.0	94.5 (+1.1)	72.1

Similar performance improvements can also be seen in results from the SAR-Ship-Dataset in Table 3. The baseline YOLOv5 attains a precision of 90.6%, recall of 89.8%, AP50 of 94.7%, and AP50-95 of 56.1%. Adding Wise IoU loss slightly improves precision, recall, and AP50 by 0.1%, 0.4%, and 0.3%, respectively. Incorporating shuffle attention results in improvements across all metrics, with AP50 and AP50-95 increasing by 0.2% and 0.5%. Context Decoupled Head integration yields significant improvements, with precision, recall, AP50, and AP50-95 all increasing by 1.3%, 0.6%, 0.4%, and 1.0%, respectively. Combining Wise IoU loss and shuffle attention with the Context Decoupled Head further enhances performance. The highest overall improvements are observed in the model incorporating all three enhancements in our proposed method, with AP50 increasing by 0.8% and AP50-95 by 2.2% in comparison to the baseline network.

Table 3. Detection results on SAR-Ship-Dataset.

Baseline	+Wise IoU Loss	+Shuffle Attention	+Context Decoupled Head	Precision (%)	Recall (%)	F1 Score (%)	AP50 (%)	AP50-95 (%)
✓				90.6	89.8	90.3	94.7	56.1
✓	✓			90.7	90.2	90.5	95.0 (+0.3)	56.5
✓		✓		91.2	89.7	90.4	94.9 (+0.2)	56.6
✓			✓	91.9	90.4	91.1	95.1 (+0.4)	57.1
✓	✓	✓		91.5	89.7	90.6	95.2 (+0.5)	56.9
✓	✓		✓	92.0	90.5	91.2	95.3 (+0.6)	57.7
✓		✓	✓	92.2	90.3	91.2	95.2 (+0.5)	57.4
✓	✓	✓	✓	92.5	90.5	91.5	95.5 (+0.8)	58.3

To summarize, the ablation study illustrates the cumulative effect of integrating Wise IoU loss, shuffle attention, and the Context Decoupled Head on enhancing object detection performance across both datasets, resulting in notable improvements in precision, recall, and AP scores.

3.5. Comparative Experiments

The comparative experiment result on the HRSID dataset is shown in Table 4. Based on the comparative experiments on the HRSID dataset, we focused on the performance of various object detection models across key metrics including F1 Score, AP50, and AP50-95. YOLOv5, serving as the baseline model, demonstrates a strong performance, with an F1 Score of 88.9%, AP50 of 93.4%, and AP50-95 of 68.1%. In contrast, classic methods like Faster R-CNN and SSD show comparatively less impressive results on these metrics. YOLOv3 exhibits high performance but it is lower than the baseline model YOLOv5. The results of CenterNet are lower than those of YOLOv3. YOLOv4 performs better than YOLOv3, but it is still below our baseline, YOLOv5. YOLOX, another emerging method, exhibits a notable performance for AP50, AP50-95, and F1 Score, at 89.5%, 93.1%, and 67.7%, respectively, albeit slightly below the baseline model YOLOv5. However, our proposed method showcases superior overall performance across all key metrics, achieving an F1 Score of 90.9%, AP50 of 94.5%, and AP50-95 of 72.1%, significantly outperforming all other models. This underscores the significant advantages of our approach in object detection tasks, particularly in enhancing detection accuracy, recall, and stability.

Table 4. Detection results on HRSID.

Method	Precision (%)	Recall (%)	F1 Score (%)	AP50 (%)	AP50-95 (%)
Faster R-CNN	81.7	81.6	81.6	84.1	53.4
SSD	86.3	80.8	83.5	87.1	57.8
YOLOv3	91.5	85.7	88.5	92.7	66.5
CenterNet	90.1	84.3	87.1	91.4	63.1
CenterNet+SSE	91.1	86.2	88.6	93.0	65.0
YOLOv4	91.1	85.9	88.4	92.9	67.2
YOLOv5	91.4	86.4	88.9	93.4	68.1
FS-YOLO	92.0	87.1	89.5	93.7	68.6
GLC-DET	91.6	87.9	89.7	93.9	69.0
YOLOX	92.7	86.6	89.5	93.1	67.7
S2D	92.7	87.6	90.1	94.0	69.7
Proposed Method	92.4	89.4	90.9	94.5	72.1

Furthermore, our method achieves remarkable results compared to several other SAR image processing approaches. The core metrics of CenterNet + SSE [50], such as AP50 and AP50-95, while superior to the results of CenterNet, still fall short of those achieved by our proposed method. Although FS-YOLO [51], GLC-DET [52], and S2D [53] have shown improvements based on their chosen YOLO backbone, their performance still does not match that of our approach. Therefore, in comparison with the latest SAR object detection methods, our method continues to deliver outstanding results.

Similarly, based on the comparative experiments on the SAR-Ship-Dataset shown in Table 5, we focused on different object detection models' performance metrics such as precision, recall, F1 Score, AP50, and AP50-95. Traditional methods like Faster R-CNN and SSD demonstrate stable performance but fall short compared to the YOLO series, achieving an AP50 of 90.6% and 92.3%, respectively. Modern methods including CenterNet, YOLOv3, YOLOv4, YOLOv5, and YOLOX exhibit higher performance levels, achieving an AP50 of 92.6%, 93.9%, 94.2%, 94.7%, and 94.4%, respectively. However, our proposed method outperforms all others across all key metrics, achieving 92.5% precision, 90.3% recall, 91.5% F1 Score, as well as an AP50 of 95.4% and AP50-95 of 58.3%, significantly surpassing all other models. Meanwhile, the proposed method surpasses the latest SAR object detection methods [50–53] across a range of metrics, including F1 Score, AP50, and AP50-95. This highlights the exceptional performance of our method on the SAR-Ship-Dataset.

Table 5. Detection results on SAR-Ship-Dataset.

Method	Precision (%)	Recall (%)	F1 Score (%)	AP50 (%)	AP50-95 (%)
Faster R-CNN	85.2	88.1	86.6	90.6	47.2
SSD	87.3	87.7	87.5	92.3	49.8
YOLOv3	89.8	88.7	89.2	93.9	54.4
CenterNet	88.1	87.9	88.0	92.6	54.2
CenterNet+SSE	89.3	88.4	88.8	93.5	55.1
YOLOv4	90.2	89.3	89.7	94.2	55.4
YOLOv5	90.6	89.8	90.2	94.7	56.1
FS-YOLO	91.2	90.0	90.6	94.9	56.9
GLC-DET	92.0	89.7	90.8	95.0	57.1
YOLOX	90.7	90.2	90.4	94.4	56.6
S2D	91.4	90.3	90.8	95.0	57.4
Proposed Method	92.5	90.3	91.5	95.4	58.3

3.6. Comparison Experiment Visualization

Figure 6 below compares the performance of YOLOX, baseline YOLOv5, and the proposed algorithm in dense and complex scenes, highlighting distinct advantages of the proposed algorithm. The first row of the images depicts results from complex dock scenes in the HRSID dataset, where many port facilities resemble ships in shape and exhibit strong electromagnetic scattering, leading to false alarms and missed detections. All three algorithms incorrectly identify a ship facility as a ship, but besides that mistake, YOLOX also detects a noise signal false alarm as a ship target, while YOLOv5 misses a small ship in the bottom left corner. The second row shows detection in dense target scenes within the HRSID dataset, where the proposed algorithm exhibits fewer false alarms compared to YOLOv5 and YOLOX. In the SAR-Ship-Dataset, the advantages of the proposed algorithm are more pronounced. In the third row, YOLOv5 and YOLOX show severely missed detections in dense ship scenes, whereas the proposed algorithm achieves a better detection of dense vessels. In the fourth row, amid noisy conditions, YOLOv5 as the baseline incorrectly identifies many noise signals as ships. Lastly, in the complex port data, the proposed algorithm demonstrates the least false alarms and mistaken detections. This comparative demonstration has proved the effectiveness of our proposed approach to be superior to both the baseline YOLOv5 and methods such as YOLOX.

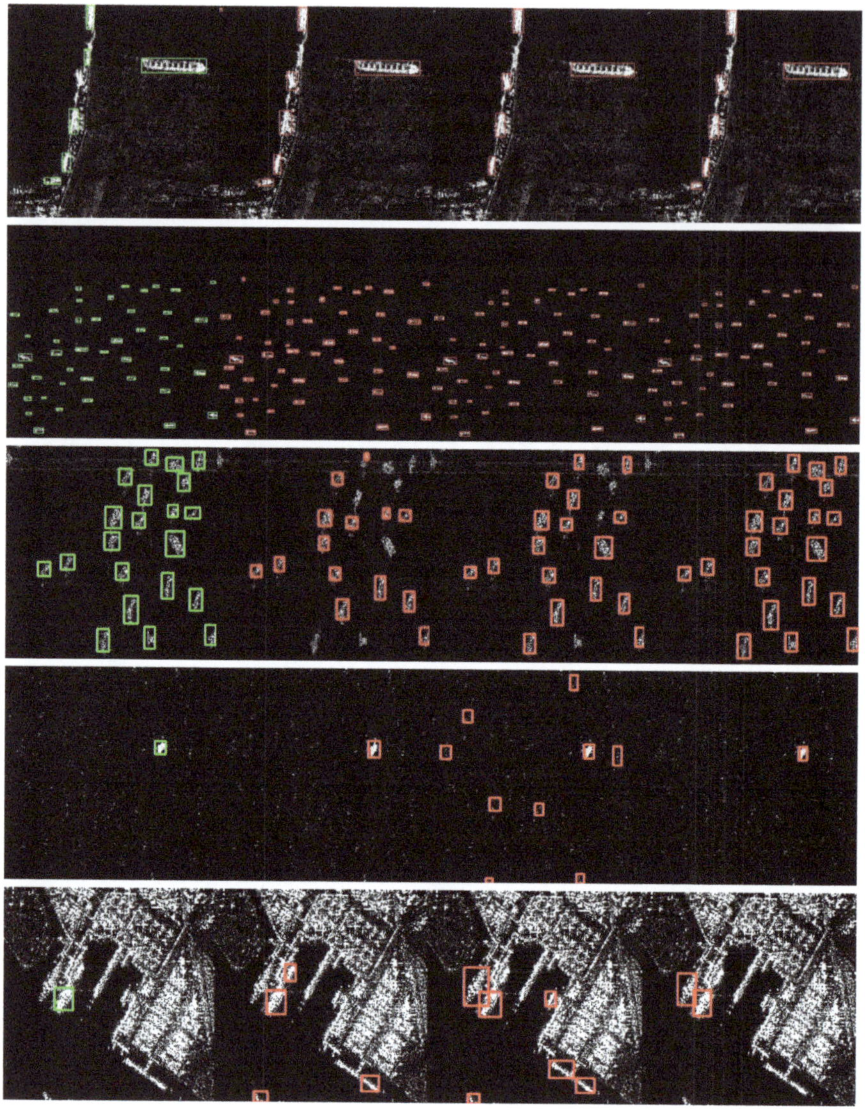

(a) (b) (c) (d)

Figure 6. Comparison figures of algorithm detection performance for SAR ship targets with various algorithms: (**a**) column represents the ground truth (GT), (**b**) column shows the performance of YOLOX algorithm, (**c**) column shows the performance of YOLOv5 as the baseline algorithm and (**d**) column displays the effectiveness of the proposed approach. Here the green box represents the targets of GT, while the red box represents the detected targets.

3.7. Visualization of Test Results in Complex Situations

Further tests are conducted to assess the robustness of the proposed method in complex scenarios, including an analysis of the model's robustness under challenging conditions. We selected high noise situations, dense ship scenarios, and complex background cases. The visualization of the experimental test results is shown below. From Figure 7, it can be seen that our method achieves excellent results in complex scenarios. The first row depicts high noise conditions; by comparing it with the ground truth, we find that our method can overcome high noise interference and correctly detect the targets. The second row illustrates dense and small target situations. From the comparison of (e) and (f), we can see that, out of 120 ship targets, we only miss one, and this missed detection was due to two ship targets being too close to distinguish. In (g) and (h), our main errors are also due to the excessive density of ship targets, making it difficult to discern the exact number of targets. Additionally, some targets are too small to differentiate from floating objects in the river, contributing to some of our errors. Nevertheless, our method successfully detects the vast majority of targets (79 targets, with 75 correctly detected and 1 false alarm). In such overly complex situations, corresponding optical remote sensing images are needed for assistance, which will be a focus of our future research. The third row depicts a situation where targets of varying sizes coexist in a complex nearshore environment, and our method successfully and accurately detects all ship targets here. The superior performance of our method in complex scenarios also demonstrates its strong robustness in handling such conditions.

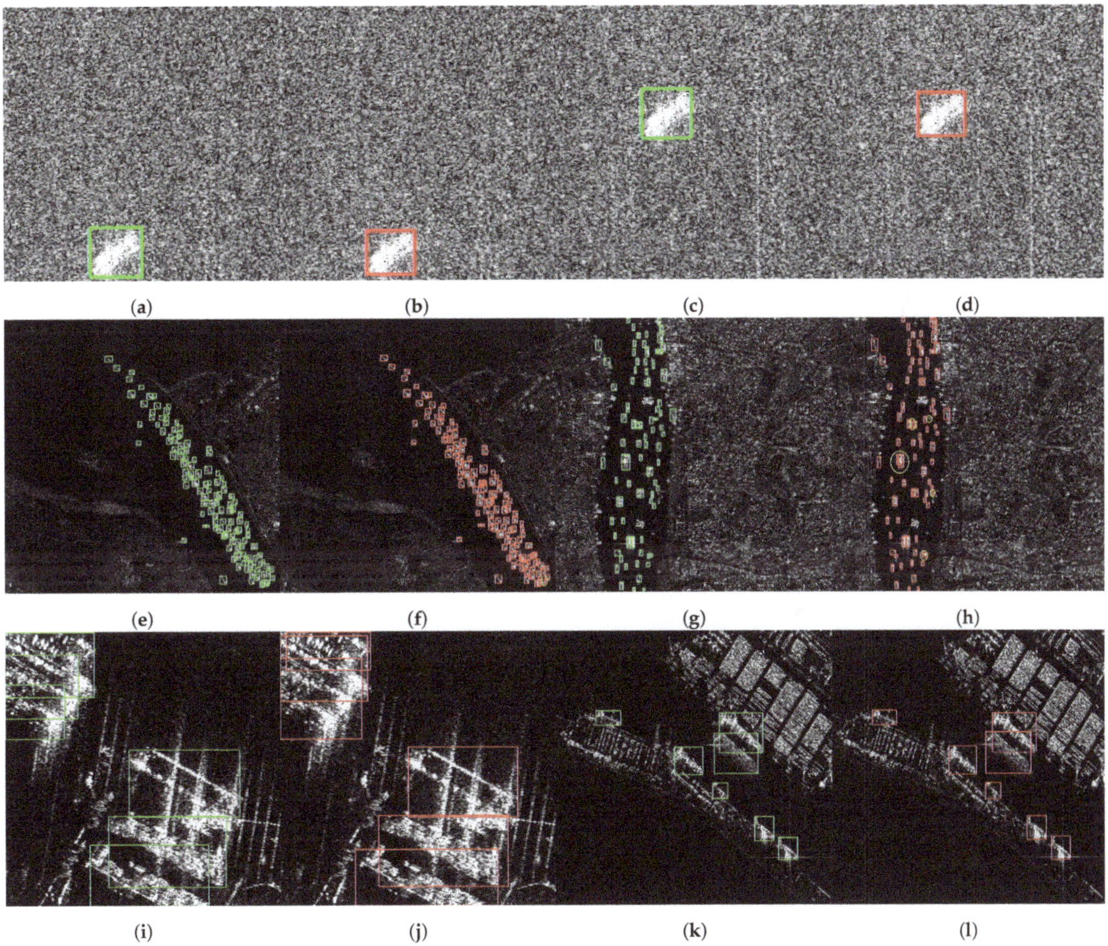

Figure 7. Test results displayed in complex scenarios. The first row shows high noise conditions, where (**a**,**c**) are the ground truth, and (**b**,**d**) are the corresponding test results; the second row presents dense and small target situations, with (**e**,**g**) as the ground truth, and (**f**,**h**) as the corresponding test results; the third row illustrates complex scenarios with multiple scales, where (**i**,**k**) are the ground truth, and (**j**,**l**) are the corresponding test results. Here the green and the red box represents the target of GT and the detected target, while the yellow circle represents the missed or incorrect detection.

4. Discussion

4.1. Attention Mechanism

The integration of shuffle attention serves as a critical enhancement in feature representation. Unlike traditional attention mechanisms that often prioritize spatial or channel-wise features in isolation, shuffle attention dynamically adjusts the attention weights across both dimensions simultaneously. This dual approach enables the model to effectively capture contextual relationships among objects and their surroundings, which is particularly beneficial in cluttered environments. By concentrating on relevant spatial features while maintaining a holistic view of the input data, the model's ability to infer object categories and their contextual significance is markedly improved. Furthermore, the adaptability of shuffle attention to multi-scale objects allows for a more nuanced understanding of features, thereby enhancing the model's overall performance across varying object sizes.

In this part, we conducted extensive experiments applying various attention mechanisms on the HRSID dataset and the SAR-Ship-Dataset, analyzing their effectiveness in object detection tasks.

Concerning the HRSID dataset, the comparative experiment results are shown in Table 6. Among the various attention mechanisms examined, shuffle attention demonstrated outstanding performance in enhancing recall, getting precision and recall rates of 92.4% and 89.4%, along with an F1 Score of 90.9%. Furthermore, it attained high levels of 94.5% and 72.1% on the AP50 and AP50-95 evaluation metrics, respectively. These results indicate that, compared with many other attention mechanisms, shuffle attention effectively elevates the network's capabilities to identify ship targets in object detection tasks.

Table 6. Detection results on HRSID.

Method	Precision (%)	Recall (%)	F1 Score (%)	AP50 (%)	AP50-95 (%)
+SE	93.7	87.4	90.4	94.1	71.5
+CBAM	92.7	87.7	90.1	94.2	71.2
+ECA	93.1	87.6	90.3	94.1	71.1
+Coordinate attention	93.2	86.9	89.9	94.3	71.3
+sim attention	92.5	87.2	89.8	94.1	70.9
+shuffle attention	92.4	89.4	90.9	94.5	72.1

Apart from shuffle attention, other attention mechanisms exhibited relatively weaker performances in recall. For instance, SE, CBAM, and Efficient Channel Attention (ECA) achieved recall rates of 87.4%, 87.7%, and 87.6%, respectively, much lower than shuffle attention's 89.4%. Additionally, coordinate attention and sim attention achieved recall rates of 86.9% and 87.2%, respectively, also lower than shuffle attention. Besides recall, other performance metrics (F1 Score, AP50, and AP50-95) also failed to surpass shuffle attention. Specifically, shuffle attention achieved relatively high levels of 90.9%, 94.5%, and 72.1% on the F1 Score, AP50, and AP50-95, respectively. In comparison, the performance of other attention mechanisms on these metrics was slightly inferior. For instance, the performance of SE, CBAM, and ECA on these metrics were 90.4%, 90.1%, and 90.3% (F1 Score), 94.1%, 94.2%, and 94.1% (AP50), and 71.5%, 71.2%, and 71.1% (AP50-95), respectively. Although their performance remains respectable, they cannot match the overall performance of shuffle attention. Thus, shuffle attention not only excels in recall rate but also achieves high levels on other crucial performance metrics, further demonstrating its superiority in object detection tasks.

Furthermore, the results in Table 7 indicate that shuffle attention also performs optimally on the SAR-Ship-Dataset. It surpasses other attention mechanisms in key performance indicators such as precision (92.5%), recall (90.5%), F1 Score (91.5%), AP50 (95.5%), and AP50-95 (58.3%). This underscores the significant advantage of shuffle attention in object detection tasks, particularly in improving recall and overall performance.

Table 7. Detection results on SAR-Ship-Dataset.

Method	Precision (%)	Recall (%)	F1 Score (%)	AP50 (%)	AP50-95 (%)
+SE	91.7	89.6	90.6	94.8	56.7
+CBAM	91.8	89.6	90.7	94.9	57.3
+ECA	91.9	89.8	90.8	95.1	56.7
+Coordinate attention	91.2	90.1	90.7	94.8	56.4
+Sim attention	92.3	90.2	91.2	95.2	58.0
+Shuffle attention	92.5	90.5	91.5	95.5	58.3

Consequently, we conclude that shuffle attention is the optimal choice among many attention mechanisms for achieving object detection on the SAR-Ship-Dataset.

4.2. Decoupled Head

In object detection, classification and localization are two main sub-tasks, but there is an inconsistency in their requirements for feature context. The localization task focuses more on boundary features to accurately regress bounding boxes, while the classification task tends to rely on a rich semantic context. Existing methods typically employ decoupled heads to address this issue, attempting to learn different feature contexts for each task. However, these decoupled heads still operate based on the same input features, resulting in an unsatisfactory balance between classification and localization. Specifically, bounding box regression requires more texture details and edge information to precisely locate the object's boundaries, whereas the classification task necessitates a stronger semantic context to identify the object's category.

This situation means that traditional decoupled head detectors cannot effectively meet the demands of these two tasks because they still share the same input feature maps, limiting their ability to select task-specific contexts. Although traditional decoupling designs achieve parameter decoupling by learning independent parameters, they still fail to fully resolve the issue, as the semantic context is largely determined by the shared input features. This leads to the phenomenon of feature redundancy in the classification task, while the localization task relies on more detailed texture and boundary information, making it difficult to achieve accurate corner predictions.

In order to demonstrate that designing decoupled heads based on different contextual semantics for classification and regression branches achieves better target detection results in SAR ship target detection than simple decoupled heads, we conducted comparative experiments using the simple decoupled head and Context Decoupled head.

The Tables 8 and 9 below present the performance metrics of the two different heads, simple decoupled head and Context Decoupled head, on the HRSID and SAR-Ship-Datasets. These methods were evaluated based on precision (Pre), recall (Rec), AP50, AP50-95, and Giga Floating-point Operations (GFLOPs).

Table 8. Comparative detection result on HRSID.

Method	Pre (%)	Rec (%)	AP50 (%)	AP50-95 (%)	GFLOPs
+simple decoupled head	91.6	88.4	94.2	70.1	7.1
+Context Decoupled head	92.4	89.4	94.5	72.1	9.8

Table 9. Comparative detection result on SAR-Ship-Dataset.

Method	Pre (%)	Rec (%)	AP50 (%)	AP50-95 (%)	GFLOPs
+simple decoupled head	91.3	90.2	94.8	57.1	7.1
+Context Decoupled head	92.5	90.5	95.5	58.3	9.8

For the simple decoupled head method, on the HRSID dataset, its precision is 91.6%, recall is 88.4%, AP50 is 94.2%, AP50-95 is 70.1%, and computational complexity is 7.1 GFLOPs.

On the SAR-Ship-Dataset, its precision is 91.3%, recall is 90.2%, AP50 is 94.8%, and AP50-95 is 57.1%, with computational complexity remaining at 7.1 GFLOPs. In contrast, the Context Decoupled head method demonstrates superior performance on both datasets. On the HRSID dataset, its precision is 92.4%, rate of recall is 89.4%, AP50 is 94.5%, AP50-95 is 72.1%, and computational complexity is 9.8 GFLOPs. On the SAR-Ship-Dataset, its precision is 92.5%, recall is 90.5%, AP50 is 95.5%, and AP50-95 is 58.3%, with computational complexity still at 9.8 GFLOPs.

These results show that the Context Decoupled head approach outperforms the simple decoupled head method regarding precision, recall, and AP on both datasets, albeit with slightly higher computational complexity.

4.3. Wise IoU Loss

The Wise IoU loss introduces a sophisticated mechanism to mitigate the negative impact of low-quality samples during training. Traditional loss functions often penalize the model heavily for geometric discrepancies, which can disproportionately affect generalization, especially in datasets with noisy annotations. By employing a distance attention mechanism alongside a dynamic focus mechanism, our loss function alleviates the penalty on well-aligned anchor boxes while downplaying the influence of poorly aligned ones. This novel approach not only fosters better training dynamics but also enhances the model's robustness against false positives and negatives. The result is a model that excels in precise localization, particularly in challenging scenarios where object overlap and occlusion are prevalent.

The comparison experiments of the loss functions on HRSID and SAR-Ship-Dataset are shown in Table 10 and Table 11, respectively.

The loss function used in the original baseline method is the CIoU loss function, while the loss function used in this paper is the Wise IoU loss. We conducted comparative experiments on the HRSID and SAR-Ship-Dataset, demonstrating the superiority of the Wise IoU algorithm.

Table 10. Detection results on HRSID.

Method	Precision (%)	Recall (%)	F1 Score (%)	AP50 (%)	AP50-95 (%)
Baseline (CIoU Loss)	91.4	86.5	88.9	93.4	68.1
+Wise IoU Loss	91.4	87.5	89.4	93.8 (+0.4)	69.5

Table 11. Detection results on SAR-Ship-Dataset.

Method	Precision (%)	Recall (%)	F1 Score (%)	AP50 (%)	AP50-95 (%)
Baseline (CIoU Loss)	90.6	89.8	90.3	94.7	56.1
+Wise IoU Loss	90.7	90.2	90.5	95.0 (+0.3)	56.5

The results from the experiments clearly demonstrate that the use of Wise IoU leads to improvements in various aspects of object detection on the HRSID and SAR-Ship-Dataset.

5. Conclusions

To sum up, this work introduces an innovative approach for ship detection in SAR imagery, addressing key challenges faced by existing methods. The proposed SAR Ship Context Decoupled Head leverages both positioning and semantic information, enhancing the network's ability to recognize multi-scale objects with greater accuracy. Also by incorporating a shuffle attention module and a Wise IoU loss function, the proposed method attains superior performance in object detection tasks, as demonstrated through extensive experiments on benchmark datasets. These contributions represent significant advancements in SAR-based ship detection algorithms, with promising implications for applications in maritime surveillance and security. While our method demonstrates promising results, it is worth noting that our proposed method comes with a higher computational cost. In later studies, we will delve into more lightweight network designs to mitigate this issue. Additionally, considerations for deploying the network on hardware devices should also be incorporated into future research efforts.

Author Contributions: Methodology, Y.T.; Software, Y.T. and J.X.; Validation, Y.T.; Investigation, Y.T. and Y.Z.; Writing—original draft, Y.T.; Writing—review & editing, Y.Z.; Supervision, Y.C.; Project administration, Z.Y. All authors have read and agreed to the published version of the manuscript.

Funding: This research was funded by Project named Three Dimensional Cross Band Multi Frequency Composite Antenna Microsystem Technology with grant number E3Z221030F.

Data Availability Statement: The original contributions presented in the study are included in the article, further inquiries can be directed to the corresponding author.

Conflicts of Interest: The authors declare no conflicts of interest.

References

1. Moreira, A.; Prats-Iraola, P.; Younis, M.; Krieger, G.; Hajnsek, I.; Papathanassiou, K.P. A tutorial on synthetic aperture radar. *IEEE Geosci. Remote. Sens. Mag.* **2013**, *1*, 6–43. [CrossRef]
2. Eldhuset, K. An automatic ship and ship wake detection system for spaceborne SAR images in coastal regions. *IEEE Trans. Geosci. Remote Sens.* **1996**, *34*, 1010–1019. [CrossRef]
3. Robey, F.C.; Fuhrmann, D.R.; Kelly, E.J.; Nitzberg, R. A CFAR adaptive matched filter detector. *IEEE Trans. Aerosp. Electron. Syst.* **1992**, *28*, 208–216. [CrossRef]
4. Henschel, M.D.; Rey, M.T.; Campbell, J.W.M.; Petrovic, D. Comparison of probability statistics for automated ship detection in SAR imagery. In Proceedings of the International Conference on Applications of Photonic Technology III: Closing the Gap between Theory, Development, and Applications, Ottawa, ON, Canada, 4 December 1998; pp. 986–991.
5. Frery, C.; Müller, H.-J.; Yanasse, C.C.F.; Sant'Anna, S.J.S. A model for extremely heterogeneous clutter. *IEEE Trans. Geosci. Remote Sens.* **1997**, *35*, 648–659. [CrossRef]
6. Schwegmann, P.; Kleynhans, W.; Salmon, B.P. Manifold adaptation for constant false alarm rate ship detection in South African oceans. *IEEE J. Sel. Topics Appl. Earth Observ. Remote Sens.* **2015**, *8*, 3329–3337. [CrossRef]
7. Qin, X.; Zhou, S.; Zou, H.; Gao, G. A CFAR detection algorithm for generalized gamma distributed background in high-resolution SAR images. *IEEE Geosci. Remote Sens. Lett.* **2013**, *10*, 806–810.
8. He, J.; Wang, Y.; Liu, H.; Wang, N.; Wang, J. A novel automatic PolSAR ship detection method based on superpixel-level local information measurement. *IEEE Geosci. Remote Sens. Lett.* **2018**, *15*, 384–388. [CrossRef]
9. Colone, F.; Filippini, F.; Pastina, D. Passive Radar: Past, Present, and Future Challenges. *IEEE Aerosp. Electron. Syst. Mag.* **2023**, *38*, 54–69. [CrossRef]
10. Li, J.; Xu, C.; Su, H.; Gao, L.; Wang, T. Deep Learning for SAR Ship Detection: Past, Present and Future. *Remote Sens.* **2022**, *14*, 2712. [CrossRef]
11. Krizhevsky, A.; Sutskever, I.; Hinton, G.E. ImageNet classification with deep convolutional neural networks. *Commun. ACM* **2012**, *60*, 84–90. [CrossRef]
12. Girshick, R.; Donahue, J.; Darrell, T.; Malik, J. Rich feature hierarchies for accurate object detection and semantic segmentation. In Proceedings of the IEEE Conference on Computer Vision and Pattern Recognition (CVPR), Columbus, OH, USA, 23–28 June 2014; pp. 580–587.
13. He, K.; Zhang, X.; Ren, S.; Sun, J. Spatial Pyramid Pooling in Deep Convolutional Networks for Visual Recognition. *IEEE Trans. Pattern Anal. Mach. Intell.* **2015**, *37*, 1904–1916. [CrossRef]
14. Girshick, R. Fast R-CNN. In Proceedings of the 2015 IEEE International Conference on Computer Vision (ICCV), Santiago, Chile, 7–13 December 2015; pp. 1440–1448. [CrossRef]
15. Ren, S.; He, K.; Girshick, R.; Sun, J. Faster R-CNN: Towards Real-Time Object Detection with Region Proposal Networks. *IEEE Trans. Pattern Anal. Mach. Intell.* **2017**, *39*, 1137–1149. [CrossRef] [PubMed]
16. Lin, T.-Y.; Dollár, P.; Girshick, R.; He, K.; Hariharan, B.; Belongie, S. Feature Pyramid Networks for Object Detection. In Proceedings of the 2017 IEEE Conference on Computer Vision and Pattern Recognition (CVPR), Honolulu, HI, USA, 2017; pp. 936–944. [CrossRef]
17. Cai, Z.; Vasconcelos, N. Cascade R-CNN: Delving Into High Quality Object Detection. In Proceedings of the 2018 IEEE/CVF Conference on Computer Vision and Pattern Recognition, Salt Lake City, UT, USA, 18–22 June 2018; pp. 6154–6162. [CrossRef]
18. He, K.; Gkioxari, G.; Dollár, P.; Girshick, R. Mask R-CNN. In Proceedings of the 2017 IEEE International Conference on Computer Vision (ICCV), Venice, Italy, 22–29 October 2017; pp. 2980–2988. [CrossRef]
19. Pang, J.; Chen, K.; Shi, J.; Feng, H.; Ouyang, W.; Lin, D. Libra R-CNN: Towards Balanced Learning for Object Detection. In Proceedings of the IEEE/CVF Conference on Computer Vision and Pattern Recognition, Long Beach, CA, USA, 16–20 June 2019.

20. Li, Z.; Peng, C.; Yu, G.; Zhang, X.Y.; Deng, Y.D.; Sun, J. Light-head r-cnn: In defense of two-stage object detector. *arXiv* **2017**, arXiv:1711.07264.
21. Redmon, J.; Divvala, S.; Girshick, R.; Farhadi, A. You Only Look Once: Unified, Real-Time Object Detection. In Proceedings of the 2016 IEEE Conference on Computer Vision and Pattern Recognition (CVPR), Las Vegas, NV, USA, 27–30 June 2016; pp. 779–788. [CrossRef]
22. Liu, W.; Anguelov, D.; Erhan, D.; Szegedy, C.; Reed, S.E.; Fu, C.; Berg, A.C. SSD: Single Shot MultiBox Detector. In Proceedings of the European Conference on Computer Vision, Santiago, Chile, 7–13 December 2015.
23. Redmon, J.; Farhadi, A. YOLO9000: Better, Faster, Stronger. In Proceedings of the 2017 IEEE Conference on Computer Vision and Pattern Recognition (CVPR), Honolulu, HI, USA, 21–26 July 2017; pp. 6517–6525. [CrossRef]
24. Redmon, J.; Farhadi, A. YOLOv3: An Incremental Improvement. *arXiv* **2018**, arXiv:1804.02767.
25. Lin, T.Y.; Goyal, P.; Girshick, R.; He, K.; Dollar, P. Focal Loss for Dense Object Detection. *IEEE Trans. Pattern Anal. Mach. Intell.* **2020**, *42*, 318–327. [CrossRef] [PubMed]
26. Law, H.; Deng, J. CornerNet: Detecting Objects as Paired Keypoints. *Int. J. Comput. Vis.* **2018**, *128*, 642–656. [CrossRef]
27. Duan, K.; Bai, S.; Xie, L.; Qi, H.; Huang, Q.; Tian, Q. CenterNet: Keypoint Triplets for Object Detection. In Proceedings of the 2019 IEEE/CVF International Conference on Computer Vision (ICCV), Seoul, Republic of Korea, 27 October–2 November 2019; pp. 6568–6577. [CrossRef]
28. Bochkovskiy, A.; Wang, C.; Liao, H.M. YOLOv4: Optimal Speed and Accuracy of Object Detection. *arXiv* **2020**, arXiv:2004.10934.
29. Zheng, Z.; Wang, P.; Liu, W.; Li, J.; Ye, R.; Ren, D. Distance-IoU Loss: Faster and Better Learning for Bounding Box Regression. In Proceedings of the AAAI Conference on Artificial Intelligence, New York, NY, USA, 7–12 February 2020; Volume 34, pp. 12993–13000. [CrossRef]
30. Liu, S.; Qi, L.; Qin, H.; Shi, J.; Jia, J. Path Aggregation Network for Instance Segmentation. In Proceedings of the 2018 IEEE/CVF Conference on Computer Vision and Pattern Recognition (CVPR), Salt Lake City, UT, USA, 18–22 June 2018; pp. 8759–8768. [CrossRef]
31. Zhang, H.; Cisse, M.; Dauphin, Y.N.; Lopez-Paz, D. MixUp: Beyond empirical risk minimization. *arXiv* **2017**, arXiv:1710.09412.
32. Ge, Z.; Liu, S.; Wang, F.; Li, Z.; Sun, J. YOLOX: Exceeding YOLO Series in 2021. *arXiv* **2021**, arXiv:2107.08430.
33. Jocher, G.; Nishimura, K.; Mineeva, T.; Vilariño, R. YOLOv5 by Ultralytics. Code Repository. 2020. Available online: https://github.com/ultralytics/yolov5 (accessed on 4 October 2022).
34. Li, J.; Qu, C.; Shao, J. Ship detection in SAR images based on an improved faster R-CNN. In Proceedings of the Sar in Big Data Era: Models, Methods & Applications, Beijing, China, 13–14 November 2017.
35. Wang, Y.; Wang, C.; Zhang, H.; Dong, Y.; Wei, S.L. A SAR Dataset of Ship Detection for Deep Learning under Complex Backgrounds. *Remote Sens.* **2019**, *11*, 765. [CrossRef]
36. Wei, S.; Zeng, X.; Qu, Q.; Wang, M.; Su, H.; Shi, J. HRSID: A High-Resolution SAR Images Dataset for Ship Detection and Instance Segmentation. *IEEE Access* **2020**, *8*, 2031. [CrossRef]
37. Zhang, C.; Zhang, X.; Gao, G.; Lang, H.; Liu, G.; Cao, C.; Song, Y.; Guan, Y.; Dai, Y. Development and Application of Ship Detection and Classification Datasets: A Review. *IEEE Geosci. Remote Sens. Mag.* **2024**, 2–36. [CrossRef]
38. Wang, Y.; Wang, C.; Zhang, H.; Zhang, C.; Fu, Q. Combing Single Shot Multibox Detector with transfer learning for ship detection using Chinese Gaofen-3 images. In Proceedings of the 2017 Progress in Electromagnetics Research Symposium-Fall (PIERS-FALL), Singapore, 19–22 November 2017.
39. Khan, H.M.; Cai, Y. Ship detection in SAR Image using YOLOv2. In Proceedings of the 2018 37th Chinese Control Conference (CCC), Wuhan, China, 25–27 July 2018.
40. Lin, Z.; Ji, K.; Leng, X.; Kuang, G. Squeeze and Excitation Rank Faster R-CNN for Ship Detection in SAR Images. *IEEE Geosci. Remote Sens. Lett.* **2019**, *16*, 751–755. [CrossRef]
41. Zhao, W.; Syafrudin, M.; Fitriyani, N.L. CRAS-YOLO: A Novel Multi-Category Vessel Detection and Classification Model Based on YOLOv5s Algorithm. *IEEE Access* **2023**, *11*, 11463–11478. [CrossRef]
42. Wang, Z.; Hou, G.; Xin, Z.; Liao, G.; Huang, P.; Tai, Y. Detection of SAR Image Multiscale Ship Targets in Complex Inshore Scenes Based on Improved YOLOv5. *IEEE J. Sel. Top. Appl. Earth Obs. Remote Sens.* **2024**, *17*, 5804–5823. [CrossRef]
43. Li, Q.; Xiao, D.; Shi, F. A Decoupled Head and Coordinate Attention Detection Method for Ship Targets in SAR Images. *IEEE Access* **2022**, *10*, 128562–128578. [CrossRef]
44. Tang, H.; Gao, S.; Li, S.; Wang, P.; Liu, J.; Wang, S.; Qian, J. A Lightweight SAR Image Ship Detection Method Based on Improved Convolution and YOLOv7. *Remote Sens.* **2024**, *16*, 486. [CrossRef]
45. Bai, L.; Yao, C.; Ye, Z.; Xue, D.; Lin, X.; Hui, M. A Novel Anchor-Free Detector Using Global Context-Guide Feature Balance Pyramid and United Attention for SAR Ship Detection. *IEEE Geosci. Remote Sens. Lett.* **2023**, *20*, 4003005. [CrossRef]
46. Wu, K.; Zhang, Z.; Chen, Z.; Liu, G. Object-Enhanced YOLO Networks for Synthetic Aperture Radar Ship Detection. *Remote Sens.* **2024**, *16*, 1001. [CrossRef]
47. Hu, Q.; Hu, S.; Liu, S. BANet: A Balance Attention Network for Anchor-Free Ship Detection in SAR Images. *IEEE Trans. Geosci. Remote Sens.* **2022**, *60*, 5222212. [CrossRef]
48. Ren, X.; Bai, Y.; Liu, G.; Zhang, P. YOLO-Lite: An Efficient Lightweight Network for SAR Ship Detection. *Remote Sens.* **2023**, *15*, 3771. [CrossRef]

49. Xu, Z.; Zhai, J.; Huang, K.; Liu, K. DSF-Net: A Dual Feature Shuffle Guided Multi-Field Fusion Network for SAR Small Ship Target Detection. *Remote Sens.* **2023**, *15*, 4546. [CrossRef]
50. Cui, Z.; Wang, X.; Liu, N.; Cao, Z.; Yang, J. Ship Detection in Large-Scale SAR Images Via Spatial Shuffle-Group Enhance Attention. *IEEE Trans. Geosci. Remote Sens.* **2021**, *59*, 379–391. [CrossRef]
51. Cai, S.; Meng, H.; Yuan, M.; Wu, J. FS-YOLO: A multi-scale SAR ship detection network in complex scenes. *Signal Image Video Process.* **2024**, *18*, 5017–5027. [CrossRef]
52. Wang, Z.; Wang, R.; Ai, J.; Zou, H.; Li, J. Global and Local Context-Aware Ship Detector for High-Resolution SAR Images. *IEEE Trans. Aerosp. Electron. Syst.* **2023**, *59*, 4159–4167. [CrossRef]
53. Cheng, P. Improve the Performance of SAR Ship Detectors by Small Object Detection Strategies. *Remote Sens.* **2024**, *16*, 3338. [CrossRef]
54. Zhang, X.; Gao, G.; Chen, S.-W. Polarimetric Autocorrelation Matrix: A New Tool for Joint Characterizing of Target Polarization and Doppler Scattering Mechanism. *IEEE Trans. Geosci. Remote Sens.* **2024**, *62*, 5213522. [CrossRef]
55. Gao, G.; Bai, Q.; Zhang, C.; Zhang, L.; Yao, L. Dualistic Cascade Convolutional Neural Network Dedicated to Fully PolSAR Image Ship Detection. *ISPRS J. Photogramm. Remote Sens.* **2023**, *202*, 663–681. [CrossRef]
56. Zhang, C.; Gao, G.; Liu, J.; Duan, D. Oriented Ship Detection Based on Soft Thresholding and Context Information in SAR Images of Complex Scenes. *IEEE Trans. Geosci. Remote Sens.* **2024**, *62*, 5200615. [CrossRef]
57. Zhou, Y.; Liu, H.; Ma, F.; Pan, Z.; Zhang, F. A Sidelobe-Aware Small Ship Detection Network for Synthetic Aperture Radar Imagery. *IEEE Trans. Geosci. Remote Sens.* **2023**, *61*, 5205516. [CrossRef]
58. Zhang, L.; Liu, Y.; Qu, L.; Cai, J.; Fang, J. A Spatial Cross-Scale Attention Network and Global Average Accuracy Loss for SAR Ship Detection. *Remote Sens.* **2023**, *15*, 350. [CrossRef]
59. Liu, Y.; Ma, Y.; Chen, F.; Shang, E.; Yao, W.; Zhang, S.; Yang, J. YOLOv7oSAR: A Lightweight High-Precision Ship Detection Model for SAR Images Based on the YOLOv7 Algorithm. *Remote Sens.* **2024**, *16*, 913. [CrossRef]
60. Chen, Z.; Liu, C.; Filaretov, V.F.; Yukhimets, D.A. Multi-Scale Ship Detection Algorithm Based on YOLOv7 for Complex Scene SAR Images. *Remote Sens.* **2023**, *15*, 2071. [CrossRef]
61. Yu, W.; Wang, Z.; Li, J.; Luo, Y.; Yu, Z. A Lightweight Network Based on One-Level Feature for Ship Detection in SAR Images. *Remote Sens.* **2022**, *14*, 3321. [CrossRef]
62. Hu, J.; Shen, L.; Sun, G. Squeeze-and-Excitation Networks. In Proceedings of the 2018 IEEE/CVF Conference on Computer Vision and Pattern Recognition (CVPR), Salt Lake City, UT, USA, 18–23 June 2018; pp. 7132–7141. [CrossRef]
63. Woo, S.; Park, J.; Lee, J.Y.; Kweon, I.S. Cbam: Convolutional block attention module. In Proceedings of the European Conference on Computer Vision (ECCV), Munich, Germany, 8–14 September 2018; pp. 3–19.
64. Zhang, Q.-L.; Yang, Y.-B. SA-Net: Shuffle Attention for Deep Convolutional Neural Networks. In Proceedings of the ICASSP 2021—2021 IEEE International Conference on Acoustics, Speech and Signal Processing (ICASSP), Toronto, ON, Canada, 6–11 June 2021; pp. 2235–2239. [CrossRef]
65. Zhuang, J.; Qin, Z.; Yu, H.; Chen, X. Task-Specific Context Decoupling for Object Detection. *arXiv* **2023**, arXiv:2303.01047.
66. Tong, Z.; Chen, Y.; Xu, Z.; Yu, R. Wise-IoU: Bounding Box Regression Loss with Dynamic Focusing Mechanism. *arXiv* **2023**, arXiv:2301.10051.

remote sensing

MDPI

Article

The Spectrum Difference Enhanced Network for Hyperspectral Anomaly Detection

Shaohua Liu [1], Huibo Guo [2], Shiwen Gao [2] and Wuxia Zhang [2,*]

1 Faculty of Engineering, School of Computer Science, The University of Sydney, Camperdown, NSW 2006, Australia; sliu0564@uni.sydney.edu.au

2 School of Computer Science and Technology, Xi'an University of Posts and Telecommunications, Xi'an 710121, China; huibo@stu.xupt.edu.cn (H.G.); gaoshiwen@eurasia.edu (S.G.)

* Correspondence: zhangwuxia@xupt.edu.cn

Abstract: Most deep learning-based hyperspectral anomaly detection (HAD) methods focus on modeling or reconstructing the hyperspectral background to obtain residual maps from the original hyperspectral images. However, these methods typically do not pay enough attention to the spectral similarity in the complex environment, resulting in inadequate distinction between background and anomalies. Moreover, some anomalies and background are different objects, but they are sometimes recognized as the objects with the same spectrum. To address the issues mentioned above, this paper proposes a Spectrum Difference Enhanced Network (SDENet) for HAD, which employs variational mapping and Transformer to amplify spectrum differences. The proposed network is based on the encoder–decoder structure, which contains a CSWin-Transformer encoder, Variational Mapping Module (VMModule), and CSWin-Transformer decoder. First, the CSWin-Transformer encoder and decoder are designed to supplement image information by extracting deep and semantic features, where a cross-shaped window self-attention mechanism is designed to provide strong modeling capability with minimal computational cost. Second, in order to enhance the spectral difference characteristics between anomalies and background, a randomly sampling VMModule is presented for feature space transformation. Finally, all fully connected mapping operations are replaced with convolutional layers to reduce the model parameters and computational load. The effectiveness of the proposed SDENet is verified on three datasets, and experimental results show that it achieves better detection accuracy and lower model complexity compared with existing methods.

Keywords: hyperspectral anomaly detection; variational mapping; Transformer; self-attention

1. Introduction

Hyperspectral images (HSIs) have high spatial and spectral resolution, enabling the differentiation of objects with similar physical or visual characteristics. However, they also contain significant redundant information. Hyperspectral anomaly detection (HAD) aims to identify targets with significant spectral differences from surrounding pixels or regions without relying on prior knowledge of the targets [1]. Typically, these anomalies occupy less than 10% of the image, accounting for a small proportion of the image. HAD has a wide range of real-world applications, including military reconnaissance [2], mineral exploration [3], land cover classification [4], and precision agriculture [5].

HAD can be classified into two categories: traditional HAD and deep learning-based HAD. Traditional HAD methods typically extract shallow features and often show poor performance in complex environments due to the intricate nature of HSIs. In contrast, deep learning techniques can extract abstract, hierarchical, and semantic features, allowing for a more accurate representation of the background and anomalies. This capability of deep learning to extract more complex features has led to its widespread adoption in the HAD field. Notable deep learning-based methods include the Autonomous Hyperspectral

Anomaly Detection Network (Auto-AD) [6], the Plug-and-Play Denoising Convolutional Neural Network Regularized Anomaly Detection (DeCNN-AD) [7], and the Anomaly Enhancement Transformation Network (AETNet) [8].

However, the deep learning-based methods mentioned above each have their own drawbacks. High complexity and computational cost can be prohibitive for real-time or resource-constrained applications. The challenge of spectral similarity—where both background and anomalies share similar spectral characteristics—persists, making it difficult for models to differentiate between them. Limited utilization of contextual information in hyperspectral data may result in the insufficient exploitation of spatial relationships between pixels, ultimately affecting detection accuracy. Additionally, feature loss between layers can lead to the degradation of important details as data pass through the network, negatively impacting overall performance. These limitations collectively restrict the effectiveness and efficiency of these models in practical applications.

To address the issues mentioned above, this paper proposes a HAD method based on the Spectrum Difference Enhanced Network (SDENet). First, the Cross-Shaped Window (CSWin) Transformer unit [9] is incorporated into the encoder–decoder structure as the backbone of SDENet. The CSWin Transformer uses a cross-shaped window attention mechanism to capture local features, aiming to reduce model parameters while effectively extracting background information. In addition, SDENet emphasizes the spectral difference between anomalies and background without directly computing this difference. The Variational Mapping Module (VMModule) transforms feature space into variational space, where spectrum differences are implicitly amplified. By enhancing the spectrum separation within the feature space, SDENet overcomes the spectral similarity interference issue that often hinders accurate detection in hyperspectral images. Second, a Variational Mapping Module (VMModule) is designed to connect the CSWin Transformer encoder and decoder. The extracted features from the CSWin Transformer encoder are first randomly sampled and then mapped from feature space to variational space, enhancing the differences between background and anomaly features, thereby precisely addressing the spectral similarity interference issue. Moreover, skip connections with convolutional operations are utilized in the encoder–decoder structures of SDENet to supplement semantic information. Finally, convolutional layers are used instead of fully connected layers, which helps to improve computational speed and reduce the number of model parameters.

The main contributions of this paper are summarized as follows:

(1) A CSWin Transformer-based encoder and decoder are designed to integrate the CSWin Transformer into the encoder–decoder structure, which can capture more semantic features and reduce the information loss during background reconstruction.
(2) A VMModule is proposed to transform the features extracted from the CSWin Transformer encoder into the variational space, which can increase the difference between anomalies and the background.

2. Related Work

2.1. Hyperspectral Anomaly Detection Method

HAD seeks to extract anomalies from the background without prior knowledge of the target anomalies. Since anomalies typically make up only a small portion of the HSI, most of the image consists of background information. Modeling anomalies directly is challenging and often leads to inefficiencies and suboptimal performance. As a result, algorithms that focus on accurately reconstructing the background have been developed to enhance anomaly detection.

In traditional anomaly detection techniques, the Reed–Xiaoli (RX) algorithm [10] models the background information as a Gaussian distribution and identifies anomalous pixels by calculating the Mahalanobis distance between the pixel to be identified and the background distribution. The RX algorithm has a low computational cost and can identify most anomalous targets, making it a benchmark reference method for HAD tests. However, due to the disparity in the proportion of background and anomalies in hyperspectral data, statistical methods cannot effectively separate anomalies from the background. Therefore, methods like background joint sparse representation (BJSR) [11] have been developed, which constructs an over-complete dictionary for background detection from a representation perspective.

To better separate background and anomalies, some researchers have proposed using tensor decomposition techniques. Additionally, the spectral similarity between anomalies and their surrounding background often complicates detection. Therefore, certain studies have suggested transforming data distribution from the feature space to the variational space to increase the dissimilarity between background and anomalies, thereby improving detection effectiveness. As early as 2014, Zhang et al. demonstrated a similar view with the Low-Rank and Sparse Matrix Decomposition (LRaSMD) technique [12]. The LRaSMD technique posits that the background scene has low-rank characteristics, while anomalies have sparse distribution in the image, converting the anomaly detection task into a convex optimization problem. The Collaborative-Representation-based Detector (CRD) algorithm [13] proposed by Li et al. also demonstrated similar ideas, where each pixel in the background can be approximated by other adjacent pixels in the same space, while anomaly pixels cannot. Xu et al., with their Low-Rank and Sparse Representation (LRASR) algorithm [14], separated anomalies by constructing a background dictionary. All background pixels can be approximated by the background dictionary, and the representation coefficients of all pixels can form a low-rank matrix, modeling background information with low-rank representation to achieve background separation.

However, the methods mentioned above are based on traditional techniques and lack the ability to extract nonlinear and deep features. In contrast, deep learning-based methods are able to extract abstract, hierarchical, and deep features in HSIs to better represent the anomalies and background. The Autonomous Hyperspectral Anomaly Detection Network (Auto-AD) algorithm [6] uses an autoencoder network with skip connections to obtain deep features to compensate for information loss caused by model layers. The Plug-and-Play Denoising Convolutional Neural Network Regularized Anomaly Detection (DeCNN-AD) algorithm [7] combines background dictionary construction with a Convolutional Neural Network (CNN) to enhance dictionary expression capabilities. Recently, in the Anomaly Enhancement Transformation (AETNet) algorithm [8], Li et al. introduced the Swin-Transformer structure [15] into HAD tasks. The AETNet algorithm uses a random masking technique to enhance the network's feature acquisition ability, extracting spatial context features to compensate for information loss.

2.2. Vision Transformer

Initially, the Transformer is a model designed for Natural Language Processing (NLP) [16], but its excellent performance has led to its application in other fields. The Transformer is a sequence transduction model entirely based on attention [17], using a multi-head self-attention mechanism to replace the recurrent layers commonly used in encoder–decoder architectures. The Transformer consists of an encoder and a decoder, each made up of six encoder blocks and decoder blocks, respectively. When a sentence is input, the Transformer generates an embedding for each word alongside its positional embedding, combining these to form a comprehensive representation vector for each word. The word embedding represents the word's data information, which can be obtained during pre-training or training. The positional embedding represents the relative or absolute position information of the word in the sentence, calculated through a formula. As the Transformer saw increasingly widespread use, the Vision Transformer (ViT) [18] was proposed in 2020 and applied to the field of image classification. Due to its simple architecture, effective classification performance, and excellent portability, it has become the benchmark model for using Transformers in image processing.

$$PEmb_{(pos,2i)} = sin(pos/10000^{2i/d}) \quad (1)$$

$$PEmb_{(pos,2i+1)} = cos(pos/10000^{2i/d}) \quad (2)$$

$PEmb$ represents the positional embedding information, pos indicates the word's position in the sentence, d represents the dimension of $PEmb$, $2i$ represents the even dimensions, and $2i + 1$ represents the odd dimensions. Next, the representation vectors obtained by the six encoder blocks are combined to form an encoding information matrix, which is then sent to the decoder. The decoder infers the next word based on the currently translated words until the entire sentence is translated.

ViT treats each image patch as a token, similar to words in a sentence. Each patch is assigned a positional embedding, establishing spatial context within the image. The network then applies random masking to the combination of patches and their positional embeddings, preserving essential spatial relationships while processing each patch. The patches and positional embeddings are then sent to the Transformer encoder to infer the next patch of the positional embedding until all patches are inferred. Finally, the patches are combined according to the positional embeddings to achieve classification. ViT has demonstrated excellent performance, using only the encoder from the Transformer as the classification network. This has prompted many researchers to apply ViT to various image processing tasks.

In studies on applying ViT to HAD, Xu et al. [19] presented a hyperspectral anomaly detector using a ViT with an adversarial strategy. This approach suppresses the reconstruction of anomalies and refines the detection results based on suppressed images. Ning et al. [20] proposed a unified detector (AUD-Net) inspired by few-shot learning, which generalizes across different HSIs through relation learning and uses a pooling layer to manage varying spectral sizes. Their Transformer-based memory model integrates contextual relation embeddings for anomaly detection. Wang et al. [21] presented a self-supervised HAD method using Finite Spatialwise Attention (FSA), with its core being the Self-Supervised HAD transFormer (SSHADFormer). This method reconstructs background HSIs from RGB images, enhancing semantic guidance and anomaly detection effectiveness. The FSA mechanism enlarges distinction between background and anomalies by mining the cluster structure of the background spectrum.

2.3. Variational Auto-Encoder Network

An autoencoder structure consists of two symmetrical parts: an encoder and a decoder. Data are passed through the encoder to the middle layer, where it is represented as latent features of expected values. However, using only the latent vectors or parameters from the middle layer makes it challenging to approximate and learn complex data distributions accurately. For instance, in object detection [22], features such as the blue sky, white clouds, and houses in a landscape painting need to be recognized by the network model. While an autoencoder might represent these features with specific values like 1, 2, and 3, the intensity of the blue sky, its size, and the color and dimensions of the house cannot be explicitly represented. This is where the Variational AutoEncoder (VAE) [23] comes into play.

In a VAE, the middle layer no longer directly uses the encoder's output as expected values. Instead, it uses probability values from multiple probability distribution spaces to represent the features in the middle layer. The VAE employs encoder and decoder networks to establish probabilistic models that represent data distributions. Through variational inference, the encoder maps the original data features to a probability distribution of latent vectors in the hidden layer, allowing for a more nuanced and expressive feature representation.

Wei et al. [24] proposed a Graph Regularized Variational AutoEncoder (GRVAE) in HAD tasks in which a variational autoencoder is used to reconstruct the spectral vector of the HSI. Zhang et al. [25] presented a 3D-Convolutional Variational AutoEncoder (3D-CVAE) whose encoder extracts the spectral–spatial features that are used to reconstruct the background. Anomalies are identified by the Reed–Xiaoli (RX) detector by the residual between the original input and the reconstructed background. Jiang et al. [26] proposed a Manifold constrained Multi-head Self-attention Variational AutoEncoder (MMS-VAE) method. It uses a manifold learning strategy to learn the embedded manifold to maintain the internal structure of the hyperspectral data. Multi-head self-attention captures context-related information. Anomalies are detected by considering both global and local reconstruction errors.

3. Method

The structure of the proposed SDENet is shown in Figure 1, which includes two primary modules: the CSWin Transformer-based encoder and decoder and the VMModule. The CSWin Transformer serves as the backbone of SDENet, enabling the extraction of more semantic features, minimizing information loss, and optimizing model parameters during background reconstruction. The VMModule is designed for feature space transformation between the encoder and the decoder, mapping the feature space into a variational space. This enhances the expression of the background, facilitating background reconstruction. The proposed method aims to ensure the effectiveness in the complex tasks by considering spectral similarity and the issue that the different objects are recognized as the same spectrum.

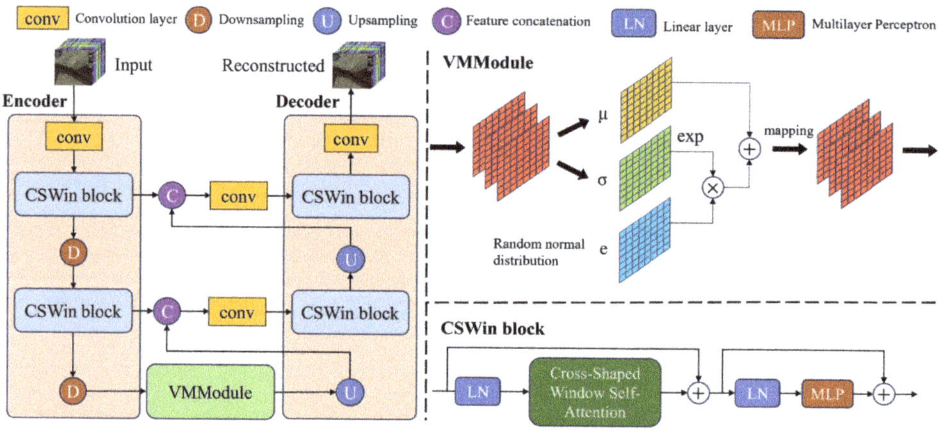

Figure 1. The structure of the Spectrum Difference Enhanced Network.

3.1. CSWin-Transformer-Based Encoder and Decoder

3.1.1. CSWin Block

The CSWin block is the main component of both the encoder and the decoder. It includes a linear layer (LN), cross-shaped window self-attention mechanism, multilayer perceptron (MLP), and feature addition operations. The structure of the CSWin block is shown in the lower-right part of Figure 1.

Typically, LN in the Transformer structure is composed of fully connected layers. However, for hyperspectral data with extensive spectral information, this can impose a significant computational burden. To enhance computational efficiency, this paper incorporates the Convolutional vision Transformer (CvT) structure proposed by Wu et al. [27], introducing convolution operations into the CSWin block to replace all linear layers. Convolutional layers are used in place of upsampling and downsampling operations in the encoder and decoder to improve spatial feature extraction. Furthermore, the depth of the MLP layer is reduced from four to two layers to avoid excessive parameters and mitigate model redundancy.

In the classic Transformer structure, attention computation is performed over the entire image. However, for hyperspectral data with hundreds of spectral channels, this approach results in high computational costs. Therefore, the cross-shaped window self-attention mechanism does not use the traditional attention calculation method but instead employs a sliding cross-shaped window approach. This reduces the complexity and computational cost by computing multi-scale features and considering the spectral similarity of local background information, thus extracting more accurate land cover distribution information.

For hyperspectral data of size $C \times H \times W$ (where C, H, and W represent depth, height, and width), denoted as X, first, input X into the cross-shaped window self-attention (CSWS). Here, X is defined as follows:

$$X = \left[X^1, \ldots\ldots, X^C\right]. \tag{3}$$

Then, the attention of the sliding window is calculated vertically and horizontally for feature stitching to form the cross-shaped attention mechanism Att_{CSWS}, as follows:

$$Att_z(X) = \left[Att(X^1W^1), \ldots\ldots, Att(X^aW^a)\right] \tag{4}$$

$$Att_h(X) = \left[Att(X^1W^1), \ldots\ldots, Att(X^bW^b)\right] \tag{5}$$

$$Att_{CSWS}(X) = concat[Att_z(X), \ldots\ldots, Att_h(X)] \tag{6}$$

where Att denotes the attention calculation. Att_z represents vertical attention. Att_h represents horizontal attention. a and b denote the width and height of the attention window. The CSWin block can be defined as follows:

$$\hat{X}^i = Att_{CSWS}(LN(X_{i-1}) + X_{i-1}) + X_{i-1} \tag{7}$$

$$X_i = MLP(LN(\hat{X}^i)) + \hat{X}^i \tag{8}$$

where $\hat{X}^i$ represents the features after the first feature addition of the i-th layer. Xi denotes the output of the CSWin block for the i-th layer or the convolution for the upper layer.

3.1.2. CSWin-Transformer Based Encoder

The encoder consists of convolutional layers, two CSWin blocks, and two downsampling layers. To ensure the consistency of input data channels, the kernel size of the convolutional layer is set to (3, 3) and the stride size to (1, 1). Traditional deep learning methods typically use fully connected layers for self-supervised learning at the spectral level, which can lead to a loss of spatial information. To better capture spatial information while changing feature dimensions, the encoder uses 2D convolution (Conv2d) for downsampling instead of channel transformation. The kernel size is set to (4, 4), the stride size to (2, 2), and the padding to (1, 1).

3.1.3. CSWin-Transformer Based Decoder

The decoder comprises convolutional layers, two CSWin blocks, and two upsampling layers. The convolutional layers and CSWin blocks in the decoder share the same parameter settings as those in the encoder, ensuring consistency in feature extraction. To efficiently increase spatial resolution while minimizing information loss, a 2D transposed convolution layer with a kernel size of (2, 2) and a stride size of (2, 2) is employed during upsampling.Unlike the encoder, the decoder processes data in a non-sequential manner by concatenating its intermediate outputs with the corresponding outputs from the CSWin blocks in the encoder. This skip connection mechanism helps preserve spatial and semantic information, improving the reconstruction quality. After feature concatenation, to align the number of channels between the concatenated features and the upsampled features, a convolution layer with a kernel size and stride size of (1, 1) is applied, ensuring efficient channel-wise integration.

3.1.4. Variational Mapping Module

This paper integrates the CSWin-Transformer structure into the autoencoder reconstruction network. However, when dealing with cases of high spectral similarity and small anomalies, this strategy does not perform ideally. Based on the idea of collaborative representation methods, elements in the background can be represented by the collaborative representation of other surrounding elements, whereas anomalies cannot.

To address these challenges, a VMModule is designed and integrated into the hidden layer of the variational autoencoder network, converting feature representations from expected values into probability distributions. This VMModule transforms the feature space, enhancing feature expression and increasing the distinction between background and anomalies, as illustrated in the upper-right corner of Figure 1.

Since different feature spaces result in varied feature distributions, the VMModule alters the overall background distribution to achieve feature space transformation. For the input background data $F_{in}([F_1, F_2, \ldots\ldots, F_n])$, it is transformed into the distribution $N(\bar{F}_{in}, \sigma(F_{in}))$ through a fully connected layer mapping. Here, $\bar{F}_{in}$ represents the mean of F_{in}, and $\sigma(F_{in})$ represents the variance of F_{in}.

Both the encoder and decoder structures are deep nonlinear networks. As the complexity of the network structure increases, the autoencoder can achieve more effective dimensionality reduction while maintaining low reconstruction loss. Theoretically, by reducing the feature dimensions with the encoder and then increasing them with the decoder, an almost-lossless reconstructed image can be obtained. However, such a high-degree-of-freedom autoencoder structure is prone to overfitting, potentially leading to an over-matching of the training data in practical applications.

Furthermore, the purpose of dimensionality reduction in the autoencoder structure is not merely to enhance the encoder's reconstruction capability, but to retain the main structural information of the features in a concise representation while reducing dimensions. In HAD tasks, the dimensionality reduction capability of the autoencoder should be aimed at extracting the primary features of the background and anomalies to the maximum extent, rather than precisely reconstructing the original data.

To address these issues, the random normal distribution is introduced as noise into the feature distribution $P(\bar{F}_{in}, \sigma(F_{in}))$ in the variational space to avoid model overfitting. Since background information constitutes the majority in hyperspectral data, this approach also ensures that the data generated in the variational space better conform to the background. The calculation process of the VMModule is as follows: the mean $\bar{F}_{in}$ and variance $\sigma(F_{in})$ of the input background data F_{in} correspond to the theoretical feature distribution $P(\bar{F}_{in}, \sigma(F_{in}))$. During each training process, a normal distribution $N(0,1)$ is randomly sampled as noise, added to the feature distribution of F_{in}, as shown in the following Equation (9):

$$\hat{F} = \sum_{i=1}^{n} (EXP(\sigma_i) \times N(0,1) + \bar{F}_{in}) \tag{9}$$

where EXP is the natural exponential function.

Finally, $\hat{F}$ is mapped to the feature space to obtain the module output F_{out}, ensuring the consistency of the channel count. The specific formula is as follows:

$$F_{\text{out}} = LN(\hat{F}). \tag{10}$$

3.2. Loss Function

The background reconstruction network aims to explore the spectral differences between anomalous targets and background pixels, rather than merely focusing on spectral reconstruction accuracy. Excessive reconstruction accuracy may lead to the misreconstruction of some anomalous targets. Therefore, multiple scales of gradients are considered to measure similarity. The reconstruction loss function L_{MGS} for the hyperspectral remote sensing image data X and the reconstructed background $\hat{X}$ can be calculated using Equation (11).

$$L_{MGS} = \frac{1}{S}\sum_{n=1}^{S}\frac{1}{H_nW_n}\sum_{a=1}^{H_n}\sum_{b=1}^{W_n}(1 - GMS_{a,b}(X^n, \hat{X}^n)). \tag{11}$$

In Equation (11), S represents the number of scales of the reconstructed background, and H_n and W_n denote the height and width of the image at the n-th scale. GMS is the multi-scale gradient similarity, and a and b represent the height and width of the current pixel coordinates. The calculation process for GMS is shown in Equation (12). To obtain more accurate gradient magnitude values, a 3 × 3 Sobel filter is used from horizontal, vertical, and diagonal dimensions, as shown in Equations (13) and (14).

$$GMS_{a,b}(X^n, \hat{X}^n) = \frac{2G_XG_{\hat{X}} + c}{{G_X}^2 + {G_{\hat{X}}}^2 + c} \tag{12}$$

$$G_X = \sqrt{(X^n \circledast s_x)^2 + (X^n \circledast s_y)^2 + (X^n \circledast s_{z1})^2 + (X^n \circledast s_{z2})^2} \tag{13}$$

$$G_{\hat{X}} = \sqrt{(\hat{X}^n \circledast s_x)^2 + (\hat{X}^n \circledast s_y)^2 + (\hat{X}^n \circledast s_{z1})^2 + (\hat{X}^n \circledast s_{z2})^2}. \tag{14}$$

In Equations (12)–(14), G represents the gradient magnitude, and c is a constant set to 0.1 to ensure numerical stability during the calculation. $\circledast$ denotes the convolution operation. s_x, s_y, s_{z1}, and s_{z2} represent the Sobel filters along the x-dimension, y-dimension, and 45° and 135° diagonals, respectively.

3.3. SDENet Training and Anomaly Detection Workflow

During the training phase, the Adam optimizer is used to optimize the iterative process of SDENet, with an initial learning rate set to 5e-6. The dimension of the hidden layer in SDENet is set to 32, and the rationale for this parameter setting is discussed in Section 4.4. The maximum number of training epochs is set to 1000, with early stopping as an option.

First, the hyperspectral remote sensing image data X is fed into SDENet to obtain the reconstructed background $\hat{X}$. Second, the anomaly score, Score, is calculated using Mahalanobis distance [28]. Third, it is determined whether Score is greater than the maximum anomaly score MaxScore. If so, Score is assigned to MaxScore and Count is reset; otherwise, Count is incremented by 1. The iteration stops when the maximum number of training epochs is reached or the anomaly score does not improve for 30 consecutive epochs. In other words, if Count is greater than or equal to 30, the iteration stops, and the optimal SDENet model is obtained. Finally, in the fourth step, the SDENet model is used to obtain the reconstructed background $\hat{X}$ and combined with the original input X, and the anomaly detection result map is obtained by using Mahalanobis distance [28]. The hyperspectral anomaly detection process based on SDENet is shown in Algorithm 1.

Algorithm 1 The process of HAD based on SDENet.

Input:

- Hyperspectral remote sensing image data X.

Initialization:

- Optimizer is Adam with a learning rate of 5e-6.
- Hidden layer dimension is 32.
- Loss function refers to Equation (11).
- Maximum training epochs is 1000.
- Initial maximum anomaly score MaxScore and counter Count are both set to 0.

Steps:

1. Input X into SDENet to obtain the reconstructed background $\hat{X}$.
2. Calculate the anomaly score (Score) between X and $\hat{X}$ using the Mahalanobis distance [28].
3. If Score $>$ MaxScore:
    MaxScore $=$ Score
    Count $= 0$
   Else:
    Count $++$
   Until: the number of training epochs reaches 1000 or Count is greater than or equal to 30 to obtain the optimal SDENet model.
4. Use the optimal SDENet model to obtain the reconstructed background $\hat{X}$. Then, combine with the original input X to calculate the anomaly detection result map using the Mahalanobis distance [28].

Output:

- Anomaly detection result map.
- The area under the curve (AUC) value.

4. Experiments and Analysis

4.1. Datasets

In HAD tasks, real datasets captured by sensors and synthetic hyperspectral datasets can both be used. To ensure the applicability of the algorithm discussed in this paper, open-source real datasets are selected for the experiments. Below is a brief introduction to the three real datasets used and the evaluation metric employed.

4.1.1. Airplane1 Dataset

This dataset comprises Airborne Visible/Infrared Imaging Spectrometer (AVIRIS) data captured over a specific area in San Diego, CA, USA. The spatial resolution of this data is 20 meters, and the spectral resolution is 10 nanometers, with a spectral wavelength range of 370 to 2510 nanometers. The spatial dimensions are 64×64, with 224 spectral bands. After removing poor or noisy bands, 189 spectral bands are retained. In the image, three airplanes are classified as anomalies, while other ground features are considered background. The visualized image of this data and its corresponding ground truth labels are shown in Figure 2. In the sub figure (b) of Figure 2, the blue regions represent the background, while the yellow regions indicate anomalies.

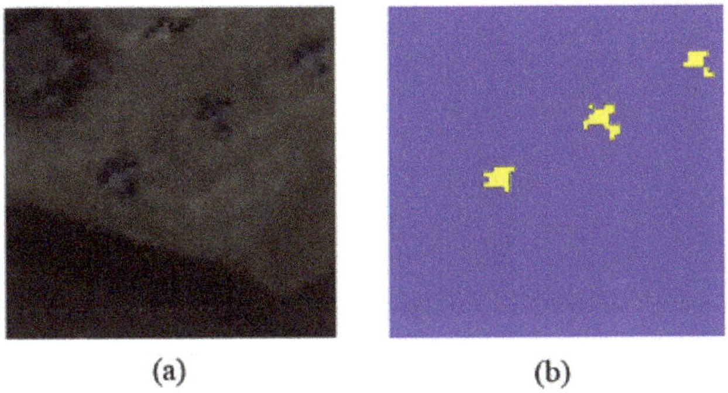

Figure 2. (a) The Airplane1 dataset. (b) The ground truth.

4.1.2. HYDICE1 Dataset

This dataset comprises Hyperspectral Digital Imagery Collection Experiment (HYDICE) urban data collected by an airborne sensor. It has spatial dimensions of 64 × 64 pixels and includes 210 spectral bands with wavelengths ranging from 400 to 2500 nanometers. After removing low signal-to-noise ratio bands and water absorption bands, 162 effective bands remain. In the dataset, man-made objects such as cars and rooftops are considered anomalies, while other ground features serve as the background. The visualized image of these data and its corresponding labels are shown in Figure 3. In the sub figure (b) of Figure 3, the blue regions represent the background, while the yellow regions indicate anomalies.

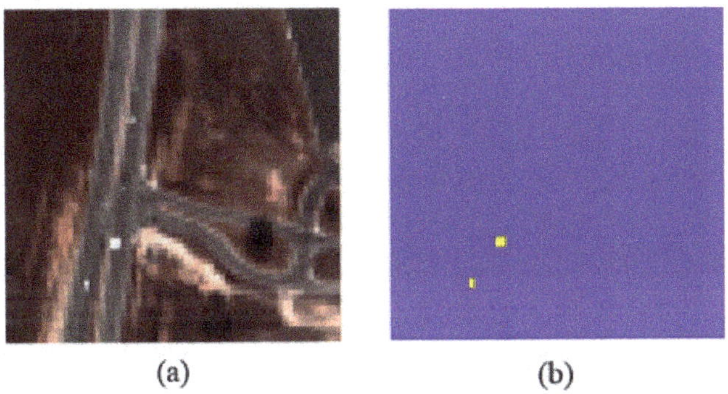

Figure 3. (a) The HYDICE1 dataset. (b) The ground truth.

4.1.3. Salinas1 Dataset

This dataset consists of Salinas scene data captured by the AVIRIS sensor over the Salinas Valley in California, USA. The image has spatial dimensions of 64 × 64 pixels and contains 224 spectral bands. Vegetables, vineyard fields, and bare soil in the Salinas scene are considered anomalies, while other ground features are regarded as background. The visualized image of the Salinas scene data and its corresponding ground truth labels are shown in Figure 4. In the sub figure (b) of Figure 4, the blue regions represent the background, while the yellow regions indicate anomalies.

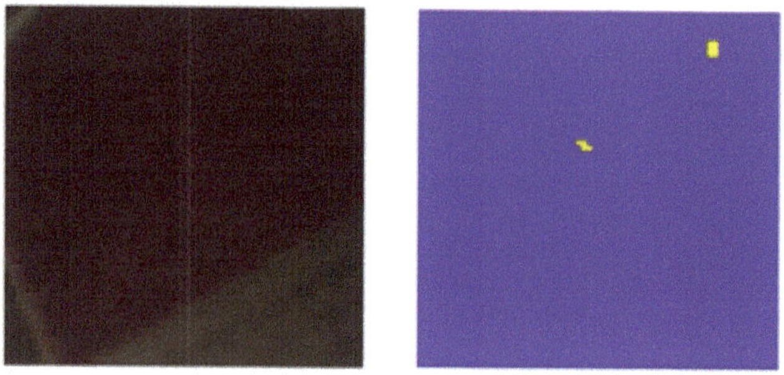

(a) (b)

Figure 4. (**a**) The Salinas1 dataset. (**b**) The ground truth.

4.2. Evaluation Criteria

We use the area under the curve (AUC) metric to compare the detection performances of different anomaly detection methods on the three datasets. The AUC of the receiver operating characteristic (ROC) curve is the most widely used evaluation tool in HAD tasks, providing a direct and quantitative measure of the algorithm's performance. A higher AUC value indicates better performance, with values close to 1 representing the best test performance.

4.3. Comparison with States of the Arts

To validate the effectiveness of the proposed SDENet on three hyperspectral datasets, seven other methods are used for comparison. The comparison methods are listed as follows:

- Auto-AD: The Autonomous Hyperspectral Anomaly Detection Network (Auto-AD) [6] uses a fully convolutional autoencoder with skip connections and an adaptive-weighted loss function to reconstruct the background and increase the contrast between anomalies and the background.
- DeCNN-AD: DeCNN-AD [7] utilizes a plug-and-play prior for representation coefficients and a CNN denoiser to leverage spatial correlation, constructing a background dictionary based on clustering to exclude anomalous pixels.
- FEBPAD: The feature extraction and background purification anomaly detection (FEBPAD) [29] method integrates fractional Fourier transform (FrFT) with row-constrained low rank and sparse matrix decomposition (RC-LRaSMD) for HAD by extracting features, separating background from noise and anomalies, and constructing a background covariance matrix for detection.
- LRSNCR: Low-Rank and Sparse Matrix Decomposition (LRSNCR) [30] enhances traditional RPCA by using non-convex regularization with Weighted Nuclear Norm Minimization (WNNM) and Capped $\ell_{2,1}$-norm.
- RGAE: Robust graph AE (RGAE) [31] integrates a robust autoencoder framework with an $\ell_{2,1}$-norm and a superpixel segmentation-based graph regularization term (SuperGraph) to resist noise and anomalies and maintain the geometric structure and spatial consistency of HSIs. The method distinguishes anomalies from the background while preserving essential spatial relationships.
- AETNet: AETNet [8] introduces a general anomaly enhancement network trained once on anomaly-free HSIs with random masks, learning spatial context characteristics and utilizing a plug-and-play model selection module to find the optimal spatial-spectral transform domain.
- GT-HAD: The Gated Transformer Network for HAD (GT-HAD) [32] leverages spatial–spectral similarity to effectively distinguish between background and anomalies by using dual-branch modeling with content similarity constraints and an adaptive

gating unit for dynamic activation, further enhanced by a Content-Matching Method (CMM) to regulate the activation states of the branches.

From a qualitative perspective, the results of each algorithm on the three datasets are visualized to directly observe their anomaly detection performance. The anomaly detection results of eight algorithms on the Airplane1 dataset are shown in Figure 5. Three airplanes are considered anomalies, while buildings, land, and other ground objects are considered background.The ground truth for the Airplane1 dataset is presented in Figure 5i. In Figure 5c, it is evident that the FEBPAD algorithm does not perform well in distinguishing between anomalies and background in the Airplane1 data, failing to separate or enhance the differences between anomalies and background effectively. In Figure 5b and Figure 5d, in comparison, the DeCNNAD and LRSNCR algorithms show better pixel-level anomaly detection, but they have a high false detection rate, with some background being incorrectly identified as anomalies in the detection results. In Figure 5a, it can be seen that the Auto-AD algorithm does not handle the contour and line information in the background well. Although it does not mistake large areas of the background for anomalies, it scores lower on contour information than the background. The detection results of the RGAE algorithm Figure 5e significantly suppress the background but do not highlight the anomaly information. From Figure 5f, Figure 5g, and Figure 5h, it can be seen that the AETNet, GT-HAD, and SDENet algorithms suppress background information more effectively. However, AETNet does not intuitively detect the middle airplane anomaly target. Despite unavoidable pixel interference, the proposed SDENet algorithm demonstrates its ability to enhance the distinction between anomalies and background by suppressing background information, thereby playing a more intuitive role in anomaly detection.

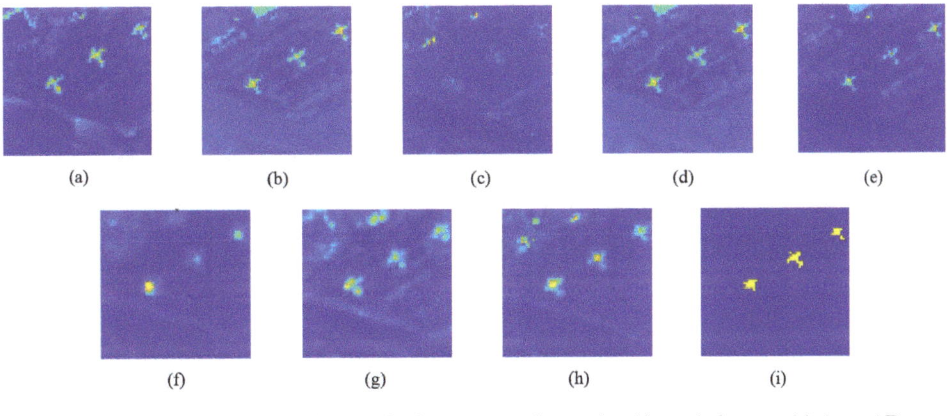

Figure 5. The visualization of anomaly detection results on the Airport1 dataset: (**a**) Auto-AD, (**b**) DeCNNAD, (**c**) FEBPAD, (**d**) LRSNCR, (**e**) RGAE, (**f**) AETNet, (**g**) GT-HAD, (**h**) SDENet (Ours), and (**i**) the ground truth.

The anomaly detection results of eight algorithms on the HYDICE1 dataset are shown in Figure 6. Two cars on the road are considered anomalies, while other objects such as roads, land, and buildings are considered background. The ground truth for the HYDICE1 data is presented in Figure 6i. Algorithms such as Auto-AD, RGAE, AETNet, and GT-HAD, which performed well on the Airplane1 dataset, fail to accurately detect anomalies in the HYDICE1 dataset, often misidentifying much of the nearby background as anomalies. Analyzing the implementation processes of these algorithms reveals that they all involve deep convolutional layer network structures. The sliding operation of convolutional kernels tends to favor the extraction of local information, potentially overlooking global information, resulting in the subpar detection of smaller anomalous targets. The LRSNCR algorithm primarily uses component analysis methods to distinguish anomalies from the background and is not affected in this manner, but it does not suppress the background, which is treated as the main component in HAD. In contrast, the DeCNNAD, FEBPAD, and SDENet algorithms show better detection performance. DeCNNAD and FEBPAD use shallow convolution operations to extract features, while the SDENet algorithm uses cross-shaped window attention to extract features in two dimensions, effectively replacing the use of global features. Although there are still some instances where background anomalies receive higher scores, the two anomaly targets are also enhanced, making them easier to detect.

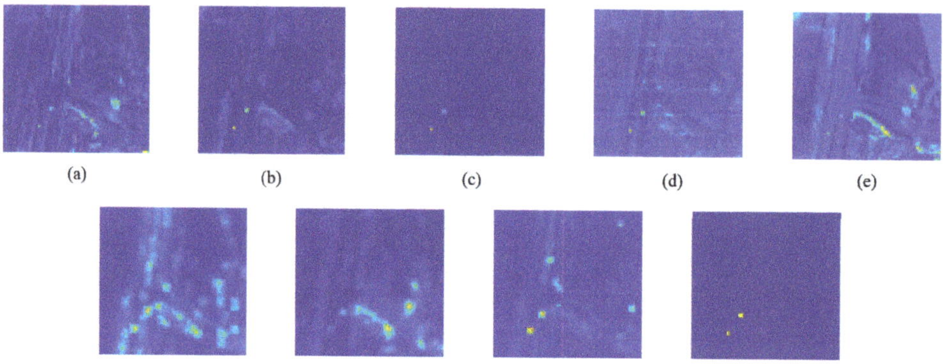

(a) (b) (c) (d) (e) (f) (g) (h) (i)

Figure 6. The visualization of anomaly detection results on the HYDICE1 dataset: (**a**) Auto-AD, (**b**) DeCNNAD, (**c**) FEBPAD, (**d**) LRSNCR, (**e**) RGAE, (**f**) AETNet, (**g**) GT-HAD, (**h**) SDENet (Ours), and (i) the ground truth.

The anomaly detection results of eight algorithms on the Salinas1 dataset are shown in Figure 7. In this dataset, vegetables, vineyard fields, and bare soil are considered anomalies, while other objects are considered background. The ground truth for the Salinas1 data is presented in Figure 7i. In the detection results of the Auto-AD and RGAE algorithms, although small and randomly distributed anomalies are detected, large areas of land are incorrectly identified as anomalies, significantly affecting the detection performance. The DeCNNAD and LRSNCR algorithms perform slightly better but still fail to clearly distinguish between anomalies and background. FEBPAD has the clearest anomaly scores, but like the AETNet algorithm, it is overly sensitive to background contours, erroneously detecting field edges and other background elements as anomalies. In contrast, the GT-HAD and SDENet algorithms can detect the anomaly targets with only a few high-score background pixels. Overall, SDENet achieves the best detection performance for both block and point anomalies across the three datasets.

From a quantitative perspective, the effectiveness of eight algorithms for HAD and the proposed SDENet algorithm is validated using AUC values on the Airplane1, HYDICE1, and Salinas1 datasets. As shown in Table 1, the proposed SDENet algorithm achieves the highest average AUC values, with scores of 0.9899, 0.9994, and 0.9597 on the respective datasets. SDENet performs well in handling different types of anomalous target distributions, whether the anomalies are block-distributed as in the Airplane1 dataset or point-distributed as in the HYDICE1 and Salinas1 datasets. The AUC values on all three datasets are above 0.95. Specifically, in processing the Salinas1 dataset, SDENet significantly enhances the differentiation between anomaly and background scores, effectively distinguishing anomalies even in contour and edge pixels, which is crucial for HAD tasks.

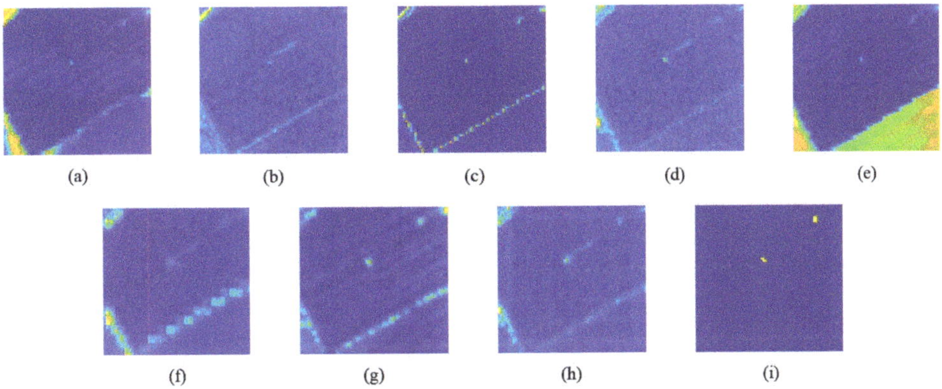

Figure 7. The visualization of anomaly detection results on the Salinas1 dataset: (**a**) Auto-AD, (**b**) DeCNNAD, (**c**) FEBPAD, (**d**) LRSNCR, (**e**) RGAE, (**f**) AETNet, (**g**) GT-HAD, (**h**) SDENet (Ours), and (**i**) the ground truth.

Table 1. The AUC values for the three datasets on the comparison methods.

Dataset	Airplane1	HYDICE1	Salinas1	Avg AUC
Auto-AD	0.9858	0.9534	0.9405	0.9599
DeCNNAD	0.9934	0.9990	0.7504	0.9143
FEBPAD	0.9563	1.0000	0.9756	0.9773
LRSNCR	0.9936	0.9980	0.9563	0.9826
RGAE	0.9901	0.9183	0.7843	0.8976
AETNet	0.9892	0.9986	0.8657	0.9509
GT-HAD	0.9849	0.9535	0.9896	0.9760
SDENet (ours)	0.9899	0.9994	0.9597	0.9830

4.4. Algorithm Time Cost

To evaluate the performance of the proposed SDENet algorithm compared with the other seven algorithms, this section conducts experiments to measure their time overhead. Table 2 shows the time overhead for anomaly detection on the three datasets.

According to Table 2, the detection times of the SDENet algorithm on the three datasets are 4.90, 4.93, and 5.40 s, respectively. In comparison, algorithms such as Auto-AD, DeCNNAD, and RGAE involve training and testing processes, so their time overhead includes both training and inference times. Therefore, when comparing these algorithms, only the anomaly detection inference time is considered. Among these algorithms, SDENet has the lowest average time on the three datasets, indicating that SDENet has an advantage in terms of time overhead compared with the other algorithms.

Table 2. The time overhead of different methods on three datasets (in seconds).

Method	Airplane1	HYDICE1	Salinas1	Avg Time
Auto-AD	55.93	59.34	61.51	58.93
DeCNNAD	28.88	27.67	57.77	38.11
FEBPAD	5.61	4.91	6.48	5.67
LRSNCR	9.00	10.02	16.47	11.83
RGAE	217.73	201.80	243.48	221.01
AETNet	5.22	4.99	10.62	6.94
GT-HAD	25.20	18.42	20.73	21.45
SDENet (ours)	4.90	4.93	5.40	5.08

4.5. Parameter Setup

To ensure that the encoder and decoder effectively extract and retain the main feature information of hyperspectral data during the feature compression and restoration process, experiments are designed to explore the appropriate dimension of the hidden layer between the encoder and the decoder. SDENet is tested on the Airplane1, HYDICE1, and Salinas1 datasets, and the results are analyzed to determine the optimal hidden layer dimension setting.

Figure 8 shows the AUC values for anomaly detection using SDENet with different dimensions of the hidden layer. Blue, red, and green represent the experimental results when the latent dimension (latent dim) is 16, 32, and 64, respectively.

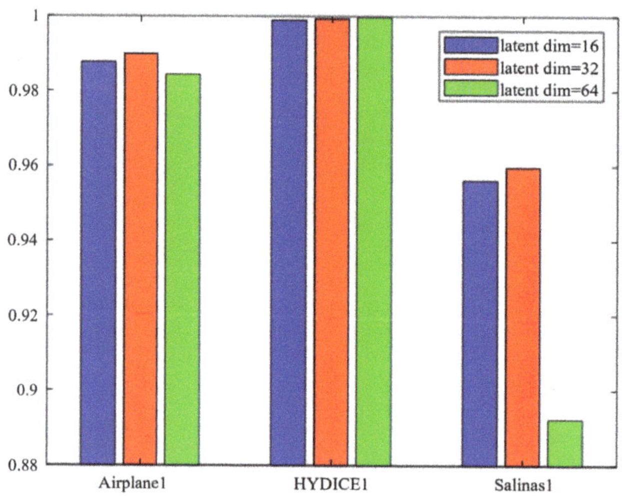

Figure 8. Anomaly detection results of SDENet on three datasets with varying latent dimensions.

On the Airplane1 dataset, as the latent dim increased, the AUC values for anomaly detection reached 0.9878, 0.9899, and 0.9843, respectively. By treating the latent dim as the independent variable and the AUC value as the dependent variable, the AUC exhibits an initial increase followed by a decrease, resembling a convex function. Based on the properties of continuous curves, where the derivative between two points can change from positive to negative, there must be a maximum within the interval [16, 64]. Since the derivative is positive at a latent dim of 16 and negative at 32, the maximum occurs within this range. Given that the latent dim values are powers of two, the optimal value is 32, yielding the best anomaly detection performance.

In the Salinas1 dataset, the AUC values are 0.9562, 0.9597, and 0.8922 for latent dim values of 16, 32, and 64, respectively. Similar to the Airplane1 dataset, the AUC follows a convex trend, with the optimal performance at a latent dim of 32.

For the HYDICE1 dataset, as the latent dim increases, the AUC values are 0.9990, 0.9994, and 0.9997, respectively. Unlike the other datasets, the function is increasing across the interval [16, 64], indicating no extremum or maximum.

Based on the analysis of the anomaly detection performance on the datasets, the AUC values in the Airplane1, HYDICE1, and Salinas1 datasets when the network's latent dim is 16, 32, and 64, respectively, are shown in Table 3.

Table 3. AUC values of SDENet on three datasets with varying latent dimensions (latent dim).

Dataset	Latent Dim = 16	Latent Dim = 32	Latent Dim = 64
Airplane1	0.9878	0.9899	0.9843
HYDICE1	0.9990	0.9994	0.9997
Salinas1	0.9562	0.9597	0.8922
Average AUC	0.9810	0.9830	0.9587

When the latent dim is set to 16, 32, and 64, the average AUC values across the three datasets are 0.9810, 0.9830, and 0.9587, respectively. As the latent dim changes, the average AUC follows a convex trend. Thus, it can be concluded that the optimal latent dim for SDENet is 32, providing the best overall anomaly detection performance across the datasets.

4.6. Ablation Study

This section involves a series of experiments to verify the impact of the innovative modules in the SDENet algorithm on HAD tasks. These experiments include designs where innovative modules are removed or replaced to assess their effect on algorithm performance.

4.6.1. Effectiveness of CSWin Block

First, we replace the CSWin block in the background reconstruction network based on variational mapping and Transformer to verify its impact on the anomaly detection task. Keeping the network structure unchanged, the CSWin block is replaced with the Swin block from the Swin Transformer network structure, noted as "SDENet wo CSWin". The cut Airplane1, HYDICE1, and Salinas1 datasets are used as network inputs. The experimental results are shown in Figure 9. The SDENet wo CSWin algorithm is shown in blue, and the SDENet algorithm is shown in red.

The AUC values of the SDENet wo CSWin algorithm on the Airplane1, HYDICE1, and Salinas1 datasets are 0.9892, 0.9986, and 0.8657, respectively. The SDENet algorithm achieves AUC values of 0.9899, 0.9994, and 0.9597 on the three datasets. It can be observed that after replacing the CSWin block, the AUC values of the SDENet algorithm (SDENet wo CSWin) decreased by 0.0007, 0.0008, and 0.0940 on the three datasets, respectively. Although both the CSWin block and the Swin block are Transformer structures, the results show that the cross-shaped window attention mechanism in the CSWin block is more suitable for HAD tasks. Especially on the Salinas1 dataset, the detection effect is more significant. This proves that the CSWin block has a stronger detection capability for handling small and randomly distributed anomalous targets.

4.6.2. Effectiveness of the VMModule

Next, we replace the VMModule to verify its effectiveness. Keeping the network structure unchanged, the VMModule is replaced with a CSWin block, noted as "SDENet wo VMModule". The Airplane1, HYDICE1, and Salinas1 datasets are still used as inputs, and the results are shown in Figure 10. The SDENet wo VMModule algorithm is shown in blue, and the SDENet algorithm is shown in red.

The AUC values of the SDENet wo VMModule algorithm for anomaly detection on the Airplane1, HYDICE1, and Salinas1 datasets are 0.9814, 0.9991, and 0.9232, respectively. The SDENet algorithm achieves AUC values of 0.9899, 0.9994, and 0.9597 on the three datasets. Replacing the VMModule with the CSWin block in the SDENet wo VMModule algorithm results in AUC values decreasing by 0.0085, 0.0003, and 0.0365 on the three datasets, respectively. Notably, even in the SDENet wo VMModule algorithm, the AUC values for anomaly detection on the three datasets still reach above 0.92. However, replacing the VMModule allows the SDENet algorithm to further improve the AUC values by 3 percentage points on each dataset. This indicates that the VMModule provides a stable improvement in the expression ability of anomalies after feature space transformation, enhancing the final anomaly detection effect.

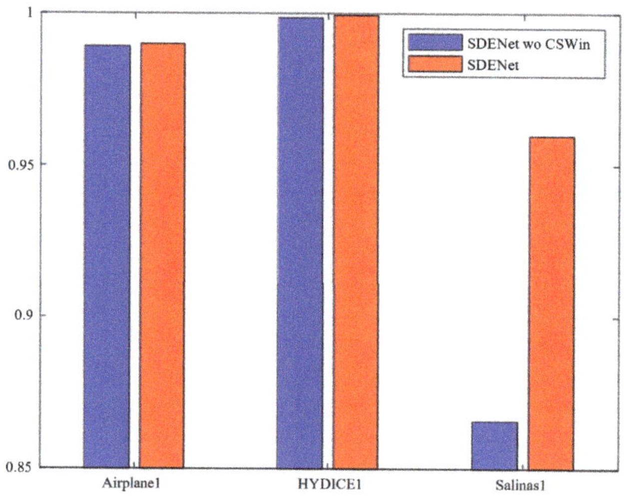

Figure 9. AUC values of SDENet wo CSWin and SDENet algorithms on three datasets.

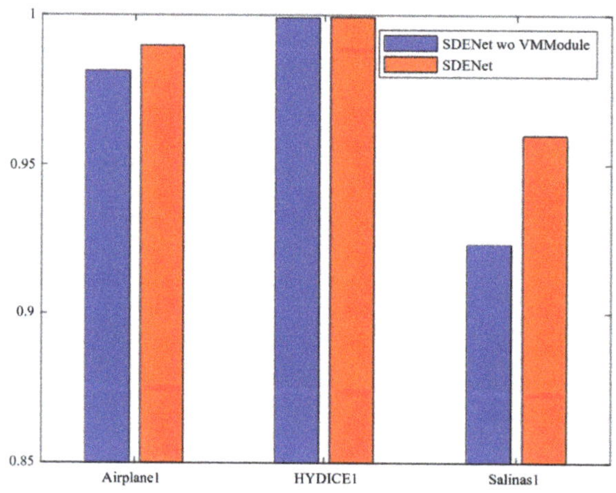

Figure 10. AUC values of SDENet wo VMModule and SDENet algorithms on three datasets.

4.7. Model Complexity Evaluation

To evaluate the complexity of the models, this paper analyzes the Floating Point Operations (FLOPs) and the number of parameters (Params) of the network models before and after the ablation of the innovative modules. As shown in Table 4, FLOPs represent the total number of floating point operations in the network model, which approximately indicates the overall computational load. For the same task, a lower computational load signifies a more streamlined and efficient network. Params indicate the total number of parameters in the current network model. Fewer parameters mean less hardware resource usage and lower dependency on hardware devices.

Table 4. FLOPs and Params of algorithms in ablation experiments.

Parameters	SDENet wo CSWin	SDENet wo VMModule	SDENet
FLOPs	13903.74	8990.47	8363.41
Params (Unit: M)	0.51	0.46	0.34

The FLOPs and Params of the SDENet wo CSWin algorithm are 13,903.74 and 0.51 M, respectively, while those of the SDENet algorithm are 8363.41 and 0.34 M, respectively. Clearly, SDENet uses fewer resources, showing lower dependency on the hardware. The primary reason for this difference lies in the attention mechanism's calculation methods. The attention calculation in the SDENet wo CSWin algorithm is based on the weights of a rectangular sliding window, while the attention calculation in the SDENet algorithm is based on the weights of a cross-shaped sliding window. For the same bounding rectangle size, the cross-shaped window requires fewer weight calculations than the rectangular sliding window, which is the main reason for the increase in FLOPs and Params after replacing the CSWin block in the SDENet wo CSWin algorithm.

The main difference between the SDENet wo VMModule algorithm and the SDENet algorithm lies in the CSWin block and the Var-mapping block. The CSWin block is deeper than the VMModule, and the convolution kernel used in the VMModule is a (1, 1) convolution layer as the mapping operation. One reason for this design is that convolution layers can reduce the number of parameters compared with commonly used fully connected mapping layers. Another reason is that the sliding calculation method of the convolution kernel is conducive to extracting local features, providing good separation for small anomaly targets. The FLOPs and Params of SDENet are minimized to 8363.41 and 0.34 M, respectively, indicating that the algorithm has a low computational cost and can achieve satisfactory detection results without over-relying on hardware devices.

5. Conclusions

In this paper, we propose a Spectrum Difference Enhanced Network named SDENet for HAD tasks, which aims to enhance the expression of anomalies and increases the spectrum difference between anomalies and the background. SDENet consists of a CSWin-Transformer encoder, a CSWin-Transformer decoder, and a Variational Mapping Module. The CSWin-Transformer encoder and decoder supplement image information by extracting deep and semantic features, where a cross-shaped window self-attention mechanism provides a strong modeling capability with minimal computational cost. A randomly sampling VMModule enhances the spectral difference characteristics between anomalies and background through feature space transformation. First, the encoder uses convolutional layers, CSWin blocks, and downsampling operations to reduce the dimensionality of the data, obtaining a concise representation that retains the main features. Then, the VMModule maps the feature space to the variational space, thereby increasing the difference between anomaly features and background features. Moreover, the decoder reconstructs the background using a structure composed of convolutional layers, CSWin blocks, and upsampling operations. The reconstruction process is enhanced by concatenating the features extracted from the corresponding CSWin blocks in the encoder with the features to be reconstructed. Finally, the residual map is obtained based on the Mahalanobis distance.

Experiments are conducted on three real-world datasets to compare SDENet with seven other SOTA methods, including ablation and parameter experiments. On the Airplane1, HYDICE1, and Salinas1 datasets, the SDENet algorithm achieves AUC values of 0.9899, 0.9994, and 0.9597, respectively. The average AUC value across these datasets is 0.9830, significantly higher than that of the other methods. Additionally, SDENet achieves the lowest test inference time, FLOPs, and number of parameters among all the algorithms tested. In terms of quantitative and qualitative results, inference time, and model complexity, the SDENet algorithm outperforms the others, showcasing its superior performance in HAD tasks.

Author Contributions: S.L., H.G., S.G. and W.Z. made contributions to proposing the method, performing the experiments and analyzing the result. S.L., H.G., S.G. and W.Z. are involved in the preparation and revision of the manuscript. All authors have read and agreed to the published version of the manuscript.

Funding: This work was supported in part by National Natural Science Foundation of China General Program 62471389 and in part by the Shaanxi Provincial Key Research and Develop Programme General Project under Grant 2024SF-YBXM-572.

Data Availability Statement: The raw data supporting the conclusions of this article will be made available by the authors on request.

Conflicts of Interest: The authors declare no conflicts of interest.

References

1. Su, H.; Wu, Z.; Zhang, H.; Du, Q. Hyperspectral Anomaly Detection: A survey. *IEEE Geosci. Remote Sens. Mag.* **2022**, *10*, 64–90. [CrossRef]
2. Shimoni, M.; Haelterman, R.; Perneel, C. Hypersectral imaging for military and security applications: Combining myriad processing and sensing techniques. *IEEE Geosci. Remote Sens. Mag.* **2019**, *7*, 101–117. [CrossRef]
3. Hörig, B.; Kühn, F.; Oschütz, F.; Lehmann, F. HyMap hyperspectral remote sensing to detect hydrocarbons. *Int. J. Remote Sens.* **2001**, *22*, 1413–1422. [CrossRef]
4. Cheng, G.; Xie, X.; Han, J.; Guo, L.; Xia, G.S. Remote sensing image scene classification meets deep learning: Challenges, methods, benchmarks, and opportunities. *IEEE J. Sel. Top. Appl. Earth Obs. Remote Sens.* **2020**, *13*, 3735–3756. [CrossRef]
5. Goel, P.K.; Prasher, S.O.; Patel, R.M.; Landry, J.A.; Bonnell, R.; Viau, A.A. Classification of hyperspectral data by decision trees and artificial neural networks to identify weed stress and nitrogen status of corn. *Comput. Electron. Agric.* **2003**, *39*, 67–93. [CrossRef]
6. Wang, S.; Wang, X.; Zhang, L.; Zhong, Y. Auto-AD: Autonomous hyperspectral anomaly detection network based on fully convolutional autoencoder. *IEEE Trans. Geosci. Remote Sens.* **2021**, *60*, 1–14. [CrossRef]
7. Fu, X.; Jia, S.; Zhuang, L.; Xu, M.; Zhou, J.; Li, Q. Hyperspectral anomaly detection via deep plug-and-play denoising CNN regularization. *IEEE Trans. Geosci. Remote Sens.* **2021**, *59*, 9553–9568. [CrossRef]
8. Li, Z.; Wang, Y.; Xiao, C.; Ling, Q.; Lin, Z.; An, W. You only train once: Learning a general anomaly enhancement network with random masks for hyperspectral anomaly detection. *IEEE Trans. Geosci. Remote Sens.* **2023**, *61*, 1–18. [CrossRef]
9. Dong, X.; Bao, J.; Chen, D.; Zhang, W.; Yu, N.; Yuan, L.; Chen, D.; Guo, B. Cswin transformer: A general vision transformer backbone with cross-shaped windows. In Proceedings of the IEEE/CVF Conference on Computer Vision and Pattern Recognition, New Orleans, LA, USA, 18–24 June 2022; pp. 12124–12134.
10. Reed, I.S.; Yu, X. Adaptive multiple-band CFAR detection of an optical pattern with unknown spectral distribution. *IEEE Trans. Acoust. Speech Signal Process.* **1990**, *38*, 1760–1770. [CrossRef]
11. Li, J.; Zhang, H.; Zhang, L.; Ma, L. Hyperspectral anomaly detection by the use of background joint sparse representation. *IEEE J. Sel. Top. Appl. Earth Obs. Remote Sens.* **2015**, *8*, 2523–2533. [CrossRef]
12. Zhang, Y.; Du, B.; Zhang, L.; Wang, S. A low-rank and sparse matrix decomposition-based Mahalanobis distance method for hyperspectral anomaly detection. *IEEE Trans. Geosci. Remote Sens.* **2015**, *54*, 1376–1389. [CrossRef]
13. Li, W.; Du, Q. Collaborative representation for hyperspectral anomaly detection. *IEEE Trans. Geosci. Remote Sens.* **2014**, *53*, 1463–1474. [CrossRef]
14. Xu, Y.; Wu, Z.; Li, J.; Plaza, A.; Wei, Z. Anomaly detection in hyperspectral images based on low-rank and sparse representation. *IEEE Trans. Geosci. Remote Sens.* **2015**, *54*, 1990–2000. [CrossRef]
15. Liu, Z.; Lin, Y.; Cao, Y.; Hu, H.; Wei, Y.; Zhang, Z.; Lin, S.; Guo, B. Swin transformer: Hierarchical vision transformer using shifted windows. In Proceedings of the IEEE/CVF International Conference on Computer Vision, Montreal, QC, Canada, 10–17 October 2021; pp. 10012–10022.
16. Han, K.; Wang, Y.; Chen, H.; Chen, X.; Guo, J.; Liu, Z.; Tang, Y.; Xiao, A.; Xu, C.; Xu, Y.; et al. A survey on vision transformer. *IEEE Trans. Pattern Anal. Mach. Intell.* **2022**, *45*, 87–110. [CrossRef]
17. Vaswani, A.; Shazeer, N.; Parmar, N.; Uszkoreit, J.; Jones, L.; Gomez, A.N.; Kaiser, Ł.; Polosukhin, I. Attention is all you need. *Adv. Neural Inf. Process. Syst.* **2017**, *30*.
18. Dosovitskiy, A.; Beyer, L.; Kolesnikov, A.; Weissenborn, D.; Zhai, X.; Unterthiner, T.; Dehghani, M.; Minderer, M.; Heigold, G.; Gelly, S.; et al. An image is worth 16 × 16 words: Transformers for image recognition at scale. *arXiv* **2020**, arXiv:2010.11929.
19. Xu, Y.; Zhao, K.; Zhang, L.; Zhu, M.; Zeng, D. Hyperspectral anomaly detection with vision transformer and adversarial refinement. *Int. J. Remote Sens.* **2023**, *44*, 4034–4057. [CrossRef]
20. Huyan, N.; Zhang, X.; Quan, D.; Chanussot, J.; Jiao, L. AUD-Net: A unified deep detector for multiple hyperspectral image anomaly detection via relation and few-shot learning. *IEEE Trans. Neural Netw. Learn. Syst.* **2022**, *35*, 6835–6849. [CrossRef]
21. Wang, Z.; Ma, D.; Yue, G.; Li, B.; Cong, R.; Wu, Z. Self-supervised Hyperspectral Anomaly Detection Based on Finite Spatial-wise Attention. *IEEE Trans. Geosci. Remote Sens.* **2023**, *62*, 5502918.

22. Zhao, M.; Li, W.; Li, L.; Hu, J.; Ma, P.; Tao, R. Single-frame infrared small-target detection: A survey. *IEEE Geosci. Remote Sens. Mag.* **2022**, *10*, 87–119. [CrossRef]
23. Kingma, D.P.; Welling, M. Auto-encoding variational bayes. *arXiv* **2013**, arXiv:1312.6114.
24. Wei, J.; Zhang, J.; Xu, Y.; Xu, L.; Wu, Z.; Wei, Z. Hyperspectral anomaly detection based on graph regularized variational autoencoder. *IEEE Geosci. Remote Sens. Lett.* **2022**, *19*, 1–5. [CrossRef]
25. Zhang, J.; Xu, Y.; Zhan, T.; Wu, Z.; Wei, Z. Anomaly detection in hyperspectral image using 3D-convolutional variational autoencoder. In Proceedings of the 2021 IEEE International Geoscience and Remote Sensing Symposium IGARSS, Brussels, Belgium, 11–16 July 2021; IEEE: Piscataway, NJ, USA, 2021; pp. 2512–2515.
26. Jiang, H. A manifold constrained multi-head self-attention variational autoencoder method for hyperspectral anomaly detection. In Proceedings of the 2021 International Conference on Electronic Information Technology and Smart Agriculture (ICEITSA), Huaihua, China, 10–12 December 2021; IEEE: Piscataway, NJ, USA, 2021; pp. 11–17.
27. Wu, H.; Xiao, B.; Codella, N.; Liu, M.; Dai, X.; Yuan, L.; Zhang, L. Cvt: Introducing convolutions to vision transformers. In Proceedings of the IEEE/CVF International Conference on Computer Vision, Montreal, QC, Canada, 10–17 October 2021; pp. 22–31.
28. De Maesschalck, R.; Jouan-Rimbaud, D.; Massart, D.L. The mahalanobis distance. *Chemom. Intell. Lab. Syst.* **2000**, *50*, 1–18. [CrossRef]
29. Ma, Y.; Fan, G.; Jin, Q.; Huang, J.; Mei, X.; Ma, J. Hyperspectral anomaly detection via integration of feature extraction and background purification. *IEEE Geosci. Remote Sens. Lett.* **2020**, *18*, 1436–1440. [CrossRef]
30. Yao, W.; Li, L.; Ni, H.; Li, W.; Tao, R. Hyperspectral Anomaly Detection Based on Improved RPCA with Non-Convex Regularization. *Remote Sens.* **2022**, *14*, 1343. [CrossRef]
31. Fan, G.; Ma, Y.; Mei, X.; Fan, F.; Huang, J.; Ma, J. Hyperspectral Anomaly Detection With Robust Graph Autoencoders. *IEEE Trans. Geosci. Remote Sens.* **2022**, *60*, 5511314. [CrossRef]
32. Lian, J.; Wang, L.; Sun, H.; Huang, H. GT-HAD: Gated Transformer for Hyperspectral Anomaly Detection. *IEEE Trans. Neural Netw. Learn. Syst.* **2024**, 1–15. [CrossRef]

remote sensing

MDPI

Article

Remote Sensing Cross-Modal Text-Image Retrieval Based on Attention Correction and Filtering

Xiaoyu Yang [1], Chao Li [1], Zhiming Wang [1], Hao Xie [2], Junyi Mao [3] and Guangqiang Yin [1,2,4,*]

1 School of Information and Software Engineering, University of Electronic Science and Technology of China, Chengdu 611731, China; yangxy@std.uestc.edu.cn (X.Y.); 202012090915@std.uestc.edu.cn (C.L.); zmwang@std.uestc.edu.cn (Z.W.)

2 Shenzhen Institute for Advanced Study, University of Electronic Science and Technology of China, Shenzhen 518110, China; 202222280115@std.uestc.edu.cn

3 Faculty of Information Technology, Monash University, Melbourne, VIC 3800, Australia; jmao0023@student.monash.edu

4 Kashgar Regional Electronic Information Industry Technology Research Institute, Kashi 844000, China

* Correspondence: yingq@uestc.edu.cn

Abstract: Remote sensing cross-modal text-image retrieval constitutes a pivotal component of multi-modal retrieval in remote sensing, central to which is the process of learning integrated visual and textual representations. Prior research predominantly emphasized the overarching characteristics of remote sensing images, or employed attention mechanisms for meticulous alignment. However, these investigations, to some degree, overlooked the intricacies inherent in the textual descriptions accompanying remote sensing images. In this paper, we introduce a novel cross-modal retrieval model, specifically tailored for remote sensing image-text, leveraging attention correction and filtering mechanisms. The proposed model is architected around four primary components: an image feature extraction module, a text feature extraction module, an attention correction module, and an attention filtering module. Within the image feature extraction module, the Visual Graph Neural Network (VIG) serves as the principal encoder, augmented by a multi-tiered node feature fusion mechanism. This ensures a comprehensive understanding of remote sensing images. For text feature extraction, both the Bidirectional Gated Recurrent Unit (BGRU) and the Graph Attention Network (GAT) are employed as encoders, furnishing the model with an enriched understanding of the associated text. The attention correction segment minimizes potential misalignments in image-text pairings, specifically by modulating attention weightings in cases where there's a unique correlation between visual area attributes and textual descriptors. Concurrently, the attention filtering segment diminishes the influence of extraneous visual sectors and terms in the image-text matching process, thereby enhancing the precision of cross-modal retrieval. Extensive experimentation carried out on both the RSICD and RSITMD datasets, yielded commendable results, attesting to the superior efficacy of the proposed methodology in the domain of remote sensing cross-modal text-image retrieval.

Keywords: cross-modal retrieval; remote sensing; attention weight

1. Introduction

In recent years, the rapid development and application of remote sensing technology have led to an exponential increase in the quantity of optical remote sensing images [1]. Yet, the challenge arises when faced with the task of efficiently extracting invaluable insights from such vast repositories of data. Automatic remote sensing cross-modal retrieval has become a key area of research due to the exponential growth of optical remote sensing data. The increasing role of text in human-computer interactions has further heightened interest in cross-modal text-image retrieval for remote sensing applications.

Historically, remote sensing image retrieval predominantly relied on manual annotations to label each image, utilizing query text to match these annotations [2]. Given the exponential increase in remote sensing images, manual annotation has become increasingly labor-intensive. This shift has prompted a heightened interest in automated image captioning [3,4]. For instance, to derive more nuanced descriptions, Zhao et al. [5] introduced an approach grounded in fine-grained and structured attention, aimed at harnessing the structural attributes of semantic content in remote sensing imagery. Despite the advancements in automated subtitle generation, challenges persist. Primarily, two-stage retrieval models often encounter substantial information attrition in the intermediary phase [6], thereby compromising the retrieval's precision and completeness. Furthermore, captions generated by machines may inadequately encapsulate unique semantic nuances and intricacies of remote sensing images [7]. This raises the question of whether there exist more optimal methodologies than the conventional remote sensing text-image retrieval techniques for cross-modal retrieval tasks.

Historically, when the Image-Text Retrieval challenge first gained traction, the academic community primarily aimed to map text and images into a shared subspace using an end-to-end approach. Yet, recent developments have charted new territories. For instance, SCAN [8] employs region-level and word-level feature encoding for images and text respectively, subsequently utilizing stacked cross-modal attention for affinity computations. CAMP [9] masterfully orchestrates the cross-modal messaging flow, ensuring meticulous cross-modal interactions and adeptly managing discordant pairs and non-essential data through an adaptive gating strategy. VSRN [10] devises visual representations by inferring regional relationships and global semantic connotations. This enhanced representation aptly captures pivotal objects and semantic motifs in scenes, facilitating superior alignment with associated text. SGM [11] leverages dual scene graph modalities for text and images: visual and textual scene graphs. It introduces a scene graph alignment model and harnesses two graph encoders to derive object-level and relation-level features for image-text alignment.

However, it's imperative to note that the above strategies, tailored for natural scenes, falter when applied to remote sensing imagery [12]. Yuan et al. [12] attempted to fine-tune remote sensing images using methodologies from [8,9] and related works. The results were suboptimal, leading them to formulate a multi-scale visual self-attention module to sift through extraneous image features and deploy cross-modal guidance protocols for enhanced multi-modal representations. To forge a more direct nexus between remote sensing imagery and corresponding text, Cheng et al. [13] utilized attention and gating mechanisms, optimizing data characteristics to extract more potent feature representations. Recognizing the dearth of fine-grained object perception in existing remote sensing retrieval frameworks, Yuan et al. [14] recognized the lack of fine-grained object perception in existing remote sensing retrieval frameworks. They proposed an integrated approach that combines both global and granular data through a multi-tier information fusion module. This strategy enabled a deeper understanding of objects and their interrelations, thereby improving retrieval performance.

Notwithstanding the achievements in remote sensing image-text retrieval, there remain pertinent challenges warranting further exploration. Firstly, remote sensing imagery markedly contrasts with natural scenes. Natural scenes typically feature fewer, larger, and more distinctive objects, whereas remote sensing images are characterized by numerous, smaller, and less distinct entities. As a result, extracting regional features from remote sensing images using target detection methods, and then aligning them with textual word features, becomes paramount. Although this strategy excels in natural scene datasets, the extraction of pertinent image regional features remains an outstanding challenge. Secondly, prevalent methodologies employ Bidirectional Gated Recurrent Unit (BGRU) for textual word feature extraction, which predominantly factors in immediate positional word relationships. This overlooks distant word relationships, which could offer significant insights. Lastly, while numerous scholars have championed attention mechanism strategies for discerning granular alignment between images and text, current iterations of these mechanisms warrant refinements. Specifically, the current focus with regard to merely granular alignments may be myopic, potentially obscuring cases of partial alignments in discordant sample pairs. In congruent pairs, not all attention weights bear significance. The prevailing methodologies indiscriminately treat all attention weights, inadvertently incorporating inconsequential textual prepositions.

To address the aforementioned challenges, this study introduces a cross-modal retrieval algorithm for remote sensing image text based on similarity correction and filtering (ACF). The principal contributions of this research are outlined below:

- Enhanced Image Comprehension: To bolster the model's proficiency in deciphering remote sensing images, we have adopted the visual graph neural network (VIG) [15], as the primary image feature extraction mechanism. Moreover, a multi-tier node feature fusion module has been instituted, enabling the model to understand remote sensing images both at varied granularities and in their entirety.
- Optimized Text Understanding: This study leverages the BGRU model to extract word-level vector features from the text. Subsequently, the graph attention network (GAT) is employed to compute M word-level features that represent positional relationships. The culmination of this process involves the utilization of pooling to capture the overarching features of the textual content.
- Attention Correction Unit: We introduce a novel attention correction unit. Herein, the visual area features coupled with the textual word features are processed via the cross-attention module to generate attention weights. Subsequently, global similarity metrics are employed to rectify these attention weights. A distinct attention threshold is incorporated to recalibrate the attention weight, substantially mitigating the propensity for misalignment in discordant image-text pairs, especially when such misalignments arise from specific correlations between visual area attributes and textual words.
- Attention Filtering Unit: Recognizing that not all attention-derived information holds relevance, we propose an attention filtering unit. This study aims to discern the most pertinent attention weight, resonating with the visual area features and textual word attributes, and employs a secondary attention threshold to filter out inconsequential attention. This strategic approach attenuates the influence of non-essential visual zones and words when aligning image-text pairs, thus amplifying the likelihood of accurate matches.

To substantiate the superiority of the ACF approach, we orchestrated a series of comparative experiments across two remote sensing cross-modal retrieval datasets. Furthermore, a range of ablation studies were executed to dissect the efficacy of each individual module. The ensuing sections are structured as follows: Section 2 provides an overview of related work in remote sensing image text retrieval. Section 3 delves deep into the intricacies of the proposed modules. Section 4 is dedicated to a comprehensive presentation of our experimental validations, demonstrating the potency of our proposed methodology. Finally, Section 5 draws conclusions based on the research findings.

2. Related Work

2.1. Cross-Modal Text-Image Retrieval

Cross-modal retrieval is the process by which data from one modality is utilized to retrieve semantically consistent modal information from another modality [16]. Using the image and text modality as an illustration, images retrieve related texts that fall under the same category or topic. Image-text retrieval primarily follows two research trajectories: global matching and regional matching.

Global matching is designed to seamlessly embed both images and texts into a shared subspace, subsequently learning their semantic alignment through optimization using a ranking loss. Canonical correlation analysis is employed by both CCA [17] and DCCA [18] to ascertain the semantic representation of images and their corresponding texts. Given the exceptional performance of convolutional neural networks in image processing [19] and the superior performance of LSTM [20] and GRU [21] in the realm of natural language processing, R. Kiros et al. [22] innovatively introduced the CNN-LSTM architecture for the purpose of learning combined image-text embeddings. Following the advancements achieved by pre-trained models in Natural Language Processing(NLP), exemplified by BERT [23] and GPT [24], TOD-Net [25], introduced in 2021, refines text representations. This method overlays a pre-existing embedding system, altering the embedding space based on specific parameters.

Drawing inspiration from generative adversarial networks [26], analogous generative and adversarial learning strategies can be adopted for image-text matching tasks. This approach seeks to bridge the divergence between the two modalities. Tools like ACMR [27] and CM-GANs [28] incorporate a modal discriminator to discern the modal data of features, leveraging a traditional bidirectional network. When discrimination becomes unfeasible, the disparity between the two modalities is deemed to have been resolved. Additionally, GXN [29] exploits either text or visual features to produce images or captions, aiding in the diminishment of cross-modal informational gaps. Wen et al. [30] presented a cross-memory network equipped with pair recognition, designed to encapsulate shared knowledge across image and text modalities.

Furthermore, specialized mechanisms have been incorporated within global matching. DAN [31] implements an attention mechanism fortified by visual and textual elements. In the context of MTFN [32], Wang et al. conceived a reordering strategy to refine the ranking accuracy during test phases. In pursuit of holistic matching, MFM [33] employs a multifaceted representation of both images and texts, facilitating a comprehensive understanding and subsequently discerning the congruence between both modalities from various perspectives. Ji et al. [34] unveiled the Saliency-Guided Attention Network (SAN), which capitalizes on visual saliency detection, emphasizing visually significant regions or entities in images based on textual content.

The aforementioned methodologies primarily encode an entire image or text into a singular vector, and are thus categorized under global image-text matching methods. However, these techniques predominantly focus on the alignment of the overarching context of either the image or text, often neglecting the congruence between specific image regions and textual elements. This oversight is addressed by the subsequent regional image-text matching methodology.

Regional matching offers a nuanced approach to image-text pairing, associating distinct regions within an image to specific words in a text, as opposed to solely aligning overarching semantics. This method capitalizes on target detection [35] for image object identification, diverging from the conventional CNN for image feature extraction. Concurrently, the output from the text encoder transitions from a singular sentence vector to a word-centric matrix. Pioneering this approach in 2015, Karpathy et al. [36] presented a technique to identify objects in images, embedding them within a subspace. The associated similarity is determined by the cumulative similarities of each region-word pairing. This approach to determining image-text congruence has been further refined by subsequent studies [8,9,37,38], which have employed attention mechanisms to delineate the regional congruence between visual and linguistic elements. Specifically, BFAN [37] selectively omits irrelevant segments from mutual semantics, directing focus towards pertinent segments. PFAN [38] amplifies this by incorporating regional location data, introducing an integration strategy that emphasizes object location hints, augmenting the learning of visual-textual joint embeddings, and thereby achieving superior alignment. Several other studies [9,39–43] have further contributed to refining the outcomes of image-text retrieval.

A unique proposition involves constructing inherent structures and relationships among fragments within their individual modalities, and subsequently identifying distinct inter-structural semantic correlations between visual and textual elements. Specifically, relationships between visual and textual fragments are modeled by developing both a visual context-aware tree encoder (VCS-Tree) and a textual context-aware tree encoder (TCS-Tree) with mutual labels. This facilitates the concurrent learning and optimization of both visual and textual features.

Graphical structures adeptly depict object-centric relationships. However, a plethora of visual data cannot consistently be represented in grid-like formats such as visual graphs. This led to the introduction of graph neural networks (GNN) [44] as extensions of recurrent neural networks, enabling them to directly process graphs. This was further expanded upon with the introduction of the Graph Convolutional Network (GCN) [45] tailored for capturing visual relationships. Several contemporary studies [10,11,46–49] have further expanded on this foundational work, aiming to enhance either visual or textual features in the context of image-text alignment. For instance, SCG [46] develops a scene concept graph by extracting frequently co-occurring concept pairings as intrinsic scene knowledge. Subsequently, this base is expanded to incorporate additional semantic concepts, selectively merging them to enhance an image's semantic representation. CVSE [47] harnesses consensus data by calculating statistical co-occurrence correlations among semantic concepts within image datasets, employing the constructed concept correlation graph to produce consensus-aware concept representations. Meanwhile, GSMN [48] distinctly models objects, relationships, and attributes as a structured phrase. This not only identifies the correlations among objects, relationships, and attributes but also aids in recognizing the intricate congruences among structured phrases.

2.2. Remote Sensing Cross-Modal Text-Image Retrieval

RSCTIR involves using text to retrieve corresponding remote-sensing images. The heterogeneity-induced semantic gap renders the RSCTIR task particularly challenging. In terms of implementation, RSCTIR approaches can be broadly categorized into subtitle-based methods and embedding-based methods.

Subtitle-based methods are essentially two-stage retrieval approaches. In this approach, annotations are typically generated for each remote sensing (RS) image in the database through a subtitle generator. Subsequently, during the retrieval phase, the BLEU [50] metric is utilized to compute the similarity between the query text and the generated annotations. Qu et al. [51] employed multi-modal deep networks for the semantic understanding of high-resolution remote sensing images. To enhance the characterization of remote sensing images, Shi et al. [52] introduced a Deep Learning-based Remote Sensing Image Captioning (RSIC) framework, employing fully convolutional networks to semantically decompose terrestrial elements at various scales. Lu et al. [53] presented a large-scale RSIC dataset and conducted an extensive review to promote the RSIC mission. Sumbul et al. [54] introduced a summary-driven RSIC technique to address information deficits and evaluated its influence across several RS text-image datasets. Li et al. [4] formulated a truncated cross-entropy loss to mitigate the overfitting issue in RSIC. Addressing the computational demands of contemporary subtitle generators, Genc et al. [55] designed a support vector machine-based decoder that proves efficient with limited training samples. While subtitle-based RSCTIR methods [5,56–58] have matured, their two-stage nature inevitably introduces noise, potentially compromising retrieval accuracy.

Embedding-based RSCTIR techniques entail mapping RS images and text into a shared high-dimensional space. The cross-modal similarity is then ascertained using appropriate distance metrics. Abdullah et al. [59] introduced a deep bidirectional triplet network that derives joint encoding between multiple modalities and yields more robust embeddings. They implemented an average fusion approach to amalgamate features from multiple text-image pairings. Addressing multi-scale scarcity and target redundancy challenges in RSCITR, Yuan et al. [12] designed an asymmetric multi-modal feature matching network (AMFMN) and contributed a fine-grained RS image-text dataset for this task. Investigating potential associations between RS images and text, Cheng et al. [13] devised a semantic alignment module to capture more discriminative feature representations. Lv et al. [60] proposed a fusion-based correlation learning model for RS image-text retrieval, this approach bridges the heterogeneity gap by leveraging knowledge distillation. Alternatively, Yuan et al. [14] suggested a lightweight text-image retrieval model was designed to expedite RS cross-modal retrieval by employing knowledge extraction and contrastive learning, thereby improving retrieval performance.

3. Method

This section elucidates the Attention Correction and Filtering algorithm tailored for cross-modal retrieval in remote sensing image-text contexts. The comprehensive workflow is depicted in Figure 1.

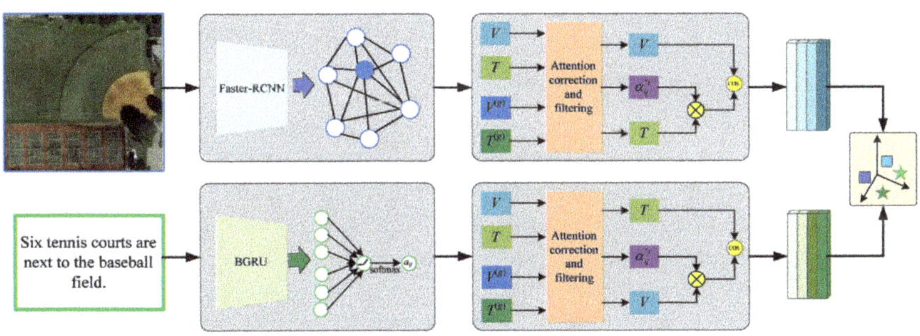

Figure 1. Overview of the proposed ACF.

Initially, in the context of image processing, the VIG is employed to extract image features. Building on this foundation, the fusion of low-level and mid-level node information produces N node details, which are subsequently treated as visual area features via the multi-scale fusion module.

For handling the textual aspect of remote sensing, a BGRU is employed to distill word-level vectors from the text. Following this, the Graph Attention Module is harnessed to derive M word-level attributes.

Subsequently, leveraging the features derived from the preceding two modules, a weight matrix is procured through the cross-attention module. This weight matrix is then scaled using global similarity metrics. To address information redundancy, only relevant weight details are retained. As such, the attention filtering module is employed to sieve out attention weights that are inconsequential to either the image or the text. To culminate, the model's training process synergistic ally integrates the Triplet loss function with global similarity measures.

3.1. Feature Extraction

3.1.1. Image Feature Extraction

Due to the complexity and particularity of remote sensing images, the object features obtained through the target detection algorithm need to be more representative. In order to extract valuable features from these object features, complex redundant operations are required, which undoubtedly increases the time required for retrieval. Process complexity. As a more flexible backbone network, the VIG [9] divides images into many blocks and treats them as nodes. Building graphs based on these nodes can better represent irregular and complex objects in the wild.

The intrinsic advantages of VIG address the challenges of meticulously extracting object features from remote sensing images. Therefore, this study adopts VIG as the backbone network for extracting remote sensing image features. Initially, each image is divided into 7 × 7 patches. Based on this, a multi-level node information fusion module is designed. The fusion of low-level and mid-level node features from the VIG results in 49 node features, which are used as visual region features. This approach enables the model to achieve a multi-level and comprehensive understanding of remote sensing images, as illustrated in Figure 2.

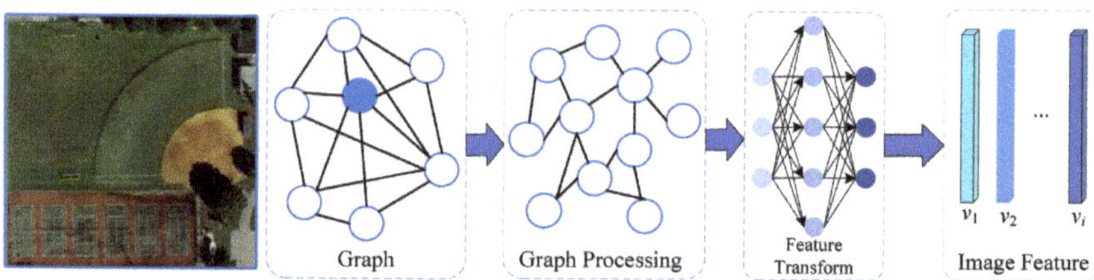

Figure 2. Image feature extraction module.

Within this module, node information from disparate levels is perceived as objects of varying dimensions. This data is then amalgamated, treating these object details as local insights. This approach compensates for the inadequacies of purely global perspectives, leading to the derivation of richer visual features, as represented in Equation (1). Subsequent to this, a global pooling mechanism is deployed to yield the visual global feature $V^{(g)}$. This feature is then synergized with the terminal layer attributes of the VIG, as depicted in Equation (2).

$$v_i = VIG(x_l, x_m), i \in [1, k] \tag{1}$$

$$v^{(g)} = VIG(x_l, x_m) \times x_t \tag{2}$$

3.1.2. Text Feature Extraction

To achieve a word-level representation of text, this study employs both the BGRU and the GAT as encoders, as depicted in Figure 3. For a specific text S, comprising m words, we represent these words using word vectors e_j. Acknowledging the significance of positional data within the sentence structure, these word vectors are channeled into the Bidirectional GRU network. This yields word feature representations, which are subsequently introduced into the GAT. This network is responsible for discerning and learning inter-word correlations, culminating in the final word features, denoted as h_j. This computational procedure is detailed in Equation (2). Subsequent to this phase, an average pooling strategy is employed to extract the global text feature, $T^{(g)}$ as elaborated upon in Equation (4).

$$h_j = GAT(\frac{\overrightarrow{GRU}(e_j, \overrightarrow{h}_{j-1}) + \overrightarrow{GRU}(e_j, \overrightarrow{h}_{j+1})}{2}), j \in [1, m] \tag{3}$$

$$T^{(g)} = \frac{1}{m} \sum\nolimits_{j=1}^{m} h_j \tag{4}$$

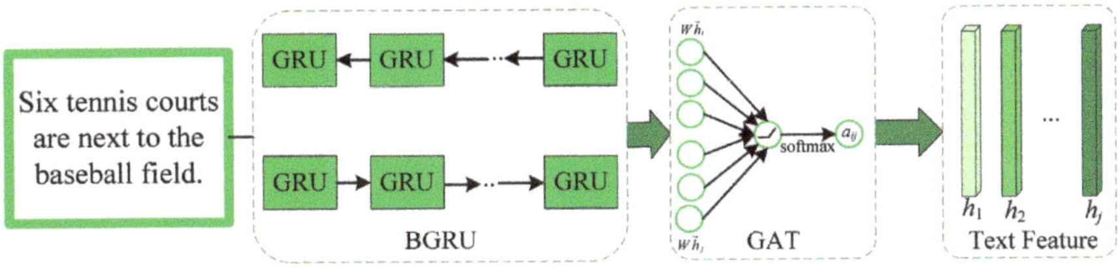

Figure 3. Text feature extraction module.

3.2. Attention Correction and Filtering

The focus of the attention mechanism should be appropriately directed towards the pertinent regions in images or relevant segments in text. The Attention Correction and Filtering module is structured in three sequential stages:

1. Cross-Attention Generation: In this phase, an attention weight matrix is derived using the cross-attention mechanism. This matrix characterizes the relationships between elements in the image and text modalities.
2. Attention Correction via Global Similarity: The initial attention weights are refined using a measure of global similarity.
   This refinement ensures that the attention mechanism is focused on semantically consistent areas of the image and corresponding segments of the text.
3. Attention Filtering for Relevance Determination: This stage identifies and retains only the most relevant attention weights. By concentrating on highly relevant areas, it eliminates non-essential regions or segments, thereby reducing noise in the attention mechanism.

The complete procedure is visually depicted in Figure 4. It's crucial to note that the aforementioned stages are bidirectional in nature. This means that the mechanism can operate in two modes: from images to text and vice versa (text-to-image). To facilitate a clearer understanding, the subsequent sections will elaborate on the image-to-text procedure, detailing each stage comprehensively.

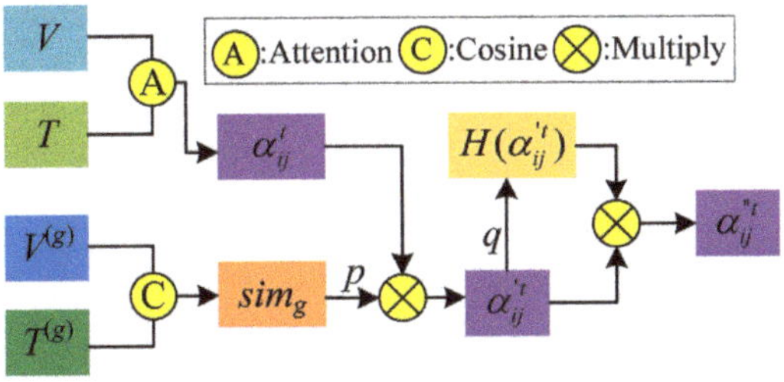

Figure 4. Attention correction and filtering flow chart.

3.2.1. Base Attention

In order to obtain the image-to-text attention weight s_{ij}, first calculate the similarity matrix between image-text pairs, which is obtained by calculating the cosine similarity between the image region feature v_i and the text word feature w_j, as shown in Equation (5).

$$s_{ij} = \frac{v_i^T w_j}{||v_i|| \, ||w_j||}, i \in [1,k], j \in [1,m] \tag{5}$$

Then regularize it to get $\overline{s_{ij}} = \frac{[s_{ij}]_+}{\sqrt{\sum_{i=1}^{k} [s_{ij}]_+^2}}$, where $[x]_+ = Max(x,0)$. The similarity matrix α_{ij}^t is then used to calculate the attention score of each region, as shown in Equation (6).

$$\alpha_{ij}^t = \frac{\exp(\lambda \overline{s_{ij}})}{\sum_{j=1}^{m} \exp(\lambda \overline{s_{ij}})} \tag{6}$$

where λ is the inverse temperature of similarity.

3.2.2. Attention Correction Unit

This study employs the similarity between the global features of images and text as a constraint for attention weights. This approach aims to diminish attention to irrelevant visual areas or text segments and instead prioritize semantically relevant regions in both images and text. The mathematical representation for this global similarity sim_g is provided in Equation (7).

$$sim_g = sim(v^{(g)}, T^{(g)}) = \frac{v^{(g)T} T^{(g)}}{||v^{(g)}|| \, ||T^{(g)}||} \tag{7}$$

This study introduces an attention weight threshold, denoted as p, to evaluate the magnitude of the global similarity. By multiplying this threshold with the attention matrix, we derive a new normalized attention weight matrix $\alpha_{ij}^{'t}$. This process is mathematically represented in Equations (8) and (9).

$$\overline{\alpha}_{ij}^t = (sim_g - p) \times \alpha_{ij}^t \tag{8}$$

$$\alpha_{ij}^{'t} = \frac{\overline{\alpha}_{ij}^t}{\sum_{j=1}^{m} \overline{\alpha}_{ij}^t} \tag{9}$$

Should the global similarity prove substantial, the local similarity will be proportionally amplified following the attention correction module. Conversely, if the global similarity is minimal, the local similarity will be proportionally diminished post-attention correction. In essence, the attention correction module mitigates the potential for mismatched image-text pairings that might arise from alignments between specific image areas and distinct text words.

3.2.3. Attention Filtering Unit

Given the redundancy in attention weights, it's evident that not all attention-weight data holds significance. This study seeks to identify the attention most pertinent to the text word features, namely, the visual area features with the highest attention weight. As a foundational step, we introduce an attention weight ratio threshold, denoted as q. This threshold evaluates the relationship between a given attention weight value and the maximal attention weight value. Any weight values below this threshold q are nullified. Following this, we derive a refreshed attention weight matrix post-normalization $\alpha_{ij}^{''t}$, as illustrated in Equations (10) and (11).

$$H(\alpha_{ij}^{'t}) = \begin{cases} \alpha_{ij}^{'t}, \left|\alpha_{ij}^{'t} - Max(\alpha_i^{'t})\right| < q \\ 0, other \end{cases} \tag{10}$$

$$\alpha_{ij}^{''t} = \frac{\alpha_{ij}^{'t} H(\alpha_{ij}^{'t})}{\sum_{j=1}^{m} \alpha_{ij}^{'t} H(\alpha_{ij}^{'t})} \tag{11}$$

In corresponding text-image pairs, the attention filtering module minimizes the impact of unrelated areas and words, ensuring that the attention weight predominantly concentrates on the matching visual areas and relevant words.

3.3. Loss Function

In the Attention Correction and Filtering section, attention is directed towards relevant words or visual areas. Subsequently, the final text vector α_i^t and image vector α_j^v are determined as illustrated in Equations (12) and (13).

$$\alpha_i^t = \sum\nolimits_{j=1}^{m} \alpha_{ij}^{''t} w_j \tag{12}$$

$$\alpha_j^v = \sum\nolimits_{i=1}^{k} \alpha_{ij}^{''t} v_i \tag{13}$$

The matching scores of text and image can then be derived from the two-way matching, as shown in Equation (14).

$$R(I,T) = \frac{1}{k} \sum\nolimits_{i=1}^{k} R(v_i, v_i) + \frac{1}{m} \sum\nolimits_{j=1}^{m} R(\alpha_j^v, w_j) \tag{14}$$

In remote sensing cross-modal retrieval, the triplet ranking loss function is frequently employed. In this study, we continue to use this loss function to align images and text. Furthermore, a global similarity metric is incorporated to jointly compute the loss value. The specific calculation is provided in Equation (15), where δ represents the minimum boundary value, $\widehat{I}$ denotes the remote sensing image that does not match the text T, $\widehat{T}$ represents the text that does not match the remote sensing image I, and L_g is the loss calculated based on global similarity.

$$L = [\delta - R(\widehat{I}, T) - R(I, T)]_+ + [\delta - R(I, \widehat{T}) - R(I, T)]_+ + L_g \tag{15}$$

4. Experiment

This section provides an overview of the datasets utilized, the evaluation metrics, and the specifics of the experiments conducted. We will compare and analyze two widely recognized remote sensing text-image datasets and validate the efficacy of the ACF model we've developed. Furthermore, we will conduct a series of ablation studies to delve into the underlying factors contributing to the superior performance of the ACF model.

4.1. Datasets and Evaluation Metrics

In our study, two prominent remote sensing text-image datasets, RSICD [12] and RSITMD [53], were employed. The RSICD dataset comprises 10,921 samples, with each sample containing a remote sensing image accompanied by five pertinent sentence descriptions; these images have a resolution of 224 × 224. The RSITMD dataset, on the other hand, consists of 4743 samples, and akin to the RSICD, each sample features a remote sensing image coupled with five sentence descriptions, albeit with an image resolution of 256 × 256. Notably, the RSITMD dataset offers a more intricate textual representation in comparison to the RSICD dataset, as illustrated in Figure 5. For the purposes of our experiment, the datasets were partitioned into a training set (comprising 80% of the data), a validation set (10%), and a test set (10%), in alignment with the methodology proposed by Yuan et al. [12].

To evaluate the model's efficacy, this study employs the R@K and mR metrics. R@K denotes the percentage of accurate matches within the top k retrieved results. For a comprehensive assessment, the experiment utilized R@1, R@5, and R@10 as metrics. Furthermore, mR, representing the mean value across multiple R@K values (specifically for K = 1, 5, 10), was employed to provide a holistic perspective on the model's performance.

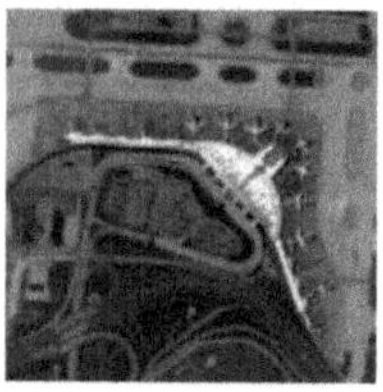

Cap1: Several buildings and green trees are around a piece of bareland.
Cap2: Some planes are parked near an airport with parking lot.
Cap3: Some planes are parked near an airport with parking lot.
Cap4: Several buildings and green trees are around a piece of bareland.
Cap5: Several buildings and green trees are around a piece of bareland.

(1)

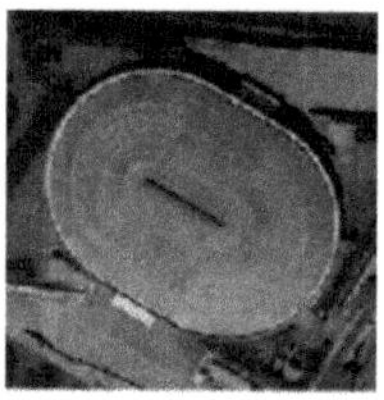

Cap1: A building with light blue roof in the middle.
Cap2: A oval building in the middle while with some intensive plants in side.
Cap3: A building in the middle while with light gray ground around.
Cap4: A oval building with light blue roof and white edge in the middle.
Cap5: An almost circle building is next to roads.

(2)

Figure 5. (1) is a sample in RSICD, and (2) is a sample in RSITMD. Each sample in both datasets contains five descriptions, but RSITMD's descriptions are more diverse.

4.2. Implementation Details

All experiments presented in this study were executed on an NVIDIA RTX8000 GPU. Despite the varying image sizes of the two primary datasets employed, for consistency, we resized all images to a dimension of 224 × 224 before feeding them into the model. To bolster the model's resilience to variations, a series of data augmentation techniques were applied to the training set's image data, including operations such as cropping and rotation.

For the extraction of textual features, the word vector's dimension was fixed at 300, while the features' dimension, used to compute the similarity between images and texts, was set at 512. Optimal thresholds for attention correction (p) and attention filtering (q) were identified through controlled parameter experimentation, settling at values of 0.3 and 0.1, respectively. As this study employs the triplet loss function, setting an appropriate margin is essential. Again, through parameter tuning, the most effective margin was determined to be 0.2.

Regarding the optimization of the model, the Adam optimizer was utilized. We adopted a batch size of 150 and set the initial learning rate at 0.001. A decay factor of 0.5 was applied every 20 epochs, and the model was trained for a total of 60 epochs. We leverage k-fold cross-validation to obtain an average result, and k is set to 5.

4.3. Parameter Experiment

This section delves into control experiments focused on three parameters: the attention correction threshold p, the attention filtering threshold q, and the triplet loss function margin δ. The baseline values for these parameters were initialized as follows: p was set at 0.1, q at 0.1, and δ at 0.2. Detailed experimental outcomes are visually represented in

Figure 6, and the specifics of each experimental run will be elucidated in the subsequent discussions.

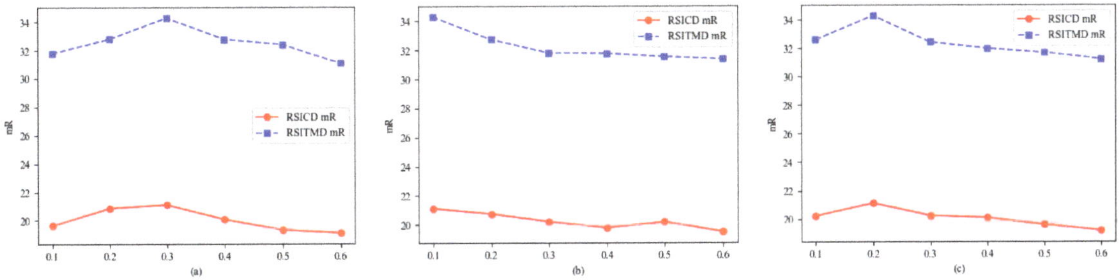

Figure 6. Parameter experiment results. (**a**) Attention correction threshold experiment results. (**b**) Attention filtering threshold experiment results. (**c**) Margin experiment results.

4.3.1. Attention Correction Threshold p

The attention correction threshold p, governs the modulation of attention weights. Its primary role is to mitigate the chances of erroneous matching in image-text pairs that are not inherently related, even if there seems to be a specific match between certain visual area features and text words. Setting p too low may render the scaling effect insignificant. Conversely, an excessively high value for p can negatively impact the matching likelihood of genuine positive samples.

To comprehensively assess the influence of p, experiments were conducted on two distinct datasets. In these experiments, the value of p was incrementally adjusted, ranging from 0.1 to 0.6. The outcomes of these experiments are tabulated in Table 1.

Table 1. Attention correction threshold experiment on RSICD dataset and RSITMD dataset.

	RSICD Dataset							**RSITMD Dataset**						
Thredhold	**Sentence Retrieval**			**Image Retrieval**			**mR**	**Sentence Retrieval**			**Image Retrieval**			**mR**
	R@1	**R@5**	**R@10**	**R@1**	**R@5**	**R@10**		**R@1**	**R@5**	**R@10**	**R@1**	**R@5**	**R@10**	
$p = 0.1$	6.92	19.76	30.34	5.94	20.82	33.94	19.62	13.72	30.31	44.47	9.87	37.12	55.66	31.78
$p = 0.2$	7.81	**20.71**	**31.88**	6.09	22.26	36.32	20.84	14.82	33.63	43.81	9.56	37.52	**57.52**	32.80
$p = 0.3$	**8.23**	20.31	30.47	**7.39**	**23.28**	**36.91**	**21.10**	**15.94**	**34.96**	**49.12**	**12.83**	37.74	55.53	**34.28**
$p = 0.4$	7.39	19.69	30.74	5.74	21.83	34.97	20.06	13.94	33.41	46.24	11.24	**38.36**	53.50	32.78
$p = 0.5$	5.95	18.21	31.47	5.58	21.06	33.65	19.32	13.32	33.54	46.28	10.90	38.18	56.69	32.40
$p = 0.6$	6.13	19.12	29.00	5.45	20.79	34.11	19.10	12.21	29.25	42.65	10.14	36.88	55.22	31.06

From Table 1, it is evident that while maintaining the initial values for the attention filtering threshold q and the triplet loss function margin δ, adjusting the attention correction threshold p to 0.3 enhances the model's performance across both datasets.

For the RSICD dataset, our model showcased superior performance in the image retrieval task across all three metrics. In the text retrieval task, we recorded the best results in R@1 and R@5. However, for R@10, there was a slight decrease of 0.4% and 1.41% respectively when compared to the results with $p = 0.2$.

On the RSITMD dataset, the model exhibited optimal performance in the text retrieval task for all three metrics. For the image retrieval task, while the model achieved the best results for R@1, there was a slight decrease of 0.62% for R@5 when compared to $p = 0.4$, and a 1.99% decrease for R@10 compared to $p = 0.2$. Despite these reductions, the model still demonstrates competitive and commendable results.

4.3.2. Attention Filtering Threshold q

When assessing the impact of the attention filtering threshold q, its primary role is to modulate the influence of unmatched or irrelevant visual areas and words in image-text pairs. By varying q within the range of 0.1 to 0.6 across the two datasets, we aim to understand its optimal value for maximum performance. The outcomes of these experiments can be found in Table 2.

Table 2. Attention filtering threshold experiment on rsicd dataset and rsitmd dataset.

Thredhold	RSICD Dataset							RSITMD Dataset						
	Sentence Retrieval			Image Retrieval			mR	Sentence Retrieval			Image Retrieval			mR
	R@1	R@5	R@10	R@1	R@5	R@10		R@1	R@5	R@10	R@1	R@5	R@10	
$q = 0.1$	**8.23**	**20.31**	30.47	**7.39**	**23.28**	**36.91**	**21.10**	**15.49**	**34.96**	49.12	**12.83**	37.74	55.53	**34.28**
$q = 0.2$	7.41	**20.04**	31.20	6.04	22.89	36.83	20.73	12.74	32.26	46.15	11.12	**38.21**	55.93	32.73
$q = 0.3$	**7.14**	20.40	**32.48**	**6.39**	**21.33**	33.39	20.19	12.65	31.06	44.78	11.30	36.78	54.31	31.81
$q = 0.4$	7.04	19.76	30.74	5.23	21.81	33.92	19.75	12.83	29.87	43.94	10.58	37.69	55.74	31.77
$q = 0.5$	7.50	20.21	31.38	6.37	21.06	34.47	20.16	12.26	30.58	43.41	10.25	36.70	**56.08**	31.54
$q = 0.6$	7.59	20.59	30.28	5.67	21.04	31.78	19.49	11.68	30.22	42.96	10.55	37.37	55.38	31.36

From Table 2, it's evident that without modifying the values of the attention correction threshold p and the triplet loss function margin δ, adjusting the attention filtering threshold q to 0.1 allows the model to excel in both retrieval directions on the RSICD dataset. In the context of image retrieval, optimal results were obtained. For text retrieval, peak results were noted in R@1 and R@5, although R@10 performance lagged slightly behind the outcomes achieved when q was set to 0.3.

For the RSITMD dataset, text retrieval metrics were all at their peak. In the image retrieval dimension, the model delivered the best results for R@1 and showed competitive performance for R@5—a mere 0.47% decline compared to when q was set to 0.2. For R@10, the performance drop was 0.55% in comparison to a q value of 0.5.

4.3.3. Margin δ

The triplet loss function optimizes the model by minimizing the distance between positive samples and maximizing the distance between negative samples. When the margin δ is small, the loss approaches 0, making it challenging to distinguish between positive and negative samples. Conversely, a larger margin δ suggests a greater expected distance between positive samples and a more substantial separation from negative samples. However, this can make network convergence more challenging.

Experiments were carried out on two datasets, adjusting the value of δ incrementally from 0.1 to 0.6. The findings of these experiments are presented in Table 3.

Table 3. Margin experiment on RSICD dataset and RSITMD dataset.

Margin	RSICD Dataset							RSITMD Dataset						
	Sentence Retrieval			Image Retrieval			mR	Sentence Retrieval			Image Retrieval			mR
	R@1	R@5	R@10	R@1	R@5	R@10		R@1	R@5	R@10	R@1	R@5	R@10	
$\delta = 0.1$	6.68	19.12	29.83	**6.92**	23.18	35.55	20.21	12.61	30.97	45.80	12.30	38.27	**55.66**	32.60
$\delta = 0.2$	**8.23**	**20.31**	30.47	**7.39**	**23.28**	**36.91**	**21.10**	**15.49**	**34.96**	**49.12**	**12.83**	**37.74**	55.53	**34.28**
$\delta = 0.3$	7.87	19.76	**31.56**	**6.68**	**21.48**	33.98	20.22	14.82	32.30	44.47	11.73	**38.41**	52.79	32.42
$\delta = 0.4$	6.68	17.38	30.56	6.62	22.78	36.45	20.08	12.70	32.03	44.16	10.31	37.31	55.38	31.98
$\delta = 0.5$	6.95	19.21	31.11	6.17	21.10	32.96	19.58	12.17	30.31	46.02	10.88	36.90	53.81	31.68
$\delta = 0.6$	5.76	17.84	28.82	5.56	21.35	35.66	19.17	11.50	31.86	45.58	9.16	36.81	52.26	31.19

From Table 3, we observe that by holding the initial values of the attention correction threshold p and the attention filtering threshold q constant, setting the triplet loss function margin δ to 0.2 enhances the model's performance in both retrieval directions. Specifically:

For the RSICD dataset: In the image retrieval tasks, the model achieves the best results. In text retrieval tasks, the model excels in R@1 and R@5 metrics. However, there is a decline of 1.09% in the R@10 metric when compared to $\delta = 0.3$.

For the RSITMD dataset: In text retrieval, the model outperforms the outcomes observed for other values of δ. Regarding the image retrieval task, the model's best performance is noted in the R@1 metric. However, there's a decrease of 0.67% in the R@5 metric relative to $\delta = 0.3$, and a 0.13% reduction in the R@10 metric compared to $\delta = 0.1$.

4.4. Comparison with the Other Methods

This study compares the performance of the ACF model with contemporary methods on the RSICD and RSITMD datasets. The results of this comparison are detailed in Table 4. The primary models under consideration include VSE++ [61], SCAN [8], CAMP [9], MTFN [32], CMFN [62], AMFMN [12] GaLR [63] and SWAN [64].

- VSE++ [61]: This model extracts image features using CNNs and text features using GRU. It employs the triplet loss function directly for model optimization.
- SCAN [8]: SCAN extracts image regional features via target detection and text word features using a bidirectional GRU. It subsequently aligns them finely using a cross-attention mechanism.
- CMAP [9]: CAMP utilizes a passing mechanism to adaptively control cross-modal information flow, producing the final result through cosine similarity.
- MTFN [23]: This model capitalizes on the fusion of various features to compute cross-modal similarity in an end-to-end manner.
- CMFN [62]: CMFN enhances retrieval performance by individually learning the feature interaction between query text and RS images and modeling the feature association between both modes, thus preventing information misalignment.
- LW-MCR [63]: This lightweight multi-scale cross-modal retrieval method leverages techniques such as knowledge distillation and contrast learning.
- AMFMN [12]: AMFMN employs a multi-scale self-attention module to derive image features. These features then guide text representation, and a dynamically variable triplet loss function optimizes the model.
- GaLR [64]: GaLR amalgamates image features from different levels using a multi-level information dynamic fusion module, eliminating redundancy in the process.
- SWAN [64]: SWAN uses a multi-scale fusion module to extract regional image features and then employs significant feature correlation to formulate a comprehensive image representation.

As presented in Table 4, the proposed ACF model achieves superior performance on the RSICD and RSITMD datasets compared to other methods. The experimental results on the RSICD dataset reveal that, in the text retrieval task, the ACF algorithm outperforms other methods in terms of R@1 and R@5 metrics, while the R@10 metric is slightly lower than that of the GaLR with MR method. In the image retrieval task, the ACF algorithm similarly surpasses other methods in R@1 and R@5 metrics, with the R@10 metric being slightly lower than that of the latest SWAN method. Notably, the ACF algorithm achieves an mR value of 21.10, demonstrating an improvement over other algorithms.

On the RSITMD dataset, the experimental results indicate that, in the text retrieval task, the ACF algorithm surpasses the latest SWAN algorithm across all metrics, achieving R@1, R@5, and R@10 values of 15.49%, 34.96%, and 49.12%, respectively. For the image retrieval task, the R@1 metric of the ACF algorithm is 1.59% higher than that of the SWAN algorithm, while the R@5 and R@10 metrics are slightly lower than the corresponding metrics of the SWAN algorithm. Finally, the ACF algorithm achieves an mR value of 34.28, representing a significant improvement over other algorithms. These results strongly validate the superiority of the ACF model and confirm the effectiveness of the attention weight correction and filtering method for cross-modal retrieval of remote sensing images and texts.

Table 4. Comparisons of retrieval performance on RSICD dataset and RSITMD dataset.

Thredhold	RSICD Dataset							RSITMD Dataset						
	Sentence Retrieval			Image Retrieval			mR	Sentence Retrieval			Image Retrieval			mR
	R@1	R@5	R@10	R@1	R@5	R@10		R@1	R@5	R@10	R@1	R@5	R@10	
VSE++	3.38	9.51	17.46	2.82	11.32	18.10	10.43	10.38	27.65	39.60	7.79	24.87	38.67	24.83
SCAN t2i	4.39	10.90	17.64	3.91	16.20	26.49	13.25	10.18	28.53	38.49	10.10	28.98	43.53	26.64
SCAN i2t	5.85	12.89	19.84	3.71	16.40	26.73	14.23	11.06	25.88	39.38	9.82	29.38	42.12	26.28
CAMP-triplet	5.12	12.89	21.12	4.15	15.23	27.81	14.39	11.73	26.99	38.05	8.27	27.79	44.34	26.20
CAMP-bce	4.20	10.24	15.45	2.72	12.76	22.89	11.38	9.07	23.01	33.19	5.22	23.32	38.36	22.03
MTFN	5.02	12.52	19.74	4.90	17.17	29.49	14.81	10.40	27.65	36.28	9.96	31.37	45.84	26.92
CMFM	5.40	18.66	28.55	5.31	18.57	30.03	17.75	10.84	28.76	40.04	10.00	32.83	47.21	28.28
LW-MCR(b)	4.57	13.71	20.11	4.02	16.47	28.23	14.52	9.07	22.79	38.05	6.11	27.74	49.56	25.55
LW-MCR(d)	3.29	12.52	19.93	4.66	17.51	30.02	14.66	10.18	28.98	39.82	7.79	30.18	49.78	27.79
AMFMN-soft	5.05	14.53	21.57	5.05	19.74	31.04	16.02	11.06	25.88	39.82	9.82	33.94	51.90	28.74
AMFMN-fusion	5.39	15.08	23.40	4.90	18.28	31.44	16.42	11.06	29.20	38.72	9.96	34.03	52.96	29.32
AMFMN-sim	5.21	14.72	21.57	4.08	17.00	30.60	15.53	10.63	24.78	41.81	11.51	34.69	54.87	29.72
GaLR *w/o* MR	6.50	18.91	29.70	5.11	19.57	31.92	18.62	13.05	30.09	42.70	10.47	36.34	53.35	31.00
GaLR with MR	6.59	19.85	**31.04**	4.69	19.48	32.13	18.96	14.82	31.64	42.48	11.15	36.68	51.68	31.41
SWAN	7.41	20.13	30.86	5.56	22.26	**37.41**	20.61	13.35	32.15	46.90	11.24	**40.40**	**60.60**	34.11
ACF (ours)	**8.23**	**20.31**	30.47	**7.39**	**23.28**	36.91	**21.10**	**15.49**	**34.96**	**49.12**	**12.83**	37.74	55.53	**34.28**

4.5. Ablation Study

In this section, we delve into ablation studies to assess the significance of each module within the proposed method. To ensure consistency, the hyperparameters were meticulously chosen based on prior parameter experiments. The series consists of five distinct experiments. The results for the RSICD dataset are documented in Table 5, whereas those for the RSITMD dataset can be found in Table 6.

Table 5. Ablation experiment on RSICD dataset.

M1	M2	M3	M4	M5	Sentence Retrieval			Image Retrieval			mR
					R@1	R@5	R@10	R@1	R@5	R@10	
					7.32	19.12	30.83	5.76	20.00	33.32	19.39
√					7.12	20.02	30.98	5.75	20.91	33.83	19.77
√	√				7.50	19.76	31.75	6.39	20.42	34.82	20.11
√	√	√			6.04	19.30	30.92	6.57	23.29	36.63	20.46
√	√	√	√		8.34	21.04	32.48	6.11	21.57	36.19	20.95
√	√	√	√	√	8.23	20.31	30.47	7.39	23.28	36.91	21.10

Table 6. Ablation experiment on RSITMD dataset.

M1	M2	M3	M4	M5	Sentence Retrieval			Image Retrieval			mR
					R@1	R@5	R@10	R@1	R@5	R@10	
					11.95	28.23	41.11	10.95	34.94	51.35	29.75
√					13.76	31.02	42.57	11.05	36.08	51.81	31.05
√	√				16.59	32.08	44.49	11.55	37.70	53.05	32.61
√	√	√			12.83	33.19	48.89	11.50	37.88	54.91	33.20
√	√	√	√		14.16	34.51	48.23	12.92	38.67	54.87	33.89
√	√	√	√	√	15.49	34.96	49.12	12.83	37.74	55.53	34.28

This detailed breakdown aims to elucidate the contribution of each module to the overall effectiveness of our approach.

- M1: Incorporates the GAT for text feature extraction.
- M2: Pertains to image feature extraction supplemented with a multi-scale fusion module.
- M3: Involves the attention correction unit.
- M4: Introduces the attention filtering unit.
- M5: Adds a global similarity component.

On the RSICD dataset:

- With the inclusion of the M1 module, there was a rise in the mR score of the model by 0.38.
- Upon the integration of the M2 module, the mR score experienced an increment of 0.72. This marked a 0.34 rise compared to the addition of M1 alone.
- Introducing the M3 module further augmented the mR score by 1.07. This denotes an enhancement of 0.35 when stacked against the combined addition of M1 and M2. Notably, at this juncture, the model topped the R@5 metric in the image retrieval task.
- The addition of the M4 module propelled the mR score by 1.56, showcasing an improvement of 0.49 over the previous configuration. This configuration yielded the best performance in the realm of text retrieval.
- Finally, with all modules incorporated, the model's mR score surged by 1.71. In terms of image retrieval, the model outperformed its peers in the R@1 and R@10 metrics.

This progression underlines the cumulative efficacy of each module and their combined influence in enhancing the model's performance.

On the RSITMD dataset:

- With the integration of the M1 module, there was an increase in the mR score of the model by 1.3.
- Upon adding the M2 module, the mR score surged by 2.86, marking an enhancement of 1.56 compared to the sole addition of M1. Remarkably, during this phase, the model achieved pinnacle performance in the R@1 metric of text retrieval.
- Introducing the M3 module further augmented the mR score to 3.45. This denotes a rise of 0.59 when juxtaposed against the cumulative addition of M1 and M2.
- The inclusion of the M4 module propelled the mR score to 4.14, showcasing an improvement of 0.69 over the prior configuration. At this stage, the model clinched the top spot in the R@1 and R@5 metrics for image retrieval.
- Ultimately, when all modules were incorporated, the model's mR score reached 4.53. It stood out in the R@10 metric for image retrieval and achieved premier results in both R@5 and R@10 metrics for text retrieval.

This trajectory highlights the combined impact of each module in driving the model's performance on the RSITMD dataset to new heights.

4.6. Visual Analysis of Retrieval Results

In the following subsection, we provide a visual analysis to offer an intuitive comparison of performance disparities across several retrieval models. We have chosen the GaLR, AMFMN, and LW-MCR models to compare against our proprietary model. These experiments were performed on the RSITMD dataset, and the comparative visuals are depicted in Figure 7. Within these visuals, a green box signifies a correct match, whereas a red box indicates an incorrect match. This distinction aids in an immediate and clear understanding of each model's efficacy in retrieval tasks.

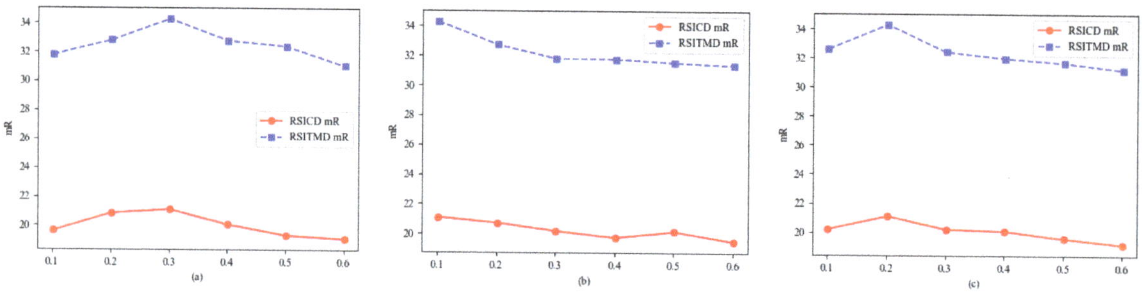

Figure 7. Visualization of retrieval results.

Based on the visualized results, it is evident that our method is proficient in retrieving accurate results even within intricate RS scenes. Our model's overall visualization underscores its ability to discern detailed and exhaustive correlations between images and textual sentences, thanks to the attention correction and filtering mechanisms. When juxtaposed with the GaLR, AMFMN, and LW-MCR models, our approach demonstrates superior retrieval outcomes.

5. Conclusions

This study introduces a novel cross-modal retrieval model tailored for remote-sensing image-text associations, leveraging attention correction and filtering. The model is structured around four primary components: an image feature extraction module, a text feature extraction module, an attention correction unit, and an attention filtering unit. The image feature extraction module utilizes the VIG as its encoder, this module incorporates a multi-level node feature fusion design. This ensures the model's comprehensive understanding of remote-sensing images across multiple layers. The text feature extraction module employs both BGRU and the GAT as encoders, this module enhances the model's depth of textual comprehension. The attention correction unit addresses mismatches in image-text pairings caused by specific alignments between visual features and textual words. It accomplishes this by adjusting the attention weights. The attention filtering unit enhances the precision of cross-modal retrieval by reducing the influence of unrelated visual zones and text, thereby streamlining the matching process within image-text pairs. Experimental evaluations conducted on the RSICD and RSITMD datasets underscore the excellence of the ACF model. Furthermore, ablation studies affirm the individual effectiveness of each module.

Author Contributions: X.Y.: Conceptualization, Methodology, Software; C.L.: Software; Z.W.: Formal analysis; H.X.: Validation; J.M.: Formal analysis; G.Y.: Data curation, Supervision, Writing original draft, Writing review editing. All authors have read and agreed to the published version of the manuscript.

Funding: This research was funded and supported by Kashgar Science and Technology Plan Project (KS2023024).

Data Availability Statement: Please check the details through this link: https://github.com/Huey-uestc/ACF (accessed on 20 January 2025).

Conflicts of Interest: The authors declare no conflicts of interest.

References

1. Li, Y.; Ma, J.; Zhang, Y. Image retrieval from remote sensing big data: A survey. *Inf. Fusion* **2021**, *67*, 94–115. [CrossRef]
2. Shyu, C.R.; Klaric, M.; Scott, J.G. GeoIRIS: Geospatial information retrieval and indexing system—Content mining, semantics modeling, and complex queries. *IEEE Trans. Geosci. Remote Sens.* **2007**, *45*, 839–852. [CrossRef]
3. Kandala, H.; Saha, S.; Banerjee, B. Exploring transformer and multilabel classification for remote sensing image captioning. *IEEE Geosci. Remote Sens. Lett.* **2022**, *19*, 1–5. [CrossRef]

4. Li, X.; Zhang, X.; Huang, W. Truncation cross entropy loss for remote sensing image captioning. *IEEE Trans. Geosci. Remote Sens.* **2020**, *59*, 5246–5257. [CrossRef]
5. Zhao, R.; Shi, Z.; Zuo, Z. High-resolution remote sensing image captioning based on structured attention. *IEEE Trans. Geosci. Remote Sens.* **2021**, *60*, 1–14. [CrossRef]
6. Hoxha, G.; Melgani, F.; Demir, B. Toward remote sensing image retrieval under a deep image captioning perspective. *IEEE J. Sel. Top. Appl. Earth Observ. Remote Sens.* **2020**, *13*, 4462–4475. [CrossRef]
7. Hoxha, G.; Melgani, F.; Demir, B. Retrieving images with generated textual descriptions. In Proceedings of the IGARSS 2019—2019 IEEE International Geoscience and Remote Sensing Symposium, Yokohama, Japan, 28 July–2 August 2019; pp. 5812–5815.
8. Lee, K.H.; Chen, X.; Hua, G.; Hu, H.; He, X. Stacked cross attention for image-text matching. In Proceedings of the Computer Vision—ECCV 2018: 15th European Conference, Munich, Germany, 8–14 September 2018; pp. 201–216.
9. Wang, Z.; Liu, X.; Li, H.; Sheng, L.; Yan, J.; Wang, X.; Shao, J. CAMP: Cross-modal adaptive message passing for textimage retrieval. In Proceedings of the IEEE/CVF International Conference on Computer Vision (ICCV), Seoul, Republic of Korea, 27 October–2 November 2019; pp. 5764–5773.
10. Li, K.; Zhang, Y. Visual semantic reasoning for image-text matching. In Proceedings of the IEEE/CVF International Conference on Computer Vision (ICCV), Seoul, Republic of Korea, 27 October–2 November 2019; pp. 4654–4662.
11. Wang, S.; Wang, R.; Yao, Z. Cross-modal scene graph matching for relationship-aware image-text retrieval. In Proceedings of the 2020 IEEE Winter Conference on Applications of Computer Vision (WACV), Snowmass, CO, USA, 1–5 March 2020; pp.1508–1517.
12. Yuan, Z.; Zhang, W.; Fu, K. Exploring a Fine-Grained Multiscale Method for Cross-Modal Remote Sensing Image Retrieval. *arXiv* **2022**, arXiv:2204.09868. [CrossRef]
13. Cheng, Q.; Zhuo, Y.; Fu, P. A deep semantic alignment network for the cross-modal image-text retrieval in remote sensing. *IEEE J. Sel. Top. Appl. Earth Observ. Remote Sens.* **2021**, *14*, 4284–4297. [CrossRef]
14. Yuan, Z.; Zhang, W.; Tian, C. Remote sensing cross-modal text-image retrieval based on global and local information. *IEEE Trans. Geosci. Remote Sens.* **2022**, *60*, 1–16. [CrossRef]
15. Han, K.; Wang, Y.; Guo, J. Vision GNN: An Image is Worth Graph of Nodes. In Proceedings of the 36th International Conference on Neural Information Processing Systems, New Orleans, LA, USA, 28 November–9 December 2022; pp. 1–16.
16. Peng, Y.; Huang, X.; Zhao, Y. An overview of cross-media retrieval: Concepts, methodologies, benchmarks, and challenges. *IEEE Trans. Circuits Syst. Video Technol.* **2017**, *28*, 2372–2385. [CrossRef]
17. Hardoon, D.R.; Szedmak, S.; Shawe, J. Canonical correlation analysis: An overview with application to learning methods. *Neural Comput.* **2004**, *16*, 2639–2664. [CrossRef] [PubMed]
18. Andrew, G.; Arora, R.; Bilmes, J. Deep canonical correlation analysis. In Proceedings of the 30th International Conference on Machine Learning, Atlanta, GA, USA, 16–21 June 2013; pp. 1247–1255.
19. Krizhevsky, A.; Sutskever, I.; Hinton, G.E. Imagenet classification with deep convolutional neural networks. *Commun. ACM* **2017**, *60*, 84–90. [CrossRef]
20. Hochreiter, S.; Schmidhuber, J. Long short-term memory. *Neural Comput.* **1997**, *9*, 1735–1780. [CrossRef] [PubMed]
21. Cho, K.; Merrienboer, B.V.; Gulcehre, C. Learning phrase representations using RNN encoder-decoder for statistical machine translation. *Comput. Sci.* **2014**, *1*, 1–15.
22. Kiros, R.; Salakhutdinov, R.; Zemel, R.S. Unifying visual-semantic embeddings with multimodal neural language models. *arXiv* **2014**, arXiv:1411.2539.
23. Devlin, J.; Chang, M.W.; Lee, K. Bert: Pre-training of deep bidirectional transformers for language understanding. *arXiv* **2018**, arXiv:1810.04805.
24. Radford, A.; Narasimhan, K.; Salimans, T. Improving Language Understanding by Generative Pre-Training. 2018. Available online: https://hayate-lab.com/wp-content/uploads/2023/05/43372bfa750340059ad87ac8e538c53b.pdf (accessed on 25 January 2025).
25. Matsubara, T. Target-oriented deformation of visual-semantic embedding space. *IEICE Trans. Inf. Syst.* **2021**, *104*, 24–33. [CrossRef]
26. Goodfellow, I.; Pouget, J.; Mirza, M. Generative adversarial networks. *Commun. ACM* **2020**, *63*, 139–144. [CrossRef]
27. Wang, B.; Yang, Y.; Xu, X. Adversarial cross-modal retrieval. In Proceedings of the ACM Multimedia Conference, Mountain View, CA, USA, 23–27 October 2017; pp. 154–162.
28. Peng, Y.; Qi, J. CM-GANs: Cross-modal generative adversarial networks for common representation learning. *ACM Trans. Multimed. Comput. Commun. Appl.* **2019**, *15*, 1–24. [CrossRef]
29. Gu, J.; Ha, J.C.; Joty, S.R. Look, imagine and match: Improving textual-visual cross-modal retrieval with generative models. In Proceedings of the 2018 IEEE/CVF Conference on Computer Vision and Pattern Recognition (CVPR), Salt Lake City, UT, USA, 18–23 June 2018; pp. 7181–7189.
30. Wen, X.; Han, Z.; Liu, Y.S. CMPD: Using cross memory network with pair discrimination for image-text retrieval. *IEEE Trans. Circuits Syst. Video Technol.* **2020**, *31*, 2427–2437. [CrossRef]
31. Nam, H.; Ha, J.W.; Kim, J. Dual attention networks for multimodal reasoning and matching. In Proceedings of the 2017 IEEE Conference on Computer Vision and Pattern Recognition (CVPR), Honolulu, HI, USA, 21–26 July 2017; pp. 299–307.

32. Wang, T.; Xu, X.; Yang, Y. Matching images and text with multi-modal tensor fusion and re-ranking. In Proceedings of the 27th ACM International Conference on Multimedia, Nice, France, 21–25 October 2019; pp. 12–20.
33. Ma, L.; Jiang, W.; Jie, Z. Matching image and sentence with multi-faceted representations. *IEEE Trans. Circuits Syst. Video Technol.* **2019**, *30*, 2250–2261. [CrossRef]
34. Ji, Z.; Wang, H.; Han, J. Saliency-guided attention network for image-sentence matching. In Proceedings of the IEEE/CVF International Conference on Computer Vision (ICCV), Seoul, Republic of Korea, 27 October–2 November 2019; pp. 5754–5763.
35. Ren, S.; He, K.; Girshick, R. Faster rcnn: Towards real-time object detection with region proposal networks. *IEEE Trans. Pattern Anal. Mach. Intell.* **2016**, *39*, 1137–1149. [CrossRef]
36. Karpathy, A.; Li, F.F. Deep visual-semantic alignments for generating image descriptions. In Proceedings of the 2015 IEEE Conference on Computer Vision and Pattern Recognition (CVPR), Boston, MA, USA, 7–12 June 2015; pp. 3128–3137.
37. Liu, C.; Mao, Z.; Liu, A. Focus your attention: A bidirectional focal attention network for image-text matching. In Proceedings of the 27th ACM International Conference on Multimedia, Nice, France, 21–25 October 2019; pp. 3–11.
38. Wang, Y.; Yang, H.; Qian, X. Position focused attention network for image-text matching. *arXiv* **2019**, arXiv:1907.09748.
39. Zhang, Q.; Lei, Z.; Zhang, Z. Context-aware attention network for image-text retrieval. In Proceedings of the IEEE/CVF Conference on Computer Vision and Pattern Recognition (CVPR), Seattle, WA, USA, 13–19 June 2020; pp. 3536–3545.
40. Chen, H.; Ding, G.; Liu, X. Imram: Iterative matching with recurrent attention memory for cross-modal image-text retrieval. In Proceedings of the IEEE/CVF Conference on Computer Vision and Pattern Recognition (CVPR), Seattle, WA, USA, 13–19 June 2020; pp. 12655–12663.
41. Ji, Z.; Chen, K.; Wang, H. Step-wise hierarchical alignment network for image-text matching. *arXiv* **2021**, arXiv:2106.06509.
42. Liu, Y.; Wang, H.; Meng, F. Attend, Correct And Focus: A Bidirectional Correct Attention Network For Image-Text Matching. In Proceedings of the 2021 IEEE International Conference on Image Processing (ICIP), Anchorage, AK, USA, 19–22 September 2021; pp. 2673–2677.
43. Ge, X.; Chen, F.; Jose, J.M. Structured multi-modal feature embedding and alignment for image-sentence retrieval. In Proceedings of the 29th ACM International Conference on Multimedia, Virtual, 20–24 October 2021; pp. 5185–5193.
44. Scarselli, F.; Gori, M.; Tsoi, A.C. The graph neural network model. *IEEE Trans. Neural Netw.* **2008**, *20*, 61–80. [CrossRef]
45. Kipf, T.N.; Welling, M. Semi-supervised classification with graph convolutional networks. *arXiv* **2016**, arXiv:1609.02907.
46. Shi, B.; Ji, L.; Lu, P. Knowledge Aware Semantic Concept Expansion for Image-Text Matching. In Proceedings of the Twenty-Eighth International Joint Conference on Artificial Intelligence (IJCAI-19), Macao, China, 10–16 August 2019; pp. 5182–5189.
47. Wang, H.; Zhang, Y.; Ji, Z. Consensus-aware visual-semantic embedding for image-text matching. In Proceedings of the 2020 European Conference on Computer Vision, Glasgow, UK, 23–28 August 2020; pp. 18–34.
48. Liu, C.; Mao, Z.; Zhang, T. Graph structured network for image-text matching. In Proceedings of the IEEE/CVF Conference on Computer Vision and Pattern Recognition (CVPR), Seattle, WA, USA, 13–19 June 2020; pp. 10921–10930.
49. Nguyen, M.D.; Nguyen, B.T.; Gurrin, C. A deep local and global scene-graph matching for image-text retrieval. *arXiv* **2021**, arXiv:2106.02400.
50. Papineni, K.; Roukos, S.; Ward, T.; Zhu, W.J. BLEU: A method for automatic evaluation of machine translation. In Proceedings of the 40th Annual Meeting on Association for Computational Linguistics, Philadelphia, PA, USA, 7–12 July 2002; pp. 311–318.
51. Qu, B.; Li, X.; Tao, D.; Lu, X. Deep semantic understanding ofhigh resolution remote sensing image. In Proceedings of the 2016 International Conference on Computer, Information and Telecommunication Systems (CITS), Kunming, China, 6–8 July 2016; pp. 1–5.
52. Shi, Z.; Zou, Z. Can a machine generate humanlike language descriptions for a remote sensing image? *IEEE Trans. Geosci. Remote Sens.* **2017**, *55*, 3623–3634. [CrossRef]
53. Lu, X.; Wang, B.; Zheng, X. Exploring models and data for remote sensing image caption generation. *IEEE Trans. Geosci. Remote Sens.* **2017**, *56*, 2183–2195. [CrossRef]
54. Sumbul, G.; Nayak, S.; Demir, B. SD-RSIC: Summarization-driven deep remote sensing image captioning. *IEEE Trans. Geosci. Remote Sens.* **2020**, *59*, 6922–6934. [CrossRef]
55. Hoxha, G.; Melgani, F. A novel SVM-based decoder for remote sensing image captioning. *IEEE Trans. Geosci. Remote Sens.* **2021**, *60*, 1–14. [CrossRef]
56. Wang, Q.; Huang, W.; Zhang, X. Word–sentence framework for remote sensing image captioning. *IEEE Trans. Geosci. Remote Sens.* **2020**, *59*, 10532–10543. [CrossRef]
57. Wang, B.; Zheng, X.; Qu, B. Retrieval topic recurrent memory network for remote sensing image captioning. *IEEE J. Sel. Top. Appl. Earth Observ. Remote Sens.* **2020**, *13*, 256–270. [CrossRef]
58. Zhang, Z.; Zhang, W.; Yan, M. Global visual feature and linguistic state guided attention for remote sensing image captioning. *IEEE Trans. Geosci. Remote Sens.* **2021**, *60*, 1–16. [CrossRef]
59. Abdullah, T.; Bazi, Y.; Rahhal, M.M.A.; Mekhalfi, M.L.; Rangarajan, L.; Zuair, M. TextRS: Deep bidirectional triplet network for matching text to remote sensing images. *Remote Sens.* **2021**, *12*, 405. [CrossRef]

60. Lv, Y.; Xiong, W.; Zhang, X. Fusion-based correlation learning model for cross-modal remote sensing image retrieval. *IEEE Geosci. Remote Sens. Lett.* **2021**, *19*, 1–5. [CrossRef]
61. Faghri, F.; Fleet, D.J.; Kiros, J.R.; Fidler, S. Vse++: Improving visual-semantic embeddings with hard negatives. *arXiv* **2017**, arXiv:1707.05612.
62. Yu, H.; Yao, F.; Lu, W. Text-Image Matching for Cross-Modal Remote Sensing Image Retrieval via Graph Neural Network. *IEEE J. Sel. Top. Appl. Earth Observ. Remote Sens.* **2023**, *16*, 812–824. [CrossRef]
63. Yuan, Z. A lightweight multi-scale crossmodal text-image retrieval method in remote sensing. *IEEE Trans. Geosci. Remote Sens.* **2021**, *60*, 1–19. [CrossRef]
64. Pan, J.; Ma, Q.; Cong, B. Reducing Semantic Confusion: Scene-aware Aggregation Network for Remote Sensing Cross-modal Retrieval.. In Proceedings of the 2023 ACM International Conference on Multimedia Retrieval, Thessaloniki, Greece, 12–15 June 2023; pp. 398–406.

remote sensing

MDPI

Article

A Lightweight and Adaptive Image Inference Strategy for Earth Observation on LEO Satellites

Bo Wang, Yuhang Fang, Dongyan Huang *, Zelin Lu and Jiaqi Lv

School of Information and Communication, Guilin University of Electronic Technology, Guilin 541004, China; wangbo@guet.edu.com (B.W.); 1972564665@mails.guet.edu.cn (Y.F.); lzl90648@mails.guet.edu.cn (Z.L.); ljq576453618@mails.guet.edu.cn (J.L.)
* Correspondence: huangdongyan@guet.edu.cn

Abstract: Low Earth Orbit (LEO) satellite equipped with image inference capabilities (LEO-IISat) offer significant potential for Earth Observation (EO) missions. However, the dual challenges of limited computational capacity and unbalanced energy supply present significant obstacles. This paper introduces the Accuracy-Energy Efficiency (AEE) index to quantify inference accuracy unit of energy consumption and evaluate the inference performance of LEO-IISat. It also proposes a lightweight and adaptive image inference strategy utilizing the Markov Decision Process (MDP) and Deep Q Network (DQN), which dynamically optimizes model selection to balance accuracy and energy efficiency under varying conditions. Simulations demonstrate a 31.3% improvement in inference performance compared to a fixed model strategy at the same energy consumption, achieving a maximum inference accuracy of 91.8% and an average inference accuracy of 89.1%. Compared to MDP-Policy Gradient and MDP-Q Learning strategies, the proposed strategy improves the AEE by 12.2% and 6.09%, respectively.

Keywords: LEO satellites; EO; image inference; energy efficiency; lightweight models

1. Introduction

Low Earth Orbit (LEO) satellite networks (LSNs) are a foundational enabler for achieving global seamless coverage in the sixth-generation mobile communication network (6G) [1]. With the rapid advancement of technology and the continuous expansion of application scenarios, LSNs have gradually transformed from traditional communication network forms into integrated networks that combine communication, sensing, and computing functions [2].

In this context, the use of LEO satellites equipped with image inference capabilities (LEO-IISat) offers significant advantages for Earth Observation (EO) [3]. Traditional EO approaches require transmitting observation data to ground stations for image inference, which consumes communication resources and results in high latency [4]. By performing image inference directly on LEO-IISat, only critical results need to be transmitted [5]. This approach reduces bandwidth pressure and inference latency, thereby improving real-time performance and operational efficiency [6].

Although LEO-IISat has significant advantages in EO, it still faces two major challenges. First, due to the limited physical size of LEO-IISat, their computational resources are relatively constrained, making the execution of high-complexity convolutional neural network (CNN) image inference tasks on LEO-IISat highly challenging [7]. Second, LEO-IISat rely on solar panels for power, and their energy supply is subject to limitations. Furthermore, because LEO-IISat alternate between sunlit and shadowed regions during their orbital operation, their energy supply experiences periodic fluctuations, which can lead to interruptions or instability in image inference tasks, further complicating resource allocation and task scheduling [8].

To address the challenge of limited on-board computational resources, Reference [9] introduced a lightweight deep neural network (DNN) based on U-Net for satellite cloud detection tasks. By compressing the dataset, the processing time was reduced from 5.408 s per million pixels to 0.12 s, while average memory consumption decreased by approximately 30%. Similarly, Reference [10] focused on real-time images classification for meteorological satellites. By reducing the neural network depth and the number of parameters, inference time was reduced to 3.3 milliseconds, achieving 93.6% accuracy.

To address energy constraints and unstable supply, Reference [11] reduced energy consumption by optimizing images distribution and compression parameters in real-time, ultra-high-resolution EO scenarios. This optimization doubled the number of supported images processing tasks and reduced energy use by 11% for volcanic imaging missions. Reference [12] proposed an algorithm capable of minimizing satellite energy consumption while meeting latency constraints, achieving up to 18% energy savings. However, References [9–12] focus primarily on individual challenges, and comprehensive studies on optimizing EO missions under the dual constraints of LEO-IISat computational and energy resources are still limited.

In this study, we employ MDP-QL and MDP-PG as benchmark methods to evaluate the performance of MDP-DQN in satellite inference optimization. MDP-QL, as a value-based reinforcement learning approach, is well-suited for discrete decision tasks in low-dimensional settings, making it applicable to basic satellite operations such as mode selection and module activation [13]. However, as the complexity of inference increases, the high-dimensional state space exacerbates the "curse of dimensionality", leading to slow convergence and instability [14].

Meanwhile, MDP-PG, as a policy gradient method, is effective in continuous action spaces but lacks efficiency when dealing with discrete optimization problems. Its reliance on stochastic gradient estimation and high sample complexity leads to inefficient resource utilization [15]. Furthermore, MDP-PG requires significant computational resources and extensive hyperparameter tuning, which is impractical for real-time, resource-constrained LEO satellite applications [16].

To overcome these limitations, we propose MDP-DQN, which leverages deep neural networks to handle high-dimensional state spaces efficiently while maintaining stability and fast convergence [17]. Its discrete action framework naturally aligns with satellite inference tasks, making it a more suitable and efficient approach in this context [18].

This paper focuses on optimizing Earth Observation (EO) missions in LEO-IISat, addressing the dual challenges of limited computational capacity and unbalanced energy supply. The main contributions are as follows: First, a lightweight and adaptive image inference strategy, MDP-DQN, combining Markov Decision Process (MDP) and Deep Q Network (DQN), is proposed to effectively handle these constraints. Second, simulation results demonstrate that compared to a fixed model strategy, the adaptive strategy significantly enhances inference performance. Moreover, MDP-DQN outperforms baseline strategies (MDP-QL and MDP-PG), particularly when evaluated using the Accuracy-Energy Efficiency (AEE) index. Finally, under high-load conditions, a performance analysis of the accuracy and energy efficiency metrics of MDP-DQN, MDP-QL, and MDP-PG in LEO satellite image inference tasks was conducted, along with an evaluation of their training stability, providing effective insights for optimizing intelligent inference in future satellite applications.

2. System Models and Mathematical Methods

2.1. LEO-IISat Orbital Model

In Figure 1, the operational orbit of the LEO-IISat and its support for EO applications are depicted. The LEO-IISat alternately passing through sunlit and shadow regions along its orbit [19]. In both of these regions, the LEO-IISat is capable of capturing EO images and utilizing multiple inference models for data processing and inference tasks, supporting various EO applications [20].

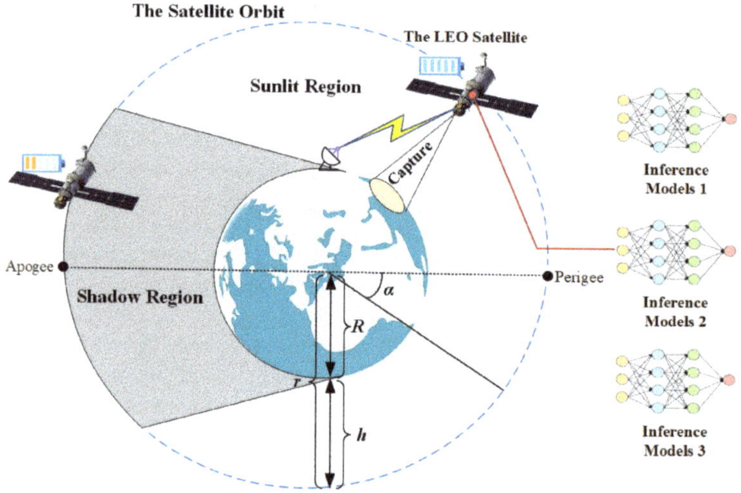

Figure 1. LEO-IISat operational orbit and EO application support.

The orbital equation of the LEO-IISat is represented as [21]:

$$r(t) = (R + h)[1 - e \cdot cos(\alpha(t))] \tag{1}$$

where $r(t)$ represents the orbital radius of the LEO-IISat at a given time t, which is the distance of the satellite from the Earth's center. R is the Earth's radius, h is the orbital altitude, e is the orbital eccentricity, and $\alpha(t)$ is the true anomaly, which is the angle between the LEO-IISat's current position and the perigee.

The orbital period of the LEO-IISat is given by [22]:

$$T_s = 2\pi\sqrt{\frac{(R+h)^3}{GM_e}} \tag{2}$$

where G is the gravitational constant and M_e is the Earth's mass.

2.2. LEO-IISat Energy Model

Figure 2 illustrates the energy distribution of the LEO-IISat in both sunlit and shadow regions. In the sunlit region, the solar panels generate electricity by absorbing sunlight, and the Electrical Power System (EPS) distributes this energy to the images capture, image inference, and communication modules, enabling LEO-IISat to efficiently execute image inference tasks [23]. At the same time, the EPS stores any surplus energy in the onboard batteries. In the shadow region, where sunlight is unavailable, the power system relies on the energy stored in the onboard batteries to provide energy to all modules [24].

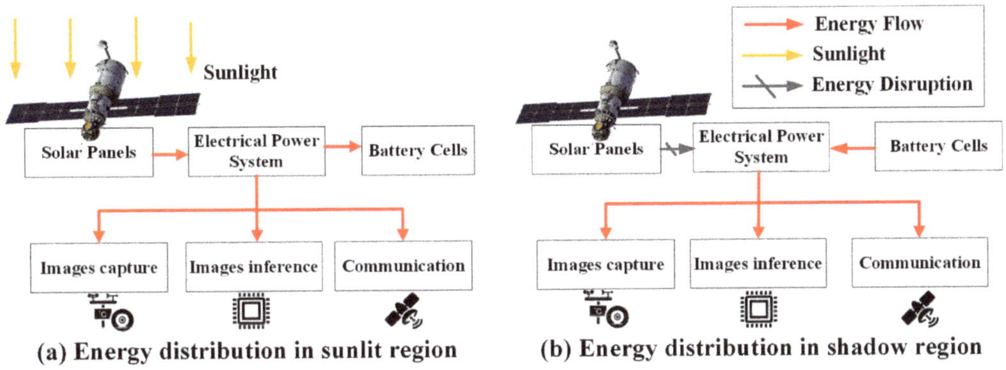

Figure 2. LEO-IISat energy distribution in sunlit and shadow regions.

Let the initial battery energy of the LEO-IISat upon entering the sunlit region be E_B^o, the maximum battery capacity be $E_B^{\max}$, and the minimum battery energy required for LEO-IISat operation be $E_B^{\min}$. Prior to entering the shadow region, the LEO-IISat must charge its battery to $E_B^{\max}$ to ensure sufficient energy availability.

The orbital period T_s is divided into N equal time slots, with Δt representing the duration of each time interval. The sequence of time slots is denoted as $\mathcal{T} = \{t_1, \ldots, t_i, \ldots, t_N\}$, where t_i represents any time slot.

Let $P_r(t)$ be the solar radiation received per square meter of the solar panel, given by:

$$P_r(t) = \begin{cases} P_{max} \exp\left[-\frac{(2t-\mu)^2}{8\sigma^2}\right], & 0 \le t \le \mu T_s \\ 0, & \mu T_s < t \le T_s \end{cases} \tag{3}$$

where $P_{\max}$ is the peak power received per square meter, μ is the fraction of time in the sunlit region during the orbital period, and σ is the parameter controlling radiation intensity distribution.

If t_i is within the sunlit region, $1 \le i \le \mu N$, the energy captured in t_i is:

$$E_i^c = \eta D \int_{(i-1)\cdot\Delta t}^{i\cdot\Delta t} P_r(t)dt \tag{4}$$

where η is the efficiency of solar energy conversion, and D is the solar panel area.

A fixed battery charging mechanism is used, where each time slot adds the same average energy to the battery. The charging energy during t_i is:

$$E_i^r = \frac{(E_B^{max} - E_B^o)}{\mu N} \tag{5}$$

The available energy for image inference during t_i is:

$$E_i^u = E_i^c - E_i^r \tag{6}$$

If t_i is within the shadow region, $\mu N < i \le N$, a cyclic averaging mechanism is used. Initially, the energy per time slot is averaged to determine the available energy for inference. After deducting the inference energy, the average is recalculated for the next slot. This process continues iteratively until the final time slot in the shadow region.

The available energy for image inference during t_i is:

$$E_i^u = \frac{E_B^{max} - E_B^{min} - \sum_{v=\mu N}^{i-1} E_v}{N - i + 1} \tag{7}$$

where E_v represents the energy consumption for any time slot from μN to $i-1$.

2.3. LEO-IISat Inference Model

LEO-IISat conducts EO missions based on its orbital operations, enabling real-time collection of high-resolution imagery data for aerial, maritime, and terrestrial infrastructure. This provides crucial support for achieving integrated air-sea-land traffic management [25]. To accomplish the image classification task—that is, the automatic recognition and classification of various objects in the collected images, LEO-IISat deploys M lightweight candidate CNN models, denoted as $\mathcal{M} = \{m_1, \ldots, m_j, \ldots, m_M\}$, where m_j represents any candidate CNN model [26].

Figure 3 illustrates image inference workflow on LEO-IISat.

Stage 1: Image Preprocessing. In this stage, the LEO-IISat captures raw remote sensing images, which are subsequently segmented into smaller sub-images [27].

Stage 2: Image Inferencing. In this stage, the preprocessed sub-images are fed into the onboard candidate CNN models for analysis. These models extract images features and identify the target object categories within the images [28].

Stage 3: Information Feedback. In this stage, once the image inference process is completed, the results, which include the identified target object categories, are transmitted to the ground station for further analysis, while irrelevant information is discarded [29].

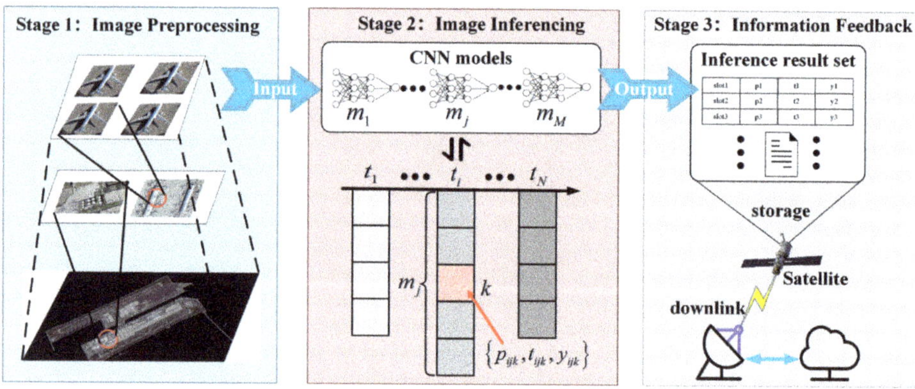

Figure 3. Image inference workflow on LEO-IISat.

The xView dataset, a widely recognized benchmark in remote sensing images analysis, is used in this paper as the source of raw remote sensing images during the images preprocessing stage [30].

The segmentation process of the raw remote sensing images is as follows: First, a sliding window cropping technique was used to segment the raw high-resolution images (3000 × 3000 pixels) into smaller sub-images (224 × 224 pixels) [31]. Then, min-max normalization was applied to scale the pixel values of the segmented sub-images from the range [0, 255] to [0, 1], ensuring a consistent input scale across all images. To enhance the diversity of the dataset and improve the robustness of the model, random flipping and random rotation were performed during preprocessing, simulating potential images transformations encountered in real-world applications. Finally, the images were standardized using mean and standard deviation, ensuring that the pixel values for each channel follow a consistent distribution [32].

Figure 4 displays four representative target object categories from the xView dataset, covering critical categories in aerial, maritime, and terrestrial transportation [33]. The identification of fixed-wing aircraft (a) helps track air traffic and assist in aviation safety management. The recognition of ferries (b) aids in monitoring maritime traffic, optimizing ferry routes, and ensuring safe operations in port areas. For buildings (c) and storage tanks (d), LEO-IISat can identify and assess the condition of urban infrastructure and industrial sites [34].

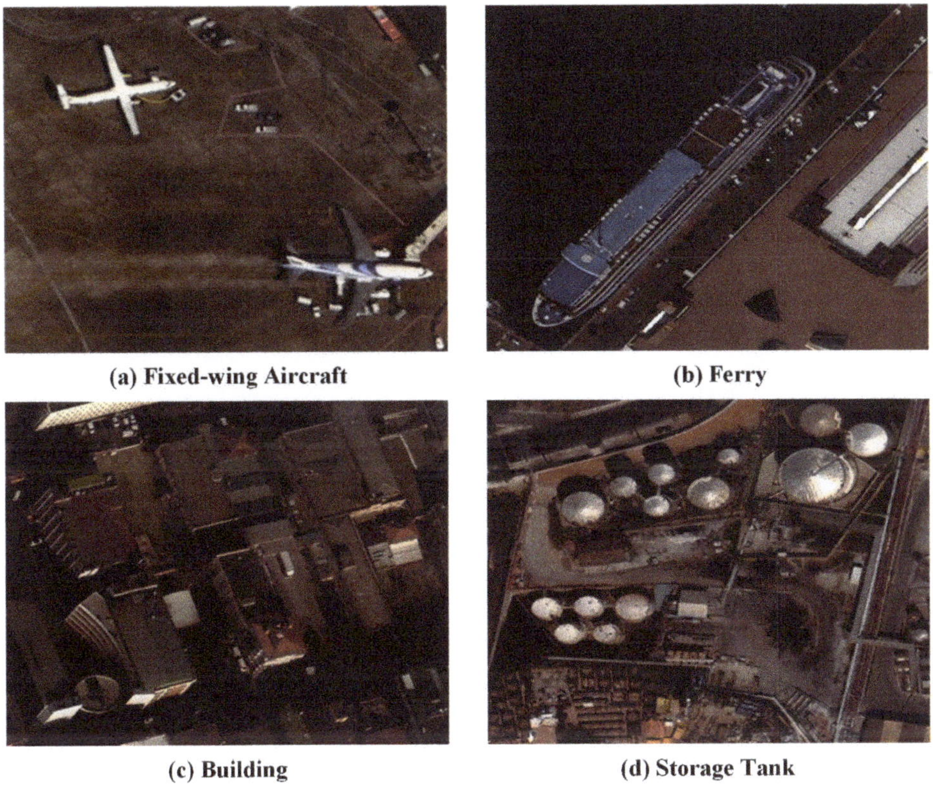

Figure 4. Representative target object categories from the xView dataset.

Let the number of images to be processed at t_i follow a Poisson distribution, as given by:

$$Q(P_i = n_i) = \frac{e^{-\lambda_i} {\lambda_i}^{n_i}}{n_i!} \tag{8}$$

where n_i represents the number of images in t_i, and λ_i is the average number of images in t_i.

The sequence of images in any time slot to be processed is denoted as $\mathcal{I} = \{I_1, \ldots, I_k, \ldots\}$, where I_k represents any image.

The performance set for inferring the k-th image with model m_j during t_i is:

$$\mathcal{P}_{\mathcal{S}} = \left\{p_{ijk}, t_{ijk}, y_{ijk}\right\}, 1 \leq i \leq N, 1 \leq j \leq M \tag{9}$$

where p_{ijk} is the inference power for the k-th image during t_i using m_j, t_{ijk} is the inference time for the k-th image during t_i using m_j, and y_{ijk} is the inference result label for the k-th image during t_i using m_j.

Figure 5 demonstrates the aforementioned performance data set (P_{ijk}, t_{ijk}, y_{ijk}) in a 3D coordinate system, along with its relationships to the time slots ($\mathcal{T}$), models ($\mathcal{M}$), and image sequences ($\mathcal{I}$). Here, the axes i, j, and k correspond to the time slots ($\mathcal{T}$), models ($\mathcal{M}$), and image sequences ($\mathcal{I}$), respectively.

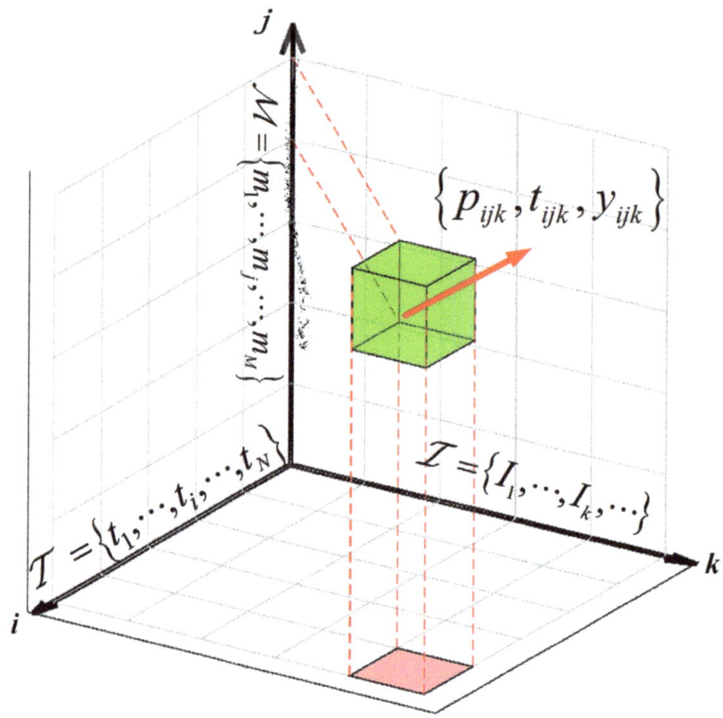

Figure 5. The performance data set for inferring in a 3D coordinate system.

The average image inference energy consumption using m_j during t_i is:

$$\overline{E_{ij}} = \frac{\sum_{k=1}^{n_i} p_{ijk} \cdot t_{ijk}}{n_i}, 1 \le i \le N, 1 \le j \le M \tag{10}$$

The image inference accuracy using model m_j during t_i is:

$$A_{ij} = \frac{\sum_{k=1}^{n_i} 1(y_{ijk} = x_{ijk})}{n_i} \tag{11}$$

where x_{ijk} is the ground truth label, $1(y_{ijk} = x_{ijk})$ is an indicator function that equals 1 if $y_{ijk} = x_{ijk}$ is satisfied, and 0 otherwise.

2.4. Problem Formulation

To quantify both accuracy and energy consumption, the AEE index is defined as follows:

$$AEE = \frac{Accuracy}{Energy} \tag{12}$$

where *Accuracy* denote the inference accuracy (expressed as %), defined as the ratio of correctly classified images to the total number of tested images. *Energy* represent the energy consumed during inference (measured in Joules). The AEE represents the inference accuracy per unit of energy consumed, expressed in terms of Accuracy per Joule (Accuracy/Joule)

In this paper, the AEE_{ij} is derived from the basic formula of AEE, representing the AEE value of selecting model m_j in time slot t_i. The formula is given by:

$$AEE_{ij} = \frac{A_{ij}}{\overline{E_{ij}}} = \frac{\sum_{k=1}^{n_i} 1(y_{ijk} = x_{ijk})}{\sum_{k=1}^{n_i} (P_{ijk} \cdot t_{ijk})} \tag{13}$$

Since our study aims for general applicability and is not focused on a specific category or domain, and the experiments are conducted on a dataset with a relatively balanced class distribution, the accuracy A_{ij} represents the unweighted average across different image categories.

Assume there are two models, m_1 and m_2, which are selected in time slot t_1. m_1 has an accuracy of 92% while consuming 0.8 J of energy; m_2 has an accuracy of 88% while consuming 0.5 J of energy. The AEE values of m_1 and m_2 in time slot t_1 are represented as:

$$AEE_{11} = \frac{0.92}{0.8} = 1.15, \quad AEE_{12} = \frac{0.88}{0.5} = 1.76 \tag{14}$$

Although in time slot t_1, m_1 has a higher accuracy, its higher energy consumption results in a lower AEE value compared to m_2, thereby highlighting the advantage of m_2 in time slot t_1.

The objective function and constraints are as follows:

$$\max \sum_{i=1}^{N} \sum_{j=1}^{M} 1(m_j = m_j^{\text{opt}} | t_i) \cdot AEE_{ij} \tag{15}$$

$$\text{s.t.} \quad A_{ij} \geq A_i^{min} \tag{16}$$

$$n_i \cdot \overline{E_{ij}} \leq E_i^{u} \tag{17}$$

$$\forall t_i, \ \exists! m_j \tag{18}$$

where $1(m_j = m_j^{\text{opt}} \mid t_i)$ is a conditional indicator function. It equals 1 if m_j is optimal during t_i; otherwise, it is 0.

Function (16) represents the inference accuracy constraint, where A_i^{min} is the minimum required inference accuracy during t_i. Function (17) refers to the inference energy consumption constraint. Function (18) ensures that for each t_i, only one model m_j is selected.

2.5. Problem Solving

The overall process of our adaptive model selection strategy for satellite inference is as follows: First, we select a set of initial candidate models. Subsequently, these candidate models are trained on a unified remote sensing dataset (the xView dataset). After training, each model is evaluated on a fixed test subset of the xView dataset using key performance metrics. We formalize the model selection problem as a Markov Decision Process (MDP), treating each discrete time slot within the satellite's orbital period as a decision point. In each time slot, a Deep Q-Network (DQN) dynamically selects the optimal model from the pre-trained candidate pool to adapt to the satellite's current energy level, inference task requirements, and expected inference accuracy.

The above problem is modeled as a Markov Decision Process [35].

The MDP consists of the tuple (S, A, T, r, γ):

- $S = \{E_i^u, I_i\}$ is the state space, where the state element E_i^u represents the available energy for inference in t_i, and the state element I_i represents the task distribution in t_i.
- $A = \mathcal{M} = \{m_1, \cdots, m_j, \cdots, m_M\}$ is the action space, representing the choices for the adaptive strategy, which are the different CNN models.
- $T = \{T_i^E, T_i^I\}$ is the state transition function, where T_i^E represents the energy state transition function, and T_i^I represents the task state transition function.
- $r(i,j)$ is the reward function, representing the reward obtained by selecting CNN model m_j in t_i, as follows:

$$r(i,j) = \delta_1 AEE_{ij} + \delta_2 (A_{ij} - A_i^{min}) \tag{19}$$

  where δ_1 is the weight coefficient for accuracy-energy efficiency, and δ_2 is the coefficient for the deviation from the minimum accuracy.
- γ is the discount factor, determining long-term rewards.

The MDP problem is solved using the DQN, in which the optimal strategy is learned and the optimal CNN model is selected for each time slot.

Figure 6 illustrates workflow of the MDP-DQN strategy, with the specific steps described as follows:

Step 1: Initialization. The MDP framework is initialized, including the state space ($S = \{E_i^u, I_i\}$), which represents environment states (E_i^u) and internal states (I_i); the action space ($A = \mathcal{M}$), representing all possible actions; the reward function ($r(i,j)$), which measures the feedback of actions; and the state transition function ($T = \{T_i^E, T_i^I\}$), which defines how states change based on actions.

Step 2: Input Current State into DQN. The current state $S = \{E_i^u, I_i\}$ is fed into the Deep Q-Network (DQN), representing the state of the MDP environment at time t.

Step 3: Action Selection. Based on the current state S, the DQN selects an optimal action $a \in A$ using the ϵ-greedy strategy to maximize the expected cumulative reward. Subsequently, the selected action a is executed, and the feedback reward $r(i,j)$ is received. The system state is then updated to S_{t+1} according to the state transition function $T = \{T_i^E, T_i^I\}$.

Step 4: Execute Action and Receive Feedback. Based on the reward $r(i,j)$ and the Q-value $Q_{\text{target}}(s', a')$ from the target Q-network, the target Q-value is calculated as follows:

$$y = r + \gamma \max_{a'} Q_{\text{target}}(s', a') \tag{20}$$

where $Q_{\text{target}}(s', a')$ is the Q-value computed by the target Q-network, and γ is the discount factor.

Step 5: Store Experience. The experience tuple (S_t, A_t, r_t, S_{t+1}) (current state, action, reward, next state) is stored in the replay memory buffer for future training. Then, a batch of experiences is randomly sampled from the replay buffer, and the behavioral Q-network is trained by minimizing the mean squared error (MSE) through gradient descent. The loss function is optimized as follows [36]:

$$\theta \leftarrow \theta - \beta \nabla_\theta \mathbb{E}\left[(y - Q(s, a; \theta))^2\right] \tag{21}$$

where θ represents the parameters of the Q-network, β is the learning rate, ∇_θ denotes the gradient with respect to the parameters θ, $\mathbb{E}$ is expectation value, and $Q(s, a; \theta)$ is the Q-value function of the current Q-network.

Step 6: Experience Sampling and Training. Through continuous updates of the network parameters θ, the DQN is progressively optimized to select the optimal model m_j at each time step t_i, ensuring the maximization of the target Q-value.

Step 7: Task Completion Check. The system checks whether the task has been completed. If the task is completed, the results are output, and the process terminates. Otherwise, the state is updated, and the process returns to Step 2, continuing the loop until the task is completed.

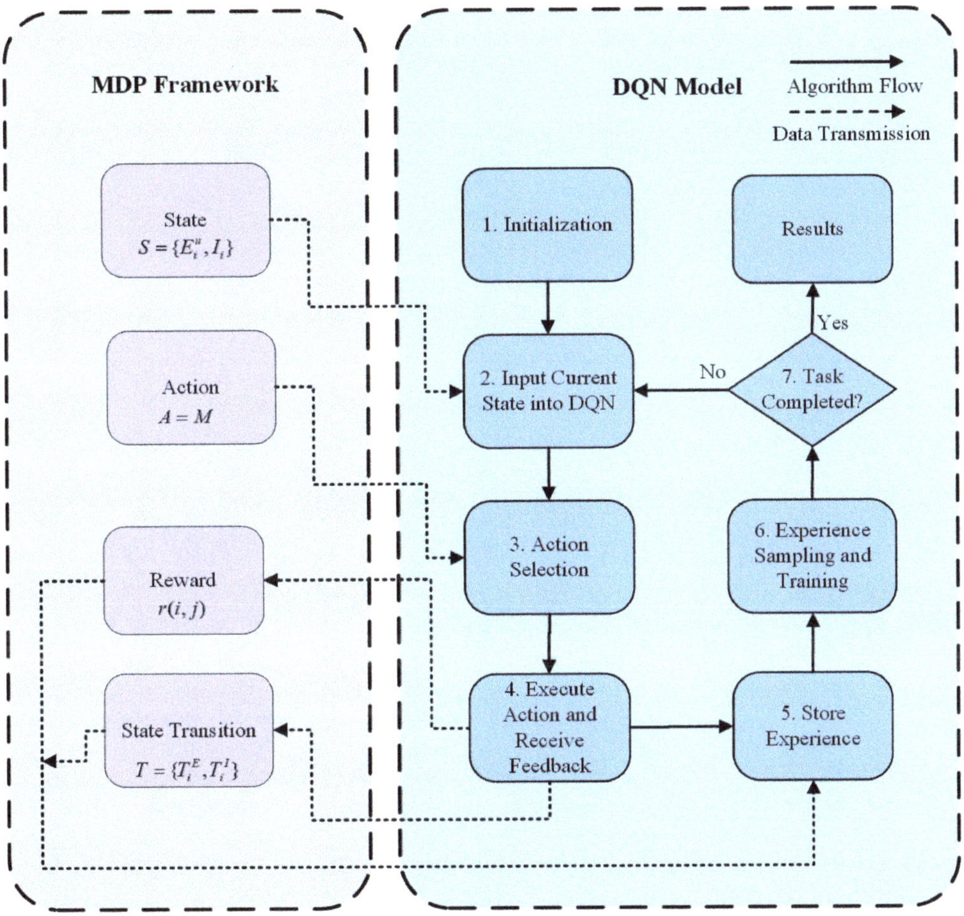

Figure 6. MDP-DQN strategy workflow.

3. Results

3.1. Simulation Parameters

Table 1 presents the simulation parameters for the LEO-IISat used in Earth observation missions, with an orbital altitude h of 500 km. The orbital period T_s is 5670 s, divided into 30 time slots [37]. During one orbital period, approximately 70% of the time is spent in the sunlit region. The LEO-IISat is equipped with 100 m^2 solar panels, with an energy conversion efficiency of 25% [38]. The solar panels are capable of generating a peak power of 1.36 kW [39]. the maximum battery capacity $E_B^{\max}$ is 10 kWh, while the minimum battery energy required for LEO-IISat operation $E_B^{\min}$ is 2 kWh.

Table 1. LEO-IISat parameters.

Parameter	Value	Parameter	Value
h	500 km	η	25%
T_s	5670 s	$P_{\max}$	1.36 kW
N	30	E_B^{max}	10 kWh
μ	70%	E_B^{min}	2 kWh
D	100 m^2		

Table 2 summarizes the image inference environment parameters used in the LEO-IISat mission. The LEO-IISat incorporates three candidate CNN models: MobileNet_v3, MobileNet_v2, and ResNet18, selected for their low computational complexity, which makes them well-suited for resource-constrained LEO-IISat environments [40]. The onboard computing device is the NVIDIA Jetson AGX Orin. The raw images from the xView dataset are segmented into multiple sub-images in the preprocessing phase, providing input data for the simulation experiments [41]. The LEO-IISat processes between $5 \times 10^4 \sim 5 \times 10^5$ images per time slot, simulating the task distribution on LEO-IISat, with the exact number depending on the complexity of the tasks and operational requirements [42].

Table 2. Image inference environment parameters.

Parameter Name	Parameter Value
Candidate CNN models	MobileNet_v3; MobileNet_v2; ResNet18
Onboard computing device	NVIDIA Jetson AGX Orin
Raw image dataset	xView Dataset
Number of images processed per t_i	$5 \times 10^4 \sim 5 \times 10^5$

Table 3 compares the performance of candidate CNN models used in the LEO-IISat, focusing on accuracy, energy consumption, and delay, and these data serve as experimental parameters for the subsequent adaptive selection strategy in this study [43]. These performance metrics are obtained through actual measurements. The ranges for accuracy, energy consumption, and delay were obtained by testing 1000 segmented images 100 times. The ranges shown for accuracy, energy consumption, and delay represent the minimum and maximum values observed across these tests. Energy consumption is measured per image, and delay does not include any additional overhead (such as model loading time, data transmission time, etc.); it represents the pure inference delay. MobileNet_v3 offers the best accuracy with a delay ranging from 3.5 to 4.5 ms, making it ideal for tasks that require high precision and real-time performance; however, its higher energy consumption may limit its use in power-constrained LEO-IISat EO missions. In comparison, MobileNet_v2 strikes a better balance between accuracy and energy efficiency with a delay of 4 to 5 ms, making it a good choice for EO missions where some loss in accuracy is acceptable. Finally, while ResNet18 has the lowest accuracy, it is the most energy-efficient, with a delay ranging from 6 to 8 ms, making it suitable for energy-constrained EO missions where delay is not as critical.

Table 3. Comparison of Accuracy, Energy, Delay, and EDP/A of candidate CNN models.

CNN Models	Accuracy (%)	Energy (J)	Delay (ms)	EDP/A (J · ms/%)
MobileNet_v3	85.7∼92.4	0.87∼1.04	3.5∼4.5	3.30∼5.46
MobileNet_v2	75.3∼91.7	0.79∼0.9	4∼5	3.45∼5.98
ResNet18	72.2∼89.5	0.69∼1.0	6∼8	4.63∼11.08

To further evaluate these models, we introduce the Energy-Delay-Product per Accuracy (EDP/A) metric, defined as:

$$EDP/A = \frac{Energy \times Delay}{Accuracy}$$

This metric provides a comprehensive assessment by considering the trade-off between energy consumption, processing delay, and accuracy. Lower EDP/A values indicate better overall efficiency. The EDP/A values for the three models were calculated based on the experimental data presented in Table 3.

According to the data in Table 3, we have plotted a boxplot to visually compare the performance of different CNN models across multiple metrics, including Accuracy, Energy, Delay, and EDP/A, as shown in Figure 7.

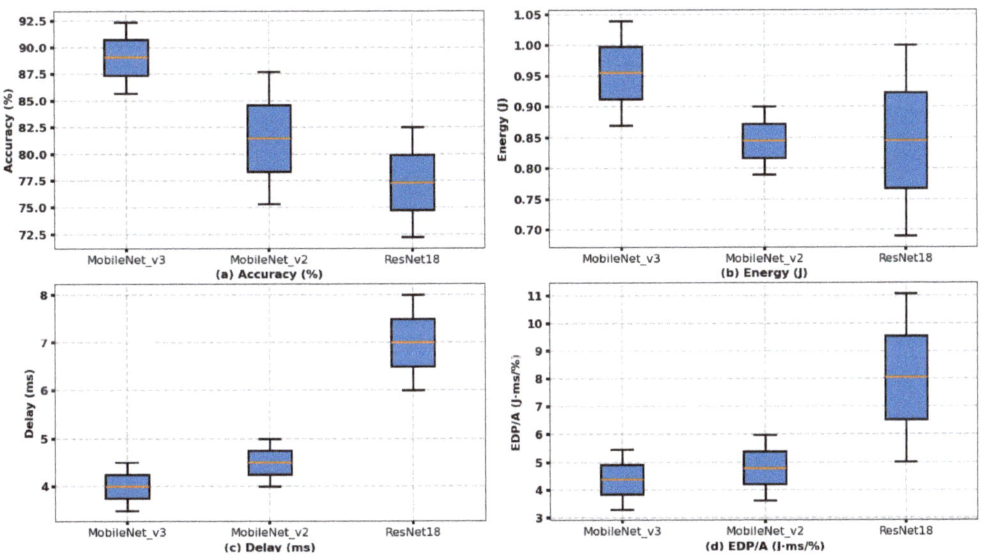

Figure 7. Comparison of CNN model performance across multiple metrics.

Table 4 presents the parameters for the MDP-DQN strategy applied to LEO-IISat. Here, the weight coefficient for accuracy-energy efficiency δ_1 is set to 1.5; the coefficient for the deviation from the minimum accuracy δ_2 is set to 10; the number of training episodes κ is set to 2000; the learning rate β is set to 0.001, which helps stabilize the training process; the discount factor for future rewards γ is set to 0.99, placing greater emphasis on future rewards; and the initial exploration rate ϵ is set to 0.9, which encourages more exploration in the early stages of training [44].

Table 4. MDP-DQN strategy parameters.

Parameter	Value	Parameter	Value	Parameter	Value
δ_1	1.5	κ	2000	γ	0.99
δ_2	10	β	0.001	ϵ	0.9

3.2. MDP-DQN Strategy Results

Figure 8 presents the curves of available energy for inference, the adaptive model selection, and the AEE index performance curves for different time slots during an orbital period. The available energy for inference first increases in the sunlight region, reaching a maximum of approximately 5.8×10^6 joules at the subsolar point (the 15th time slot), and then begins to decrease. In the shadow region, the available energy for inference remains relatively stable at approximately 3.2×10^6 joules. Under high-energy condition (i.e., $3.7 \times 10^6 \sim 6 \times 10^6$ J), MobileNet_v3 is prioritized, supplemented by MobileNet_v2, with MobileNet_v3 accounting for 70% and MobileNet_v2 for 30%. Under low-energy condition (i.e., $0.4 \times 10^6 \sim 3.7 \times 10^6$ J), MobileNet_v2 and ResNet18 exhibit competitiveness.

Moreover, under high-energy conditions, the transient fluctuations in model selection can be attributed to our adaptive inference strategy, which not only considers the available energy level but also accounts for variations in the number of images processed in each time slot. Changes in the number of images affect the AEE values, and since the image count in each time slot follows a Poisson distribution, occasional variations in model selection may occur even under high-energy conditions.

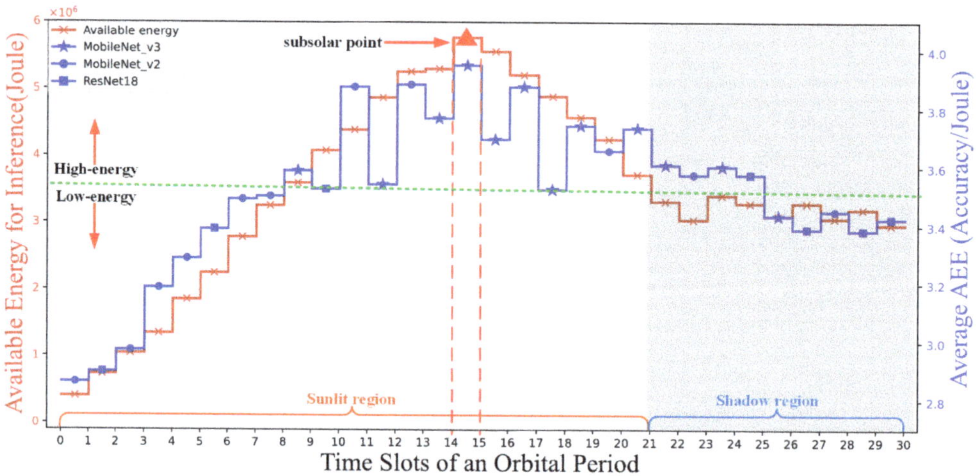

Figure 8. Available inference energy versus average AEE index in different time slots of an orbital period, and only one model is selected per time slot.

3.3. Comparison Results of Different Strategies

To validate the performance of the proposed strategy, the following baseline strategies are considered for comparison experiments, all of which are solutions based on the MDP:

- The MDP-Q Learning strategy (MDP-QL): The Q-learning updates the Q-values of state-action pairs to learn the optimal strategy [45].
- The MDP-Policy gradient strategy (MDP-PG): The policy gradient strategy directly optimizes the policy parameters to maximize cumulative rewards [46].

Both of these strategies are classical reinforcement learning algorithms widely used to solve the MDP problem [47]. They enable a comprehensive evaluation of the MDP-DQN strategy in terms of accuracy, convergence speed, and stability [48].

Figure 9 presents the relationship between the average number of images per time slot and the AEE index for different strategies. As the average number of images per time slot increases, the AEE index values of all strategies gradually decrease. This is because processing more images with the same energy supply reduces accuracy, thereby lowering the AEE index values. This indicates that in energy-limited situations, a balance between task load and model complexity is necessary. Under low-load conditions (i.e., $0.5 \times 10^5 \sim 1.5 \times 10^5$), the performance gap between MDP-DQN and MDP-QL is small; however, under high-load conditions (i.e., $1.5 \times 10^5 \sim 5 \times 10^5$), the MDP-DQN strategy estimates Q-values more accurately and performs better.

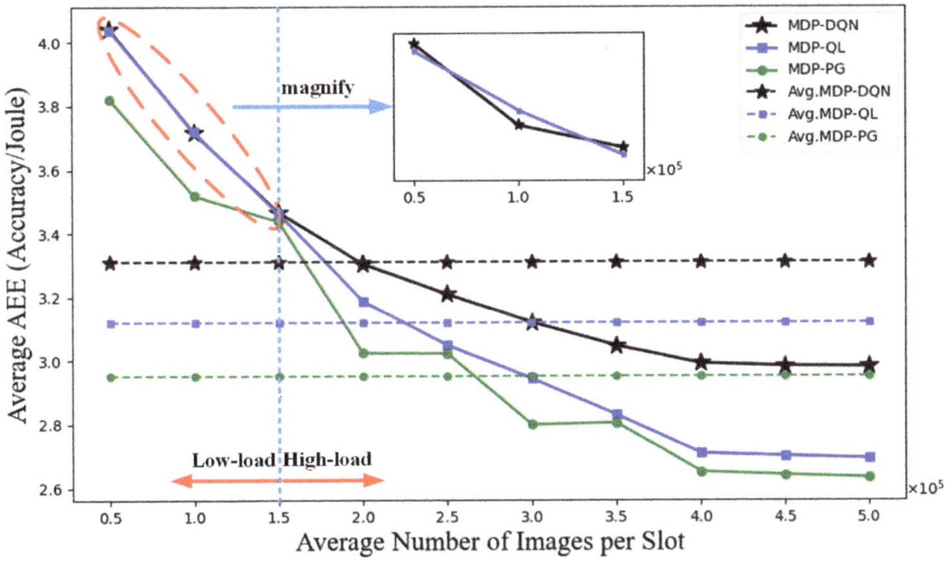

Figure 9. Average number of images per slot versus average AEE index for different strategies.

To quantify measurement uncertainty, we conducted 30 independent experiments under all load conditions and computed the 95% confidence intervals (CIs) using the standard error of the mean. Across all load conditions ($0.5 \times 10^5 \sim 1.5 \times 10^5$), the average AEE index values are 3.31 (95% CI: 3.26–3.36) for MDP-DQN, 3.12 (95% CI: 3.07–3.17) for MDP-QL, and 2.95 (95% CI: 2.92–2.98) for MDP-PG. Consequently, MDP-DQN improves the AEE index by approximately 6.1% and 12.2% relative to MDP-QL and MDP-PG.

Figure 10 illustrates the comparison of cumulative AEE scores between the MDP-DQN adaptive strategy and the fixed model over 30 time slots within an orbital period. The MDP-DQN strategy adaptively selects among three candidate models (MobileNet_v3, MobileNet_v2, and ResNet18), while the fixed model consistently employs MobileNet_v2. The final cumulative score for the MDP-DQN adaptive strategy is 142.34, while that for the fixed model is 108.41. Therefore, compared to the fixed model, the AEE index of MDP-DQN is improved by approximately 31.3%.

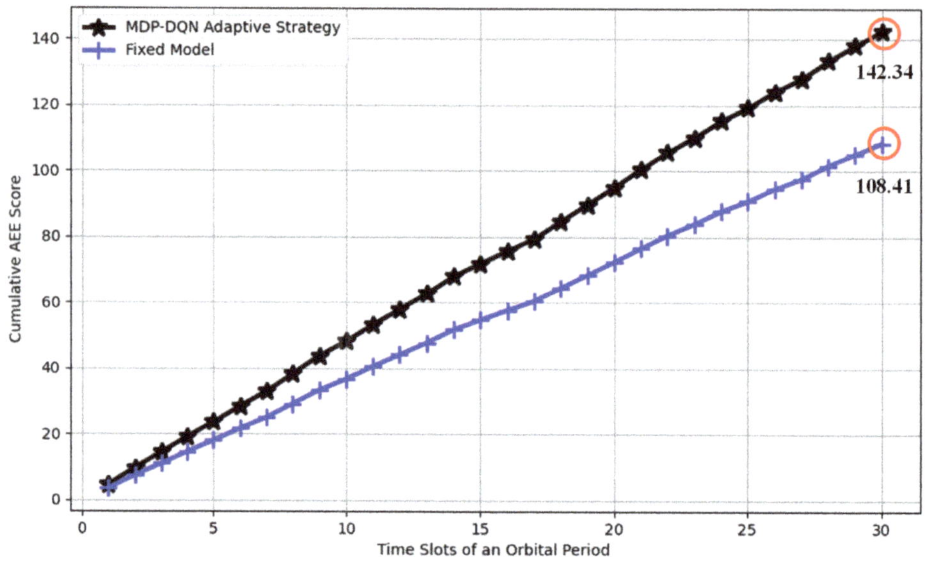

Figure 10. Comparison of cumulative AEE scores between the MDP-DQN adaptive strategy and the fixed model over orbital period time slots.

Finally, we repeated the experiments of the adaptive selection strategy over 30 complete orbital cycles, and the results showed that the strategy achieved a maximum inference accuracy of 91.8% and an average inference accuracy of 89.1%.

Figure 11 illustrates the performance trends of three different algorithms (MDP-DQN, MDP-QL, and MDP-PG) as the average AEE index evolves with the increase in training episodes. The x-axis represents the number of training episodes, while the y-axis measures the algorithm's performance metric—average AEE index. Overall, as the number of training episodes increases, the performance of all algorithms improves, but their improvement rates, final performance, and stability exhibit noticeable differences. A critical focal point is observed at approximately (860, 3.62), where the performance of all three algorithms converges. At this stage, the average AEE index values of MDP-DQN, MDP-QL, and MDP-PG are similar, indicating a transitional phase in their performance trends. Beyond this focal point, the trajectories of the algorithms diverge significantly. From the analysis, MDP-PG performs best in the early training phase (0–500 episodes), with rapid and stable increases in average AEE index. However, after the focal point, its performance plateaus, with no significant improvement. In contrast, MDP-DQN demonstrates superior performance in the middle and late stages of training, eventually stabilizing at the highest average AEE index value, making it the most effective algorithm among the three. Additionally, while MDP-QL shows rapid improvement, it suffers from high volatility throughout the training process, particularly beyond the focal point, indicating a lack of stability.

Table 5 compares the variance of the AEE index across the three strategies (MDP-DQN, MDP-QL, and MDP-PG) during training, with the variance calculated based on the average of the previous and next sampling points (as shown in Figure 11). As shown in Table 5, MDP-DQN exhibits the lowest variance and higher stability. The fluctuations in the training process are mainly due to two factors: first, the transitional regions between sunlit and shadow lead to abnormal energy fluctuations; second, the number of images processed in each time slot varies irregularly.

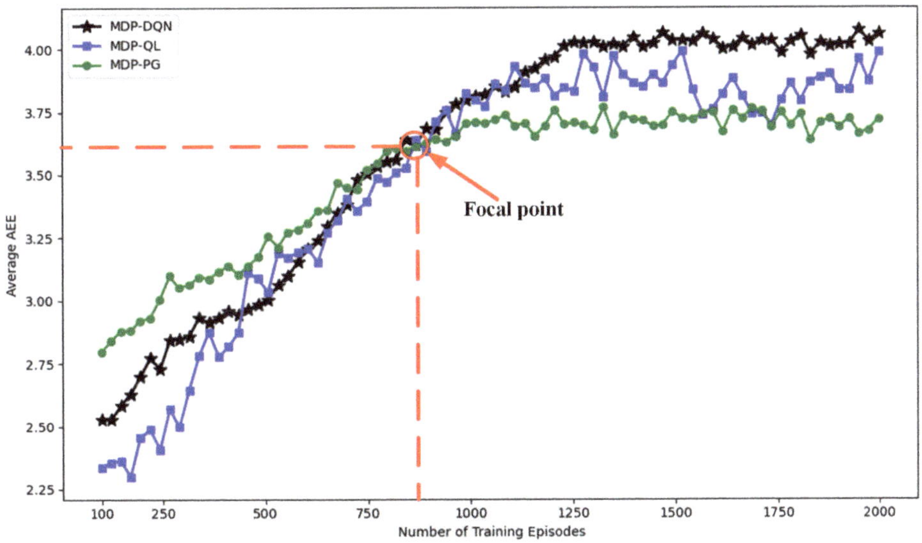

Figure 11. Different training episodes versus average AEE index for different strategies.

Table 5. Comparison of the average variance values of three strategies during training.

Strategies	MDP-DQN	MDP-QL	MDP-PG
Variance	0.023	0.061	0.032

Figure 12 shows the Average AEE index of MDP-DQN, MDP-QL, and MDP-PG under different learning rates and discount factors. The left panel (a) illustrates the Average AEE index of the algorithms under varying learning rates (10^{-4} to 10^{-2}). MDP-DQN achieves its highest AEE index at a learning rate of 10^{-3}, marked as the Optimal Point. MDP-QL and MDP-PG remain relatively stable and exhibit lower AEE index values compared to MDP-DQN.The right panel (b) presents the Average AEE index under different discount factors (0.90 to 1.00). MDP-DQN achieves its optimal value near a discount factor of 1.0, marked again as the Optimal Point. MDP-QL shows a consistent trend across all discount factors, while MDP-PG demonstrates a slight upward trend as the discount factor increases.

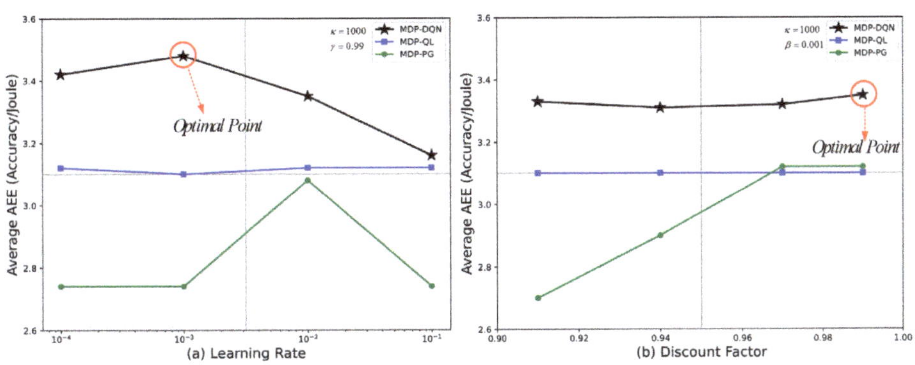

Figure 12. Average AEE index under different learning rates and discount factors for different strategies.

Figure 13 illustrates the normalized performance comparison of MDP-DQN, MDP-QL, and MDP-PG across four key metrics: AEE index, stability, memory usage, and training time. MDP-DQN excels in AEE index and stability, indicating high accuracy and robustness, but incurs higher memory usage and training time. MDP-QL shows balanced performance across all metrics, while MDP-PG performs efficiently in memory usage and training time, but lags behind in AEE index and stability. This visualization highlights the trade-offs among the algorithms for different application priorities.

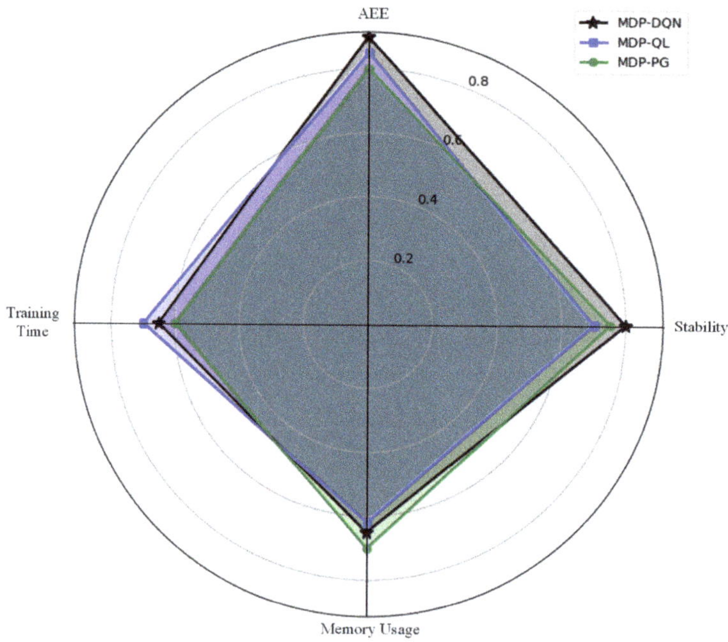

Figure 13. Normalized performance comparison of different strategies across four key metrics.

Table 6 presents the time complexity of the three algorithms, where L is the number of network layers, N_e is the number of neurons per layer, $|S|$ is the size of the state space, and $|A|$ is the size of the action space. Both the MDP-DQN and the MDP-PG use deep neural networks, resulting in a similar time complexity of $O(L \times {N_e}^2)$ [49]. As the complexity of the network structures increases, so does the time complexity. In contrast, the MDP-QL has a time complexity of $O(|S| \times |A|)$, directly related to the size of the state and action spaces [50]. This algorithm performs well when the state and action spaces are small, but the computing load increases as these spaces expand.

Table 6. Time complexity analysis of algorithms.

Algorithms	DQN	QL	PG
Time complexity	$O(L \times N_e^2)$	$O(\|S\| \times \|A\|)$	$O(L \times N_e^2)$

4. Discussion

From an overall perspective, the AEE index value shows a positive correlation with the available energy for inference. But under high energy condition, the AEE index performance of the models fluctuates significantly, reaching a maximum of approximately 3.94 and a minimum of 3.42. This is due to variations in the number of images (as illustrated in Figure 8) and the tendency to select complex models with numerous parameters and high-dimensional features, making them more susceptible to randomness and noise.

During the Table 3 evaluation, MobileNet_v3 demonstrated excellent accuracy (85.7% to 92.4%), making it particularly suitable for complex and high-precision task scenarios, such as disaster detection or urban development monitoring. While its energy consumption (0.87 to 1.04 J/image) was slightly higher, its performance on the Jetson AGX Orin remained highly efficient, making it ideal for high-performance operational modes. In contrast, MobileNet_v2 achieved high classification accuracy (75.3% to 91.7%) with lower energy consumption (0.79 to 0.9 J/image), making it an ideal choice for resource-constrained tasks, such as micro-satellite missions or scenarios requiring continuous operation over extended periods. Meanwhile, ResNet18 exhibited balanced performance in terms of energy consumption (0.69 to 1.0 J/image) and accuracy (72.2% to 89.5%), making it suitable for large-scale, rapid screening tasks or secondary tasks requiring high real-time processing efficiency [51].

From the results presented in Table 4 and Figure 12 , it is evident that the performance of the DQN algorithm is highly sensitive to key parameters, such as learning rate and discount factor. Regarding the impact of the learning rate, DQN achieves optimal energy efficiency (maximum AEE) when the learning rate is set to 10^{-3}, indicating that this value strikes a balance between stable convergence and rapid updates. In contrast, higher learning rates (e.g., 10^{-1}) result in a decline in performance, potentially due to unstable convergence caused by overly aggressive parameter updates. Additionally, in terms of the discount factor, DQN performs best at $\gamma = 0.99$, demonstrating its ability to balance short-term and long-term rewards during the optimization process [52]. This also highlights DQN's advantage in handling long-term temporal dependencies in complex tasks. In comparison, the performance of QL and PG shows less sensitivity to these parameters but remains significantly inferior to DQN overall. These results further underscore the superiority of deep reinforcement learning in energy efficiency optimization and decision-making accuracy, particularly in resource-constrained environments such as satellite edge computing networks [53].

From Figure 11, it is evident that MDP-DQN excels in the later stages of training, making it well-suited for tasks that require high stability and optimal final performance. This robust performance can be attributed to the incorporation of experience replay and target network mechanisms, which help smooth out fluctuations in Q-value estimates as training progresses. In contrast, MDP-PG demonstrates rapid convergence during the initial phase, rendering it more suitable for scenarios that demand quick progress. However, its performance tends to plateau in later stages, suggesting that further tuning may be necessary to maintain long-term stability. Meanwhile, MDP-QL shows rapid improvement at the outset but suffers from significant volatility throughout the training process, likely due to challenges inherent in Q-learning when operating in high-dimensional state spaces. This indicates that MDP-QL might benefit from additional modifications or adaptive parameter adjustments to achieve a stability level comparable to that of MDP-DQN.

The training process of MDP-DQN exhibits a certain degree of volatility. As shown in Figure 6, the training relies on several random factors: the intermittent energy supply of the satellite introduces randomness in state transitions, and fluctuations in the number of input data within each time slot result in inherent uncertainty in the reward feedback. However, optimizing the learning rate and discount factor can help the model better cope with these random factors in the environment. Therefore, to overcome these issues and stabilize the training process, we selected the optimal learning rate and discount factor as the experimental parameters for the adaptive selection strategy, as illustrated in Figure 12. Finally, based on the convergence trend shown in Figure 11, MDP-DQN has essentially converged after approximately 1200 training episodes, exhibiting minimal fluctuations with a variance of 0.023.

5. Conclusions

This paper introduces the AEE index to quantify inference accuracy unit of energy consumption and evaluate the inference performance of LEO-IISat. The proposed MDP-DQN strategy successfully integrates lightweight models and adaptive inference frameworks, dynamically balancing computational and energy resources to address the challenges in LEO-IISat for EO missions. The simulation results demonstrate the superiority of this strategy, achieving a 31.3% improvement in inference performance compared to a fixed model strategy at the same energy consumption, and achieves improvements over MDP-PG and MDP-QL strategies, enhancing the AEE index by 12.2% and 6.09%, respectively.

The MDP-DQN strategy has substantial applications in real-time disaster monitoring, precise climate analysis, and military reconnaissance. Future research will focus on improving CNN architectures to adapt to diverse mission scenarios, optimizing real-time images batch processing techniques, and enhancing system robustness under dynamic task conditions. These advancements will further solidify the role of LEO-IISat as a cornerstone for next-generation EO missions.

Author Contributions: Conceptualization, B.W.; Methodology, B.W.; Software, Y.F.; Validation, D.H.; Formal analysis, Y.F.; Investigation, Y.F.; Resources, Z.L. and J.L.; Data curation, J.L.; Writing—original draft preparation, Y.F.; Writing—review and editing, D.H.; Visualization, B.W.; Supervision, D.H.; Funding acquisition, D.H. All authors have read and agreed to the published version of the manuscript.

Funding: This research was funded by Guangxi Natural Science Foundation for Youths (No. 2022GXNSFBA035645) and Guangxi Natural Science Foundation General Project (No. 2025GXNSFAA069685)

Institutional Review Board Statement: Not applicable.

Data Availability Statement: The xView dataset used in this study is publicly available and can be accessed at https://xviewdataset.org. The pre-trained models used, including MobileNetV2, MobileNetV3, and ResNet18, are publicly available and can be found in their respective repositories. However, the DQN network trained for this study is part of ongoing research and, therefore, we are unable to make it publicly available at this time.

Acknowledgments: The authors would like to thank the developers of MobileNet_v3, MobileNet_v2, and ResNet18 for providing the foundational models utilized in this research. These models served as the basis for our experiments and significantly contributed to the results presented in this manuscript. Additionally, we acknowledge the xView dataset, which provided essential data for the training and evaluation of our models. The availability of high-quality open-source models and datasets like these has been invaluable to the advancement of this work.

Conflicts of Interest: The authors declare that they have no financial or non-financial conflicts of interest related to the research, authorship, and publication of this article. No competing interests exist that could have influenced the results or interpretation of this study.

References

1. Banafaa, M.; Shayea, I.; Din, J.; Azmi, M.H.; Alashbi, A.; Daradkeh, Y.I.; Alhammadi, A. 6G Mobile Communication Technology: Requirements, Targets, Applications, Challenges, Advantages, and Opportunities. *Alex. Eng. J.* **2023**, *64*, 245–274. [CrossRef]
2. Dwivedi, Y.K.; Hughes, L.; Ismagilova, E.; Aarts, G.; Coombs, C.; Crick, T.; Duan, Y.; Dwivedi, R.; Edwards, J.; Eirug, A.; et al. Artificial Intelligence (AI): Multidisciplinary Perspectives on Emerging Challenges, Opportunities, and Agenda for Research, Practice, and Policy. *Int. J. Inf. Manag.* **2021**, *57*, 101994. [CrossRef]

3. Bedi, R. In-Orbit Artificial Intelligence and Machine Learning On-Board Processing Solutions for Space Applications: Edge-Based and Versal Space Reference Designs: First Design-In Experiences. In Proceedings of the 2023 European Data Handling & Data Processing Conference (EDHPC), Juan Les Pins, France, 2–6 October 2023; pp. 1–4. [CrossRef]
4. He, C.; Dong, Y.; Li, H.; Liew, Y. Reasoning-Based Scheduling Method for Agile Earth Observation Satellite with Multi-Subsystem Coupling. *Remote Sens.* **2023**, *15*, 1577. [CrossRef]
5. Cui, G.; Duan, P.; Xu, L.; Wang, W. Latency Optimization for Hybrid GEO–LEO Satellite-Assisted IoT Networks. *IEEE Internet Things J.* **2023**, *10*, 6286–6297. [CrossRef]
6. Zhu, X.; Jiang, C. Integrated Satellite-Terrestrial Networks toward 6G: Architectures, Applications, and Challenges. *IEEE Internet Things J.* **2021**, *9*, 437–461. [CrossRef]
7. Wang, W.; Chen, W.; Luo, Y.; Long, Y.; Lin, Z.; Zhang, L.; Lin, B.; Cai, D.; He, X. Model Compression and Efficient Inference for Large Language Models: A Survey. *arXiv* **2024**, arXiv:2402.09748. [CrossRef]
8. Malaviya, P.; Sarvaiya, V.; Shah, A.; Thakkar, D.; Shah, M. A Comprehensive Review on Space Solar Power Satellite: An Idiosyncratic Approach. *Environ. Sci. Pollut. Res.* **2022**, *29*, 42476–42492. [CrossRef]
9. Miralles, P.; Thangavel, K.; Scannapieco, A.F.; Jagadam, N.; Baranwal, P.; Faldu, B.; Abhang, R.; Bhatia, S.; Bonnart, S.; Bhatnagar, I.; et al. A Critical Review on the State-of-the-Art and Future Prospects of Machine Learning for Earth Observation Operations. *Adv. Space Res.* **2023**, *71*, 4959–4986. [CrossRef]
10. Shang, S.; Zhang, J.; Wang, X.; Wang, X.; Li, Y.; Li, Y. Faster and Lighter Meteorological Satellite Image Classification by a Lightweight Channel-Dilation-Concatenation Net. *IEEE J. Sel. Top. Appl. Earth Obs. Remote Sens.* **2023**, *16*, 2301–2317. [CrossRef]
11. Leyva-Mayorga, I.; Martinez-Gost, M.; Moretti, M.; Pérez-Neira, A.; Vázquez, M.Á; Popovski, P.; Soret, B. Satellite Edge Computing for Real-Time and Very-High Resolution Earth Observation. *IEEE Trans. Commun.* **2023**, *71*, 6180–6194. [CrossRef]
12. Gost, M.M.; Leyva-Mayorga, I.; Pérez-Neira, A.; Vázquez, M.Á.; Soret, B.; Moretti, M. Edge Computing and Communication for Energy-Efficient Earth Surveillance with LEO Satellites. In Proceedings of the 2022 IEEE International Conference on Communications Workshops (ICC Workshops), Seoul, Republic of Korea, 16–20 May 2022; pp. 556–561. [CrossRef]
13. Khalek, N.A.; Tashman, D.H.; Hamouda, W. Advances in machine learning-driven cognitive radio for wireless networks: A survey. *IEEE Commun. Surv. Tutor.* **2024**, *26*, 1201–1237. [CrossRef]
14. Yin, L.; Cao, X. Inspired lightweight robust quantum Q-learning for smart generation control of power systems. *Appl. Soft Comput.* **2022**, *131*, 109804. [CrossRef]
15. Bhandari, J.; Russo, D. Global optimality guarantees for policy gradient methods. *Oper. Res.* **2024**, *72*, 1906–1927. [CrossRef]
16. Ali, Y.A.; Awwad, E.M.; Al-Razgan, M.; Maarouf, A. Hyperparameter search for machine learning algorithms for optimizing the computational complexity. *Processes* **2023**, *11*, 349. [CrossRef]
17. Wang, Z.; Zhao, W.; Zhai, A.; He, P.; Wang, D. DQN based single-pixel imaging. *Opt. Express* **2021**, *29*, 15463–15477. [CrossRef]
18. Luo, J.; Li, F.; Jiao, J. A dynamic multiobjective recommendation method based on soft actor-critic with discrete actions. *J. King Saud Univ. Comput. Inf. Sci.* **2025**, *37*, 1. [CrossRef]
19. Alavipanah, S.K.; Karimi Firozjaei, M.; Sedighi, A.; Fathololoumi, S.; Zare Naghadehi, S.; Saleh, S.; Naghdizadegan, M.; Gomeh, Z.; Arsanjani, J.J.; Makki, M.; et al. The Shadow Effect on Surface Biophysical Variables Derived from Remote Sensing: A Review. *Land* **2022**, *11*, 2025. [CrossRef]
20. Persello, C.; Wegner, J.D.; Hänsch, R.; Tuia, D.; Ghamisi, P.; Koeva, M.; Camps-Valls, G. Deep Learning and Earth Observation to Support the Sustainable Development Goals: Current Approaches, Open Challenges, and Future Opportunities. *IEEE Geosci. Remote Sens. Mag.* **2022**, *10*, 172–200. [CrossRef]
21. Wang, Z.; Li, Z.; Wang, L.; Wang, N.; Yang, Y.; Li, R.; Zhang, Y.; Liu, A.; Yuan, H.; Hoque, M. Comparison of the Real-Time Precise Orbit Determination for LEO between Kinematic and Reduced-Dynamic Modes. *Measurement* **2022**, *187*, 110224. [CrossRef]
22. Prol, F.S.; Ferre, R.M.; Saleem, Z.; Välisuo, P.; Pinell, C.; Lohan, E.S.; Elsanhoury, M.; Elmusrati, M.; Islam, S.; Çelikbilek, K.; et al. Position, Navigation, and Timing (PNT) through Low Earth Orbit (LEO) Satellites: A Survey on Current Status, Challenges, and Opportunities. *IEEE Access* **2022**, *10*, 83971–84002. [CrossRef]
23. Liu, W.; Lai, Z.; Wu, Q.; Li, H.; Zhang, Q.; Li, Z.; Li, Y.; Liu, J. In-Orbit Processing or Not? Sunlight-Aware Task Scheduling for Energy-Efficient Space Edge Computing Networks. In Proceedings of the IEEE INFOCOM 2024—IEEE Conference on Computer Communications, Vancouver, BC, Canada, 20–23 May 2024; pp. 881–890. [CrossRef]
24. Pathak, A.D.; Saha, S.; Bharti, V.K.; Gaikwad, M.M.; Sharma, C.S. A Review on Battery Technology for Space Application. *J. Energy Storage* **2023**, *61*, 106792. [CrossRef]
25. Hong, D.; Hu, J.; Yao, J.; Chanussot, J.; Zhu, X.X. Multimodal remote sensing benchmark datasets for land cover classification with a shared and specific feature learning model. *ISPRS J. Photogramm. Remote Sens.* **2021**, *178*, 107–122. [CrossRef] [PubMed]
26. Chen, Z.; Jiang, Y.; Zhang, X.; Zheng, R.; Qiu, R.; Sun, Y.; Zhao, C.; Shang, H. ResNet18DNN: Prediction Approach of Drug-Induced Liver Injury by Deep Neural Network with ResNet18. *Brief. Bioinform.* **2022**, *23*, bbab503. [CrossRef]

27. Kazmi Policht, N.F.; Brooks, T.N.; North, P. Characterization and Classification of Low-Resolution LEO and GEO Satellites with Electro-Optical Fiducial Markers. In Proceedings of the AIAA SCITECH 2024 Forum, Orlando, FL, USA, 8–12 January 2024; p. 2267. [CrossRef]
28. Abraham, K.; Abdelwahab, M.; Abo-Zahhad, M. Classification and Detection of Natural Disasters Using Machine Learning and Deep Learning Techniques: A Review. *Earth Sci. Inform.* **2024**, *17*, 869–891. [CrossRef]
29. Meimetis, D.; Papaioannou, S.; Katsoni, P.; Lappas, V. An Architecture for Early Wildfire Detection and Spread Estimation Using Unmanned Aerial Vehicles, Base Stations, and Space Assets. *Drones Auton. Veh.* **2024**, *1*, 10006. [CrossRef]
30. Sun, X.; Wang, P.; Yan, Z.; Xu, F.; Wang, R.; Diao, W.; Chen, J.; Li, J.; Feng, Y.; Xu, T.; et al. FAIR1M: A Benchmark Dataset for Fine-Grained Object Recognition in High-Resolution Remote Sensing Imagery. *ISPRS J. Photogramm. Remote Sens.* **2022**, *184*, 116–130. [CrossRef]
31. Turkoglu, M.O.; D'Aronco, S.; Perich, G.; Liebisch, F.; Streit, C.; Schindler, K.; Wegner, J.D. Crop Mapping from Image Time Series: Deep Learning with Multi-Scale Label Hierarchies. *Remote Sens. Environ.* **2021**, *264*, 112603. [CrossRef]
32. Yousif, M.J. Enhancing the accuracy of image classification using deep learning and preprocessing methods. *Artif. Intell. Robot. Dev. J.* **2023**, *3*, 348. [CrossRef]
33. Lam, D.; Kuzma, R.; McGee, K.; Dooley, S.; Laielli, M.; Klaric, M.; Bulatov, Y.; McCord, B. xView: Objects in Context in Overhead Imagery. *arXiv* **2018**, arXiv:1802.07856. [CrossRef]
34. Qiao, Y.; Teng, S.; Luo, J.; Sun, P.; Li, F.; Tang, F. On-Orbit DNN Distributed Inference for Remote Sensing Images in Satellite Internet of Things. *IEEE Internet Things J.* **2024**, *12*, 5687–5703. [CrossRef]
35. He, Z.; Tran, K.P.; Thomassey, S.; Zeng, X.; Xu, J.; Yi, C. Multi-Objective Optimization of the Textile Manufacturing Process Using Deep-Q-Network Based Multi-Agent Reinforcement Learning. *J. Manuf. Syst.* **2022**, *62*, 939–949. [CrossRef]
36. Park, S.; Yoo, Y.; Pyo, C.W. Applying DQN Solutions in Fog-Based Vehicular Networks: Scheduling, Caching, and Collision Control. *Veh. Commun.* **2022**, *33*, 100397. [CrossRef]
37. Edwards, M.R.; Holloway, T.; Pierce, R.B.; Blank, L.; Broddle, M.; Choi, E.; Duncan, B.N.; Esparza, Á.; Falchetta, G.; Fritz, M.; et al. Satellite Data Applications for Sustainable Energy Transitions. *Front. Sustain.* **2022**, *3*, 910924. [CrossRef]
38. Myyas, R.E.N.; Al-Dabbasa, M.; Tostado-Véliz, M.; Jurado, F. A Novel Solar Panel Cleaning Mechanism to Improve Performance and Harvesting Rainwater. *Solar Energy* **2022**, *237*, 19–28. [CrossRef]
39. Chen, H.; Zhang, X.; Wang, L.; Xing, L.; Pedrycz, W. Resource-Constrained Self-Organized Optimization for Near-Real-Time Offloading Satellite Earth Observation Big Data. *Knowl.-Based Syst.* **2022**, *253*, 109496. [CrossRef]
40. Chen, B.; Liu, L.; Zou, Z.; Shi, Z. Target Detection in Hyperspectral Remote Sensing Image: Current Status and Challenges. *Remote Sens.* **2023**, *15*, 3223. [CrossRef]
41. Ferreira, B.; Silva, R.G.; Iten, M. Earth Observation Satellite Imagery Information-Based Decision Support Using Machine Learning. *Remote Sens.* **2022**, *14*, 3776. [CrossRef]
42. Zhou, X.; Liang, W.; Yan, K.; Li, W.; Wang, K.I.K.; Ma, J.; Jin, Q. Edge-Enabled Two-Stage Scheduling Based on Deep Reinforcement Learning for Internet of Everything. *IEEE Internet Things J.* **2022**, *10*, 3295–3304. [CrossRef]
43. Yang, Z.; Wang, T.; Lin, Y.; Chen, Y.; Zeng, H.; Pei, J.; Wang, J.; Liu, X.; Zhou, Y.; Zhang, J.; et al. A Vision Chip with Complementary Pathways for Open-World Sensing. *Nature* **2024**, *629*, 1027–1033. [CrossRef]
44. Yang, X.; Shi, Y.; Liu, W.; Ye, H.; Zhong, W.; Xiang, Z. Global Path Planning Algorithm Based on Double DQN for Multi-Tasks Amphibious Unmanned Surface Vehicle. *Ocean Eng.* **2022**, *266*, 112809. [CrossRef]
45. Tan, T.; Xie, H.; Xia, Y.; Shi, X.; Shang, M. Adaptive Moving Average Q-Learning. *Knowl. Inf. Syst.* **2024**, *66*, 7389–7417. [CrossRef]
46. Huang, C.; Wang, G.; Zhou, Z.; Zhang, R.; Lin, L. Reward-Adaptive Reinforcement Learning: Dynamic Policy Gradient Optimization for Bipedal Locomotion. *IEEE Trans. Pattern Anal. Mach. Intell.* **2022**, *45*, 7686–7695. [CrossRef]
47. Shakya, A.K.; Pillai, G.; Chakrabarty, S. Reinforcement Learning Algorithms: A Brief Survey. *Expert Syst. Appl.* **2023**, *231*, 120495. [CrossRef]
48. Li, D.; Yang, Q.; Ma, L.; Wang, Y.; Zhang, Y.; Liao, X. An Electrical Vehicle-Assisted Demand Response Management System: A Reinforcement Learning Method. *Front. Energy Res.* **2023**, *10*, 1071948. [CrossRef]
49. Vashist, A.; Shanmugham, S.V.V.; Ganguly, A.; Manoj, S. DQN Based Exit Selection in Multi-Exit Deep Neural Networks for Applications Targeting Situation Awareness. In Proceedings of the 2022 IEEE International Conference on Consumer Electronics (ICCE), Las Vegas, NV, USA, 7–9 January 2022; pp. 1–6. [CrossRef]
50. Rodrigues, F.F.C. Supergame, A System with Data Collection to Support Game Recommendation: Creating a Recommender System for Casual Games. Master's Thesis, Universidade de Evora, Évora, Portugal, 2023.
51. Goriparthi, R.G. Deep Learning Architectures for Real-Time Image Recognition: Innovations and Applications. *Rev. Intel. Artif. Med.* **2024**, *15*, 880–907. Available online: https://redcrevistas.com/index.php/Revista/article/view/219 (accessed on 14 February 2025).

52. Zhang, Y.; Cheng, Y.; Zheng, H.; Tao, F. Long-/Short-Term Preference Based Dynamic Pricing and Manufacturing Service Collaboration Optimization. *IEEE Trans. Ind. Inform.* **2022**, *18*, 8948–8956. [CrossRef]
53. Nabi, A.; Baidya, T.; Moh, S. Comprehensive Survey on Reinforcement Learning-Based Task Offloading Techniques in Aerial Edge Computing. *Internet Things* **2024**, *28*, 101342. [CrossRef]

remote sensing

MDPI

Article

Adaptive Conditional Reasoning for Remote Sensing Visual Question Answering

Yiqun Gao, Zongwen Bai *, Meili Zhou, Bolin Jia, Peiqi Gao and Rui Zhu

School of Physics and Electronic Information, Yan'an University, Yan'an 716000, China; gaoyq@yau.edu.cn (Y.G.); zml@yau.edu.cn (M.Z.); jbl@yau.edu.cn (B.J.); gaopq@yau.edu.cn (P.G.); zxr14106@yau.edu.cn (R.Z.)

* Correspondence: ydbzw@yau.edu.cn

Abstract: Remote Sensing Visual Question Answering (RS-VQA) is a research task that combines remote sensing image processing and natural language understanding. The increasing complexity and diversity of question types in Remote Sensing Visual Question Answering (RS-VQA) pose significant challenges for unified multimodal reasoning within a single model architecture. Therefore, we propose the Adaptive Conditional Reasoning (ACR) network, a novel framework that dynamically tailors reasoning pathways to question semantics through type-aware feature fusion. The ACR module selectively applies different reasoning strategies depending on whether the question is open-ended or closed-ended, thereby tailoring the reasoning process to the specific nature of the question. In order to enhance the multimodal fusion process of different types of questions, the ACR model further integrates visual and textual features by leveraging type-guided cross-attention. Meanwhile, we use a Dual-Reconstruction Feature Enhancer that mitigates spatial and channel redundancy in remote sensing images via spatial and channel reconstruction convolution, enhancing discriminative feature extraction for key regions. Experimental results demonstrate that our method achieves 78.5% overall accuracy on the EarthVQA dataset, showcasing the effectiveness of adaptive reasoning in remote sensing application.

Keywords: remote sensing visual question answering; multimodal fusion; visual and question reasoning

1. Introduction

Remote Sensing Visual Question Answering (RS-VQA) is an emerging research area that bridges the fields of computer vision and remote sensing, where the goal is to comprehend complex remote sensing images and provide answers to natural language questions related to those images. With the advent of advanced satellite imaging technologies and the vast volume of remotely sensed data, RS-VQA has gained significant attention due to its potential applications in environmental monitoring [1], disaster management [2], and agricultural surveillance [3]. However, despite recent advancements, RS-VQA still faces significant challenges due to the complexity of remote sensing images, which often contain diverse objects, intricate spatial relationships, and varying scales of features. Remote sensing images often contain diverse and intricate information at multiple spatial and temporal scales. These images typically feature heterogeneous objects, such as buildings, roads and water, with varying textures, shapes, and sizes. Additionally, the vast amount of geospatial data captured from satellites or drones can present difficulties in effectively extracting relevant features that are essential for answering specific questions. For instance, questions related to land cover type recognition may involve differentiating between water, forest, and urban areas, while those focused on environmental changes might require temporal analysis of image sequences. The dynamic nature of these tasks makes RS-VQA a challenging problem, as it demands both precise image understanding and the ability to reason about spatial and contextual relationships between objects in the scene. Furthermore, the inherent multimodal nature of RS-VQA tasks—where both visual content and natural language need to be processed simultaneously—compounds the difficulty of achieving robust and accurate performance.

Recent research in RS-VQA has largely followed the trend of adapting deep learning-based approaches originally designed for image captioning and Visual Question Answering (VQA) to the remote sensing domain [4]. These methods typically rely on convolutional neural networks (CNNs) for visual feature extraction and recurrent neural networks (RNNs) for language understanding. These methods often struggle to effectively handle complex problems that require multi-step reasoning or fine-grained relationship analysis. They tend to perform better when dealing with simpler problems (such as determining the presence of an object), but lack sufficient flexibility and accuracy when it comes to tasks that involve complex reasoning processes (such as dynamic changes in spatial relationships). These methods typically rely on static architectures and fixed spatial hierarchies, which cannot dynamically adjust based on the semantic or contextual dependencies of the problem. They are also unable to automatically adjust the weight of visual features or switch reasoning paths according to the different intents of the problem.

While these models have shown promise, they often struggle to effectively integrate the diverse, multi-scale, and highly detailed information embedded in remote sensing images. Furthermore, existing approaches tend to apply a one-size-fits-all reasoning process across different question types, which may limit their ability to perform nuanced reasoning for complex or context-dependent questions. Existing unified frameworks employ static fusion strategies (e.g., concatenation or fixed attention) that indiscriminately process all question types, leading to suboptimal performance for context-dependent or multi-step queries. For example, a closed-ended question like 'Is there a hospital near the river?' requires simple object co-occurrence detection, whereas an open-ended question like 'How does the distribution of residential areas correlate with road networks in this region?' demands hierarchical spatial reasoning and semantic grounding. Traditional frameworks fail to distinguish these fundamentally different reasoning requirements, resulting in feature misalignment (e.g., over-emphasizing irrelevant regions for closed-ended tasks) or insufficient interaction depth (e.g., shallow fusion for open-ended tasks).

The unified reasoning framework of traditional VQA struggles to dynamically adjust the feature interaction methods for different types of questions, leading to limited generalization ability of the model for complex questions. Adaptive type judgment alleviates the mismatch between heterogeneous question types and a single reasoning mode by customizing reasoning paths. To address these issues, we propose Adaptive Conditional Reasoning (ACR), which aims to improve the flexibility and precision of reasoning in RS-VQA tasks. Our method consists of two key components: a Type-Driven Conditioned Reasoning module and a Text–Image Cross-Modal Reasoning module based on the type of question. The Type-Driven Conditioned Reasoning module employs Transformer-based type classification before multimodal fusion to adaptively route reasoning procedures based on semantic intent. And the Text–Image Cross-Modal Reasoning module enables fine-grained visual–linguistic interaction through attention-driven joint reasoning. Moreover, to mitigate spatial and channel redundancy in remote sensing images, we utilize Dual-Reconstruction Feature Enhancer (DRE) to enhance visual feature extraction. By leveraging cross-modal attention and adaptive reasoning strategies, our model is capable of providing more accurate, interpretable, and context-sensitive answers. Specifically, our approach excels in handling complex spatial and relational queries, which are common in remote sensing applications. Experimental results on the EarthVQA dataset demonstrate that our method significantly outperforms existing approaches, highlighting the effectiveness of adaptive reasoning in improving the performance of the RS-VQA system.

The key contributions of this paper can be summarized as follows:

(1) We propose an Adaptive Conditional Reasoning process which involves a Type-Driven Conditioned Reasoning module and a text–image cross-modal reasoning method based on the type of question. Before the fusion of multimodal features, incorporating a type judgment process enables adaptive selection of reasoning procedures corresponding to different types of questions. By using image–text and text–image attention, the module achieves symmetric interaction between visual and text features.

(2) In order to mitigate spatial redundancy and channel redundancy during image feature extraction, we employ spatial reconstruction convolution and channel reconstruction convolution, which enhance the model's ability to focus on key areas in remote sensing images.

(3) To demonstrate the superiority of our proposed framework, we conducted an evaluation, comparing it with the other methods on the EarthVQA dataset. The results confirm the substantial improvement and advancement achieved by the Adaptive Conditional Reasoning framework in Remote Sensing Visual Question Answering tasks.

2. Related Work

2.1. Visual Question Answering

Visual Question Answering (VQA) is a challenging task that requires joint image and language understanding to answer questions about given photographs. Recent research has focused on developing innovative models to improve the performance of VQA systems. Ref. Antol et al. [5] introduced the concept of neural module networks, which compose collections of jointly trained neural modules into deep networks for question answering. By applying this approach, they achieved state-of-the-art results on challenging datasets for VQA, including the VQA natural image dataset and a dataset of complex questions about abstract shapes. The prevalent framework for the general VQA domain is joint embedding [5]. This framework encompasses four key components: an image encoder, question encoder, feature fusion, and answer component tailored to task requirements. Established convolutional neural network (CNN) backbones, such as VGGNet [6] and ResNet [7], function as image feature extractors. For the question encoder, widely adopted language encoding models like LSTM [8] and GRU [9] are employed. Feature encoding models are typically initialized with pre-trained weights and fine-tuned in an end-to-end manner during training for enhanced performance. The fusion of question features and image features is achieved through an attention mechanism. The answer component commonly consists of a neural network classifier.

In summary, the majority of studies employ a transfer learning approach, where models like VGGNet and ResNet are pre-trained on extensive natural image datasets and subsequently fine-tuned using specific data.

2.2. Remote Sensing Visual Question Answering

Remote Sensing Visual Question Answering (RS-VQA) has emerged as a critical area of research, leveraging the synergy between remote sensing imagery and natural language processing to facilitate intelligent interpretation of geospatial data. Numerous advances in deep learning and multimodal reasoning have been pivotal in the development of RS-VQA systems.

Early work [10] introduced an automatic method for generating a dataset for RS-VQA using OpenStreetMap data. This innovative approach utilized deep learning techniques to establish a foundational framework for training models capable of answering questions based on remote sensing images. Expanding on this idea, they developed two distinct RS-VQA datasets containing image–question–answer triplets, derived from both low- and high-resolution satellite imagery. This expansion provided a broader range of data types, facilitating deeper exploration into how image quality impacts the performance of RS-VQA systems. Building upon the need for improved attention mechanisms in deep learning models, Zheng et al. [4] proposed the Mutual Attention Inception Network (MAIN) for RS-VQA. Their approach focused on enhancing the attention mechanism to better fuse visual and textual information, a critical aspect for accurate question answering in remote sensing contexts. Additionally, Lobry et al. [11] introduced a large-scale RS-VQA dataset by extracting image–question–answer triplets from the BigEarthNet dataset. This work highlighted the scalability of deep learning models for RS-VQA tasks, enabling more robust evaluations and improving model generalization across different types of remote sensing data.

In terms of model architectures, recent research has explored more sophisticated approaches to improve performance. Bazi et al. [12] proposed a bimodal Transformer-based approach to RS-VQA. This method utilized contextual representations from both the image and the question, allowing the model to capture intricate relationships between the visual content and the linguistic queries. Similarly, Siebert et al. [13] introduced a multimodal fusion Transformer that learned joint representations of the image and the question modalities, addressing the challenge of aligning and understanding the intricate relations between these two sources of information. In addition to question answering, Zhan et al. [14] explored the task of visual grounding for remote sensing data, focusing on the localization of objects within remote sensing images using natural language queries. Their work extended the idea of integrating language with visual data to not only answer questions but also provide spatial context and precise localization in satellite imagery. This added a layer of complexity to the task, emphasizing the need for fine-grained visual reasoning.

To improve spatial reasoning in RS-VQA systems, Zhang et al. [15] proposed a Spatial Hierarchical Reasoning Network (SHRNet). Their approach enhanced the system's ability to perform visual–spatial reasoning by breaking down the image into different spatial hierarchies, thus improving model performance on publicly available datasets and facilitating more accurate spatial interpretations in response to complex questions. The application of RS-VQA in specialized domains, such as post-disaster damage assessment, has also garnered attention. Sarkar et al. [16] presented a supervised attention-based VQA model designed for evaluating post-disaster damage from remote sensing imagery. Their approach emphasized the importance of efficient response and recovery strategies following natural disasters, where accurate interpretation of satellite images could significantly aid in emergency management and resource allocation. To extract useful landform information from remote sensing images, many studies use semantic segmentation methods for preprocessing, labeling different landform categories. This process helps the question answering system more accurately locate regions related to the question, thereby improving the relevance and accuracy of the answers. Ran et al. [17] proposed a novel Dual-Domain Image Fusion (DDF) strategy, which leverages original remote sensing images, style-transferred images, and intermediate domain information to enhance the self-training method.

Recent advancements in large-scale vision–language models have begun to influence the field of RS-VQA. Bazi et al. [18] introduced RS-LLaVA, a remote sensing-specific adaptation of the Large Language and Vision Assistant (LLaVA) model. By integrating large-scale vision–language pre-training into the analysis of remote sensing imagery, RS-LLaVA demonstrated substantial improvements in understanding complex remote sensing scenarios. This work showcases the potential of applying cutting-edge multimodal models, like LLaVA, to the specific challenges posed by remote sensing imagery, marking a significant step forward in the development of more powerful and scalable RS-VQA systems. However, the era of large models also brings forth several challenges and issues. For instance, the substantial volume of parameters in training models poses highly demanding research conditions.

2.3. Multimodal Fusion and Reasoning

Multimodal fusion is a key aspect in various fields such as emotion recognition, human activity recognition, affective computing, and sentiment analysis. Different studies have explored the effectiveness of various fusion strategies in improving recognition performance and robustness in multimodal tasks. Jiang et al. [19] conducted a snapshot research on multimodal information fusion for data-driven emotion recognition. They highlighted the importance of integrating multiple modalities to enhance emotion recognition accuracy. Gadzicki et al. [20] compared early vs. late fusion in multimodal convolutional neural networks for human activity recognition. They utilized RGB video, optical flow, and skeleton data as modalities, emphasizing the significance of fusion timing in improving recognition outcomes. Mai et al. [21] proposed a locally confined modality fusion network with a global perspective for multimodal human affective computing. Their framework incorporated bidirectional multiconnected LSTM to address the multimodal affective computing problem, focusing on both local and global fusion for comprehensive information understanding. Huang et al. [22] utilized the Transformer model for multimodal fusion in continuous emotion recognition, showcasing the superiority of model-level fusion over other strategies on the AVEC 2017 database. Additionally, Zhao et al. [23] proposed a Text-guided Coarse-to-Fine Fusion Network for robust RS-VQA, which leverages semantic relationships between question text and multi-source images for feature-level fusion guidance.

Multimodal reasoning is a significant area of research in artificial intelligence, aiming to integrate different modes of information processing to solve complex problems. Zhao et al. [24] proposed a framework that combines case-based reasoning, rule-based reasoning, and information retrieval to address challenges in evidence-based medical practice. Marling et al. [25] further explored the role of case-based reasoning in multimodal reasoning integrations, highlighting the various roles that case-based reasoning components can fulfill in integrated systems. Nam et al. [26] introduced Dual-Attention Networks for multimodal reasoning and matching, allowing visual and textual attentions to collaborate during inference tasks like Visual Question Answering. Lippe et al. [27] and Zellers et al. [28] delved into the detection of hateful memes and multimodal script knowledge models, respectively, showcasing the need for joint visual and language understanding in multimodal reasoning. Recent advancements in multimodal reasoning include the development of Socratic Models and MM-REACT [29], which leverage language as an intermediate representation to combine knowledge from different pre-trained models for various tasks. Additionally, Zheng et al. [30] introduced Duty-Distinct Chain-of-Thought Prompting for multimodal reasoning in language models, aiming to mimic human thinking processes in AI systems. These studies collectively highlight the evolving landscape of multimodal reasoning research and its applications across different domains [17].

3. Methods

Currently, the questions in Remote Sensing Visual Question Answering (RS-VQA) are becoming more complex, and the types of questions are no longer uniform. As a result, it is necessary to unify different types of questions within a single model architecture. In response, we propose the Adaptive Conditioned Reasoning (ACR) network (Figure 1), which incorporates type classification during the multimodal feature fusion process to adaptively select the reasoning process for different question types. This approach enables the RS-VQA model to better understand and adapt to the characteristics of diverse question types, thereby enhancing the efficiency and accuracy of the model during multimodal feature integration. Through this mechanism, the model can more precisely select appropriate features and reasoning strategies, ultimately improving the overall performance of the question answering system. The framework consists of three key components: (1) a Dual-Reconstruction Feature Enhancer module for mitigating spatial and channel redundancy in remote sensing images, (2) a Type-Driven Conditional Reasoning module to dynamically select a reasoning procedure based on question semantic, and (3) a Text–Image Cross-Modal Reasoning module for joint visual-linguistic interaction.

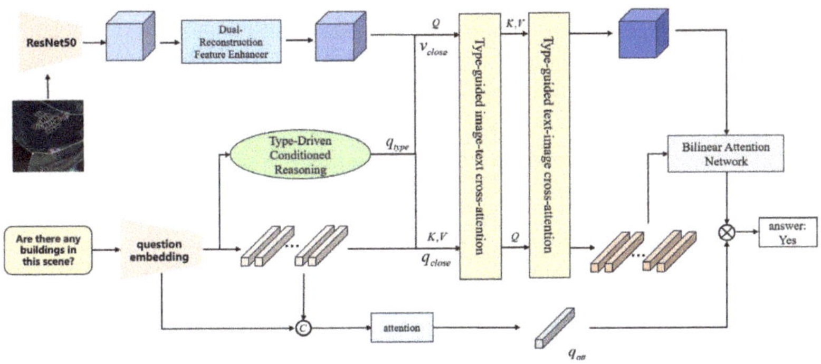

Figure 1. The framework of the proposed Adaptive Conditional Reasoning module (ACR). We utilize a type judgment process which enables adaptive selection of reasoning procedures corresponding to different types of questions. Then, we use a type-guided cross-attention module with image–text and text–image attention to enhance the representation of visual features and textual features.

3.1. Type-Driven Conditional Reasoning

The Type-Driven Conditional Reasoning module is the core component of our proposed method, designed to dynamically adjust the fusion of visual features based on the semantic content of different types of questions.

Elevating the model's understanding capability is achievable by leveraging task-specific skills tailored to different tasks. The model enhances multi-level reasoning capabilities through adaptive handling of different tasks based on its judgment of various questions. The structure of the Type-Driven Conditional Reasoning module is shown in Figure 2.

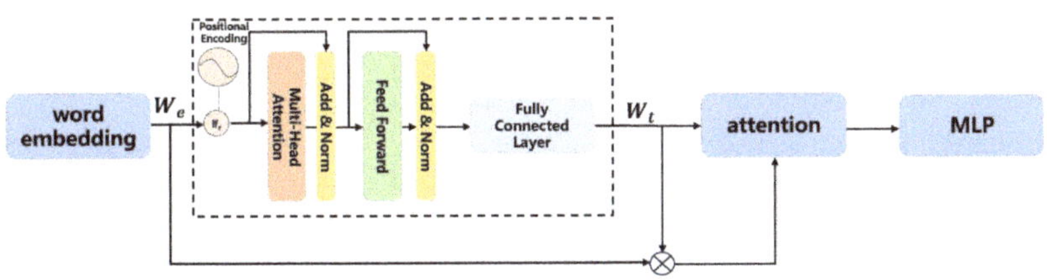

Figure 2. Type-Driven Conditional Reasoning module.

The role of the question encoding module is to transform natural language questions into high-dimensional semantic vectors, facilitating effective interaction with image features. This semantic vector serves as the input to the Adaptive Conditional Reasoning module, which integrates with the image features to perform subsequent reasoning. The question string is initially converted into a word embedding sequence.

$$W_e = word\ embedding(w) = [q_1, q_2, ..., q_l] \quad (1)$$

where q_i represents the word embedding of the ith word.

For the word embedding sequence, we further process it to obtain efficient question embedding, facilitating effective feature extraction.

$$W_t = encoder([q_1, q_2, ..., q_l]) = (\theta_1, \theta_2, ..., \theta_n) \quad (2)$$

The encoder relies on self-attention mechanisms to process input sequences in parallel, overcoming the sequential nature of RNNs. This architecture is particularly effective for word embedding, as it can simultaneously attend to all words in a sentence, capturing complex relationships between them without relying on sequential processing. The Transformer Encoder consists of multiple stacked layers, each composed of two main components:

The self-attention mechanism enables the model to weigh the importance of each word relative to the others in the input sequence. Specifically, for each word w_i in the input sequence, self-attention computes a weighted sum of all words in the sentence, based on their relevance to w_i. The attention weights are calculated as follows:

$$\alpha_{i,j} = \frac{e^{\frac{Q_i K_j^T}{\sqrt{d_k}}}}{\sum_{k=1}^{N} e^{\frac{Q_i K_k^T}{\sqrt{d_k}}}} \quad (3)$$

where Q_i and K_j are the query and key vectors of words i and j, respectively, and d_k is the dimension of the key vectors. The output is a context-sensitive representation of each word.

After applying self-attention, the output is passed through a fully connected feed-forward network. The feed-forward network helps introduce non-linearity, allowing for a richer transformation of the word representations. Each encoder layer also includes residual connections and layer normalization to stabilize training and improve the flow of gradients.

Due to the RS-VQA model's limited ability to perform multi-layer reasoning, we adopt separate reasoning modules to process closed-ended and open-ended questions.

Closed-ended questions typically start with verbs such as "Is", "Are", or "Does", while open-ended questions usually begin with question words like "How", "Where", or "What". Different question types (such as open-ended questions and closed-ended questions) require different processing approaches. The distinction between these two types can be captured through the use of question embedding. So, the Type-Driven Conditional Reasoning module is responsible for selecting the appropriate reasoning strategy based on the question type. It first classifies the question and then adopts different reasoning paths based on the classification results. Specifically, the module takes the question as input and outputs its question type (either closed-ended or open-ended).

For questions, we utilize the question feature extractor to obtain semantic features. With the multi-head self-attention mechanism as the core, it effectively captures the dependency relationships and semantic information among words in the questions, avoiding long-term dependency on context from a global perspective. Therefore, it can better model the semantics of questions. After extracting question features, an attention mechanism is used to assign important weights to different words to further emphasize the important parts of each problem, such as "What is the area of buildings?". Then, we further incorporate an attention mechanism:

$$\widetilde{W} = W_e \otimes W_t \tag{4}$$

where $\widetilde{W}$ represents the concatenation of embedded features and question features along the dimension.

$$\begin{cases} Y = tanh(W_1\widetilde{W}) \\ \widetilde{Y} = \sigma(W_2\widetilde{W}) \\ G = Y \odot \widetilde{Y} \end{cases} \tag{5}$$

where $\odot$ represents the Hadamard product. Next, add attention information to the features:

$$\alpha = softmax((W_\alpha G)^T) \tag{6}$$

where α represents the attention score.

$$q_{att} = W_t\alpha \tag{7}$$

q_{att} is the question feature with attention information. The question encoder in the module reduces the long-term dependency of the question context, which is beneficial for subsequent reasoning processes. The obtained question embedding q_{att} is passed through an MLP to map it to a classification score. The classification probabilities are denoted as p, where p_0 represents the probability of the question being a closed-ended question, and p_1 represents the probability of the question being an open-ended question. If $p_0 > p_1$, it indicates that the question is closed-ended. This can be represented by

$$T(q) = \begin{cases} 0, \ p_0 > p_1 \\ 1, \ else \end{cases} \tag{8}$$

where $T(q)$ represents the probability that the question is an open-ended question versus a closed-ended question. A $T(q)$ of 0 indicates that a question is closed-ended, and a $T(q)$ of 1 indicates that a question is open-ended. The visual features and question features are then subjected to corresponding multimodal fusion based on the classification results. The network trains a module effective for open-ended questions ($T(q) = 1$) and the network trains a module effective only for closed-ended questions ($T(q) = 0$). Through this module, the model can determine the probability that the input question is an open or closed question, thereby providing guidance for the targeted feature fusion process.

3.2. Text–Image Cross-Modal Reasoning Module

If the question type is open-ended (or closed-ended), then the visual feature is v_{open} (v_{close}), and the text feature is q_{open} (q_{close}). To achieve fine-grained alignment between visual and textual modalities, we design a bidirectional cross-attention architecture shown in Figure 3:

First, map the visual feature v_0 to the query vector Q_V, with the text feature q_0 serving as the key K_L and value V_L.

$$Q_V = v_0 W_V^q \tag{9}$$

$$K_L = q_0 W_L^k \tag{10}$$

$$V_L = q_0 W_L^v \tag{11}$$

Then, calculate the cross-attention weights, allowing the visual features to focus on relevant text information and integrate the textual context into the visual features. This helps filter the visual regions that are semantically related to the text:

$$A_{v2l} = Softmax\left(\frac{Q_V K_L^\top}{\sqrt{d_k}}\right) \tag{12}$$

$$v' = A_{v2l} V_L \tag{13}$$

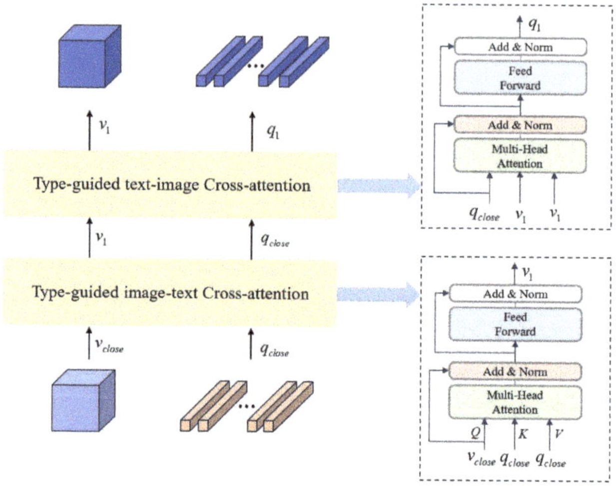

Figure 3. Text–Image Cross-Modal Reasoning module.

After the cross-attention operation, the enhanced visual feature v_1 is obtained, which contains rich information from the text modality.

Then, the text feature q_0 is mapped to the query vector Q_L, with the visual feature v_0 serving as the key K_V and value V_V.

$$Q_L = q_0 W_L^q \tag{14}$$

$$K_V = v_0 W_V^k \tag{15}$$

$$V_V = v_0 W_V^v \tag{16}$$

We calculate the cross-attention weights to optimize the semantic representation through visual features, integrating visual context information.

$$A_{l2v} = Softmax\left(\frac{Q_L K_V^\top}{\sqrt{d_k}}\right) \tag{17}$$

$$q' = A_{l2v} V_V \tag{18}$$

The cross-attention operation allows the text features to integrate visual information, thereby enhancing the representational power of the text features. After the cross-attention operation, the enhanced text feature q_1 is obtained, which contains rich information from the visual modality.

To prevent information loss, residual connections and layer normalization are added to the output of each stage:

$$v_1 = LayerNorm(v_0 + v') \tag{19}$$

$$q_1 = LayerNorm(q_0 + q') \tag{20}$$

In reasoning with the Type-Driven Conditioned Reasoning module, reasoning skill is learned by simultaneously applying importance selection to the fused feature. The module needs to dynamically adjust the handling of image features based on the semantic content of the question. Different types of questions may focus on different regions of the image, requiring the model to selectively attend to specific parts of the image. Through this process, the model can flexibly select the relevant areas of the image based on the semantic information of the question, thereby enhancing the specificity and accuracy of the reasoning.

We combine the language and image features that capture the key information in the problem to obtain a comprehensive feature representation. Specifically, we utilize a common fusion module, denoted as A, to integrate the two modalities effectively. The fused features are then fed into a classifier, denoted as D, for the final prediction.

$$s = D_{\theta_c}(A_{\theta_m}(v_1, q_1) \circ q_{att}) \tag{21}$$

where $\circ$ represents the element-wise product, s is the final predicted score, A is a commonly used fusion module, and D is the classifier. Through this approach, the Type-Driven Conditioned Reasoning module ensures that different types of questions are handled with the most suitable reasoning strategy, thereby improving both the efficiency and accuracy of the reasoning process.

The training objective minimizes cross-entropy loss for answer prediction, formulated as

$$\mathcal{L}_{\text{CE}} = -\sum_{c=1}^{C} y_{i,c} log(p_{i,c}) \tag{22}$$

where C is the number of answer classes, $y_{i,c}$ is the ground-truth one-hot label for the i-th sample, and $p_{i,c}$ is the predicted probability from the classifier D.

3.3. Dual-Reconstruction Feature Enhancer

Objects in remote sensing images often exhibit complex shapes, diverse land cover types, and rich spatial information, making the visual feature extraction module particularly critical. In this study, we employ a convolutional neural network based on the deep residual network (ResNet-50) to extract multi-scale features from the images.

In this process, drawing inspiration from [31] to address spatial and channel redundancy in image features, we devise a Dual-Reconstruction Feature Enhancer through spatial reconstruction units and channel reconstruction units.

In the process of feature extraction from remote sensing images, we incorporate the spatial and channel reconstruction convolution method to enhance the spatial and channel representation capabilities of the features. Specifically, within each residual block of the feature extraction network, spatial and channel reconstruction convolutions are applied after the convolution operation to further process the extracted feature maps. By integrating spatial and channel reconstruction convolution into the feature extraction process of remote sensing images, we can effectively mitigate the impact of redundant features and improve the deep network's ability to represent remote sensing images. This improvement aids the model in better understanding the types of ground objects, spatial structures, and various environmental features within the images.

Spatial reconstruction convolution aims to enhance the spatial information representation of an image by reconstructing the features along the spatial dimension. In the process of remote sensing image feature extraction, spatial reconstruction convolution can be applied to further process the feature maps, thereby reinforcing the spatial information in important regions and diminishing the influence of redundant areas. For instance, in the case of high-resolution details in remote sensing images, spatial reconstruction convolution enables the model to focus on fine-grained details of ground objects (e.g., buildings, roads, water), while minimizing the interference from irrelevant background regions.

The spatial and channel reconstruction convolution module in the visual feature extraction process is shown in Figure 4. Initially, the assessment of information content in different feature maps is conducted using the scaling factor in Group Normalization. This process separates feature maps with higher information content from those with lower information content.

$$X_{out} = GN(X) = \gamma \frac{X - \mu}{\sqrt{\sigma^2 + \varepsilon}} + \beta \tag{23}$$

$$W_\gamma = \frac{\gamma_i}{\sum_{j=1}^{C} \gamma_j}, i, j = 1, 2, \ldots, C \tag{24}$$

$$W = Gate(sigmoid(W_\gamma(X_{out}))) \tag{25}$$

where X_{out} represents the standardized input feature X, and W_γ obtained from Equation (24) indicates the importance of different feature mappings. The weights of the feature mappings, adjusted through W_γ, are mapped to the (0, 1) range by a sigmoid function and gated by a threshold. We set the weights above the threshold to 1, yielding the information weight W_1, and set them to 0, resulting in the non-information weight W_2.

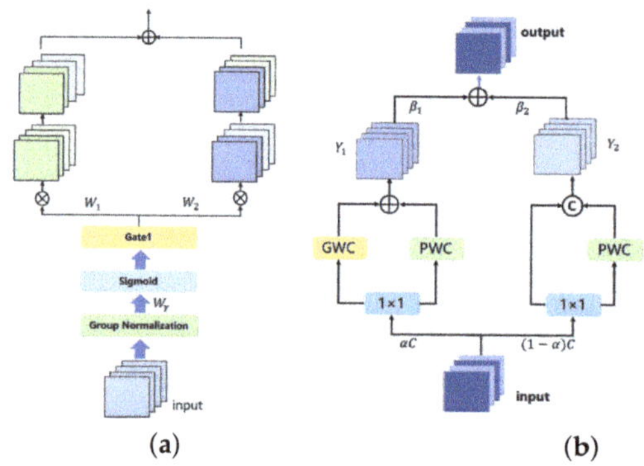

Figure 4. (**a**) Spatial reconstruction convolution and (**b**) Channel reconstruction convolution.

Subsequently, the addition of feature maps with more information and those with less information is performed to generate feature maps with more information while conserving space. The specific operation is cross-reconstruction, involving the weighted combination of two different information features, resulting in a spatially refined feature map. This approach effectively separates feature maps with higher information content from those with lower information content, thus mitigating redundant features in the spatial dimension.

$$\begin{cases} X_1^\omega = W_1 \otimes X \\ X_2^\omega = W_2 \otimes X \\ X_{11}^\omega \cup X_{22}^\omega = X^{\omega_1} \\ X_{21}^\omega \cup X_{12}^\omega = X^{\omega_2} \\ X^{\omega_1} \oplus X^{\omega_2} = X^\omega \end{cases} \tag{26}$$

where $\cup$ represents concatenation, $\otimes$ represents element-wise multiplication and $\oplus$ is element-wise summation.

Channel reconstruction convolution optimizes feature representation by reconstructing the channel dimension, thereby reducing redundancy between channels. In the context of remote sensing images, channel reconstruction convolution adjusts the weights of different feature channels, compressing or optimizing redundant channel information. For the extracted multi-scale feature maps, some feature channels may contain duplicate or overly similar information. Channel reconstruction convolution can adaptively learn which channels are most critical for the final task, automatically suppressing redundant channels, thus enhancing the expressiveness of the feature maps.

In the channel dimension, the spatially refined features of the input are split into two segments: one with αC channels and the other with $(1-\alpha)C$ channels, where α is a hyper-parameter, and $0 \leq \alpha \leq C$, 1×1 convolution kernels are employed to compress the channel numbers of the two sets of features, resulting in X_{up} and X_{low}.

We perform GWC and PWC separately, followed by adding the outputs. The fusion operation utilizes global average pooling to integrate global spatial information and channel statistics, yielding pooled S_1 and S_2.

$$S_m = Pooling(Y_m) \tag{27}$$

Then, we obtain feature weight vectors β_1 and β_2.

$$\beta_1 = \frac{e^{S_1}}{e^{S_1} + e^{S_2}}, \quad \beta_2 = 1 - \beta_1 \tag{28}$$

Finally, the output Y is acquired using the feature weight vectors, representing the channel-refined features.

$$v = Y = \beta_1 Y_1 + \beta_2 Y_2 \tag{29}$$

where Y represents the visual features extracted by the model.

4. Experiment and Results

4.1. Setting

The model is implemented using pytorch and trained on a single GPU in the Ubuntu 22.04 environment. During the model training process, the learning rate decay algorithm is employed, and the Adam [32] optimizer is used. During training, the batch size is set to 16, and the initial learning rate of the model is set to 5×10^{-5}.

The accuracy of the model's answers to questions is the most important and sole evaluation metric, which is the mainstream evaluation standard for RS-VQA models. We also use accuracy as the evaluation metric for the model, and it is calculated as follows:

$$Accuracy = \frac{S_c}{S_{all}} \times 100 \tag{30}$$

where S_c represents the number of correctly answered questions, and S_{all} represents the total number of questions.

4.2. Dataset

In this study, we use the EarthVQA [33] dataset as the primary data source for the Visual Question Answering model.

The EarthVQA dataset consists of 6000 high-resolution remote sensing images, corresponding semantic masks, and 208,593 question–answer pairs. These QA pairs are closely related to urban and rural governance requirements, covering a wide range of tasks from simple judgments and counting to more complex relational analysis. The dataset is an extension of the LoveDA dataset and includes 18 urban and rural areas from cities in China, namely Nanjing, Changzhou, and Wuhan. Similar to common Visual Question Answering (VQA) datasets, the distribution of answers in EarthVQA is imbalanced, posing additional challenges for practical applications in the Earth's environmental contexts. Figure 5 shows an example image from the EarthVQA dataset along with the corresponding QA pairs.

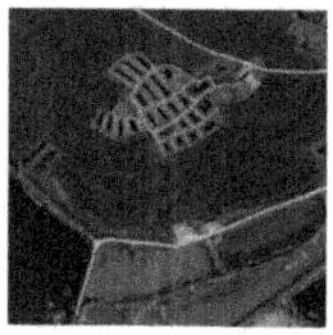

Question Type: Basic Judging Q: Are there any buildings in this scene? A: No.	**Question Type: Basic Counting** Q: What is the area of buildings? A: 0%-10%.
Question Type: Object Situation Analysis Q: What are the water types in this scene? A: There are ponds.	**Question Type: Reasoning-based Judging** Q: Is there any residential land in this scene? A: No.
Question Type: Reasoning-based Counting Q: How many eutrophic waters are in this scene? A: 0.	**Question Type: Comprehensive Analysis** Q: What are the land use types in this scene? A: There are agricultural areas.

Figure 5. Example image and corresponding QA pairs from the EarthVQA dataset.

4.3. Accuracy Evaluation with Other Methods

To better evaluate the RS-VQA model's robustness to various types of questions, the accuracy is typically analyzed from six perspectives: basic counting, relational-based counting, basic judging, relational-based judging, comprehensive analysis and object situation analysis. All types of questions encompass both open-ended and closed-ended questions. Open-ended questions are defined as question types without fixed answers, meaning that the type of answer changes with the question, while closed-ended questions are defined as question types with fixed answers, meaning that the type of answer remains the same regardless of how the question changes (e.g., yes/no).

To comprehensively evaluate the performance of the ACR module, we conducted comparative experiments with other methods on the EarthVQA dataset. Table 1 presents the results of the EarthVQA dataset. The compared models include both general VQA frameworks and specialized RS-VQA approaches:

(1) SAN [34]: SAN processes the input image and question through stacked attention mechanisms, progressively enhancing the model's focus on different visual information, thereby enabling more accurate reasoning and answering in the given visual scene.
(2) MAC [35]: MAC introduces a memory module, which is used to store and transfer relevant features of the image. The model gradually reads the image features and stores them in the "memory" for subsequent reasoning and answering.
(3) MCAN [36]: MCAN is composed of a series of Modular Co-Attention (MCA) layers. Each MCA layer is capable of modeling the attention between the image and the question.
(4) BUTD [37]: BUTD combines bottom-up and top-down attention mechanisms to compute the salient regions in the image at the object level.
(5) D-VQA [38]: D-VQA constructs branches from questions to answers and from visuals to answers, capturing the biases in language and vision, and applies two unimodal bias detection modules to explicitly identify and remove negative biases.
(6) RSVQA [39]: A baseline model constrained by its shallow CNN feature extractor in capturing high-resolution RS image details.
(7) SOBA [33]: SOBA generates object semantics using a segmentation network and aggregates internal object features through pseudo-masks.

Table 1. Accuracy of the existing methods on the EarthVQA dataset.

Methods	Bas Co	Bas Ju	Rel Co	Rel Ju	Obj An	Com An	Overall	Param. (M)
BAN	77.6	89.8	63.7	81.9	55.7	45.1	76.7	58.7
SAN	76.2	87.6	59.2	81.8	55.0	43.3	75.7	32.3
MAC	72.5	82.9	55.9	79.5	46.3	40.5	72.0	38.6
MCAN	79.8	89.6	63.8	81.8	55.6	45.0	77.0	55.2
D-VQA	77.3	89.7	64.0	82.1	55.1	43.2	76.6	37.8
SOBA	80.1	89.6	67.8	82.6	61.4	49.3	78.1	40.5
RSVQA	70.7	82.4	55.5	79.3	42.5	35.5	70.7	30.2
BUTD	77.2	90.0	60.9	82.0	56.3	42.3	76.5	34.9
ACR (ours)	79.7	89.8	68.0	83.6	61.6	49.2	78.5	47.9

Our experiments on the EarthVQA dataset demonstrate the superior performance of the proposed ACR model in Remote Sensing Visual Question Answering tasks. ACR achieves an overall accuracy of 78.5%, surpassing all baseline methods, particularly excelling in tasks requiring complex spatial relational reasoning (68.0% for relational-based counting and 83.6% for relational-based judging), outperforming the suboptimal model SOBA by +0.2% and +1.0%, respectively. With only 47.9 M parameters (81.6% of BAN's 58.7 M), ACR maintains leadership in high-level semantic tasks such as object situation analysis (61.6%) through its dynamic relational reasoning module and multimodal feature fusion strategy, achieving an optimal balance between parameter efficiency and task performance. While slightly trailing behind specialized models like BUTD in basic tasks (79.7% for counting and 89.8% for judging), ACR validates the effectiveness of its unified architecture for multi-granularity geospatial reasoning. This work establishes a new paradigm for building efficient and interpretable remote sensing QA systems.

While ACR achieves great performance in complex tasks (e.g., relational reasoning), its modest improvement in Bas Co (79.7%) compared to MCAN (79.8%) and SOBA (80.1%) stems from the inherent simplicity of basic counting tasks. These tasks often require localized object detection rather than adaptive reasoning. TCR's adaptive reasoning pathways are more impactful for open-ended or relation-heavy questions, where nuanced cross-modal interaction is critical. Future work will explore task-specific feature enhancement to better balance performance across simple and complex tasks.

Based on the experimental evaluation results, we can make the following analysis. First, the results for basic condition-type questions indicate that, in fundamental analyses of remote sensing images (such as terrain type, vegetation cover, and building presence), our method is able to effectively understand and reason about the basic condition information within the image, accurately identifying the geographic phenomena queried by the question. Secondly, for basic judging-type questions, our method achieves an accuracy of 89.8%, demonstrating its effectiveness in reasoning about simple judgments within the image (such as whether a specific feature is present or whether climatic conditions are met). In making basic judgments on remote sensing images, particularly in low-resolution images or those significantly affected by weather conditions, the model can make relatively accurate inferences by carefully processing image features. Third, relational-based counting-type questions typically involve reasoning about the relationships between multiple variables, such as identifying spatial relationships between different features in remote sensing images (e.g., the relative position of water and urban areas). Our method performs well in reasoning across complex geographical and spatial information. Finally, our method exhibits significantly higher accuracy than other methods in answering comprehensive analysis-type questions. This suggests that our approach is particularly effective in integrating multidimensional information from remote sensing images, such as considering vegetation, buildings, road networks, and climatic conditions simultaneously, to conduct comprehensive reasoning for complex questions.

Overall, our method outperforms traditional approaches such as SAN, MAC, and MCAN on the EarthVQA dataset, demonstrating strong reasoning capabilities in Remote Sensing Visual Question Answering. Remote sensing images often contain complex information related to terrain, climate, and human activities. Our method is able to effectively integrate image and question information, extracting key geographical details from these complex data, thereby enabling more accurate reasoning.

4.4. Ablation Study

In order to evaluate the effectiveness of the proposed Adaptive Conditional Reasoning network and new image feature extraction module, we conducted ablation experiments on the model by removing the Dual-Reconstruction Feature Enhancer (DRE) and the Type-Driven Conditioned Reasoning (TCR) module separately. We evaluated the performance of the model in both cases, as shown in Table 2. "DRE" represents the accuracy after adding the Dual-Reconstruction Feature Enhancer to the model. "TCR" represents the accuracy after adding the Type-Driven Conditioned Reasoning module to the model. It can be observed that removing both modules resulted in a decrease in the prediction accuracy of the model to varying degrees.

Table 2. Ablation study of the proposed modules.

DRE	TCR	Bas Co	Bas Ju	Rel Co	Rel Ju	Obj An	Com An	Overall
		78.9	89.0	64.2	82.7	57.4	47.6	77.3
✓		79.2	89.3	64.6	81.7	57.5	48.3	77.4
	✓	80.4	90.2	67.5	82.8	60.3	48.5	78.4
✓	✓	79.7	89.8	68.0	83.6	61.6	49.2	78.5

The ablation results in Table 2 reveal nuanced contributions of the Dual-Reconstruction Feature Enhancer (DRE) and Type-Driven Conditional Reasoning (TCR) modules. The results of the ablation study reveal that when the DRE module is used individually, the overall performance of the model is 77.4%. When the TCR module is enabled, the performance slightly improves to 78.4%. The DRE improves basic counting questions (+0.3% without DRE) and comprehensive analysis questions (+0.7%) by suppressing spatial–channel redundancies, which is critical for tasks requiring fine-grained localization (e.g., counting scattered buildings). However, its impact on relational-based judging questions is limited, as relational judgments rely more on cross-modal interaction than spatial refinement. TCR significantly boosts relational-based counting questions (+3.3%) and object situation analysis questions (+2.9%) by dynamically aligning visual–textual features based on question semantics. However, TCR provides minimal gains for basic judging questions (+0.9%), as closed-ended questions (e.g., 'Is there a road?') depend less on adaptive reasoning. However, when both modules are used together, the overall performance significantly increases to 78.5%. This indicates that both DRE and TCR modules contribute to performance enhancement when used individually, but their combined use demonstrates a synergistic effect, leading to a substantial optimization of the model's performance. This highlights that DRE optimizes low-level feature discriminability, while TCR governs high-level reasoning pathways—both are essential for complex tasks. Therefore, it can be concluded that all the proposed modules contribute to the performance improvement of the Remote Sensing Visual Question Answering system, with the most significant contribution coming from the conditionally adaptive reasoning module, which effectively enhances the inference capability of the Remote Sensing Visual Question Answering model.

While ACR achieves great performance in complex tasks, its modest improvement in Bas Co (79.7%) compared to MCAN (79.8%) and SOBA (80.1%) stems from the inherent simplicity of basic counting tasks. These tasks often require localized object detection rather than adaptive reasoning. TCR's adaptive reasoning pathways are more impactful for open-ended or relation-heavy questions, where nuanced cross-modal interaction is critical. Future work will explore task-specific feature enhancement to better balance performance across simple and complex tasks.

4.5. Accuracy of Different Types of Questions

To validate the adaptive reasoning capability of ACR for open-ended (closed-ended) questions, we conducted fine-grained evaluation on the EarthVQA dataset, with results shown in Figure 6 and Table 3. Case 1 corresponds to the ACR model's average answer accuracy for both open-ended and closed-ended questions, while case 2 represents the average accuracy of open-ended or closed-ended questions when the ACR module is removed. The experimental results demonstrate that the ACR model achieves improved answer accuracy for both question types, with a particularly pronounced enhancement observed for open-ended questions.

Table 3. The accuracy of different types of questions.

Types	Open-Ended	Closed-Ended	Overall Accuracy
case1	84.1	65.9	78.5
case2	82.8	64.5	77.3

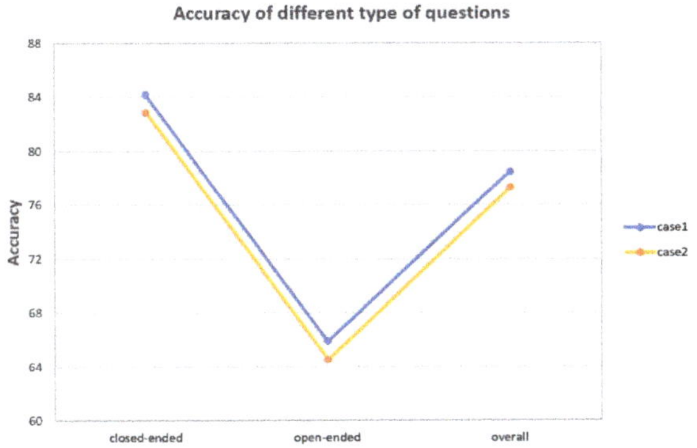

Figure 6. The accuracy of open-ended and closed-ended questions. Case 1 represents ACR model's average answer accuracy and case 2 represents the accuracy without the ACR module.

5. Discussion

A comparison of various Visual Question Answering (VQA) methods on the EarthVQA dataset reveals that the method proposed in this study outperforms others in multiple task types, particularly in relational-based judging, where it shows superior performance. Additionally, it demonstrates a relatively balanced performance in more complex tasks such as object situation analysis and comprehensive analysis, with an overall accuracy of 78.5%, surpassing SOBA [33] (78.1%). While traditional methods such as SAN, BAN, and MCAN excel in basic tasks like basic counting and basic judging, they show weaker performance in complex scenario analysis. In contrast, RSVQA [39] consistently exhibits lower accuracy across all task types, particularly struggling with more complex problem-solving tasks. Overall, the proposed method exhibits strong capabilities in handling complex VQA tasks, establishing itself as a competitive approach in the field. This indicates that our proposed framework, utilizing Adaptive Conditional Reasoning at multiple levels, enables the model to better comprehend questions during the VQA process, thereby enhancing the model's multi-level reasoning capability.

Moreover, ACR's adaptive reasoning capabilities hold significant practical value in disaster response. For instance, during post-earthquake assessments, emergency teams could input a satellite image of an affected area and ask questions like 'How many buildings show severe structural damage?' or 'Are there accessible roads connecting evacuation zones?'. ACR's ability to dynamically parse spatial relationships (e.g., collapsed buildings blocking roads) and quantify damage (e.g., counting damaged roofs) would enable rapid, actionable insights. VQA systems accelerated post-disaster damage assessment, but ACR's adaptive reasoning offers superior scalability for complex, dynamic scenarios.

5.1. Qualitative Result Visualization

In order to demonstrate the effectiveness of our proposed Adaptive Conditional Reasoning method in remote sensing image Visual Question Answering, we present six remote sensing images along with their corresponding questions, predicted results, and correct answers (Figure 7). In these examples, the predicted results are fully consistent with the correct answers, which validates the outstanding performance of our method in complex remote sensing image analysis tasks.

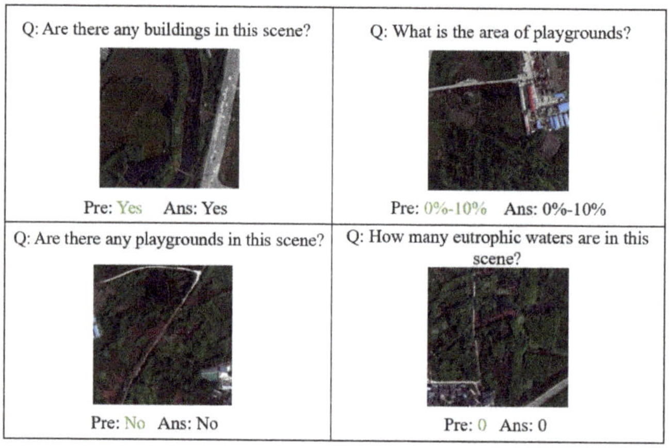

Figure 7. Qualitative result visualization on the EarthVQA dataset.

Our method introduces two key components: the question-based conditional Transformer reasoning module and the type-based conditional Transformer reasoning module. The synergy between these modules enables the model to flexibly adjust its reasoning strategy when facing different types of questions, thereby enhancing the accuracy of remote sensing image interpretation. The question-based conditional reasoning module dynamically adjusts the fusion of image features based on the semantic content of the question, allowing the model to more accurately focus on and process contextually relevant information. In remote sensing tasks, images contain vast amounts of geospatial information, and questions may concern specific geographic areas or particular object features. The question-based conditional reasoning module adapts the selection and processing of image features based on the specific requirements of the question, ensuring that the final prediction is closely aligned with the actual query.

The type-based conditional reasoning module selectively applies different reasoning strategies depending on whether the question is open-ended or closed-ended. Open-ended questions typically require the model to provide detailed explanations or reasoning processes, whereas closed-ended questions demand a clear, definitive answer. In Remote Sensing Visual Question Answering tasks, the difference in question types may involve tasks such as land cover type recognition, regional change analysis, or classification based on specific conditions. The type-based conditional reasoning module ensures that the model selects the appropriate reasoning path based on the nature of the question, thus improving both the accuracy and interpretability of the predictions.

Through the collaboration of these two modules, our method is able to flexibly adapt to the diverse demands of different questions and achieve strong performance in remote sensing image VQA tasks. In the demonstrated examples, our model successfully identifies key features in the images and performs reasonable inferences based on the content of the question, ultimately generating predictions that are consistent with the actual answers. For instance, in a remote sensing image of urban buildings, the question "How many eutrophic waters are in this scene?" is answered by the question-based conditional reasoning module, which allows the model to focus on the water bodies in the image and accurately extract relevant information. In another closed-ended question regarding buildings, the model uses the type-based conditional reasoning module to directly provide a clear answer on the presence of buildings.

5.2. Attention Visualization on the EarthVQA Dataset

To validate the effectiveness of Adaptive Conditional Reasoning in Remote Sensing Visual Question Answering tasks, we designed a multi-level attention visualization scheme to intuitively demonstrate the model's ability to model cross-modal associations (Figure 8). The first column displays the input original images, the second column shows the attention maps from the first cross-attention layer, and the third column presents the attention maps from the final layer. As illustrated in the figure, as the network depth increases, the model progressively focuses on semantically relevant regions while suppressing attention to irrelevant areas. This gradual shift in focus illustrates the model's ability to dynamically adjust its attention, ensuring that it selectively emphasizes the most pertinent visual information based on the given textual input. This observation demonstrates the effectiveness of our proposed model in Remote Sensing Visual Question Answering tasks.

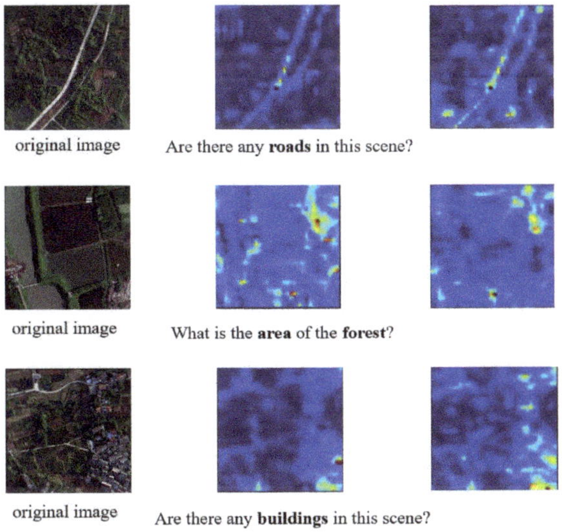

Figure 8. Attention map visualization of the EarthVQA dataset. The darker the red color, the higher the attention level in that area.

6. Conclusions

In this paper, we propose Adaptive Conditional Reasoning that effectively solves the lack of multi-level reasoning capabilities in Remote Sensing Visual Question Answering tasks. The primary goal of our research was to develop a more effective and contextually aware VQA model that can reason both with the content of images and the specific nature of the questions. Through this approach, we aim to improve the accuracy and relevance of answers provided by VQA systems, particularly for complex questions that involve various reasoning types and multiple object relationships.

Our method consists of two key components: a Type-Driven Conditioned Reasoning module and Text–Image Cross-Modal Reasoning module based on the type of question. The Type-Driven Conditioned Reasoning module employs transformer-based type classification before multimodal fusion to adaptively route reasoning procedures based on semantic intent. And the Text–Image Cross-Modal Reasoning module enables fine-grained visual–linguistic interaction through attention-driven joint reasoning. Moreover, to mitigate spatial and channel redundancy in remote sensing images, we utilize the Dual-Reconstruction Feature Enhancer to enhance visual feature extraction. By leveraging cross-modal attention and adaptive reasoning strategies, our model is capable of providing more accurate, interpretable, and context-sensitive answers.

Despite the promising results, our method has several limitations. First, the binary classification of question types (open-ended and closed-ended) may oversimplify the diversity of real-world queries, especially for ambiguous questions that blend both types. Future work will explore finer-grained question categorization. Expanding the model to handle more diverse and nuanced question types—such as those involving complex multi-step inference—would provide significant improvements in real-world applicability. Finally, we aim to investigate the generalization capability of our model across various datasets and domains, ensuring that the proposed method is robust and adaptable to different VQA tasks.

Author Contributions: Methodology, Y.G.; software, Y.G. and B.J.; investigation, Y.G., Z.B. and P.G.; writing—original draft preparation, Y.G.; writing—review and editing, Y.G. and R.Z.; supervision, Z.B. and M.Z.; project administration, Z.B.; funding acquisition, Z.B. All authors have read and agreed to the published version of the manuscript.

Funding: This research was funded by the National Key Research and Development Program of China (No. 2022YFE0138600) and the National Natural Science Foundation of China (Grant No. 62266045).

Data Availability Statement: The EarthVQA dataset was obtained from Datasets at Intelligent Data Extraction, Analysis and Applications of Remote Sensing (http://rsidea.whu.edu.cn/EarthVQA.htm accessed on 7 December 2024).

Conflicts of Interest: The authors declare no conflicts of interest.

References

1. Qing, Y.; Ming, D.; Wen, Q.; Weng, Q.; Xu, L.; Chen, Y.; Zhang, Y.; Zeng, B. Operational earthquake-induced building damage assessment using CNN-based direct remote sensing change detection on superpixel level. *Int. J. Appl. Earth Obs. Geoinf.* **2022**, *112*, 102899.
2. Lei, T.; Wang, J.; Li, X.; Wang, W.; Shao, C.; Liu, B. Flood disaster monitoring and emergency assessment based on multi-source remote sensing observations. *Water* **2022**, *14*, 2207. [CrossRef]
3. Zhu, Y.; Wu, S.; Qin, M.; Fu, Z.; Gao, Y.; Wang, Y.; Du, Z. A deep learning crop model for adaptive yield estimation in large areas. *Int. J. Appl. Earth Obs. Geoinf.* **2022**, *110*, 102828.
4. Zheng, X.; Wang, B.; Du, X.; Lu, X. Mutual attention inception network for remote sensing visual question answering. *IEEE Trans. Geosci. Remote Sens.* **2021**, *60*, 5606514.

5. Antol, S.; Agrawal, A.; Lu, J.; Mitchell, M.; Batra, D.; Zitnick, C.L.; Parikh, D. Vqa: Visual question answering. In Proceedings of the IEEE International Conference on Computer Vision, Santiago, Chile, 7–13 December 2015; pp. 2425–2433.
6. Simonyan, K.; Zisserman, A. Very deep convolutional networks for large-scale image recognition. *arXiv* **2014**, arXiv:1409.1556.
7. He, K.; Zhang, X.; Ren, S.; Sun, J. Deep residual learning for image recognition. In Proceedings of the IEEE Conference on Computer Vision and Pattern Recognition, Las Vegas, NV, USA, 27–30 June 2016; pp. 770–778.
8. Hochreiter, S.; Schmidhuber, J. Long short-term memory. *Neural Comput.* **1997**, *9*, 1735–1780. [CrossRef]
9. Chung, J.; Gulcehre, C.; Cho, K.; Bengio, Y. Empirical evaluation of gated recurrent neural networks on sequence modeling. *arXiv* **2014**, arXiv:1412.3555.
10. Lobry, S.; Tuia, D. Visual question answering on remote sensing images. In *Advances in Machine Learning and Image Analysis for GeoAI*; Elsevier: Amsterdam, The Netherlands, 2024; pp. 237–254.
11. Lobry, S.; Demir, B.; Tuia, D. RSVQA meets BigEarthNet: A new, large-scale, visual question answering dataset for remote sensing. In Proceedings of the 2021 IEEE International Geoscience and Remote Sensing Symposium IGARSS, Brussels, Belgium, 11–16 July 2021; pp. 1218–1221.
12. Bazi, Y.; Al Rahhal, M.M.; Mekhalfi, M.L.; Al Zuair, M.A.; Melgani, F. Bi-modal transformer-based approach for visual question answering in remote sensing imagery. *IEEE Trans. Geosci. Remote Sens.* **2022**, *60*, 4708011.
13. Siebert, T.; Clasen, K.N.; Ravanbakhsh, M.; Demir, B. Multi-modal fusion transformer for visual question answering in remote sensing. In *Image and Signal Processing for Remote Sensing XXVIII*; SPIE: Bellingham, WA, USA, 2022; Volume 12267, pp. 162–170.
14. Zhan, Y.; Xiong, Z.; Yuan, Y. Rsvg: Exploring data and models for visual grounding on remote sensing data. *IEEE Trans. Geosci. Remote Sens.* **2023**, *61*, 5604513. [CrossRef]
15. Zhang, Z.; Jiao, L.; Li, L.; Liu, X.; Chen, P.; Liu, F.; Li, Y.; Guo, Z. A spatial hierarchical reasoning network for remote sensing visual question answering. *IEEE Trans. Geosci. Remote Sens.* **2023**, *61*, 4400815.
16. Sarkar, A.; Chowdhury, T.; Murphy, R.R.; Gangopadhyay, A.; Rahnemoonfar, M. Sam-vqa: Supervised attention-based visual question answering model for post-disaster damage assessment on remote sensing imagery. *IEEE Trans. Geosci. Remote Sens.* **2023**, *61*, 4702716.
17. Ran, L.; Wang, L.; Zhuo, T.; Xing, Y.; Zhang, Y. DDF: A Novel Dual-Domain Image Fusion Strategy for Remote Sensing Image Semantic Segmentation with Unsupervised Domain Adaptation. *IEEE Trans. Geosci. Remote Sens.* **2024**, *62*, 4708113. [CrossRef]
18. Bazi, Y.; Bashmal, L.; Al Rahhal, M.M.; Ricci, R.; Melgani, F. Rs-llava: A large vision-language model for joint captioning and question answering in remote sensing imagery. *Remote Sens.* **2024**, *16*, 1477.
19. Jiang, Y.; Li, W.; Hossain, M.S.; Chen, M.; Alelaiwi, A.; Al-Hammadi, M. A snapshot research and implementation of multimodal information fusion for data-driven emotion recognition. *Inf. Fusion* **2020**, *53*, 209–221.
20. Gadzicki, K.; Khamsehashari, R.; Zetzsche, C. Early vs late fusion in multimodal convolutional neural networks. In Proceedings of the 2020 IEEE 23rd International Conference on Information Fusion (FUSION), Rustenburg, South Africa, 6–9 July 2020; pp. 1–6.
21. Mai, S.; Xing, S.; Hu, H. Locally confined modality fusion network with a global perspective for multimodal human affective computing. *IEEE Trans. Multimed.* **2019**, *22*, 122–137.
22. Huang, J.; Tao, J.; Liu, B.; Lian, Z.; Niu, M. Multimodal transformer fusion for continuous emotion recognition. In Proceedings of the ICASSP 2020-2020 IEEE International Conference on Acoustics, Speech and Signal Processing (ICASSP), Barcelona, Spain, 4–8 May 2020; pp. 3507–3511.
23. Zhao, Z.; Zhou, C.; Zhang, Y.; Li, C.; Ma, X.; Tang, J. Text-Guided Coarse-to-Fine Fusion Network for Robust Remote Sensing Visual Question Answering. *arXiv* **2024**, arXiv:2411.15770.
24. Bichindaritz, I.; Kansu, E.; Sullivan, K.M. Case-based reasoning in care-partner: Gathering evidence for evidence-based medical practice. In Proceedings of the European Workshop on Advances in Case-Based Reasoning, Dublin, Ireland, September 23–25 1998; Springer: Berlin/Heidelberg, Germany, 1998; pp. 334–345.
25. Marling, C.; Sqalli, M.; Rissland, E.; Muñoz-Avila, H.; Aha, D. Case-based reasoning integrations. *AI Mag.* **2002**, *23*, 69.
26. Nam, H.; Ha, J.W.; Kim, J. Dual attention networks for multimodal reasoning and matching. In Proceedings of the IEEE Conference on Computer Vision and Pattern Recognition, Honolulu, HI, USA, 21–26 July 2017; pp. 299–307.
27. Lippe, P.; Holla, N.; Chandra, S.; Rajamanickam, S.; Antoniou, G.; Shutova, E.; Yannakoudakis, H. A multimodal framework for the detection of hateful memes. *arXiv* **2020**, arXiv:2012.12871.
28. Zellers, R.; Lu, X.; Hessel, J.; Yu, Y.; Park, J.S.; Cao, J.; Farhadi, A.; Choi, Y. Merlot: Multimodal neural script knowledge models. *Adv. Neural Inf. Process. Syst.* **2021**, *34*, 23634–23651.
29. Yang, Z.; Li, L.; Wang, J.; Lin, K.; Azarnasab, E.; Ahmed, F.; Liu, Z.; Liu, C.; Zeng, M.; Wang, L. Mm-react: Prompting chatgpt for multimodal reasoning and action. *arXiv* **2023**, arXiv:2303.11381.
30. Zheng, G.; Yang, B.; Tang, J.; Zhou, H.Y.; Yang, S. Ddcot: Duty-distinct chain-of-thought prompting for multimodal reasoning in language models. *Adv. Neural Inf. Process. Syst.* **2023**, *36*, 5168–5191.

31. Li, J.; Wen, Y.; He, L. Scconv: Spatial and channel reconstruction convolution for feature redundancy. In Proceedings of the IEEE/CVF Conference on Computer Vision and Pattern Recognition, Vancouver, BC, Canada, 17–24 June 2023; pp. 6153–6162.
32. Kingma, D.P.; Ba, J. Adam: A method for stochastic optimization. *arXiv* **2014**, arXiv:1412.6980.
33. Wang, J.; Zheng, Z.; Chen, Z.; Ma, A.; Zhong, Y. Earthvqa: Towards queryable earth via relational reasoning-based remote sensing visual question answering. In Proceedings of the AAAI Conference on Artificial Intelligence, Vancouver, BC, Canada, 20–27 February 2024; Volume 38, pp. 5481–5489.
34. Yang, Z.; He, X.; Gao, J.; Deng, L.; Smola, A. Stacked attention networks for image question answering. In Proceedings of the IEEE Conference on Computer Vision and Pattern Recognition, Las Vegas, NV, USA, 27–30 June 2016; pp. 21–29.
35. Hudson, D.A.; Manning, C.D. Compositional Attention Networks for Machine Reasoning. In Proceedings of the International Conference on Learning Representations, Vancouver, BC, Canada, 30 April–3 May 2018.
36. Yu, Z.; Yu, J.; Cui, Y.; Tao, D.; Tian, Q. Deep modular co-attention networks for visual question answering. In Proceedings of the IEEE/CVF Conference on Computer Vision and Pattern Recognition, Long Beach, CA, USA, 15–20 June 2019; pp. 6281–6290.
37. Anderson, P.; He, X.; Buehler, C.; Teney, D.; Johnson, M.; Gould, S.; Zhang, L. Bottom-Up and Top-Down Attention for Image Captioning and Visual Question Answering. In Proceedings of the IEEE Conference on Computer Vision and Pattern Recognition (CVPR), Salt Lake City, UT, USA, 18–23 June 2018.
38. Wen, Z.; Xu, G.; Tan, M.; Wu, Q.; Wu, Q. Debiased Visual Question Answering from Feature and Sample Perspectives. In *Advances in Neural Information Processing Systems*; Beygelzimer, A., Dauphin, Y., Liang, P., Vaughan, J.W., Eds.; MIT Press: Cambridge, MA, USA, 2021.
39. Lobry, S.; Marcos, D.; Murray, J.; Tuia, D. RSVQA: Visual Question Answering for Remote Sensing Data. *IEEE Trans. Geosci. Remote Sens.* **2020**, *58*, 8555–8566. [CrossRef]

remote sensing

MDPI

Article

Enhancing Real-Time Aerial Image Object Detection with High-Frequency Feature Learning and Context-Aware Fusion

Xin Ge [1], Liping Qi [2,*], Qingsen Yan [1], Jinqiu Sun [3], Yu Zhu [1] and Yanning Zhang [1]

1 School of Computer Science, Northwestern Polytechnical University, Xi'an 710129, China; gxin@mail.nwpu.edu.cn (X.G.); qingsenyan@nwpu.edu.cn (Q.Y.); yuzhu@nwpu.edu.cn (Y.Z.); ynzhang@nwpu.edu.cn (Y.Z.)
2 College of Science and Technology, Hebei Agricultural University, Cangzhou 061100, China
3 School of Astronautics, Northwestern Polytechnical University, Xi'an 710072, China; sunjinqiu@nwpu.edu.cn
* Correspondence: lgqlp@hebau.edu.cn

Abstract: Aerial image object detection faces significant challenges due to notable scale variations, numerous small objects, complex backgrounds, illumination variability, motion blur, and densely overlapping objects, placing stringent demands on both accuracy and real-time performance. Although Transformer-based real-time detection methods have achieved remarkable performance by effectively modeling global context, they typically emphasize non-local feature interactions while insufficiently utilizing high-frequency local details, which are crucial for detecting small objects in aerial images. To address these limitations, we propose a novel VMC-DETR framework designed to enhance the extraction and utilization of high-frequency texture features in aerial images. Specifically, our approach integrates three innovative modules: (1) the VHeat C2f module, which employs a frequency-domain heat conduction mechanism to fine-tune feature representations and significantly enhance high-frequency detail extraction; (2) the Multi-scale Feature Aggregation and Distribution Module (MFADM), which utilizes large convolution kernels of different sizes to robustly capture effective high-frequency features; and (3) the Context Attention Guided Fusion Module (CAGFM), which ensures precise and effective fusion of high-frequency contextual information across scales, substantially improving the detection accuracy of small objects. Extensive experiments and ablation studies on three public aerial image datasets validate that our proposed VMC-DETR framework effectively balances accuracy and computational efficiency, consistently outperforming state-of-the-art methods.

Keywords: aerial images; object detection; high-frequency feature extraction; multi-scale feature fusion; contextual attention

1. Introduction

Aerial image object detection [1,2] plays a vital role in remote sensing, supporting various modern applications including drone-assisted detection, satellite remote sensing analysis, and smart city monitoring. It also significantly impacts critical areas like agricultural development [3,4], environmental monitoring [5,6], disaster assessment [7,8], and military reconnaissance [9,10], providing essential support for efficient and accurate remote sensing data analysis. However, aerial image detection inherently presents enormous challenges due to significant size variations in high-resolution imagery, abundant small objects, interference from complex backgrounds, illumination variability, motion blur, and dense overlaps among objects. These features pose severe requirements on both detection accuracy and real-time inference performance simultaneously [11].

Compared with traditional object-detection methods relying on manual features or shallow learning models, deep learning methods have demonstrated remarkable superiority in modeling accuracy due to their powerful feature representation capabilities [1,12]. Among recent deep-learning techniques, Transformer-based approaches [13] have rapidly become research hotspots thanks to their outstanding performance in global feature modeling and capturing long-distance dependencies, and are commonly referred to as Detection Transformer (DETR) in the context of object detection. Compared with CNN-based methods, Transformer architectures can more effectively capture global context information, thus significantly improving accuracy in scenarios involving occlusions and small object detection. In particular, Zhao et al. introduced RT-DETR [14,15], demonstrating the possibility of achieving real-time detection with DETR architectures.

Although Transformer modules in DETR-based methods excel at modeling non-local dependencies, their detection performance degrades significantly in aerial remote sensing scenarios. This performance gap stems from two structural limitations: (1) the inadequate capacity of CNN-based backbones to extract fine-grained local features, leading to weak initial representations of small or densely packed objects; and (2) the restricted ability of existing feature aggregation and fusion strategies to preserve and enhance these details across scales, resulting in further information degradation during multi-level integration. These challenges are further exacerbated by the fact that most state-of-the-art DETR models are trained and evaluated on natural image datasets, which differ fundamentally from aerial imagery in object scale, texture distribution, and especially in the frequency domain.

As illustrated in Figure 1, aerial images often contain numerous small, densely packed objects and exhibit concentrated high-frequency textures, whereas natural images (e.g., COCO val2017 [16]) feature more distinct object boundaries and smoother variations. The Laplacian-based frequency analysis highlights this discrepancy across datasets, including AI-TOD val [17] and VisDrone val2019 [18], confirming the unique high-frequency properties of aerial imagery. These characteristics expose real-time DETR frameworks to several practical challenges: (1) Existing studies have shown that conventional CNN-based feature extractors (e.g., ResNet [19], C3 [20], C2f [21]) tend to emphasize low-to-mid frequency components [22] and may introduce artifacts [23], hindering accurate localization of small targets. (2) The effectiveness of high-frequency extraction is highly sensitive to convolutional kernel sizes [24], and modules like ASFF [25], PAFPN [26], and BIFPN [27] fail to capture multi-scale fine details comprehensively. (3) Prior research has also indicated that simplistic fusion strategies (e.g., direct concatenation or linear weighting [28,29]) tend to mix high-frequency signals across scales indiscriminately, leading to feature aliasing and the loss of distinct texture cues critical for accurate modeling.

These observations reveal a core scientific challenge: the mismatch in high-frequency feature distributions between natural and aerial images, coupled with the inherent architectural limitations of CNN-based frameworks, results in a performance bottleneck for existing real-time DETR models in aerial object detection. To address these critical limitations, this work proposes a novel framework, VMC-DETR, which is inspired by the recent RT-DETR architecture and advancements in lightweight module design [30–32]. It explicitly enhances the extraction, aggregation, and fusion of high-frequency texture information, and incorporates three carefully designed modules: the VHeat C2f Module, the Multi-scale Feature Aggregation and Distribution Module (MFADM), and the Context Attention-Guided Fusion Module (CAGFM). Specifically, the main contributions of this work are as follows:

- VHeat C2f, which introduces frequency-domain heat conduction into the backbone. It enhances local high-frequency detail extraction, solving the problem of blurred edges and weak features in small and densely packed objects.

- MFADM, which employs large and diverse depthwise convolutions for multi-scale feature aggregation. It selectively preserves informative high-frequency features of small objects across scales, balancing detail sensitivity and redundancy in aerial images.
- CAGFM, which employs a lightweight attention mechanism to integrate contextual information across scales. It refines the representation of small and overlapping targets, improving detection accuracy in complex aerial scenes.
- Extensive comparisons with state-of-the-art real-time DNN-based methods on benchmark remote sensing datasets AI-TOD, VisDrone-2019, and TinyPerson across small object-detection tasks demonstrate that the proposed VMC-DETR framework achieves outstanding detection performance while maintaining real-time inference speed.

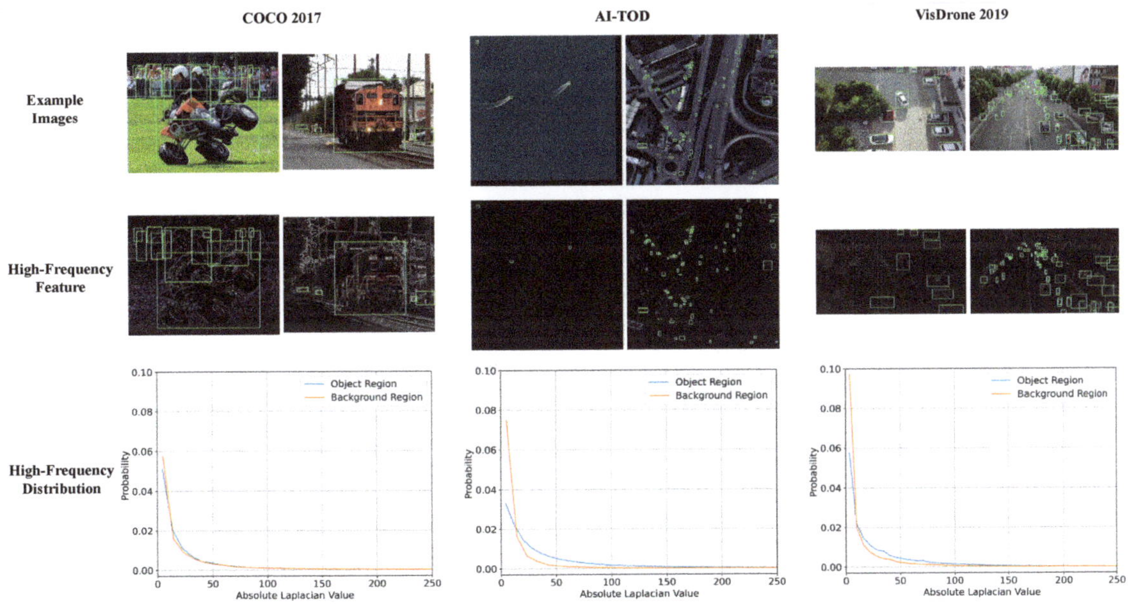

Figure 1. Comparison of frequency component distributions in object and background regions between natural and remote sensing images. The object regions annotated in the ground truth labels are marked by green rectangular boxes. High-frequency features are extracted using the Laplacian operator. The high-frequency feature maps are obtained by extracting frequency-domain responses separately from the R, G, and B channels, where brighter colors indicate stronger high-frequency components. The frequency distribution plots are computed from grayscale images, and larger x-axis values correspond to higher-frequency features.

2. Related Work

Relevant prior work includes one-stage and two-stage object-detection algorithms for aerial image object detection, as well as DETR-based algorithms.

2.1. CNN-Based One-Stage Object-Detection Methods

One-stage object-detection algorithms have shown high detection efficiency in aerial image object detection and have achieved a series of improvements in recent studies. For example, EL-YOLO [33] designs a sparsely connected progressive feature pyramid network and a cross-space learning multi-head attention mechanism based on YOLOv5 [20], which eliminates cross-layer interference during feature fusion and enhances contextual connections between object scales. It is deployed on an embedded platform, demonstrating the model's real-time performance. FCOSR [34] introduces a novel label assignment strategy tailored to the characteristics of aerial images, significantly improving the detection of overlapping objects and enhancing the model's robustness in complex scenes. Drone-TOOD [35] introduces an explicit visual center module in the neck network to capture local object information, boosting the model's capability to detect dense objects and achieving outstanding performance in aerial image object detection in crowded scenes. SDSDet [36] proposes a neighborhood erasing module that optimizes the learning of multi-scale features and improves detection accuracy by preventing redundant gradient feedback between adjacent scales.

However, these one-stage methods usually focus on optimizing the multi-scale feature fusion strategy of the feature pyramid and improving the label assignment strategy. Despite these advances, they do not make full use of the feature extraction stage and fail to distinguish edge information between objects and backgrounds effectively. The weak foundation not only limits the object feature information that can be used in the subsequent feature fusion and detection stages but also allows excessive background information to interfere when fusing contextual feature information. As a result, they still struggle to flexibly and effectively handle high-density aerial images with complex backgrounds, and the detection results remain suboptimal. These limitations highlight the need to pave the way for subsequent feature fusion through more effective feature extraction and refinement of small object features, thus shaping our research direction for VMC-Net to address the shortcomings of these aerial object-detection methods.

2.2. CNN-Based Two-Stage Object-Detection Methods

Two-stage object-detection algorithms have stronger feature extraction capabilities in aerial image object detection and have achieved a series of optimizations in recent studies. For example, TARDet [37] introduces a feature refinement module and an aligned convolution module, which are used to aggregate and enhance contextual information, respectively, achieving outstanding performance in the task of rotational object detection in aerial images with large-scale variations. AFOD [38] integrates spatial and channel attention modules into the Faster R-CNN network, enhancing the network's ability to perceive object features in remote sensing images and improving detection accuracy in complex scenes. Another work [39] incorporates a dynamic detection head into the Oriented R-CNN framework, effectively addressing the problem of object occlusion in aerial images. MSA R-CNN [40] proposes an enhanced feature extraction method that optimizes the feature processing process and reduces information loss in the FPN, thereby improving the detection performance of multi-scale objects.

However, these two-stage methods typically come with high computational costs and time complexity, especially when processing high-resolution aerial images. This limits their real-time performance, making them less suitable for time-sensitive applications. While recent studies introduce modules that enhance feature extraction and contextual awareness, these improvements often increase computational demands. These issues highlight the need for detection methods to balance object feature richness and computational overhead, which leads us to design VMC-DETR as a lightweight yet effective aerial object detector.

2.3. Transformer-Based One-Stage Object-Detection Methods

It is worth noting that DETR (DEtection TRansformer) and its variants belong to the category of one-stage object detectors, as they directly predict objects from image features without relying on a region proposal stage. Therefore, we reorganize the related work accordingly, separating CNN-based methods and Transformer-based methods while clearly categorizing DETR as a one-stage method. The DETR series of object-detection algorithms has the advantage of global information modeling in aerial image object detection and has made breakthroughs in many aspects in recent studies. For example, OVA-DETR [41], inspired by the concept of text alignment, introduces a region-text contrastive loss and a bidirectional vision-language fusion module to address the limitations of DETR models in open-world object detection. QETR [42] incorporates query alignment and a scale controller to enhance the ability of local queries to capture object information, thereby improving detection performance in aerial images. Another work [43] based on DINO designs a backbone network that combines CNN and ViT, leveraging the local feature extraction capabilities of CNNs and the global modeling strengths of ViTs, thus enhancing the network's ability to extract both global and local features. AODet [44] first uses RoI to remove background areas that do not contain objects, then employs a Transformer to integrate the contextual information of the foreground regions, enabling effective detection in aerial images with sparse objects.

However, these DETR-based methods often struggle with slow convergence and poor handling of high-frequency details and multi-scale features, limiting their effectiveness in aerial images with densely occluded objects. Although recent work introduces improvements such as region-text contrastive loss, query alignment, and hybrid backbones combining CNN and ViT, these approaches still have difficulty processing fine-grained features across different scales efficiently. Additionally, their reliance on large-scale global modeling makes it challenging to detect small, overlapping objects in complex scenes. These limitations emphasize the need for VMC-DETR to not only make full use of information about objects of different scales in aerial images to more accurately detect objects with dense occlusions but also to improve the convergence speed of the detector for practical deployment.

3. Method

3.1. The Overall Architecture of VMC-DETR

VMC-DETR is a one-stage object-detection framework. Its overall architecture is shown in Figure 2. In the feature extraction stage, VMC-DETR employs a C2f backbone network based on visual heat conduction operations [45] to refine the feature map. This unique backbone enables the model to enhance its ability to capture high-frequency features that represent fine-grained details, improving its effectiveness in handling small-scale objects. After extracting features from the input image, these features are passed to the attention-based intrascale feature interaction (AIFI) module [14], which is responsible for facilitating effective interactions between features of different scales. This module ensures that the model can balance the contextual information across scales, thus providing robust feature representations that are essential for accurate detection.

In the neck network, VMC-DETR leverages two MFADM blocks. These modules operate at the P4 layer, aggregating and distributing features from the P3, P4, and P5 layers to improve multi-scale feature fusion. By using the MFADM modules, VMC-DETR is able to achieve efficient integration of features at different resolutions, which is crucial for detecting objects of varying sizes. Additionally, four CAGFM blocks replace standard feature fusion methods in the neck. These CAGFM modules use contextual attention mechanisms to guide the fusion of features, enhancing the model's ability to leverage the rich contextual information present in the aerial images.

Finally, the VMC-DETR framework employs an IoU-aware query selection mechanism for label matching and detection. This process ensures that the final detection results are not only precise but also robust against overlapping objects and complex scenarios. By incorporating these advanced modules, VMC-DETR provides a powerful and efficient framework for aerial object detection, capable of handling both small-scale and large-scale objects with high accuracy.

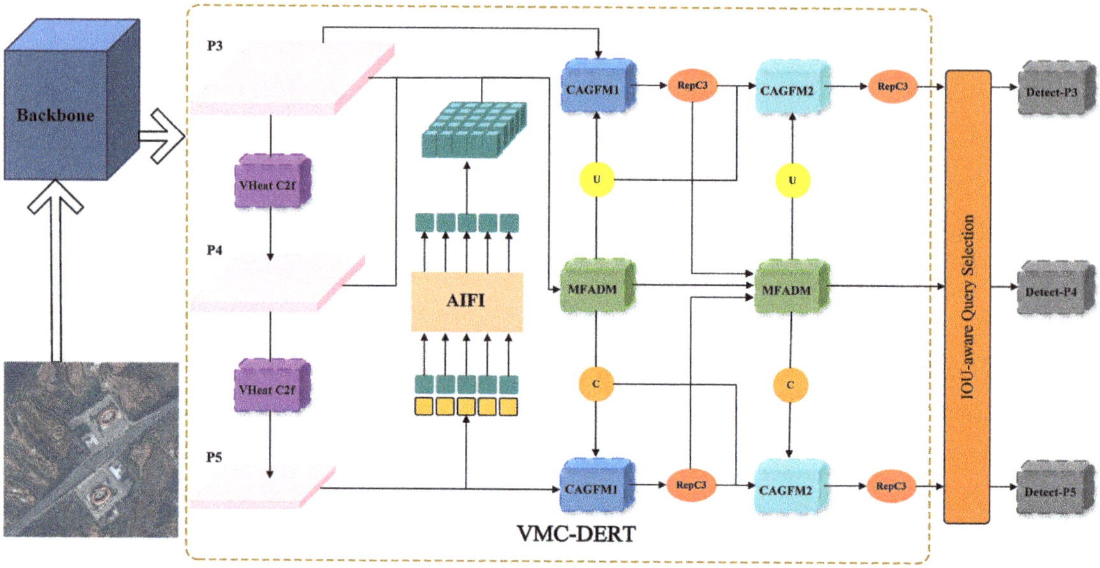

Figure 2. The overall architecture of the proposed VMC-DETR framework consists mainly of three modules: the VHeat C2f module, which is based on visual heat conduction; the MFADM, a multi-scale feature aggregation distribution module; and the CAGFM, a contextual attention guided fusion module, where CAGFM1 refers to the dual-branch CAGFM and CAGFM2 refers to the triple-branch CAGFM. The remaining modules include U, which handles upsampling operations; C, responsible for downsampling using ADown [46]; AIFI, an attention-based intrascale feature interaction module; and RepC3 [14], designed for reparameterization convolution.

3.2. Visual Heat Conduction C2f Module

In the task of object detection in aerial images, traditional backbone networks exhibit notable limitations in extracting high-frequency features that convey critical detail cues. Figure 3 illustrates the feature maps of ResNet [19], C3 [20], C2f [21], and the proposed VHeat C2f backbone network across various scenarios. Observations indicate that ResNet performs relatively poorly in capturing the details of small objects in high-resolution aerial images, resulting in blurred object edges and details in the feature maps. C3 improves upon ResNet by better capturing edges and textures, but is more susceptible to interference in scenes with densely arranged or overlapping objects, leading to boundary confusion among objects. Compared with C3, C2f further enhances the distribution and capture of features, generating feature maps with more intricate details. However, in complex backgrounds, C2f has limited noise suppression capabilities and remains susceptible to background interference.

These deficiencies can be partially attributed to the intrinsic properties of high-frequency features. Characterized by fine textures and sharp edges, high-frequency components are inherently difficult for CNNs to capture accurately, particularly in complex aerial scenes. Papyan et al. [47] demonstrated that CNNs can be interpreted as learning convolutional sparse-coded representations, implying that the receptive field size of convolutional kernels significantly influences their ability to extract high-frequency information. Lin et al. [22] further observed that in classification and detection tasks, convolutional kernels larger than 1×1 in ResNet tend to prioritize medium-to-low frequency texture learning. Consequently, the 1×1 convolutions employed in modules such as C3 and C2f can forcibly extract high-frequency features. However, Tomen et al. [24] pointed out that overly small kernels may introduce severe high-frequency artifacts, ultimately reducing the robustness of the extracted high-frequency representations. This observation is consistent with the phenomenon illustrated in Figure 3.

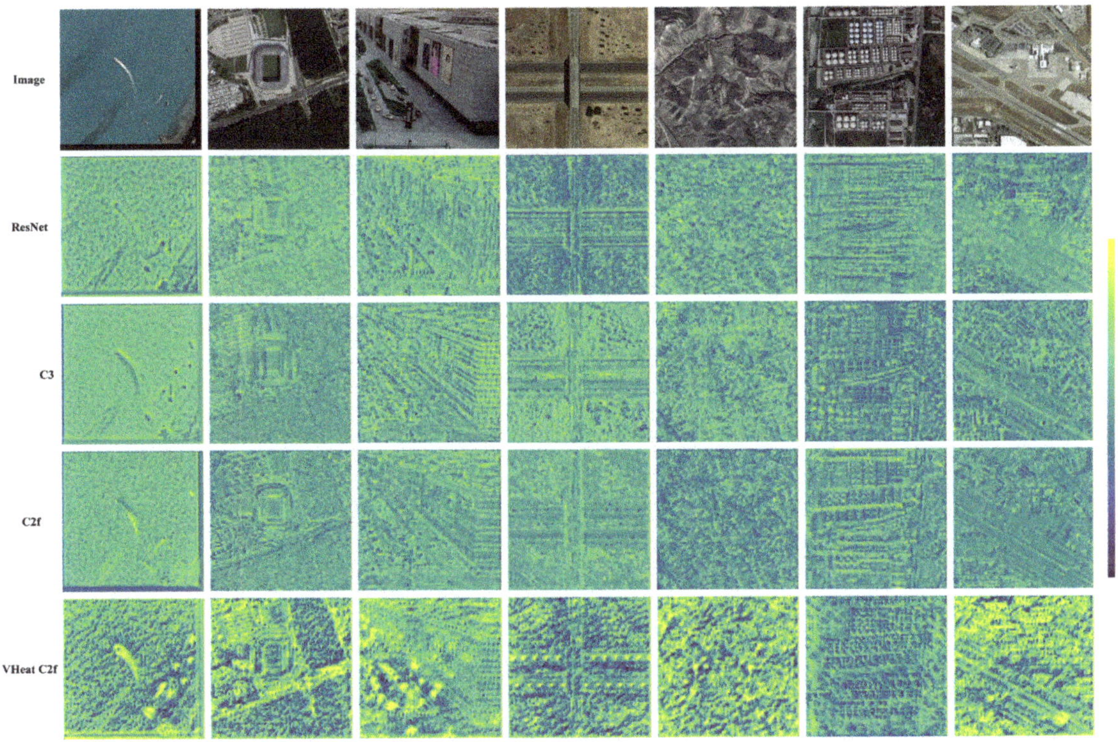

Figure 3. Visual comparison of feature maps from traditional backbone networks (ResNet, C3, and C2f) and the proposed VHeat C2f backbone on aerial images from various categories and scenes. The colormap encodes the strength of feature responses, where yellow corresponds to high response values, often associated with salient texture or edge information, while dark green represents weaker responses. Variations in response strength allow for intuitive observation of how different backbone networks capture high-frequency features with varying levels of precision and accuracy.

To address these challenges comprehensively, we introduce the VHeat [45] module to improve the robustness of the C2f backbone by fine-tuning features in the frequency domain [30,48], significantly improving its capacity to handle high-frequency features and manage the complexities associated with aerial image object-detection tasks during feature extraction.

Figure 4 presents the detailed implementation of the proposed VHeat C2f module. In the original C2f module, where the number of channels between P3, P4, and P5 is 256, 512, and 1024, respectively. The Bottleneck block, composed of simple convolutions, is replaced by the Heat block from the VHeat module, which enhances the backbone's capability to extract and utilize high-frequency texture features that are critical for precise object detection.

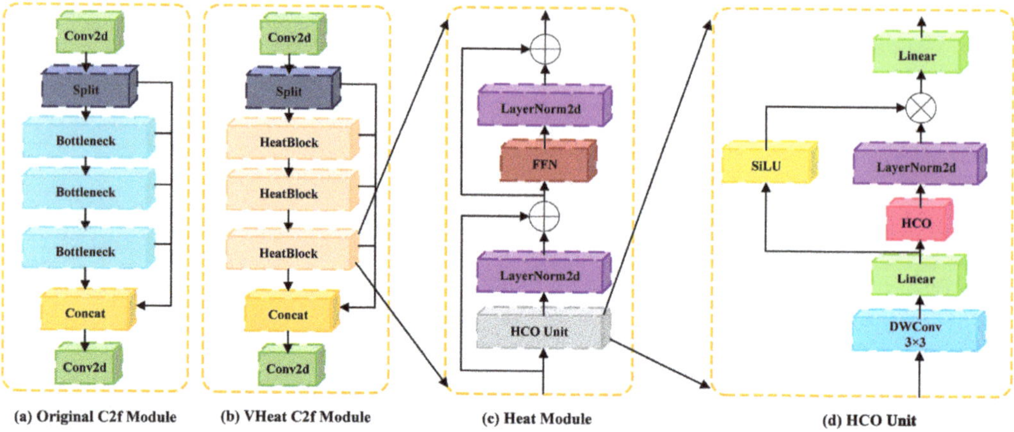

Figure 4. Detailed architecture of the VHeat C2f module used in the backbone network. (**a**) Original C2f module, which consists of a convolutional layer, a split-branch structure, and three sequential Bottleneck blocks followed by concatenation. (**b**) Modified VHeat C2f module, where Bottleneck blocks are replaced with HeatBlocks to enhance high-frequency feature learning. (**c**) Heat Module, which introduces frequency-domain processing with residual connections and normalization layers. (**d**) HCO Unit, which performs the heat conduction operation using discrete cosine transforms, simulating spatial-frequency energy propagation. Here, ⊗ denotes the Hadamard product and ⊕ represents element-wise addition. HCO in (**d**) stands for Heat Conduction Operation.

3.2.1. Heat Block

Heat block is the core unit of the VHeat C2f module, consisting of a series of feature enhancements and information processing steps. It begins with a heat conduction operation, where the input feature map and learning frequency are used as parameters to simulate the physical heat diffusion process, dynamically extracting the spatial and frequency information of the feature map. This is followed by two-layer normalization processes, a feedforward layer, and two residual connections to further enhance the framework's feature representation capabilities.

3.2.2. Heat Conduction Operator Unit

The Heat Conduction Operator (HCO) unit primarily simulates the heat conduction process. It performs a series of operations on the input features, including convolution, frequency mapping, and weighting, to achieve fine-grained feature adjustments. First, a depthwise convolution (DWConv [49]) with a 3×3 kernel size is applied, followed by a linear layer to extract the local spatial information from the feature map while retaining the channel features. Then, the feature map is split into two parts: one for the heat conduction operation and the other for frequency embedding. The HCO is grounded in the general solution of the heat equation in the spatial domain of the inverse Fourier transform ($\mathcal{F}^{-1}$), as shown in Equation (1).

$$u(x,y,t) = \mathcal{F}^{-1}\left(\tilde{f}(\omega_x,\omega_y)e^{-k(\omega_x^2+\omega_y^2)t}\right). \quad (1)$$

The two-dimensional temperature distribution ($u(x,y,t)$) is extended to the channel dimension, with the input and output being $U(x,y,c,0)$ and $U(x,y,c,t)$, respectively. Based on Equation (1), this concept is applied to the field of computer vision, and the resulting formula can be expressed as (2).

$$U^t = \mathcal{F}^{-1}\left(\mathcal{F}(U^0)e^{-k(\omega_x^2+\omega_y^2)t}\right). \tag{2}$$

Among them, U^0 represents $U(x,y,c,0)$, and U^t represents $U(x,y,c,t)$. Since visual images are generally rectangular, HCO replaces the two-dimensional discrete Fourier transform (2D DFT) and the two-dimensional inverse discrete Fourier transform (2D IDFT) with the two-dimensional discrete cosine transform (2D DCT) and the two-dimensional inverse discrete cosine transform (2D IDCT), as shown below:

$$U^t = \mathrm{IDCT}_{2\mathrm{D}}\left(\mathrm{DCT}_{2\mathrm{D}}(U^0)e^{-k(\omega_x^2+\omega_y^2)t}\right). \tag{3}$$

Here, $\mathrm{DCT}_{2\mathrm{D}}$ and $\mathrm{IDCT}_{2\mathrm{D}}$ represent the discrete cosine transform and inverse discrete cosine transform, respectively. The HCO unit is similar to the self-attention mechanism in ViT [50], dynamically propagating energy to capture object features within the image. In HCO, the cosine weight matrix required for $\mathrm{DCT}_{2\mathrm{D}}$ is first initialized to transform the feature map from the spatial domain to the frequency domain and to initialize the attenuation matrix that simulates the diffusion effect in the heat conduction process. In the frequency domain, HCO regards the object pixels in the image as heat sources according to the heat diffusion formula $e^{-k(\omega_x^2+\omega_y^2)t}$, and weights the frequency components of the feature map to propagate information. Among them, frequency embedding (FVEs) is a learnable shared parameter, similar to the absolute position embedding in ViT, which is used to adjust the frequency attenuation in heat conduction. The parameters k and t are both fixed hyperparameters, which are jointly controlled by FVEs and the output image resolution (1600 between P3 and P4 layers, 400 between P4 and P5 layers). k is used to control the attenuation rate of heat conduction, and t is used to simulate the time change during heat conduction.

HCO can be regarded as an adaptive filter. Representative objects as high-frequency components will accumulate more energy and higher temperatures, while irrelevant objects and backgrounds as low-frequency components are the opposite. In addition, adjacent areas of the image have similar features. HCO can continuously propagate heat source information to enhance the boundary contour feature extraction of high-frequency component areas and suppress the interference of irrelevant information features in low-frequency component areas. After applying the heat diffusion formula, the transformed feature map is returned to the spatial domain through the inverse transform $\mathrm{IDCT}_{2\mathrm{D}}$. The time complexity of the HCO operation is $\mathcal{O}(N^{1.5})$, where N is the number of input image patches. Since HCO's frequency domain filtering can affect all patches in the image, it is less complex than the ViT self-attention mechanism (with a complexity of $\mathcal{O}(N^2)$) that calculates the similarity between image patches. Finally, the cosine map feature map obtained by HCO is fused with the frequency embedding feature map, and a nonlinear activation (SiLU) is applied to produce the final output.

Through comparative analysis (as shown in Figure 3), the VHeat C2f module significantly improves the quality of high-frequency feature extraction and makes up for the shortcomings of the traditional backbone network. In response to the problem of blurred details of small objects in ResNet, VHeat C2f refines the object area features through HCO, generates clearer edges and richer textures, and solves the problem of distinguishing small objects. At the same time, compared with the shortcomings of C3 in boundary confusion in high-density or overlapping object scenes, VHeat C2f uses energy propagation characteristics to enhance the object boundary distinction and adapt to complex scenes. In addition, it effectively suppresses background noise through frequency domain filtering, makes up for the shortcomings of C2f, improves the overall quality of feature maps, and achieves efficient calculation with a lower time complexity of $\mathcal{O}(N^{1.5})$, has stronger adaptability and robustness, and can better cope with the diverse needs of aerial image object detection tasks.

3.3. *Multi-Scale Feature Aggregation and Distribution Module*

At present, many mainstream and well-established multi-scale feature fusion methods exhibit strong performance in natural image object-detection tasks but perform suboptimally when applied to aerial imagery. This performance gap is primarily due to the unique aerial perspective, where the extraction of abundant high-frequency cues is beneficial for detecting dense and tiny objects. However, modules such as VHeat C2f extract high-frequency features indiscriminately, and these redundant or irrelevant high-frequency components have been shown to compromise the robustness of detection networks [51,52], leading to a high rate of false positives. As shown in Figure 5, we visualize the heatmaps of ASFF [25], PAFPN [26], BIFPN [27], and the proposed MFADM under six key challenges in aerial object detection. It can be observed that the first three methods exhibit varying degrees of missed detections and false positives, indicating their limited effectiveness in handling such extreme aerial scenarios.

Specifically, both ASFF and BIFPN utilize weighted feature fusion mechanisms, which tend to overreact to high-frequency regions. For example, ASFF frequently misclassifies streetlights, traffic lights, noise artifacts, and trees as valid objects, while BIFPN often falsely detects streetlights, building windows, traffic lights, wall graffiti, road centerlines, and trees. Additionally, both methods tend to miss larger objects within densely populated scenes. This behavior proves beneficial when high-frequency information is limited, as the fusion mechanism can enhance detection accuracy. However, when paired with modules like VHeat C2f that extract abundant high-frequency features, this tendency leads to a surge in false positives.

In contrast, PAFPN, which does not adopt a weighted feature fusion strategy, demonstrates a lower false-detection rate. Nonetheless, it still occasionally misidentifies high-frequency regions such as wall textures, signal lights, streetlights, and trees as objects. This may be due to the use of relatively small convolutional kernels in PAFPN, which limits its ability to effectively filter high-frequency features across different levels [53].

To overcome the limitations of these classic multi-scale feature fusion approaches in aerial object detection, and to better leverage the spatial and semantic information extracted by the VHeat-enhanced C2f backbone, we propose the Multi-level Feature Aggregation and Distribution Module (MFADM). This module integrates the strengths of both PAFPN and KPI Modules [31], leveraging large convolutional kernels of varying sizes to capture rich contextual information across hierarchical feature maps. Moreover, MFADM ensures precise and efficient propagation of high-frequency information at every detection scale. As a result, it significantly improves the accuracy of anchor box localization and object classification. The implementation details of MFADM are illustrated in Figure 6.

3.3.1. The First Feature Aggregation Stage

MFADM can process input features of different scales from P3, P4, and P5 using a customized feature aggregation module. For the 80×80 feature map of the P3 layer, we employ the ADown module from YOLOv9c and YOLOv9e within the YOLOv9 [46] family. This module integrates maximum pooling, average pooling, and standard convolution operations. Compared to ordinary 2D convolution downsampling, it retains more original information and provides more comprehensive object features for subsequent operations. For the 40×40 feature map of the P4 layer and the 20×20 feature map of the P5 layer, standard 2D convolution and upsampling are used to adjust the number of channels, which are then concatenated with the P3 layer along the channel dimension.

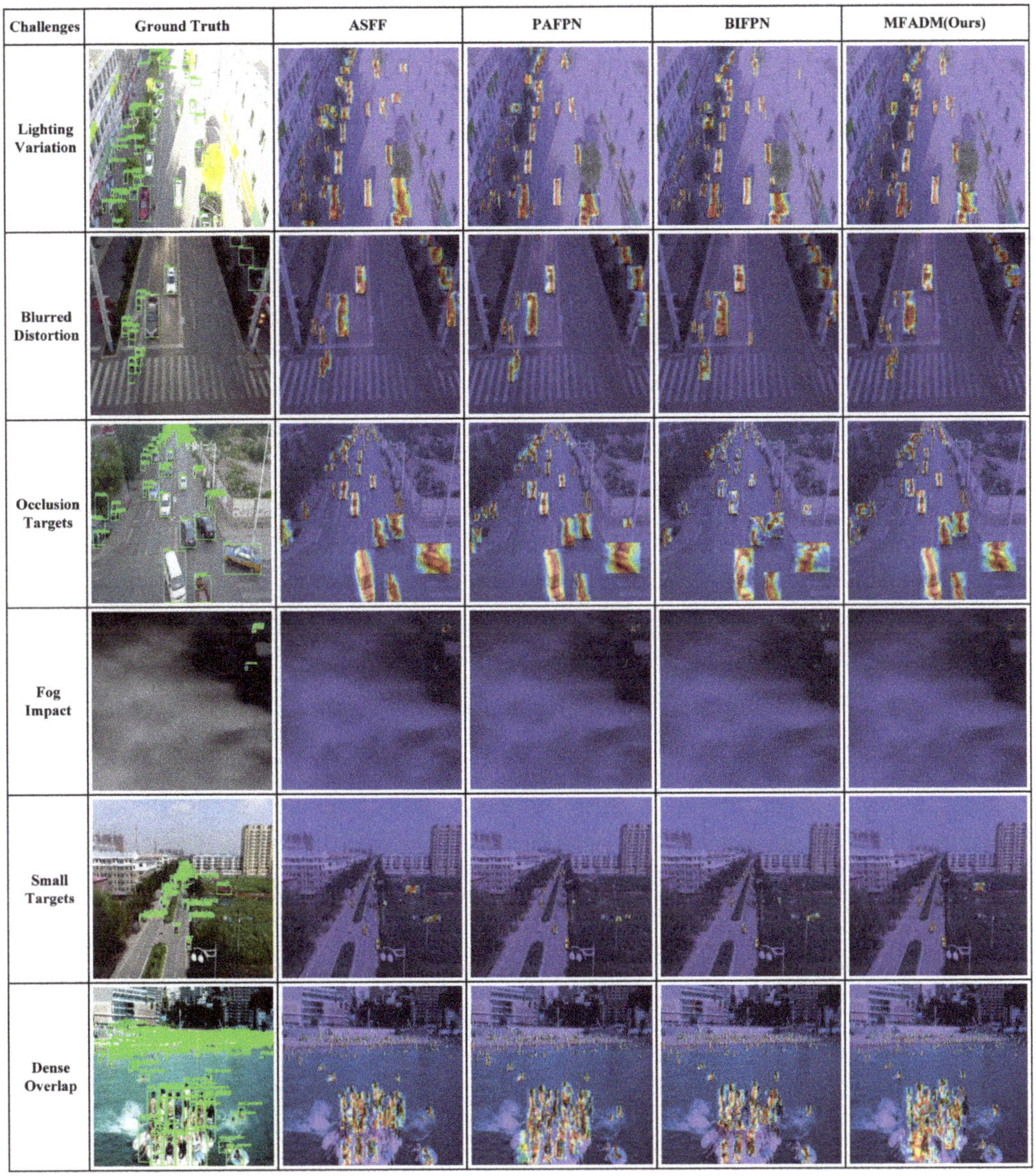

Figure 5. Comparison of heatmap activations under typical challenges in aerial object detection using different multi-scale feature fusion methods, including ASFF, PAFPN, BIFPN, and the proposed MFADM. The colormap highlights feature response intensity, where red and yellow regions indicate strong attention and blue denotes weak response. The green bounding boxes in the Ground Truth column denote annotated object locations. Despite minor visual overlap, all target areas remain clearly identifiable and do not hinder scientific interpretation.

3.3.2. Feature Distribution and Second Aggregation Stage

After the first feature aggregation stage of MFADM, we introduced the PKI Module from PKINet to perform the feature distribution operation. The PKI Module employs deep convolutions of sizes $5 \times 5, 7 \times 7, 9 \times 9$, and 11×11 in parallel (the selection of kernel sizes will be discussed in Section 5.2.3), along with an identity mapping, to transform the global information of the extracted features into various forms of local information for distribution. A 1×1 convolution is then used for channel fusion. Finally, a residual connection is established with the feature information prior to distribution, allowing the network to effectively retain both global and local feature information of objects at different scales across each layer. The complete formula for the DWConv module, including depthwise convolutions and the 1×1 convolution for channel fusion, is expressed as follows:

$$F = X + \text{Conv}_{1\times1}\left(X + \sum_{k\in\{5,7,9,11\}} (X * DW_k)\right), \tag{4}$$

where DW_k represents the weights of the depthwise convolution with kernel size k, and $*$ denotes the convolution operation, $\text{Conv}_{1\times1}$ is the 1×1 convolution used for channel fusion.

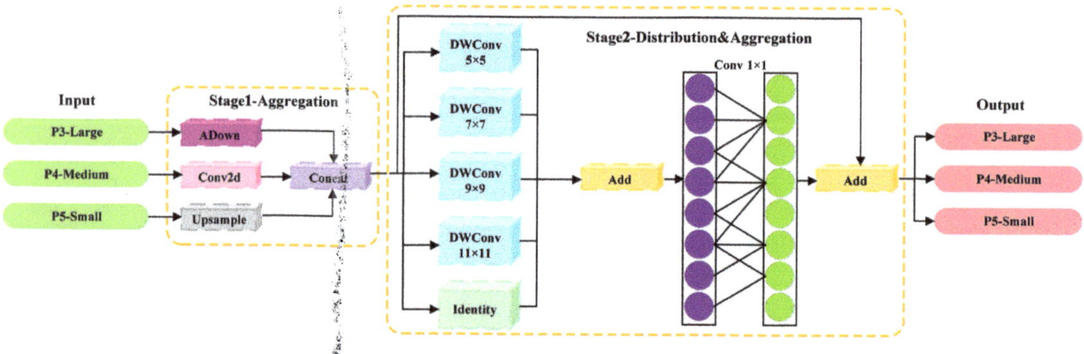

Figure 6. The detailed process of the MFADM module: ADown denotes the downsampling module of YOLOv9, DWConv represents the depthwise convolution, and Identity refers to the identity mapping.

Finally, according to the comparison of the heat map results in Figure 5, MFADM effectively solves the defects of other methods. For example, under conditions of changing lighting, MFADM combines deep convolutions of different kernel sizes with identity mapping to prevent excessive response at a single scale and adaptively suppress interference caused by strong light. For example, in the case of motion blur, MFADM more effectively classifies the semantic information of the extracted object features during the downsampling process using ADown, and combines the feature distribution of deep convolutions of different kernel sizes. This method enhances the model's ability to identify blurred objects. For example, in the case of densely overlapping objects, MFADM uses convolution kernels of different sizes to enhance the receptive field and effectively capture the global and local features of dense objects. Its aggregation and distribution strategy dynamically adjusts the contribution of features at different layers, significantly reducing background sensitivity.

3.4. Contextual Attention Guided Fusion Module

In aerial image object detection, feature fusion plays a critical role in enhancing the performance of multi-scale object detection. High-frequency features extracted from different scales carry rich information and are highly sensitive to spatial variations [54,55]. However, conventional feature fusion methods typically rely on simple concatenation or linear weighting operations. Such simplistic strategies often lead to the blending or compression of essential high-frequency cues, resulting in the loss of contextual information, redundancy, and insufficient exploitation of multi-scale representations. These issues adversely affect detection accuracy, especially for small objects.

To address these issues, we propose the Context Attention Guided Fusion Module (CAGFM), as illustrated in Figure 7. The pseudocode of CAGFM for aerial image processing within the VMC-DETR framework is provided in Algorithm 1. By effectively preserving and integrating high-frequency contextual information, CAGFM significantly enhances the robustness and precision of multi-scale feature fusion.

Algorithm 1 Applying CAGFM for Aerial Image Processing in VMC-DETR Framework

Input: Aerial image dataset with images of size (h, w, c), number of epochs N
Output: Enhanced feature maps of P3 and P5 layers after contextual attention guided fusion
for $i = 1$ to N **do**
    Loop over each training epochs and load image I_i and extract feature maps at scales P3, P4, P5 with channels c_k for each layer
    Step 1: Dual-Branch CAGFM on P3 **Layer,** $k = 3$
    if The number of channels of P3 and P4 do not match after the first MFDAM **then**
        Adjust channels of P3 and P4 to c_k via 1×1 Conv
    end if
    Concatenate P3 and P4 along the channel dimension to obtain $[\mathrm{P3}, \mathrm{P4}]$.
    Apply ESE Attention: $\mathrm{P3}_{\mathrm{concat}} = \mathrm{ESE}([\mathrm{P3}, \mathrm{P4}])$, refine features by global mean and adaptive gating
    Split $\mathrm{P3}_{\mathrm{concat}}$ into weighted components for P3 and P4 layers
    Fuse weighted features: $\mathrm{P3}' = [\mathrm{weighted}(\mathrm{P3}) + \mathrm{P4}, \mathrm{weighted}(\mathrm{P4}) + \mathrm{P3}]$
    Step 2: Dual-Branch CAGFM on P5 **Layer,** $k = 5$
    Repeat Step 1 for P5 and P4 to obtain $\mathrm{P5}'$, focusing on larger object regions in complex scenes
    Step 3: Triple-Branch CAGFM on P3 **Layer,** $k = 3$
    if The number of channels in $\mathrm{P3}'$, $\mathrm{P4}'$ after the second MFADM and P4 after the first MFDAM do not match **then**
        Adjust channels of $\mathrm{P3}'$, P4 and $\mathrm{P4}'$ to c_k via 1×1 Conv
    end if
    Concatenate $\mathrm{P3}', \mathrm{P4}, \mathrm{P4}'$ along the channel dimension to obtain $[\mathrm{P3}', \mathrm{P4}, \mathrm{P4}']$
    Apply ESE Attention: $\mathrm{P3}'_{\mathrm{concat}} = \mathrm{ESE}([\mathrm{P3}', \mathrm{P4}, \mathrm{P4}'])$, enhance small object features by computing channel mean and scaling
    Split $\mathrm{P3}'_{\mathrm{concat}}$ into weighted components for $\mathrm{P3}'$, P4 and $\mathrm{P4}'$ layers
    Fuse weighted features: $\mathrm{P3}_{\mathrm{final}} = [\mathrm{weighted}(\mathrm{P3}') + \mathrm{P4} + \mathrm{P4}', \mathrm{weighted}(\mathrm{P4}) + \mathrm{P3} + \mathrm{P4}', \mathrm{weighted}(\mathrm{P4}') + \mathrm{P3}' + \mathrm{P4}']$
    Step 4: Triple-Branch CAGFM on P5 **Layer,** $k = 5$
    Repeat Step 3 for $\mathrm{P5}', \mathrm{P4}, \mathrm{P4}'$ to obtain $\mathrm{P5}_{\mathrm{final}}$, focusing on broader contextual elements
    Store enhanced feature maps $\mathrm{P3}_{\mathrm{final}}, \mathrm{P5}_{\mathrm{final}}$ for image I_i
end for
return Enhanced feature maps for all dataset images used in the final detection stage

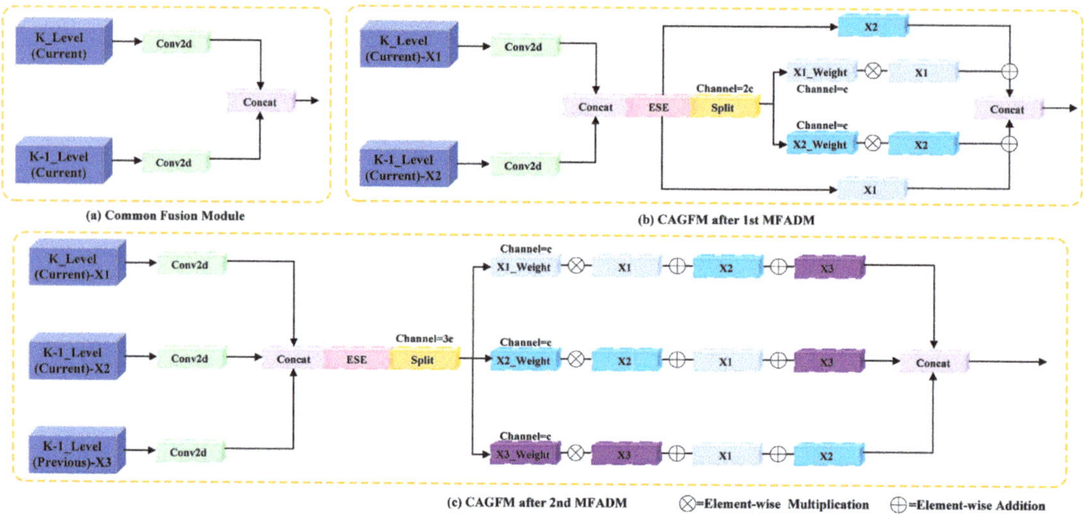

Figure 7. Specific details of the CAGFM module implementation: ESE stands for the effective squeeze and extraction attention mechanism. (**a**) Standard feature fusion operation, (**b**) dual-branch CAGFM, (**c**) triple-branch CAGFM. X_1, X_2, and X_3 represent input feature maps from different scales or stages. The terms X_{1_Weight}, X_{2_Weight}, and X_{3_Weight} denote the channel-wise attention weights computed via the contextual attention mechanism (ESE [56]), adjusting the contributions of each feature map in the fusion process.

3.4.1. Dual-Branch CAGFM

The dual-branch CAGFM is applied to the P5 and P3 layers, respectively, after the first MFADM module, where the corresponding features in these two layers are fused. For the P5 layer, small object detection in aerial images is a critical challenge. Since the P5 layer contains more small-scale features and has a higher number of channels, it is essential to fully utilize the features of this layer. Therefore, in the dual-branch CAGFM, we fuse the P5 and P4 layers during the current fusion stage. To ensure the complete transmission of information from the P5 layer, the number of channels in the P4 layer is first increased to match that of the P5 layer, aligning the feature dimensions required for the fusion operation. This strategy preserves rich multi-scale information and enhances the accuracy of small object detection. For the P3 layer, to strike a balance between detection accuracy and computational efficiency, the fusion process reduces the number of channels in the P4 feature map to match that of the P3 layer. In this manner, the dual-branch CAGFM effectively utilizes features of different scales during fusion while avoiding excessive computational overhead in the P3 layer, thereby optimizing the overall performance of the network.

Subsequently, the Effective Squeeze and Extraction (ESE [32]) mechanism is employed as an attention module to effectively capture global contextual information from the input features. The core idea of ESE is to dynamically adjust the channel-wise importance of the feature map through a channel attention mechanism, thereby enhancing key channels and suppressing redundant ones. Specifically, the input feature map $X_{\text{div}} \in \mathbb{R}^{C \times H \times W}$

first undergoes a global average pooling operation $\mathcal{G}_{\text{gap}}(\cdot)$, which compresses the spatial dimensions to 1×1 and retains only the channel-wise information:

$$\mathcal{G}_{\text{gap}}(X_{\text{div}}) = \frac{1}{H \cdot W} \sum_{i=1}^{H} \sum_{j=1}^{W} X_{\text{div}}^{c,i,j}, \quad c \in [1, C]. \tag{5}$$

The obtained channel vector $S \in \mathbb{R}^{C}$ is fed into a fully connected layer, whose weight is $W_{\text{ESE}} \in \mathbb{R}^{C \times C'}$, where C' is the size of the intermediate dimension. Subsequently, the normalized channel attention weight is generated by the Sigmoid activation function σ:

$$A_{\text{ESE}} = \sigma(W_{\text{ESE}} \cdot \mathcal{G}_{\text{gap}}(X_{\text{div}})). \tag{6}$$

Finally, we perform element-wise multiplication operation $\otimes$ on the generated channel attention weight $A_{\text{ESE}} \in \mathbb{R}^{C}$ and the original feature map X_{div} to obtain the enhanced feature map X_{refine}:

$$X_{\text{refine}} = A_{\text{ESE}} \otimes X_{\text{div}}. \tag{7}$$

This process not only preserves the semantic information between channels but also enhances the overall performance of the framework through dynamic weighting. Compared with the traditional squeeze and extract (SE [56]) attention, it only uses one fully connected layer, which not only reduces the channel information loss but also improves the computational efficiency. After the ESE attention mechanism, each layer can adaptively adjust the weight of the input feature map through feature weight segmentation. Finally, after interactive fusion, the two feature maps are weighted based on the weight mapping. The weighted features are then added and concatenated to form a new output feature. For more details, please refer to the following section on the Triple-Branch CAGFM.

3.4.2. Triple-Branch CAGFM

A triple-branch CAGFM is deployed at both the P3 and P5 layers. Although the two modules do not share parameters, their inputs and outputs are represented using the same variables for notational convenience.

Specifically, the triple-branch CAGFM integrates features from three different layers (X_{P_3}, X_{P_4}, and X_{P_5}). Unlike separately computing channel-wise attention weights for each layer, the CAGFM jointly computes the attention through a concatenation of all three feature maps($X_{P_{\text{concat}}}$), as formulated below:

$$A_{\text{ESE}}^{(i)} = \text{Split}(\sigma(W_{\text{ESE}} \cdot \mathcal{G}_{\text{gap}}(X_{P_{\text{concat}}})), i), \quad i \in \{3, 4, 5\}, \tag{8}$$

where $A_{\text{ESE}}^{(i)}$ denotes the attention weights for layer P_i, and W_{ESE} represents the learnable parameters. The function $\text{Split}(\cdot, i)$ extracts the portion of the concatenated attention vector that corresponds to X_{P_i} based on its channel allocation.

Then, the weighted feature fusion across three scales is explicitly formulated as follows:

$$X_{\text{fusion}}^{(i)} = A_{\text{ESE}}^{(i)} \otimes X_{P_i} + \sum_{k \neq i} X_{P_k}, \quad i, k \in \{3, 4, 5\}, \tag{9}$$

where $X_{\text{fusion}}^{(i)}$ is the fused feature at the current object scale P_i.

Finally, the three enhanced features $X_{\text{fusion}}^{(i)}$ are concatenated to form X_{fusion}, which is then processed by the RepC3 module before being passed to the detection head:

$$X_{\text{out}} = \text{RepC3}(X_{\text{fusion}}). \tag{10}$$

4. Experiments and Results

To validate the effectiveness of the proposed VMC-DETR framework, we adopt RT-DETR with a ResNet-18 backbone (RT-DETR-R18 [14]) as the baseline. This framework employs the same AIFI and RepC3 modules in the neck and maintains a comparable level of computational complexity. We conduct both comparative and ablation experiments on three aerial image datasets—AI-TOD, VisDrone-2019, and TinyPerson—and visualize representative detection results to facilitate comprehensive analysis.

4.1. Datasets

The first dataset we use is the AI-TOD [17] dataset, which was proposed by Wuhan University in 2020. It is an aerial image dataset, where 87.7% of the objects are smaller than 32 × 32 pixels. The mean and standard deviation of the absolute size are 12.8 pixels and 5.9 pixels, respectively. These values are much smaller than those found in other natural image and aerial image datasets. The AI-TOD dataset contains eight categories, namely airplanes (Air), bridges (Bri), persons (Per), ships (Shi), storage-tanks (Sto), swimming pools (Swi), vehicles (Veh), and windmills (Win). The dataset consists of images with 800 × 800 pixels and contains 700,621 labeled objects. It is split into 11,214 images for training and 2804 images for testing.

The second dataset we use is the VisDrone-2019 [18] dataset, which is released by the AISKYEYE team at Tianjin University. This dataset is designed for object detection in UAV-captured images of diverse remote sensing scenes, including urban areas, residential regions, and rural environments. The VisDrone-2019 dataset presents challenges such as dense object distribution, scale variation, and complex backgrounds. The dataset contains ten categories: awning-tricycle (Awn), bicycle (Bic), bus (Bus), car (Car), motorcycle (Mot), pedestrian (Ped), people (Peo), tricycle (Tri), truck (Tru), and van (Van). In total, the dataset consists of 8629 images with a variety of weather conditions, lighting, and viewpoints. It is divided into three subsets: 6471 images for training, 548 images for validation, and 1610 images for testing.

The third dataset we use is the TinyPerson [57] dataset, proposed by the University of the Chinese Academy of Sciences in 2019. This dataset is constructed using high-resolution aerial images, originally gathered from various websites. The researchers extract frames from videos captured at different seaside locations at 50-frame intervals, removing duplicates to compile a diverse collection of aerial scenes. The TinyPerson dataset is characterized by very small human object s, significant aspect ratio variations, and dense distributions, all within complex seaside environments. It includes two categories: people on the sea (Sp), such as swimmers or surfers, and people on earth (Ep), including beachgoers. In total, the dataset comprises 1610 images and 72,651 labeled instances of people. For our experiments, we use 794 images for training and 816 images for testing.

Figure 8 summarizes the detailed statistics of the three datasets, including object categories, the number of images, instance counts, and other relevant attributes. In addition, following the MS COCO [16] definition of small objects (i.e., objects smaller than 32 × 32 pixels), we compute the proportion of small objects within each category across the three datasets. This information is also shown in Figure 8, enabling a more intuitive analysis in the subsequent experiments of the VMC-DETR framework's detection performance on small objects in aerial images.

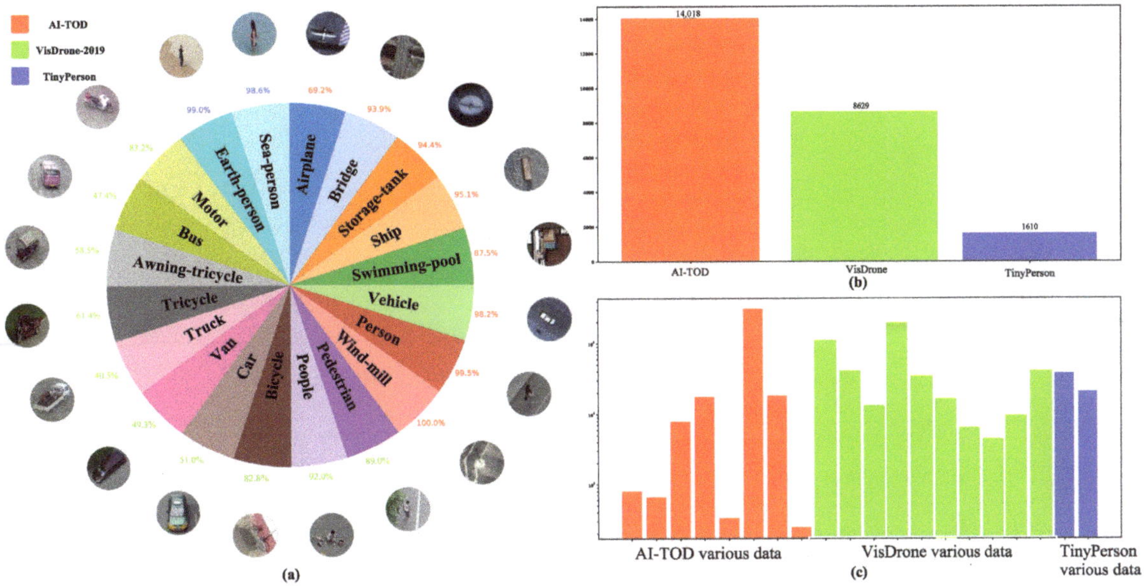

Figure 8. (**a**) Object category names, image examples, and the proportion of small objects across the three datasets. (**b**) The number of images in each of the three datasets. (**c**) The number of instances for each object category across the three datasets.

4.2. Experimental Setup

The hardware configuration of our experimental environment includes: CPU: Intel(R) Xeon(R) CPU E5-2682 v4 @ 2.50 GHz 64-core processor, GPU: NVIDIA GeForce RTX 3090 × 1, video memory: 24G. The software environment includes: Ubuntu 20.04.3 LTS, python 3.8.16, Torch 1.13.1. Tables 1 and 2 provide detailed information on the hyperparameter configuration and data augmentation techniques used throughout the experimental process.

Table 1. The hyperparameters and their corresponding values used in the experiments. Adam denotes the adaptive moment estimation optimizer, and IoU represents intersection over union.

Hyperparameters	Values
Learning Rate	0.0001
Batch Size	8
Optimizer	Adam
Epochs	150
Input Image Size	640 × 640
Weight Decay	0.0001
Momentum	0.9
IoU Threshold	0.7

To evaluate the performance of the framework, this experiment uses precision (Pre), recall (Rec), average precision (mAP), frames per second (FPS), gigaflop operations (GFLOPs), inference time per image (IT), and model memory usage (MU) as evaluation metrics. The formulas for the first three evaluation indicators are as follows:

$$\text{Pre} = \frac{\text{TP}}{\text{TP} + \text{FP}}, \tag{11}$$

$$\text{Rec} = \frac{\text{TP}}{\text{TP} + \text{FN}}, \tag{12}$$

$$\text{mAP} = \frac{1}{N}\sum_{i=1}^{N} \text{AP}_i, \tag{13}$$

where TP, FP, and FN represent the numbers of true positives, false positives, and false negatives, respectively; N denotes the total number of object categories; and AP_i is the average precision for the i-th category, computed as follows:

$$\text{AP}_i = \int_0^1 p_i(r)\, dr, \tag{14}$$

where $p_i(r)$ denotes the precision-recall curve for class i as a function of recall r.

Table 2. Data augmentation techniques and their application ratios used in the experiment.

Data Augmentation	Ratios
Hue	0.015
Saturation	0.7
Value	0.4
Translate	0.1
Scale	0.5
Flip Left-Right	0.5

4.3. Quantitative Evaluation of Detection Results

We use mainstream CNN-based and Transformer-based object-detection algorithms from the past three years, including medium-sized models from DDOD, TOOD, DAB-DETR, DINO, RTMDET, LD, ConvNeXt, Gold-YOLO, YOLOv9, and YOLOv10 detection frameworks. Specifically, we employ the "Medium" models from the YOLO series and other models with ResNet50 as the backbone network to conduct comparative experiments on three aerial image datasets. Considering that several recent methods such as RingMoE [11], QETR [58], and OVA-DETR [59] focus on different problem settings, including multi-modal fusion, open-vocabulary detection, and large-scale pretraining, they are not directly comparable to our work, which emphasizes single-modality input, lightweight architecture, and real-time performance. Therefore, we exclude them from our comparative experiments, while still acknowledging their contributions in Sections 1 and 2.

Table 3 presents the results of our comparative experiments on the AI-TOD aerial image dataset. The proposed VMC-DETR framework achieves the best overall performance, with mAP50 and mAP50:95 scores of 45.6% and 19.3%, respectively. Compared to other mainstream detection frameworks such as DDOD, TOOD, and ConvNeXt, VMC-DETR significantly outperforms them—for instance, achieving gains of 11.4%, 17.4%, and 20.1% in mAP50, respectively. Furthermore, VMC-DETR obtains the highest accuracy in five of the eight object categories and demonstrates superior capability in detecting densely overlapping targets such as "Veh" (69.7%) and "Sto" (79.3%). This performance is largely attributed to the proposed VHeat C2f module, which draws inspiration from the heat conduction mechanism to refine feature maps and enhance object-level feature representation. As a result, VMC-DETR is better equipped to distinguish between foreground and background in complex aerial scenes, outperforming other frameworks in the feature extraction stage.

Table 3. Comparison experiments with current mainstream methods on the AI-TOD dataset. Each object category and mAP are expressed as percentages (%), IT represents the inference time for a single image (ms), and MU denotes peak memory usage during model runtime (MB). **Bold** numbers indicate the best results among all compared methods.

Method	Air	Bri	Per	Shi	Sto	Swi	Veh	Win	mAP50	mAP50:95	FPS	GFLOPs	IT	MU
DDOD-R50 [60]	28.8	9.3	14.3	50.6	52.4	0.1	48.4	0.0	25.5	10.9	32.2	111	29.4	371
TOOD-R50 [61]	35.8	31.0	20.0	57.6	56.2	10.9	51.2	10.6	34.2	14.9	28.6	124	35.0	365
Dab-DETR-R50 [62]	22.3	2.9	9.2	33.9	18.5	2.1	17.0	11.8	14.7	4.3	25.3	72.4	39.5	412
DINO-R50 [63]	45.4	**48.0**	29.7	65.8	74.9	10.9	62.4	16.0	44.1	15.5	19.8	179	50.5	437
RTMDET-M [64]	50.0	25.4	20.4	54.5	59.7	**26.9**	53.7	4.9	36.9	16.0	36.7	**39.7**	27.2	315
LD-R50 [65]	21.0	0.0	10.9	40.6	34.5	5.3	30.6	0.0	17.9	7.5	**40.6**	128	24.6	567
ConvNeXt-R50 [66]	48.0	33.1	12.5	42.0	33.4	15.6	33.3	7.7	28.2	12.4	27.8	189	36.0	1031
Gold-YOLO-M [67]	46.0	33.9	24.0	64.5	77.2	17.7	69.0	10.2	42.8	18.3	27.4	79.3	8.7	338
YOLOv9-M [46]	**52.7**	37.7	24.9	64.6	77.2	13.9	69.1	8.6	43.6	19.0	31.8	77.9	8.5	290
YOLOv10-M [68]	50.0	29.9	24.1	64.7	78.4	7.0	68.6	11.5	41.8	18.7	38.8	64.0	**8.2**	284
Baseline [14]	31.1	42.4	28.3	69.9	76.7	2.8	67.7	7.0	40.7	16.8	37.6	66.1	9.0	**277**
Ours	42.0	42.9	**30.7**	**70.8**	**79.3**	12.8	**69.7**	**16.5**	**45.6**	**19.3**	36.8	70.5	9.2	302

In terms of computational efficiency and real-time processing, VMC-DETR ranks fourth in both FPS and GFLOPs, with a single image processing time of 9.2 ms. Although it slightly lags behind the YOLO series models, it outperforms other CNN and Transformer-based models, demonstrating excellent detection accuracy while maintaining high computational efficiency and real-time processing capabilities. This meets the real-time performance requirements of one-stage object detection algorithms. Additionally, the VMC-DETR framework uses 302 MB of memory, making it compatible with the memory constraints of most edge computing devices and positioning it as a lightweight model.

Table 4 presents the results of our comparative experiments on the VisDrone-2019 drone dataset. Our proposed VMC-DETR framework achieves the best performance, with mAP50 and mAP50:95 scores of 45.9% and 27.9%, respectively. Compared to the excellent YOLOv9 and YOLOv10 medium models proposed in 2024, VMC-DETR framework outperforms them by 3.9% in mAP50 and by 2.7% and 2.6% in mAP50:95, respectively. Notably, it demonstrates the highest accuracy not only for small objects like "Peo" (47.9%) but also for large objects such as "Van" (49.9%), while maintaining strong performance across other categories. This superior outcome is attributed to the integration of MFADM in the neck network. By effectively aggregating and distributing multi-scale features across the P3, P4, and P5 layers, MFADM enhances the VMC-DETR framework's detection accuracy for objects of various sizes, enabling it to consistently outperform other mainstream methods in complex aerial imagery.

Table 5 presents the results of our comparative experiments on the TinyPerson dataset. Our proposed VMC-DETR framework achieves the best performance, with mAP50 and mAP50:95 scores of 25.4% and 7.5%, respectively, surpassing the best Transformer-based method, DINO, by 1.1% and 0.7%. Additionally, VMC-DETR framework achieves the highest accuracy in the categories "Ep" (19.3%) and "Sp" (31.5%), demonstrating its effectiveness in handling tiny objects in aerial images. This outstanding performance is attributed to the integration of the CAGFM. By utilizing an optimized feature fusion strategy and attention mechanism, CAGFM effectively guides and enhances the fused features, allowing the framework to fully leverage the contextual information in the image. This capability significantly improves the detection accuracy of small objects in aerial images.

Table 4. Comparison experiments with current mainstream methods on the VisDrone-2019 dataset. All values are expressed as percentages (%). **Bold** numbers indicate the best results for each metric across all methods.

Method	Year	Awn	Bic	Bus	Car	Mot	Ped	Peo	Tri	Tru	Van	mAP50	mAP50:95
DDOD-R50	2021	14.2	18.2	58.5	78.8	47.5	47.4	34.9	27.5	41.0	45.4	40.7	24.8
TOOD-R50	2021	14.2	19.8	56.4	79.3	49.2	46.8	35.4	27.2	40.9	45.6	38.8	24.3
Dab-DETR-R50	2022	15.3	12.7	57.5	66.7	26.2	21.4	14.3	19.7	39.3	38.2	31.1	15.5
DINO-R50	2022	18.0	18.3	61.2	83.9	51.2	58.1	44.3	30.7	38.5	49.6	45.4	26.7
RTMDET-M	2022	14.6	12.1	56.1	75.2	40.4	34.2	28.3	25.1	36.3	41.4	36.4	21.5
LD-R50	2022	7.6	5.1	29.6	68.4	24.5	33.5	18.3	12.9	21.7	31.3	25.3	14.7
ConvNeXt-R50	2022	17.2	21.7	60.5	75.2	42.5	39.4	32.6	32.8	44.0	49.8	41.6	24.7
Gold-YOLO-M	2023	18.8	14.4	59.8	80.4	46.6	43.5	34.2	30.3	40.9	45.5	41.4	25.0
YOLOv9-M	2024	17.7	15.5	62.2	80.8	47.4	43.5	34.3	31.8	39.6	46.9	42.0	25.2
YOLOv10-M	2024	16.8	16.2	59.0	81.3	47.2	46.0	36.1	31.1	38.7	47.2	42.0	25.3
Baseline	2023	11.8	13.3	52.2	81.9	49.7	45.4	39.0	28.2	27.8	46.3	39.6	23.7
Ours	-	**18.9**	19.1	59.8	**84.2**	**56.4**	54.0	**47.9**	**33.1**	36.1	**49.9**	**45.9**	**27.9**

Table 5. Comparison experiments with current mainstream methods on the TinyPerson dataset. All values are expressed as percentages (%). **Bold** numbers indicate the best performance for each metric across all methods.

Method	Ep	Sp	mAP50	mAP50:95
DDOD-R50	11.6	24.3	18.0	5.9
TOOD-R50	13.0	26.1	19.5	6.1
Dab-DETR-R50	3.2	10.1	6.6	1.8
DINO-R50	18.0	30.5	24.3	6.8
RTMDET-M	14.6	26.3	20.4	6.7
LD-R50	5.9	12.7	9.3	2.7
ConvNeXt-R50	7.1	16.2	11.6	3.6
Gold-YOLO-M	18.3	30.1	24.2	6.9
YOLOv9-M	17.1	29.0	23.1	7.2
YOLOv10-M	15.0	23.1	19.0	5.7
Baseline	17.9	26.1	22.0	6.6
Ours	**19.3**	**31.5**	**25.4**	**7.5**

In all three datasets, VMC-DETR exhibits a strong trade-off between detection accuracy, speed, and memory footprint. It maintains top-tier performance across both anchor-based and anchor-free models, including two-stage (e.g., DAB-DETR, RTMDet) and one-stage (e.g., YOLOv8-M, YOLOv10-M) detectors, highlighting its generalization ability under varied aerial scenarios.

4.4. Visualization of Detection Results

Figure 9 shows the visualization results of all comparison methods on the AI-TOD dataset. For clarity, these errors are highlighted using red and yellow circles. Red circles indicate missed detections, where actual objects in the scene are not detected, leading to false negatives. Yellow circles, on the other hand, indicate false detections, where the model identifies objects that do not exist in the scene, resulting in false positives.

As shown in Figure 9, our framework (l) produces results that are nearly identical to the ground truth (a), demonstrating the high accuracy and stability of our approach in object detection in aerial images. In contrast, other methods (shown in (b) to (k)) exhibit varying degrees of error. Notably, the image is taken at night, where objects are densely distributed and overlapping, and all object instances are small—factors that pose significant challenges in aerial object detection. Our method effectively addresses these issues. Specifically, VHeat C2f enhances the feature extraction capability, enabling clearer distinction between objects and backgrounds under low-light conditions. MFADM expands the receptive field through multi-scale deep convolution kernels to capture dense object regions effectively, while CAGFM enhances the weight of small objects through contextual attention and adaptive fusion. As a result, the VMC-DETR framework significantly reduces both false detections and missed detections, offering more reliable and robust detection performance compared to other advanced frameworks.

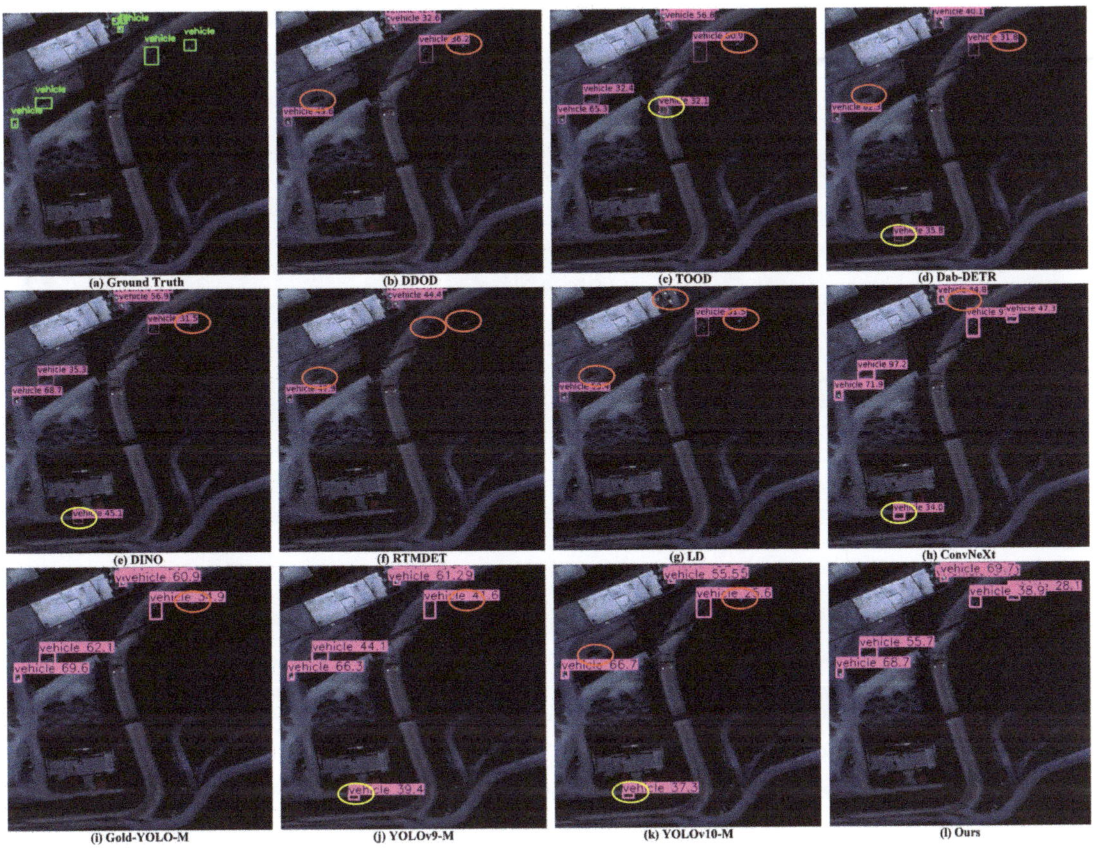

Figure 9. Visualization of all comparison methods on the AI-TOD dataset. (**a**) shows the ground truth bounding boxes. (**b**–**h**) are detection results visualized using MMDetection version 3.3.0, while (**i**–**l**) are generated using Ultralytics version 8.0.201. Red circles highlight false positive detections, and yellow circles mark missed detections.

Figure 10 presents the visualization results on the VisDrone-2019 dataset, comparing our framework (c) with the baseline (b). Similar to before, red circles indicate missed detections, and yellow circles represent false positives. In this dataset, baseline methods often miss multiple objects or generate false detections in crowded urban scenes, especially along roadsides where occlusions from trees, vehicles, and buildings are frequent. In contrast, our framework accurately detects both large and small vehicles as well as partially occluded pedestrians and cyclists. This improvement is largely due to the MFADM module, which incorporates the ADown structure to enhance the model's capacity to distinguish objects in complex spatial hierarchies. These visual results further confirm the robustness of VMC-DETR in dense urban environments with challenging occlusion and clutter.

(a)
(b)
(c)

Figure 10. Comparison of visualization effects with baseline methods on the VisDrone-2019 dataset, implemented using Ultralytics version 8.0.201. (**a**) shows the ground truth annotations, (**b**) presents detection results from the baseline model, and (**c**) displays the results of our proposed method. Yellow circles highlight missed detections or false classifications made by the baseline method.

5. Analysis and Discussion

5.1. Module Contribution Analysis of VMC-DETR

To verify the contribution of each module in VMC-DETR framework, we conduct an ablation study on three datasets: AI-TOD, VisDrone-2019, and TinyPerson. The modules involved include VHeat C2f, MFADM, and CAGFM. Below, we provide a detailed analysis of the results.

5.1.1. Effectiveness Validation on AI-TOD Dataset

The results in Table 6 show that the VMC-DETR framework achieves a significant performance improvement on the AI-TOD dataset, with final mAP50 and mAP50:95 scores of 45.6% and 19.3%, respectively, compared to 40.7% and 16.8% for the baseline model. Introducing the VHeat C2f module alone raises mAP50 from 40.7% to 42.2% and Rec from 42.0% to 44.1%. This result demonstrates the effectiveness of VHeat C2f in addressing the challenges posed by varying object scales and motion blur in the AI-TOD dataset. Through a heat conduction mechanism, VHeat C2f enables precise spatial adjustments in the feature map, enhancing the model's ability to distinguish objects at different scales and capture finer details in blurred conditions.

Table 6. Ablation experiment results on the AI-TOD dataset. All values are expressed as percentages (%). **Bold** numbers indicate the best performance for each metric across all variants.

Method	Pre	Rec	mAP50	mAP50:95
Baseline	47.9	42.0	40.7	16.8
VHeat C2f	54.1	44.1	42.2	18.1
CAGFM	52.7	43.4	41.0	17.1
MFADM	47.9	45.2	41.8	17.3
VHeat C2f + CAGFM	**61.3**	42.4	42.5	18.1
VHeat C2f + MFADM	51.2	46.5	43.4	17.7
MFADM+CAGFM	55.0	42.8	42.9	18.1
Ours	55.4	**47.8**	**45.6**	**19.3**

Further combining VHeat C2f with CAGFM or MFADM yields even more significant performance gains. For instance, the combination of VHeat C2f and CAGFM achieves a Pre of 61.3% and mAP50 of 42.5%, highlighting the ability of the contextual attention mechanism to fusion key information in complex backgrounds. In the AI-TOD dataset, background information greatly exceeds the object. CAGFM focuses on the object area through contextual clues, identifies the object location, and filters the background noise. In addition, the multi-scale feature fusion and distribution mechanism of MFADM enables the model to effectively handle the problem of changes in object details caused by changes in fog conditions, improving the VMC-DETR framework's ability to resist light interference. Together, the modules in the VMC-DETR framework greatly enhance the model's robustness in tackling diverse challenges within the AI-TOD dataset.

5.1.2. Effectiveness Validation on VisDrone-2019 Dataset

The results in Table 7 indicate that the VMC-DETR framework performs exceptionally well on the VisDrone-2019 dataset, achieving final mAP50 and mAP50:95 scores of 45.9% and 27.9%, respectively, significantly surpassing the baseline model's scores of 39.6% and 23.7%. Introducing the MFADM alone raises Rec from 37.9% to 38.2% and mAP50 from 39.6% to 40.0%. This demonstrates MFADM's advantage in handling object overlap and occlusion issues in the VisDrone-2019 dataset. Through multi-scale feature aggregation and distribution, MFADM enables flexible feature allocation across scales, enhancing the model's ability to distinguish densely packed and occluded objects.

Table 7. Ablation experiment results on the VisDrone-2019 dataset. All values are expressed as percentages (%). **Bold** numbers indicate the best performance for each metric across all ablation variants.

Method	Pre	Rec	mAP50	mAP50:95
Baseline	53.7	37.9	39.6	23.7
VHeat C2f	56.4	40.4	42.4	25.5
CAGFM	55.2	40.1	41.2	24.6
MFADM	55.0	38.2	40.0	23.8
VHeat C2f + CAGFM	56.5	41.5	43.1	25.9
VHeat C2f + MFADM	57.5	41.9	43.4	26.3
MFADM+CAGFM	57.3	41.4	42.9	25.2
Ours	**59.6**	**44.7**	**45.9**	**27.9**

Combining MFADM with VHeat C2f or CAGFM further boosts model performance. For example, the combination of MFADM and CAGFM achieves an mAP50 of 42.9%, showcasing the synergy between contextual attention and multi-scale feature fusion. In the VisDrone-2019 dataset, small objects are densely packed, and some images are significantly affected by lighting conditions. CAGFM improves the model's ability to locate small objects in complex lighting environments by focusing on the contextual information around the small objects. Additionally, the VHeat C2f module enhances the model's detail recognition when addressing lighting variations and dense distributions. With all three modules combined, the VMC-DETR framework demonstrates robust detection performance, effectively tackling the challenges of density, occlusion, and lighting variations.

5.1.3. Effectiveness Validation on TinyPerson Dataset

The results in Table 8 show that the VMC-Net framework achieves a significant performance improvement on the TinyPerson dataset, with final mAP50 and mAP50:95 scores of 25.4% and 7.6%, respectively, representing a clear improvement over the baseline model's scores of 22.0% and 6.6%. Using the CAGFM module alone increases Pre from 37.6% to 39.4% and mAP50 from 22.0% to 23.2%. This result highlights CAGFM's ability to fusion information effectively in the complex scenes of the TinyPerson dataset. By leveraging contextual attention, CAGFM enhances the model's capacity to perceive and fuse small and overlapping objects, allowing for more accurate object recognition within aerial images.

Table 8. Ablation experiment results on the TinyPerson dataset. All values are expressed as percentages (%). **Bold** numbers indicate the best performance in each column.

Method	Pre	Rec	mAP50	mAP50:95
Baseline	37.6	28.9	22.0	6.6
VHeat C2f	41.4	30.2	23.8	6.9
CAGFM	39.4	30.0	23.2	6.9
MFADM	37.6	31.5	23.9	7.2
VHeat C2f + CAGFM	40.9	31.5	24.2	7.3
VHeat C2f +MFADM	**42.6**	30.1	24.4	7.4
MFADM+CAGFM	40.6	31.1	24.0	7.2
Ours	41.4	**31.6**	**25.4**	**7.6**

Further combining CAGFM with VHeat C2f or MFADM leads to additional performance gains. For example, the combination of CAGFM and VHeat C2f achieves an mAP50 of 24.4%, demonstrating the synergy between fine-grained feature extraction and contextual attention. In the TinyPerson dataset, small objects are often densely packed within complex backgrounds. The VHeat C2f module, through its heat conduction mechanism, effectively captures detailed features, while MFADM's multi-scale feature fusion and distribution mechanism improves the model's adaptability to overlapping and variably sized objects. With all three modules working in tandem, the VMC-DETR framework achieves comprehensive enhancements in detecting overlapping objects within complex scenes on the TinyPerson dataset.

5.1.4. Discussion on Module Contributions

The ablation study clearly shows that each module in the VMC-DETR framework contributes to improving detection performance. The VHeat C2f module effectively enhances the framework's ability to capture detailed object features, MFADM ensures efficient feature fusion across different scales, and CAGFM leverages contextual information to further strengthen the fused features. The combination of these modules achieves superior performance across all datasets, especially for small and densely overlapping objects in complex aerial images. The mAP curves in Figure 11 show the mAP trends for different modules across the three datasets, providing an intuitive illustration of the incremental improvements brought by each module, and highlighting the effectiveness and necessity of each component in achieving optimal performance.

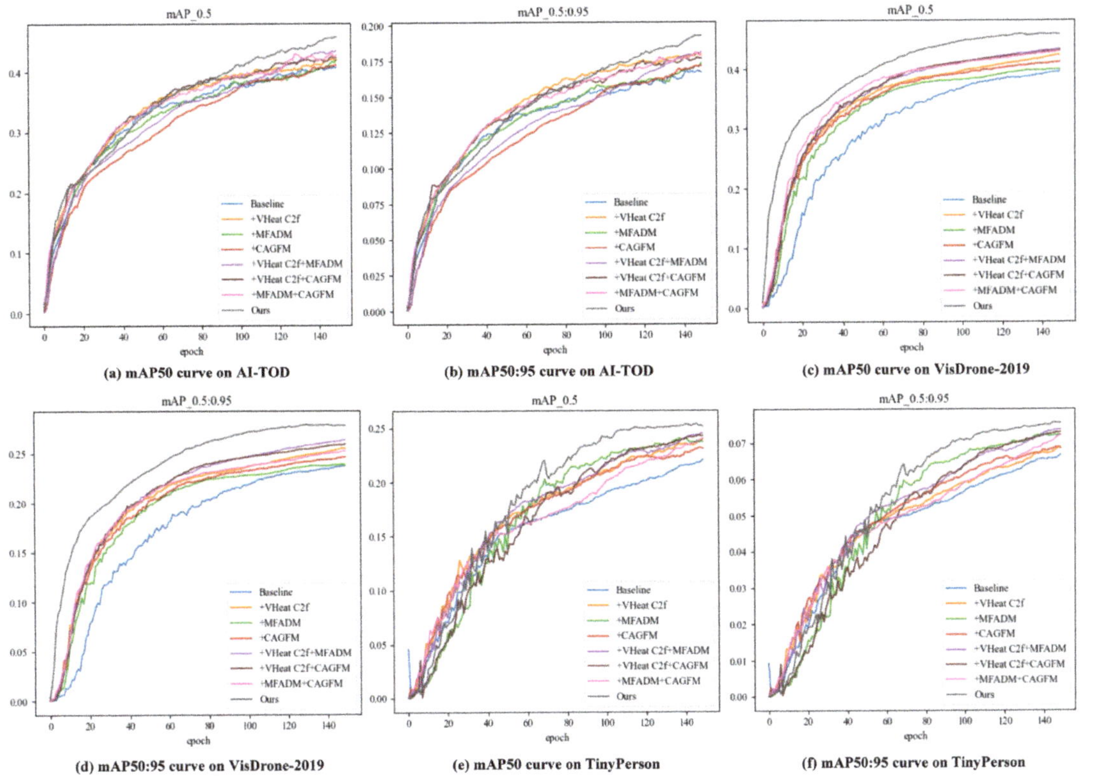

Figure 11. mAP curves from ablation experiments on the AI-TOD, VisDrone-2019, and TinyPerson datasets, showing the performance impact of each module.

However, the VMC-DETR framework also has certain limitations. Although VMC-DETR is optimized for aerial imagery datasets, it may struggle to adapt to non-aerial or highly diverse scenes. The reliance on multi-scale feature fusion and attention mechanisms could also make the framework sensitive to hyperparameter settings and model configurations, potentially reducing its generalizability to other tasks.

5.2. Module Configurations Analysis in VMC-DETR

To ensure the completeness of the experiment and thoroughly examine the impact of the internal design details of the proposed module on performance, we conduct ablation experiments on the three modules of the VMC-DETR framework using the AI-TOD, VisDrone-2019, and TinyPerson datasets.

5.2.1. Ablation Study on the Design of the VHeat C2f Module

As shown in Figure 12, in terms of Pre, Rec, mAP50, and mAP50:95 metrics, the "All" configuration, which uses the VHeat C2f module in all positions, shows varying degrees of improvement over the "No" configuration, which uses only the standard C2f module, across all three datasets. This demonstrates that the VHeat C2f module effectively enhances the extraction of feature information for small objects in aerial images by refining feature maps. Additionally, the FPS results indicate that the computational complexity of using the VHeat C2f module is nearly identical to that of the standard C2f module, showing that the VHeat C2f module improves detection accuracy while maintaining the model's inference speed.

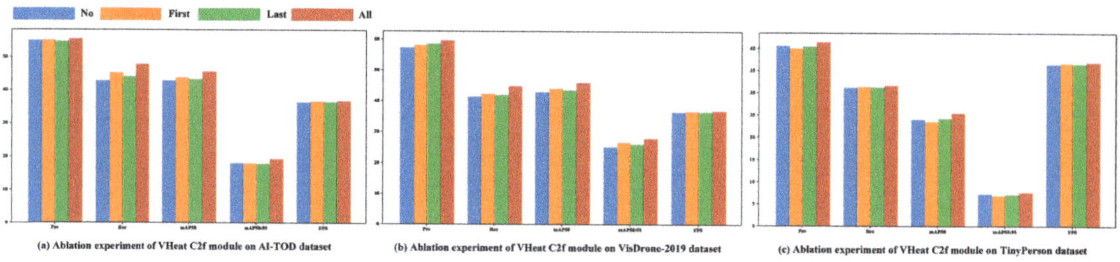

Figure 12. Effect of varying frequency and placement of the VHeat C2f module across the AI-TOD, VisDrone-2019, and TinyPerson datasets. "First" indicates that the VHeat C2f module is used only between the P3 and P4 layers, "Last" indicates that it is used only between the P4 and P5 layers, "No" indicates that the standard C2f module is used in both locations, and "All" indicates that the VHeat C2f module is used in both locations.

For the AI-TOD and VisDrone-2019 datasets, the "First" configuration—using the VHeat C2f module between P3 and P4—performs better than the "Last" configuration using the VHeat C2f module between P4 and P5. This suggests that for aerial image data with complex scenes and large-scale variations, using the VHeat C2f module at a lower level strengthens the spatial distribution and fine-grained high-frequency features of the object earlier, allowing more irrelevant background information to be filtered out for subsequent layers. For the TinyPerson dataset, the results of "Last" and "No" are nearly identical, while "First" performs lower than "No" in most metrics except for Rec. This indicates that for extremely small objects, it remains challenging to extract low-level feature information effectively, as these objects rely more on high-level semantic information with richer channels. Using the VHeat C2f module alone has limited impact, and better results are achieved when it is used in combination with other configurations.

5.2.2. Ablation Study on the First Aggregation Stage of MFADM

According to the ablation experiment results in Table 9, ADown, used in the first feature aggregation stage of MFADM, achieves the best overall performance in terms of Pre, Rec, mAP50, and mAP50:95 across the three datasets. Specifically, mAP50 and mAP50:95 are improved by 0.5%, 0.5%, 0.8%, 0.7%, 0.8%, and 0.4% on the three datasets, respectively, compared to the second-best Conv2d. Although the Rec values on the AI-TOD and TinyPerson datasets are 0.4% lower than those of Conv2d, this has minimal impact on the overall strong performance of the ADown module.

In addition, for aerial images with densely overlapping small objects, interpolation downsampling and average pooling have poor overall effects. This is because the absence of convolution operations leads to excessive loss of spatial structural information, making it difficult for the model to distinguish between objects and backgrounds, and preventing accurate object localization, ultimately resulting in reduced accuracy. Overall, the ADown module offers distinct advantages in processing aerial images. By preserving the smoothness of downsampled features, it retains more multi-scale feature information through a rich and diverse combination of convolution and pooling operations.

Table 9. Ablation experiments on the AI-TOD, VisDrone-2019, and TinyPerson datasets using different downsampling methods in the first feature aggregation stage of the MFADM module, including Interpolation, AvgPool2d, Conv2d, and ADown. **Bold** numbers indicate the best performance in each column.

Method	FPS	AI-TOD				VisDrone-2019				TinyPerson			
		Pre	Rec	mAP50	mAP50:95	Pre	Rec	mAP50	mAP50:95	Pre	Rec	mAP50	mAP50:95
Interpolation	35.2	54.2	47.9	44.5	18.3	58.5	43.6	44.6	26.9	39.6	30.1	23.2	6.8
AvgPool2d	**37.9**	53.9	47.7	44.3	18.2	58.7	43.5	44.9	27.2	39.8	30.1	23.9	7.1
Conv2d	36.5	54.6	**48.2**	45.1	18.8	58.9	44.1	45.1	27.2	40.7	**32.0**	24.6	7.2
ADown [46]	36.8	**55.4**	47.8	**45.6**	**19.3**	**59.6**	**44.7**	**45.9**	**27.9**	**41.4**	31.6	**25.4**	**7.6**

Finally, the FPS of the ADown module is similar to that of other methods, indicating that there is no significant increase in computational overhead, and it maintains high efficiency. Therefore, downsampling using ADown in the first stage of MFADM is necessary for the overall VMC-DETR framework.

5.2.3. Ablation Study on the Distribution and Second Aggregation Stage of MFADM

We conduct ablation experiments on the distribution operation in the third stage of MFADM using different numbers, strides, and sizes of deep convolution kernel combinations. The experimental results are shown in Table 10. The (5, 7, 9, 11) deep convolution kernel combination used in our MFADM performs the best across all three accuracy indicators on the three datasets.

Table 10. Ablation experiments on three datasets for different numbers, strides, and sizes of deep convolutional kernels used in the distribution operation in the third stage of the MFADM module. **Bold** numbers indicate the best performance in each column.

Design	Numbers	Strides	FPS	GFLOPs	AI-TOD			VisDrone-2019			TinyPerson		
					Pre	Rec	mAP50	Pre	Rec	mAP50	Pre	Rec	mAP50
(5, 7, 9)	3	2	**37.1**	**68.9**	55.5	45.8	43.7	58.6	42.2	44.1	39.3	29.2	23.5
(7, 9, 11)	3	2	37.0	69.6	55.1	45.9	45.3	59.0	42.8	44.8	40.0	29.2	24.1
(9, 11, 13)	3	2	36.8	70.3	53.7	45.1	43.2	59.0	44.9	45.5	37.8	28.9	23.4
(3, 7, 11, 15)	4	4	36.8	70.8	53.8	43.3	43.3	58.7	42.2	44.2	36.1	29.9	22.7
(3, 5, 7, 9)	4	2	36.9	69.9	53.4	45.7	43.5	59.3	43.1	44.5	38.3	29.7	23.3
(7, 9, 11, 13)	4	2	36.7	71.0	**55.6**	45.3	45.5	**60.2**	42.9	45.0	41.3	30.0	25.2
(9, 11, 13, 15)	4	2	36.6	71.6	54.0	45.4	44.1	58.4	41.8	43.5	38.6	29.5	24.0
(5, 7, 9, 11)-Ours	4	2	36.8	70.5	55.4	**47.8**	**45.6**	59.6	**44.7**	**45.9**	**41.4**	**31.6**	**25.4**

The fusion strategy using four deep convolution kernels consistently outperforms the one using only three kernels in terms of all evaluation metrics. This suggests that employing a greater number of deep convolution kernels enables more effective and comprehensive integration of high-frequency object features across multiple scales. In contrast, the (3, 7, 11, 15) kernel combination with a stride of 4 performs poorly on all datasets. Compared with the (5, 7, 9, 11) setting, the mAP50 drops by 2.3%, 1.7%, and 2.7% on the respective datasets. These results indicate that using an excessively large stride during the distribution process can lead to the loss of important high-frequency details—particularly around object boundaries—thus weakening the model's ability to localize objects accurately.

Moreover, using overly small depthwise convolution kernels (e.g., 3×3) may lead to missed features of large-scale objects due to the limited receptive field. At the same time, high-frequency features extracted with small kernels tend to be more vulnerable to interference and exhibit poor robustness. In contrast, employing excessively large kernels (e.g., 13 × 13 or 15 × 15) often results in the loss of critical high-frequency cues essential for accurate detection, retaining primarily mid- and low-frequency components. Both scenarios ultimately compromise detection accuracy.

This observation is consistent with findings from adversarial attack studies on deep neural networks, which indicate that the extraction of high-frequency features is highly sensitive to the choice of convolution kernel size [24,53,69]. To address this issue, MFADM adopts a multi-scale depthwise convolution kernel combination of (5, 7, 9, 11), which serves as a compromise strategy. This design effectively balances sensitivity to fine-grained high-frequency details and robustness against noise and perturbations, thereby achieving optimal detection performance.

Regarding computational complexity, increasing the kernel size and the number of kernels inevitably introduces additional computational overhead. However, the overall impact on inference efficiency remains minimal, making this trade-off acceptable for practical applications.

5.2.4. Ablation Study on MFADM and Classic Multi-Scale Feature Fusion Methods

We conduct ablation experiments on the proposed MFADM and classic multi-scale feature fusion strategies, including ASFF, PAFPN, and BIFPN. To ensure the exclusivity of MFADM as the sole variable in the ablation experiments, we use VHeat C2f as the backbone network and replace the normal concatenation operation in the neck with CAGFM when evaluating the other three methods.

In addition, to clearly demonstrate the experimental effects of different methods on objects of varying sizes, we use two thresholds, an area of 16 × 16 = 256 pixels and an area of 32 × 32 = 1024 pixels, to categorize object sizes. The objects are divided into three groups: extremely small objects with an area less than 256 pixels, small objects with an area between 256 and 1024 pixels, and medium objects with an area greater than 1024 pixels. Additionally, two object categories are selected from each group to display experimental results: Sp from the TinyPerson dataset, Win and Sto from the AI-TOD dataset, and Mot, Van, and Tru from the VisDrone-2019 dataset.

Figure 13 shows the experimental results, demonstrating that MFADM achieves significant advantages in two key metrics: Rec and mAP50. Across six object categories of varying sizes—including extremely small, small, and medium object—MFADM consistently delivers the best performance. This highlights the effectiveness and robustness of MFADM's ADown-based feature fusion and multi-scale large-kernel depthwise convolution distribution strategy in aerial image object detection.

Despite its strong overall performance in terms of Pre and mAP50:95 across most categories, MFADM exhibits suboptimal results on the small object class "Sto" (area: 298.90 pixels) and the medium object class "Van" (area: 3663.10 pixels), with "Van" even ranking last in the Pre metric. This suggests that although MFADM excels in detecting smaller objects, it still faces limitations when handling medium or larger objects. A potential reason lies in the design of the feature distribution stage, where multiple large-sized depthwise convolutions are applied. While this design effectively filters high-frequency features of extremely small and small objects, it may also lead to the excessive attenuation of limited high-frequency details in larger objects, ultimately resulting in significant bounding box regression loss.

In general, aerial image object detection mainly focuses on detecting small objects. MFADM performs well on extremely small and small objects and solves the shortcomings of several classic multi-scale feature fusion methods in some extreme cases, as shown in Figure 5.

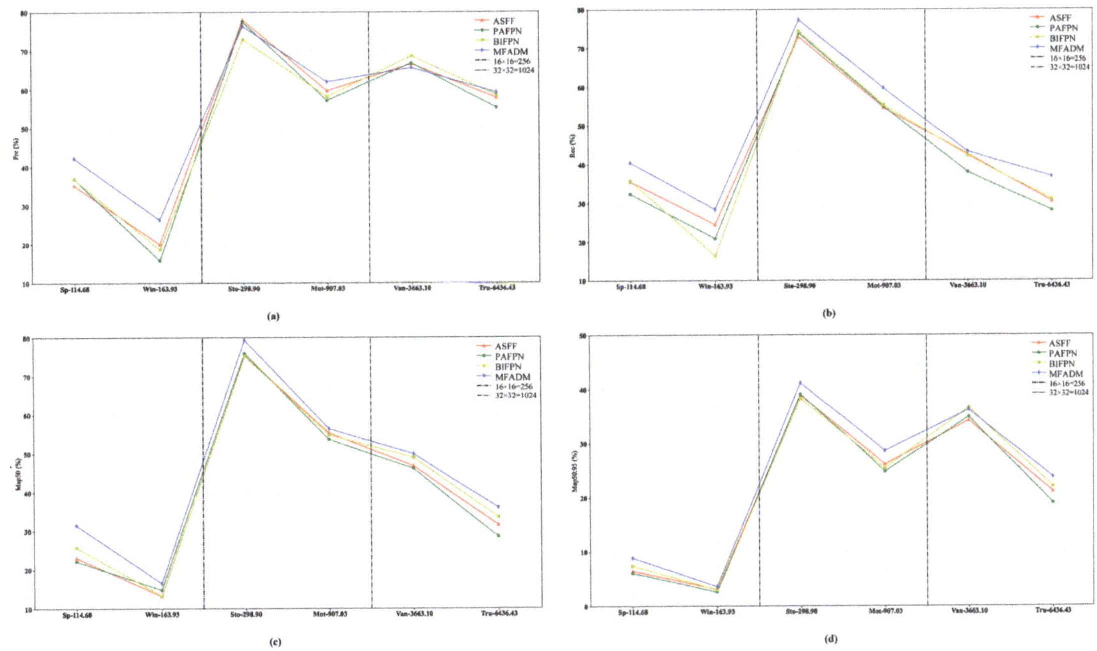

Figure 13. The comparison between the proposed MFADM and classic multi-scale feature fusion strategies on aerial image object-detection datasets is presented. The vertical axes in (**a**), (**b**), (**c**), and (**d**) represent the performance metrics of Pre, Rec, mAP50, and mAP50:95, respectively, while the horizontal axes indicate the average area of object instances in pixels.

5.2.5. Ablation Study on the Design of CAGFM

We conduct experiments on the AI-TOD, VisDrone-2019, and TinyPerson datasets, using various attention mechanisms with similar computational complexity for context guided fusion in CAGFM, including CA [70], SE [56], SimAM [71], CBAM [72], ELA [73], and ESE [32], as used in this paper. The results are shown in Figure 14. CAGFM with the ESE attention mechanism achieves the best results on the mAP50 and mAP50:95 metrics across all three datasets, with the most notable effect on the VisDrone-2019 dataset. This is because ESE more effectively highlights the object regions of various categories in the image through an efficient attention mechanism, thereby enhancing the quality of the feature fusion process, especially for small object detection in dense, light-affected scenes in the VisDrone-2019 dataset.

In addition, for the GFLOPs metric, ESE is relatively lightweight among the six attention mechanisms, significantly lower than ELA, which ranks second in accuracy. This demonstrates that ESE reduces redundant operations through effective parameter-sharing mechanisms and efficient feature selection strategies. Compared to other mainstream attention mechanisms, it maintains a lightweight model structure while effectively enhancing contextual information interaction between multi-scale objects in aerial images.

5.3. Small Object Detection Performance Analysis

Due to the frequent occurrence of densely distributed and low-resolution objects in aerial imagery, this study focuses on the task of small object detection. As illustrated in Figure 8, and following the MS COCO definition, objects smaller than 32×32 pixels are categorized as small objects. To better evaluate the effectiveness of the proposed VMC-

DETR in this context, we analyze its performance on three benchmark datasets: AI-TOD (as shown in Table 3), VisDrone-2019 (as shown in Table 4), and TinyPerson (as shown in Table 5).

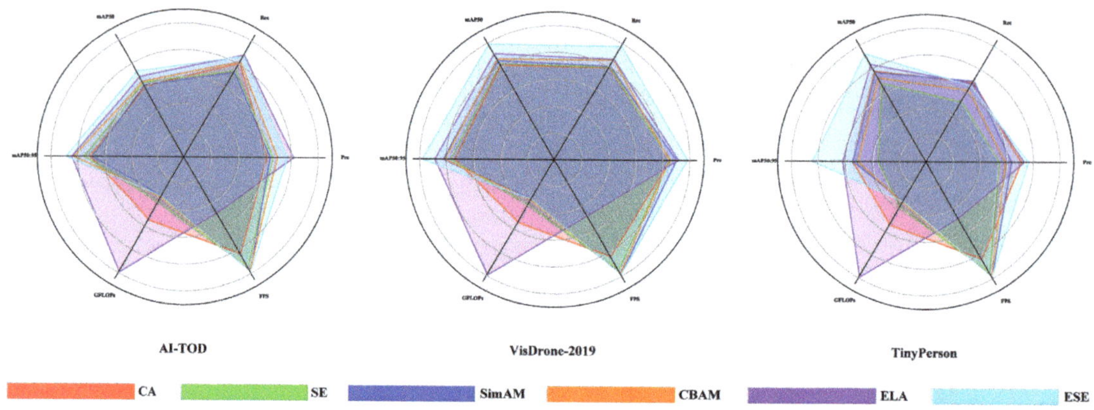

Figure 14. Effect of different attention mechanisms in CAGFM on context-guided fusion, evaluated through ablation experiments across the AI-TOD, VisDrone-2019, and TinyPerson datasets. Higher Pre, Rec, mAP50, and mAP50:95 indicate greater model accuracy, higher FPS represents faster inference, and lower GFLOPs imply a more lightweight model.

In the AI-TOD dataset, more than 87.7% of objects are considered small, with a mean object size of only 12.8 pixels. VMC-DETR achieves the highest AP in small-object dominant categories such as Air, Per, and Veh, with scores of 42.0%, 30.7%, and 69.7%, respectively, indicating strong robustness in dense aerial scenes.

The VisDrone-2019 dataset contains a high proportion of small targets in categories like Peo, Ped, and Mot. In these categories, our method outperforms other baselines with up to 47.9% AP on Peo, clearly demonstrating improved sensitivity to small-scale object features.

The TinyPerson dataset consists almost entirely of extremely small human instances. VMC-DETR achieves AP scores of 19.3% and 31.5% for the Ep and Sp categories, outperforming the best baseline method by 1.4% and 1.0%, respectively.

These results affirm that the high-frequency feature enhancement and multi-scale context-aware design of VMC-DETR are particularly beneficial for small object detection, which is critical for real-world aerial applications.

5.4. Computational Complexity Analysis

The proposed VMC-DETR framework introduces three modules—VHeat C2f, MFADM, and CAGFM—each designed to enhance performance while maintaining computational efficiency. This section provides a theoretical analysis of their complexity characteristics. The actual effectiveness of this design is quantitatively demonstrated in Table 3 and through the ablation experiments presented in this section.

VHeat C2f Module: By integrating frequency-domain heat conduction into the backbone, the module leverages a HCO based on DCT. This operator operates with a time complexity of $\mathcal{O}(N^{1.5})$, where N denotes the number of spatial locations. This is more efficient than traditional attention mechanisms ($\mathcal{O}(N^2)$), and the frequency filtering is applied selectively to balance precision and overhead.

MFADM Module: The MFADM utilizes depthwise separable convolutions with large kernels (5×5 to 11×11) to capture multi-scale spatial context. Depthwise convolutions significantly reduce computational load compared to standard convolutions, and their parallel arrangement introduces only marginal cost while substantially expanding the receptive field.

CAGFM Module: The CAGFM applies a lightweight attention mechanism, ESE (Effective Squeeze and Extraction), which uses a single fully connected layer without dimensional expansion. This module avoids expensive multi-head attention and maintains linear complexity relative to channel count, adding negligible burden to the overall model.

In summary, all modules are constructed based on lightweight design principles, with their computational complexity strictly controlled to ensure real-time inference capability. Naturally, the integration of multiple modules introduces additional computational overhead, as shown in Table 3. VMC-DETR achieves 36.8 FPS, 70.5 GFLOPs, 9.2 IT, and 302 MU, which are slightly lower than those of the baseline model and YOLO series in terms of real-time performance and memory efficiency. Nevertheless, VMC-DETR strikes a well-considered balance between detection accuracy and computational efficiency. It is compatible with mainstream edge computing platforms such as the Raspberry Pi 4B and NVIDIA Jetson Nano, making it suitable for real-time aerial applications under resource-constrained conditions, although it may encounter limitations on lower-end smartphones or older mobile devices.

6. Conclusions and Future Work

6.1. Conclusions

This paper proposes the VMC-DETR framework for object detection in aerial images, targeting key challenges such as small objects, complex backgrounds, and overlapping or occluded targets that are common in remote sensing scenarios. VMC-DETR integrates three novel modules—Visual-frequency Heat-enhanced C2f (VHeat C2f), Multi-scale Feature Aggregation and Distribution Module (MFADM), and Context Attention Guided Fusion Module (CAGFM)—to improve feature extraction and multi-scale feature fusion. These modules enhance both the backbone and neck stages of the network, leading to performance improvements across three public datasets: AI-TOD, VisDrone-2019, and TinyPerson. Ablation experiments confirm the individual and combined contributions of these modules, and visualization results demonstrate their effectiveness in reducing false positives and negatives in complex aerial scenes. VMC-DETR shows strong potential in practical applications such as urban planning, environmental monitoring, disaster management, and drone-based surveillance. Its accurate detection of small and dense objects supports critical tasks in real-time remote sensing systems and contributes to data-driven decision-making in diverse application domains.

6.2. Future Work

While VMC-DETR achieves excellent results on standard aerial image datasets, its application in real-world scenarios still presents several important challenges and opportunities for further research.

First, the current evaluation is limited to offline inference on high-performance GPUs. To realize the full potential of VMC-DETR in time-sensitive or mobile sensing tasks—such as drone-based monitoring or embedded remote sensing systems—future work should focus on hardware-level deployment. This includes porting the model to resource-constrained platforms (e.g., NVIDIA Jetson Nano, Orin, or ARM-based SoCs) and addressing the trade-off between accuracy, latency, and energy consumption. Quantization, pruning, and neural architecture search tailored to embedded environments will be key to enabling efficient on-device inference.

Second, although VMC-DETR is optimized for aerial RGB imagery, real-world applications often involve heterogeneous sensor data such as infrared, SAR, or multi-spectral inputs. Extending the current framework to multi-modal data fusion—while preserving high-frequency detail and spatial context across modalities—remains a crucial research direction. This would improve robustness under varying lighting, weather, or occlusion conditions.

Third, the proposed modules are currently fixed in structure and configuration. In dynamic environments or evolving mission tasks, a static architecture may struggle to adapt. Future efforts may explore adaptive computation mechanisms, such as dynamic receptive fields, runtime scale selection, or attention-based pruning strategies. These approaches could endow the model with the ability to self-adjust according to scene complexity or device constraints, improving generalizability and sustainability.

Finally, the real-world deployment of aerial detection models also raises concerns around model robustness, adversarial safety, and long-term maintenance. Investigating continual learning strategies, edge-cloud collaborative inference pipelines, and security-aware optimization will further enhance the readiness of VMC-DETR for operational use.

Author Contributions: Conceptualization, X.G. and L.Q.; methodology, X.G. and L.Q.; software, L.Q.; validation, X.G., L.Q., and Q.Y.; formal analysis, X.G. and Q.Y.; investigation, Y.Z. (Yu Zhu); data curation, L.Q.; writing—original draft preparation, L.Q. and X.G.; writing—review and editing, X.G. and J.S.; visualization, X.G. and L.Q.; supervision, Y.Z. (Yanning Zhang). All authors have read and agreed to the published version of the manuscript.

Funding: This research was funded by the National Science Foundation of China under grant no. 62301432, 62306240; the Natural Science Basic Research Program of Shaanxi, no. 2023-JC-QN-0685, QCYRCXM-2023-057; the Fundamental Research Funds for the Central Universities, China, no. D5000220444; the Natural Science Basic Research Program of Shaanxi under grant 2024JC-YBMS-464; the National Engineering Laboratory for Integrated Aero-Space-Ground-Ocean Big Data Application Technology; the Second Batch of Collaborative Innovation Projects for Teachers and Students of Bohai Campus, Hebei Agricultural University (2024-BHXT-07); and the Basic Research Program of Provincial Universities in Hebei Province (KY2022060).

Data Availability Statement: All data used in this study are obtained from publicly available datasets.

Acknowledgments: The College of Science and Technology at Hebei Agricultural University is acknowledged for providing engineering support for this research.

Conflicts of Interest: The authors declare no conflicts of interest.

References

1. Liao, D.; Zhang, J.; Tao, Y.; Jin, X. ATBHC-YOLO: Aggregate transformer and bidirectional hybrid convolution for small object detection. *Complex Intell. Syst.* **2025**, *11*, 38. [CrossRef]
2. Hua, C.; Zhong, B.; Song, W.; Yang, J. Circular coding: A technique for visual localization in urban areas. *Displays* **2022**, *75*, 102299. [CrossRef]
3. Tian, Y.; Zhang, K.; Hu, X.; Lu, Y. Crop type recognition of VGI road-side images via hierarchy structure based on semantic segmentation model Deeplabv3+. *Displays* **2024**, *81*, 102574. [CrossRef]
4. Maurya, K.; Mahajan, S.; Chaube, N. Remote sensing techniques: Mapping and monitoring of mangrove ecosystem—A review. *Complex Intell. Syst.* **2021**, *7*, 2797–2818. [CrossRef]
5. Chen, W.; Wang, H.; Li, H.; Li, Q.; Yang, Y.; Yang, K. Real-time garbage object detection with data augmentation and feature fusion using SUAV low-altitude remote sensing images. *IEEE Geosci. Remote Sens. Lett.* **2021**, *19*, 6003005. [CrossRef]
6. Baur, J.; Dewey, K.; Steinberg, G.; Nitsche, F.O. Modeling the Effect of Vegetation Coverage on Unmanned Aerial Vehicles-Based Object Detection: A Study in the Minefield Environment. *Remote Sens.* **2024**, *16*, 2046. [CrossRef]
7. Yue, M.; Lu, Z.; Ding, C.; Haolei, Z.; Yitong, Z.; Shiyong, Y. Inversion of reservoir parameters for oil extraction based on deformation monitoring with InSAR. *IEEE J. Sel. Top. Appl. Earth Obs. Remote Sens.* **2024**, *17*, 10559–10568.

8. Han, Q.; Yin, Q.; Zheng, X.; Chen, Z. Remote sensing image building detection method based on Mask R-CNN. *Complex Intell. Syst.* **2021**, *8*, 1847–1855. [CrossRef]
9. Wenqi, Y.; Gong, C.; Meijun, W.; Yanqing, Y.; Xingxing, X.; Xiwen, Y.; Junwei, H. MAR20: A benchmark for military aircraft recognition in remote sensing images. *Natl. Remote Sens. Bull.* **2024**, *27*, 2688–2696.
10. Sree Soumya, D.; Aishwarya, C.; Vasavi, S. FPGA-based military vehicles detection and classification from drone videos using YOLOV5. In *International Conference on Energy Systems, Drives and Automations*; Springer: Singapore, 2021; pp. 265–276.
11. Bi, H.; Feng, Y.; Tong, B.; Wang, M.; Yu, H.; Mao, Y.; Chang, H.; Diao, W.; Wang, P.; Yu, Y.; et al. RingMoE: Mixture-of-Modality-Experts Multi-Modal Foundation Models for Universal Remote Sensing Image Interpretation. *arXiv* **2025**, arXiv:2504.03166.
12. Wang, H.; Wu, X.; Huang, Z.; Xing, E.P. High-frequency component helps explain the generalization of convolutional neural networks. In Proceedings of the IEEE/CVF Conference on Computer Vision and Pattern Recognition, Seattle, WA, USA, 14–19 June 2020; pp. 8684–8694.
13. Vaswani, A.; Shazeer, N.; Parmar, N.; Uszkoreit, J.; Jones, L.; Gomez, A.N.; Kaiser, Ł.; Polosukhin, I. Attention is all you need. In Proceedings of the Advances in Neural Information Processing Systems, Long Beach, CA, USA, 4–9 December 2017; Volume 30.
14. Zhao, Y.; Lv, W.; Xu, S.; Wei, J.; Wang, G.; Dang, Q.; Liu, Y.; Chen, J. Detrs beat yolos on real-time object detection. In Proceedings of the IEEE/CVF Conference on Computer Vision and Pattern Recognition, Seattle, WA, USA, 17–18 June 2024; pp. 16965–16974.
15. Lv, W.; Zhao, Y.; Chang, Q.; Huang, K.; Wang, G.; Liu, Y. Rt-detrv2: Improved baseline with bag-of-freebies for real-time detection transformer. *arXiv* 2024, arXiv:2407.17140.
16. Lin, T.Y.; Maire, M.; Belongie, S.; Hays, J.; Perona, P.; Ramanan, D.; Dollár, P.; Zitnick, C.L. Microsoft coco: Common objects in context. In Proceedings of the Computer Vision–ECCV 2014: 13th European Conference, Zurich, Switzerland, 6–12 September 2014; proceedings, part v 13; Springer: Cham, Switzerland, 2014; pp. 740–755.
17. Wang, J.; Yang, W.; Guo, H.; Zhang, R.; Xia, G.S. Tiny object detection in aerial images. In Proceedings of the 2020 25th International Conference on Pattern Recognition (ICPR), Milan, Italy, 10–15 January 2021; IEEE: Piscataway, NJ, USA, 2021; pp. 3791–3798.
18. Du, D.; Zhu, P.; Wen, L.; Bian, X.; Lin, H.; Hu, Q.; Peng, T.; Zheng, J.; Wang, X.; Zhang, Y.; et al. VisDrone-DET2019: The vision meets drone object detection in image challenge results. In Proceedings of the IEEE/CVF International Conference on Computer Vision Workshops, Seoul, Republic of Korea, 27–28 October 2019.
19. He, K.; Zhang, X.; Ren, S.; Sun, J. Deep residual learning for image recognition. In Proceedings of the IEEE Conference on Computer Vision and pattern Recognition, Las Vegas, NV, USA, 27–30 June 2016; pp. 770–778.
20. Jocher, G.; Stoken, A.; Borovec, J.; Liu, C.; Hogan, A.; Diaconu, L.; Poznanski, J.; Yu, L.; Rai, P.; Ferriday, R.; et al. Ultralytics/yolov5: v3.0. *Zenodo* **2020**. Available online: https://github.com/ultralytics/yolov5 (accessed on 15 May 2020).
21. Jocher, G.; Chaurasia, A.; Qiu, J. Ultralytics YOLOv8. *Ultralytics* **2023**. Available online: https://github.com/ultralytics/ultralytics (accessed on 10 January 2023).
22. Lin, Z.; Gao, Y.; Sang, J. Investigating and Explaining the Frequency Bias in Image Classification. In Proceedings of the 31st International Joint Conference on Artificial Intelligence (IJCAI), Vienna, Austria, 23–29 July 2022.
23. Ge, X.; Zhu, Y.; Qi, L.; Hu, Y.; Sun, J.; Zhang, Y. Enhancing Border Learning for Better Image Denoising. *Mathematics* **2025**, *13*, 1119. [CrossRef]
24. Tomen, N.; van Gemert, J.C. Spectral leakage and rethinking the kernel size in cnns. In Proceedings of the IEEE/CVF International Conference on Computer Vision, Montreal, BC, Canada, 11–17 October 2021; pp. 5138–5147.
25. Liu, S.; Huang, D.; Wang, Y. Learning spatial fusion for single-shot object detection. *arXiv* **2019**, arXiv:1911.09516.
26. Liu, S.; Qi, L.; Qin, H.; Shi, J.; Jia, J. Path aggregation network for instance segmentation. In Proceedings of the IEEE Conference on Computer Vision and pattern Recognition, Salt Lake City, UT, USA, 18–22 June 2018; pp. 8759–8768.
27. Tan, M.; Pang, R.; Le, Q.V. Efficientdet: Scalable and efficient object detection. In Proceedings of the IEEE/CVF Conference on Computer Vision and Pattern Recognition, Seattle, WA, USA, 14–19 June 2020; pp. 10781–10790.
28. Wang, Z.; Wang, J.; Wu, Y.; Xu, J.; Zhang, X. UNFusion: A unified multi-scale densely connected network for infrared and visible image fusion. *IEEE Trans. Circuits Syst. Video Technol.* **2021**, *32*, 3360–3374. [CrossRef]
29. Yan, Q.; Wang, H.; Ma, Y.; Liu, Y.; Dong, W.; Woźniak, M.; Zhang, Y. Uncertainty estimation in HDR imaging with Bayesian neural networks. *Pattern Recognit.* **2024**, *156*, 110802. [CrossRef]
30. Chen, Y.; Ren, Q.; Yan, J. Rethinking and improving robustness of convolutional neural networks: A shapley value-based approach in frequency domain. *Adv. Neural Inf. Process. Syst.* **2022**, *35*, 324–337.
31. Cai, X.; Lai, Q.; Wang, Y.; Wang, W.; Sun, Z.; Yao, Y. Poly kernel inception network for remote sensing detection. In Proceedings of the IEEE/CVF Conference on Computer Vision and Pattern Recognition, Seattle, WA, USA, 16–22 June 2024; pp. 27706–27716.
32. Lee, Y.; Park, J. Centermask: Real-time anchor-free instance segmentation. In Proceedings of the IEEE/CVF Conference on Computer Vision and Pattern Recognition, Seattle, WA, USA, 14–19 June 2020; pp. 13906–13915.
33. Xue, C.; Xia, Y.; Wu, M.; Chen, Z.; Cheng, F.; Yun, L. EL-YOLO: An efficient and lightweight low-altitude aerial objects detector for onboard applications. *Expert Syst. Appl.* **2024**, *256*, 124848. [CrossRef]

34. Li, Z.; Hou, B.; Wu, Z.; Ren, B.; Yang, C. FCOSR: A simple anchor-free rotated detector for aerial object detection. *Remote Sens.* **2023**, *15*, 5499. [CrossRef]
35. Ou, K.; Dong, C.; Liu, X.; Zhai, Y.; Li, Y.; Huang, W.; Qiu, W.; Wang, Y.; Wang, C. Drone-TOOD: A lightweight task-aligned object detection algorithm for vehicle detection in UAV images. *IEEE Access* **2024**, *12*, 41999–42016. [CrossRef]
36. Liu, J.; Zheng, K.; Liu, X.; Xu, P.; Zhou, Y. SDSDet: A real-time object detector for small, dense, multi-scale remote sensing objects. *Image Vis. Comput.* **2024**, *142*, 104898. [CrossRef]
37. Dai, L.; Chen, H.; Li, Y.; Kong, C.; Fan, Z.; Lu, J.; Chen, X. TARDet: Two-stage anchor-free rotating object detector in aerial images. In Proceedings of the IEEE/CVF Conference on Computer Vision and Pattern Recognition, New Orleans, LA, USA, 18–24 June 2022; pp. 4267–4275.
38. Fu, L.; Deng, J.; Zhu, B.; Li, Z.; Liao, X. AFOD: Two-stage object detection based on anchor-free remote sensing photos. *Open Comput. Sci.* **2024**, *14*, 20230105. [CrossRef]
39. Wang, H.; Zhang, J. Enhancing object detection for remote sensing with dynamic heads in Oriented R-CNN. In Proceedings of the International Conference on Remote Sensing, Mapping, and Image Processing (RSMIP 2024), SPIE, Xiamen, China, 19–21 January 2024; Volume 13167, pp. 150–156.
40. Sagar, A.S.; Chen, Y.; Xie, Y.; Kim, H.S. MSA R-CNN: A comprehensive approach to remote sensing object detection and scene understanding. *Expert Syst. Appl.* **2024**, *241*, 122788. [CrossRef]
41. Wei, G.; Yuan, X.; Liu, Y.; Shang, Z.; Yao, K.; Li, C.; Yan, Q.; Zhao, C.; Zhang, H.; Xiao, R. OVA-DETR: Open vocabulary aerial object detection using image-text alignment and fusion. *arXiv* **2024**, arXiv:2408.12246.
42. Ma, X.; Lv, P.; Zhong, Y. QETR: A query-enhanced transformer for remote sensing image object detection. *IEEE Geosci. Remote Sens. Lett.* **2024**, *21*, 6005905. [CrossRef]
43. Lu, W.; Niu, C.; Lan, C.; Liu, W.; Wang, S.; Yu, J.; Hu, T. High-quality object detection method for uav images based on improved dino and masked image modeling. *Remote Sens.* **2023**, *15*, 4740. [CrossRef]
44. Wang, X.; Chen, H.; Chu, X.; Wang, P. AODet: Aerial Object Detection Using Transformers for Foreground Regions. *IEEE Trans. Geosci. Remote Sens.* **2024**, *62*, 4106711. [CrossRef]
45. Wang, Z.; Liu, Y.; Liu, Y.; Yu, H.; Wang, Y.; Ye, Q.; Tian, Y. vheat: Building vision models upon heat conduction. *arXiv* **2024**, arXiv:2405.16555.
46. Wang, C.Y.; Yeh, I.H.; Mark Liao, H.Y. Yolov9: Learning what you want to learn using programmable gradient information. In *European Conference on Computer Vision*; Springer: Cham, Switzerland, 2024; pp. 1–21.
47. Papyan, V.; Romano, Y.; Elad, M. Convolutional neural networks analyzed via convolutional sparse coding. *J. Mach. Learn. Res.* **2017**, *18*, 1–52.
48. Yan, Q.; Hu, T.; Wu, P.; Dai, D.; Gu, S.; Dong, W.; Zhang, Y. Efficient Image Enhancement with A Diffusion-Based Frequency Prior. *IEEE Trans. Circuits Syst. Video Technol.* 2025, *early access*.
49. Howard, A.G.; Zhu, M.; Chen, B.; Kalenichenko, D.; Wang, W.; Weyand, T.; Andreetto, M.; Adam, H. Mobilenets: Efficient convolutional neural networks for mobile vision applications. *arXiv* **2017**, arXiv:1704.04861.
50. Dosovitskiy, A.; Beyer, L.; Kolesnikov, A.; Weissenborn, D.; Zhai, X.; Unterthiner, T.; Dehghani, M.; Minderer, M.; Heigold, G.; Gelly, S.; et al. An image is worth 16x16 words: Transformers for image recognition at scale. *arXiv* **2020**, arXiv:2010.11929.
51. Yin, D.; Gontijo Lopes, R.; Shlens, J.; Cubuk, E.D.; Gilmer, J. A fourier perspective on model robustness in computer vision. In Proceedings of the Advances in Neural Information Processing Systems, Vancouver, BC, Canada, 8–14 December 2019; Volume 32.
52. Yucel, M.K.; Cinbis, R.G.; Duygulu, P. Hybridaugment++: Unified frequency spectra perturbations for model robustness. In Proceedings of the IEEE/CVF International Conference on Computer Vision, Paris, France, 1–6 October 2023; pp. 5718–5728.
53. Grabinski, J.; Keuper, J.; Keuper, M. As large as it gets-studying infinitely large convolutions via neural implicit frequency filters. *Trans. Mach. Learn. Res.* **2024**, *2024*, 1–42.
54. Yan, Q.; Hu, T.; Sun, Y.; Tang, H.; Zhu, Y.; Dong, W.; Van Gool, L.; Zhang, Y. Toward high-quality HDR deghosting with conditional diffusion models. *IEEE Trans. Circuits Syst. Video Technol.* **2023**, *34*, 4011–4026. [CrossRef]
55. Yan, Q.; Yang, K.; Hu, T.; Chen, G.; Dai, K.; Wu, P.; Ren, W.; Zhang, Y. From dynamic to static: Stepwisely generate HDR image for ghost removal. *IEEE Trans. Circuits Syst. Video Technol.* **2024**, *35*, 1409–1421. [CrossRef]
56. Hu, J.; Shen, L.; Sun, G. Squeeze-and-excitation networks. In Proceedings of the IEEE Conference on Computer Vision and Pattern Recognition, Salt Lake City, UT, USA, 18–22 June 2018; pp. 7132–7141.
57. Yu, X.; Gong, Y.; Jiang, N.; Ye, Q.; Han, Z. Scale match for tiny person detection. In Proceedings of the IEEE/CVF Winter Conference on Applications of Computer Vision, Waikoloa, HI, USA, 1–5 March 2020; pp. 1257–1265.
58. Zhang, L.; Yu, H.; Chen, M. QETR: Query-Enhanced Transformer for Dense Remote Sensing Object Detection. *arXiv* **2025**, arXiv:2502.07841.
59. Li, J.; Wang, B.; Gao, X. OVA-DETR: Open-Vocabulary Aerial Detection Transformer for Remote Sensing. *arXiv* **2025**, arXiv:2501.02179.

60. Chen, Z.; Yang, C.; Li, Q.; Zhao, F.; Zha, Z.J.; Wu, F. Disentangle your dense object detector. In Proceedings of the 29th ACM International Conference on Multimedia, Virtual, 20–24 October 2021; pp. 4939–4948.
61. Feng, C.; Zhong, Y.; Gao, Y.; Scott, M.R.; Huang, W. Tood: Task-aligned one-stage object detection. In Proceedings of the 2021 IEEE/CVF International Conference on Computer Vision (ICCV), Montreal, BC, Canada, 11–17 October 2021; IEEE Computer Society: Piscataway, NJ, USA, 2021; pp. 3490–3499.
62. Liu, S.; Li, F.; Zhang, H.; Yang, X.; Qi, X.; Su, H.; Zhu, J.; Zhang, L. DAB-DETR: Dynamic Anchor Boxes are Better Queries for DETR. In Proceedings of the International Conference on Learning Representations, Virtual, 25–29 April 2022.
63. Zhang, H.; Li, F.; Liu, S.; Zhang, L.; Su, H.; Zhu, J.; Ni, L.; Shum, H.Y. DINO: DETR with Improved DeNoising Anchor Boxes for End-to-End Object Detection. In Proceedings of the The Eleventh International Conference on Learning Representations, Kigali, Rwanda, 1–5 May 2023.
64. Lyu, C.; Zhang, W.; Huang, H.; Zhou, Y.; Wang, Y.; Liu, Y.; Zhang, S.; Chen, K. Rtmdet: An empirical study of designing real-time object detectors. *arXiv* **2022**, arXiv:2212.07784.
65. Zheng, Z.; Ye, R.; Wang, P.; Ren, D.; Zuo, W.; Hou, Q.; Cheng, M.M. Localization distillation for dense object detection. In Proceedings of the IEEE/CVF Conference on Computer Vision and Pattern Recognition, New Orleans, LA, USA, 18–24 June 2022; pp. 9407–9416.
66. Liu, Z.; Mao, H.; Wu, C.Y.; Feichtenhofer, C.; Darrell, T.; Xie, S. A convnet for the 2020s. In Proceedings of the IEEE/CVF Conference on Computer Vision and Pattern Recognition, New Orleans, LA, USA, 18–24 June 2022; pp. 11976–11986.
67. Wang, C.; He, W.; Nie, Y.; Guo, J.; Liu, C.; Wang, Y.; Han, K. Gold-YOLO: Efficient object detector via gather-and-distribute mechanism. *Adv. Neural Inf. Process. Syst.* **2023**, *36*, 51094–51112.
68. Wang, A.; Chen, H.; Liu, L.; Chen, K.; Lin, Z.; Han, J.; Ding, G. Yolov10: Real-time end-to-end object detection. *Adv. Neural Inf. Process. Syst.* **2024**, *37*, 107984–108011.
69. Chen, H.; Zhang, Y.; Feng, X.; Chu, X.; Huang, K. Revealing the Dark Secrets of Extremely Large Kernel ConvNets on Robustness. In Proceedings of the Forty-First International Conference on Machine Learning, Vienna, Austria, 21–27 July 2024.
70. Hou, Q.; Zhou, D.; Feng, J. Coordinate attention for efficient mobile network design. In Proceedings of the IEEE/CVF Conference on Computer Vision and Pattern Recognition, Nashville, TN, USA, 20–25 June 2021; pp. 13713–13722.
71. Yang, L.; Zhang, R.Y.; Li, L.; Xie, X. Simam: A simple, parameter-free attention module for convolutional neural networks. In Proceedings of the International conference on machine learning. PMLR, Virtual, 18–24 July 2021; pp. 11863–11874.
72. Woo, S.; Park, J.; Lee, J.Y.; Kweon, I.S. Cbam: Convolutional block attention module. In Proceedings of the European Conference on Computer Vision (ECCV), Munich, Germany, 8–14 September 2018; pp. 3–19.
73. Xu, W.; Wan, Y. ELA: Efficient local attention for deep convolutional neural networks. *arXiv* **2024**, arXiv:2403.01123.

remote sensing

MDPI

Article

DWTMA-Net: Discrete Wavelet Transform and Multi-Dimensional Attention Network for Remote Sensing Image Dehazing

Xin Guan [1], Runxu He [1], Le Wang [2], Hao Zhou [2], Yun Liu [3] and Hailing Xiong [4,*]

1 College of Computer and Information Science, Southwest University, Chongqing 400715, China; guanxin2020@email.swu.edu.cn (X.G.); hrx221226@email.swu.edu.cn (R.H.)
2 School of Computer Science and Technology, Anhui University of Technology, Ma'anshan 243032, China; wangle@ahut.edu.cn (L.W.); haozhou@ahut.edu.cn (H.Z.)
3 College of Artificial Intelligence, Southwest University, Chongqing 400715, China; yunliu@swu.edu.cn
4 College of Electronic and Information Engineering, Southwest University, Chongqing 400715, China
* Correspondence: xionghl@swu.edu.cn

Abstract: Haze caused by atmospheric scattering often leads to color distortion, reduced contrast, and diminished clarity, which significantly degrade the quality of remote sensing images. To address these issues, we propose a novel network called DWTMA-Net that integrates discrete wavelet transform with multi-dimensional attention, aiming to restore image information in both the frequency and spatial domains to enhance overall image quality. Specifically, we design a wavelet transform-based downsampling module that effectively fuses frequency and spatial features. The input first passes through a discrete wavelet block to extract frequency-domain information. These features are then fed into a multi-dimensional attention block, which incorporates pixel attention, Fourier frequency-domain attention, and channel attention. This combination allows the network to capture both global and local characteristics while enhancing deep feature representations through dimensional expansion, thereby improving spatial-domain feature extraction. Experimental results on the SateHaze1k, HRSD, and HazyDet datasets demonstrate the effectiveness of the proposed method in handling remote sensing images with varying haze levels and drone-view scenarios. By recovering both frequency and spatial details, our model achieves significant improvements in dehazing performance compared to existing state-of-the-art approaches.

Keywords: remote sensing; image dehazing; wavelet transformation; attention

1. Introduction

The quality of remote sensing imagery is often compromised by complex atmospheric interferences, including haze and semi-transparent clouds. Not only do these detrimental factors weaken the signal quality, but they also distort visual information and obscure important details, thereby limiting large-scale data collection and real-time monitoring. Therefore, it becomes challenging to restore the information of remote sensing images. High-quality and clear images can provide richer and more accurate visual information, which is essential to improve the performance and reliability of various downstream tasks [1–4] (in areas such as temporal variation analysis, hazard assessment, ecological evaluation, and defense-related observations).

Existing image dehazing solutions can be grouped into two fundamental paradigms: prior-informed algorithms and data-driven learning approaches. In the early stages of research, prior-based methods were proposed to reduce the impact of haze on images. These methods typically rely on the atmospheric scattering model (ASM) [5] to reconstruct clear images. Nevertheless, these methods frequently lack robustness and fail to effectively adapt to the highly variable haze characteristics present in diverse imaging scenarios, thereby limiting their real-world applicability.

Deep learning-powered dehazing techniques [6–17] have emerged as highly effective alternatives, exhibiting superior generalization and enhanced performance when compared to prior-guided methods. Through the use of comprehensive datasets, such techniques can autonomously map hazy to clear imagery, bypassing reliance on predefined physical models. This allows them to excel even in variable atmospheric conditions, as they effectively capture intricate features and trends from the data. Although early deep learning-based dehazing methods [18,19] were designed based on the atmospheric scattering model, their practical application in real-world haze scenes remains challenging. This is mainly because the physical scattering model cannot fully capture the complexity and diversity of real atmospheric conditions, limiting the effectiveness of these methods in complex environments.

To bypass the limitations of traditional learning-based dehazing techniques, recent approaches have adopted end-to-end learning architectures that aim to completely eliminate the dependence on physical modeling. Among these approaches, multi-scale convolutional neural networks (CNNs) [20,21] have gained significant attention, as they can directly learn the mapping from hazy images to their clear counterparts. The effectiveness of these methods largely stems from their ability to automatically extract rich and discriminative features through stacked convolution layers. However, a fundamental limitation of convolution operations is their inherently local nature, which restricts the model's ability to capture long-range dependencies and global contextual information. In response to this issue, researchers have employed hierarchical feature extraction techniques, along with adaptive focus modules, to enhance the model's ability to capture scene-wide information during haze removal. A notable example is FFA-Net [22], which employs a channel-wise attention mechanism to model non-local dependencies across different image regions, thereby effectively enhancing the network's ability to incorporate global information and improve dehazing performance.

The field of image dehazing has seen rapid progress in recent years, including Transformer-based networks [23–25], the Mamba paradigm [26], and diffusion-based frameworks [27–29], all of which have contributed to notable improvements through novel architectural designs. By utilizing self-attention, Transformer networks are capable of modeling distant spatial dependencies, addressing the limitations inherent in convolutional structures with restricted receptive scopes. Modeling global context allows the dehazing network to capture the holistic structure of the scene, thereby producing outputs with higher fidelity and visual consistency. The Mamba framework further enhances dehazing accuracy and detail recovery by incorporating multi-scale learning and efficient feature fusion strategies. This framework leverages a multi-scale feature extraction network, allowing it to effectively handle haze at varying intensities while maintaining robustness in complex scenes. Diffusion models, as generative models, have also shown great potential for image dehazing by simulating a gradual denoising process. These models learn to reverse the noise process, helping to recover clear images while preserving finer details and structural information, making them well-suited for addressing complex haze and visual impairments. Together, Transformer-based methods, the Mamba framework, and diffusion models provide more precise and flexible solutions for image dehazing.

This paper proposes a dehazing network called DWTMA-Net, which is designed to restore both frequency- and spatial-domain information in remote sensing images. Built on a

U-shaped architecture, the model consists of three key modules: the Discrete Wavelet Block (DWB), the Multi-dimensional Attention Block (MAB), and the Wavelet Downsampling Module (WDM). The DWB uses the Haar Discrete Wavelet Transform (DWT) to decompose features into four frequency components, where low-frequency features are processed by a small AOD network for feature extraction, and high-frequency features are refined using dilated residual blocks. The inverse wavelet transform is then applied to reconstruct spatial information. The MAB employs depthwise separable convolutions for deep feature extraction, followed by convolutions with various kernel sizes to enhance feature diversity. It further applies channel attention, pixel attention, and Fourier frequency attention, integrating them into a multi-dimensional attention mechanism to capture both global and local features. Meanwhile, the WDM leverages the Haar DWT for downsampling, combining frequency information from the wavelet transform with spatial information from convolutional downsampling for improved feature representation.

Main Contributions of This Paper

- A novel model is proposed that combines frequency-domain information from the discrete wavelet transform (DWT) with spatial-domain features from convolution. Validation using the complex SateHaze1k [30], HRSD [31], and HazyDet [32] datasets confirms its effectiveness in enhancing detail and visual quality.
- To enhance spatial-domain feature information, a novel multi-dimensional attention module is proposed, applying different attention mechanisms to various features extracted through different convolutions.
- To achieve frequency-domain processing, a novel frequency processing module is proposed, which extracts and refines features from four distinct frequency components generated by the Haar discrete wavelet transform (DWT).
- To capture both frequency- and spatial-domain features, a novel downsampling method is proposed, combining Haar wavelet transform and convolution for effective downsampling.

2. Related Works

2.1. Prior-Guided Image Dehazing Methods

Traditional image dehazing methods based on prior knowledge typically utilize statistical assumptions and physical constraints derived from haze characteristics to infer the transmission map and estimate atmospheric illumination. Among the earliest contributions, Tan et al. [33] exploited the contrast difference between hazy and haze-free images to enhance visibility in degraded scenes. The technique focuses on amplifying local contrast to boost image visibility and reconstruct haze-free content. He et al. [34] used the dark channel prior to estimate the transmission map, assuming that haze-free images contain at least one color channel with low intensity in most non-sky regions. It then applies the atmospheric scattering model to recover clear images. Fattal [35] utilized the observation that color lines in the RGB space remain invariant in hazy images and applied this property to estimate the transmission map and recover clear images. Tang et al. [36] advanced prior-driven dehazing by fusing diverse priors related to haze appearance, including edge sharpness, color richness, and contrast, and utilized a random forest regressor to learn the transmission map estimation process. Zhu et al. [37] relied on the observation that haze causes a color attenuation effect, particularly in the blue channel, and utilized this prior to estimate the transmission map and restore clear images efficiently. According to Berman et al. [38], haze induces the transformation of pixel clusters in clear images into haze-like structures. They leveraged this phenomenon to propose a non-local prior aimed at representing clean image characteristics.

By analyzing the haze formation process and simulating its physical characteristics, the physical prior-based method reconstructs clear images from hazy ones. The foundation of this approach is the atmospheric scattering model detailed below:

$$I(x) = J(x)t(x) + A(1 - t(x)) \tag{1}$$

In this model, $I(x)$ denotes the hazy image captured by the camera, while $J(x)$ represents the corresponding clear image. The transmission map ($t(x)$) characterizes how much light from the scene directly reaches the camera, and A stands for the global atmospheric illumination. Accurate estimation of $t(x)$ and A allows for the recovery of the original scene radiance ($J(x)$), thereby producing a haze-free image.

2.2. Data-Driven Approaches for Image Dehazing

These data-driven techniques typically utilize deep learning architectures to either predict transmission and atmospheric components informed by physical scattering mechanisms or transform hazy images into their dehazed versions through end-to-end learning, bypassing the need for handcrafted physical assumptions. The first strategy incorporates the principles of atmospheric scattering to guide the training procedure, whereas the second directly establishes a haze-to-clear transformation pipeline, eliminating the reliance on traditional physical formulations. In one of the earliest works using CNNs for haze removal, Cai et al. [18] developed DehazeNet, which processes hazy images through a learnable architecture to estimate the corresponding transmission maps. Li et al. [39] proposed an all-in-one dehazing network with the aim of simultaneously estimating both the atmospheric light and the transmission map, directly producing haze-free images. It uses an adaptive network structure to improve the accuracy and efficiency of haze removal in a unified framework. Liu et al. [20] employed an attention-based multi-scale network for image dehazing, incorporating grid-based attention mechanisms to focus on haze-affected regions. This approach enables the model to effectively capture both global and local features, improving haze removal across varying densities. Qin et al. [22] utilized a feature fusion attention network that combines multi-scale feature fusion with attention mechanisms to enhance haze removal while preserving important image details. Lu et al. [40] employed a mixed-structure block that integrates multiple network components to capture both global and local features, improving the performance of image dehazing. Similarly, Cui et al. [41] used an omni-kernel convolutional approach that combines multiple kernel sizes in a unified framework to capture diverse image features. This method allows the network to effectively handle various image restoration tasks, including dehazing, by adapting to different spatial structures. Sui et al. [42] proposed a U-shaped dual attention network based on the Vision Mamba architecture, which utilizes multi-scale feature extraction and attention mechanisms to effectively remove haze from satellite remote sensing images.

3. Method

As shown in Figure 1, the overall structure of DWTMA-Net adopts a U-shaped design and is divided into five levels. Each level embeds a Frequency Feature Extraction Block (FFEB), which integrates the proposed DWB and MAB modules in series. The input and output dimensions of the DWB and MAB modules are $B \times C \times H \times W$ for the first and fifth levels, $B \times 2C \times \frac{H}{2} \times \frac{W}{2}$ for the second and fourth levels, and $B \times 4C \times \frac{H}{4} \times \frac{W}{4}$ for the third level. The SK fusion module serves as an adaptive mechanism for fusing multi-scale or cross-level features, aiming to enhance detail and structural information in dehazed images. The WDM module employs the Haar discrete wavelet transform (DWT) to reduce feature resolution by half and combines it with convolutional downsampling to capture both frequency- and spatial-domain information. The DWB module transforms features into the frequency domain and applies customized processing strategies to different frequency components. The MAB module leverages multiple attention mechanisms to process spatial information and dynamically capture edge details, global context, and multi-dimensional features.

This network achieves multi-scale feature fusion through an encoder–decoder architecture with skip connections, balancing the need for global haze distribution modeling and local detail preservation. The core innovation lies in the dual-branch wavelet downsampling module: the Haar wavelet branch explicitly decomposes frequency-domain sub-bands (LL/LH/HL/HH), effectively preventing the loss of high-frequency information typically caused by traditional downsampling; meanwhile, the parallel convolutional branch extracts spatial-domain features, enhancing adaptability to the spatial distribution of haze. The two branches are fused via element-wise addition to achieve complementary modeling between the frequency and spatial domains. Combined with the wavelet processing block (for frequency-domain feature enhancement) and the multi-dimensional attention block (for dynamic feature recalibration), this forms a collaboratively optimized feature representation mechanism. The inverse wavelet transform further ensures lossless reconstruction during the decoding phase.

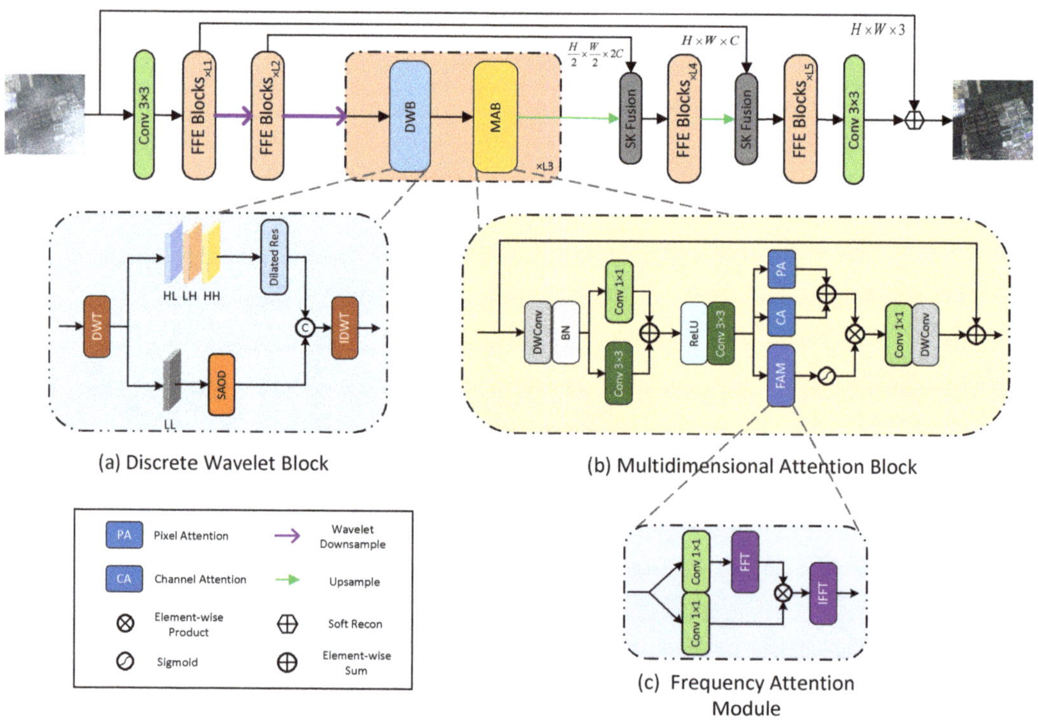

Figure 1. Structure of discrete wavelet transform and multi-dimensional attention.

3.1. *Wavelet Downsampling Module*

Our WDM extends traditional downsampling by incorporating discrete wavelet transform (DWT) to capture frequency information, in contrast to conventional methods that rely solely on convolutions for feature size reduction. By integrating the sampled spatial and frequency information, the WDM performs an additive fusion of convolutional downsampling and wavelet transform, as shown in Figure 2.

$$\widehat{x} = \text{Conv}(x) \oplus \text{Conv}(\text{DWT}(x)). \quad (2)$$

where $\widehat{x}$ represents the output of downsampling; x represents the input of the previous stage; and $\text{Conv}(\cdot)$ and $\text{DWT}(\cdot)$ represent the convolution and wavelet transform processing of the input of the previous stage, respectively.

Our downsampling module is designed with a dual-branch architecture to effectively capture both frequency-domain and spatial-domain information, enhancing the representational capacity of the network. The first branch applies a Haar wavelet transform to the input feature map, decomposing it into four sub-bands: LL, LH, HL, and HH. The LL subband retains low-frequency components that represent the overall structure and contours of the image, while the LH, HL, and HH sub-bands extract directional high-frequency details such as edges and textures. This branch enables explicit modeling of multi-scale and multi-directional frequency features, which is particularly beneficial for capturing fine details and haze boundaries. The second branch employs a standard convolution with a stride of 2 to perform spatial downsampling, preserving local context and semantic structure in the spatial domain. The outputs of the two branches are fused via element-wise addition, allowing the network to integrate complementary features from both domains. This design improves the network's ability to perceive structural and textural details, leading to more effective dehazing in complex remote sensing scenarios.

In the network design, we innovatively improve the encoder's downsampling process by introducing a self-developed dual-branch wavelet downsampling module in the downsampling layers, replacing the traditional max pooling or strided convolution operations. This module integrates a multi-scale frequency-domain feature extraction mechanism, significantly enhancing the network's ability to represent detailed image features while maintaining efficient downsampling.

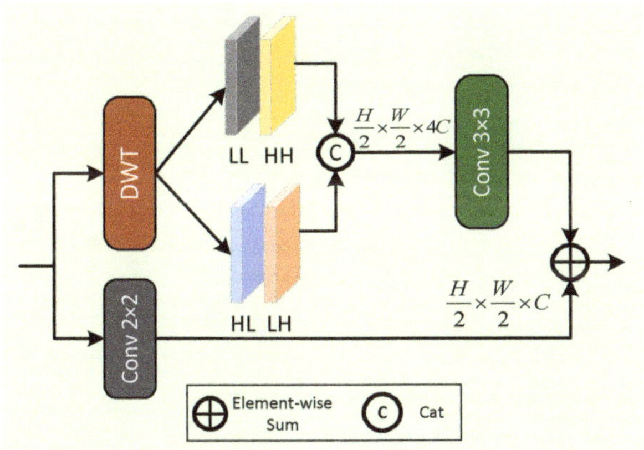

Figure 2. Structure of WDM.

3.2. Discrete Wavelet Block

Our FFEB first extracts features in the frequency domain from the wavelet-downsampled features, then performs spatial-domain feature extraction before producing the final output, as shown in Figure 1.

Wavelet transform can reduce the spatial dimensions by half with each transformation without sacrificing information, unlike other techniques, such as Fast Fourier Transform

(FFT) and Discrete Cosine Transform (DCT), which may result in information loss. Haar wavelet transform converts the input into four sub-bands, i.e.,

$$f_{LL}, f_{HL}, f_{LH}, f_{HH} = \text{DWT}(\widehat{x}). \tag{3}$$

In the discrete wavelet block (DWB), we first apply the Haar discrete wavelet transform to obtain four sub-band frequency features. The LL sub-band typically contains most of the signal energy, while the other three sub-bands capture edge and detail information. The LL sub-band is processed using a small AOD network for feature extraction, while the other three sub-bands undergo refinement using dilated residual blocks to enhance high-frequency features. Finally, the inverse wavelet transform is applied to produce the output feature map.

Drawing inspiration from AOD [39], we designed a lightweight Small AOD Dehazing Block (SAOD) grounded in the analytical formulation presented in Equation (4), with its structural details illustrated in Figure 3. First, according to the physical model, the clear image (J) is expressed as follows:

$$\begin{aligned} J(x) &= K(x)I(x) - K(x) + b \\ K(x) &= \frac{\frac{1}{t(x)}(I(x) - A) + (A - b)}{I(x) - 1} \end{aligned} \tag{4}$$

In the equation, $K(x)$ represents a parameter that fuses $t(x)$ and A from the atmospheric scattering model into a single term, and b denotes the bias term.

Considering b as a bias, we adopt a learning-based approach to estimate this bias. To begin with, we employ global average pooling to compress the feature dimensions and filter out repetitive or non-informative content from the representation space. GAP computes the average value of the feature map across its spatial dimensions, resulting in a one-dimensional feature vector that aligns with the characteristics of the bias value. This vector then undergoes a 1×1 convolution for feature transformation, followed by sigmoid activation to obtain the bias (b). The estimated b is represented as follows:

$$b = \sigma(\text{Conv}(\text{LeakyRelu}(\text{Conv}(\text{GAP}(f_{LL}))))). \tag{5}$$

However, since the transmission map (K) is non-homogeneous, applying GAP would result in information loss. Consequently, we employ stacked convolutional layers with a 3×3 kernel size to facilitate feature learning, as elaborated below:

$$K = \sigma(\text{Conv}(\text{LeakyRelu}(\text{Conv}(\text{Conv}(f_{LL}))))). \tag{6}$$

Therefore, through SAOD, we obtain the f'_{LL} feature as follows:

$$f'_{LL} = K \otimes f_{LL} \ominus K \oplus b \tag{7}$$

For the remaining three sub-bands, we employ dilated residual blocks to refine the features. These blocks use dilated convolutions with dilation rates of 1, 2, and 1; a kernel size of 3; and a stride of 1, as illustrated in Figure 3. Subsequently, the refined features are restored to the spatial domain using the inverse wavelet transform, as described below:

$$\begin{aligned} f'_{HL}, f'_{LH}, f'_{HH} &= \text{DilateRes}(f_{HL}, f_{LH}, f_{HH}), \\ \widehat{x} &= \text{IDWT}(f'_{LL}, f'_{HL}, f'_{LH}, f'_{HH}). \end{aligned} \tag{8}$$

In this formulation, $\sigma(\cdot)$ is the sigmoid nonlinearity, and $\text{Conv}(\cdot)$ indicates a standard convolutional layer. While 1×1 convolutions are designed for manipulation of channel-wise information and scaling dimensions, 3×3 kernels are favored for their efficiency in extracting spatial context and identifying localized features, including edge and texture patterns.

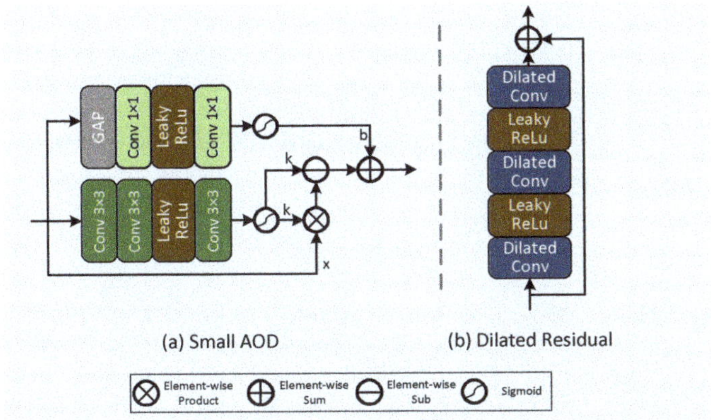

Figure 3. Structure of SAOD and dilated residual block.

3.3. Multi-Dimensional Attention Block

Within the MAB framework, a depthwise convolution (DWConv) is first applied, ensuring the preservation of feature details while improving computational efficiency. We then apply normalization to ensure consistent feature scales and facilitate more rapid network training. To enhance feature diversity, we use convolutions with a kernel size of 1 and 3 to increase the number of channels. The convolution with a kernel size of 1 mainly handles channel transformation and dimensional adjustment, while the convolution with a kernel size of 3 captures local patterns. After extracting and normalizing the features, they are fused to provide a more comprehensive input representation. Finally, another convolution with a kernel sizeof 3 is applied to further refine the features.

$$\begin{aligned} x_0 &= \text{BN}(\text{DWConv}(\hat{x})), \\ x_1 &= \text{Conv3}(\text{Relu}(\text{Conv}(x_0) \oplus \text{Conv}(x_0))). \end{aligned} \tag{9}$$

According to FFA-Net [22], pixel attention is essential for isolating scale-relevant structures through the enhancement of significant pixel information. Pixel-level attention is designed to pinpoint and enhance critical spatial areas within an image—an ability especially valuable in dehazing tasks, where preserving local visibility is vital. To complement this, we incorporate a Channel Attention (CA) module operating in parallel. While the spatial branch emphasizes localized clarity, the channel branch selectively boosts haze-relevant responses based on global contextual cues. This combined attention strategy enables the model to effectively integrate detailed textures with high-level semantic features.

$$\begin{aligned} x_a &= \text{PA}(x_1) \oplus \text{CA}(x_1), \\ x_b &= \sigma(\text{FAM}(x_1)). \end{aligned} \tag{10}$$

The outputs from the dual attention modules are fused through element-wise summation, yielding a richer and more informative feature representation. Inspired by the strategy proposed by Ma et al. [43], we apply a frequency-aware modulation using a Frequency Attention Module (FAM) scaled via a sigmoid activation to adaptively adjust the feature intensity and improve representational expressiveness. To further refine the features, a 1 × 1 convolution is employed to reduce dimensionality, condense critical information, and mitigate overfitting risks. This is followed by a 3 × 3 convolution to expand contextual understanding, alongside a residual connection that preserves the original signal. The final output effectively combines both refined enhancements and retained inputs, ensuring robustness for downstream tasks.

$$y_{out} = \mathrm{DWConv}(\mathrm{Conv}(x_a \otimes x_b)) \oplus \hat{x}. \tag{11}$$

In this expression, $\sigma(\cdot)$ denotes the sigmoid activation, while $\otimes$ indicates an element-wise multiplication. The sigmoid operation is mathematically defined as follows:

$$\sigma(x) = \frac{1}{1+e^{-x}} \tag{12}$$

3.4. Loss Function

While L_2 loss is widely adopted in dehazing tasks, empirical results from recent image restoration studies reveal that L_1 loss can achieve more favorable performance, particularly in terms of PSNR and SSIM. Therefore, we adopt the simpler L_1 loss as our primary objective. To further enhance the restoration of frequency details, we introduce a frequency loss by applying Fourier Transform (FT) to both the output and ground-truth images and computing the L_1 loss between their real and imaginary components.

$$Loss = \|J - GT\|_1 + \lambda \cdot \left[\|J_{real} - GT_{real}\|_1 + \left\|J_{imag} - GT_{imag}\right\|_1\right] \tag{13}$$

where J denotes the output remote sensing image after dehazing by DWTMA-Net; GT refers to its corresponding ground-truth counterpart; J_{real} represents the real part of the generated image; GT_{real} represents the real part of the ground-truth image; J_{imag} represents the imaginary part of the generated image; GT_{imag} represents the imaginary part of the ground-truth image; and λ represents the weight, which is 0.1.

4. Results

4.1. Datasets

We evaluate the performance of the proposed DWTMA-Net on two synthetic remote sensing (RS) haze datasets—SateHaze1k [30] and HRSD [31]—as well as one real-world UAV-based hazy dataset, HazyDet [32]. SateHaze1k is divided into three subsets corresponding to different haze densities: thin, moderate, and thick. Each subset includes 320 training samples and 45 testing images. Thin haze scenes are generated using haze masks extracted from real cloud formations, while moderate haze images blend characteristics of mist and medium haze. Thick haze is simulated using transmittance maps to represent dense atmospheric conditions.

The HRSD dataset consists of two subsets: LHID and DHID. LHID contains 30,517 training images and 500 test images, generated through the atmospheric scattering model to simulate varying levels of haze, thereby improving the model's robustness across different haze intensities. In comparison, DHID includes 14,990 images that are synthesized using real haze maps, offering a more authentic representation of haze characteristics. Among these, 14,490 images are designated for training, while 500 are reserved for testing. The inclusion of both synthetic and real haze features in these subsets provides a comprehensive platform for evaluating the dehazing capabilities of DWTMA-Net.

In order to showcase the generalization ability of our model in practical settings, we assess its performance using the newly introduced HazyDet dataset, which consists of drone-captured images affected by haze. The dataset consists of a training set with 8000 images, a validation set with 1000 images, and a test set with 2000 images. It contains a mix of authentic hazy images captured under natural fog conditions, as well as artificially created hazy images generated through the Atmospheric Scattering Model (ASM). Additionally, HazyDet features a dedicated real hazy drone detection test set (RDDTS) designed to assess model robustness in practical scenarios. Figure 4 provides examples of training samples from the dataset.

Figure 4. Example of training samples from the HazyDet dataset.

4.2. Implementation Details

Our DWTMA-Net was trained and tested using the PyTorch framework (version 1.13.1) on a system equipped with four NVIDIA GeForce GTX 1080 Ti GPUs. To enhance the training data, we applied random rotations of 90°, 180°, and 270°, as well as horizontal flipping. The input images were RGB remote sensing data resized to 240 × 240 pixels. For the FFEB, we set the configuration as [N1, N2, N3, N4, N5] = [2, 2, 4, 2, 2], with respective embedding channels of [24, 48, 96, 48, 24]. The batch size was set to 16 for each sub-dataset. The initial learning rate was initialized at 2.0×10^{-4} and reduced progressively to zero using a cosine annealing scheduler.

We assessed the generalization capacity and performance of DWTMA-Net through comprehensive comparisons across various tasks. To maintain consistency, we utilized the official codebases released by the respective authors during the training process.

4.3. Quantitative Evaluations

The quantitative evaluation results on the HRSD and SateHaze1k datasets are shown in Tables 1 and 2, with performance assessed using PSNR and SSIM metrics, as well as the average results across various haze density levels. Additionally, Table 3 presents the results on the HazyDet dataset, further highlighting the model's ability to generalize for UAV-based image dehazing tasks.

Table 1. Comparative analysis on the **SateHaze1k** dataset, where **bold** indicates the optimal method and underline signifies the second best.

Method	Thin Haze			Moderate Haze			Thick Haze			Average		
	PSNR	SSIM	NIQE	PSNR	SSIM	NIQE	PSNR	SSIM	NIQE	PSNR	SSIM	NIQE
DCP [34]	20.15	0.8645	17.98	20.51	0.8932	17.09	15.77	0.7117	17.73	18.81	0.8241	17.60
AOD-Net [39]	15.97	0.8169	18.66	15.39	0.7442	17.28	14.44	0.7013	17.91	15.27	0.7541	17.95
FCTF-Net [44]	19.13	0.8532	18.77	22.32	0.9107	17.75	17.78	0.7617	18.14	19.74	0.8419	18.22
GridDehaze-Net [20]	19.81	0.8556	18.77	22.75	0.9085	16.35	17.94	0.7551	18.69	20.17	0.8397	17.94
FFA-Net [22]	24.04	0.9130	17.09	25.62	0.9336	16.80	21.70	0.8422	17.35	23.79	0.8963	17.08
MixDehaze-Net [40]	22.12	0.8822	18.04	23.92	0.9040	**16.08**	19.96	0.7950	17.94	22.00	0.8604	17.35
OK-Net [41]	20.68	0.8860	17.78	25.39	0.9406	17.47	20.21	0.8186	18.57	22.09	0.8817	17.94
Dehazeformer [24]	24.90	0.9104	16.88	27.13	0.9431	16.70	22.68	0.8497	17.64	24.90	0.9011	17.07
VmambaIR [26]	20.81	0.8753	18.28	24.34	0.9132	16.61	20.04	0.8045	17.96	21.73	0.8643	17.62
FCDM [27]	18.94	0.8486	18.08	17.36	0.8753	16.81	16.97	0.7530	18.09	17.76	0.8256	17.66
MMPD-Net [45]	25.16	0.9227	16.76	27.30	0.9454	16.76	22.85	0.8571	17.96	25.10	0.9084	17.16
DWTMA-Net	**25.59**	**0.9229**	**16.71**	**27.53**	**0.9459**	16.80	**22.88**	**0.8576**	**17.33**	**25.33**	**0.9088**	**16.95**

Table 2. Comparative analysis on the **HRSD** dataset, where **bold** indicates the optimal method and underline signifies the second best.

Method	LHID			DHID			Average		
	PSNR	SSIM	NIQE	PSNR	SSIM	NIQE	PSNR	SSIM	NIQE
DCP [34]	21.34	0.7976	19.84	19.15	0.8195	18.99	20.25	0.8086	19.42
AOD-Net [39]	21.91	0.8144	19.53	16.03	0.7291	18.91	18.97	0.7718	19.22
FCTF-Net [44]	28.55	0.8727	19.27	22.43	0.8482	18.61	25.49	0.8605	18.94
GridDehaze-Net [20]	25.80	0.8584	19.54	26.77	0.8851	18.93	26.29	0.8718	19.24
FFA-Net [22]	29.33	0.8755	19.02	24.62	0.8657	18.50	26.98	0.8706	18.76
MixDehaze-Net [40]	29.47	0.8631	19.26	27.36	0.8864	18.89	28.42	0.8748	19.08
OK-Net [41]	29.03	0.8766	18.73	27.80	0.8973	18.17	28.42	0.8870	18.45
MMPD-Net [45]	29.76	0.8771	18.98	28.23	0.8977	18.29	29.00	0.8874	18.64
FCDM [27]	15.16	0.6459	18.79	17.13	0.6978	20.43	16.15	0.6719	19.61
DWTMA-Net	**29.86**	**0.8828**	**18.70**	**28.34**	**0.8981**	**18.15**	**29.10**	**0.8905**	**18.43**

Table 3. Comparative analysis on the **HazyDet** dataset, where **bold** indicates the optimal method and underline signifies the second best.

Method	HazyDet		
	PSNR	SSIM	NIQE
DCP [34]	17.03	0.8024	12.30
AOD-Net [39]	18.99	0.7808	12.27
FCTF-Net [44]	24.89	0.8552	12.23
GridDehaze-Net [20]	26.66	0.8801	11.33
FFA-Net [22]	27.12	0.8782	11.31
MixDehaze-Net [40]	28.75	0.9068	11.30
OK-Net [41]	27.76	0.8875	11.36
DWTMA-Net	**29.02**	**0.9108**	**11.23**

As shown in Table 1, our proposed DWTMA-Net achieves significant PSNR and SSIM improvements across different haze levels, including light, moderate, and dense conditions. Since dense haze severely degrades image quality, presenting particularly difficult restoration challenges for remote sensing data, our method exhibits marginally lower performance in such conditions. Traditional methods such as DCP and AOD-Net perform poorly overall, while FFA-Net, MixDehaze-Net, OK-Net, and Dehazeformer demonstrate moderate performance. MMPD-Net achieves relatively strong results. Nevertheless, DWTMA-Net still outperforms other models on several key metrics. Notably, our method shows excellent performance, with average PSNR and average SSIM gains of 0.23 and 0.0004 higher than the second-ranked MMPD-Net, respectively. These findings confirm DWTMA-Net's effectiveness and robustness in addressing remote sensing image dehazing challenges.

Table 2 demonstrates DWTMA-Net's superior performance on two benchmark synthetic datasets (LHID and DHID). On LHID, it outperforms MMPD-Net (previous state of the art), with gains of 0.1 dB in PSNR and 0.0057 in SSIM. On the DHID dataset, PSNR is increased by 0.11 dB and SSIM by 0.0004. It is worth noting that MMPD-Net ranks second across all metrics, with results close to ours, which may be attributed to its use of multi-scale convolutions and feature dimensionality expansion. Overall, these results demonstrate the strong dehazing capability and robust performance of DWTMA-Net in remote sensing image dehazing tasks.

To demonstrate that the model not only performs well on specific datasets but also adapts to more complex and diverse data from real-world applications, showcasing its strong adaptability, robustness, and generalization ability, we added a UAV-based image dataset for comparison. As shown in Table 3, our model achieves significantly superior performance across all metrics. Significant quality improvements are observed, with our model exceeding the second-best method's performance by 0.27 dB PSNR and 0.0233 SSIM.

We use two key metrics to evaluate the computational efficiency and memory requirements of the proposed model: FLOPs and the number of parameters. FLOPs represent the number of floating-point operations required for a single forward pass, reflecting the computational cost. The number of parameters indicates the total trainable weights, reflecting memory usage. Fewer FLOPs and fewer parameters make the model more suitable for deployment in resource-constrained or real-time scenarios, as shown in Table 4. Our SAOD is a simplified version of AOD, with 170.66M FLOPs and 684B parameters.

Table 4. Comparison of **FLOPs** and **parameters** across models.

Method	FLOPs	Parameters
DCP	-	-
AOD-Net	457.70 (M)	1.76 (K)
FCTF-Net	40.19 (G)	163.48 (K)
GridDehaze-Net	85.72 (G)	955.75 (K)
FFA-Net	624.20 (G)	4.68 (M)
MixDehaze-Net	114.30 (G)	3.17 (M)
OK-Net	158.20 (G)	4.43 (M)
MMPD-Net	298.19 (G)	8.66 (M)
DWTMA-Net	188.72 (G)	8.34 (M)

4.4. *Qualitative Evaluations*

The experiments utilize three benchmark datasets covering satellite (SateHaze1k), surface (HRSD), and aerial (HazyDet) hazy scenarios.

A performance comparison of various dehazing approaches on the light-haze test set is presented in Figure 5. The figure reveals that DCP and AOD-Net demonstrate constrained dehazing capability, leaving substantial haze remnants and apparent chromatic aberrations in output images. GridDehaze-Net and OK-Net are able to remove most of the haze, but a small amount still lingers. Although FFA-Net and MixDehaze-Net achieve better dehazing results, they fall short in color restoration. In particular, the areas highlighted by red boxes fail to accurately reproduce the colors of the reference images. In contrast, both MMPD-Net and DWTMA-Net demonstrate strong dehazing capabilities and produce results that closely resemble the ground truth. Specifically, in the red-box regions, DWTMA-Net achieves more accurate color recovery, whereas MMPD-Net tends to render the grass and trees with slightly lighter tones compared to the reference image. The quantitative metrics displayed below the images further highlight the differences in performance among the methods. Overall, our method outperforms the others in terms of dehazing effectiveness, color fidelity, and frequency information restoration, resulting in images that are more visually aligned with real-world scenes.

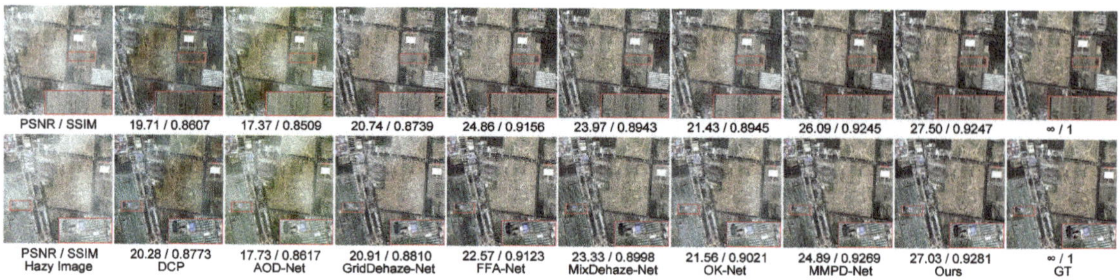

Figure 5. Qualitative analysis of two lightly hazy samples from the Haze1k-thin collection.

Figure 6 evaluates multiple dehazing approaches using moderately hazy remote sensing imagery, where atmospheric interference significantly degrades image features. While DCP fails to adequately remove haze residues, AOD-Net partially restores visibility but introduces undesirable darkening effects. In contrast, GridDehaze-Net, FFA-Net, MixDehaze-Net, OK-Net, and MMPD-Net show substantially improved restoration quality. However, noticeable differences from the ground truth still exist. For instance, in the second image, the region highlighted by the red box in the result from GridDehaze-Net appears blurred and faded, and the high-frequency details in the first image are not well restored. In contrast, FFA-Net, MixDehaze-Net, OK-Net, and MMPD-Net deepen the high-frequency features in the red-box region of the first image but show varying degrees of color distortion in the red-box region of the second image. According to the performance metrics displayed below each image, our method demonstrates the best dehazing performance. Overall, our approach exhibits superior dehazing capability and more accurate color restoration in high-frequency regions, which is largely attributed to the incorporation of our frequency information enhancement module.

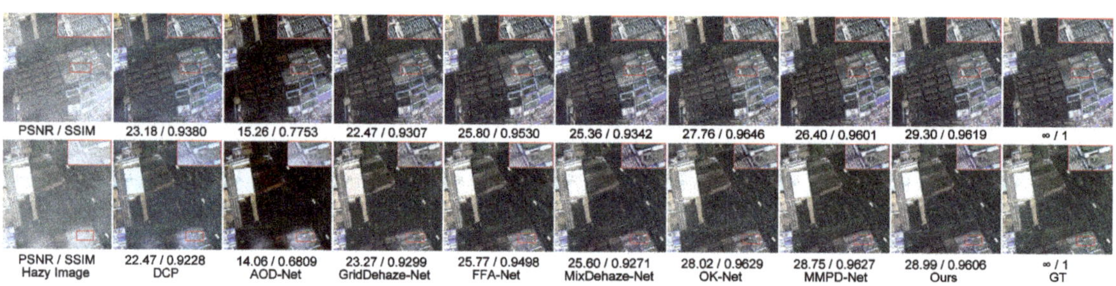

Figure 6. Qualitative analysis of two moderately hazy samples from the Haze1k-moderate collection.

Figure 7 compares restoration results across different approaches using severely degraded images from the dense-haze dataset. Due to the severe impact of dense haze, a significant amount of frequency information and fine details is lost in this dataset. DCP and AOD-Net fail to completely eliminate atmospheric interference, leaving substantial haze contamination and introducing significant chromatic aberrations in the processed images. GridDehaze-Net and OK-Net introduce noticeable color shifts in their outputs; for example, compared to the reference image, the green lawns in the two restored images appear either overly darkened or overly lightened. Color fidelity analysis reveals that FFA-Net, MMPD-Net, and MixDehaze-Net all introduce chromatic aberrations, rendering lawns in un-naturally pale or oversaturated green tones. In contrast, our method demonstrates consistently robust performance across all dehazing indicators in both images, producing results that closely resemble the ground truth in terms of overall structure, frequency details, and spatial information.

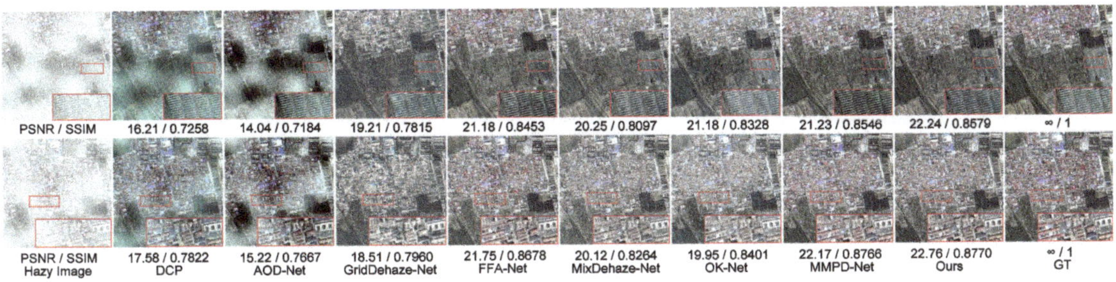

Figure 7. Qualitative analysis of two densely hazy samples from the Haze1k-thick collection.

Figure 8 compares the performance of multiple dehazing algorithms on the LHID dataset. DCP's output displays excessive color saturation, resulting in critical detail loss, whereas AOD-Net generates underexposed reconstructions that degrade visual clarity. Although GridDehaze-Net, FFA-Net, MixDehaze-Net, OK-Net, and MMPD-Net achieve perceptually reasonable results, their PSNR/SSIM scores indicate substantial deviations from reference data. The proposed DWTMA-Net outperforms these approaches by effectively restoring haze-obscured high-frequency components, delivering superior sharpness and enhanced image quality.

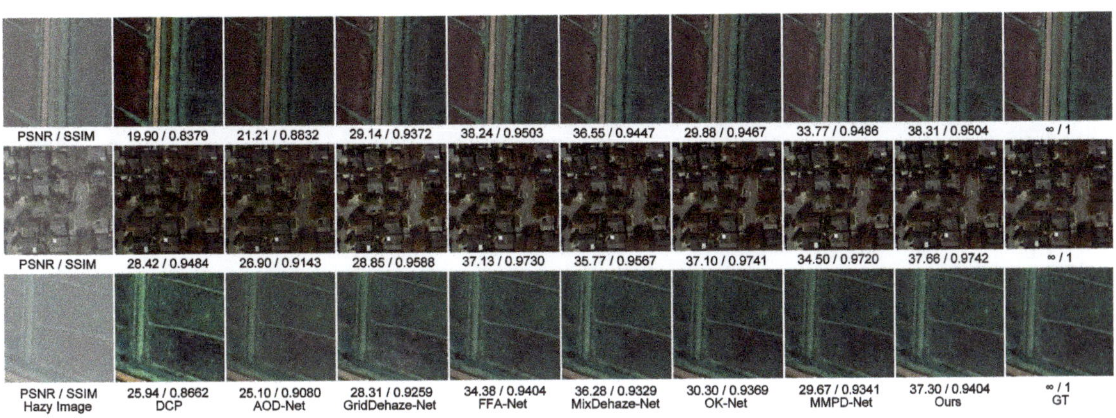

Figure 8. Qualitative analysis of three samples from the LHID collection.

Figure 9 benchmarks dehazing performance on the DHID dataset, featuring uniformly dense haze in remote sensing imagery. DCP's reconstructions exhibit severe luminance suppression and detail loss, failing to recover critical high-frequency components. AOD-Net produces even darker outputs, with a noticeable black mask overlaying the images. Although GridDehaze-Net, MixDehaze-Net, OK-Net, FFA-Net, and MMPD-Net are capable of effectively removing haze and largely restoring the overall scene, their outputs still exhibit subtle black artifacts in fine-detail regions when compared to the reference images. In contrast, our proposed DWTMA-Net demonstrates superior performance in both color accuracy and high-frequency detail restoration, particularly in areas such as roads and rooftops, as further confirmed by the quantitative metrics shown below the images.

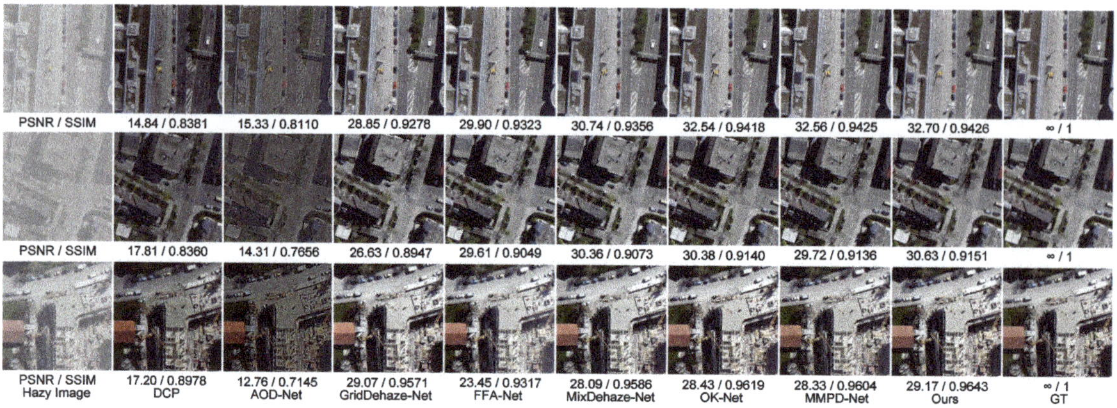

Figure 9. Qualitative analysis of three samples from the DHID collection.

Figure 10 benchmarks dehazing performance across UAV imagery under varying atmospheric conditions, from light to dense haze. In these examples, light haze slightly obscures critical information in UAV images, affecting recognition and tracking accuracy. Moderate haze interferes with the identification of certain regions of the UAV, while heavy haze severely hampers information extraction, significantly impacting the UAV's operational capabilities. Therefore, effective haze removal from UAV images is of great importance.

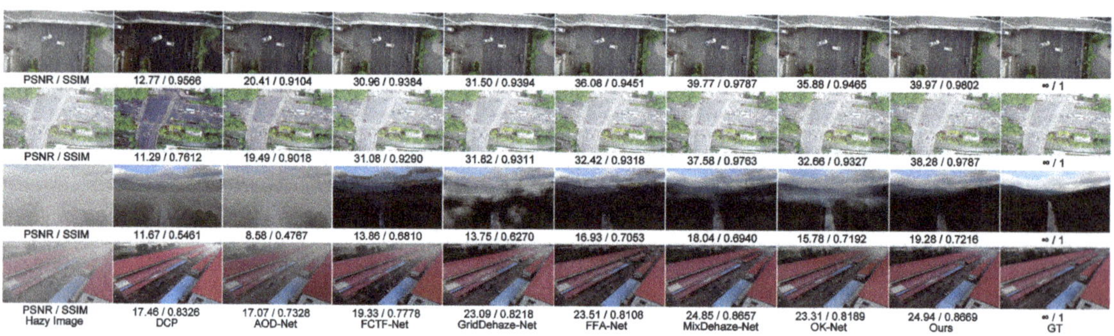

Figure 10. Qualitative analysis of four samples from the HazyDet collection.

As for the results, DCP performs poorly, introducing noticeable color distortion and leaving substantial residual haze in the third and fourth images. AOD-Net shows limited performance under light haze and fails to remove haze effectively in the third and fourth images. GridDehaze-Net and OK-Net perform relatively well in the first and second images but leave obvious haze residues in the third and fourth images, indicating incomplete dehazing. Although FCTF-Net and FFA-Net manage to remove haze in the third image, the resulting images become heavily blurred, making it difficult to recognize objects. MixDehaze-Net successfully removes a large portion of the haze and preserves the original features, yet a small amount of haze remains in the third image.

In contrast, our proposed method achieves the best dehazing performance across all haze levels. It nearly restores all image details under light haze, effectively recovers obscured information under moderate haze, and successfully reconstructs images under heavy haze conditions, producing visually impressive results. These outcomes highlight the strong generalization ability and robustness of our method across various haze intensities.

To demonstrate the dehazing performance of our network in real-world scenarios, we conducted tests on a real hazy remote sensing dataset provided in [46]. As shown in Figure 11, our method effectively removes haze while preserving edge and texture details. This test effectively evaluates the robustness and dehazing capability of our method in practical environments.

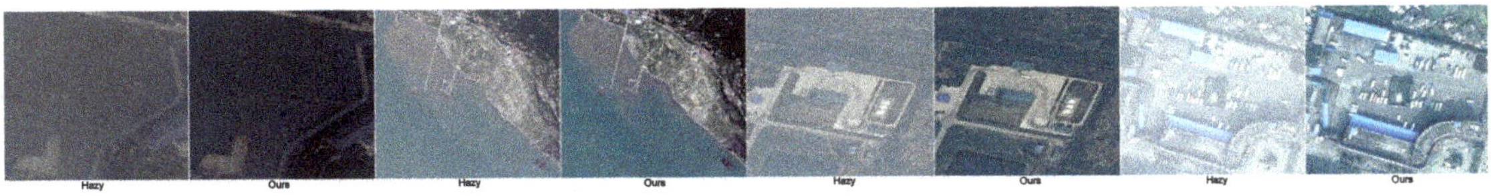

Figure 11. Visual comparison of four images within the real dataset.

4.5. Ablation Study

To validate the contributions of our proposed components, we performed a comprehensive ablation analysis using the light-haze dataset, evaluating the individual and combined effects of three key modules: the wavelet downsampling module (WDM), Discrete Wavelet Block (DWB), and multi-scale attention block (MAB). For computational efficiency during training, we processed 80 × 80 pixel image patches sampled from the original RGB inputs while maintaining hyperparameters and training protocols identical to those of our complete model implementation.

Our baseline architecture builds upon the fundamental structure of Star [43], incorporating its core modules and basic attention mechanisms as the foundational learning blocks. In our modified design, the original DM module is replaced with the proposed WDM, and the DWB module is removed. Table 5 quantitatively evaluates the individual contributions of all proposed components (WDM, DWB, and MAB), with each module showing statistically significant performance improvements that confirm their design efficacy. Figure 12 visually compares the ablation results of different modules, providing a clearer and more intuitive illustration of each module's role and contribution in enhancing the overall network performance.

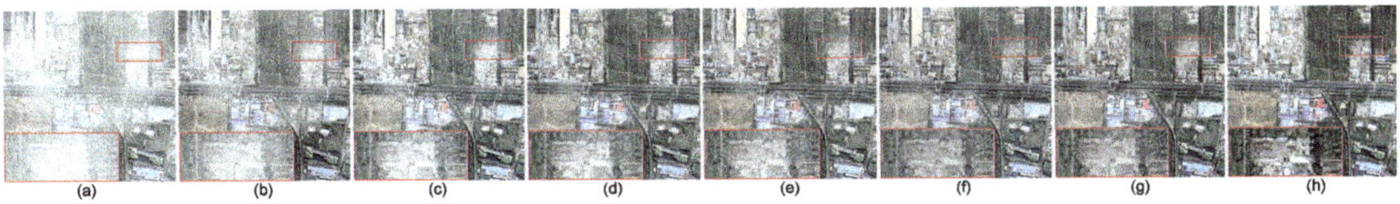

Figure 12. Visual comparison of ablation experiments on the thin dataset. (**a**) Hazy image; (**b**) Base(DM); (**c**) Base(DM) + DWB; (**d**) Base(DM) + MAB; (**e**) Base(DM) + DWB + MAB; (**f**) Base + MAB + WDM; (**g**) Base + DWB + MAB + WDM; (**h**) ground truth.

When the model is in the base state with standard downsampling, the image quality is the poorest, with the lowest PSNR and SSIM values. The red-box regions are heavily obscured by haze, and the overall image appears noticeably pale. Introducing the DWB module to the base network significantly improves image quality, increasing the PSNR by 2.06 and SSIM by 0.0349. Similarly, integrating the MAB module brings substantial enhancement, with a PSNR increase of 3.37 and an SSIM improvement of 0.0291, resulting in clearer details in the red-box areas. Further combining DWB and MAB in the FFEB module leads to additional gains in performance, with improved color restoration and a notable enhancement in overall visual quality. Although minor blurring and slight whitening still remain, FFEB effectively recovers both frequency and spatial information. The contribution of DWB is clearly demonstrated in quantitative form, as the PSNR and SSIM values drop significantly when this module is removed. To objectively assess the WDM's superiority, we replaced standard downsampling layers with our wavelet-based module in identical network architectures. The results show a further PSNR gain of 0.82 and an SSIM increase of 0.0103, with significant visual enhancement in the red-box areas. The resulting images are noticeably sharper, demonstrating the effectiveness of the WDM in extracting frequency and spatial features and improving overall image quality.

Table 5. The ablation experiments performed on the thin-haze subset reveal comparative method effectiveness, with optimal results highlighted in boldface.

Method	Thin Haze	
	PSNR	SSIM
Base(DM)	18.47	0.8547
Base(DM) + DWB	20.53	0.8896
Base(DM) + MAB	21.84	0.8838
Base(DM) + DWB + MAB	22.87	0.8940
Base + MAB + WDM	21.64	0.8860
Base + DWB + MAB + WDM	**23.69**	**0.9043**

The MAB module contains different attention mechanisms. To analyze their impact, we conducted ablation experiments, as shown in Table 6.

Table 6. The ablation experiments conducted on the light-haze subset reveal the impacts of different attention mechanisms in the MAB.

Method	Thin Haze	
	PSNR	SSIM
DWTMA-Net - CA	23.16	0.8966
DWTMA-Net - PA	20.04	0.8905
DWTMA-Net - FA	22.66	0.8910

5. Discussion

This paper proposes a network that combines frequency-domain and spatial-domain processing to address the issues of blurring and information loss in remote sensing images. Experimental validation on aerial imagery (UAV dataset) confirms the model's strong transferability, with quantitatively significant haze removal results.

Although the proposed model achieves significantly better dehazing performance compared to existing lightweight methods, it also incurs a relatively higher computational cost. It is particularly well-suited for applications that demand high image clarity and detail preservation, such as remote sensing under adverse weather conditions or UAV-based surveillance. However, to enable efficient deployment on resource-constrained edge devices, further model optimization is necessary. Future work will focus on techniques such as network pruning, quantization, and knowledge distillation to develop a more lightweight and efficient variant. By seeking a balanced trade-off between performance and complexity, this study lays a solid foundation for both practical deployment and future scalability of the model.

6. Conclusions

DWTMA-Net consists of a series of frequency feature extraction modules designed to simultaneously capture both frequency and spatial information. We designed an innovative downsampling method that combines Haar discrete wavelet transform to extract frequency-domain features and convolution operations to capture spatial-domain features. The extracted features are then processed separately in the frequency and spatial domains. The discrete wavelet block handles the frequency-domain information, decomposing the features into four sub-band frequency characteristics using wavelet transform. Different recovery and refinement strategies are applied to each sub-band. Next, we apply a multi-dimensional attention mechanism to enhance the spatial-domain features. This mechanism extracts fine details through deep convolution layers and captures diverse features by expanding the number of channels. These diverse features are further optimized using channel attention, pixel attention, and Fourier frequency-domain attention, enhancing both local and global information, which improves image quality and strengthens the network's robustness. Experimental results show that our method achieves excellent performance on the SateHaze-1K, HRSD, and HazyDet datasets, effectively recovering image details in complex environments. However, under heavy haze conditions, the network still faces challenges in information recovery. To advance this research direction, two key objectives will be pursued: (1) the development of an enhanced lightweight architecture specifically optimized for remote sensing image dehazing under challenging conditions and (2) the construction of a comprehensive benchmark dataset addressing top-down imaging artifacts to facilitate community-wide progress.

Author Contributions: Methodology, L.W.; Validation, Y.L.; Resources, R.H.; Writing—original draft, X.G.; Writing—review & editing, H.Z.; Supervision, H.X. All authors have read and agreed to the published version of the manuscript.

Funding: This work was supported by the National Natural Science Foundation of China (62401012) and the Fundamental Research Funds for the Central Universities of China (SWU2009107).

Data Availability Statement: The StateHaze1k dataset, HRSD dataset, and HazyDet dataset are publicly available for research use only. For more information, please refer to the following links: StateHaze1k https://www.dropbox.com/s/k2i3p7puuwl2g59/Haze1k.zip?dl=0 (accessed on 7 June 2025), HRSD https://github.com/Shan-rs/DCI-Net (accessed on 7 June 2025), and HazyDet https://github.com/GrokCV/HazyDet (accessed on 7 June 2025).

Conflicts of Interest: The authors declare no conflict of interest.

References

1. Kumar, P.; Singh, S.; Pandey, A.; Singh, R.K.; Srivastava, P.K.; Kumar, M.; Dubey, S.K.; Sah, U.; Nandan, R.; Singh, S.K.; et al. Multi-level impacts of the COVID-19 lockdown on agricultural systems in India: The case of Uttar Pradesh. *Agric. Syst.* **2021**, *187*, 103027. [CrossRef]
2. Amaro García, A. Relationship between blue economy, cruise tourism, and urban regeneration: Case study of Olbia, Sardinia. *J. Urban Plan. Dev.* **2021**, *147*, 05021029. [CrossRef]
3. Li, S.; Fang, H.; Zhang, Y. Determination of the leaf inclination angle (LIA) through field and remote sensing methods: Current status and future prospects. *Remote Sens.* **2023**, *15*, 946. [CrossRef]
4. Yan, Q.; Yang, K.; Hu, T.; Chen, G.; Dai, K.; Wu, P.; Ren, W.; Zhang, Y. From dynamic to static: Stepwisely generate HDR image for ghost removal. *IEEE Trans. Circuits Syst. Video Technol.* **2025**, *35*, 1409–1421. [CrossRef]
5. McCartney, E. *Optics of the Atmosphere: Scattering by Molecules and Particles*; John Wiley & Sons Inc.: Hoboken, NJ, USA, 1976.
6. Yan, Q.; Zhang, L.; Liu, Y.; Zhu, Y.; Sun, J.; Shi, Q.; Zhang, Y. Deep HDR imaging via a non-local network. *IEEE Trans. Image Process.* **2020**, *29*, 4308–4322. [CrossRef]
7. Kulkarni, A.; Phutke, S.S.; Vipparthi, S.K.; Murala, S. C2AIR: Consolidated Compact Aerial Image Haze Removal. In Proceedings of the IEEE/CVF Winter Conference on Applications of Computer Vision, Waikoloa, HI, USA, 3–8 January 2024; pp. 749–758.
8. Ali, A.; Sarkar, R.; Chaudhuri, S.S. Wavelet-based Auto-Encoder for simultaneous haze and rain removal from images. *Pattern Recognit.* **2024**, *150*, 110370. [CrossRef]
9. Wang, T.; Tao, G.; Lu, W.; Zhang, K.; Luo, W.; Zhang, X.; Lu, T. Restoring vision in hazy weather with hierarchical contrastive learning. *Pattern Recognit.* **2024**, *145*, 109956. [CrossRef]

10. Yan, Q.; Wang, H.; Ma, Y.; Liu, Y.; Dong, W.; Woźniak, M.; Zhang, Y. Uncertainty estimation in HDR imaging with Bayesian neural networks. *Pattern Recognit.* **2024**, *156*, 110802. [CrossRef]
11. Zhou, H.; Chen, Z.; Liu, Y.; Sheng, Y.; Ren, W.; Xiong, H. Physical-priors-guided DehazeFormer. *Knowl.-Based Syst.* **2023**, *266*, 110410. [CrossRef]
12. Liu, Y.; Wang, X.; Hu, E.; Wang, A.; Shiri, B.; Lin, W. VNDHR: Variational single nighttime image dehazing for enhancing visibility in intelligent transportation systems via hybrid regularization. *IEEE Trans. Intell. Transp. Syst.* 2025, *early access*.
13. Liu, Y.; Yan, Z.; Tan, J.; Li, Y. Multi-purpose oriented single nighttime image haze removal based on unified variational retinex model. *IEEE Trans. Circuits Syst. Video Technol.* **2022**, *33*, 1643–1657. [CrossRef]
14. Liu, Y.; Yan, Z.; Chen, S.; Ye, T.; Ren, W.; Chen, E. Nighthazeformer: Single nighttime haze removal using prior query transformer. In Proceedings of the 31st ACM International Conference on Multimedia, Ottawa, ON, Canada, 29 October–3 November 2023; pp. 4119–4128.
15. Li, C.; Hu, E.; Zhang, X.; Zhou, H.; Xiong, H.; Liu, Y. Visibility restoration for real-world hazy images via improved physical model and Gaussian total variation. *Front. Comput. Sci.* **2024**, *18*, 181708. [CrossRef]
16. Li, T.; Liu, Y.; Ren, W.; Shiri, B.; Lin, W. Single Image Dehazing Using Fuzzy Region Segmentation and Haze Density Decomposition. *IEEE Trans. Circuits Syst. Video Technol.* 2025, *early access*.
17. Chen, G.; Jia, Y.; Yin, Y.; Fu, S.; Liu, D.; Wang, T. Remote sensing image dehazing using a wavelet-based generative adversarial networks. *Sci. Rep.* **2025**, *15*, 3634. [CrossRef] [PubMed]
18. Cai, B.; Xu, X.; Jia, K.; Qing, C.; Tao, D. Dehazenet: An end-to-end system for single image haze removal. *IEEE Trans. Image Process.* **2016**, *25*, 5187–5198. [CrossRef]
19. Pang, Y.; Xie, J.; Li, X. Visual haze removal by a unified generative adversarial network. *IEEE Trans. Circuits Syst. Video Technol.* **2018**, *29*, 3211–3221. [CrossRef]
20. Liu, X.; Ma, Y.; Shi, Z.; Chen, J. Griddehazenet: Attention-based multi-scale network for image dehazing. In Proceedings of the IEEE/CVF International Conference on Computer Vision, Seoul, Republic of Korea, 27 October– 2 November 2019; pp. 7314–7323.
21. Dong, H.; Pan, J.; Xiang, L.; Hu, Z.; Zhang, X.; Wang, F.; Yang, M.H. Multi-scale boosted dehazing network with dense feature fusion. In Proceedings of the IEEE/CVF Conference on Computer Vision and Pattern Recognition, Seattle, WA, USA, 13–19 June 2020; pp. 2157–2167.
22. Qin, X.; Wang, Z.; Bai, Y.; Xie, X.; Jia, H. FFA-Net: Feature fusion attention network for single image dehazing. In Proceedings of the AAAI Conference on Artificial Intelligence, New York, NY, USA, 7–12 February 2020; Volume 34, pp. 11908–11915.
23. Wang, Z.; Cun, X.; Bao, J.; Zhou, W.; Liu, J.; Li, H. Uformer: A general u-shaped transformer for image restoration. In Proceedings of the IEEE/CVF Conference on Computer Vision and Pattern Recognition, New Orleans, LA, USA, 18–24 June 2022; pp. 17683–17693.
24. Song, Y.; He, Z.; Qian, H.; Du, X. Vision transformers for single image dehazing. *IEEE Trans. Image Process.* **2023**, *32*, 1927–1941. [CrossRef]
25. Nie, J.; Xie, J.; Sun, H. Remote Sensing Image Dehazing via a Local Context-Enriched Transformer. *Remote Sens.* **2024**, *16*, 1422. [CrossRef]
26. Shi, Y.; Xia, B.; Jin, X.; Wang, X.; Zhao, T.; Xia, X.; Xiao, X.; Yang, W. Vmambair: Visual state space model for image restoration. *arXiv* **2024**, arXiv:2403.11423. [CrossRef]
27. Wang, J.; Wu, S.; Yuan, Z.; Tong, Q.; Xu, K. Frequency compensated diffusion model for real-scene dehazing. *Neural Netw.* **2024**, *175*, 106281. [CrossRef]
28. Huang, Y.; Xiong, S. Remote sensing image dehazing using adaptive region-based diffusion models. *IEEE Geosci. Remote. Sens. Lett.* **2023**, *20*, 8001805. [CrossRef]
29. Yan, Q.; Hu, T.; Wu, P.; Dai, D.; Gu, S.; Dong, W.; Zhang, Y. Efficient Image Enhancement with A Diffusion-Based Frequency Prior. *IEEE Trans. Circuits Syst. Video Technol.* 2025, *early access*.
30. Huang, B.; Zhi, L.; Yang, C.; Sun, F.; Song, Y. Single satellite optical imagery dehazing using SAR image prior based on conditional generative adversarial networks. In Proceedings of the IEEE/CVF Winter Conference on Applications of Computer Vision, Snowmass Village, CO, USA, 1–5 March 2020; pp. 1806–1813.
31. Zhang, L.; Wang, S. Dense haze removal based on dynamic collaborative inference learning for remote sensing images. *IEEE Trans. Geosci. Remote. Sens.* **2022**, *60*, 5631016. [CrossRef]
32. Feng, C.; Chen, Z.; Kou, R.; Gao, G.; Wang, C.; Li, X.; Shu, X.; Dai, Y.; Fu, Q.; Yang, J. HazyDet: Open-source Benchmark for Drone-view Object Detection with Depth-cues in Hazy Scenes. *arXiv* **2024**, arXiv:2409.19833.
33. Tan, R.T. Visibility in bad weather from a single image. In Proceedings of the 2008 IEEE Conference on Computer Vision and Pattern Recognition, Anchorage, AK, USA, 23–28 June 2008; pp. 1–8.
34. He, K.; Sun, J.; Tang, X. Single image haze removal using dark channel prior. *IEEE Trans. Pattern Anal. Mach. Intell.* **2010**, *33*, 2341–2353. [PubMed]
35. Fattal, R. Dehazing using color-lines. *Acm Trans. Graph. (TOG)* **2014**, *34*, 1–14. [CrossRef]

36. Tang, K.; Yang, J.; Wang, J. Investigating haze-relevant features in a learning framework for image dehazing. In Proceedings of the IEEE Conference on Computer Vision and Pattern Recognition, Columbus, OH, USA, 23–28 June 2014; pp. 2995–3000.
37. Zhu, Q.; Mai, J.; Shao, L. A fast single image haze removal algorithm using color attenuation prior. *IEEE Trans. Image Process.* **2015**, *24*, 3522–3533.
38. Berman, D.; Avidan, S. Non-local image dehazing. In Proceedings of the IEEE Conference on Computer Vision and Pattern Recognition, Las Vegas, NV, USA, 27–30 June 2016; pp. 1674–1682.
39. Li, B.; Peng, X.; Wang, Z.; Xu, J.; Feng, D. Aod-net: All-in-one dehazing network. In Proceedings of the IEEE International Conference on Computer Vision, Venice, Italy, 22 –29 October 2017; pp. 4770–4778.
40. Lu, L.; Xiong, Q.; Xu, B.; Chu, D. Mixdehazenet: Mix structure block for image dehazing network. In Proceedings of the 2024 International Joint Conference on Neural Networks (IJCNN), Yokohama, Japan, 30 June–5 July 2024; pp. 1–10.
41. Cui, Y.; Ren, W.; Knoll, A. Omni-Kernel Network for Image Restoration. In Proceedings of the AAAI Conference on Artificial Intelligence, Vancouver, Canada, 20–27 February 2024; Volume 38, pp. 1426–1434.
42. Sui, T.; Xiang, G.; Chen, F.; Li, Y.; Tao, X.; Zhou, J.; Hong, J.; Qiu, Z. U-Shaped Dual Attention Vision Mamba Network for Satellite Remote Sensing Single-Image Dehazing. *Remote Sens.* **2025**, *17*, 1055. [CrossRef]
43. Ma, X.; Dai, X.; Bai, Y.; Wang, Y.; Fu, Y. Rewrite the Stars. In Proceedings of the IEEE/CVF Conference on Computer Vision and Pattern Recognition, Seattle, WA, USA, 16–22 June 2024; pp. 5694–5703.
44. Li, Y.; Chen, X. A coarse-to-fine two-stage attentive network for haze removal of remote sensing images. *IEEE Geosci. Remote Sens. Lett.* **2020**, *18*, 1751–1755. [CrossRef]
45. Zhou, H.; Wang, L.; Li, Q.; Guan, X.; Tao, T. Multi-Dimensional and Multi-Scale Physical Dehazing Network for Remote Sensing Images. *Remote Sens.* **2024**, *16*, 4780. [CrossRef]
46. Liu, B.; Chen, S.B.; Wang, J.X.; Tang, J.; Luo, B. An Oriented Object Detector for Hazy Remote Sensing Images. *IEEE Trans. Geosci. Remote Sens.* **2024**, *62*, 1001711. [CrossRef]

remote sensing

MDPI

Article

Remote Sensing Image-Based Building Change Detection: A Case Study of the Qinling Mountains in China

Lei Fu [1,2], Yunfeng Zhang [2,3], Keyun Zhao [1], Lulu Zhang [1], Ying Li [1,*], Changjing Shang [4] and Qiang Shen [4]

1 School of Computer Science, Northwestern Polytechnical University, Xi'an 710129, China; bobyfly@mail.nwpu.edu.cn (L.F.); kyzhao@mail.nwpu.edu.cn (K.Z.); zzhanglull@mail.nwpu.edu.cn (L.Z.)
2 Shaanxi Satellite Application Center for Natural Resources, Xi'an 710065, China; yunfengzhang@mail.nwpu.edu.cn
3 School of Software, Northwestern Polytechnical University, Xi'an 710129, China
4 Department of Computer Science, Aberystwyth University, Aberystwyth SY23 3DB, UK; cns@aber.ac.uk (C.S.); qqs@aber.ac.uk (Q.S.)
* Correspondence: lybyp@nwpu.edu.cn

Abstract

With the widespread application of deep learning in Earth observation, remote sensing image-based building change detection has achieved numerous groundbreaking advancements. However, differences across time periods caused by temporal variations in land cover, as well as the complex spatial structures in remote sensing scenes, significantly constrain the performance of change detection. To address these challenges, a change detection algorithm based on spatio-spectral information aggregation is proposed, which consists of two key modules: the Cross-Scale Heterogeneous Convolution module (CSHConv) and the Spatio-Spectral Information Fusion module (SSIF). CSHConv mitigates information loss caused by scale heterogeneity, thereby enhancing the effective utilization of multi-scale features. Meanwhile, SSIF models spatial and spectral information jointly, capturing interactions across different spatial scales and spectral domains. This investigation is illustrated with a case study conducted with the real-world dataset QL-CD (Qinling change detection), acquired in the Qinling region of China. The work includes the construction of QL-CD, which includes 12,724 pairs of images captured by the Gaofen-1 satellite. Experimental results demonstrate that the proposed approach outperforms a wide range of state-of-the-art algorithms.

Keywords: building change detection; spatio-spectral information fusion; cross-scale heterogeneous convolution; building change detection dataset

1. Introduction

Building change detection involves conducting analysis on remote sensing data acquired at different time points over the same location, to determine whether new buildings have been constructed or existing ones have been demolished. With continuous advancements in Earth observation technologies, state-of-the-art remote sensing sensors can now provide high-resolution imagery at meter- or even sub-meter-level precision. As a result, utilizing remote sensing imagery for large-scale building change detection has become a crucial Earth observation approach. Widely utilized in practice [1], it supports applications such as urban planning [2,3], natural resource conservation [4], disaster evaluation [5], and tracking land use and land cover changes [6].

Traditional change detection methods can be broadly categorized into two types: pixel-based methods and object-based methods. Pixel-based methods use individual pixels as detection units, extracting change information by analyzing spectral differences on a per-pixel basis. Common approaches in this category such as image differencing [7], statistical regression modeling [8], change vector analysis (CVA) [9,10], and principal component analysis (PCA) [11]. Object-based methods, on the other hand, analyze objects as fundamental units, allowing them to capture both spectral information and spatial context. Representative methods include those based on conditional random fields (CRFs) [12] and Markov random fields (MRFs) [13,14]. While these traditional methods offer advantages in detection efficiency and perform well in specific application scenarios, they involve significant dependence on human-designed feature representations. This dependency limits their effectiveness in complex environments.

The swift advancement of deep learning has attracted widespread interest, achieving remarkable success in many high-level interpretation tasks [15–20]. Due to the translation invariance of convolutional operations, convolutional neural networks (CNNs) exhibit robust feature representation capacity when processing image data. Thus, numerous CNN-based methods targeting change detection have been presented, including single-stream and dual-stream structures. The former merge bi-temporal images before processing, treating them as a unified entity. Daudt et al. [21], for instance, introduced a method grounded in a fully convolutional network architecture (FC-EF) [17], while Peng et al. [22] introduced a UNet++-based [23] algorithm that employs dense skip connections to capture features at multiple scales. However, these single-stream methods lack deep modeling of land cover features, which can introduce prediction bias and limit change detection accuracy. To address this issue, researchers have developed dual-stream structures, which extract bi-temporal features separately before computing their differences. Chen et al. [24] employed a Siamese architecture for feature extraction and measured feature differences using Euclidean distance. Liu et al. [25] introduced a Siamese network constrained by dual tasks, while Li et al. [26] improved upon UNet++ and introduced the Siam-NestedUNet model. Jiang et al. [27] developed PGA-SiamNet, a Siamese network utilizing pyramid feature-based attention. These dual-stream architectures enable independent modeling of features from images, while maintaining the same parameter efficiency as single-stream networks through shared weights. This significantly enhances change detection performance.

Different from CNNs that treat all regions of an image with equal importance, the attention mechanism dynamically adjusts the weights of different regions [28,29]. Various attention-based approaches have been developed. Zhang et al. [30] employed spatial attention mechanisms [31] and channel attention mechanisms [32] to integrate deep hierarchical features and bi-temporal difference features. Song et al. [33] proposed an attention-guided network, which enhances the distinction by leveraging both spatial and channel information. Chen et al. [34] introduced DASNet, which captures long-range dependencies using dual attention mechanisms. Fang et al. [35] designed an integrated attention module to refine multi-level semantic feature information, extracting the most representative features. In addition, many attention-based methods have also achieved certain performance [36–39].

Given the vast land cover information and the complex structural in remote sensing images, single-level feature fusion often fails to effectively model the intricate relationships among different land cover types. To overcome this, multi-level feature fusion strategies [40–42] are developed. An alternative approach involves employing spatial or channel attention mechanisms [34,36,38,43–45] to highlight key information. However, multi-scale feature integration may cause loss of fine details, producing smoothed features. Although many deep learning change detection methods apply spatial and channel attention—sometimes combined—they often neglect the synergy between spatial and spectral features. Moreover, these methods usually introduce many parameters, increasing computational cost and limiting practical use.

The scale, quality, and completeness of datasets influence deep learning detection performance by enhancing model generalization and representation. Thus, large-scale, high-quality datasets are vital for remote sensing progress. Public datasets like LEVIR-CD [24], WHU-Building [46], S2Looking [47], and CDD [48] exist but mainly cover single-scene scenarios with limited geographic and environmental diversity, restricting model adaptability and representation of complex land cover.

To address the aforementioned challenges, SSA-Net is herein proposed on the basis of spatio-spectral information aggregation, and a diverse large-scale dataset is established. First, a Cross-Scale Heterogeneous Convolution module is developed to effectively utilize multi-scale information and mitigate information loss caused by scale differences. Second, a Spatio-Spectral Information Aggregation module is developed, which efficiently captures and integrates spatio-spectral information across different scales. Finally, a change detection study is conducted in the Qinling region, constructing a large-scale dataset that encompasses diverse scenarios, including mountain ranges, forests, rural areas, and nature reserves.

The primary contributions are outlined below:

(1) A Cross-Scale Heterogeneous Convolution (CSHConv) module is introduced to precisely capture key change information across multiple scales.
(2) A Spatio-Spectral Information Aggregation (SSIF) module is designed to comprehensively model the complex spatial–spectral relationships between land cover features.
(3) An extensive experimental study is conducted in the real-world Qinling region, resulting in a new change detection dataset, consisting of 12,724 pairs of images captured by the Gaofen-1 satellite. This dataset covers diverse landscapes, including mountains, forests, rural areas, and nature reserves, providing a valuable resource for future research.

The remainder of this paper is organized as follows: Section 2 provides a detailed introduction to the dataset. Section 3 presents an in-depth explanation of the proposed SSA-Net. Section 4 describes the experiments and analysis. Section 5 discusses the computational complexity of different methods. Finally, Section 6 summarizes the study and discusses future research directions.

2. Dataset

As deep learning is inherently data-driven, its performance largely depends on the scale, quality, and completeness of the training dataset. Consequently, there is an increasing demand for large-scale, high-quality change detection datasets. To address the challenges posed by existing building change detection datasets, a well-annotated dataset regarding the region over the Qinling Mountains, QL-CD, is constructed. This dataset consists of 12,724 pairs of satellite images with a spatial resolution of 2 m and a patch size of 256 × 256 pixels. Below is a detailed introduction to QL-CD, including the area covered, annotation process, and preprocessing methods, followed by a comprehensive statistical analysis.

2.1. Study Regions

The Qinling Mountains are located in central China, extending across southern Shaanxi Province. They serve as a critical climatic transition zone between northern and southern China and form the watershed between the Yangtze River and the Yellow River basins. The QL-CD dataset covers the central segment of the Qinling Mountains within Shaanxi Province, spanning a geographical range of 106°03′–110°00′E, 32°4′–34°33′N, with a total area of approximately 58,000 km^2. As illustrated in Figure 1, the dataset encompasses 39 districts and counties across Baoji, Xi'an, Hanzhong, Ankang, and Shangluo.

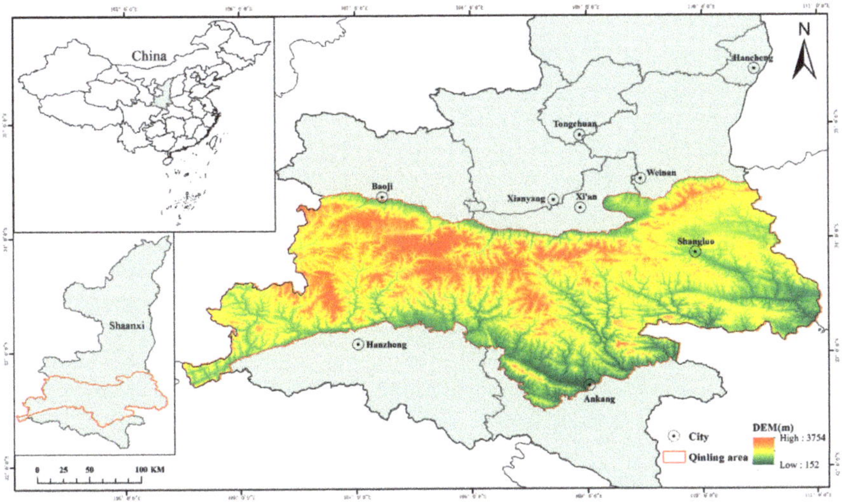

Figure 1. Location of study area.

The topography of the central Qinling region is highly rugged. The northern slopes are steep and characterized by deep valleys, while the southern slopes are more gradual, exhibiting a distinct north-steep–south-gentle mountain morphology. The region has an average elevation exceeding 1000 m, with certain peaks surpassing 3000 m. This complex terrain structure introduces significant spatial heterogeneity in human settlement distribution and building change dynamics. The selected study areas feature diverse and unique landscapes with a wide range of land cover types, including mountains, forests, rural settlements, and nature reserves. These geographical and environmental characteristics present both challenges and opportunities for building change detection systems to work in mountainous regions.

In this study, the dataset is derived from very-high-resolution (VHR) satellite imagery captured by Gaofen-1 (GF-1). The bi-temporal images were acquired in 2018 and 2022, covering the Qinling region and its surrounding areas. The imagery has a spatial resolution of 2 m and consists of three visible spectral bands (red, green, and blue).

2.2. Data Annotation and Preprocessing

Annotation: Compared to single-temporal image annotation, labeling multi-temporal remote sensing datasets is a significantly more complex task. Not only does it require annotating a larger number of change targets, but it also involves extensive cross-temporal region comparisons, increasing the overall workload. Moreover, the complex topography of mountainous regions and variations in imaging conditions across different acquisition times introduce additional challenges. In the Qinling region, the appearance and geographic characteristics of buildings can undergo substantial changes due to seasonal and weather variations, further complicating the annotation process.

To address these challenges, a refined annotation workflow is designed that ensures both high accuracy and efficiency. The annotation process carried out consists of multiple stages, each incorporating strict quality control measures to maintain the trustworthiness of the resulting dataset.

To manage the complexity of multi-temporal dataset annotation, a phased annotation strategy was adopted. Particularly, a 15-member professional annotation team was assembled, each with extensive experience in remote sensing image interpretation. The team received specialized training focused on mountainous terrain characteristics and building change patterns to enhance their expertise. Using professional GIS tools such as ArcGIS, annotators carefully delineated building change areas, based on their training and domain knowledge. In cases where images exhibited partial occlusion or distortion, the team leveraged external references, such as Google Maps and other Geographic Information Systems (GIS) resources, for cross-validation.

To further enhance annotation accuracy and consistency, a rigorous quality control framework was implemented, consisting of three key verification steps: (1) Each annotation result was reviewed by a second annotator, ensuring the detection of potential errors or omissions and maintaining high inter-annotator consistency. (2) Upon completion of the annotation process, domain experts conducted random spot checks to verify the correctness and completeness of the labeled data. (3) By integrating cross-validation, expert auditing, and iterative refinements, errors were significantly minimized, ensuring the high reliability of the final dataset.

Through such a systematic and meticulous annotation process, a highly accurate dataset tailored for building change detection is produced in mountainous environments. It lays a strong groundwork for future remote sensing image interpretation and model training over complex landscapes.

Preprocessing: To ensure consistency and usability of the dataset, a structured preprocessing pipeline was applied, which includes vector-to-raster conversion, image tiling, geographic metadata preservation, and secondary quality checks. Specifically, the precisely annotated vector files were converted into binary raster masks, where changed areas were assigned a value of 255, and unchanged areas were set to 0. The original high-resolution remote sensing images were segmented into separate 256 $\times$ 256 GeoTIFF blocks, ensuring compatibility with modern GPUs and deep learning frameworks. No overlap was introduced between image patches, facilitating efficient processing while maintaining spatial integrity. Geographic coordinates were preserved for each image patch, allowing them to be reassembled into a full reference map when needed. Each image block was sequentially numbered, providing a structured format for large-scale mapping and further applications. To enhance dataset relevance and precision, irrelevant regions were manually filtered out, ensuring that the final dataset focuses strictly on meaningful change areas.

Despite the rigorous quality control implemented during annotation, minor errors might still be present. To address this issue, a secondary review was conducted through cross-validation by multiple reviewers. This process effectively identified and removed images with unclear or incorrect annotations, ensuring high accuracy and reliability in the final dataset. By applying the aforementioned meticulous preprocessing steps, a well-structured, high-quality dataset optimized for building change detection is created for remote sensing applications.

Through this systematic processing workflow, the work implemented has not only ensured the high quality of the dataset but also provided an efficient and standardized input for subsequent building change detection models. The meticulous operations applied during the image tiling and filtering stages significantly enhance their effectiveness. Moreover, the systematic approach adopted in building this dataset lays a strong groundwork for remote sensing image analysis and change detection, promoting progress in both scholarly research and practical applications.

2.3. Dataset Analysis

Compared to existing building change detection datasets, QL-CD offers significant advantages in terms of coverage area, scene diversity, background complexity, and illumination variations. The key advantages of QL-CD are further emphasized as follows:

(1) Extensive Geographic Coverage: The QL-CD dataset encompasses 12,724 image pairs collected over a vast 58,000 km^2 area. Compared to existing datasets, QL-CD covers a significantly larger geographic region, making it one of the most comprehensive datasets in this domain. Specifically, the dataset represents a ground area of over 3300 km^2, with change regions covering approximately 367 km^2. Each image pair captures rich land cover variations, posing a more challenging benchmark for evaluating model performance in detecting change regions. This extensive coverage enhances the dataset's utility for performing real-world change detection tasks across diverse environments.

(2) Diverse Scene Coverage: As shown in Figure 2, the QL-CD dataset includes rich scene types, such as urban regions, suburban regions, rural settlements, hills, and rivers. This scene diversity poses a greater challenge for change detection algorithms, as it requires strong adaptability to model variations in complex environments. Additionally, it can be expected to help enhance the generalization capability of models trained on this dataset. This is because compared to existing datasets like LEVIR-CD and CDD, QL-CD not only provides a more comprehensive diversity of scenes but also serves as a multi-layered data resource for in-depth research and analysis. Such an extended scene coverage ensures that models developed using QL-CD are adaptable to more real-world scenarios.

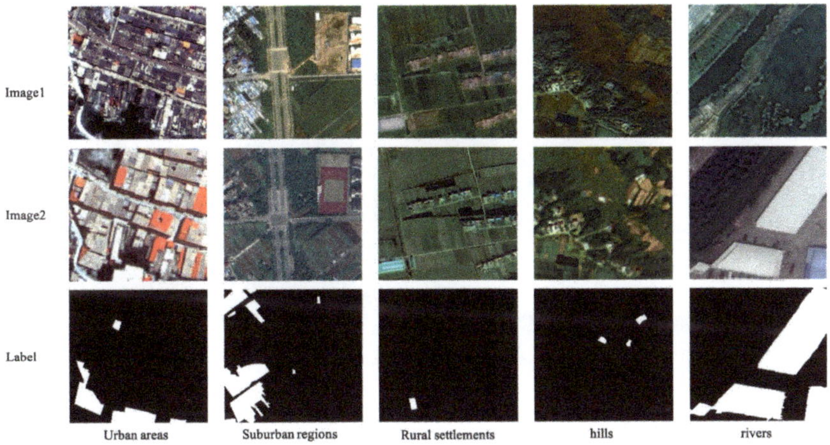

Figure 2. Diverse scene coverage of QL-CD.

(3) High Background Complexity: Most existing change detection datasets primarily focus on specific urban areas, where buildings are typically present against simplistic backgrounds such as streets and roads. In contrast, the QL-CD dataset not only retains these urban elements but also significantly expands the variety of background types, including lakes, grasslands, farmland, low vegetation, and bare land. This diverse background complexity, as illustrated in Figure 3, introduces additional challenges for change detection algorithms, requiring them to distinguish between building-related changes and natural environmental variations. The inclusion of such varied backgrounds enhances the dataset's practical value, making it a more realistic and robust benchmark for real-world applications.

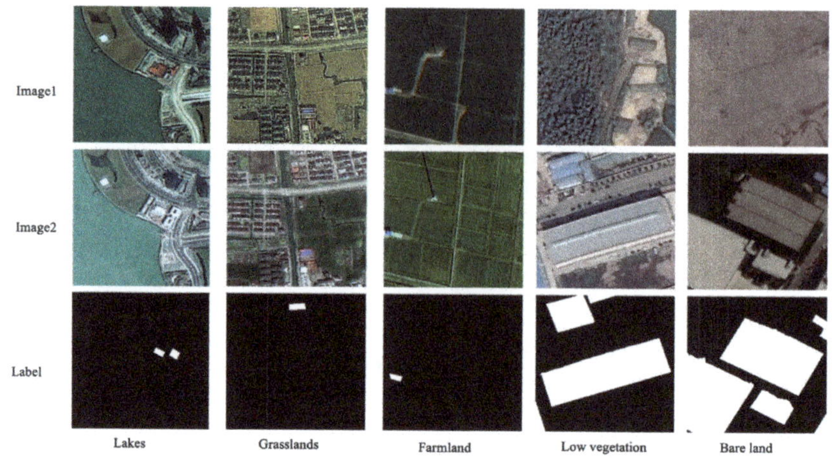

Figure 3. High background complexity of QL-CD.

(4) Illumination Heterogeneity: As shown in Figure 4, the QL-CD dataset exhibits significant illumination heterogeneity, with noticeable variations in brightness, saturation, contrast, and overall image style between the two temporal images. Unlike conventional datasets captured under uniform lighting conditions, QL-CD introduces a greater degree of illumination variability, making it more representative of real-world remote sensing scenarios. This heterogeneity enables models to better capture dynamic surface changes, including seasonal transitions, meteorological variations, and natural events that impact land cover. Additionally, illumination-induced pseudo-changes present an extra challenge for algorithms, requiring them to distinguish actual building changes from lighting variations. As a result, models trained on QL-CD can be expected to achieve greater robustness with improved generalization.

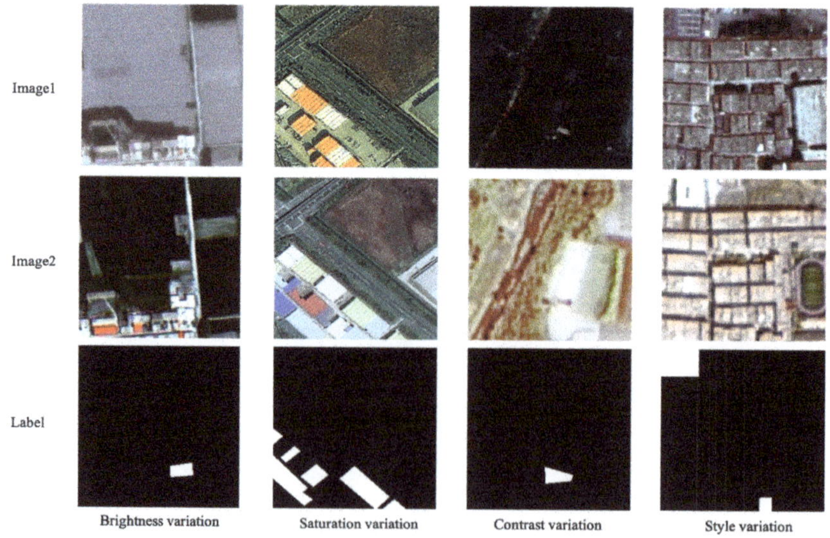

Figure 4. Illumination heterogeneity of QL-CD.

3. Methodology

To enhance the performance, a Spatio-Spectral Information Aggregation Change Detection Network (SSA-Net) is proposed, as illustrated in Figure 5. Unlike traditional networks, SSA-Net incorporates two novel modules:

1. Cross-Scale Heterogeneous Convolution (CSHConv) module
2. Spatio-Spectral Information Fusion (SSIF) module

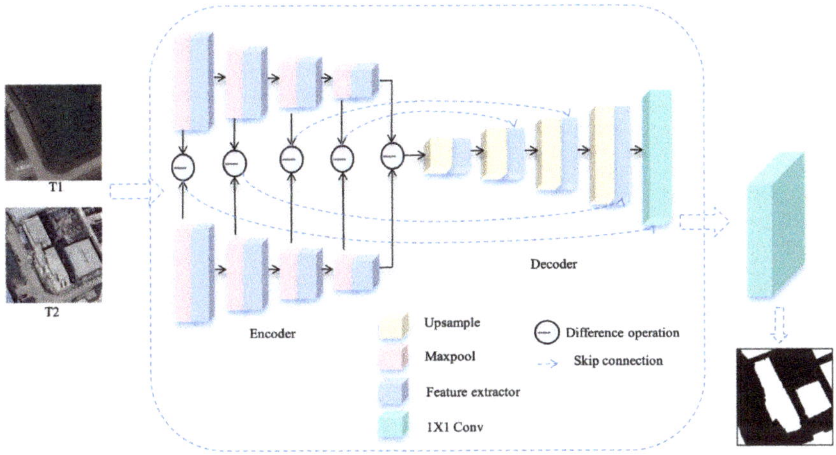

Figure 5. The architecture schematic of SSA-Net.

The CSHConv module mitigates information degradation caused by scale heterogeneity in standard convolutional kernels when processing land cover changes in remote sensing images. Meanwhile, recognizing the interdependencies between spatial and spectral channel information, the SSIF module is employed to facilitate feature fusion, effectively capturing cross-scale and cross-channel interactions. This enhanced information aggregation significantly improves model accuracy in detecting building changes.

3.1. Overview

A U-shaped network with a non-shared pseudo-Siamese structure [49] is adopted as the backbone of SSA-Net. The introduction of a non-weight-sharing encoder enhances flexibility in learning feature representations, while skip connections facilitate the interaction of temporal difference information between bi-temporal images. Bi-temporal images are first fed into the encoder, where four successive downsampling steps are performed to progressively extract multi-level features.

Instead of traditional convolutions, the Cross-Scale Heterogeneous Convolution (CSHConv) module is employed, which integrates different receptive fields to effectively capture multi-scale change information. Meanwhile, the Spatio-Spectral Information Fusion (SSIF) module is utilized to aggregate spatial and spectral information, ensuring a comprehensive representation of image features and an efficient encoding of semantic information. Using different convolutional operations at each stage, SSA-Net gradually extracts rich semantic, spatial, and spectral channel information, facilitating improved recognition and representation of change objects by the network in bi-temporal images. The decoder is designed to be approximately symmetric to the encoder, supporting effective upsampling of feature maps. This balanced structure helps keep the high-level multi-scale features acquired during encoding, preserving fine object details and structural integrity. The decoder applies four successive transposed convolutions to restore spatial resolution, followed by a final refinement step using a 1×1 convolution combined with an activation function to fine-tune the feature representations and generate the final change map. This architecture allows SSA-Net to effectively capture, analyze, and reconstruct change information, entailing high accuracy in building change detection.

3.2. Cross-Scale Heterogeneous Convolution Module

Traditional convolutional neural networks (CNNs) utilize single-scale convolutional kernels, meaning that kernels of the same size compute feature information within the same spatial region. Due to this design limitation, the extracted features may lack comprehensiveness and completeness. As a result, CNNs may struggle to effectively model complex multi-scale variations present in remote sensing images. To overcome this limitation, we propose the Cross-Scale Heterogeneous Convolution (CSHConv) module, which addresses the information loss caused by scale heterogeneity in traditional convolutional kernels when processing land surface changes in remote sensing imagery. By incorporating multiple receptive fields, CSHConv enables more effective capture of multi-scale changes, which improves both accuracy and robustness in detection models.

Figure 6 illustrates the basic architecture of CSHConv. In CSHConv, the input feature f is first processed using a 1×1 convolution, which reduces the channel dimension by half, thereby obtaining the initial feature representation. This operation can be mathematically expressed as follows:

$$O_1 = \sigma(Conv_{1\times1}(f)) \tag{1}$$

where $\sigma(\cdot)$ represents the ReLU activation function, $Conv_{1\times1}$ denotes the 1×1 convolution operation, and O_1 is the feature map obtained after convolution. Subsequently, O_1 passes through heterogeneous convolution to obtain multi-scale feature information. The design of heterogeneous convolution involves the operation with different kernel sizes, where a portion of the kernels are 3×3, and the rest are 1×1. This design allows the network to extract local fine-grained details (with 3×3 kernels) while preserving global semantic information (with 1×1 kernels), effectively addressing the scale heterogeneity issue in remote sensing images.

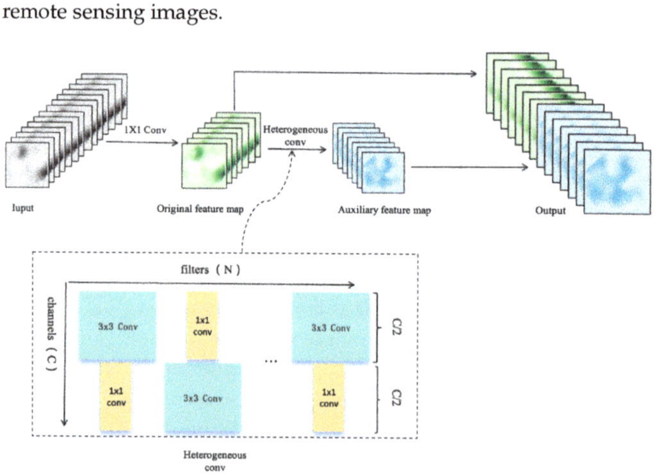

Figure 6. Cross-Scale Heterogeneous Convolution module.

Formally, the heterogeneous convolution operation can be mathematically expressed as follows:

$$O_2 = Conv_{3\times3}(O_1) + Conv_{1\times1}(O_1) \tag{2}$$

Also, the 3×3 convolution operation in the CSHConv module can be expressed by

$$Conv_{3\times3}(x,y,o) = \sum_{i=0}^{I/G-1} \sum_{j=0}^{K-1} \sum_{k=0}^{K-1} X(x+j, y+k, i+o \times I/G) \times kernel(j,k,i,o) \quad (3)$$

where X represents the input tensor, which corresponds to O_1; (x,y) denotes the spatial coordinates of the feature; K is the kernel size, defining the spatial extent of the convolution; I is the number of input channels in the feature map; G indicates how many groups are in the grouped convolution; I/G represents the input channel number per group in grouped convolution; $kernel(j,k,i,o)$ represents the convolution kernel's weight parameters, with j, k indicating the spatial offsets of the kernel, representing its position in the convolution window (i.e., row and column offsets), i is the index of the channel group, with $(i + o \times I/G)$ being the input channel index, denoting which input channel the kernel operates on, and o being the output channel index, specifying the feature map's corresponding output channel.

Each convolution kernel consists of a set of trainable weights that perform a weighted summation over different input channels and spatial positions. This operation generates an element of the output tensor, by computing a local weighted sum across the corresponding receptive field. The obtained feature information is then concatenated with the original feature map to produce the final prediction. This process can be formally summarized as follows:

$$O_{ans} = concat(\sigma(O_2), O_1) \quad (4)$$

The CSHConv module serves as a compact feature extraction unit, replacing the standard convolution operations in the encoder–decoder structure. It aims to obtain multi-scale representations of change objects, helping deep learning models effectively detect variations at multiple scales. The design of CSHConv leverages heterogeneous convolution, which incorporates various kernel sizes (e.g., some kernels are 3×3 while others are 1×1). The core idea behind this heterogeneous convolution is to leverage multiple receptive fields, enabling the network to extract multi-scale contextual information and enhance feature learning for change detection. By integrating varied convolutional kernels, CSHConv preserves fine information details while capturing broader spatial structures, making it particularly suitable for detecting complex and multi-scale changes.

3.3. Spatial and Spectral Information Fusion Module

As previously noted, straightforward fusion of auxiliary and original feature maps might cause information loss in complex scenes. To resolve this, the Spatio-Spectral Information Fusion (SSIF) module is proposed, which refines the feature fusion process by explicitly modeling interactions across different spatial scales and spectral channels. This design ensures that the network effectively captures and integrates complementary information.

Typically, attention mechanisms include three main components: Query (Q), Key (K), and Value (V). These elements work together to establish strong correlations between intent (query) and target (key). In this context, the query represents the system's intent, while the key represents the regions of interest in the image. The attention mechanism enhances feature representation by calculating the interaction between query and key, then applying this to the corresponding value, allowing the system to concentrate on important image regions.

To compute the correlation between query and key, following the Nadaraya–Watson kernel regression [50], a novel spatio-spectral information aggregation strategy is proposed.

Specifically, it utilizes Gaussian kernel-based spatio-spectral information aggregation, implementing the strategy below:

$$Y = sigmoid(\sum_{i=1}^{n=2} \frac{(Q_i - K)^2}{2\sigma_i^2} + \frac{1}{2}) \times V \tag{5}$$

where the Gaussian kernel function is used to measure the similarity between the query Q_i and the key K, with σ_i controlling the sensitivity of similarity computation. By performing a weighted summation across all similarity scores, the final similarity measure is obtained. This formulation is commonly applied, particularly in Nadaraya–Watson kernel regression, which is often used for non-parametric estimation of relationships between variables. In machine learning and statistics, employing such kernel functions helps capture complex dependencies between input variables, thereby increasing the model's effectiveness in learning complex patterns [51].

Figure 7 illustrates the detailed process of the Spatio-Spectral Information Fusion (SSIF) module. In this framework, both K(Key) and V(Value) originate from the input feature map $X \in \mathbb{R}^{C \times H \times W}$, where C, H, and W represent the channel dimension, height, and width of the feature map, respectively. Channel-wise Query Q_1 is extracted from the channel information, represented as the mean of X along the channel axis, denoted as $X \in \mathbb{R}^{C \times 1 \times 1}$. Spatial-wise Query Q_2 is extracted from the spatial dimension, represented as the mean of X along the spatial axis, denoted as $X \in \mathbb{R}^{1 \times H \times W}$. Additionally, the variances σ_1^2 and σ_2^2 are computed for the channel and spatial information, respectively. These variance values play a crucial role in controlling the richness of feature representations: a greater variance σ_i^2 indicates greater variance, meaning that the feature map contains richer contextual information. This formulation allows the model to capture attention relationships across different dimensions, leveraging both spatial and channel statistics.

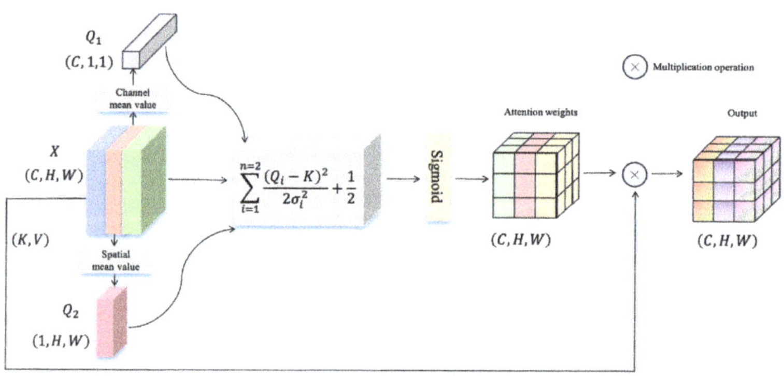

Figure 7. Spatial and Spectral Information Fusion module.

To ensure that attention weights positively contribute to feature learning, the following regularization steps are applied: (1) A bias term $\frac{1}{2}$ is added to the raw attention scores to stabilize the attention values. (2) To normalize attention scores, a Sigmoid activation is used, allowing weights to reflect the relevance of diverse regions in the feature map. The computed attention weights are then multiplied with the input feature map X to generate the final output feature map Y.

Figure 8 illustrates the structural diagram of integrating SSIF into CSHConv, demonstrating their synergistic effect. CSHConv effectively captures multi-scale features, refining the representation of changed objects with greater precision. Simultaneously, SSIF efficiently aggregates spectral information across different channels, leveraging spectral dependencies to provide a more accurate depiction of surface changes. Combining SSIF with CSHConv strengthens the model's capacity to represent and capture input data, which is especially beneficial for complex scenes and multi-scale information.

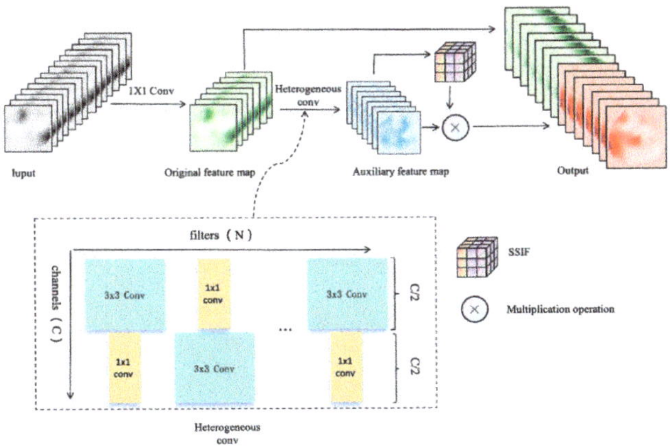

Figure 8. Architecture schematic of integrating SSIF into CSHConv.

3.4. Loss Function of SSA-Net

Change detection is commonly formulated as a pixel-wise binary classification problem, where the Binary Cross-Entropy (BCE) loss function is used to measure the discrepancy between the model's predictions and ground truth labels. However, due to the class imbalance issue (where the proportion of changed regions is significantly smaller than that of unchanged regions), BCE loss alone may lead to biased learning, favoring the majority class (unchanged pixels). To address this, a mixed loss function is used, inspired by A2Net [52], which combines BCE [53] and Dice Loss [54]. This hybrid approach balances the impact of both loss components, ensuring that the model learns effectively from both changed and unchanged regions.

For each sample, the BCE Loss and the Dice Loss are, respectively, computed as follows:

$$L(y, \hat{y}) = -\frac{1}{N}\sum_{i=1}^{N}[y_i \cdot log(\hat{y_i}) + (1 - y_i) \cdot \log(1 - \hat{y}_i)] \tag{6}$$

$$L_{dice}(y, \hat{y}) = 1 - \frac{2\sum_{i=1}^{N} y_i \hat{y}_i}{\sum_{i=1}^{N} {y_i}^2 + \sum_{i=1}^{N} {\hat{y}_i}^2 + \epsilon} \tag{7}$$

where N is the total number of pixels in the image, y_i is the ground truth label for the i-th pixel, $\hat{y}_i$ is the predicted probability of change for the i-th pixel output by the network, and ϵ is a small constant to prevent division by zero.

The overall loss for SSA-Net is computed by summing BCE and Dice losses, defined as follows:

$$L_{loss}(y, \hat{y}) = L(y, \hat{y}) + L_{dice} \tag{8}$$

4. Experimental Studies

4.1. Implementation Setup

SSA-Net is fully implemented using PyTorch 2.1.0 and all experiments are conducted on two American Nvidia RTX 4090 GPUs (Santa Clara, CA, USA). The Adam optimizer is used for training, with momentum set to 0.9 and weight decay set to 0.0005 as typically performed in the relevant literature. A polynomial decay learning rate scheduler (lr_scheduler) is applied, with a decay cycle of 50 epochs. The initial learning rate is set to 1×10^{-4}. The max epoch number is set to 200. The batch size is set to 8 for all methods.

4.2. Evaluation Metrics

To quantitatively assess different models, researchers typically rely on a set of commonly used evaluation metrics. These metrics not only help in understanding the accuracy of an algorithm but also serve as objective standards for comparing different methods across various datasets.

As stated before, change detection is considered as a binary classification task. For evaluation, performance metrics are derived from the confusion matrix. Table 1 shows the standard binary classification confusion matrix, dividing all pixels into four categories based on the comparison between model predictions and ground truth labels: True Positive (TP), False Positive (FP), True Negative (TN), and False Negative (FN).

Table 1. Confusion matrix.

Prediction\Ground Truth	Positive	Negative
Positive	TP	FP
Negative	FN	TN

Based on confusion matrices, four commonly used evaluation metrics are herein adopted to assess the accuracy of the change detection results: Precision, Recall, F1-score, and Intersection over Union (IoU). Their mathematical formulations are as follows:

$$Precision = \frac{\mathrm{TP}}{\mathrm{TP} + \mathrm{FP}} \tag{9}$$

$$Recall = \frac{\mathrm{TP}}{\mathrm{TP} + \mathrm{FN}} \tag{10}$$

$$F1 = \frac{2 \times Precision \times Recall}{Precision + Recall} \tag{11}$$

$$IoU = \frac{\mathrm{TP}}{\mathrm{TP} + \mathrm{FN} + \mathrm{FP}} \tag{12}$$

4.3. Methods Compared

To comprehensively evaluate SSA-Net, 12 change detection methods are compared, including three widely applied classic algorithms: FC-EF [21], FC-Siam-Conc [21], and FC-Siam-Diff [21]; six high-performing recent algorithms evaluated on public datasets: STANet and its two derivatives (STANet_BAM and STANet_PAM) [24], SNUNet [35], A2Net [52], and HANet [55]; and three Transformer-based methods: BIT [56], Changer [57], and ChangeFormer [58]. These methods are briefly introduced below for academic completeness.

FC-EF merges bi-temporal images early and utilizes a Fully Convolutional Network for detecting changes; FC-Siam-Conc integrates features from both times through skip connections in a Siamese FCN for long-range mapping; FC-Siam-Diff detects changes by computing differences between features in a Siamese network setup. STANet series [24] introduces a spatiotemporal attention module into a Siamese network and employs a pyramid attention mechanism to leverage spatiotemporal dependencies, generating more expressive region change features. SNUNet [35] designs a densely connected U-shaped Siamese network, incorporating a channel attention module to optimize different semantic features. A2Net [52] utilizes a lightweight backbone and enhances change information through attention mechanisms. HANet [55] adopts a progressive sampling approach balanced toward the foreground, which improves the model's early-stage change identification and detection accuracy. BIT [56] presents a Transformer encoder that captures spatiotemporal relationships using context-aware token representations to extract high-level semantic features. Changer [57] presents a general change detection framework, improving detection performance through feature interaction and fusion strategies. ChangeFormer [58] integrates a hierarchical Transformer in Siamese architecture, enabling stronger multi-scale information modeling capability.

4.4. Experimental Results on QL-CD

Table 2 presents the quantitative results of running different methods across five evaluation metrics: Precision, Recall, F1, IoU, and Kappa, with the highest scores highlighted in bold. The experimental results demonstrate that FC-EF, FC-Siam-Conc, and FC-Siam-Diff exhibit relatively poor performance. In contrast, algorithms such as STANet, Changer, and ChangeFormer achieve better performance by employing distinct feature fusion approaches and attention mechanisms. Compared with the 12 existing change detection methods, the proposed SSA-Net attains the best performance on the two comprehensive metrics of F1 and IoU, achieving scores of 84.15% and 74.64%, respectively, surpassing the second-best algorithm (STANet_PAM) by 2.65% and 3.44%. Furthermore, SSA-Net also achieves the highest Kappa coefficient of 82.43%, significantly outperforming STANet_PAM's 79.54% by 2.89%. This superior Kappa score reinforces the model's overall effectiveness in achieving high agreement beyond chance, aligning with its leading performance in F1 and IoU. Notably, from an application perspective, the F1 metric holds greater significance as it requires a balanced performance between Recall and Precision to ensure robust and effective detection results.

Table 2. Performance of different methods on QL-CD.

Method	Precision (%)	Recall (%)	F1 (%)	IoU (%)	Kappa (%)
FC-EF	47.64	46.36	46.99	30.71	40.99
FC-Siam-Conc	68.43	37.03	48.06	31.63	44.00
FC-Siam-Diff	82.49	26.08	39.63	24.72	36.49
STANet	65.14	76.97	70.56	54.51	66.86
STANet_BAM	75.58	85.21	79.22	68.28	77.67
STANet_PAM	79.25	84.34	81.50	71.20	79.54
SNUNet	87.23	74.64	79.27	69.04	78.39
HANet	77.09	55.06	64.23	47.31	60.88
A2Net	88.96	72.81	80.08	66.78	78.04
BIT	70.93	69.25	70.04	59.23	66.69
Changer	71.92	70.35	71.09	60.22	67.85
ChangeFormer	79.39	69.21	72.86	62.34	71.19
SSA-Net	88.70	80.04	84.15	72.64	82.43

Figure 9 qualitatively illustrates the prediction results of the proposed method and other approaches on the QL-CD test set images. Here, T1 and T2 represent a pair of multi-temporal images to be analyzed. "GT" denotes the ground truth. As shown in the figure, for scenarios where the multi-temporal images exhibit consistent styles and simple backgrounds, all methods can roughly localize changed buildings. However, the proposed method demonstrates highly consistent edge details between predictions and ground truth labels. In complex scenes with cluttered backgrounds, other algorithms show limitations in handling the continuity of change regions and edge details, accompanied by missed or false detections. In contrast, SSA-Net effectively addresses such incoherent cases, accurately localizes changed objects, and robustly suppresses background interference across bi-temporal images. For scenarios with inconsistent imaging styles between multi-temporal phases, SSA-Net significantly outperforms all comparison methods, achieving the best performance by precisely localizing change regions, which benefits from its domain consistency constraints.

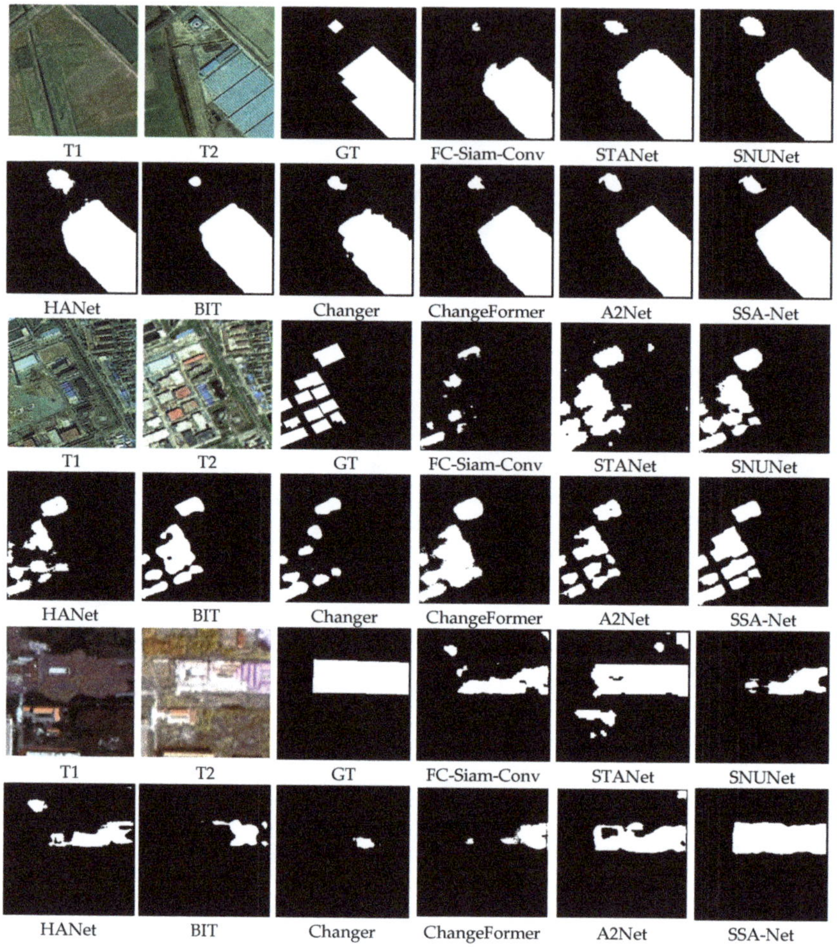

Figure 9. Change detection results on QL-CD.

4.5. Ablation Investigation

To further investigate the value of the proposed CSHConv and SSIF modules in SSA-Net, ablation studies are carried out on the QL-CD dataset. The experimental protocol involves incrementally integrating each module into the backbone and evaluating the resulting accuracy improvements. Table 3 shows the outcomes.

Table 3. Ablation experiment of SSA-Net on QL-CD.

Methods	Precision (%)	Recall (%)	F1 (%)	IoU (%)	Kappa (%)
Backbone	86.11	75.32	80.35	70.62	78.26
Backbone + CSHConv	86.93	76.07	81.13	71.50	79.13
Backbone + SSIF	83.85	79.14	81.14	68.87	79.36
SSA-Net	88.70	80.04	84.15	72.64	82.43

The first step is to verify whether the design of CSHConv enhances building change detection performance. This module addresses the issue of information loss caused by scale heterogeneity when using traditional designs. By replacing standard convolutions with heterogeneous convolutions, CSHConv captures multi-scale feature representations of change objects, enabling the deep learning model to more effectively learn multi-scale change information. Experimental results demonstrate that utilizing CSHConv leads to a modest overall improvement in network performance.

The second step is to show that the SSIF module aggregates spectral information from different bands without introducing any additional parameters. Experimental results indicate that SSIF significantly boosts the model's change detection capability, with the Recall metric increasing by nearly 4%.

Moreover, to intuitively demonstrate the roles of CSHConv and SSIF within the network, we visualized the intermediate feature activation maps from the encoder, as shown in Figure 10. As observed, when only the baseline is used, the model mistakenly focuses on many unchanged regions. With the introduction of CSHConv, the attention becomes more aligned with the actual change areas, though some discontinuities along class boundaries and missed detections remain. Finally, SSA-Net, incorporating both CSHConv and SSIF, effectively focuses on the truly changed regions in the images.

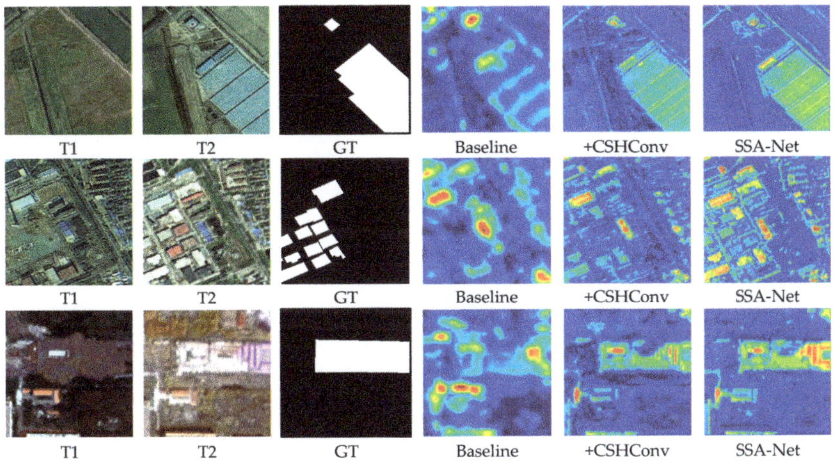

Figure 10. Feature activation maps of different models.

These ablation results demonstrate that the proposed CSHConv and SSIF modules improve various network metrics, leading to superior detection performance. The integration of both modules enhances the network's IoU and F1-scores. This indicates that, for the change detection task, these two innovative modules enable the network to more effectively extract change features from bi-temporal images, focusing on regions with potential changes and fusing multi-scale features efficiently.

5. Discussion

Parameter and computation efficiency are critical for real-world deployment. As shown in Table 4, SSA-Net achieves exceptional efficiency with only 3.54M parameters and 6.65G FLOPs—close to lightweight FC variants (1.29–1.93M Params) but surpassing them by >44% in F1. This demonstrates that our architecture eliminates redundant parameters without sacrificing accuracy.

Notably, SSA-Net outperforms all high-accuracy competitors in efficiency, it reduces parameters by 79% versus similarly accurate STANet_PAM while maintaining equivalent computation (6.65G vs. 6.58G). Compared to BIT, SSA-Net uses nearly identical parameters but cuts computation by 37% and improves F1 by13.41%. In terms of inference time, SSA-Net also achieves competitive performance. This optimal balance establishes SSA-

Net as a practical solution for resource-constrained scenarios requiring high-precision change detection.

Table 4. Complexity comparison of different methods.

Method	Params (M)	Flops (G)	Times (S)
FC-EF	1.93	4.55	60
FC-Siam-Conc	1.75	3.99	57
FC-Siam-Diff	1.29	2.92	52
STANet	12.28	25.69	165
STANet_BAM	16.93	14.4	154
STANet_PAM	16.93	6.58	159
SNUNet	28.34	97.87	191
HANet	3.03	14.07	102
A2Net	3.78	6.02	120
BIT	3.55	10.6	244
Changer	11.39	11.89	184
ChangeFormer	20.75	11.35	80
SSA-Net	3.54	6.65	84

6. Conclusions

This paper has presented a novel system, SSA-Net, for remote sensing change detection. It leverages the CSHConv module to integrate multi-scale receptive field information through heterogeneous convolutions, thereby precisely capturing critical features of change objects across varying scales. Furthermore, the SSIF module is employed to deeply explore complex interdependencies between spatial and channel-wise spectral features in the input data. The system enables efficient global context modeling without introducing additional parameters, refining features to suppress interference from irrelevant regions and extract more accurate change information. Additionally, a case study has been carried out with data regarding China's Qinling Mountains region, including the creation of a comprehensive QL-CD change detection dataset. Experimental results demonstrate that SSA-Net achieves competitive performance in change detection. For future work, it would be interesting to prioritize lightweight network design and incorporate weakly supervised learning, thereby reducing the approach's reliance on extensive labeled samples, alleviating annotation complexity. It is also worth exploring multi-modal data fusion to enhance building change detection by leveraging diverse data sources.

Author Contributions: Conceptualization, L.F. and L.Z.; methodology, L.F. and Y.Z.; validation, L.F. and Y.Z.; writing—original draft preparation, L.F.; writing—review and editing, C.S. and Q.S.; visualization, Y.Z. and K.Z.; supervision, Y.L. and Q.S.; funding acquisition, Y.L. All authors have read and agreed to the published version of the manuscript.

Funding: This research was funded by the National Natural Science Foundation of China (62271400).

Data Availability Statement: Data will be made available on request.

Conflicts of Interest: The authors declare no conflicts of interest.

References

1. Shafique, A.; Cao, G.; Khan, Z.; Asad, M.; Aslam, M. Deep Learning-Based Change Detection in Remote Sensing Images: A Review. *Remote Sens.* **2022**, *14*, 871. [CrossRef]
2. Bouziani, M.; Goïta, K.; He, D.-C. Automatic change detection of buildings in urban environment from very high spatial resolution images using existing geodatabase and prior knowledge. *ISPRS J. Photogramm. Remote Sens.* **2010**, *65*, 143–153. [CrossRef]
3. Huang, X.; Han, X.; Ma, S.; Lin, T.; Gong, J. Monitoring ecosystem service change in the City of Shenzhen by the use of high-resolution remotely sensed imagery and deep learning. *Land Degrad. Dev.* **2019**, *30*, 1490–1501. [CrossRef]

4. Wang, J.; Yang, D.; Detto, M.; Nelson, B.W.; Chen, M.; Guan, K.; Wu, S.; Yan, Z.; Wu, J. Multi-scale integration of satellite remote sensing improves characterization of dry-season green-up in an Amazon tropical evergreen forest. *Remote Sens. Environ.* **2020**, *246*, 111865. [CrossRef]
5. Zheng, Z.; Zhong, Y.; Wang, J.; Ma, A.; Zhang, L. Building damage assessment for rapid disaster response with a deep object-based semantic change detection framework: From natural disasters to man-made disasters. *Remote Sens. Environ.* **2021**, *265*, 112636. [CrossRef]
6. Lv, Z.; Zhong, P.; Wang, W.; You, Z.; Falco, N. Multi-scale attention network guided with change gradient image for land cover change detection using remote sensing images. *IEEE Geosci. Remote Sens. Lett.* **2023**, *20*, 2501805.
7. Turner, H. A comparison of some methods of slope measurement from large-scale air photos. *Photogrammetria* **1977**, *32*, 209–237. [CrossRef]
8. Ludeke, A.K.; Maggio, R.C.; Reid, L.M. An analysis of anthropogenic deforestation using logistic regression and GIS. *J. Environ. Manag.* **1990**, *31*, 247–259. [CrossRef]
9. Chen, J.; Gong, P.; He, C.; Pu, R.; Shi, P. Land-use/land-cover change detection using improved change-vector analysis. *Photogramm. Eng. Remote Sens.* **2003**, *69*, 369–379. [CrossRef]
10. Bayarjargal, Y.; Karnieli, A.; Bayasgalan, M.; Khudulmur, S.; Gandush, C.; Tucker, C. A comparative study of NOAA–AVHRR derived drought indices using change vector analysis. *Remote Sens. Environ.* **2006**, *105*, 9–22. [CrossRef]
11. Deng, J.; Wang, K.; Deng, Y.; Qi, G. PCA-based land-use change detection and analysis using multitemporal and multisensor satellite data. *Int. J. Remote Sens.* **2008**, *29*, 4823–4838. [CrossRef]
12. Kasetkasem, T.; Varshney, P.K. An image change detection algorithm based on Markov random field models. *IEEE Trans. Geosci. Remote Sens.* **2002**, *40*, 1815–1823. [CrossRef]
13. Benedek, C.; Szirányi, T. Change detection in optical aerial images by a multilayer conditional mixed Markov model. *IEEE Trans. Geosci. Remote Sens.* **2009**, *47*, 3416–3430. [CrossRef]
14. Bruzzone, L.; Prieto, D.F. An MRF approach to unsupervised change detection. In Proceedings of the 1999 International Conference on Image Processing (Cat. 99CH36348), Kobe, Japan, 24–28 October 1999; pp. 143–147.
15. Li, Y.; Zhang, H.; Xue, X.; Jiang, Y.; Shen, Q. Deep learning for remote sensing image classification: A survey. *Wiley Interdiscip. Rev. Data Min. Knowl. Discov.* **2018**, *8*, e1264. [CrossRef]
16. Li, Y.; Zhang, H.; Shen, Q. Spectral–spatial classification of hyperspectral imagery with 3D convolutional neural network. *Remote Sens.* **2017**, *9*, 67. [CrossRef]
17. Long, J.; Shelhamer, E.; Darrell, T. Fully convolutional networks for semantic segmentation. In Proceedings of the IEEE Conference on Computer Vision and Pattern Recognition, Boston, MA, USA, 7–12 June 2015; pp. 3431–3440.
18. Ren, S.; He, K.; Girshick, R.; Sun, J. Faster R-CNN: Towards real-time object detection with region proposal networks. *IEEE Trans. Pattern Anal. Mach. Intell.* **2016**, *39*, 1137–1149. [CrossRef]
19. Hou, X.; Bai, Y.; Xie, Y.; Zhang, Y.; Fu, L.; Li, Y.; Shang, C.; Shen, Q. Self-supervised multimodal change detection based on difference contrast learning for remote sensing imagery. *Pattern Recognit.* **2025**, *159*, 111148. [CrossRef]
20. Hou, X.; Bai, Y.; Li, Y.; Shang, C.; Shen, Q. High-resolution triplet network with dynamic multiscale feature for change detection on satellite images. *ISPRS J. Photogramm. Remote Sens.* **2021**, *177*, 103–115. [CrossRef]
21. Daudt, R.C.; Le Saux, B.; Boulch, A. Fully convolutional siamese networks for change detection. In Proceedings of the 2018 25th IEEE international conference on image processing (ICIP), Athens, Greece, 7–10 October 2018; pp. 4063–4067.
22. Peng, D.; Zhang, Y.; Guan, H. End-to-end change detection for high resolution satellite images using improved UNet++. *Remote Sens.* **2019**, *11*, 1382. [CrossRef]
23. Zhou, Z.; Rahman Siddiquee, M.M.; Tajbakhsh, N.; Liang, J. Unet++: A nested u-net architecture for medical image segmentation. In Proceedings of the Deep Learning in Medical Image Analysis and Multimodal Learning for Clinical Decision Support: 4th International Workshop, DLMIA 2018, and 8th International Workshop, ML-CDS 2018, Held in Conjunction with MICCAI 2018, Granada, Spain, 20 September 2018; pp. 3–11.
24. Chen, H.; Shi, Z. A spatial-temporal attention-based method and a new dataset for remote sensing image change detection. *Remote Sens.* **2020**, *12*, 1662. [CrossRef]
25. Liu, Y.; Pang, C.; Zhan, Z.; Zhang, X.; Yang, X. Building change detection for remote sensing images using a dual-task constrained deep siamese convolutional network model. *IEEE Geosci. Remote Sens. Lett.* **2020**, *18*, 811–815. [CrossRef]
26. Li, K.; Li, Z.; Fang, S. Siamese NestedUNet networks for change detection of high resolution satellite image. In Proceedings of the 2020 1st International Conference on Control, Robotics and Intelligent System, Xiamen, China, 27–29 October 2020; pp. 42–48.
27. Jiang, H.; Hu, X.; Li, K.; Zhang, J.; Gong, J.; Zhang, M. PGA-SiamNet: Pyramid feature-based attention-guided Siamese network for remote sensing orthoimagery building change detection. *Remote Sens.* **2020**, *12*, 484. [CrossRef]
28. Vaswani, A.; Shazeer, N.; Parmar, N.; Uszkoreit, J.; Jones, L.; Gomez, A.N.; Kaiser, Ł.; Polosukhin, I. Attention is all you need. *Adv. Neural Inf. Process. Syst.* **2017**, 6000–6010.

29. Guo, M.-H.; Xu, T.-X.; Liu, J.-J.; Liu, Z.-N.; Jiang, P.-T.; Mu, T.-J.; Zhang, S.-H.; Martin, R.R.; Cheng, M.-M.; Hu, S.-M. Attention mechanisms in computer vision: A survey. *Comput. Vis. Media* **2022**, *8*, 331–368. [CrossRef]
30. Zhang, C.; Yue, P.; Tapete, D.; Jiang, L.; Shangguan, B.; Huang, L.; Liu, G. A deeply supervised image fusion network for change detection in high resolution bi-temporal remote sensing images. *ISPRS J. Photogramm. Remote Sens.* **2020**, *166*, 183–200. [CrossRef]
31. Wang, H.; Fan, Y.; Wang, Z.; Jiao, L.; Schiele, B. Parameter-free spatial attention network for person re-identification. *arXiv* **2018**, arXiv:1811.12150.
32. Hu, J.; Shen, L.; Sun, G. Squeeze-and-excitation networks. In Proceedings of the IEEE Conference on Computer Vision and Pattern Recognition, Salt Lake City, UT, USA, 18–23 June 2018; pp. 7132–7141.
33. Song, K.; Jiang, J. AGCDetNet: An attention-guided network for building change detection in high-resolution remote sensing images. *IEEE J. Sel. Top. Appl. Earth Obs. Remote Sens.* **2021**, *14*, 4816–4831. [CrossRef]
34. Chen, J.; Yuan, Z.; Peng, J.; Chen, L.; Huang, H.; Zhu, J.; Liu, Y.; Li, H. DASNet: Dual attentive fully convolutional Siamese networks for change detection in high-resolution satellite images. *IEEE J. Sel. Top. Appl. Earth Obs. Remote Sens.* **2020**, *14*, 1194–1206. [CrossRef]
35. Fang, S.; Li, K.; Shao, J.; Li, Z. SNUNet-CD: A densely connected Siamese network for change detection of VHR images. *IEEE Geosci. Remote Sens. Lett.* **2021**, *19*, 8007805. [CrossRef]
36. Shi, Q.; Liu, M.; Li, S.; Liu, X.; Wang, F.; Zhang, L. A deeply supervised attention metric-based network and an open aerial image dataset for remote sensing change detection. *IEEE Trans. Geosci. Remote Sens.* **2021**, *60*, 5604816. [CrossRef]
37. Woo, S.; Park, J.; Lee, J.-Y.; Kweon, I.S. Cbam: Convolutional block attention module. In Proceedings of the European Conference on Computer Vision (ECCV), Munich, Germany, 8–14 September 2018; pp. 3–19.
38. Wang, D.; Chen, X.; Jiang, M.; Du, S.; Xu, B.; Wang, J. ADS-Net: An Attention-Based deeply supervised network for remote sensing image change detection. *Int. J. Appl. Earth Obs. Geoinf.* **2021**, *101*, 102348.
39. Zheng, H.; Gong, M.; Liu, T.; Jiang, F.; Zhan, T.; Lu, D.; Zhang, M. HFA-Net: High frequency attention siamese network for building change detection in VHR remote sensing images. *Pattern Recognit.* **2022**, *129*, 108717. [CrossRef]
40. Ren, W.; Wang, Z.; Xia, M.; Lin, H. MFINet: Multi-scale feature interaction network for change detection of high-resolution remote sensing images. *Remote Sens.* **2024**, *16*, 1269. [CrossRef]
41. Yu, X.; Fan, J.; Zhang, P.; Han, L.; Zhang, D.; Sun, G. Multi-scale convolutional neural network for remote sensing image change detection. In Proceedings of the Geoinformatics in Sustainable Ecosystem and Society: 7th International Conference, GSES 2019, and First International Conference, GeoAI 2019, Guangzhou, China, 21–25 November 2019; pp. 234–242.
42. Yu, X.; Fan, J.; Chen, J.; Zhang, P.; Zhou, Y.; Han, L. NestNet: A multiscale convolutional neural network for remote sensing image change detection. *Int. J. Remote Sens.* **2021**, *42*, 4898–4921. [CrossRef]
43. Ren, H.; Xia, M.; Weng, L.; Hu, K.; Lin, H. Dual attention-guided multiscale feature aggregation network for remote sensing image change detection. *IEEE J. Sel. Top. Appl. Earth Obs. Remote Sens.* **2024**, *17*, 4899–4916. [CrossRef]
44. Yin, H.; Weng, L.; Li, Y.; Xia, M.; Hu, K.; Lin, H.; Qian, M. Attention-guided siamese networks for change detection in high resolution remote sensing images. *Int. J. Appl. Earth Obs. Geoinf.* **2023**, *117*, 103206. [CrossRef]
45. Ding, Q.; Shao, Z.; Huang, X.; Altan, O. DSA-Net: A novel deeply supervised attention-guided network for building change detection in high-resolution remote sensing images. *Int. J. Appl. Earth Obs. Geoinf.* **2021**, *105*, 102591. [CrossRef]
46. Ji, S.; Wei, S.; Lu, M. Fully convolutional networks for multisource building extraction from an open aerial and satellite imagery data set. *IEEE Trans. Geosci. Remote Sens.* **2018**, *57*, 574–586. [CrossRef]
47. Shen, L.; Lu, Y.; Chen, H.; Wei, H.; Xie, D.; Yue, J.; Chen, R.; Lv, S.; Jiang, B. S2Looking: A Satellite Side-Looking Dataset for Building Change Detection. *Remote Sens.* **2021**, *13*, 5094. [CrossRef]
48. Lebedev, M.; Vizilter, Y.V.; Vygolov, O.; Knyaz, V.A.; Rubis, A.Y. Change detection in remote sensing images using conditional adversarial networks. *Int. Arch. Photogramm. Remote Sens. Spat. Inf. Sci.* **2018**, *42*, 565–571. [CrossRef]
49. Lei, T.; Geng, X.; Ning, H.; Lv, Z.; Gong, M.; Jin, Y.; Nandi, A.K. Ultralightweight Spatial–Spectral Feature Cooperation Network for Change Detection in Remote Sensing Images. *IEEE Trans. Geosci. Remote Sens.* **2023**, *61*, 4402114. [CrossRef]
50. Demir, S.; Toktamiş, Ö. On the adaptive Nadaraya-Watson kernel regression estimators. *Hacet. J. Math. Stat.* **2010**, *39*, 429–437.
51. Hofmann, T.; Schölkopf, B.; Smola, A.J. Kernel methods in machine learning. *Ann. Statist.* **2008**, *36*, 1171–1220. [CrossRef]
52. Li, Z.; Tang, C.; Liu, X.; Zhang, W.; Dou, J.; Wang, L.; Zomaya, A.Y. Lightweight remote sensing change detection with progressive feature aggregation and supervised attention. *IEEE Trans. Geosci. Remote Sens.* **2023**, *61*, 5602812. [CrossRef]
53. Ruby, U.; Yendapalli, V. Binary cross entropy with deep learning technique for image classification. *Int. J. Adv. Trends Comput. Sci. Eng.* **2020**, *9*. [CrossRef]
54. Milletari, F.; Navab, N.; Ahmadi, S.-A. V-Net: Fully convolutional neural networks for volumetric medical image segmentation. In Proceedings of the 2016 Fourth International Conference on 3D Vision (3DV), Stanford, CA, USA, 25–28 October 2016; pp. 565–571.
55. Han, C.; Wu, C.; Guo, H.; Hu, M.; Chen, H. HANet: A hierarchical attention network for change detection with bitemporal very-high-resolution remote sensing images. *IEEE J. Sel. Top. Appl. Earth Obs. Remote Sens.* **2023**, *16*, 3867–3878. [CrossRef]

56. Chen, H.; Qi, Z.; Shi, Z. Remote sensing image change detection with transformers. *IEEE Trans. Geosci. Remote Sens.* **2021**, *60*, 5900318. [CrossRef]
57. Fang, S.; Li, K.; Li, Z. Changer: Feature interaction is what you need for change detection. *IEEE Trans. Geosci. Remote Sens.* **2023**, *61*, 5610111. [CrossRef]
58. Bandara, W.G.C.; Patel, V.M. A transformer-based siamese network for change detection. In Proceedings of the IGARSS 2022—2022 IEEE International Geoscience and Remote Sensing Symposium, Kuala Lumpur, Malaysia, 17–22 July 2022; pp. 207–210.

remote sensing

MDPI

Article

Cross Attention Based Dual-Modality Collaboration for Hyperspectral Image and LiDAR Data Classification

Khanzada Muzammil Hussain [1,†], Keyun Zhao [1,†], Yang Zhou [1,†], Aamir Ali [2] and Ying Li [1,*]

[1] School of Computer Science, Northwestern Polytechnical University, Xi'an 710129, China; muz1@mail.nwpu.edu.cn (K.M.H.); kyzhao@mail.nwpu.edu.cn (K.Z.); zy4637@mail.nwpu.edu.cn (Y.Z.)
[2] School of Artificial Intelligence, Xidian University, Xi'an 710129, China; aamirali@stu.xidian.edu.cn
* Correspondence: lybyp@nwpu.edu.cn
† These authors contributed equally to this work.

Abstract

Advancements in satellite sensor technology have enabled access to diverse remote sensing (RS) data from multiple platforms. Hyperspectral Image (HSI) data offers rich spectral detail for material identification, while LiDAR captures high-resolution 3D structural information, making the two modalities naturally complementary. By fusing HSI and LiDAR, we can mitigate the limitations of each and improve tasks like land cover classification, vegetation analysis, and terrain mapping through more robust spectral–spatial feature representation. However, traditional multi-scale feature fusion models often struggle with aligning features effectively, which can lead to redundant outputs and diminished spatial clarity. To address these issues, we propose the Cross Attention Bridge for HSI and LiDAR (CAB-HL), a novel dual-path framework that employs a multi-stage cross-attention mechanism to guide the interaction between spectral and spatial features. In CAB-HL, features from each modality are refined across three progressive stages using cross-attention modules, which enhance contextual alignment while preserving the distinctive characteristics of each modality. These fused representations are subsequently integrated and passed through a lightweight classification head. Extensive experiments on three benchmark RS datasets demonstrate that CAB-HL consistently outperforms existing state-of-the-art models, confirm that CAB-HL consistently outperforms in learning deep joint representations for multimodal classification tasks.

Keywords: hyperspectral image; cross attention; LiDAR data; dual-modality fusion; remote sensing fusion; spatial spectral representation; deep learning

1. Introduction

In recent years, the integration of hyperspectral and LiDAR data has become critical for improving land cover classification tasks. Recent innovations, such as joint convolutional networks, have further refined this process, offering significant improvements in classification accuracy and robustness. This multimodal fusion has proven superior performance in applications such as land cover classification and vegetation analysis, particularly by enhancing the ability to distinguish between spectrally similar land cover classes [1]. Meanwhile, with the development of sensor technology, remote sensing imaging methods exhibit a diversified trend [2]. Despite the availability of extensive multi-source data, remote sensing data from each source captures just one or a restricting their ability to fully characterize complex terrestrial scenes, which fail to comprehensively depict the observed scenes [3].

with self-calibrated convolution to extract features from diverse receiving domains, thereby augmenting the model's capacity to represent multimodal data; ref. [21] proposed a novel Glt-Net that extracts multiscale local spatial features and performs an adaptive linear weighted fusion of multimodal features. Additionally, multiscale features are incorporated with spectral features of HS data; ref. [22] proposed a multiscale pseudo-Siamese network with attention mechanism (MA-PSNet) and provided a multiscale feature learning module to comprehensively extract features at various scales.

Despite the compensatory advantages of multiscale feature input over single scale characteristics, many challenges persist. Different land cover categories possess varying requirements across scales, indicating that the contribution of multiscale features to classification performance is not uniform. Consequently, it is essential to calibrate the respective weights of each characteristic, a laborious and inherently imprecise operation. Conversely, merely amalgamating multimodal features from various scales via cascading may intensify high-dimensional issues, while high-dimensional data can result in the curse of dimensionality in the model when labeled data is inadequate, potentially compromising the accuracy of the final classification of multimodal data. Consequently, the selection of suitable scale features from multiscale characteristics and the proper utilization of multiscale feature information to prevent overly high dimensionality are critical challenges that require immediate attention.

2.2. Attention Mechanism

The attention mechanism (AM) [23] has been a subject of investigation in neurology for some decades. The AM is an important part of human vision and has become a research hotspot in the past few years [24]. The human visual system does not perceive external objects in their entirety; instead, it selectively focuses on significant elements based on necessity, subsequently synthesizing these disparate components to create a comprehensive impression of the observed entities. The AM is critically significant since it enhances the performance and accuracy of DNNs [25]. The AM can provide varying weights to relevant components of each input, enabling the model to concentrate on extracting the most critical and significant content, thus facilitating more precise decisions. Simultaneously, the implementation of AM does not impose additional burdens on model storage and processing, which is a significant factor contributing to its widespread utilization [26]. The AM has been extensively utilized in visual tasks by augmenting the features; ref. [27] propose a hierarchical CNN and transformer architecture for combined categorization of hyperspectral imagery and LiDAR data. The approaches for attention can be found in [28].

The AM has been widely applied in the visual tasks by enhancing the ability of network to perceive the effective information and enables the model to focus on the pivotal parts of the features [29]. Woo et al. [30] proposed a convolutional block attention module (CBAM) that can enhance the features in both the channel and spatial domains. Dosovitskiy et al. [31] presented a VIT (Vision Transformer) based on the traditional transformer model and applied self-attention mechanism to extract image features, achieving results comparable to those of CNNs. The success of AM in computer vision has introduced new concepts to the field of RS image processing. Zhu et al.'s [32] proposed end-to-end residual spectral spatial attention network (RSSAN) utilizes CBAM to search for empty spectral features connected to target pixel points and assign different weights to them, resulting in more discriminative features and improved classification accuracy. Wang et al. [33] proposed a full-scale linked Unet network based on spatial–spectral joint perceptual attention for HS image and multispectral image fusion.

2.3. Hyperspectral and LiDAR Fusion Classification

The integration of LiDAR and hyperspectral data has seen numerous advancements with deep learning models, such as CNNs, that effectively extract spatial and spectral features [34]. Furthermore, ref. [14] introduced a two-branch multiscale network that enhances spectral–spatial feature extraction, providing a solid foundation for multimodal classification tasks. In recent years, many researchers combined HSI with LiDAR images for classification. Typical networks are dual-branch CNN [34] and HRWN (Hyperspectral and LiDAR Wide Network). The former designs a unique network, which has two branches, to extract HSI features and LiDAR image features, respectively. Specifically, 2D convolution structure and 1D convolution are applied in HSI feature extraction to capture spectral and spatial features simultaneously. Also, a cascade block is utilized in LiDAR feature extraction for feature reusing. Finally, the features are stacked and classified in the classifier. Based on the two-branch network, HRWN applies the pixel affinity approach to the LiDAR branch. In addition, a hierarchical random walk module is designed in the classifier to fuse the features of different sources and obtain more significant classification results. Moreover the FusAtNet [35] applies the attention mechanism for land-cover classification. In the feature extraction part, the self-attention method is adopted to collect HSI and LiDAR features, and then this network links multimodal data with cross-attention. The coupled CNN [36] also achieves satisfactory outcomes. This network adopts the approach of sharing parameters when extracting features from different sources, greatly reducing the number of operation parameters, and designs a decision fusion module to better adapt to the features of multisource data. Different from the above methods, the proposed method adopts an exceptional feature fusion approach and achieves a better classification performance.

3. Methodology

3.1. Overall Architecture

The overall architecture of the proposed CAB-HL model is shown in Figure 1. The proposed framework uses both HSI and LiDAR data for classification in a dual-modality manner. The HSI data was first transformed into a data cube through PCA dimensionality reduction and fed through multipath 3D convolutional layers to extract spectral–spatial features. To extract spatial features effectively, LiDAR data is passed through multipath depthwise separable 2D convolutional layers. The extracted features from both modalities are then fused using CAM in two stages to enable feature matching and interaction. The last fused features are then classified to produce accurate land-cover maps to take advantage of the synergistic relationship between HSI and LiDAR, integrating hyperspectral imaging (HSI) and LiDAR modalities. The model leverages complementary spatial and spectral features from HSI and spatial features from LiDAR to achieve robust classification. The pipeline consists of the following steps:

- HSI Feature Extraction: A multipath 3D convolutional block is used to extract spectral–spatial features from the HSI data.
- LiDAR Feature Extraction: A multipath depthwise 2D convolutional block processes the LiDAR data to extract spatial features at multiple scales
- Cross-Attention Fusion: The extracted features from HSI and LiDAR are fused using a cross-attention mechanism in two stages.
- Classification: The fused features are passed through fully connected layers and a softmax activation function to generate class predictions.

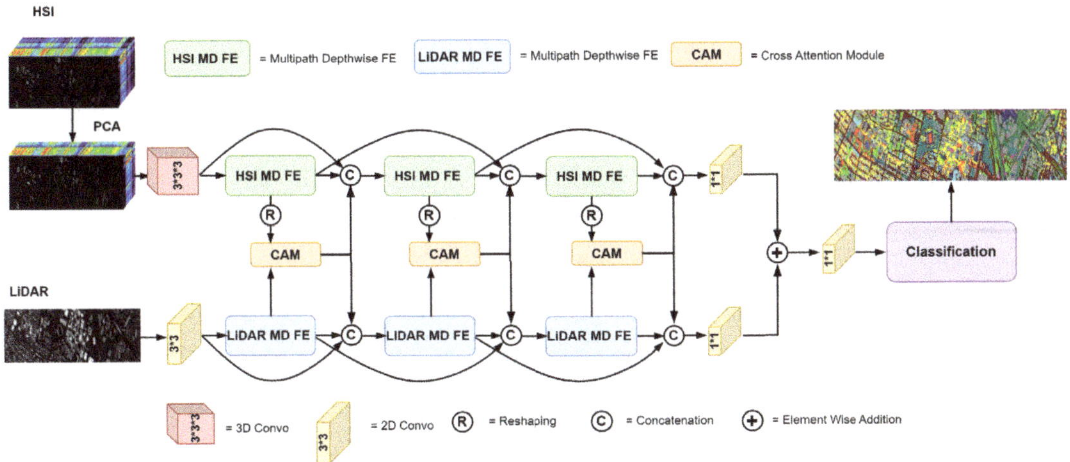

Figure 1. Architecture of the proposed cross-attention bridge for the HSI and LiDAR (CAB-HL) models.

3.2. Multipath Convolutional Blocks (CAB-HL)

The HSI feature extraction module employs multipath 3D convolutional layers to extract spectral–spatial features at multiple scales, as illustrated in Figure 2. The block utilizes three parallel pathways to record multi-scale spectral–spatial characteristics. Each pathway initiates with a Conv3D layer, employing varying kernel sizes ($7 \times 7 \times 7, 5 \times 5 \times 5$, and $3 \times 3 \times 3$), generating feature maps with channel dimensions of 8, 16, and 32, correspondingly. The Conv3D layers with $1 \times 1 \times 1$ kernels further enhance these features, augmenting the channels to 16, 32, and 64 for improved feature representations. The outputs from all pathways are concatenated and integrated using a Conv3D layer with a $3 \times 3 \times 3$ kernel, resulting in a final output with b channels. A skip connection directly incorporates the block's input into the output via element-wise summation, facilitating robust spectral–spatial feature learning and fast gradient propagation. The methodology includes the following:

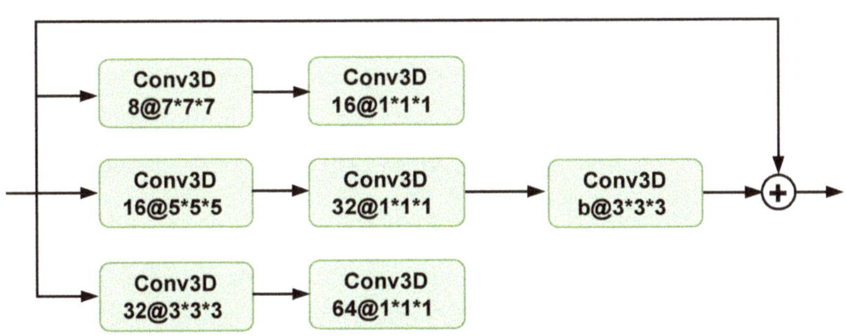

Figure 2. Structure of the multipath 3D convolutional block for HSI feature extraction in the CAB-HL model.

- Multi-Scale Convolutions: Different kernel sizes ($7 \times 7 \times 7, 5 \times 5 \times 5, 3 \times 3 \times 3$) are applied to capture features at varying scales.

$$\mathbf{F}_p = \text{Conv3D}_{k_p \times k_p \times k_p}(\mathbf{X}_{\text{HSI}}), \quad p \in \{1,2,3\} \tag{1}$$

- Channel Refinement: Pointwise convolutions refine the extracted features by reducing the number of channels:

$$\mathbf{F}'_p = \text{Conv3D}_{1\times1\times1}(\mathbf{F}_p). \tag{2}$$

- Feature Fusion and Skip Connections: The refined features are concatenated and passed through another 3D convolutional layer. A skip connection adds the input back to the processed features:

$$\mathbf{F}_{\text{Final}} = \text{Conv3D}_{3\times3\times3}(\text{Concat}(\mathbf{F}'_1, \mathbf{F}'_2, \mathbf{F}'_3)) + \mathbf{X}_{\text{HSI}}. \tag{3}$$

The LiDAR feature extraction module uses multipath depthwise convolutional blocks, as depicted in Figure 3. The block consists of three parallel paths, with Conv2D layers using different kernel sizes ($7 \times 7, 5 \times 5$, and 3×3) to extract multi-scale spatial features, producing feature maps with 8, 16, and 32 channels, respectively. Each pathway incorporates a depthwise separable Conv2D (3×3) and a 1×1 Conv2D to enhance the computing efficiency and optimize features. The outputs are concatenated and integrated via a Conv2D ($3 \times 3 \times 3$) layer, followed by a skip connection to enhance feature learning and gradient propagation. The methodology includes the following:

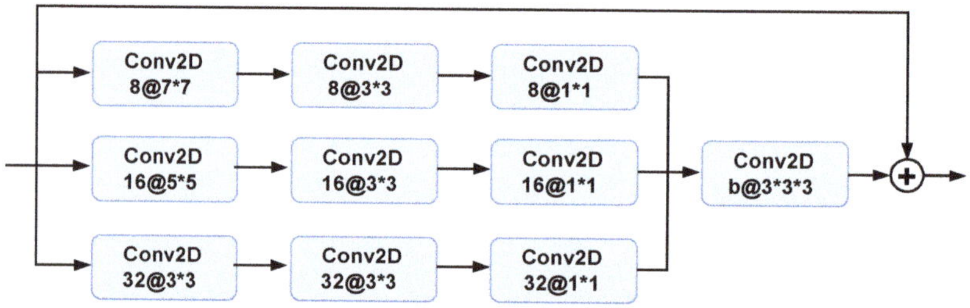

Figure 3. Structure of the multipath depthwise convolutional block for LiDAR feature extraction in the CAB-HL model.

- Multi-Scale Convolutions: Convolutions with kernel sizes ($7 \times 7, 5 \times 5, 3 \times 3$) extract features at different spatial scales:

$$\mathbf{F}_p = \text{Conv2D}_{k_p\times k_p}(\mathbf{X}_{\text{LiDAR}}), \quad p \in \{1,2,3\}. \tag{4}$$

- Depthwise Separable Convolutions: Depthwise convolutions followed by pointwise convolutions refine the spatial features:

$$\mathbf{F}'_p = \text{DepthwiseConv2D}_{3\times3}(\mathbf{F}_p) \tag{5}$$

$$\mathbf{F}''_p = \text{Conv2D}_{1\times1}(\mathbf{F}'_p). \tag{6}$$

- Feature Fusion and Skip Connections: The refined features are concatenated and processed further, with the input added back to preserve the original information:

$$\mathbf{F}_{\text{Final}} = \text{Conv2D}_{3\times3\times3}(\text{Concat}(\mathbf{F}''_1, \mathbf{F}''_2, \mathbf{F}''_3)) + \mathbf{X}_{\text{LiDAR}}. \tag{7}$$

3.3. Cross-Attention Mechanism

The CAM serves as the core of the proposed CAB-HL framework, facilitating effective feature fusion between HSI data and LiDAR data. HSI data, which are inherently 3D, provide detailed spectral–spatial information, while LiDAR data, which are primarily 2D, focus on spatial elevation details. CAM is designed to align and integrate these heterogeneous features by dynamically adjusting attention weights between the modalities, ensuring effective information exchange.

The architecture of CAM, shown in Figure 4, aligns and fuses the HSI and LiDAR features in two stages. For each stage k, the fusion process is defined as follows:

$$\mathbf{F}_{\text{Cross}}^{(k)} = \text{CAM}(\mathbf{F}_{\text{HSI}}^{(k)}, \mathbf{F}_{\text{LiDAR}}^{(k)}), \quad k \in \{1,2,3\} \tag{8}$$

We first reshape each input so that the spatial dimensions are flattened:

$$\mathbf{F}'_{HSI} = \text{reshape}(\mathbf{F}_{HSI}) \in \mathbb{R}^{B\times(HW)\times C_{\text{HSI}}} \tag{9}$$

$$\mathbf{F}'_{LiDAR} = \text{reshape}(\mathbf{F}_{LiDAR}) \in \mathbb{R}^{B\times(HW)\times C_{\text{LiDAR}}} \tag{10}$$

The HSI input tensor is denoted as $\mathbf{F}_{HSI} \in \mathbb{R}^{B\times C_{\text{HSI}}\times H\times W}$, and the LiDAR input tensor is denoted as $\mathbf{F}_{LiDAR} \in \mathbb{R}^{B\times C_{\text{LiDAR}}\times H\times W}$.

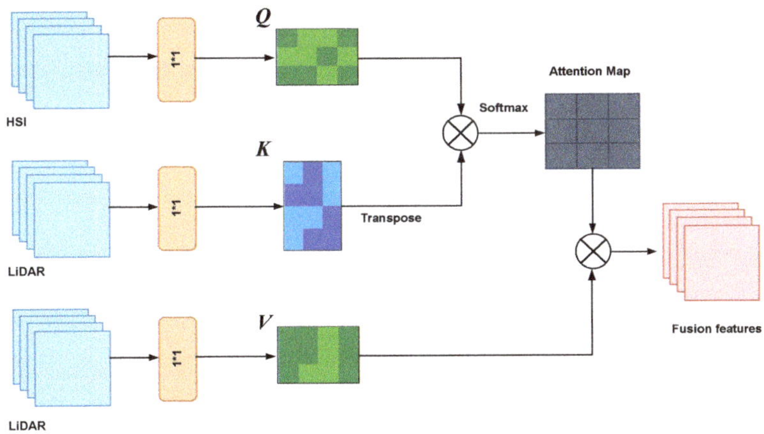

Figure 4. Cross-attention module.

Here, B is the batch size, C_{HSI} and C_{LiDAR} are the channel dimensions of the respective modalities, while H and W are the spatial dimensions, where (HW) is the sequence length. In the computational framework of CAM, the query serves as the core information for generating attention scores. When processing joint HSI and LiDAR datasets, we posit that the spectral features derived from HSI exhibit superior discriminative power compared to spatial and elevation features, thus warranting higher prioritization. Spectral information inherently captures fine-grained physical properties and spectral responses of ground objects, making it especially effective for discriminative tasks, such as land-cover classification and change detection. In contrast, while the spatial and elevation data provided by LiDAR play a critical role in characterizing object morphology and structural attributes, their discriminative capacity remains relatively limited. We project $\mathbf{F}'_{HSI}$ to queries and $\mathbf{F}'_{LiDAR}$ to keys and values, respectively:

$$\mathbf{Q} = \mathbf{F}'_{HSI} \times W_Q \tag{11}$$

$$\mathbf{K} = \mathbf{F}'_{LiDAR} \times W_K \tag{12}$$

$$\mathbf{V} = \mathbf{F}'_{LiDAR} \times W_V \tag{13}$$

$$\textbf{Attention} = \text{Softmax}(\frac{\mathbf{Q} \times \mathbf{K}^T}{\sqrt{k}})\mathbf{V} \tag{14}$$

$$\text{CAM}(\mathbf{F}_{HSI}, \mathbf{F}_{LiDAR}) = \text{Cat}(\mathbf{Attention}^{(\text{h})}) \times \mathbf{W}_{\text{O}} \tag{15}$$

where W_Q, W_K, and W_V are the projection matrices for the three spaces, respectively. Q represents the queries, K represents the keys, V represents the values, h represents the number of heads, $Attention^{(h)}$ represents the output of the h-th head, and W_O represents the output transform matrix.

3.4. Classification and Optimization

The fused features from the cross-attention mechanism are passed through fully connected layers for classification. A softmax activation function generates the final class probabilities:

$$\mathbf{Y} = \text{Softmax}(\text{FC}(\mathbf{F}^{(2)}_{\text{Cross}})) \tag{16}$$

To optimize the CAB-HL model, the cross-entropy loss is minimized:

$$\mathcal{L} = -\sum_{i=1}^{C} y_i \log(\hat{y}_i) \tag{17}$$

where y_i is the ground truth label, and $\hat{y}_i$ is the predicted probability for class i. An Adam optimizer is employed for training.

3.5. Algorithm

The overall training strategy of the CAB-HL framework is outlined in Algorithm 1. This algorithm encapsulates the end-to-end process, including preprocessing, feature extraction, cross-attention fusion, and final classification. Equations (1)–(17) correspond to key steps for spectral–spatial integration of HSI and LiDAR data. Refer to Algorithm 1 for the detailed procedural steps.

Algorithm 1 Multimodal classification pipeline with cross-attention

Require: HSI data X_{HSI}, LiDAR data X_{LiDAR}
Ensure: Classified results Y
Preprocess Input Data
Apply PCA on X_{HSI} for dimensionality reduction.
Normalize LiDAR data X_{LiDAR}.
Feature Extraction
Extract features with 3×3 convolutions:

$$F_{\text{HSI}} = \text{Conv3D}_{3\times3\times3}(X_{\text{HSI}}), \quad F_{\text{LiDAR}} = \text{Conv2D}_{3\times3}(X_{\text{LiDAR}})$$

Cross-Attention Mechanism (CAM)
Generate Query (Q), Key (K), and Value (V) from HSI and LiDAR features:

$$\text{Attention Map} = \text{Softmax}(Q \cdot K^{\top}) \; F_{\text{fused}} = \text{Attention Map} \cdot V$$

Feature Fusion
Concatenate and reshape fused features:

$$F_{\text{final}} = \text{Concat}(F_{\text{HSI}}, F_{\text{LiDAR}})$$

Apply element-wise addition:

$$F_{\text{final}} = F_{\text{fused}} + F_{\text{previous}}$$

Final Refinement and Classification
Apply 1×1 convolutions and softmax:

$$Y = \text{Softmax}(\text{FC}(F_{\text{final}}))$$

return Y

4. Experimental Results

4.1. Datasets

To assess the effectiveness of the proposed approach, three publicly accessible multi-sensor remote sensing image classification datasets are utilized as experimental datasets: the Houston2013 dataset, the Trento dataset, and the Augsburg dataset. Comprehensive parameters are shown in Table 1.

Table 1. Dataset description.

Dataset	Houston2013 [37]		Trento [11]		Augsburg [38]	
Location	Houston, Texas, USA		Trento, Italy		Augsburg, Germany	
Sensor Type	HSI	LiDAR	HSI	LiDAR	HSI	LiDAR
Image Size	349 × 1905	349 × 1905	600 × 166	600 × 166	332 × 485	332 × 485
Spatial Resolution	2.5 m	2.5 m	1 m	1 m	30 m	30 m
Number of Bands	144	1	63	1	180	1
Wavelength Range	0.38–1.05 m	/	0.42–0.99 m	/	0.4–2.5 m	/
Sensor Name	CASI-1500	/	AISA Eagle	Optech ALTM 3100EA	HySpex	DLR-3 K

Augsburg dataset: The Augsburg dataset consists of paired HSI and LiDAR DSM data, where the HSI data was collected using the HySpex sensor, and the LiDAR DSM data was obtained with the DLR-3 K sensor. This dataset was acquired over Augsburg, Germany, which is an urban environment. The spatial dimensions of the Augsburg dataset are 332 × 485, with a spatial resolution of approximately 30 m. The HSI data includes 180 spectral bands, spanning the wavelength range of 0.4 to 2.5 μm. The LiDAR DSM data provides 3D elevation information for surface features. The detailed number of samples for each category is listed in Table 2.

Houston2013 dataset: The Houston2013 dataset was captured using the ITERS CASI-1500 sensor over the University of Houston campus and its surrounding urban area in Houston, Texas, USA, in 2012. This dataset includes both HSI and LiDAR DSM data. The spatial dimensions of the dataset are 349 × 1905, with a spatial resolution of approximately 2.5 m. The HSI data consists of 144 spectral bands, covering the wavelength range from 380 to 1050 nm. The LiDAR data provides elevation information for ground features. The land cover is categorized into 15 types: Healthy grass, Stressed grass, Synthetic grass, Trees, Soil, Water, Residential, Commercial, Road, Highway, Railway, Parking Lot 1, Parking Lot 2, Tennis Court, and Running Track. The sample counts for each class are listed in Table 3.

Trento Dataset: The Trento dataset is an HSI-LiDAR pair dataset, where the HSI data were collected by an AISA Eagle sensor, and the LiDAR digital surface model (DSM) data were acquired by an Optech ALTM 3100EA sensor. The dataset is captured over a rural area south of the city of Trento, Italy. The Trento dataset has a spatial dimension of 166 × 600 with a spatial resolution of approximately 1 m. The HSI data in the Trento dataset consists of 63 spectral bands, with wavelengths ranging from 420 to 990 nm. The LiDAR DSM data provides elevation information of ground features. The land cover is classified into six categories: Apple trees, Buildings, Ground, Woods, Vineyard, and Roads. The number of samples for each category is provided in Table 4.

Table 2. Classification accuracy description with Augsburg dataset.

No.	Class (Train/Test)	MDL-RS [13]	EndNet [11]	CALC [39]	CCR-Net [40]	ExViT [41]	DHViT [42]	SAL2RN [43]	MS2CANet [44]	DSHF [45]	Proposed
1	Forest (146/13361)	84.97	89.70	94.16	93.47	91.83	90.45	96.58	96.40	97.60	98.74
2	Residential-Area (264/30065)	91.56	86.75	95.32	96.86	95.38	90.87	97.69	97.90	92.94	98.24
3	Industrial-Area (21/3830)	8.17	24.26	86.18	82.56	43.32	61.20	53.44	48.79	87.13	78.09
4	Low-Plants (248/36609)	78.07	76.77	95.57	84.45	91.13	82.82	92.84	96.47	96.38	97.59
5	Allotment (52/523)	26.00	34.42	0.00	44.36	41.11	21.80	38.62	44.55	64.05	96.94
6	Commercial-Area (7/1638)	2.14	9.46	6.05	0.00	26.01	23.50	15.14	13.43	2.50	11.9
7	Water (23/1507)	36.30	46.78	55.96	40.48	42.07	7.43	12.47	49.90	48.77	58.33
	OA% (761/77533)	79.11	78.25	91.46	87.82	87.82	83.06	89.85	91.65	91.67	94.5
	AA%	46.74	52.29	61.89	63.17	61.41	54.01	58.11	63.92	69.91	77.12
	Kappa×100	67.52	68.11	88.04	82.48	82.44	75.91	85.26	88.22	88.12	92.1

Table 3. Classification accuracy description with Houston2013 dataset.

No.	Class (Train/Test)	MDL-RS [13]	EndNet [11]	CALC [39]	CCR-Net [40]	ExViT [41]	DHViT [42]	SAL2RN [43]	MS2CANet [44]	DSHF [45]	Proposed
1	Health grass (198/1053)	83.10	96.24	82.24	83.00	91.55	81.01	82.71	82.62	97.44	99.62
2	Stressed grass (190/1064)	81.58	93.46	83.93	84.87	85.15	85.15	85.15	82.04	85.15	99.44
3	Synthetic grass (192/505)	100.00	96.44	93.47	100	98.61	93.47	100.00	92.67	97.62	100
4	Trees (188/1056)	99.72	98.51	98.86	92.14	98.61	80.40	92.80	98.67	100	99.91
5	Soil (186/1056)	99.81	96.25	99.72	99.81	100.00	99.53	100.00	100.00	100	100
6	Water (182/143)	95.10	96.53	98.60	95.80	98.60	95.80	93.00	100.00	100	100
7	Residential (196/1072)	90.02	98.03	90.21	95.34	88.90	92.16	94.86	94.30	88.34	98.6
8	Commercial (191/1053)	87.94	95.53	81.58	81.39	93.35	92.21	90.97	89.74	82.15	96.87
9	Road (193/1059)	81.59	79.80	84.99	84.14	89.52	81.78	94.14	93.20	89.61	98.21
10	Highway (191/1036)	86.68	77.53	68.15	63.22	65.54	68.73	71.42	82.04	99.32	100
11	Railway (181/1054)	89.37	86.40	95.16	90.32	95.83	79.60	91.93	98.29	80.17	100
12	Parking lot 1 (192/104)	85.69	87.02	93.56	93.08	90.39	94.81	97.79	94.90	98.75	99.9
13	Parking lot 2 (184/285)	83.16	79.64	87.37	88.42	90.53	88.42	84.21	92.28	92.98	100
14	Tennis court (181/247)	100.00	98.71	99.60	96.36	99.60	100.00	99.59	87.85	100	100
15	Running track (187/473)	98.73	99.38	99.58	99.37	89.85	71.25	100.00	99.78	100	100
	OA% (2832/12197)	89.60	90.77	88.91	88.15	90.62	85.82	91.08	91.99	92.88	99.35
	AA%	90.83	91.96	90.47	89.89	91.76	86.95	91.90	92.56	94.10	99.5
	Kappa×100	88.75	89.98	87.98	87.19	89.83	84.61	90.32	91.37	92.27	99.3

Table 4. Classification accuracy description with Trento dataset.

No.	Class (Train/Test)	MDL-RS [13]	EndNet [11]	CALC [39]	CCR-Net [40]	ExViT [41]	DHViT [42]	SAL2RN [43]	MS2CANet [44]	DSHF [45]	Proposed
1	Apple trees (129/3905)	88.58	88.19	97.26	100.00	99.56	98.36	99.74	99.84	99.49	99.95
2	Building (125/2778)	95.86	98.49	100.00	98.88	98.13	99.06	96.76	98.52	98.74	99.21
3	Ground (105/374)	93.58	95.19	89.57	79.68	76.47	67.65	83.68	86.36	99.73	97.59
4	Woods (154/8969)	99.22	99.30	100.00	100.00	100.00	100.00	99.21	99.98	100	99.99
5	Vineyard (184/10317)	83.82	91.96	99.75	94.79	99.93	98.89	99.97	100.00	100	100
6	Roads (122/3052)	76.51	90.14	87.45	88.07	93.84	87.98	88.99	92.92	93.45	98.2
	OA% (819/29395)	90.65	94.17	98.16	96.57	98.80	98.00	98.06	98.92	99.13	99.7
	AA%	89.60	93.88	95.68	93.57	94.66	92.16	94.72	96.27	98.57	99.16
	Kappa×100	86.28	92.22	97.48	95.43	98.39	97.31	97.40	98.56	98.83	99.59

4.2. Parameter Tuning

In this article, we use Python 3.10 to create our programs and PyTorch 2.1.2 to implement the convolutional neural network component. Every test was carried out on a PC running Windows 10, an Intel Core i7-10870 h, and a GeForce RTX 4060ti with Max-Q Design.

4.3. Parameter Setting

The experiments use multiple batch sizes of 8, 16, 32, 48, and 64; encompass 150 epochs; and employ the cross-entropy loss function. The proposed CAB-HL model is implemented using the PyTorch deep learning framework, with all program development conducted in Python 3.10. The experiments are executed on a workstation configured with an Intel Core i5-13490F CPU, 96 GB of RAM, and an NVIDIA GeForce RTX 4060 Ti GPU, operating under the Windows 10 environment. To ensure objective and reproducible performance evaluation, three commonly adopted metrics are employed: overall accuracy (OA), average accuracy (AA), and the Kappa coefficient. These metrics facilitate a comprehensive comparison between the predicted classification results and the corresponding ground truth maps across all benchmark datasets.

4.4. Effect of Patch Size and PCA Components on OA

In the proposed method, the CAB-HL component applies CNN as its backbone. The feature extraction efficacy of CNNs is considerably affected by the dimensions of the input patches. Smaller patch sizes emphasize intricate features in the image, including texture and edges; nevertheless, overly diminutive patches may neglect contextual information. On the other hand, greater neighborhood patch sizes can incorporate rich data from nearby pixels, which improves the ability to capture contextual associations. Excessively large patches, however, could mask crucial local information. Thus, choosing the neighborhood patch size necessitates striking a balance between local detail preservation and information integration. Patch and PCA comparison has been shown in Figure 5.

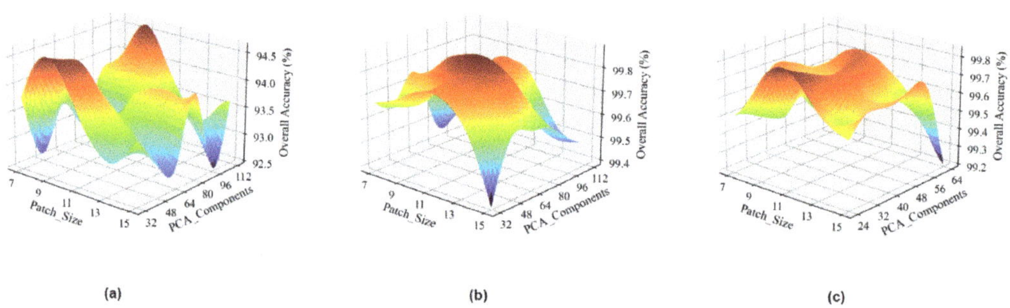

Figure 5. Comparison of different models various parameters: (**a**) Augsburg. (**b**) Houston2013. (**c**) Trento.

4.5. Learning-Rate Comparison

The learning rate is a crucial hyperparameter in the deep learning process. The main goal is to control the network's mass by calculating and implementing the gradient of the loss function. An excessively high learning rate may cause parameter updates to exceed the optimal value. This consequently causes variations in the loss function value throughout parameter tuning, ultimately leading to the failure of network convergence. A learning rate that is excessively low may cause the network parameters to become ensnared in a high local minimum during the parameter search, hindering the exploration of superior local minima that are more likely to be global.

4.6. Comparison and Analysis of Classification Performance

The classification efficacy of the proposed CAB-HL model is evaluated utilizing three standard benchmark datasets: Augsburg, Trento, and Houston2013, in comparison to nine cutting-edge models: MDL-RS [13], EndNet [11], CALC [39], CCR-Net [40], ExViT [41], DHViT [42], SAL2RN [43], MS2CANet [44], and DSHF [45]. The assessment is conducted utilizing OA, AA, and the Kappa Coefficient, in addition to class-specific accuracy evaluations. Our proposed CAB-HL model consistently surpasses all rival method, demonstrating substantial enhancements across all datasets. The model attains OA, AA, and Kappa coefficients, illustrating its efficacy in managing intricate spectral–spatial fluctuations. The classification maps (Figures 6–8) visibly validate the enhanced efficacy of CAB-HL, demonstrating fewer classification errors and superior boundary delineation relative to alternative models. In Figures 6–8, the black pixels in the ground truth label image represent background or unlabeled regions, which are intentionally excluded from both training and evaluation. This visualization follows established practices in recent benchmark studies, such as S3F2Net [46], DSHFNet [45] and AM3Net [47], ensuring consistency and fairness in comparative analysis. Among the competing methodologies, DSHF ranks as the second-best performer, succeeded by MS2CANet and SAL2RN, whereas models like CCR-Net, DHViT, and MDL-RS demonstrate inferior classification performance due to their inadequacy in effectively distinguishing spectrally identical land-cover categories. A comprehensive analysis of classification outcomes for each dataset is presented below:

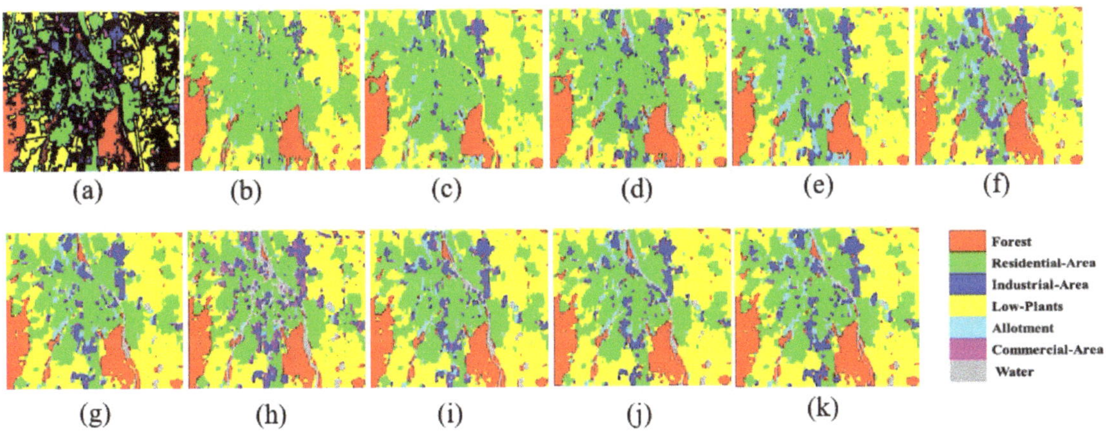

Figure 6. Classification maps utilizing several methodologies for the Augsburg dataset: (**a**) Ground-truth map; (**b**) MDL-RS (89.60%); (**c**) CALC (98.16%); (**d**) CCR-Net (88.15%); (**e**) EndNet (88.52%); (**f**) ExViT (90.62%); (**g**) DHViT (85.82%); (**h**) Sal2RN (91.08%); (**i**) MS2CANet (91.99%); (**j**) DSHF (92.88%); (**k**) Proposed (94.5%).

4.6.1. Classification Performance on the Augsburg Dataset

The Augsburg dataset comprises natural and artificial land cover types, presenting difficulties due to the existence of spectrally analogous urban structures and vegetation. Table 2 delineates the categorization performance of each model.

- CAB-HL achieved the highest accuracy, with an OA of 94.5%, AA of 77.12%, and a Kappa coefficient of 92.1%.
- DSHF follows as the second-best model with an OA of 92.88%, benefiting from its spectral–spatial fusion capability but struggling with shadowed urban areas.
- MS2CANet (91.67%) and SAL2RN (89.85%) perform relatively well but fail to fully exploit spatial dependencies in the dataset.

- MDL-RS, EndNet, and DHViT exhibit a lower classification accuracy, particularly in urban areas where mixed pixels reduce their effectiveness.

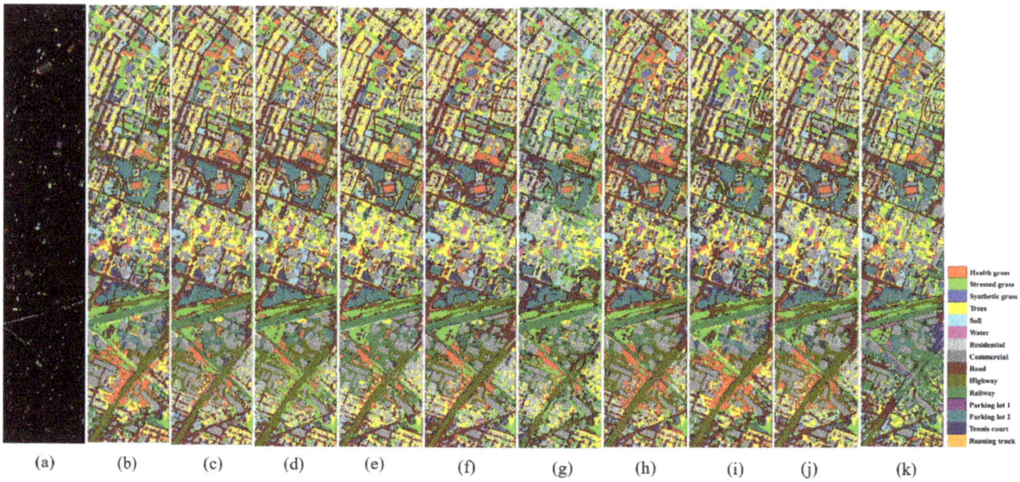

Figure 7. Classification maps utilizing several methodologies for the Houston2013 dataset: (**a**) Ground-truth map; (**b**) MDL-RS (89.60%); (**c**) CALC (98.16%); (**d**) CCR-Net (88.15%); (**e**) EndNet (88.52%); (**f**) ExViT (90.62%); (**g**) DHViT (85.82%); (**h**) Sal2RN (91.08%); (**i**) MS2CANet (91.99%); (**j**) DSHF (92.88%); (**k**) Proposed (99.35%).

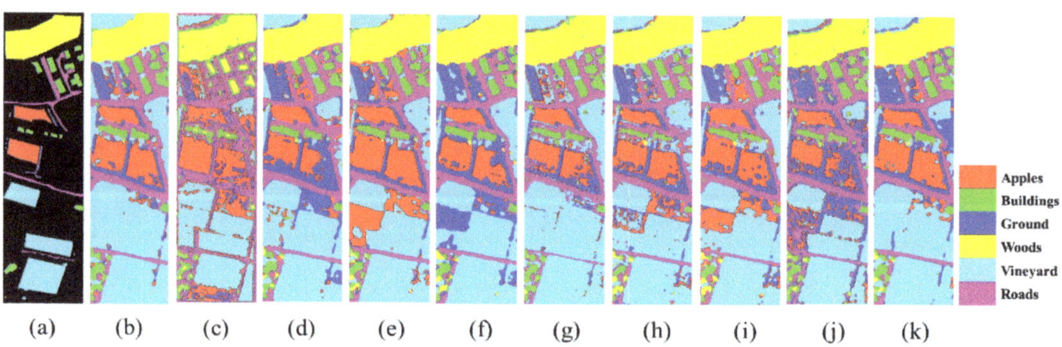

Figure 8. Classification maps utilizing several methodologies for the Trento dataset: (**a**) Ground-truth map; (**b**) MDL-RS (89.60%); (**c**) CALC (98.16%); (**d**) CCR-Net (88.15%); (**e**) EndNet (88.52%); (**f**) ExViT (90.62%); (**g**) DHViT (85.82%); (**h**) Sal2RN (91.08%); (**i**) MS2CANet (91.99%); (**j**) DSHF (92.88%); (**k**) Proposed (99.7%).

The classification maps in Figure 6 provide a visual confirmation of the superior performance of CAB-HL, where misclassification in urban areas is significantly reduced compared to other models. Competing models exhibit difficulty in differentiating between vegetative and constructed environments, whereas CAB-HL provides more accurate boundary delineation.

4.6.2. Classification Performance on the Houston2013 Dataset

The Houston2013 dataset is widely recognized in hyperspectral image classification research due to its diverse set of urban and vegetation classes, making it a highly challenging benchmark. The composition includes intricate urban formations, aquatic environments, and flora, necessitating advanced spectral–spatial learning for optimal categorization precision.

- CAB-HL markedly surpasses all alternative approaches, attaining OA of 99.35%, an AA of 99.5%, and a Kappa coefficient of 99.3.
- DSHF achieved an overall accuracy of 92.88%, ranking second in performance, although it demonstrates misclassification in metropolitan areas characterized by significant spectral mixing.
- MS2CANet (91.99%) and SAL2RN (91.08%) yield robust findings; nevertheless, they do not sustain classification consistency across various land cover types.
- MDL-RS and EndNet exhibit modest performance; nevertheless, their classification maps indicate increased noise and misclassification in vegetative areas.
- CCR-Net and DHViT demonstrate the poorest performance, especially in differentiating residential, business, and road networks due to spectral overlap.

Figure 7 illustrates classification maps that underscore the superior performance of CAB-HL, demonstrating more precise and refined separation of urban and vegetation areas relative to rival models. The CAB-HL approach significantly mitigates misclassification in aquatic and urban regions, hence enhancing accuracy in land cover classification.

4.6.3. Classification Performance on the Trento Dataset

The Trento dataset predominantly consists of agricultural and urban areas, posing difficulties due to the significant spectral resemblance among various land cover categories, especially in vineyards and roadways.

- CAB-HL attains an OA of 99.7%, an AA of 99.6%, and a Kappa coefficient of 99.59, illustrating its exceptional proficiency in identifying agricultural and urban areas.
- DSHF (98.3%) and MS2CANet (97.9%) demonstrate competitive efficacy; nevertheless, they inadequately capture fine-grained spatial information, resulting in misclassification within mixed land cover areas.
- SAL2RN (97.6%) and CCR-Net (96.4%) exhibit difficulty in distinguishing between vineyard and ground classes, thus affecting their total classification accuracy.
- DHViT and ExViT demonstrate the poorest performance, mostly because to their constrained capacity to capture long-range dependencies in agricultural regions.

Figure 8 demonstrates that the classification map produced by CAB-HL closely corresponds with the ground-truth data, whereas alternative approaches exhibit significant classification noise. Competing models demonstrate misclassification at field boundaries and road networks, but CAB-HL effectively maintains spatial continuity in agricultural areas. In all three datasets (Augsburg, Trento, and Houston2013), our proposed CAB-HL model consistently surpasses current state-of-the-art approaches regarding OA, AA, and Kappa measures. The enhancements in classification accuracy are due to CAB-HL's sophisticated spectral–spatial feature extraction and hierarchical learning methodology, which adeptly catches intricate nuances and complex land cover patterns.

The classification maps (Figures 6–8) further substantiate the efficacy of our approach, demonstrating a notable decrease in misclassification errors relative to alternative methods. Specifically, in densely populated metropolitan regions and agricultural environments, CAB-HL exhibits distinct benefits in maintaining spatial coherence and minimizing categorization noise.

These findings highlight the capability of CAB-HL as a formidable hyperspectral image classification framework, facilitating enhanced land cover mapping applications in urban planning, agriculture, and environmental monitoring.

4.7. Multiscale Input Patch Size Comparison

The determination of the optimal patch size is critical in picture categorization, since a large patch size incorporates superfluous information, but a small patch size may obscure essential details. In multiscale feature inputs, the patch size is crucial, as varying patch sizes produce distinct imaging outcomes. Figure 7 depicts the effect of input patch sizes λ varying from 2 to 10. The findings indicate that 8 is the ideal parameter for the Houston2013 dataset, whereas 6 is optimal for the other two datasets. This variation is ascribed to the varying spatial scale dimensions among the various datasets.

4.8. Learning-Rate Comparison

The learning rate is a crucial hyperparameter in the deep learning process (Figure 6). The main goal is to control the network's mass by calculating and implementing the gradient of the loss function. An excessively high learning rate may cause parameter updates to exceed the optimal value. This consequently causes variations in the loss function value throughout parameter tuning, ultimately leading to the failure of network convergence. A learning rate that is excessively low may cause the network parameters to become ensnared in a high local minimum during the parameter search, hindering the exploration of superior local minima that are more likely to be global. The classification results with learning rates varying from 0.001 to 0.0001. The findings indicate that 0.0001 is the best parameter for three datasets.

5. Ablation Study: Evaluating the Impact of Key Components in the CAB-HL Model

In this ablation study, we examine various iterations and combinations of input modalities and modules in order to assess the efficacy of the cross attention module (CAM) in the CAB-HL model. Three benchmark datasets, Houston2013, Augsburg, and Trento, were used in the trials to evaluate how each component affects the model performance. The findings for various configurations, such as HSI, LiDAR, and CAMs, are displayed in Table 5, along with the OA, AA, and Kappa coefficient.

The introduction of the cross attention module (CAM) significantly improves the performance of the CAB-HL model across all datasets. The HSI + LiDAR + CAM configuration yields the maximum overall accuracy (OA) of 99.91 percent in the Trento dataset, 99.89 percent in Houston2013, and 99.91 percent in Augsburg. This signifies that the CAM proficiently integrates spatial and spectral data from both HSI and LiDAR, enhancing the model's capacity to capture complementing attributes. The improvement in performance is due to the model's capacity to dynamically focus on the most informative information from both modalities, hence enhancing the overall representation.

Table 5. Ablation Study.

Module			Metrics	Datasets		
HSI	LiDAR	CAM		Houston2013	Augsburg	Trento
√	×	×	OA (%)	98.98	93.79	98.88
			AA (%)	99.22	75.44	98.19
			Kappa (%)	98.9	91.06	98.5
√	√	×	OA (%)	99.57	94.50	99.63
			AA (%)	99.67	77.12	99.02
			Kappa (%)	99.54	92.10	99.5
√	×	√	OA (%)	99.76	93.93	99.63
			AA (%)	99.81	79.27	99.43
			Kappa (%)	99.74	91.32	99.51
√	√	√	OA (%)	99.89	93.51	99.83
			AA (%)	99.91	75.76	99.70
			Kappa (%)	99.88	90.69	99.77

When the CAM is excluded and the model uses only HSI and LiDAR features for fusion, we observe a drop in performance. The OA diminishes to 99.57% for Houston2013, 99.54% for Augsburg, and 99.74 percent for Trento, as seen in the HSI-with-LiDAR row in the table. The lack of the CAM restricts the model's capacity to concentrate on the most pertinent features from each modality, leading to a less effective fusion process. This setup underscores the significance of attention methods for enhanced feature alignment and integration, notwithstanding the model's continued strong performance.

6. Conclusions

In conclusion, a major development in multimodal data fusion for remote sensing applications is the suggested cross attention bridge for the HSI and LiDAR (CAB-HL) framework. CAB-HL achieves greater integration of spectral and spatial information by utilizing a single-stage fusion technique and a cross-attention mechanism, which overcomes conventional constraints in feature clarity and spatial context. Its efficacy is demonstrated by experimental results on a variety of real-world datasets, which show improved performance in vegetation analysis, topography mapping, and land cover categorization. These results highlight CAB-HL's potential to improve resource management and environmental monitoring, opening the door for further advancements in remote sensing technology.

Author Contributions: Conceptualization, K.M.H. and Y.L.; Methodology, K.M.H., Y.Z. and A.A.; Validation, K.Z.; Resources, Y.L.; Data curation, A.A.; Writing—original draft, K.M.H.; Writing—review & editing, K.Z. and Y.Z.; Visualization, A.A.; Supervision, Y.L. All authors have read and agreed to the published version of the manuscript

Funding: This research received no funding.

Data Availability Statement: Datasets and Code can be provided on request.

Conflicts of Interest: The authors declare no conflicts of interest.

References

1. Xu, H.; Zheng, T.; Liu, Y.; Zhang, Z.; Xue, C.; Li, J. A joint convolutional cross ViT network for hyperspectral and light detection and ranging fusion classification. *Remote Sens.* **2024**, *16*, 489. [CrossRef]
2. Sun, W.; Yang, G.; Chen, C.; Chang, M.; Huang, K.; Meng, X.; Liu, L. Development status and literature analysis of China's earth observation remote sensing satellites. *J. Remote Sens.* **2020**, *24*, 479–510. [CrossRef]
3. Hong, D.; Gao, L.; Yao, J.; Zhang, B.; Plaza, A.; Chanussot, J. Graph convolutional networks for hyperspectral image classification. *IEEE Trans. Geosci. Remote Sens.* **2020**, *59*, 5966–5978. [CrossRef]
4. Wang, L.; Wang, X. Dual-coupled cnn-gcn-based classification for hyperspectral and lidar data. *Sensors* **2022**, *22*, 5735. [CrossRef]
5. Yang, J.X.; Wang, J.; Sui, C.H.; Long, Z.; Zhou, J. HSLiNets: Hyperspectral Image and LiDAR Data Fusion Using Efficient Dual Linear Feature Learning Networks. *arXiv* **2024**, arXiv:2412.00302.
6. Yu, C.; Han, R.; Song, M.; Liu, C.; Chang, C.I. A simplified 2D-3D CNN architecture for hyperspectral image classification based on spatial–spectral fusion. *IEEE J. Sel. Top. Appl. Earth Obs. Remote Sens.* **2020**, *13*, 2485–2501. [CrossRef]
7. Hao, J.; Dong, F.; Wang, S.; Li, Y.; Cui, J.; Men, J.; Liu, S. Combined hyperspectral imaging technology with 2D convolutional neural network for near geographical origins identification of wolfberry. *J. Food Meas. Charact.* **2022**, *16*, 4923–4933. [CrossRef]
8. Liu, D.; Han, G.; Liu, P.; Yang, H.; Sun, X.; Li, Q.; Wu, J. A novel 2D-3D CNN with spectral-spatial multi-scale feature fusion for hyperspectral image classification. *Remote Sens.* **2021**, *13*, 4621. [CrossRef]
9. Zhao, J.; Wang, G.; Zhou, B.; Ying, J.; Liu, J. Exploring an application-oriented land-based hyperspectral target detection framework based on 3D–2D CNN and transfer learning. *EURASIP J. Adv. Signal Process.* **2024**, *2024*, 37. [CrossRef]
10. Wang, Q.; Zhou, B.; Zhang, J.; Xie, J.; Wang, Y. Joint Classification of Hyperspectral Images and LiDAR Data Based on Dual-Branch Transformer. *Sensors* **2024**, *24*, 867. [CrossRef]
11. Hong, D.; Gao, L.; Hang, R.; Zhang, B.; Chanussot, J. Deep encoder–decoder networks for classification of hyperspectral and LiDAR data. *IEEE Geosci. Remote Sens. Lett.* **2020**, *19*, 5500205. [CrossRef]
12. Ghamisi, P.; Höfle, B.; Zhu, X.X. Hyperspectral and LiDAR data fusion using extinction profiles and deep convolutional neural network. *IEEE J. Sel. Top. Appl. Earth Obs. Remote Sens.* **2016**, *10*, 3011–3024. [CrossRef]

13. Hong, D.; Gao, L.; Yokoya, N.; Yao, J.; Chanussot, J.; Du, Q.; Zhang, B. More diverse means better: Multimodal deep learning meets remote-sensing imagery classification. *IEEE Trans. Geosci. Remote Sens.* **2020**, *59*, 4340–4354. [CrossRef]
14. Ali, A.; Mu, C.; Zhang, Z.; Zhu, J.; Liu, Y. A two-branch multiscale spectral-spatial feature extraction network for hyperspectral image classification. *J. Inf. Intell.* **2024**, *2*, 224–235. [CrossRef]
15. Choi, E.; Lee, C. Optimizing feature extraction for multiclass problems. *IEEE Trans. Geosci. Remote Sens.* **2001**, *39*, 521–528. [CrossRef]
16. Zheng, Q.; Sun, J. Effective point cloud analysis using multi-scale features. *Sensors* **2021**, *21*, 5574. [CrossRef] [PubMed]
17. Gao, H.; Wu, H.; Chen, Z.; Zhang, Y.; Zhang, Y.; Li, C. Multiscale spectral-spatial cross-extraction network for hyperspectral image classification. *IET Image Process.* **2022**, *16*, 755–771. [CrossRef]
18. Pan, H.; Gao, F.; Dong, J.; Du, Q. Multiscale adaptive fusion network for hyperspectral image denoising. *IEEE J. Sel. Top. Appl. Earth Obs. Remote Sens.* **2023**, *16*, 3045–3059. [CrossRef]
19. Wang, K.; Bai, F.; Li, J.; Liu, Y.; Li, Y. MashFormer: A novel multiscale aware hybrid detector for remote sensing object detection. *IEEE J. Sel. Top. Appl. Earth Obs. Remote Sens.* **2023**, *16*, 2753–2763. [CrossRef]
20. Xue, Z.; Yu, X.; Tan, X.; Liu, B.; Yu, A.; Wei, X. Multiscale deep learning network with self-calibrated convolution for hyperspectral and LiDAR data collaborative classification. *IEEE Trans. Geosci. Remote Sens.* **2021**, *60*, 5514116. [CrossRef]
21. Ding, K.; Lu, T.; Fu, W.; Li, S.; Ma, F. Global–local transformer network for HSI and LiDAR data joint classification. *IEEE Trans. Geosci. Remote Sens.* **2022**, *60*, 5541213. [CrossRef]
22. Song, D.; Gao, J.; Wang, B.; Wang, M. A multi-scale pseudo-siamese network with an attention mechanism for classification of hyperspectral and lidar data. *Remote Sens.* **2023**, *15*, 1283. [CrossRef]
23. Meng, Q.; Zhao, M.; Zhang, L.; Shi, W.; Su, C.; Bruzzone, L. Multilayer feature fusion network with spatial attention and gated mechanism for remote sensing scene classification. *IEEE Geosci. Remote Sens. Lett.* **2022**, *19*, 6510105. [CrossRef]
24. Geng, Z.; Guo, M.H.; Chen, H.; Li, X.; Wei, K.; Lin, Z. Is attention better than matrix decomposition? *arXiv* **2021**, arXiv:2109.04553. [CrossRef]
25. Mnih, V.; Heess, N.; Graves, A.; Kavukcuoglu, K. Recurrent models of visual attention. *Adv. Neural Inf. Process. Syst.* **2014**, *27*. [CrossRef]
26. Vaswani, A. Attention is all you need. *Adv. Neural Inf. Process. Syst.* **2017**. [CrossRef]
27. Hu, J.; Shen, L.; Sun, G. Squeeze-and-excitation networks. In Proceedings of the IEEE Conference on Computer Vision and Pattern Recognition, Salt Lake City, UT, USA, 18–23 June 2018; pp. 7132–7141.
28. Li, H.C.; Hu, W.S.; Li, W.; Li, J.; Du, Q.; Plaza, A. A 3 clnn: Spatial, spectral and multiscale attention convlstm neural network for multisource remote sensing data classification. *IEEE Trans. Neural Netw. Learn. Syst.* **2020**, *33*, 747–761. [CrossRef]
29. He, K.; Sun, W.; Yang, G.; Meng, X.; Ren, K.; Peng, J.; Du, Q. A dual global–local attention network for hyperspectral band selection. *IEEE Trans. Geosci. Remote Sens.* **2022**, *60*, 5527613. [CrossRef]
30. Woo, S.; Park, J.; Lee, J.Y.; Kweon, I.S. Cbam: Convolutional block attention module. In Proceedings of the European Conference on Computer Vision (ECCV), Munich, Germany, 8–14 September 2018; pp. 3–19.
31. Dosovitskiy, A.; Beyer, L.; Kolesnikov, A.; Weissenborn, D.; Zhai, X.; Unterthiner, T.; Dehghani, M.; Minderer, M.; Heigold, G.; Gelly, S.; et al. An image is worth 16x16 words: Transformers for image recognition at scale. *arXiv* **2020**, arXiv:2010.11929.
32. Zhu, M.; Jiao, L.; Liu, F.; Yang, S.; Wang, J. Residual spectral–spatial attention network for hyperspectral image classification. *IEEE Trans. Geosci. Remote Sens.* **2020**, *59*, 449–462. [CrossRef]
33. Wang, X.; Wang, X.; Zhao, K.; Zhao, X.; Song, C. Fsl-unet: Full-scale linked unet with spatial–spectral joint perceptual attention for hyperspectral and multispectral image fusion. *IEEE Trans. Geosci. Remote Sens.* **2022**, *60*, 5539114. [CrossRef]
34. Xu, X.; Li, W.; Ran, Q.; Du, Q.; Gao, L.; Zhang, B. Multisource remote sensing data classification based on convolutional neural network. *IEEE Trans. Geosci. Remote Sens.* **2017**, *56*, 937–949. [CrossRef]
35. Mohla, S.; Pande, S.; Banerjee, B.; Chaudhuri, S. Fusatnet: Dual attention based spectrospatial multimodal fusion network for hyperspectral and lidar classification. In Proceedings of the IEEE/CVF Conference on Computer Vision and Pattern Recognition Workshops, Seattle, WA, USA, 14–19 June 2020; pp. 92–93.
36. Hang, R.; Li, Z.; Ghamisi, P.; Hong, D.; Xia, G.; Liu, Q. Classification of hyperspectral and LiDAR data using coupled CNNs. *IEEE Trans. Geosci. Remote Sens.* **2020**, *58*, 4939–4950. [CrossRef]
37. Debes, C.; Merentitis, A.; Heremans, R.; Hahn, J.; Frangiadakis, N.; van Kasteren, T.; Liao, W.; Bellens, R.; Pižurica, A.; Gautama, S.; et al. Hyperspectral and LiDAR data fusion: Outcome of the 2013 GRSS data fusion contest. *IEEE J. Sel. Top. Appl. Earth Obs. Remote Sens.* **2014**, *7*, 2405–2418. [CrossRef]
38. Hong, D.; Hu, J.; Yao, J.; Chanussot, J.; Zhu, X.X. Multimodal remote sensing benchmark datasets for land cover classification with a shared and specific feature learning model. *ISPRS J. Photogramm. Remote Sens.* **2021**, *178*, 68–80. [CrossRef] [PubMed]
39. Lu, T.; Ding, K.; Fu, W.; Li, S.; Guo, A. Coupled adversarial learning for fusion classification of hyperspectral and LiDAR data. *Inf. Fusion* **2023**, *93*, 118–131. [CrossRef]

40. Wu, X.; Hong, D.; Chanussot, J. Convolutional neural networks for multimodal remote sensing data classification. *IEEE Trans. Geosci. Remote Sens.* **2021**, *60*, 5517010. [CrossRef]
41. Yao, J.; Zhang, B.; Li, C.; Hong, D.; Chanussot, J. Extended vision transformer (ExViT) for land use and land cover classification: A multimodal deep learning framework. *IEEE Trans. Geosci. Remote Sens.* **2023**, *61*, 5514415. [CrossRef]
42. Xue, Z.; Tan, X.; Yu, X.; Liu, B.; Yu, A.; Zhang, P. Deep hierarchical vision transformer for hyperspectral and LiDAR data classification. *IEEE Trans. Image Process.* **2022**, *31*, 3095–3110. [CrossRef]
43. Li, J.; Liu, Y.; Song, R.; Li, Y.; Han, K.; Du, Q. Sal^{2}rn: A spatial–spectral salient reinforcement network for hyperspectral and lidar data fusion classification. *IEEE Trans. Geosci. Remote Sens.* **2022**, *61*, 5500114. [CrossRef]
44. Wang, X.; Zhu, J.; Feng, Y.; Wang, L. MS2CANet: Multiscale spatial–spectral cross-modal attention network for hyperspectral image and LiDAR classification. *IEEE Geosci. Remote Sens. Lett.* **2024**, *21*, 5501505. [CrossRef]
45. Feng, Y.; Song, L.; Wang, L.; Wang, X. DSHFNet: Dynamic scale hierarchical fusion network based on multiattention for hyperspectral image and LiDAR data classification. *IEEE Trans. Geosci. Remote Sens.* **2023**, *61*, 5522514. [CrossRef]
46. Wang, X.; Song, L.; Feng, Y.; Zhu, J. S3F2Net: Spatial-Spectral-Structural Feature Fusion Network for Hyperspectral Image and LiDAR Data Classification. *IEEE Trans. Circuits Syst. Video Technol.* **2025**, *35*, 4801–4815. [CrossRef]
47. Wang, J.; Li, J.; Shi, Y.; Lai, J.; Tan, X. AM^{3}Net: Adaptive mutual-learning-based multimodal data fusion network. *IEEE Trans. Circuits Syst. Video Technol.* **2022**, *32*, 5411–5426. [CrossRef]

remote sensing

MDPI

Article

Hybrid-SegUFormer: A Hybrid Multi-Scale Network with Self-Distillation for Robust Landslide InSAR Deformation Detection

Wenyi Zhao [1,2,3], Jiahao Zhang [1], Jianao Cai [1] and Dongping Ming [1,4,5,6,*]

1 School of Artificial Intelligence, China University of Geosciences (Beijing), Beijing 100083, China; 3004220005@email.cugb.edu.cn (W.Z.); 1002234112@email.cugb.edu.cn (J.Z.); 2004210022@email.cugb.edu.cn (J.C.)
2 China Institute of Geo-Environment Monitoring, Beijing 100081, China
3 Technology Innovation Center for Geohazard Monitoring and Risk Early Warning, Ministry of Natural Resources, Beijing 100081, China
4 Hebei Key Laboratory of Geospatial Digital Twin and Collaborative Optimization, Beijing 100083, China
5 Frontier Science Center for Deep-Time Digital Earth, China University of Geosciences (Beijing), Beijing 100083, China
6 State key Laboratory of Geological Processes and Mineral Resources, Beijing 100083, China
* Correspondence: mingdp@cugb.edu.cn

Highlights

What are the main findings?

- Hybrid-SegUFormer achieves effective landslide InSAR deformation detection performance (IoU: 66.74%, F1-score: 80.05%) through synergistic integration of segFormer encoder, multi-scale decoder and self-distillation mechanism.
- Hybrid-SegUFormer demonstrates exceptional multi-scale adaptability with minimal performance degradation and strong cross-regional generalization capability, maintaining superior metrics on unseen datasets and demonstrating its practical utility.

What are the implications of the main findings?

- This study offers a reliable and efficient solution for large-area landslide deformation zone detection using InSAR data in rugged terrains.
- By demonstrating strong cross-regional generalization, Hybrid-SegUFormer reduces the need for localized data collection, facilitating more efficient large-area landslide early warning and risk mitigation.

Abstract

Landslide deformation monitoring via InSAR is crucial for assessing the risk of hazards. Quick and accurate detection of active deformation zones is crucial for early warning and mitigation planning. While the application of deep learning has substantially improved the detection efficiency, several challenges still persist, such as poor multi-scale perception, blurred boundaries, and limited model generalization. This study proposes Hybrid-SegUFormer to address these limitations. The model integrates the SegFormer encoder's efficient feature extraction with the U-Net decoder's superior boundary restoration. It introduces a multi-scale fusion decoding mechanism to enhance context perception structurally and incorporates a self-distillation strategy to significantly improve generalization capability. Hybrid-SegUFormer achieves detection performance (98.79% accuracy, 80.05% F1-score) while demonstrating superior multi-scale adaptability (IoU degradation of only 6.99–8.83%) and strong cross-regional generalization capability. The synergistic integration of its core modules enables an optimal balance between precision and recall, making it

https://doi.org/10.3390/rs17213514

particularly effective for complex landslide detection tasks. This study provides a new approach for intelligent interpretation of InSAR deformation in complex mountainous areas.

Keywords: landslides; active deformation zone; detection; InSAR; Multi-Scale Decoder; Self Distillation

1. Introduction

Landslides refer to the phenomenon where rock, soil, or debris masses on a slope move downward or outward under the influence of gravity, typically triggered by earthquakes, rainfall, or human activities [1,2]. According to the Global Fatal Landslide Database (GFLD, formerly termed the Durham Fatal Landslide Database), spatiotemporal analysis of global fatal non-seismic landslides from 2004 to 2016 revealed that a total of 55,997 people died in 4862 distinct landslide events, with Asia being the high-incidence region. Situated on the eastern edge of the Eurasian Plate, China is significantly influenced by the movements of the Pacific Plate, Indian Ocean Plate, and Eurasian Plate. Its complex topography, geological conditions, and intense tectonic and seismic activity contribute to a high frequency of landslide disasters [2]. In recent years, the continuation of an active seismic period, an increase in extreme rainfall events, and escalating intensity of human engineering activities have further exacerbated landslide risks, making the disaster prevention and reduction situation severe [3–6].

Deformation magnitude is a key physical quantity characterizing landslide stability and movement state [7]. It can intuitively reveal the deformation evolution process of a slope and serves as a crucial precursor signal for landslide instability. Therefore, deformation monitoring is the most direct and effective means to reveal landslide evolution mechanisms [8], and it is also the critical basis for conducting landslide hazard risk assessment and early warning forecasting. Currently, common surface deformation monitoring methods include ground-based point monitoring techniques such as crack gauges, GNSS (Global Navigation Satellite System), rain gauges, inclinometers, and accelerometers. Among these, GNSS is the most widely applied in landslide monitoring due to its global coverage, all-weather operation capability, millimeter-level 3D accuracy, and automation capacity [9,10]. However, ground-based point monitoring methods like GNSS are limited to the locations where equipment is installed, making it difficult to achieve areal coverage. This results in blind spots when monitoring large-scale landslides or risk zones, failing to meet the urgent need for large-scale, high-density monitoring of geological hazards.

The Interferometry Synthetic Aperture Radar (InSAR) technology developed in recent years possesses capabilities for large-scale, long time-series, and high-temporal-resolution surface deformation monitoring. The abundant availability of SAR satellite data and increasingly mature InSAR processing techniques provide massive deformation information for high-precision monitoring of landslide hazards, serving as critical data support for large-scale geo-hazard monitoring, with accuracy reaching centimeter to millimeter levels. Furthermore, deformation field data acquired through InSAR is crucial for the early identification of potential landslides, serving as a key basis for determining potential landslides, especially in the identification of high-altitude and concentrated distributed landslide hazards [11].

Primary radar satellite methods for landslide deformation monitoring include Differential InSAR (D-InSAR), InSAR Stacking, Multi-Temporal InSAR (MT InSAR), and Pixel Offset Tracking (POT), each playing vital roles in tracking different stages of landslide evolution [12–14]. Among these, D-InSAR technology is the earliest application of InSAR and forms the theoretical basis for multi-baseline interferometric measurement methods like PS-InSAR and SBAS-InSAR. As a data approach with relatively simple procedures, SBAS-InSAR has been broadly used in landslide monitoring based on "comprehensive remote sensing" [15–17].

Extensive InSAR-based landslide monitoring aims to enhance risk detection accuracy and prevention effectiveness. Quickly and accurately identifying areas of significant deformation is crucial for early warning and mitigation planning [18,19]. Current extraction methods mainly involve manual delineation and threshold segmentation: (1) Manual delineation uses time-series InSAR analysis followed by expert visual interpretation to define deformation zones. This method is subjective, labor-intensive, and inefficient due to dependence on expert judgment [11,20,21]; (2) Threshold segmentation detects deformation areas by applying rate thresholds to coherent targets with spatial clustering. While it allows semi-automated extraction, this approach is sensitive to InSAR noise and limited by region-specific threshold applicability [22]. Therefore, intelligent techniques that balance accuracy and efficiency are urgently needed to fully utilize InSAR data advantages in landslide risk management.

In recent years, deep learning techniques (particularly Convolutional Neural Networks, CNN) have been progressively applied to InSAR deformation area identification and segmentation [23–29]. Mainstream models such as Mask R-CNN, DeepLabv3+, U-Net, and SegFormer demonstrate notable effectiveness: Mask R-CNN combines object detection and instance segmentation capabilities, generating pixel-level masks to precisely extract landslide deformation boundaries [30,31]; DeepLabv3+ integrates an encoder-decoder structure with an Atrous Spatial Pyramid Pooling (ASPP) module, employing dilated convolutions to expand the receptive field. This effectively balances local edge features with global topographic context, enhancing deformation zone contour segmentation accuracy [32–34]. Given frequent vegetation/topographic occlusion and satellite revisit limitations in InSAR data—where significant surface deformation remains uncommon—U-Net maintains superior segmentation performance even with limited annotated samples. Its encoder-decoder architecture with skip connections preserves both low-level edge details and high-level semantic features, proving particularly adaptive for extracting vague-boundary, irregularly shaped deformation patches [35,36]; SegFormer employs a Transformer-based architecture featuring a multi-scale encoder and lightweight decoder, significantly reducing computational complexity. Its transformer encoder excels at modeling long-range dependencies, enabling efficient perception of multi-scale terrain features while accurately capturing local edges and global spatial relationships within deformation zones—critical for segmenting complex landslide deformation patterns [37–39]. The limitation of CNNs in capturing long-range dependencies was addressed through the pioneering integration of the Transformer architecture [40]. A BiFusion module was introduced to enable multi-level feature fusion, forming the TransFuse framework. Building upon this, the novel FSRNet model was developed in 2025, wherein a Feature Symbiosis Coupling (FSC) strategy was employed to combine ResNet50 with a Swin Transformer [41]. The local detail representation of CNNs and the global dependency modeling of Transformers were effectively leveraged, leading to significantly enhanced segmentation accuracy and inference efficiency in orchard extraction tasks. The Mean-Teacher self-distillation framework constructs a teacher network through an exponential moving average (EMA) of the student model's historical parameters, eliminating dependence on external pre-trained models or additional inference overhead. This framework has been widely adopted in remote sensing applications, such as utilizing the Mean Teacher model to generate pseudo-labels for enhancing model generalization under limited labeled data [42], and developing multi-granularity domain adaptation teacher models to address unsupervised domain adaptation challenges in remote sensing object detection tasks [43].

Despite significant progress in deep learning-based detection of InSAR deformation zones, existing models remain limited in three critical aspects: (1) inadequate perception of landslides with high scale heterogeneity, (2) blurred restoration of deformation boundaries caused by complex slope structures, and (3) limited generalization capability across diverse geological settings. To address these gaps, this study proposes Hybrid-SegUFormer, a novel architecture that integrates a SegFormer encoder with a U-Net–inspired decoder, augmented by a multi-scale decoding mechanism and self-distillation. Our framework introduces two key innovations: first, a hierarchical multi-scale decoder (MSD) that enhances sensitivity to landslides of varying spatial extents and improves boundary precision; and second, a self-distillation strategy that strengthens cross-regional generalization without requiring additional labeled data. Furthermore, we introduce a multi-source auxiliary data preprocessing strategy to suppress non-landslide deformation signals, thereby reducing false detections. Validated on SBAS-InSAR datasets from Zayu County and the Upper Jinsha River, our approach demonstrates superior performance over benchmarks such as Mask R-CNN, DeepLabv3+, U-Net, and SegFormer, offering a more reliable solution for landslide risk monitoring systems.

2. Study Area and Data

2.1. Study Area

The study areas comprise two representative high-risk geological hazard zones (Figure 1):

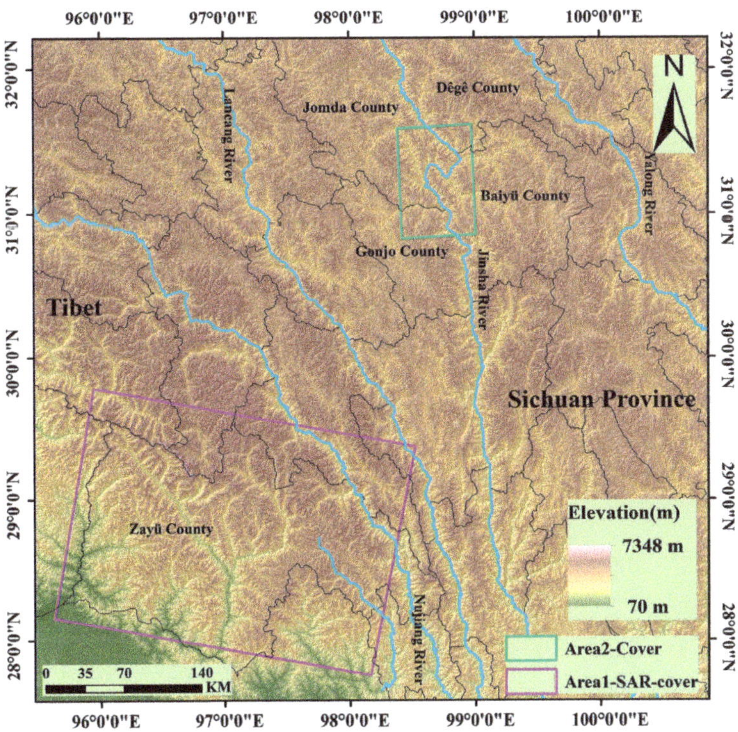

Figure 1. Location of the study area.

(1) Area 1 (Zayu County): Located in the southeastern Tibet Autonomous Region (average elevation: 2800 m), this area features higher topography in the northwest descending southeastward, with relative relief reaching 3600 m. Dominated by deeply incised V-shaped valleys, it exhibits characteristic high-mountain canyon and fluvial landforms. Controlled by the Jiali-Nujiang Fault Zone, surface cover consists of loose sediments (porosity >35%). Strong precipitation during the rainy season, coupled with tectonic activity, triggers frequent landslides and debris flows [44]. This region was used for model training, validation, and testing.

(2) Area 2 (The Upper Reach (Baiyu-Tange reach section) of the Jinsha River): Situated within the Jinsha River tectonic suture zone at the southeastern margin of the Tibetan Plateau (elevation: 2500–4400 m). NW-trending main faults and secondary faults dissect bedrock, forming steep-dipping bank slopes (>45°). It is prone to high-positioned rock landslides (e.g., Bage landslide volume >240 million m^3). This area served to validate the model's cross-regional transfer capability.

2.2. Data

2.2.1. SAR Data and Ancillary Data

This study collected 80 scenes of C-band Sentinel-1A imagery over Area 1, spanning the period from January 2020 to November 2022. The detailed parameters are listed in Table 1. The Interferometric Synthetic Aperture Radar (InSAR) data processing employed the European Space Agency (ESA) Precise Orbit products, the 30-m-resolution Shuttle Radar Topography Mission (SRTM) DEM, and Generic Atmospheric Correction Online Service (GACOS) products [45–47].

Table 1. Detailed parameters of the SAR imagery over Area 1.

Sensor	Polarization	Acquisition Mode	Wavelength	Spatial Resolution	Timespan	Direction	Path	Number of Images
Sentinel-1A	VV	IW	5.6 cm (C band)	5 m × 20 m	2020.01~2022.11	Descending	106	80

InSAR technology, constrained by the side-looking imaging geometry of SAR sensors, is susceptible to geometric distortions like layover, foreshortening, and shadow in high mountainous canyon areas. To address unreliable deformation values in these regions, this study simulated and calculated the geometric distortion distribution using Sentinel-1A orbital parameters, imaging geometry, and SRTM 30 m DEM. The identified layover, foreshortening, and shadow regions are illustrated in Figure 2a. Additionally, 66 scenes of C-band Sentinel-1A imagery over Area 2 were collected to validate the model's cross-region transferability. Detailed imagery parameters are provided in Table 2.

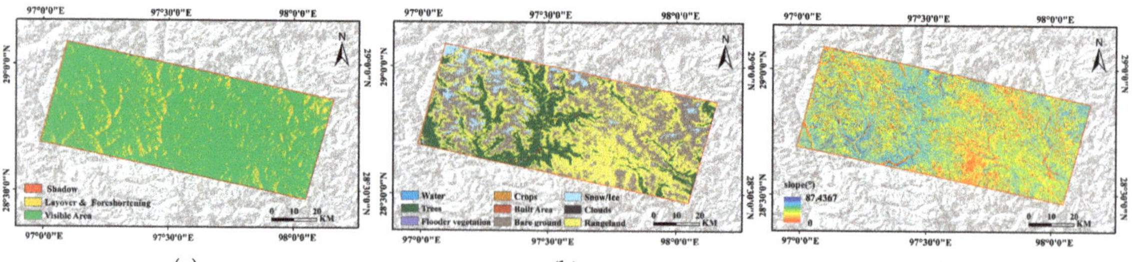

Figure 2. (**a**) Sentinel-L geometric distortion map; (**b**) Land cover; (**c**) Slope.

Table 2. Detailed parameters of the SAR imagery over Area 2.

Sensor	Polarization	Acquisition Mode	Wavelength	Spatial Resolution	Timespan	Direction	Path	Number of Images
Sentinel-1A	VV	IW	5.6 cm (C band)	5 m × 20 m	2017.04~2019.06	Ascending	99	66

2.2.2. Multi-Source Geo-Data for Eliminating Non-Landslide Deformation Areas

To accurately identify landslide deformation areas, this study utilized multi-source geoscience data to eliminate zones affected by non-landslide factors. Both surface disturbances (e.g., land use changes, vegetation dynamics) and radar geometric distortions can mislead the interpretation of deformation signals. The data sources included land cover from the official ArcGIS website, NDVI data sourced from Google Earth Engine (GEE), and slope information derived from DEM calculations. Figure 2b,c display the land cover and slope, respectively.

3. Methods

To address the limitations of current deep learning models in identifying Landslide InSAR Deformation Detection, including constrained multi-scale object perception, insufficient boundary detail restoration, and weak model generalizability, this study proposes a novel Hybrid-SegUFormer model. Compared with the conventional SegFormer–U-Net hybrid architecture, the proposed model refines the skip-connection mechanism and enhances the decoder design and training stability, enabling more efficient multi-scale feature fusion. Specifically, diagonally-linked skip connections between encoder–decoder pairs allow the decoder to recover full spatial resolution at the D_1 stage, where high-resolution semantic features are directly integrated into the multi-scale decoder (MSD). This design improves spatial detail preservation and boundary reconstruction. The integrated MSD further aggregates semantic features from all decoding stages (D_4–D_1), enhancing cross-scale feature interaction and global-to-local alignment. Moreover, a self-distillation mechanism based on an exponential moving average (EMA) teacher model introduces an auxiliary distillation loss alongside the primary supervised loss, guiding the student model to learn continuously from the teacher's soft predictions and improving training stability and segmentation accuracy. The model's effectiveness is validated using SBAS-InSAR surface deformation datasets from the study area. Additionally, multi-source auxiliary data are incorporated to mitigate interference from non-landslide deformations and reduce the misidentification rate of pseudo-landslide deformation areas. The comprehensive technical workflow of Hybrid-SegUFormer for landslide InSAR deformation identification is illustrated in Figure 3 and comprises the following key steps:

Step 1: Acquire Sentinel-1A data and multi-source auxiliary data for the study area, and invert surface deformation rates using GACOS-assisted SBAS-InSAR technology.

Step 2: Integrate the SegFormer and U-Net architectures by combining an MSD with a self-distillation mechanism to construct the Hybrid-SegUFormer model. Train and validate the model using surface deformation rate data from the study area, evaluating its performance through five metrics: accuracy, precision, recall, Intersection over Union (IoU), and F1-score. After testing and assessing the pre-trained model on the test dataset, preliminary extraction of landslide-induced significant deformation areas is conducted based on Hybrid-SegUFormer, followed by further elimination of non-landslide deformation regions using multi-source auxiliary data.

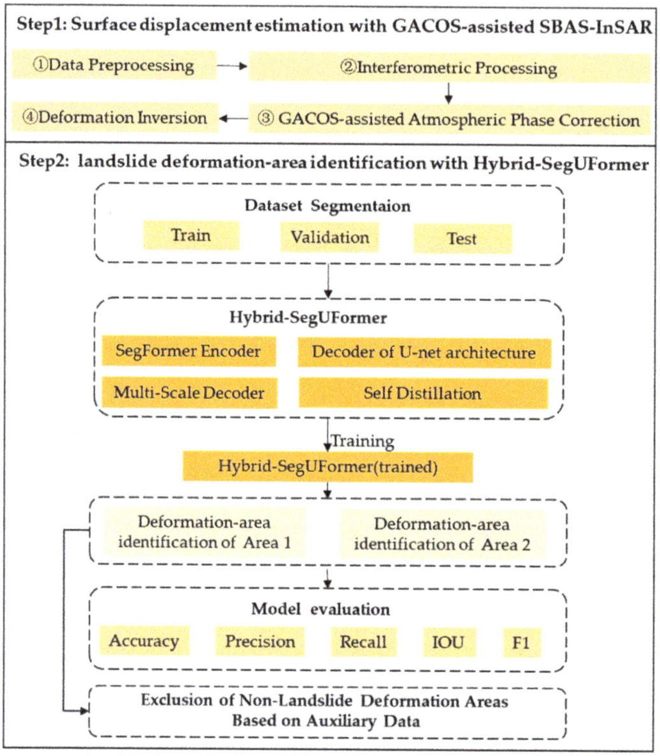

Figure 3. Hybrid-SegUFormer workflow for landslide deformation identification from InSAR data.

3.1. Surface Displacement Estimation with GACOS-Assisted SBAS-InSAR

To address atmospheric disturbances and spatiotemporal decorrelation caused by rugged terrain and dense vegetation, we used GACOS-assisted SBAS-InSAR for surface displacement estimation. The data processing workflow included the following steps:

(1) Data Preprocessing: Processed Sentinel-1A Single Look Complex (SLC) images using GAMMA software with precise orbit products. Performed SAR image co-registration and terrain phase elimination using a 30-meter Digital Elevation Model (DEM).

(2) Interferometric Processing: Set the temporal-spatial baseline threshold and generate the interferogram using Goldstein adaptive filtering [48].

(3) Conducted atmospheric phase correction using GACOS products for each interferogram. Executed phase unwrapping via the Minimum Cost Flow (MCF) algorithm [49]; Eliminated topographic residuals through linear regression of the unwrapped phase and vertical baseline.

(4) Deformation Inversion: Inverted pixel-wise time-series deformation using Least Squares (LS) with Singular Value Decomposition (SVD) [50].

3.2. Structure of Hybrid-SegUFormer

Hybrid-SegUFormer combines the advantages of the SegFormer and U-Net architectures. It incorporates an MSD and a self-distillation mechanism within a four-stage cascade architecture (Figure 4).

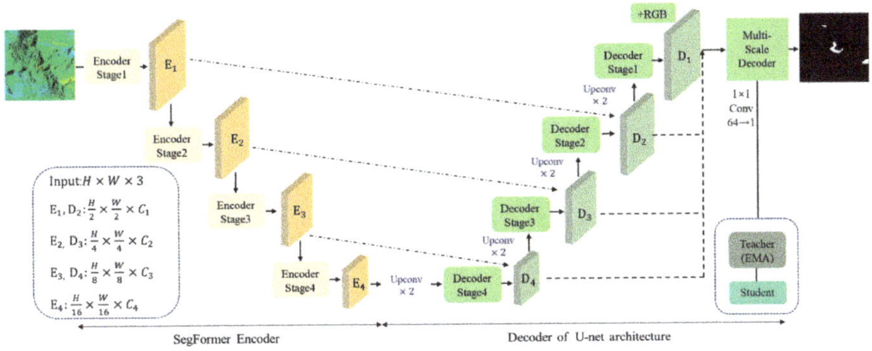

Figure 4. Structure of Hybrid-SegUFormer.

(1) SegFormer Encoder Layer: A PyTorch-based SegFormer encoder (PySegFormer-Backbone) is implemented to extract multi-level features from the input imagery.

(2) U-Net Decoder Layer: Spatial resolution is restored and boundary details are retained through skip connections and layer-wise upsampling.

(3) Multi-Scale Decoder (MSD): Multi-scale semantic features are uniformly projected and fused to generate high-resolution semantic predictions.

(4) Self-Distillation Optimization Layer: A Teacher-Student self-distillation loop is constructed by using the exponential moving average of the student model's parameters to update the teacher network. This loop compresses prediction errors and enhances the generalization ability. The complete processing workflow can be expressed as Figure 5.

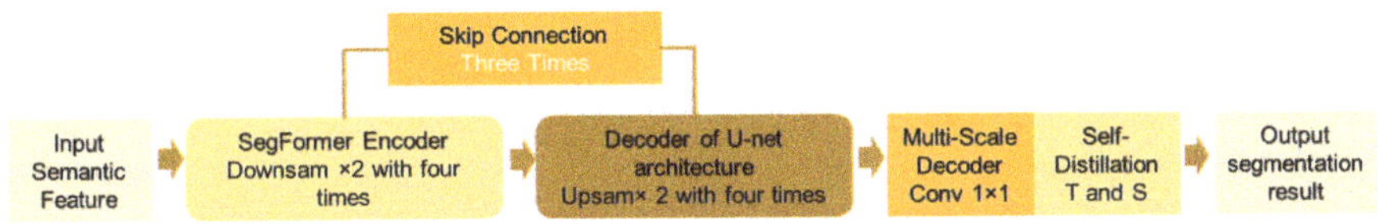

Figure 5. Complete workflow.

The nomenclature explanation for the Hybrid-SegUFormer model is provided in Table 3.

Table 3. Nomenclature of Hybrid-SegUFormer.

Components	Nomenclature
Hybrid	"Hybrid" signifies that the model integrates multiple architectures (Transformer + CNN), incorporates MSD and self-distillation mechanism, thereby highlighting its architectural hybridity.
Seg	"Seg" denotes application to semantic segmentation tasks (Segmentation).
U	"U" embodies the incorporation of the U-Net decoder architecture.
Former	"Former" signifies the Transformer encoder (from the SegFormer series).

3.3. Encoder

The PyTorch-implemented PySegFormerBackbone encoder uses a four-stage hybrid architecture that combines convolutional downsampling for local feature extraction, lightweight multi-head self-attention for global context modeling, and feed-forward networks (FFNs) for feature refinement. The overall decoding process is illustrated in Figure 6, where F1′, F2′, and F3′ denote the nodes of the skip connections. In each stage, convolutional blocks first reduce spatial dimensions and capture local receptive fields, then flatten feature maps into sequences processed by Transformer blocks to establish long-range dependencies, thereby synthesizing CNN's computational efficiency with Transformer's global representation capabilities. The convolutional block at the *l*-th decoder level includes a single 3 × 3 convolution with a stride of 2, performing the mapping defined in Equation (1):

$$X_l = \sigma(\mathrm{BN}(W_l^{\mathrm{conv}} * X_{l-1})),\ W_l^{\mathrm{conv}} \in R^{C_l \times C_{l-1} \times 3 \times 3} \tag{1}$$

where $*$ denotes convolution, X_l and X_{l-1} represent the output feature maps at levels l and $l-1$, respectively. $\mathrm{BN}(\cdot)$ is batch normalization. $\sigma(\cdot)$ the nonlinear activation, and W_l^{conv} the convolutional kernel parameters. Channel dimensions $C_l = \{64, 128, 320, 512\}$ ensure exponential channel growth while halving spatial resolution per level, generating pyramidal features.

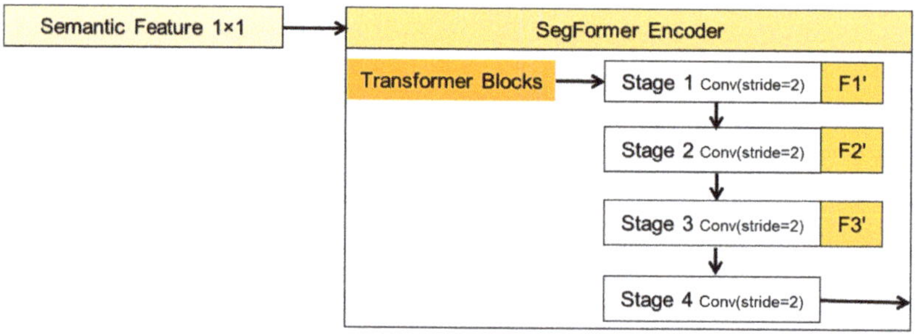

Figure 6. Processing flow of the encoder.

The resulting tensor $X_l \in R^{B \times C_l \times H_l \times W_l}$ is reshaped according to Equation (2) before Transformer processing:

$$Z_l = \mathrm{reshape}(X_l) \rightarrow R^{B \times N_l \times C_l},\ N_l = H_l W_l \tag{2}$$

where N_l represents flattened token count, H_l the feature map height, W_l the feature map width, and Z_l the reshaped 3D tensor. This implementation eliminates explicit positional encoding by leveraging convolution-derived implicit location information. This not only reduces parameters and computation but also maintains SegFormer's position-agnostic design. Subsequently, the flattened features are subjected to multi-head self-attention (Equation (3)):

$$\mathrm{MHSA}(Q, K, V) = \mathrm{Concat}(h_1, \ldots, h_H)W^O,\ h_i = \mathrm{softmax}\left(\frac{Q_i K_i^\top}{\sqrt{d_k}}\right)V_i \tag{3}$$

where Q_i, V_i, K_i are query/key/value vectors for head I, d_k the key dimension, h_i head output, W^O projection matrix, and $H = C/64$ head count. Subsequent feed-forward networks (Equation (4)) apply:

$$\mathrm{FFN}(z) = W_2\, \sigma(W_1 z) \tag{4}$$

where z represents input features, W_1 and W_2 are the linear weights. The complete Transformer block integrates GELU activation, residual connections, and layer normalization. The encoder ultimately outputs four-level features B, C_1, H_1, W_1, combining convolutional local perception with self-attention global representation.

3.4. Hierarchical U-Net Decoder

The Hybrid-SegUFormer decoder incorporates U-Net's paradigm of "Upsampling-Concatenation-Convolution", constructing four decoding stages ($D_4 \rightarrow D_1$) for quad-level encoder features (Figure 7). At each level, transposed convolution ($ConvTrans_{2\times 2,s=2}$) doubles spatial resolution, followed by skip connections with the same-resolution encoder features for semantic-detail alignment and fusion. The final decoder stage fuses with bilinearly upsampled original path features, integrating low-level texture details. This structure maintains deep semantics while gradually restoring fine-grained edges through shallow layers, achieving a unified resolution and semantics.

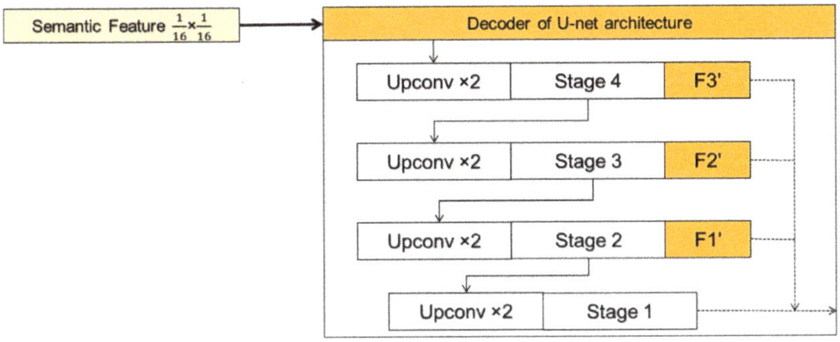

Figure 7. Processing flow of the decoder.

3.5. Multi-Scale Decoder

Due to the significant cross-scale variations in spatial patterns of landslide deformation areas, single-scale semantic features struggle to capture both macro and micro targets simultaneously. To address this limitation, Hybrid-SegUFormer includes the MSD (Figure 8). This module performs channel projection and convolutional fusion across different semantic hierarchies while maintaining a uniform output resolution, ultimately generating scale-sensitive yet spatially consistent prediction maps. The four-level features derived from the U-Net decoder still exhibit scale and channel discrepancies, specifically: $D_4 \in R^{B\times C_4\times H\times W}$, $D_3 \in R^{B\times C_3\times H\times W}$, $D_2 \in R^{B\times C_2\times H\times W}$, $D_1 \in R^{B\times C_1\times H\times W}$.

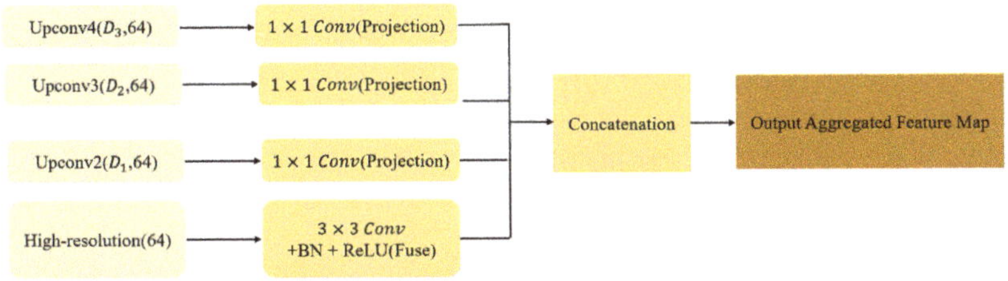

Figure 8. Core technical workflow of the multi-scale decoder.

The MSD first projects all feature scales to 64 channels using 1 × 1 convolutions. Subsequently, all multi-scale feature maps are upsampled to match the spatial resolution of the input image and concatenated along the channel dimension to fuse multi-scale information.

The integrated feature is obtained through 3 × 3 convolutional fusion, followed by projection to a single-channel segmentation map via 1 × 1 convolution. This design explicitly models diverse receptive fields, significantly enhancing detection capabilities for multi-scale targets (Large-scale landslides and Slender slope toes).

3.6. Online Self-Distillation Mechanism

To mitigate overfitting risks in landslide deformation area extraction under limited annotated samples, this study integrates a Mean Teacher self-distillation framework (Figure 9) into the Hybrid-SegUFormer backbone, enhancing model generalization. This framework constructs the teacher network via an exponential moving average (EMA) of student model parameters, offering dual advantages:

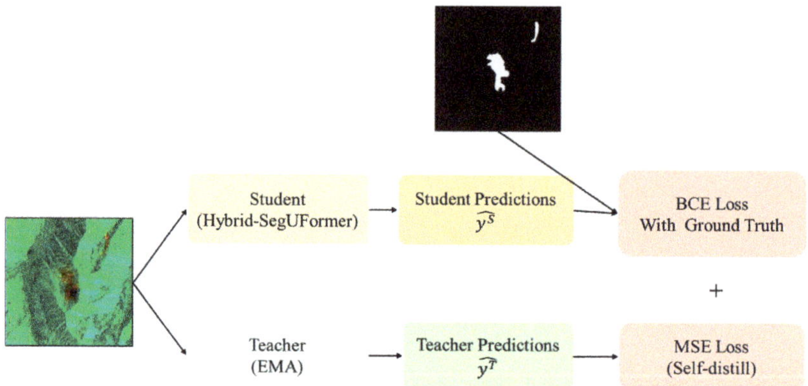

Figure 9. Self-Distillation Architecture Schematic.

(1) Pre-training Independence: The teacher network is constructed via the exponential moving average (EMA) of historical student parameters, thereby eliminating dependence on external pre-trained models. Builds the teacher network through EMA of historical student parameters, eliminating reliance on external pre-trained models;

(2) Zero Inference Overhead: The teacher network operates solely during training, adding no computational burden during inference.

The teacher model's predictions serve as stable soft labels, enforcing consistency constraints on the student model. This introduces an adaptive distillation consistency loss alongside traditional hard-label supervised loss, with the joint loss function formulated as follows (Equation (5)):

$$L = \underbrace{\mathrm{BCE}\left(\hat{y^S}, y\right)}_{\text{Primary Task Loss}} + \lambda_d \underbrace{\mathrm{MSE}\left(\sigma\left(\hat{y^S}\right), \sigma\left(\hat{y^T}\right)\right)}_{\text{Distillation Consistency}}, \ \lambda_d = 0.1 \tag{5}$$

where $\sigma(\cdot)$ is the Sigmoid function, $\hat{y^S}$ and $\hat{y^T}$ process the prediction outputs of the student and teacher networks, respectively. Teacher model weights θ_T are updated via the exponential moving average (EMA) of student parameters θ_S, without direct backpropagation.

InSAR deformation maps fundamentally differ from natural images: they contain multiplicative speckle, spatially varying coherence (γ), atmospheric phase-screen residuals, and phase-wrapping discontinuities that obscure deformation boundaries and produce sparse, noise-prone labels. The model employs a self-distillation mechanism, in which an EMA-based teacher (α = 0.99) generates temporally averaged soft masks, while the student is optimized using a BCE loss against binary labels together with an MSE consistency term to the teacher's outputs. The teacher's smoothed predictions suppress speckle-induced fluctuations and capture uncertainty in low-coherence regions, guiding the student toward spatially coherent deformation patterns. This mechanism reduces false detections in decorrelated or layover–shadow areas, preserves boundary continuity along interferometric fringes, and enhances cross-pair generalization under varying baselines and atmospheric conditions.

3.7. Evaluation Metrics

To assess the performance of the recognition method, this study uses five metrics: accuracy, precision, recall, Intersection over Union (IoU), and F1-score. Accuracy measures the proportion of correctly predicted pixels out of the total pixels. Precision quantifies the percentage of true deformation pixels among those predicted as salient deformation areas. Recall represents the fraction of actual deformation pixels that were correctly identified. IoU evaluates the overlap between predicted and ground-truth deformation regions. The F1-score is the harmonic mean of precision and recall, providing a comprehensive reflection of the model's precision and completeness in identifying salient deformation areas. The formulae for each metric are provided below.

$$Accuracy = \frac{TP + TN}{TP + TN + FP + FN} \tag{6}$$

$$Precision = \frac{TP}{TP + FP} \tag{7}$$

$$Recall = \frac{TP}{TP + FN} \tag{8}$$

$$IOU = \frac{TP}{TP + FP + FN} \tag{9}$$

$$F1\ score = \frac{2}{\frac{1}{Recall} + \frac{1}{Precision}} \tag{10}$$

where:

TP (True Positives): Correctly predicted landslide deformation pixels;
TN (True Negatives): Correctly predicted non-landslide pixels;
FP (False Positives): Non-landslide pixels misclassified as deformation;
FN (False Negatives): Landslide deformation pixels missed by the prediction.

4. Results and Analysis

4.1. Results of the SBAS-InSAR Deformation Estimation

The annual line-of-sight (LOS) deformation velocity under periodic color mapping was shown in Figure 10 (Area 1) and (Area 2).

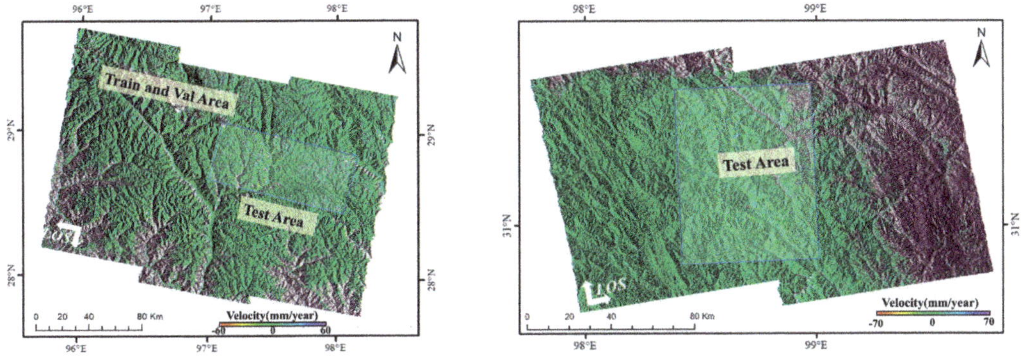

(a) (b)

Figure 10. Surface deformation velocity map. (**a**) is for Area 1 and (**b**) for Area 2.

Figure 10a illustrates the surface deformation monitoring results of Zayu County. Positive deformation velocity indicates ground movement toward the radar sensor, whereas negative deformation indicates movement away from it. The results show that during the period from 2 January 2020, to 23 November 2022, the maximum annual deformation velocity away from the LOS reached approximately 170 mm/y, while that toward the LOS reached approximately 110 mm/y. Overall, the applicability of InSAR in Zayu County is higher in the eastern region than in the western region, and higher in the northern region than in the southern region. This spatial variation was primarily attributed to the dense vegetation in the western and southern areas. The abundant vegetation caused multiple scattering, occlusion effects, and seasonal growth variations, resulting in complex phase changes of the C-band radar signal during propagation. Consequently, maintaining phase coherence between radar echoes acquired at different times and locations became difficult, ultimately leading to decorrelation.

Figure 10b presents the surface deformation estimation results for Area-2. The maximum deformation velocity away from the sensor reached 134 mm/y, while the maximum deformation velocity toward the sensor reached 52 mm/y. Owing to the sparse vegetation in this area, a high density of monitoring points is observed. Notably, the landslide deformation zone in this area exhibits a chair-shaped pattern, characterized by pronounced deformation features and clearly defined spatial boundaries.

4.2. Sample Preparation

Using Google Earth optical imagery as a supplementary reference along with InSAR deformation phase maps, we extracted significant landslide deformation areas on the ArcGIS platform. Initial interferometric processing of the study-area SAR imagery produced deformation phase and average velocity maps. Deformation-concentrated zones were identified through overlay analysis and visual interpretation. These areas were then vectorized using ArcGIS tools to create polygon vector datasets of significant deformation regions (Figure 11), providing high-quality sample labels for subsequent landslide detection. To manage GPU memory constraints during training, deformation phase images were cropped into 256 × 256-pixel samples (total: 1975 samples). The dataset was partitioned into 5:1 (train: test) and 8.5:1 (train: val) ratios, with sample ground truths comprising InSAR significant deformation areas and background values.

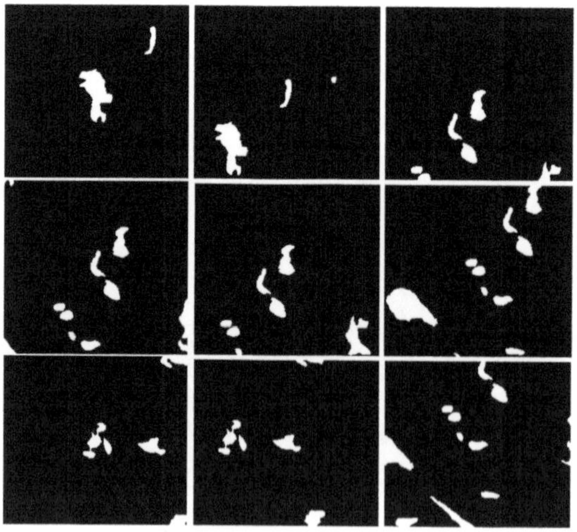

Figure 11. Examples of deformation area masks.

4.3. Model Comparative Experiments

To assess model performance, we compared Hybrid-SegUFormer with several mainstream semantic segmentation models, including U-Net, DeepLabV3+, Mask R-CNN, and Seg-Former. The results of landslide deformation area identification across these models are illustrated in Figure 12, with quantitative evaluation metrics provided in Tables 4 and 5. Both Figure 12 and Tables 4 and 5 show that Hybrid-SegUFormer outperforms the others in both qualitative visual assessment and quantitative metrics.

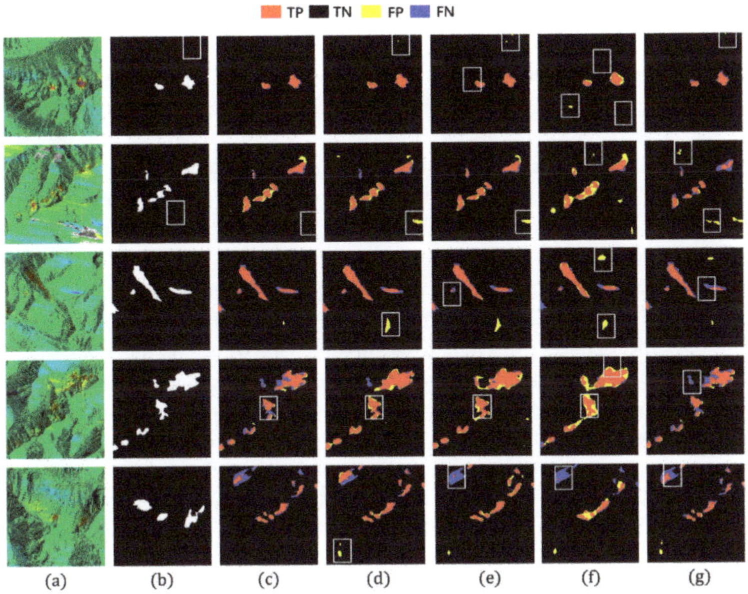

Figure 12. Detection results of different detection models. (**a**) InSAR displacement velocity map; (**b**) Ground truth label; (**c**) Hybrid-SegUFormer; (**d**) U-net; (**e**) DeepLabV3+; (**f**) Mask R-CNN; (**g**) SegFormer.

Table 4. Evaluation metrics of Hybrid-SegUFormer across multiple runs.

Number	Accuracy (%)	Precision (%)	Recall (%)	IOU (%)	F1 (%)
①	98.79	81.78	78.39	66.74	80.05
②	98.71	80.39	78.95	66.20	79.66
③	98.69	79.62	79.53	66.08	79.57
④	98.72	80.37	79.52	66.59	79.94
Average Value	98.73	80.54	79.10	66.40	79.81
Standard Deviation	0.04	0.90	0.54	0.31	0.23
Average Range	98.73 ± 0.04	80.54 ± 0.90	79.10 ± 0.54	66.40 ± 0.31	79.81 ± 0.23

Table 5. Evaluation metrics of Hybrid-SegUFormer and other models on the dataset.

Model	Accuracy (%)	Precision (%)	Recall (%)	IOU (%)	F1 (%)
Hybrid-SegUFormer	98.79	81.78	79.52	66.74	80.05
U-net	98.65	75.89	82.52	65.38	79.06
DeepLabv3+	98.66	78.25	78.56	64.48	78.40
Mask R-CNN	98.22	64.57	80.25	55.71	71.56
SegFormer	98.69	79.34	77.37	64.40	78.34

To verify the stability of the proposed model, we conducted four independent training experiments to obtain four distinct pre-trained weights. The corresponding performance data and statistical metrics are summarized in Table 4. As shown, the deviations across all evaluation indicators are minimal, indicating that the model consistently achieves comparable performance across multiple runs. This experiment provides strong evidence of the model's stability and confirms that its performance improvement is reproducible rather than incidental. Among these four trained versions, the model achieving the best test performance was selected for comparison with other benchmark methods, as presented in Table 5.

Comparative experimental analysis (Figure 12 and Table 5):

(1) Based on a comprehensive evaluation of metrics (Table 5), the proposed Hybrid-SegUFormer achieves optimal overall performance, attaining the highest scores in accuracy (98.79%), IoU (66.74%), precision (81.78%), and F1-score (80.05%), which reflects superior detection precision, the lowest false positive rate, and an optimal balance between precision and recall. Although U-Net exhibits a slightly higher recall (82.52%), its lower precision may increase false alarms. Overall, Hybrid-SegUFormer outperforms other models in accuracy, segmentation detail, and reliability.

(2) Both DeepLabv3+ and SegFormer exhibit considerable missed detections within landslide deformation zones (blue-highlighted regions in Figure 12e,g), along with inadequate boundary localization precision. Their lower recall values further corroborate these models' limitations in effectively identifying positive samples. Architectural analysis indicates that DeepLabv3+ suffers from progressive decay of critical semantic information throughout the encoder–decoder process, largely due to the absence of an efficient multi-scale feature fusion mechanism and explicit boundary modeling. This results in distorted reconstructions of landslide spatial morphology. Although SegFormer leverages a Transformer-based architecture to capture global contextual information, it remains deficient in recovering fine-grained spatial details.

(3) Both U-Net and Mask R-CNN generate a significant number of false detections in non-landslide areas (yellow-marked areas in Figure 12d,f), primarily stemming from their insufficient ability to discriminate between background and target features. U-Net's symmetric encoder–decoder design lacks sufficient global contextual understanding, leading to frequent misclassification of spectrally similar background textures as landslides. Meanwhile, Mask R-CNN, dependent on region proposal mechanisms and RoI-based feature extraction, shows reduced sensitivity to landslides with ambiguous boundaries or irregular geometries. This results in a pronounced increase in false positive rates under noisy imaging conditions.

Meanwhile, we have also added comparative experiments to evaluate the computational costs of different models (Table 6). While the proposed Hybrid-SegUFormer has a slower inference speed (125.27 ms) than lightweight models like U-Net and SegFormer, it achieves a superior balance between performance and efficiency. Its parameter count (12.55 M) and computational cost (32.56 G FLOPs) are significantly lower than those of larger models like DeepLabV3+ and Mask R-CNN. This strategic trade-off is enabled by its core design: a dual-branch hybrid encoder and an attention-guided multi-scale decoder. This architecture effectively captures richer multi-scale contextual features and finer boundary details without excessive computational overhead. The result is substantially improved segmentation accuracy and robustness in complex scenarios, affirming Hybrid-SegUFormer's advanced and well-balanced design.

Table 6. Comparative analysis of model complexity and inference performance.

Targets	Hybrid-SegUFormer	U-net	DeepLabv3+	Mask R-CNN	SegFormer
Params(M)	12.55	7.77	39.63	43.92	27.35
Flops(G)	32.56	13.75	164.12	133.92	16.77
Inference Time (Ms/Img)	125.27	7.4	105.54	84.14	18.04

4.4. Ablation Studies

To validate the contributions of individual modules in Hybrid-SegUFormer, ablation studies demonstrate that the complete model (c) achieves the best overall balance, attaining the highest scores in accuracy, recall, IoU, and F1. Notably, the F1-score reaches as high as 80.05%, confirming that the synergistic effect of these three components achieves the best overall performance balance. Although its precision is not the single highest value, it remains well-balanced with recall. This indicates that the model produces fewer false positives and missed detections in practical applications, making it more suitable for robust recognition requirements in complex scenarios. The visualization results in Figure 13 provide intuitive corroboration of the model's advantage in reducing both false detection phenomena.

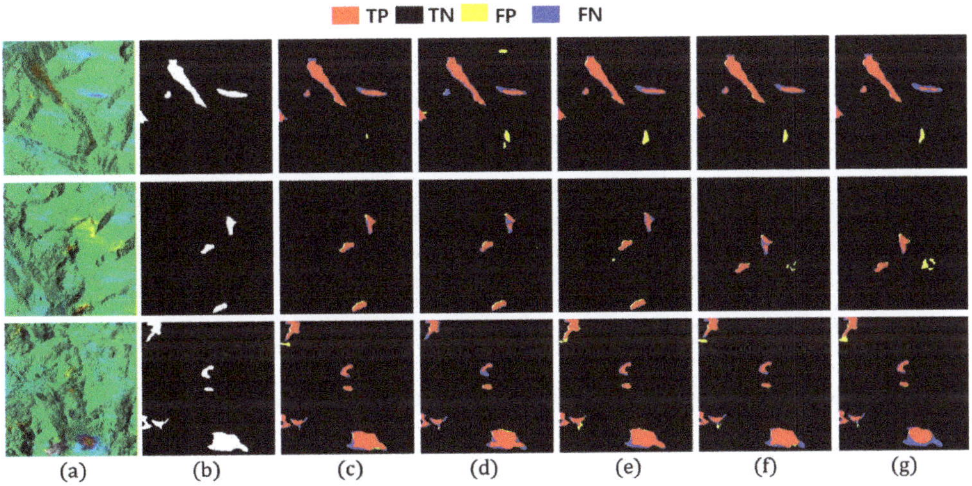

Figure 13. Ablation study results. (**a**) InSAR displacement velocity map; (**b**) Landslide label; (**c**) Hybrid-SegUFormer; (**d**) w/o SegFormer encoder (using U-net encoder instead); (**e**) w/o MSD; (**f**) w/o self-distillation; (**g**) w/o MSD and self-distillation.

The ablation study systematically analyzes the impact of each submodule in Hybrid-SegUFormer on landslide deformation area identification, demonstrating that all modules effectively enhance performance (Table 7). Comparing Figure 13e (w/o MSD) with Figure 13c (complete model) reveals that the MSD improves precision by 0.81 percentage points to 81.78% while significantly reducing false detection areas, proving its effectiveness in refining detailed segmentation. A comparison between configurations (c) and (f) demonstrates the specific contribution of the self-distillation module. While recall remains virtually unchanged (78.39% vs. 78.30%), removing this module causes a notable precision decrease from 81.78% to 80.14%, ultimately reducing both F1-score (80.05% to 79.21%) and IoU (66.74% to 65.58%). This indicates that the self-distillation module primarily enhances model performance by effectively suppressing false positives, thus playing a crucial role in maintaining the optimal precision-recall balance in the complete model. The comparison between Figure 13g (w/o MSD and self-distillation) and Figure 13e (w/o MSD) shows that the self-distillation module increases recall from 75.33% to 77.64%, with visually observable reductions in missed detection areas. This indicates its primary contribution lies in enhancing model generalization and detection sensitivity for potential landslides to reduce omissions, though it has a limited impact on precision improvement.

Table 7. Evaluation metrics for ablation study.

Figure Label	Submodule			Evaluation Metrics				
	SegFormer Encoder	MSD	Self-Distill	Accuracy (%)	Precision (%)	Recall (%)	IoU (%)	F1 (%)
(c)	√	√	√	98.79	81.78	78.39	66.74	80.05
(d)		√	√	98.74	81.49	76.87	65.44	79.11
(e)	√		√	98.74	80.97	77.64	65.54	79.18
(f)	√	√		98.73	80.14	78.30	65.58	79.21
(g)	√			98.78	83.49	75.33	65.57	79.20

A further comparison between Figure 13c (complete model) and Figure 13d (U-Net encoder replacing SegFormer) reveals that the model employing the SegFormer encoder demonstrates significantly superior performance across all five evaluation metrics. Visually, Figure 13c exhibits fewer false detections and missed identifications, along with more precise delineation of landslide boundaries. These observations collectively demonstrate that the SegFormer encoder effectively enhances the model's global contextual awareness, and the most significant improvements in fine boundary delineation are attributed to the synergistic interaction between the SegFormer encoder and our proposed decoder architecture.

It is noteworthy that when configured with only the SegFormer encoder (without the MSD and self-distillation), the model achieves its highest precision of 83.49% (the best among all configurations), demonstrating its extremely conservative prediction of foreground areas and effective suppression of false positives. However, this configuration shows suboptimal recall (75.33%) and IoU (65.57%), revealing significant missed detection issues (false negatives). This reflects the model's strong conservatism: it sacrifices detection completeness in pursuit of high precision. Mechanistically, while SegFormer's global attention mechanism can abstract semantic information and suppress background noise to reduce false alarms, the absence of boundary detail supplementation from the MSD and feature enhancement for weak semantic regions through self-distillation results in the model only recognizing the most prominent and definite landslide areas, consequently exacerbating missed detections.

4.5. Evaluation of Multi-Scale Perception Capabilities Across Models

This section demonstrates Hybrid-SegUFormer's multi-scale perception capability and its advantages over comparative models. Models with robust multi-scale perception typically exhibit three key characteristics: (1) higher recall and F1-scores for small-scale targets; (2) relative insensitivity of IoU metrics to target size variations; and (3) extensive spatial distribution of true positive (TP) regions, indicating strong spatial consistency between predictions and ground truth annotations. To quantitatively evaluate this capability, we selected sample images from Figures 14 and 15, calculating recall, IoU, and F1-scores for each case. The corresponding quantitative results are systematically summarized in Tables 8–10.

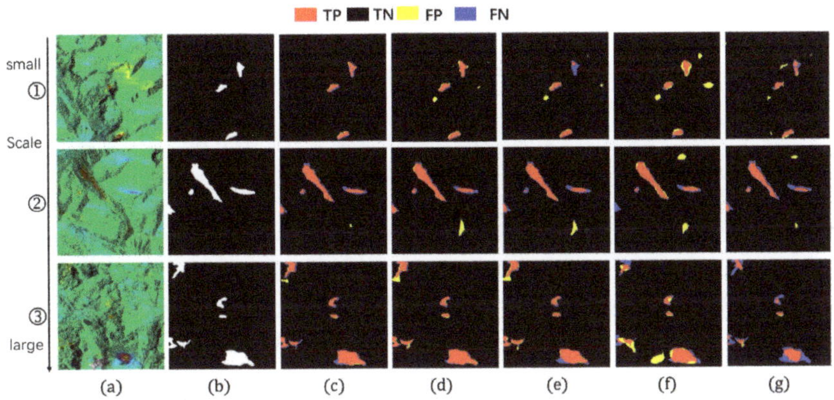

Figure 14. Detection images at different scales (group1). (**a**) InSAR displacement velocity map; (**b**) Landslide ground truth; (**c**) Hybrid-SegUFormer; (**d**) U-net; (**e**) DeepLabV3+; (**f**) Mask R-CNN; (**g**) SegFormer.

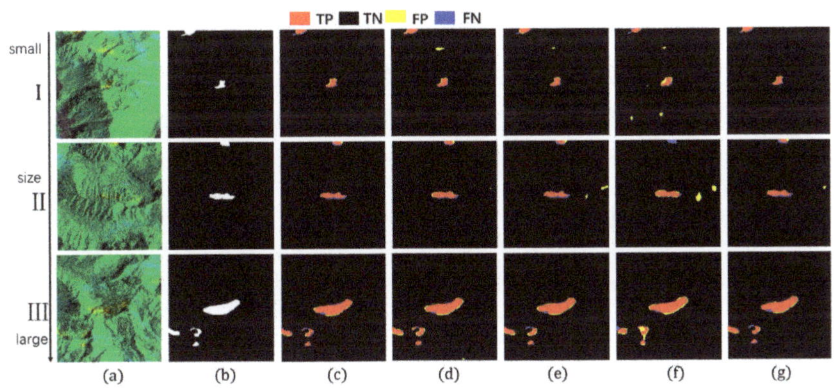

Figure 15. Detection images at different scales (group2). (**a**) InSAR displacement velocity map; (**b**) Landslide ground truth; (**c**) Hybrid-SegUFormer; (**d**) U-net; (**e**) DeepLabV3+; (**f**) Mask R-CNN; (**g**) SegFormer.

Table 8. IoU range across scales (%) for Hybrid-SegUFormer and other models on the dataset.

Image	Hybrid-SegUFormer	U-net	DeepLabV3+	Mask R-CNN	SegFormer
③	77.89	79.10	73.79	61.62	67.93
②	76.28	71.98	68.27	60.13	62.02
①	70.90	67.30	45.87	45.47	58.90
Range	6.99	11.80	27.92	16.15	19.03
III	81.03	76.63	77.64	69.67	80.95
II	74.43	76.06	62.60	48.96	68.05
I	72.20	64.88	73.22	50.31	74.31
Range	8.83	11.75	15.04	20.71	12.90

Table 9. Multi-scale recall comparison (%).

Image	Hybrid-SegUFormer	U-net	DeepLabV3+	Mask R-CNN	SegFormer
③	83.44	91.69	85.05	81.48	57.26
②	78.14	82.99	76.59	78.10	65.77
①	81.70	94.66	59.94	89.22	74.68
III	91.14	95.43	93.22	93.99	93.02
II	79.10	89.11	77.34	78.18	77.56
I	86.87	93.71	90.47	87.10	87.41

Table 10. Multi-scale F1-score comparison (%).

Image	Hybrid-SegUFormer	U-net	DeepLabV3+	Mask R-CNN	SegFormer
③	87.57	88.33	84.92	76.25	62.95
②	86.55	83.71	81.15	75.10	76.56
①	82.97	67.30	62.90	62.51	72.53
III	89.52	86.77	87.41	82.12	89.47
II	85.34	86.40	62.60	65.73	80.99
I	83.85	78.70	84.54	66.94	85.26

In the evaluation of IoU metrics (Table 8), all models exhibited performance degradation as target scales decreased, but with markedly different attenuation magnitudes. Hybrid-SegUFormer demonstrated significantly lower total IoU attenuation (6.99% and 8.83% respectively) compared to benchmark models: U-Net (11.80%/11.75%), DeepLabV3+ (27.92%/15.04%), Mask R-CNN (16.15%/20.71%), and SegFormer (19.03%/12.90%). These results indicate that Hybrid-SegUFormer maintains superior stability and robustness across scales, exhibiting more effective adaptation to varying landslide sizes while preserving higher segmentation accuracy for small targets—a compelling validation of its multi-scale fusion architecture's efficacy.

The recall analysis (Table 9) reveals significant disparities among models in detecting small targets (Image ①). While U-Net demonstrates high sensitivity to small targets with a 94.66% recall rate, its substantially degraded IoU and F1-scores indicate that this high recall comes at the cost of significant false positives. In contrast, Hybrid-SegUFormer maintains a balanced detection capability, achieving both considerable recall (81.70%) and segmentation accuracy (IoU/F1). DeepLabV3+ (59.94%) and SegFormer (74.68%), however, show markedly lower recall rates for small targets, reflecting their inadequate recognition capacity for small-scale landslide areas.

The F1-score effectively balances recall and precision. Hybrid-SegUFormer maintains consistently high F1-scores across all scales (peaking at 89.52% with a minimum of 82.97%, Table 10), demonstrating minimal performance decline and superior overall capability for multi-scale target recognition. In contrast, while U-Net achieves higher recall rates (Table 9), its F1-score drops to 67.30% on Image ①, indicating significant false positive issues with small targets. SegFormer, although showing less F1-score degradation, has generally lower absolute values (Table 10), highlighting the inherent limitations of single-scale architectures in managing target size variability.

By integrating these analyses (Tables 8–10), this study systematically compares Hybrid-SegUFormer with benchmark models (U-Net, DeepLabV3+, Mask R-CNN, SegFormer) across multiple scales using IoU, recall, and F1 metrics. It conclusively validates Hybrid-SegUFormer's superior multi-scale perception capability. The proposed model not only achieves outstanding performance across all target scales but also strikes an optimal balance between precision and recall, effectively addressing the critical limitations of comparative models in handling varying target sizes.

4.6. Ablation Study on Multi-Scale Perception Capabilities

To systematically evaluate the multi-scale perception capability of the proposed Hybrid-SegUFormer in detecting landslide deformation areas, a comparative ablation experiment was conducted with a focus on the multi-scale decoder module. The experiment utilized 20 landslide deformation velocity maps, comprising 10 large-scale and 10 small-scale images, to comprehensively assess performance across varying spatial extents. For each image, the IoU, recall, and F1-score were calculated, and the average values for each scale category were summarized to provide a robust statistical comparison, as presented in Tables 11–13. This multi-faceted evaluation with aggregated metrics verifies that the performance enhancement of the proposed model in multi-scale perception is not occasional or limited to specific cases.

Table 11. IMulti-scale IoU comparison of Hybrid-SegUFormer with or without the self-distillation module

Image	Hybrid-SegUFormer	w/o Self-Distillation
Big Scale	77.57	76.95
Small Scale	75.21	73.87
Range	2.36	3.08

Table 12. Recall range across scales (%) for different models.

Image	Hybrid-SegUFormer	w/o Self-Distillation
Big Scale	89.13	90.30
Small Scale	84.85	88.47
Range	4.28	1.83

Table 13. F1 range across scales (%) for different models.

Image	Hybrid-SegUFormer	w/o Self-Distillation
Big Scale	87.34	86.93
Small Scale	85.72	84.31
Range	1.62	2.62

The results in Table 11 (IoU across scales) demonstrate the model's stability. The complete Hybrid-SegUFormer model exhibits a smaller performance range (2.36%) between large and small scales compared to the variant without the multi-scale decoder (3.08%) in the first set, indicating superior scale robustness.

Analysis of Table 12 (recall across scales) reveals a nuanced role of the multi-scale decoder. In the first set, the complete model achieves lower recall on both large (89.13%) and small scales (84.85%) compared to the ablated version. This indicates that the multi-scale decoder's primary contribution is not necessarily to increase raw detection sensitivity but potentially to refine the quality of detections.

The data in Table 13 (F1-score across scales) provides the most critical insight into overall performance. The complete Hybrid-SegUFormer achieves higher F1-scores on both large (87.34%) and small (85.72%) scales than its counterpart, alongside a smaller performance range between scales (1.62% vs. 2.62%). This conclusively demonstrates that the integration of the multi-scale decoder enhances the model's comprehensive performance and ensures more consistent and reliable detection across diverse spatial scales.

In summary, the ablation study confirms that while the multi-scale decoder may not uniformly boost individual metrics like recall, it plays an indispensable role in achieving a superior balance between precision and recall. This is evidenced by the higher and more stable F1-scores across scales, validating its effectiveness in enabling robust multi-scale landslide detection. The synergistic integration of the multi-scale decoder is thus crucial for handling the complex multi-scale characteristics inherent in landslide deformation areas.

4.7. Model Transferability Validation

To evaluate the generalization capability of the Hybrid-SegUFormer model, the pre-trained model was transferred to Study Area II (the Baige-Tangge section of the Jinsha River), which is geographically distant from the original training area. The landslide deformation area identification results based on the Hybrid-SegUFormer model are presented in Figure 16 and Table 14.

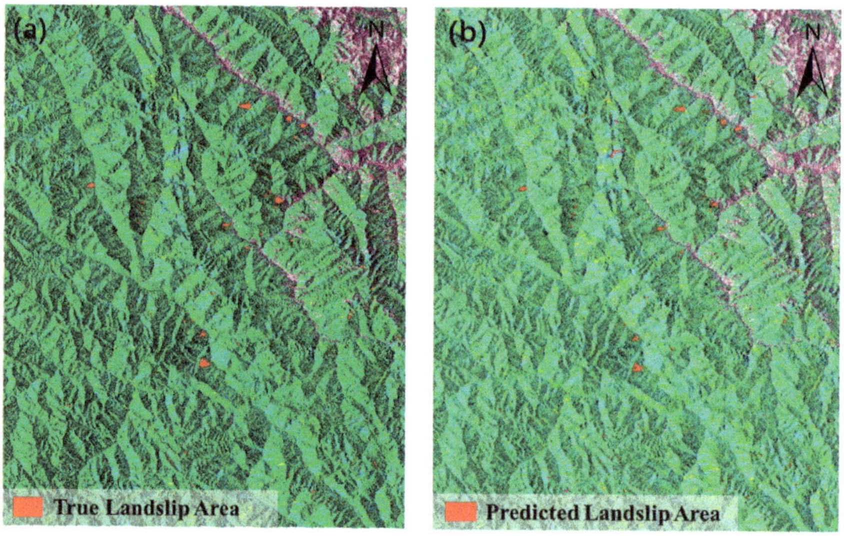

Figure 16. Partial identification of migrated dataset compared with the true value. (**a**) Ground truth of the test dataset, (**b**) Prediction part of the test dataset.

Table 14. Evaluation metrics for different detection models.

Model	Accuracy (%)	Precision (%)	Recall (%)	IOU (%)	F1 (%)
Hybrid-SegUFormer	98.92	89.81	75.42	69.47	81.99
U-net	98.90	88.15	76.47	69.34	81.89
DeepLabv3+	98.85	90.87	71.94	67.09	80.31
Mask R-CNN	98.84	87.91	74.59	67.66	80.71
SegFormer	98.45	87.88	60.76	56.06	71.84

The training results and statistical metrics of the proposed model over four independent runs are summarized in Table 15 below. As observed, although certain training iterations exhibited a slight decline in overall performance, the variations among different runs remain minor. These consistent outcomes substantiate the stability and robustness of the proposed model, indicating that its performance is not sensitive to random initialization or training variations.

Table 15. Multiple-run parameters and statistical parameters of Hybrid-SegUFormer.

Number	Accuracy (%)	Precision (%)	Recall (%)	IOU (%)	F1 (%)
①	98.92	89.81	75.42	69.47	81.99
②	98.90	88.00	76.68	69.42	81.95
③	98.85	88.11	75.12	68.21	81.10
④	98.90	88.33	76.64	69.59	82.07
Average Value	98.89	88.56	75.97	69.17	81.78
Standard Deviation	0.03	0.84	0.81	0.65	0.45
Average Range	98.89 ± 0.03	88.56 ± 0.84	75.97 ± 0.81	69.17 ± 0.65	81.78 ± 0.45

Evaluation results on the newly migrated landslide dataset (Table 13) demonstrate Hybrid-SegUFormer's significant advantages: it achieves top performance in both IoU (69.47%) and F1-score (81.99%), surpassing classical models U-Net (IoU 69.34%, F1 81.89%) and DeepLabV3+ (IoU 67.09%, F1 80.31%). Notably, compared to the widely used Transformer model SegFormer (IoU 56.06%, F1 71.84%), Hybrid-SegUFormer shows remarkable improvements of 13.41% in IoU and 10.15% in F1-score, highlighting its exceptional generalization capability. Furthermore, the model maintains an optimal balance between precision (89.81%) and recall (75.42%), indicating more balanced control over false positives and missed detections. These comprehensive metrics conclusively validate Hybrid-SegUFormer's effectiveness and robustness for transferred landslide recognition tasks.

4.8. Exclusion of Non-Landslide Deformation Areas Based on Auxiliary Data

In landslide deformation area identification, study areas often contain various non-landslide surface disturbance sources (such as agricultural activities, seasonal vegetation variations, construction activities, and radar geometric distortions), which can easily lead to misinterpretations. To improve identification accuracy and practical utility, this study uses a systematic procedure for removing non-landslide deformation areas based on multi-source auxiliary data, after initially extracting prominent landslide deformation regions using Hybrid-SegUFormer. The specific steps of this procedure include the following: ① combining land cover data to exclude human-disturbed areas such as permanent croplands, water bodies, and construction zones; ② incorporating NDVI (Normalized Difference Vegetation Index) data to exclude regions with high vegetation coverage (threshold greater than 0.5), thereby reducing false deformation signals caused by normal seasonal vegetation changes or forest dynamics; ③ using radar geometric distortion data to identify and exclude observation-unreliable areas such as layover and shadow zones; and finally, applying slope information to filter out areas with excessively gentle slopes, minimizing false alarms due to insufficient topographic relief. This systematic elimination strategy reduces the proportion of false landslide deformation areas, significantly decreases misjudgments, and provides crucial data preprocessing support for building a highly reliable automated monitoring system for geological hazards.

Before implementing the aforementioned filtering procedures, the patch-based predictions generated by the Hybrid-SegUFormer model are first mosaicked into large-scale GeoTIFF images with precise geospatial coordinates (as illustrated in Figure 17). This critical preprocessing step establishes the foundation for subsequent multi-source data spatial registration and overlay analysis.

The Python script was then employed to extract white significant deformation areas from the landslide mask and convert them into Shapefile format for ArcGIS 10.8 integration. We run the script in Python 3.11. Subsequently, multi-source auxiliary data were incorporated to eliminate non-significant deformation areas through the editing of Shapefile attributes, with the refined results presented in Figure 18.

Figure 17. (**a**) Landslide deformation area identification results; (**b**) Landslide deformation area mask.

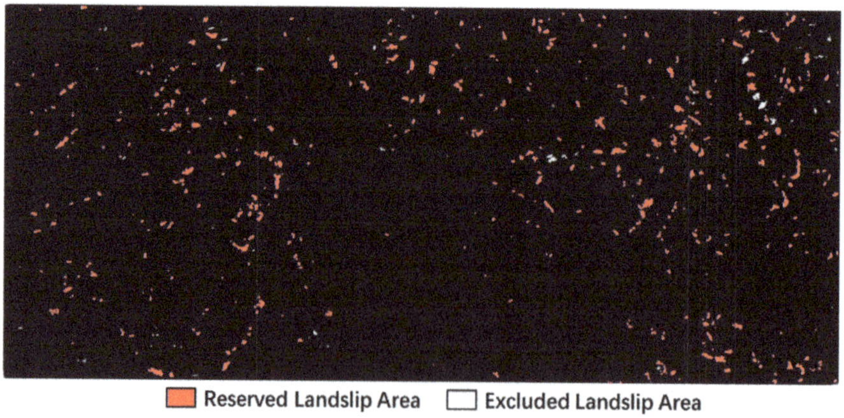

Figure 18. Results before/after non-landslide deformation area excluded.

5. Discussion

This study addresses the challenges of multi-scale target perception, boundary detail restoration, and insufficient model generalization performance in the detection of landslide InSAR Deformation areas. We propose the Hybrid-SegUFormer model, which integrates a SegFormer encoder, a U-Net decoder structure, an MSD, and a self-distillation mechanism. Through systematic experimental validation, Hybrid-SegUFormer demonstrates superior performance in complex landslide scenarios, and an in-depth analysis of its advantages is provided.

5.1. Superiority of Model Performance

Comparative experiments with mainstream semantic segmentation models (U-Net, DeepLabV3+, Mask R-CNN, SegFormer) show that Hybrid-SegUFormer performs excellently in both qualitative and quantitative evaluations. Specifically, DeepLabV3+ and SegFormer exhibit significant missed detections and boundary localization deviations; U-Net and Mask R-CNN suffer from high false detection rates due to insufficient background discrimination ability. In contrast, Hybrid-SegUFormer effectively balances missed and false detections through its hybrid architecture, achieving more accurate identification of landslide deformation areas and boundary characterization. This capability offers essential geometric parameters for volume estimation and kinematic analysis, thereby greatly improving the utility of InSAR data in landslide risk assessment.

5.2. Synergistic Contribution of Core Modules

Ablation studies quantify the contribution of each module to the model's performance. The full model (F1: 80.05%) achieves the best overall balance, attaining the highest scores in accuracy, recall, IoU, and F1, verifying the importance of the synergistic effects of the SegFormer encoder, MSD, and self-distillation module. Among them, the SegFormer encoder significantly enhances the model's global context modeling capability and generalization performance; the MSD effectively improves the segmentation precision of detailed regions (especially boundaries); the self-distillation module strengthens the model's generalization ability and detection sensitivity to potential landslide areas, effectively reducing the missed detection rate. The three together form a "global-local-knowledge distillation" closed-loop optimization, breaking through the performance limitations of individual modules.

5.3. Exceptional Multi-Scale Perception Ability

The experimental results demonstrate Hybrid-SegUFormer's competent multi-scale perception capability for landslide detection. While all models showed performance degradation with decreasing target scales, Hybrid-SegUFormer exhibited relatively attenuated performance reduction (IoU range: 6.99–8.83% versus 11.80–27.92% in benchmarks), indicating better scale adaptability. The model maintains a balance between detection sensitivity and accuracy, achieving reasonable recall (81.70% for small targets) while avoiding the significant false positive issues observed in U-Net. The ablation study further reveals that the multi-scale decoder contributes to performance stability across scales (F1-range: 1.62% versus 2.62% without decoder), though its impact varies across different metrics. These consistent results across multiple evaluation metrics suggest that Hybrid-SegUFormer's architecture effectively addresses scale variance challenges in landslide detection tasks.

5.4. Validation of Model Transferability

Evaluation results on the newly constructed transfer landslide dataset demonstrate that Hybrid-SegUFormer exhibits exceptional cross-regional recognition capability. It outperforms all comparison models in two key metrics: Intersection over Union (IoU: 69.47%) and F1-score (81.99%). Particularly when compared to the SegFormer model, it achieves significant improvements (13.41% increase in IoU and 10.15% increase in F1-score). Furthermore, the model maintains an excellent balance between precision (89.81%) and recall (75.42%), indicating more balanced control over false positives and missed detections for landslide targets. These results strongly validate the effectiveness and robustness of the model in transfer landslide identification tasks. This generalization ability can reduce dependency on extensive, region-specific data collection, thereby accelerating large-scale regional landslide screening and geohazard assessment.

5.5. Comparative Analysis with Related Studies

Compared to related studies, the innovations and distinctive features of this model are mainly reflected in three aspects: In terms of architectural fusion, it creatively combines the SegFormer's advantages in global long-range context modeling with the U-Net decoder's ability to restore fine-grained local features; in module enhancement, the introduction of the MSD significantly improves perception ability for multi-scale landslide areas in complex terrain, and the self-distillation mechanism further enhances boundary precision and model robustness; in multi-source information utilization, it effectively integrates multi-source auxiliary data (geometric distortion, terrain slope, NDVI, land use type), and by incorporating non-visual prior information, it accurately filters out non-landslide areas, significantly reducing the false detection rate and improving the reliability and practicality of the results.

5.6. Limitations and Future Work

While Hybrid-SegUFormer demonstrates strong multi-scale perception and cross-regional transferability, several limitations persist. First, the model's performance remains constrained by input data quality, including SAR coherence/resolution and DEM accuracy, where poor-quality inputs in rugged terrain can introduce artifacts and reduce boundary precision. Second, detection challenges remain for small, elongated, or blurry-boundary landslides due to Transformers' local detail constraints, error propagation in self-distillation, and inherent InSAR resolution limits. Finally, the lack of comprehensive ground-truth validation in truly unseen regions hinders the precise quantification of operational performance in new geological settings.

Based on these limitations, our future work will pursue three key directions: (1) optimizing the model through lightweight Transformers and boundary-focused loss functions to enhance efficiency and detail capture; (2) rigorously validating generalization capability across diverse terrains and data qualities; (3) advancing transfer learning techniques while initiating field campaigns for ground-truth collection, ultimately bridging the gap toward operational landslide monitoring systems; (4) integrating multi-source data (e.g., LiDAR-derived topography and SAR coherence) to enhance feature discrimination and improve model robustness against vegetation, shadows, and complex terrain.

6. Conclusions

Hybrid-SegUFormer is proposed to address the challenges of multi-scale target perception, inadequate recovery of boundary details, and limited generalization capability in the identification of landslide InSAR deformation areas. The model integrates a SegFormer encoder, a U-Net-based decoder, a multi-scale feature decoding module, and a self-distillation mechanism. Through systematic experiments and comprehensive evaluation, the following key conclusions are drawn:

(1) Comprehensive evaluation demonstrated that Hybrid-SegUFormer achieves state-of-the-art performance in landslide deformation area identification, outperforming benchmark models (U-Net, DeepLabV3+, Mask R-CNN, SegFormer) across key metrics, including accuracy (98.79%), IoU (66.74%), and F1-score (80.05%). While maintaining reasonable computational efficiency, the model effectively addresses critical limitations observed in comparative approaches: reducing false detections through enhanced global context understanding, improving boundary precision via multi-scale feature fusion, and maintaining robust performance across multiple training runs. The results confirm Hybrid-SegUFormer's superior capability in balancing segmentation accuracy, operational efficiency, and operational stability for complex landslide detection tasks.

(2) Ablation studies confirm that the complete Hybrid-SegUFormer achieves optimal performance balance (F1-score: 80.05%) through synergistic module integration. The multi-scale decoder enhances precision (81.78%) and reduces false detections, while the self-distillation module effectively suppresses false positives and maintains precision-recall balance. The SegFormer encoder provides superior global contextual awareness, though its standalone use yields high precision (83.49%) at the cost of significantly reduced recall (75.33%). These findings demonstrated that the architectural components collectively address both boundary precision and detection sensitivity, with their integration being crucial for robust landslide identification.

(3) Comprehensive evaluations demonstrated Hybrid-SegUFormer's superior multi-scale perception capability, showing significantly smaller IoU degradation across scales (6.99–8.83%) compared to benchmark models (11.80–27.92%). While maintaining balanced recall-precision trade-offs, the model achieves consistently high F1-scores (82.97–89.52%) across all target sizes. Ablation studies further confirm the multi-scale decoder's crucial role in enhancing performance stability, yielding improved F1-scores (85.72–87.34%) and reduced performance variance (1.62% range) across scales. These results collectively validate the architecture's effectiveness in handling scale variations while maintaining robust detection accuracy for landslide identification tasks.

(4) Evaluation results on a transferred landslide dataset indicate that Hybrid-SegUFormer possesses strong cross-regional recognition capability. Its IoU and F1-score are significantly higher than those of comparative models, demonstrating that the model can effectively adapt to different geographical environments and data distributions, highlighting its considerable practical value and potential for broad application.

Author Contributions: Conceptualization, W.Z. and D.M.; methodology, W.Z. and D.M.; software, J.Z.; validation, W.Z. and J.C.; formal analysis, W.Z.; investigation, J.Z.; resources, W.Z.; data curation, J.C.; writing—original draft preparation, W.Z.; writing—review and editing, D.M.; visualization, W.Z. and J.Z.; supervision, D.M.; project administration, D.M.; funding acquisition, D.M. All authors have read and agreed to the published version of the manuscript.

Funding: This research was funded by the Geological Survey Program "Support for Geo-hazard monitoring, early warning and prevention" (DD20230085) and the National Natural Science Foundation of China (42371379).

Data Availability Statement: The data are available on request from the corresponding author.

Acknowledgments: The authors want to thank the ESA for providing the satellite radar data.

Conflicts of Interest: The authors declare no conflicts of interest.

References

1. Hungr, O.; Leroueil, S.; Picarelli, L. The Varnes Classification of Landslide Types, an Update. *Landslides* **2014**, *11*, 167–194. [CrossRef]
2. Huang, R. Large-scale landslides and their sliding mechanisms in china since the 20th century. *Chin. J. Rock Mech. Eng.* **2007**, *26*, 433–454.
3. Yin, Y.; Wang, F.; Ping, S. Landslide Hazards Triggered by the 2008 Wenchuan Earthquake, Sichuan, China. *Landslides* **2009**, *6*, 139–151. [CrossRef]
4. Kirschbaum, D.; Kapnick, S.B.; Stanley, T.; Pascale, S. Changes in Extreme Precipitation and Landslides Over High Mountain Asia. *Geophys. Res. Lett.* **2020**, *47*, e2019GL085347. [CrossRef]
5. Zeng, T.; Guo, Z.; Wang, L.; Jin, B.; Wu, F.; Guo, R. Tempo-Spatial Landslide Susceptibility Assessment from the Perspective of Human Engineering Activity. *Remote Sens.* **2023**, *15*, 5549. [CrossRef]
6. Hürlimann, M.; Guo, Z.; Puig-Polo, C.; Medina, V. Impacts of Future Climate and Land Cover Changes on Landslide Susceptibility: Regional Scale Modelling in the Val d'Aran Region (Pyrenees, Spain). *Landslides* **2022**, *19*, 99–118. [CrossRef]
7. Yin, Y.; Wang, H.; Gao, Y.; Li, X. Real-Time Monitoring and Early Warning of Landslides at Relocated Wushan Town, the Three Gorges Reservoir, China. *Landslides* **2010**, *7*, 339–349. [CrossRef]

8. Xu, Q.; Zhu, X.; Li, W.; Dong, X.; Dai, K.; Jiang, Y.; Lu, H.; Guo, C. Technical Progress of Space-Air Ground Collaborative Monitoring of Landslide. *Acta Geodaetica Cartogr. Sin.* **2022**, *51*, 1416–1436. [CrossRef]
9. Zhao, W.; Zhang, M.; Ma, J.; Qi, G.; Zhu, S.; Huang, Z. Research, Development, and Field Trial of the Universal Global Navigation Satellite System Receivers. *IOP Conf. Ser. Earth Environ. Sci.* **2020**, *570*, 62048. [CrossRef]
10. Zhao, W.; Zhang, M.; Ma, J.; Han, B.; Ye, S.; Huang, Z. Application of CORS in Landslide Monitoring. *IOP Conf. Ser. Earth Environ. Sci.* **2021**, *861*, 42049. [CrossRef]
11. Li, X.; Zhou, L.; Su, F.; Wu, W. Application of InSAR Technology in Landslide Hazard: Progress and Prospects. *Natl. Remote Sens. Bull.* **2021**, *25*, 614–629. [CrossRef]
12. Vern, S.; Pierre-Jean, A.; Rejean, C.; Valentin, P. InSAR Monitoring of Landslides on Permafrost Terrain in Canada. In Proceedings of the IEEE International Geoscience and Remote Sensing Symposium (IGARSS 2007), Barcelona, Spain, 23 July 2007.
13. Antoni, W.; Zbigniew, P.; Ramon, H. InSAR Analyses of Terrain Deformation near the Wieliczka Salt Mine, Poland. *Eng. Geol.* **2009**, *106*, 58–67. [CrossRef]
14. Wang, G.; Xie, M.; Chai, X.; Wang, L.; Dong, C. Application of D-InSAR Technique to Landslide Monitoring in Wide Reservoir Area. *China Min. Mag.* **2011**, *20*, 94–101.
15. Lu, H.; Li, W.; Xu, Q.; Dong, X.; Dai, C.; Wang, D. Early Detection of Landslides in the Upstream and Downstream Areas of the Baige Landslide, the Jinsha River Based on Optical Remote Sensing and InSAR Technologies. *Geomat. Inf. Sci. Wuhan Univ.* **2019**, *44*, 1342–1354. [CrossRef]
16. Yin, Y.; Xu, S.; Wang, J.; Hu, K. Identification and Time Series Monitoring of Hidden Dangers of Geological Hazards in the Typical Loess Hilly Regions. *Hydrogeol. Eng. Geol.* **2023**, *50*, 141–149. [CrossRef]
17. Liu, X.; Zhao, C.; Zhang, Q.; Lu, Z.; Li, Z.; Yang, C.; Zhu, W.; Liu-Zeng, J.; Chen, L.; Liu, C. Integration of Sentinel-1 and ALOS/PALSAR-2 SAR Datasets for Mapping Active Landslides along the Jinsha River Corridor, China. *Eng. Geol.* **2021**, *284*, 106033. [CrossRef]
18. Mondini, A.C.; Guzzetti, F.; Chang, K.-T.; Monserrat, O.; Martha, T.R.; Manconi, A. Landslide Failures Detection and Mapping Using Synthetic Aperture Radar: Past, Present and Future. *Earth-Sci. Rev.* **2021**, *216*, 103574. [CrossRef]
19. Cai, J.; Zhang, L.; Dong, J.; Dong, X.; Li, M.; Xu, Q.; Liao, M. Detection and Characterization of Slow-Moving Landslides in the 2017 Jiuzhaigou Earthquake Area by Combining Satellite SAR Observations and Airborne Lidar DSM. *Eng. Geol.* **2022**, *305*, 106730. [CrossRef]
20. Zhang, L.; Liao, M.; Dong, J.; Xu, Q.; Gong, J. Early Detection of Landslide Hazards in Mountainous Areas of West China Using Time Series SAR Interferometry-A Case Study of Danba, Sichuan. *Geomat. Inf. Sci. Wuhan Univ.* **2018**, *43*, 2039–2049. [CrossRef]
21. Tomás, R.; Pagán, J.I.; Navarro, J.A.; Cano, M.; Pastor, J.L.; Riquelme, A.; Cuevas-González, M.; Crosetto, M.; Barra, A.; Monserrat, O.; et al. Semi-Automatic Identification and Pre-Screening of Geological–Geotechnical Deformational Processes Using Persistent Scatterer Interferometry Datasets. *Remote Sens.* **2019**, *11*, 1675. [CrossRef]
22. Liao, M.; Dong, J.; LI, M.; Ao, M.; Zhang, L.; Shi, X. Radar Remote Sensing for Potential Landslides Detection and Deformation Monitoring. *Natl. Remote Sens. Bull.* **2021**, *25*, 332–341. [CrossRef]
23. Anantrasirichai, N.; Biggs, J.; Kelevitz, K.; Sadeghi, Z.; Wright, T.; Thompson, J.; Achim, A.M.; Bull, D. Detecting Ground Deformation in the Built Environment Using Sparse Satellite InSAR Data With a Convolutional Neural Network. *IEEE Trans. Geosci. Remote Sens.* **2021**, *59*, 2940–2950. [CrossRef]
24. Wu, Q.; Ge, D.; Yu, J.; Zhang, L.; Li, M.; Liu, B.; Wang, Y.; Ma, Y.; Liu, H. Deep Learning Identification Technology of InSAR Significant Deformation Zone of Potential Landslide Hazard at Large Scale. *Acta Geod. Cartogr. Sin.* **2022**, *51*, 2046–2055.
25. Qin, S.; Guo, X.; Sun, J.; Qiao, S.; Zhang, L.; Yao, J.; Cheng, Q.; Zhang, Y. Landslide Detection from Open Satellite Imagery Using Distant Domain Transfer Learning. *Remote Sens.* **2021**, *13*, 3383. [CrossRef]
26. Li, Z.; Shi, A.; Li, X.; Dou, J.; Li, S.; Chen, T.; Chen, T. Deep Learning-Based Landslide Recognition Incorporating Deformation Characteristics. *Remote Sens.* **2024**, *16*, 992. [CrossRef]
27. Zhang, T.; Zhang, W.; Cao, D.; Yi, Y.; Wu, X. A New Deep Learning Neural Network Model for the Identification of InSAR Anomalous Deformation Areas. *Remote Sens.* **2022**, *14*, 2690. [CrossRef]
28. Ashutosh, T.; Manoochehr, S. A Novel Machine Learning and Deep Learning Semi-Supervised Approach for Automatic Detection of InSAR-Based Deformation Hotspots. *Int. J. Appl. Earth Obs. Geoinf.* **2023**, *126*, 103611. [CrossRef]
29. Liu, X.; Zhang, Y.; Shan, X.; Wang, Z.; Gong, W.; Zhang, G. Deep Learning for Automatic Detection of Volcanic and Earthquake-Related InSAR Deformation. *Remote Sens.* **2025**, *17*, 686. [CrossRef]
30. Jiang, W.; Xi, J.; Li, Z.; Ding, M.; Yang, L.; Xie, D. Landslide Detection and Segmentation Using Mask R-CNN with Simulated Hard Samples. *Geomat. Inf. Sci. Wuhan Univ.* **2023**, *48*, 1931–1942. [CrossRef]
31. Wan, C.; Gan, J.; Chen, A.; Acharya, P.; Li, F.; Yu, W.; Liu, F. A Novel Method for Identifying Landslide Surface Deformation via the Integrated YOLOX and Mask R-CNN Model. *Int. J. Comput. Intell. Syst.* **2024**, *17*, 255. [CrossRef]
32. Chen, L.-C.; Zhu, Y.; Papandreou, G.; Schroff, F.; Adam, H. Encoder-Decoder with Atrous Separable Convolution for Semantic Image Segmentation. *Lect. Notes Comput. Sci.* **2018**, *11211*, 833–851. [CrossRef]
33. Li, Y. The Research on Landslide Detection in Remote Sensing Images Based on Improved DeepLabv3+ Method. *Sci. Rep.* **2025**, *15*, 7957. [CrossRef]

34. Wang, W.; Zhang, Z.; Zhu, X.; Yang, S. Semantic Segmentation of Landslide Image Using DeepLabv3+ and Completed Local Binary Pattern. *J. Appl. Remote Sens.* **2024**, *19*, 14502. [CrossRef]
35. Vega, J.; Palomino-Ángel, S.; Hidalgo, C. Exploring U-Net Deep Learning Model for Landslide Detection Using Optical Imagery, Geo-Indices, and SAR Data in a Data Scarce Tropical Mountain Region. *PFG-J. Photogramm. Remote Sens. Geoinf. Sci.* **2025**, *93*, 251–283. [CrossRef]
36. Wang, H.; Liu, J.; Zeng, S.; Xiao, K.; Yang, D.; Yao, G.; Yang, R. A Novel Landslide Identification Method for Multi-Scale and Complex Background Region Based on Multi-Model Fusion: YOLO + U-Net. *Landslides* **2024**, *21*, 901–917. [CrossRef]
37. Yang, S.; Wang, Y.; Zhao, K.; Liu, X.; Mu, J.; Zhao, X. Partial Convolution-Simple Attention Mechanism-SegFormer: An Accurate and Robust Model for Landslide Identification. *Eng. Appl. Artif. Intell.* **2025**, *151*, 110612. [CrossRef]
38. Lv, J.; Zhang, R.; Wu, R.; Bao, X.; Liu, G. Landslide Detection Based on Pixel-Level Contrastive Learning for Semi-Supervised Semantic Segmentation in Wide Areas. *Landslides* **2025**, *22*, 1087–1105. [CrossRef]
39. Opara, J.; Moriwaki, R.; Chun, P. Automated Landslide Mapping in Japan Using the Segformer Model: Enhancing Accuracy and Efficiency in Disaster Management. *Intell. Inform. Infrastruct.* **2023**, *4*, 75–86. [CrossRef]
40. Zhang, Y.; Liu, H.; Hu, Q. Transfuse: Fusing transformers and cnns for medical image segmentation. In Proceedings of the International Conference on Medical Image Computing and Computer-Assisted Intervention, Strasbourg, France, 27 September 2021.
41. Dong, B.; Wang, Z.; Chen, C.; Wang, K.; Zhang, J. An Improved Backbone Fusion Neural Network for Orchard Extraction. *IEEE J. Sel. Top. Appl. Earth Obs. Remote Sens.* **2025**, *18*, 17961–17974. [CrossRef]
42. Mao, Z.; Tong, X.; Luo, Z. Semi-Supervised Remote Sensing Image Change Detection Using Mean Teacher Model for Constructing Pseudo-Labels. In Proceedings of the ICASSP 2023–2023 IEEE International Conference on Acoustics, Speech and Signal Processing (ICASSP), Rhodes Island, Greece, 4 June 2023.
43. Fang, F.; Kang, J.; Li, S.; Tian, P.; Liu, Y.; Luo, C.; Zhou, S. Multi-Granularity Domain-Adaptive Teacher for Unsupervised Remote Sensing Object Detection. *Remote Sens.* **2025**, *17*, 1743. [CrossRef]
44. Cai, J.; Ming, D.; Zhao, W.; Ling, X.; Zhang, Y.; Zhang, X. Integrated Remote Sensing-Based Hazard Identification and Disaster-Causing Mechanisms of Landslides in Zayu County. *Remote Sens. Nat. Resour.* **2024**, *36*, 128–136. [CrossRef]
45. Yu, C.; Li, Z.; Penna Nigel, T.; Crippa, P. Generic Atmospheric Correction Model for Interferometric Synthetic Aperture Radar Observations. *J. Geophys. Res. Solid Earth* **2018**, *123*, 9202–9222. [CrossRef]
46. Yu, C.; Penna, N.T.; Li, Z. Generation of Real-Time Mode High-Resolution Water Vapor Fields from GPS Observations. *J. Geophys. Res. Atmos.* **2017**, *122*, 2008–2025. [CrossRef]
47. Xiao, R.; Chen, Y.; Li, Z.; He, X. Statistical Assessment Metrics for InSAR Atmospheric Correction: Applications to Generic Atmospheric Correction Online Service for InSAR (GACOS) in Eastern China. *Int. J. Appl. Earth Obs. Geoinf.* **2021**, *96*, 102289. [CrossRef]
48. Goldstein, R.; Werner, C. Radar Interferogram Filtering for Geophysical Applications. *Geophys. Res. Lett.* **1998**, *25*, 4035–4038. [CrossRef]
49. Costantini, M. A Novel Phase Unwrapping Method Based on Network Programming. *IEEE Trans. Geosci. Remote Sens.* **1998**, *36*, 813–821. [CrossRef]
50. Berardino, P.; Fornaro, G.; Lanari, R. A New Algorithm for Surface Deformation Monitoring Based on Small Baseline Differential SAR Interferograms. *IEEE Trans. Geosci. Remote Sens.* **2002**, *40*, 2375–2383. [CrossRef]

remote sensing

MDPI

Article

JSPSR: Joint Spatial Propagation Super-Resolution Networks for Enhancement of Bare-Earth Digital Elevation Models from Global Data

Xiandong Cai [1] and Matthew D. Wilson [1,2,*]

[1] Geospatial Research Institute, University of Canterbury, Christchurch 8140, New Zealand; xander.cai@canterbury.ac.nz

[2] School of Earth and Environment, University of Canterbury, Christchurch 8140, New Zealand

* Correspondence: matthew.wilson@canterbury.ac.nz

Highlights

What are the main findings?

- We introduce JSPSR, a depth completion approach for real-world digital elevation model (DEM) super-resolution problems, and demonstrated that it is able to enhance global DEMs by accurately predicting ground terrain elevation at fine spatial resolution, including correction for surface features.
- JSPSR was used to predict elevation at 3 m and 8 m spatial resolution from globally-available 30 m Copernicus GLO-30 DEM data and aerial guidance imagery, achieving superior performance to other methods (∼1.05 m RMSE, up to a ∼72% improvement on GLO30 and ∼18% improvement on FathomDEM), at lower computational cost (over 4× faster than EDSR).

What is the implication of the main finding?

- Studies which require high-accuracy ground terrain elevation, e.g., flood risk assessment, may utilise JSPSR to enhance global elevation data such as the Copernicus GLO30 DEM, especially where airborne data such as LiDAR are unavailable.
- The high accuracy and low computational cost of JSPSR opens the possibility to create an open-access fine spatial resolution global elevation model with good accuracy.

Abstract

(1) Background: Digital Elevation Models (DEMs) encompass digital bare earth surface representations that are essential for spatial data analysis, such as hydrological and geological modelling, as well as for other applications, such as agriculture and environmental management. However, available bare-earth DEMs can have limited coverage or accessibility. Moreover, the majority of available global DEMs have lower spatial resolutions (∼30–90 m) and contain errors introduced by surface features such as buildings and vegetation. (2) Methods: This research presents an innovative method to convert global DEMs to bare-earth DEMs while enhancing their spatial resolution as measured by the improved vertical accuracy of each pixel, combined with reduced pixel size. We propose the Joint Spatial Propagation Super-Resolution network (JSPSR), which integrates Guided Image Filtering (GIF) and Spatial Propagation Network (SPN). By leveraging guidance features extracted from remote sensing images with or without auxiliary spatial data, our method can correct elevation errors and enhance the spatial resolution of DEMs. We developed a dataset for real-world bare-earth DEM Super-Resolution (SR) problems in low-relief areas utilising open-access data. Experiments were conducted on the dataset using JSPSR and other methods to predict 3 m and 8 m spatial resolution DEMs from 30 m spatial

https://doi.org/10.3390/rs17213591

resolution Copernicus GLO-30 DEMs. (3) Results: JSPSR improved prediction accuracy by 71.74% on Root Mean Squared Error (RMSE) and reconstruction quality by 22.9% on Peak Signal-to-Noise Ratio (PSNR) compared to bicubic interpolated GLO-30 DEMs, and achieves 56.03% and 13.8% improvement on the same items against a baseline Single Image Super Resolution (SISR) method. Overall RMSE was 1.06 m at 8 m spatial resolution and 1.1 m at 3 m, compared to 3.8 m for GLO-30, 1.8 m for FABDEM and 1.3 m for FathomDEM, at either resolution. (4) Conclusions: JSPSR outperforms other methods in bare-earth DEM super-resolution tasks, with improved elevation accuracy compared to other state-of-the-art globally available datasets.

Keywords: digital elevation model; single image super-resolution; depth completion; deep learning; guided image filtering; spatial propagation network

1. Introduction

Digital Elevation Models (DEMs) encode and represent topographic elevation data in raster format, which are fundamental for the analysis of earth surface characteristics and the computational representation and quantification of natural events [1]. Nevertheless, the spatial resolution and vertical accuracy of DEMs could significantly influence the reliability of derived outputs, such as in the modelling of surface water flows [2], including flood risk assessment and flood prediction [3]. In some cases, due to the presence of surface artefacts in the data, the inundation extent may be under- [4] or over-predicted [5]. Previous studies demonstrated how the use of global DEMs in urban flood risk assessment may consistently lead to an overestimation of predicted flood extent and its associated potential damages [3,5].

Large-scale elevation data are generally acquired through satellite-based remote sensing platforms. Interferometric Synthetic Aperture Radar (InSAR) has been used to produce freely available global data (or nearly global) DEM products with coarse resolution ($\sim$1 arcsecond, approximately 30 m at the equator) and vertical accuracy of several metres [6]. More accurately, these products represent approximate DSMs (Digital Surface Models) owing to variable signal penetration characteristics in vegetated areas [7]. Global commercial elevation data are also available, including Airbus's WorldDEM Neo product, at a spatial resolution of 5 m and a specified vertical accuracy of 1.4 m, and Maxar's Precision3D elevation product, which was generated using stereophotogrammetric techniques [8], at a spatial resolution of 0.5 m and a specified vertical accuracy of 3 m.

For local or regional studies, airborne Light Detection and Ranging (LiDAR) systems have emerged as a preferred methodology for generating bare-earth DEMs, namely Digital Terrain Models (DTMs), delivering sub-meter resolution and centimetre-grade vertical accuracy [9]. However, the limited geographical coverage of LiDAR data, particularly in developing regions or sparsely populated areas, and its high acquisition cost, necessitate reliance on coarser spatial resolution global DEM datasets with lower vertical accuracy, thereby reducing the accuracy of analyses that rely on these data. Thus, there is a need for freely available, fine spatial resolution, high-accuracy DTMs at a global scale [10].

One of the most accurate open-access global DEM products available [11] is the Copernicus GLO-30 [12] (COP30) DEM dataset. It is derived from TanDEM-X InSAR and provides $\sim$1 arc-second spatial resolution. To improve its accuracy, research efforts have focused on converting the elevation into DTMs, exemplified by FABDEM [13], which was created utilising a random forest machine learning algorithm to estimate bare-earth elevations by excluding vegetation and anthropogenic structures. A later iteration, FathomDEM [14], was developed by incorporating advanced deep learning architectures, including attention mechanisms and vision transformers [15], yielding DTMs with enhanced accuracy. Those data are underpinning recent research to predict floods on a global scale at a $\sim$30 m spatial resolution [16], with flood model accuracy assessed as the highest among several DEM alternatives [4] by using FABDEM.

However, as shown by Meadows et al. [6] in their accuracy assessment of global elevation datasets, there remains room for improvement with the overall vertical error in FABDEM assessed as 2.62 m Root Mean Square Error (RMSE), the most accurate of six alternatives, but varying between 0.81 m (herbacious wetlands) to 3.75 m (tree cover) for different land cover categories, and between 1.72 m (0–1°) to 5.65 m (>25°) for different slope categories. The overall RMSE of FathomDEM is 1.67 m, with a range between 0.62 m (0–1° slopes) to 12.78 m (>40° slopes) [14]. These figures are considerably higher than the vertical accuracy target of 0.5 m suggested by Schumann and Bates [17] in their call for developing a high-accuracy, open-access global DTM. Furthermore, it should be noted that both FABDEM and FathomDEM are openly available only for non-commercial use under a share-alike licence (CC BY-NC-SA 4.0), which presents a potential barrier to use in, for example, climate impact assessments conducted by NGOs.

Recently, several studies have explored different Super-Resolution (SR) methodologies to bridge the gap between the growing demand for high-resolution DEMs and existing low-resolution global DEMs. The use of SR techniques allows the reconstruction of high-resolution DEMs from low-resolution global datasets, leveraging readily available computing resources instead of expensive remote sensing surveys. It is important to note that, as defined by Guth et al. [7], the spatial resolution is the "horizontal dimensions of the smallest feature detectable by the sensor and modified after the gridding procedure". Therefore, SR methods must increase the amount of information present within the data, rather than only reducing the pixel size. Further, the pixel size of the source elevation data is usually smaller than the spatial resolution due to oversampling to ensure that actual spatial resolution is not lost [7]. Consequently, we note that SR techniques are starting from an unknown but larger actual spatial resolution than the pixel size of the original source data.

As described in detail by Fisher & Tate [18], errors in DEMs result from a combination of sources, including instrument errors (i.e., resulting from the sensor or scanning system), geometry-induced errors (i.e., resulting from the conversion of a continuous elevation surface into a grid of discrete cells with a certain numerical precision), and errors introduced by the environment (e.g., vegetation, buildings and any other above-surface feature). The final vertical accuracy of the DEM will comprise a combination of each of these error sources. For geometry-induced errors, these are deterministic and can be expected to increase with slope and pixel size. Thus, reducing the pixel size through SR provides the opportunity to reduce these errors, if the underlying pixels closely follow the actual terrain, although our focus is on areas of low-relief where they will be lowest. Instrument and environmental errors are more randomised and are the primary target of the error corrections presented in this paper.

In general, DEM SR originates from Single Image Super-Resolution (SISR), a fundamental low-level computer vision challenge that focuses on enhancing image resolution primarily through the use of interpolation algorithms and deep learning. SISR approaches can be applied in DEM SR tasks to reconstruct high-resolution DEMs from low-resolution DEMs since DEMs are also images in terms of representation format. The emergence of Super-Resolution Convolutional Neural Networks (SRCNNs) [19], in 2014, enabled deep learning to become the predominant approach for SISR tasks. This advancement prompted the adaptation of SISR-derived methodologies for DEM SR applications, as reported by [20–22], who generated high-resolution DEMs using SISR-derived approaches. Nevertheless, little research (e.g., [23]) has been developed towards real-world DEM SR problems, as it is common for the majority of DEM SR developments to employ synthetically degraded datasets for model training and validation, potentially compromising performance in practical applications involving authentic DEM data [23]. Further, in the absence of additional guidance data, SISR algorithms may not improve the actual spatial resolution but rather only reduce the pixel size.

In addition to the above, there is the depth completion [24] approach, which utilises the corresponding RGB image to guide neural networks in predicting a dense depth map from the input sparse depth map. Since both DEMs and depth maps represent three-dimensional information, assuming that low spatial resolution DEMs are sparse depth map samples and that high spatial resolution DEMs are dense depth map ground truth, the use of depth completion approaches to solve DEM SR problems can be considered a reasonable research hypothesis.

Motivated by the above understanding, the research presented in this paper investigated real-world DEM SR problems, leveraging approaches for sparse-to-dense depth completion problems. Our primary aim was to develop the proposed Joint Spatial Propagation Super-Resolution networks (JSPSRs) for real-world DEM SR prediction with correction for surface features, utilising globally available spatially coarse elevation data supported by high-resolution guidance data (e.g., RGB aerial imagery). JSPSR leverages remote sensing image guidance (with or without optional spatial data guidance) through depth completion derived techniques, specifically deep Guided Image Filtering (GIF) and non-local Spatial Propagation Networks (SPN). The deep GIF mechanism enhances multi-modal feature fusion capabilities, while the non-local SPN architecture optimises learnable spatial propagation parameters to refine high-frequency information with guidance features in a non-local manner, resulting in high-resolution DTM predictions. Thus, in the work presented here, our aim was to both reduce the pixel size and increase the actual spatial resolution, through inclusion of information from high-resolution aerial imagery.

To substantiate the proposed networks, we developed a ready-to-analyse dataset in low-relief areas, which serves as a reference for the comparative assessment of DEM SR methods. We proposed a relative elevation log-min–max data scale method, which involves logarithmic transformation, min–max scaling, and 0-based elevation shifting, to mitigate the distribution flaw of the dataset where the elevation is skewed toward zero due to low-relief terrain. By implementing the above proposed networks, dataset, and data scale method, along with the subsidiary common components, a deep learning training and evaluation framework was established for real-world DEM SR tasks. Code is available at https://github.com/xandercai/JSPSR, accessed on 15 September 2025.

2. Related Work

In the following section, we provide a brief introduction to existing DEM SR approaches and depth completion approaches adopted in this work. DEM SR aims to improve low spatial resolution DEMs by estimating unknown elevation values based on known elevation locations [25]. The primary approach is Single Image Super-Resolution (SISR), a process designed to reconstruct an image to enhance its quality in terms of size or resolution [26]. Another potential approach is depth completion, a subdomain within the depth estimation field that aims to predict a dense, pixel-wise depth map from a highly sparse depth map captured by depth sensors (e.g., LiDARs) [27].

Traditional SISR approaches, such as bilinear [28] and bicubic [29] interpolation, are widely deployed due to their low cost and high efficiency. However, learning-based methods have become the mainstream for SISR, given their superior performance. Beginning with SRCNN [19], which reconstructs SR predictions utilising two convolutional layers and three rectified linear unit (ReLU) activation layers, many SR networks were proposed, including residual networks (e.g., EDSR [30]), recursive networks (e.g., DRCN [31]), attention-based networks (e.g., RCAN [32]), and generative adversarial networks (GANs) (e.g., SRGAN [33]). Additional applications of these networks have been implemented for other objects, such as videos and higher-dimensional data, including DEMs [34].

Learning-based SISR approaches applied to DEM SR tasks [20,35,36] have demonstrated superior performance compared to conventional spatial interpolation algorithms, particularly those using Generative Adversarial Networks (GANs) [37,38], which produce improved visual quality. To avoid relying solely on low-resolution DEMs, recent studies have incorporated multi-modal data, such as remote sensing imagery, to extract supplementary information and enhance performance. Argudo et al. [39] pioneered the use of additional remote sensing images for DEM SR, utilising a two-branch Fully Convolutional Network (FCN) to fuse multi-modal features. Xu et al. [40] applied transfer learning to leverage weights pre-trained on remote sensing images during DEM SR network training. ELSR [22] employed ensemble learning to aggregate features from diverse geographical zones, while DSMSR [41] adopted a GAN-based architecture that jointly processes remote sensing imagery and low-resolution DEMs. MTF-SR [42] further optimised output quality by incorporating terrain features derived from DEMs during network training. Despite advancements, these methods still face a critical limitation of relying on synthetically degraded DEMs rather than real-world low-resolution data. Wu et al. [23] attempted to address this gap by using SRGAN on a hybrid dataset that combines freely available and commercial DEMs, revealing that the inherent disparities between synthetic data and real-world DEMs lead to degraded performance when applying SISR methods to actual low-resolution DEMs.

Depth completion methodologies can be categorised into unguided and image-guided approaches. When processing severely sparse depth maps that lack substantial structural information (e.g., textures and edges), image-guided methods can achieve better performance by extracting complementary information from RGB image data, thereby becoming the predominant and preferred approach for depth completion problems. The network architectures of image-guided method frameworks can be split into three major components: encoder, decoder and refiner. The implementation of the major parts is diverse. Some of them extract a type of features (e.g., image features or depth map features) using a dedicated encoding branch and fuse features at the intermediate layers between these encoding branches for optimal efficiency purposes, namely "late fusion" [27] mode, such as GuideNet [43] and LRRU [44]. The theoretical underpinning of the late fusion is Guided Image Filtering (GIF) [45] or joint image filtering [46] methods. The rest of the implementations, relying on the superior capacity of the large-scale backbone networks, fuse the multi-modal feature from the first one or two layers by concatenation, namely, "early fusion" [27] mode, such as PENet [47], DySPN [48], CompletionFormer [49]. Both early fusion and late fusion modes can achieve the existing state-of-the-art performance under applicable scenarios.

The Spatial Propagation Network (SPN) [50] is used in depth estimation to iteratively update the outputs of a regression network by aggregating reference and neighbouring pixels. By doing this, the depth mixing problem (blur effect and distortion of prediction object boundaries) can be effectively alleviated. Many series of SPNs have been developed and adopted as a refiner for the networks [47,48,51–54]. The original method proposed for SPN [55] consisted of a series of pixel updates, in which each pixel is updated by three adjacent pixels from the previous row or column. The serial update process is performed in four directions individually, and the results are combined by max-pooling. To make the update process more efficient, Cheng et al. [55] proposed the Convolutional Spatial Propagation Network (CSPN), which updates all pixels simultaneously within a fixed local neighbourhood. However, the fixed-local neighbourhood implementation can introduce irrelevant pixels (i.e., pixels that do not belong to the same category). Then this issue has been addressed by the introduction of CSPN++ [56], which enables the combination of results obtained using different kernel sizes to reduce the impact of irrelevant pixels. DSPN [48] and NLSPN [53] are methods that allow for predicting a pixel by learning the offsets to the pixel in the non-local neighbourhood. DSPN obtains kernel weights by calculating the similarity between features, while NLSPN learns them via its neural networks. Furthermore, LRRU [44] proposes a lightweight NLSPN variant based on DKN [57] that directly utilises sparse depth maps as input reference features that benefit the utilisation of high-frequency information.

3. Materials and Methods

Exploiting the strengths of depth completion methods in multi-modal fusion and non-local pixel-wise refinement, we propose the Joint Spatial Propagation Super-Resolution networks (JSPSRs) to address the limitations of existing real-world DEM SR. The outline of DEM SR methods is shown in Figure 1. Unlike Single Image Super-Resolution (SISR) approaches, as shown in Figure 1a, which directly predict unknown content based on the input data without any assisting information, JSPSR leverages guidance data, such as remote sensing imagery, to enrich the information for estimation, as shown in Figure 1b. Besides the Guided Image Filtering (GIF) architecture in the JSPSR backbone for multi-modal data fusion, a key distinction from SISR-derived methods is that JSPSR incorporates a non-local Spatial Propagation Network (SPN), which reduces errors caused by mismatches between target data (input low-resolution DSM) and ground truth DTM data or other spatial inputs. Supported by further information from the guidance features and the SPN refinement, JSPSR has the potential to outperform DEM-only approaches on real-world DEM SR tasks.

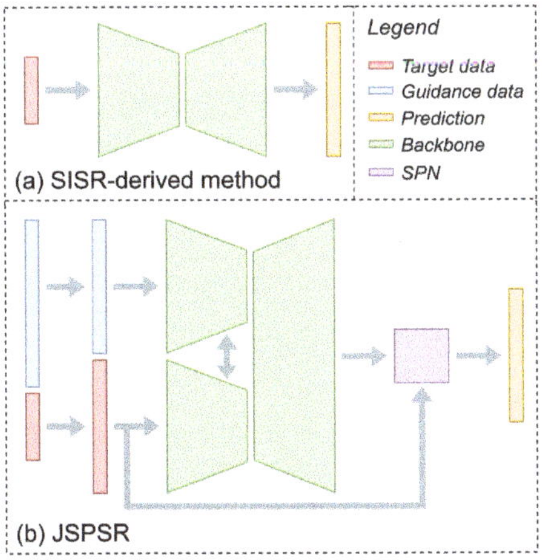

Figure 1. Outline of SISR-derived method and JSPSR. (**a**) SISR-derived method predicts SR output from target data. (**b**) JSPSR predicts SR output based on target data and fused guidance features in the SPN module.

In the following sections, an overview of the dataset developed for validating methods (Section 3.1) and the data scaling used (Section 3.2) is provided, followed by details of the

JSPSR network design in Section 3.3. Additional data processing details are included in Appendix A.1.

3.1. Dataset Development

Due to the lack of benchmark datasets for real-world DEM SR tasks, we developed a dataset to conduct experiments and compare the results of different DEM SR methods. We determined that an ideal real-world DEM SR dataset should contain the following components: high-resolution DTM samples as the ground truth, high-resolution remote sensing image samples as the guidance data, low-resolution DSM samples as the target data of SR methods, other DTM samples (existing state-of-the-art dataset is preferred) as the comparison reference for the method performance, and at least one kind of land-surface information, such as land cover masks, land use masks, canopy height data, building footprints and street maps, as the auxiliary guidance samples. All the source data should be produced in similar periods and be publicly accessible. Following the above principles, considering the location, date and quality [6], we selected (1) the Copernicus GLO-30 DEM (COP30) dataset [12] as the low-resolution DSM source, (2) the Forest And Buildings removed Copernicus DEM (FABDEM) dataset [13] and FathomDEM dataset [14] as the comparison reference DTM source, (3) the HighResCanopyHeight dataset [58] as the Canopy Height Map (CHM) source, and (4) the GRSS Data Fusion Contest 2022 (DFC2022 or grss_dfc_2022) dataset [59] as the high-resolution image, DTM and land use mask sources, to build a dataset for real-world DEM SR problems, denoted here as DFC30 (DFC2022 + FABDEM/FathomDEM + COP30, low-resolution at ∼30 m). We note that while the pixel size of GLO-30 is 30 m, and the actual spatial resolution is unknown, it is derived from 0.4 arcsecond (∼12 m) TanDEM-X data [60].

Table 1 lists DFC30 components information.

Table 1. DFC30 dataset components information.

Component	Type	Format	Pixel Size	Year	CRS	Role
DFC2022	Image	Raster	0.5 m	2012–2014	EPSG:2154	Guidance data
DFC2022	Mask	Vector	0.25 ha	2012	EPSG:2154	Auxilary guidance
DFC2022	DTM	Raster	1 m	2019–2020	EPSG:2154	Ground truth
Copernicus GLO-30	DSM	Raster	30 m	2011–2015	EPSG:4326	Target data
FABDEM	DTM	Raster	30 m	2014–2018	EPSG:4326	Comparison reference
FathomDEM	DTM	Raster	30 m	2014–2018	EPSG:4326	Comparison reference
HighResCanopyHeight	CHM	Raster	1 m	2017–2020	EPSG:3857	Auxilary guidance

EPSG codes refer to their respective standards: EPSG:2154—RGF93 v1/Lambert-93. IGN, Paris, France, 2021. See EPSG Registry 2154, https://epsg.io/2154, accessed on 15 September 2025. EPSG:3857—WGS 84/Pseudo-Mercator. IOGP/EPSG Geodetic Parameter Dataset, London, UK, 2020. See EPSG Registry 3857, https://epsg.io/3857, accessed on 15 September 2025. EPSG:4326—WGS 84. IOGP/EPSG Geodetic Parameter Dataset, London, UK, 2022. See EPSG Registry 4326, https://epsg.io/4326, accessed on 15 September 2025.

Among the DFC30 dataset components, the DFC2022 dataset was developed based on the MiniFrance dataset [61], which defined a 1 km^2 geographic bounding box for each sample. The sources of images, land use masks, and DTMs for the DFC2022 dataset are the BD ORTHO dataset [62], the UrbanAtlas 2012 dataset [63], and the IGN RGE ALTI dataset [64], respectively. DTMs of the DFC2022 dataset were derived from airborne LiDAR or correlation of aerial images at a resolution of 1 m, with a vertical accuracy of ∼0.2 m in flood or coastal areas [64]. The DFC2022 dataset comprises 3981 valid samples, each covering an area of 1 km^2 of land within the selected sixteen regions in France, with a resolution of up to 0.5 m. The DFC2022 dataset covers around 4000 km^2 in total, including urban and countryside scenes: residential areas, industrial/commercial zones, fields, forests, sea-shore, and low mountains. Based on the DFC2022 dataset sample boundary, we supplemented the samples with the same boundary from the COP30, FABDEM, FathomDEM, and HighResCanopyHeight datasets to constitute the DFC30 dataset. Figure 2 illustrates the sample locations and data distributions of the DFC30 dataset with an example region and an example sample.

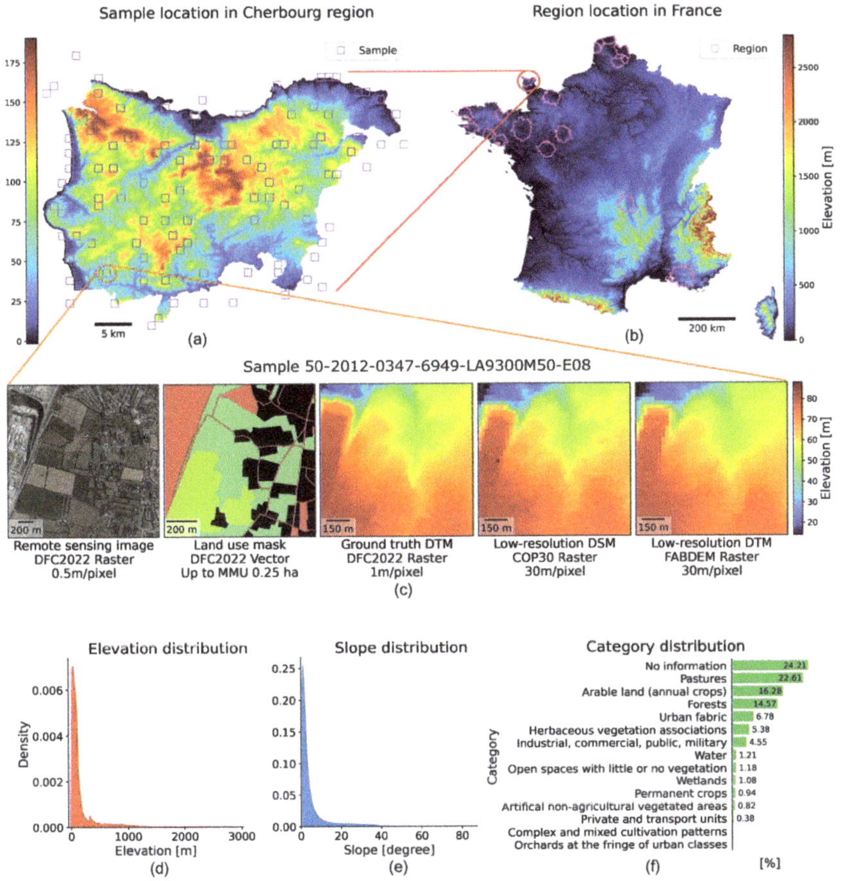

Figure 2. DFC30 dataset sample location, example, and distribution. All 3981 samples in the DFC30 dataset are located in selected sixteen regions of France. Each sample contains a high-resolution image, a high-resolution land use mask, a high-resolution CHM, a high-resolution DTM, a low-resolution DSM and two low-resolution DTMs. (**a**) The location of samples in the example region (Cherbourg); (**b**) the locations of 16 regions; (**c**) an example sample for training; (**d**) the density distribution by elevation; (**e**) the density distribution by slope; (**f**) the category distribution by percentage.

To improve data transformation efficiency during training, we preprocessed the DFC30 dataset by resampling the data to the target resolution in advance. There are several constraints in determining an appropriate target resolution:

1. Guidance information degradation: Remote sensing images (or other auxiliary spatial data) lose detail at lower resolutions. Considering road width, tree canopy radius, and residential property size, an 8 m resolution is an appropriate threshold. If the resolution is coarser than 8 m, ground features (e.g., narrow roads, individual trees, and small houses) may be lost during downsampling to the target resolution from high-resolution data.
2. Network input limitation: JSPSR only allows input tensors with shapes that are multiples of 8 (e.g., 128 × 128, 144 × 144, etc.). The input shape of 128 × 128 pixels

is the minimal adequate size for feature extraction in networks, equivalent to ∼8 m resolution.

3. Computational efficiency: training with very high resolution (e.g., 1 m resolution) data is expensive due to the vast amount of data for training, which will slow the experiment progress.

Therefore, this work selected resolutions of 8 m and 3 m as the target resolutions for experiments.

The DFC30 dataset was preprocessed to 8 m and 3 m resolution samples for network training and evaluation, denoted as DFC30-8m and DFC30-3m , respectively. More details of data processing are described in Appendix A.1.

3.2. Elevation Data Scaling

As the density plot in Figure 2d shows, the elevation distribution is close to the power law distribution, which is highly skewed towards zero elevation in an extremely narrow value range compared to the total value range, which would lead to inferior network performance [65]. Therefore, we scaled the raw elevation data to mitigate the adverse effects of data skew by converting the data distribution closer to a normal distribution using the process described here.

Assuming $\mathcal{H}^i$ is the elevation of a low-resolution DEM sample i, $\mathcal{H}^i_\alpha$ is its min–max scaling result, and a vanilla min–max data scale can be defined by the following:

$$\mathcal{H}^i_\alpha = \left(\mathcal{H}^i - \mathcal{H}_{min}\right) / (\mathcal{H}_{max} - \mathcal{H}_{min}), \tag{1}$$

where $\mathcal{H}_{min}$ and $\mathcal{H}_{max}$ are pre-defined minimum and maximum scale range parameters, respectively. The $\mathcal{H}_{min}$ is equal to or smaller than the lowest elevation in all DEMs in the dataset, and $\mathcal{H}_{max}$ is equal to or greater than the highest elevation in all DEMs in the dataset. To simplify the illustration, we assume the overall elevation range of the DEMs is $(-100, 2900)$, denoted as $\mathcal{H}_{min}$ and $\mathcal{H}_{max}$, and the elevation difference range (i.e., highest elevation subtract lowest elevation) in each DEM sample of all DEMs in the dataset is a $(-1, 399)$ range, denoted as $\mathcal{H}_{\Delta min}$ and $\mathcal{H}_{\Delta max}$.

Using a sample from the Marseille–Martigues region as an example (ID: `13-2014 0908-6289 LA93-0M50-E080`), Figure 3a shows the three-dimensional visualisation of the min–max scaled Y channel of the remote sensing image, which has a 0.2 to 0.8 data range. For comparison, Figure 3b is the min–max scaled DEM in the range $(-100, 2900)$, with a 0.1 to 0.2 data range, which is much narrower than the RGB image value range and highly skewed towards zero. Considering the fact that the features (such as slope and aspect) of a DEM will remain if changing the geoid, it will not affect the feature extraction of the networks if we shift a DEM to a 0-based relative elevation DEM, denoted as $\mathcal{H}^i_\Delta$, by subtracting the lowest elevation of the DEM:

$$\mathcal{H}^i_\Delta = \mathcal{H}^i - \min\left(\mathcal{H}^i\right). \tag{2}$$

Relative elevation helps reduce data skew by providing a smaller min–max range for scale. Each DEM can then be min–max scaled to a 0-based relative elevation, denoted as $\mathcal{H}^i_{\alpha\Delta}$, using the following:

$$\mathcal{H}^i_{\alpha\Delta} = \left(\mathcal{H}^i_\Delta - \mathcal{H}_{\Delta min}\right) / (\mathcal{H}_{\Delta max} - \mathcal{H}_{\Delta min}), \tag{3}$$

where the $\mathcal{H}_{\Delta min}$ and $\mathcal{H}_{\Delta max}$ are pre-defined minimum and maximum scale parameters of relative elevation in the whole DEMs, specifically $(-1, 399)$ as previous assumption, improved over seven times regarding the value range (i.e., from $(-100, 2900)$ to $(-1, 399)$), as Figure 3c shows. However, although the data distribution becomes more expansive, it remains skewed towards 0.

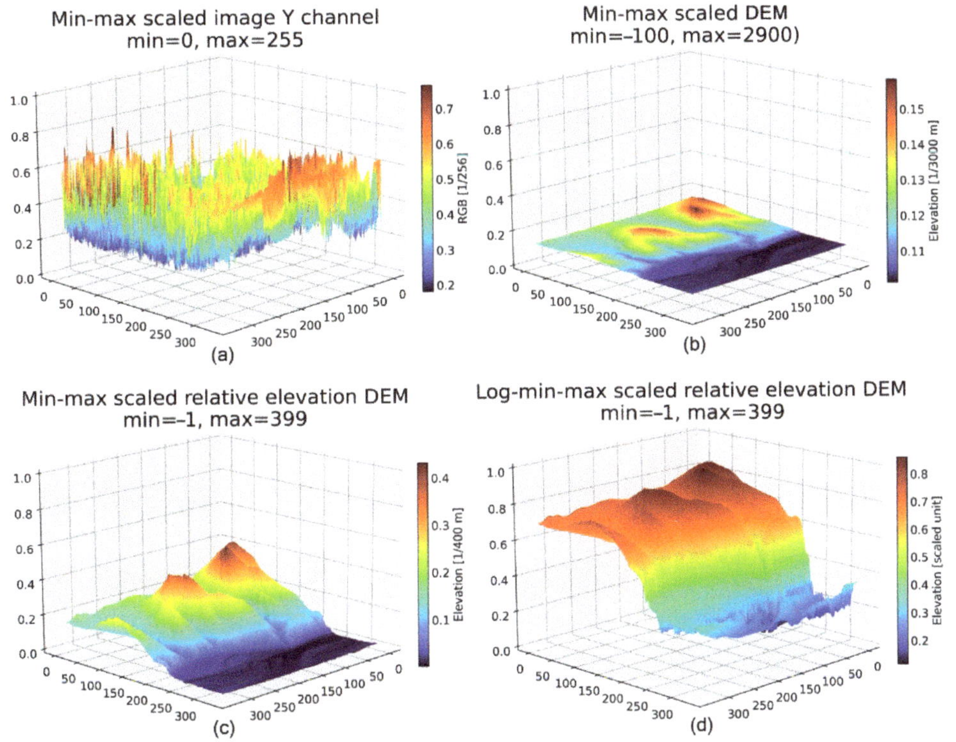

Figure 3. Data scale results of a sample: (**a**) min–max scaled image Y channel, min and max values are the 8-bit integer range; (**b**) min–max scaled DEM produced using Equation (1), min and max values are elevation min and max values of the whole dataset (−100 and 2900 in this case); (**c**) min–max scaled relative elevation DEM, min and max values are the 0-based relative elevation min and max values of the whole dataset (−1 and 399 in this case); (**d**) log-min–max scaled relative elevation DEM, min and max values are the same with (**c**). The log-min–max scale on the relative elevations (**d**) significantly extended the data distribution range and amplified the low-elevation details, which improves performance in low-relief samples but may undermine feature extraction in higher-elevation pixels.

Since the logarithmic scale generally reduces power law distribution, we applied a logarithmic operation to both the numerator and denominator in the relative elevation min–max scale from Equation (3), to provide the log-min–max scaled elevation, denoted as $\mathcal{H}^i_{\log\alpha\Delta}$:

$$\mathcal{H}^i_{\log\alpha\Delta} = \log\left(\mathcal{H}^i_\Delta - \mathcal{H}_{\Delta min}\right) / \log(\mathcal{H}_{\Delta max} - \mathcal{H}_{\Delta min}). \quad (4)$$

As shown in Figure 3d, the distribution of log-min–max scaled relative elevation DEM is less skewed and has a wider data distribution.

Figure 4 shows the distributions of the vanilla min–max scaled DEMs (Equation (1)) and the log-min–max scaled relative elevation DEMs (Equation (4)). Although the log-min–max scaled relative elevation DEM data distribution (Figure 4b) is still skewed to a particular value to a degree due to the negative elevation outliers, it mitigates the impact of the highly skewed data and, hence, is superior to the vanilla min–max scaled data distribution (Figure 4a).

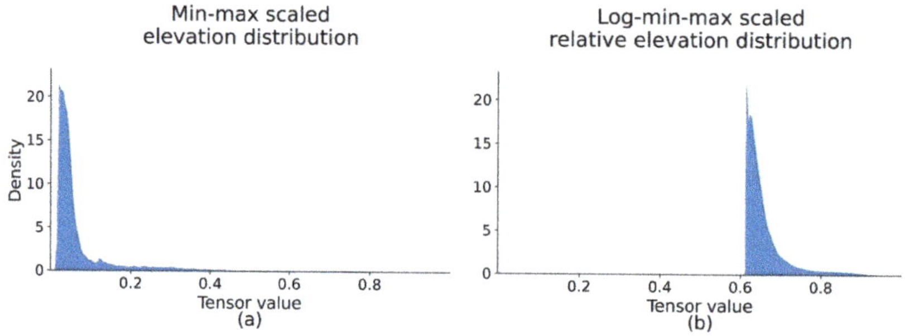

Figure 4. Scaled to [0, 1] elevation of different method: (**a**) min–max scaled elevation distribution, $\mathcal{H}_{\alpha}^{i}$, obtained using Equation (1), and (**b**) log-min–max scaled relative elevation distribution, $\mathcal{H}_{\log \alpha\Delta}^{i}$, obtained using Equation (4). The distribution of (**b**) is less skewed to 0 than that of (**a**), which benefits the performance of networks.

3.3. *Joint Spatial Propagation Super-Resolution Networks Design*

Compared to SISR methods for DEM SR that only use low-resolution DEMs as input data, the proposed JSPSRs utilise low-resolution DEMs and guidance data (with or without auxiliary guidance data), which enables the networks to extract and leverage more features from input data for regression. However, the guidance data raise challenges regarding multi-modal feature fusion [66]. Therefore, fusing data with different modalities effectively and efficiently is the primary concern for the backbone of the JSPSR networks. Furthermore, unlike popular datasets, such as DIV2k [67], which uses synthetic low-resolution images, or KITTI [68], which captures point clouds and RGB images simultaneously in the exact location, the target data (i.e., low-resolution derived DSMs), guidance data, and ground truth (i.e., high-resolution derived DTMs) are entirely independent. That means that the same coordinate pixels of different components in a sample may not necessarily be precisely matched due to time differences and system biases, which requires our network to learn features and predict output non-locally. Thus, we designed networks focusing on addressing the above two issues.

Our solution for multi-modal feature fusion is Guided Image Filtering (GIF) (Section 3.3.1). For pixel mismatch, our solution is non-local SPN methodologies (Section 3.3.2). The outline of the proposed approach is illustrated in Figure 1, which shows the coarse architecture. More details are depicted in Figure 5, which comprises a U-Net [69] structure with multi-branch encoders and a single-branch decoder, and a SPN module.

3.3.1. Guided Image Filtering

Li et al. [46] proposed the deep joint image filtering network, which sends guidance input and target input in two branches of convolutional layers separately, then concatenates the output of the two branches and extracts features again through convolutional layers to obtain the feature-fused output. This structure efficiently fuses multi-modal features (e.g., [43,44,57]). There are two main strategies for multi-modal feature fusion: early fusion and late fusion. Methods that adopt early fusion depend on the strong feature extraction ability of the encoder to fuse multi-modal features, which leads to the encoder being computationally intensive (e.g., PENet [47], with 132 million parameters, and CompletionFormer [49], with 83.5 million parameters). In contrast, methods that adopt late fusion have a dedicated branch to extract features for each input modality, making the network more efficient when the number of branches is small. However, the parameter size increases rapidly with the number of branches using later fusion. Considering SR is a low-level computer vision task that should ideally not involve high computational costs, we selected the late fusion mode referring to the guided image filtering theory, as shown in

Figure 5 (Step 2). The total parameter size of our networks with a two-branch encoder is 29.16 million, and with a three-branch encoder is 43.87 million.

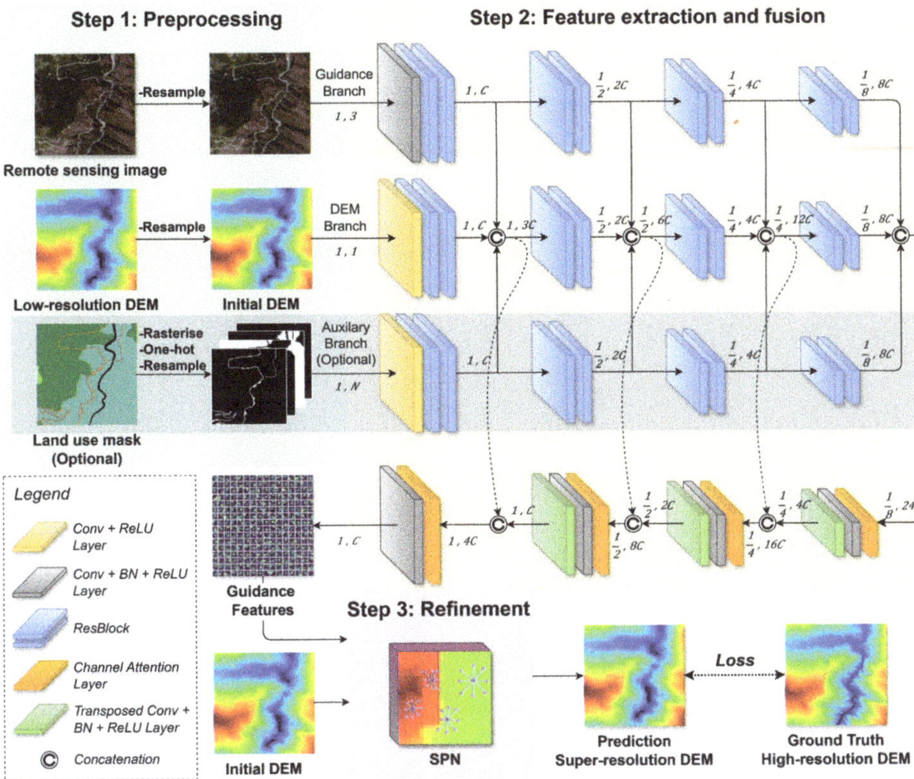

Figure 5. The architecture of JSPSR and the training workflow. The preprocessing (Step 1, described in Section 3.1) upsamples the low-resolution DSM to the target resolution as the initial DEM and sends the initial DEM with guidance image and optional auxiliary guidance data (land use mask in this case) to the corresponding branch of the backbone for multi-modal feature extraction and fusion (Step 2, described in Section 3.3.1). The refinement process (Step 3, described in Section 3.3.2) utilises a non-local SPN to tune the initial DEM based on guidance features extracted from the backbone and to estimate the SR DEM.

3.3.2. Spatial Propagation Network

The Spatial Propagation Network (SPN) was initially designed to alleviate the depth mixing problem by learning affinity from guidance features [50]. With the enhancement of the deformable convolution networks [70], non-local SPN variants have been proposed (e.g., [44,49,53,57]), which have found that the non-local SPN improves the depth accuracy on the edge of objects. This attribute could be helpful for DEM SR since our DEMs are relatively "flat" in most samples (slope smaller than 10°), which means "blur" in the RGB image perspective. During training, the SPN collects the affinity of eight neighbour pixels of each pixel to assist elevation prediction and then learns the offset (x and y directions) and weight (or confidence in some studies [49,53]) in the backpropagation stage, as shown in Figure 6. After appropriate training, the learnt SPN offset and weight can significantly contribute to the elevation prediction performance.

We built on DKN [57] and LRRU [44] to implement the non-local SPN refinement module as shown in Figure 7. The refinement module reconstructs input initial DEMs using guidance features in a deformable convolutional layer. It generates deformable convolutional kernel affinity weight parameters and sampling offset parameters for each pixel to fulfil non-local learning. It then learns the parameters during training and fine-tunes the initial DEM elevations. The refinement module has a residual connection between the initial DEM and the final output to augment high-frequency information and suppress noise. Therefore, it intrinsically learns the residual between the prediction and the ground truth. The main differences between our refinement module and the previous SPN refinement modules are:

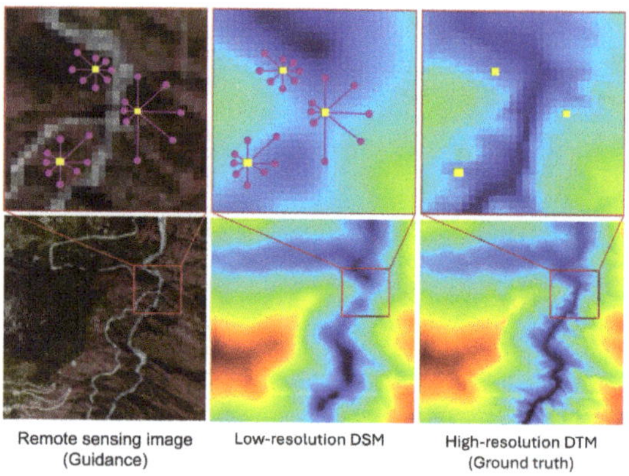

Figure 6. Example of non-local spatial propagation: three pixels (yellow) that select their most similar neighbour pixels (purple) in eight different directions to assist elevation prediction while ignoring low-similarity neighbours. This approach alleviates errors caused by pixel mismatches between the guidance image, the low-resolution derived DEM, and the high-resolution derived ground truth, as the SPN learns the similarity during training, allowing for pixel offsets in elevation prediction.

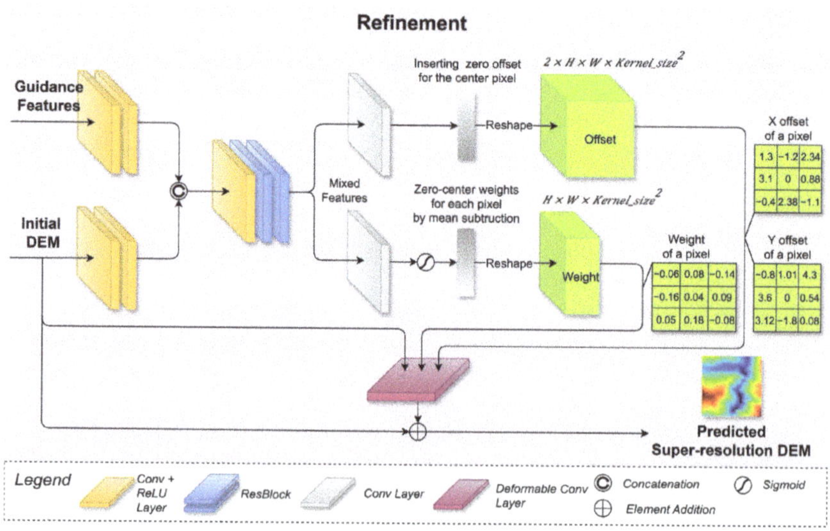

Figure 7. The refinement module structure. It first generates offset prediction and weight prediction for each pixel in the initial DEM based on mixed features. Then, it utilises a modulated deformable convolutional layer to sample neighbouring pixels based on the offset and weight to predict the SR DEM in a non-local style.

network layers and multi-iterative refinement modules, such as GuideNet [43], PENet [47], RigNet [78], CompletionFormer [49], and LRRU [44], that may be unnecessary or adverse to DEM SR tasks due to overfitting. On the contrary, JSPSR achieved superior performance with relatively fewer network parameters and a one-shot refinement, thereby reducing the computing cost.

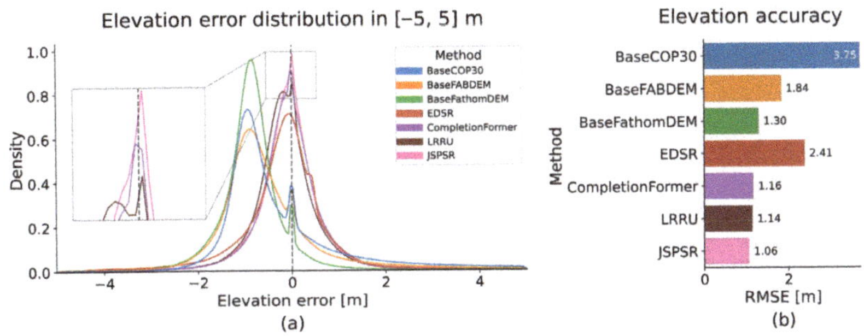

Figure 8. Comparison between baselines and the best prediction of methods. (**a**) Elevation error distribution between −5 m and 5 m. (**b**) Elevation vertical accuracy (30 m to 8 m task, best performance of a method and guidance data combination).

Table 4. Metrics of different methods on 30 m to 8 m and 30 m to 3 m SR tasks. Input data options are DEM, image, land use mask and canopy height map (CHM). The ↓, |↓|, and ↑ mean the lower, the lower absolute, and the higher value represents better performance for the metric, respectively. The red colour value is the best value of a metric in an SR task, while the blue is the second-best.

Task	Method	Input Data				Metric				
		DEM	Image	Mask	CHM	RMSE ↓	Median |↓|	NMAD ↓	LE95 ↓	PSNR↑
30 m to 8 m	BaseCOP30					3.7492	−0.587	0.8703	9.0313	47.8815
	BaseFABDEM					1.8443	−0.723	0.7232	3.2182	54.0436
	BaseFathomDEM					1.2952	−0.8614	0.4617	2.131	57.1138
	EDSR	✓				2.4101	−0.0903	0.6661	4.6267	51.7197
	CompletionFormer	✓	✓			1.9886	−0.3672	0.5926	2.8239	53.6744
	CompletionFormer	✓	✓	✓		1.2775	−0.0818	0.5637	2.2473	57.5184
	CompletionFormer	✓	✓		✓	1.1643	−0.053	0.5164	1.8621	58.0388
	LRRU	✓	✓			1.1406	−0.1391	0.5093	1.926	58.2175
	$JSPSR_{2b}$	✓	✓			1.0983	−0.0714	0.5094	1.8641	58.5463
	$JSPSR_{3b}$	✓	✓	✓		1.0596	−0.057	0.4931	1.7929	58.8572
	$JSPSR_{3b}$	✓	✓		✓	1.0644	−0.0414	0.4761	1.7939	58.8182
30 m to 3 m	BaseCOP30					3.7547	−0.587	0.8704	9.0496	47.9062
	BaseFABDEM					1.8487	−0.7235	0.7256	3.2316	54.0605
	BaseFathomDEM					1.2976	−0.8612	0.4644	2.1396	57.1345
	EDSR	✓				2.496	−0.1246	0.5945	4.7755	51.4528
	CompletionFormer	✓	✓			1.334	−0.1522	0.5058	2.1605	56.9594
	CompletionFormer	✓	✓	✓		1.4696	−0.1149	0.5241	2.3354	56.3014
	CompletionFormer	✓	✓		✓	1.2967	−0.0895	0.5375	2.0565	57.141
	LRRU	✓	✓			1.1256	−0.1039	0.5494	1.825	58.3698
	$JSPSR_{2b}$	✓	✓			1.1314	−0.1481	0.4989	1.8444	58.3255
	$JSPSR_{3b}$	✓	✓	✓		1.0851	−0.0163	0.5235	1.7975	58.6884
	$JSPSR_{3b}$	✓	✓		✓	1.104	−0.0883	0.5094	1.8271	58.5379

Metric [Unit]: RMSE [m], Median [m], NMAD [m], LE95 [m], PSNR [dB].

Beyond quantitatively comparing prediction performance, we evaluated inference time and GPU memory consumption to compare the computing cost among selected methods on the DFC30-8m dataset, as shown in Table 5. The input data resolution is 8 m, and the size is 128 × 128, with a batch size of one. PyTorch application programming interfaces (APIs) are utilised to measure the GPU inference time and memory costs precisely. We inferred all 799 test samples and calculated the average values (except for the first inference, which was affected by extra overhead from PyTorch). The experimental results indicate that JSPSR achieves the fastest inference speed and moderate memory consumption on GPUs. It is worth mentioning that our end-to-end DEM SR approach incurs an additional CPU computing cost for resampling low-resolution DEMs to the target resolution using GDAL [79], which typically takes less than 0.3 ms to resample a 128 × 128 sample using GDAL on a 4 GHz CPU core.

To visually compare the SR reconstruction quality, we selected two extreme scenarios for comparison: the most improved and the least improved cases using JSPSR. Figure 9 displays the most improved JSPSR prediction compared to BaseCOP30. In this case, the BaseCOP30 RMSE of this sample is 15.58 m, while the JSPSR prediction RMSE is 3.29 m, representing an improvement of 78.9%. EDSR and CompletionFormer appear underfit, which does not account for part of the canopy height. The predictions of LRRU and JSPSR acquire higher quality than those of other methods. However, the LRRU prediction displays signs of overfitting, as small stripes appear in pixels with very low relief.

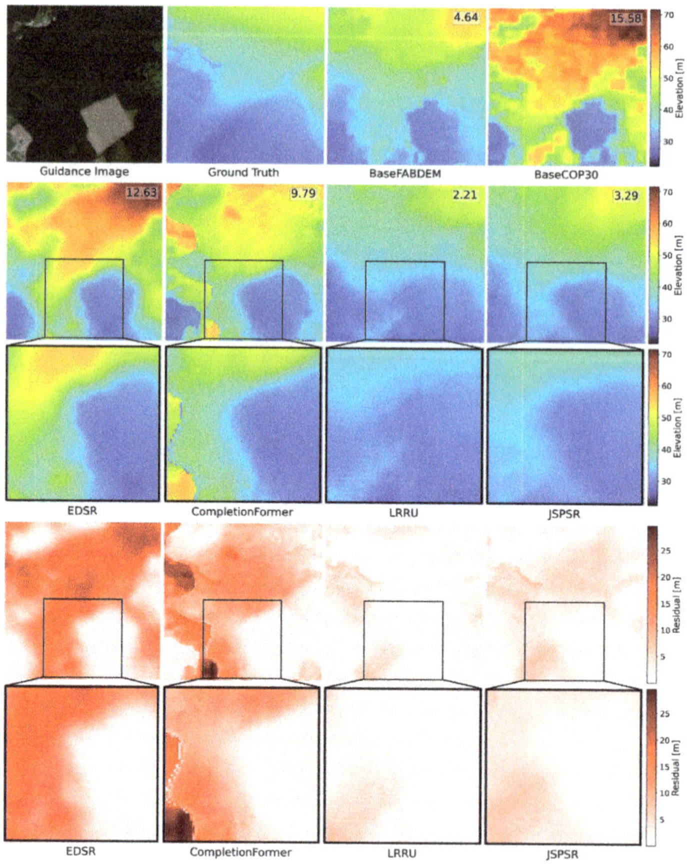

Figure 9. Comparison among predictions of different methods in the case of the most improved prediction with JSPSR compared to BaseCOP30, displayed in the format of elevations and residuals to the ground truth with partially enlarged details. The number in the top right corner is the RMSE of this sample/prediction. (30 m to 8 m SR task, image guidance only, sample ID: `Lille 59-2012-0703-7040 LA93-0M50-E080`).

On the other hand, Figure 10 displays the least improved JSPSR prediction compared to BaseCOP30. The RMSE of this BaseCOP30 sample is 2.75 m, while the JSPSR prediction RMSE is 3.39 m, increasing 23.3%. All the methods try to predict the depth of the ditch covered by vegetation. However, they all overestimate the depth of the ditch, leading to the raw input data achieving the best performance. It highlights that predicting elevation under vegetation is a challenge for all DEM SR methods in this context.

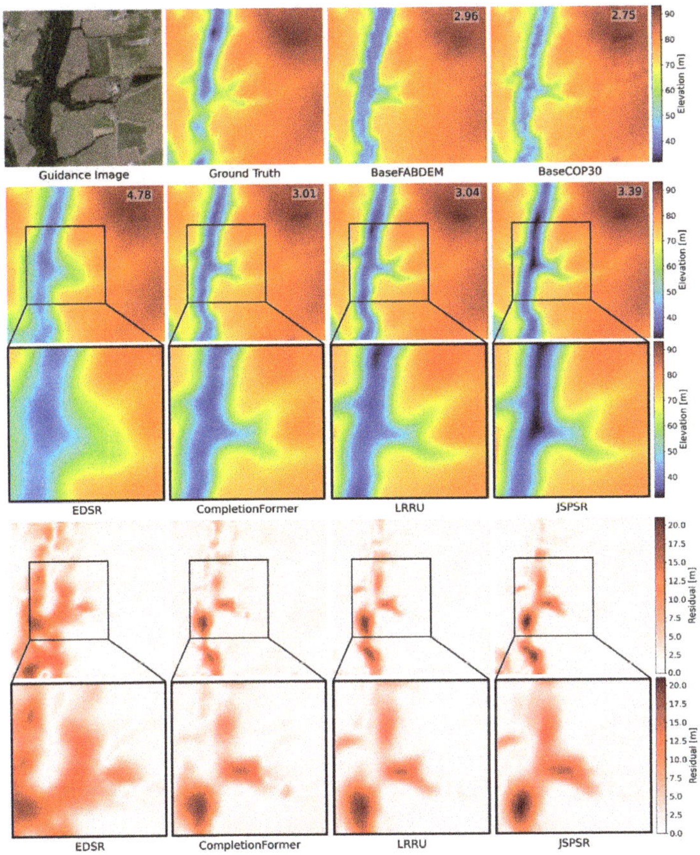

Figure 10. Comparison among predictions of different methods in the case of the least improved prediction with JSPSR compared to BaseCOP30, displayed in the format of elevations and residuals to the ground truth with partially enlarged details. The number in the top right corner is the RMSE of this sample/prediction. (30 m to 8 m SR task, image guidance only, sample ID: `Angers 49-2013-0415-6696 LA93-0M50-E080`).

Table 5. Computing cost comparison of different methods on the DFC30-8m dataset. The inference sample size is 128 × 128, and the resolution is 8 m. GPU time and GPU memory usage are the average computing costs of inferring 798 test samples. The red colour value is the best in a column, while the blue is the second-best.

Method	Parameter (MB)	Mult-Adds (G)	GPU Time (ms)	GPU Memory (MB)
EDSR	56.6	1260	18.3691	228.6
ComplitionFormer	83.7	44.8	13.9568	371.6
LRRU	20.8	68.8	5.7059	164
$JCDSR_{2b}$	29.2	66.8	3.9759	235.2
$JCDSR_{3b}$	43.9	89.4	5.1521	320.5

4.3. Ablation Studies

We conducted experiments on the DFC30-8m dataset to evaluate the effectiveness of the proposed method's components, guidance data, and generalisation.

4.3.1. Effectiveness of Proposed Data Scale Method

Data preprocessing is a fundamental factor in determining the quality of training. Before the low-resolution DSM (COP30) is transformed to tensors for training, they are interpolated to the target resolution using the bicubic algorithm, augmented with random flips and then scaled to $[0, 1]$ using a relative elevation log-min–max scale, as illustrated in Section 3.2. We conducted experiments to compare the effectiveness of the relative elevation log-min–max scale, as shown in Table 6. The RMSE decreased by 14.9% when guidance data consisted of images, and by 12.7% when guidance data consisted of images and land use masks, indicating that our relative elevation log-min–max scale method effectively improves network performance.

Table 6. RMSE comparison between with and without relative elevation and log-min–max scale in 30 m to 8 m SR task (image guidance only). The ↓ means the lower value represents better performance.

Method	Guidance Data		Relative Elevation	Log-min–max Scale	RMSE ↓
	Image	Mask			
JSPSR	✓				1.29
	✓		✓		1.1787
	✓		✓	✓	1.0983
	✓	✓			1.2136
	✓	✓	✓		1.1482
	✓	✓	✓	✓	1.0596

Metric [Unit]: RMSE [m].

4.3.2. Effectiveness of Guidance Data

The impact of different guidance data on JSPSR is reported in Table 7. We conducted experiments on EDSR and JSPSR to evaluate the significance of guidance data, including images, land-use masks, and CHMs. We also assessed JSPSR performance without image guidance, using only the land use mask or CHM auxiliary guidance. The experimental results confirm the significant enhancement of guidance images. With guidance images, EDSR performance significantly improved by over 30% compared to without guidance images. JSPSR also improved with guidance images compared to without guidance images.

Table 7. RMSE of JSPSR on 30 m to 8 m and 30 m to 3 m SR task. Input data options are DEM, image, land use mask and canopy height maps (CHM). The ↓ means the lower value represents better performance.

Method	Guidance Data				RMSE ↓	
	DEM	Image	Mask	CHM	30 m to 8 m	30 m to 3 m
EDSR	✓				2.4101	2.496
EDSR	✓	✓			1.5816	1.6258
JSPSR	✓	✓			1.0983	1.1314
JSPSR	✓		✓		1.1984	1.2231
JSPSR	✓			✓	1.0986	1.1506
JSPSR	✓	✓	✓		1.0596	1.0851
JSPSR	✓	✓		✓	1.0644	1.104

Metric [Unit]: RMSE [m].

Regarding the two types of auxiliary guidance data, their contributions are contingent upon specific conditions. Incorporating the guidance images, since CHM can be directly learnt from ground truth, the contribution of CHM is slightly less significant than that of land use masks, which contain more additional information than CHM. Without the guidance images, the networks appear less effective with auxiliary guidance land use masks than CHM.

4.3.3. Comparison of Data Fusion Operations for Guided Image Filtering (GIF)

JSPSR adopts the GIF method for feature extraction and multi-modal fusion. In general, there are three simple operations for fusing features between the encoder and decoder branches: addition, concatenation, and filtering. The addition and concatenation approaches are fundamental operations for binding features together. The addition operation adds different features element-wise, while the concatenation operation stacks different features in the channel dimension. The filtering approach uses convolutional kernel filters (e.g., LRRU [44]) or customised kernel filters (e.g., GuideNet [43]) to fuse features. Many other elaborate approaches for multi-modal data fusion have been proposed [80], but they are outside the scope of this work. We assessed the effectiveness of addition, concatenation, and convolutional kernel filtering, as shown in Table 8, which suggests that the concatenation approach achieves better performance under similar parameters and computational costs on the DFC30-8m dataset.

Table 8. RMSE comparison among different fusion operations on DFC30-8m dataset. The ↓ means the lower value represents better performance.

Method	Guidance Data		Operation			RMSE ↓
	Image	Mask	Addition	Concatenation	Filtering	
JSPSR	✓		✓			1.2649
	✓			✓		1.0983
	✓				✓	1.1527
	✓	✓	✓			1.22
	✓	✓		✓		1.0596
	✓	✓			✓	1.1592

Metric [Unit]: RMSE [m].

4.3.4. Effectiveness of Refinement Module

The refinement module is a prominent component for depth completion approaches. It is also a significant difference between the proposed JSPSR and SISR-derived methods. Table 9 compares the metrics with or without the refinement module for EDSR and JSPSR on the DFC30-8m dataset. It reported that the refinement module improved network performance remarkably (up to 48.3% on RMSE), even though the network was an SISR method (EDSR), which was enhanced by 48% on RMSE with the guidance image and refinement module.

Table 9. RMSE comparison with or without refinement module on DFC30-8m dataset. The ↓ means the lower value represents better performance.

Method	Guidance Data		Refinement	RMSE ↓
	Image	Mask		
EDSR				2.4101
EDSR	✓			1.5816
EDSR	✓		✓	1.2518
JSPSR	✓			1.4034
JSPSR	✓		✓	1.0983
JSPSR	✓	✓		2.0497
JSPSR	✓	✓	✓	1.0596

Metric [Unit]: RMSE [m].

4.3.5. Generalisation

Generalisation is a crucial ability to predict unseen data. The fixed train/test split in previous experiments cannot assess the generalisation of the proposed method. To evaluate model generalisation, we conducted experiments on different train/test splits using the k-fold cross-validation method, specifically setting each region as the test set and the rest of the fifteen regions as the training set. The results are reported in Table 10. Most regions achieved over 50% improvement compared to BaseCOP30, and over 20% improvement compared to BaseFABDEM and BaseFathomDEM. However, the two high slope regions (Nice and Marseille–Martinique) achieved underperforming results. A possible reason is that these are the only two regions (Nice and Marseille–Martinique) in the mountainous area of the DFC30 dataset, leading to the high-slope areas being under-fitted during training. Evidence is that the third high slope region (Clermont–Ferrand) achieved a 63.63% improvement compared to BaseCOP30, as the two mountainous regions are included in the training set, allowing the network to learn enough features of high slope samples, compared to learn from only one mountainous region. In general, the model generalisation of JSPSR is robust, except for high-slope regions due to the insufficiency of high-slope samples in the DFC30 dataset.

Table 10. 16-folder cross-validation on 30 m to 8 m SR task (image guidance only). The region name indicates that the region serves as the test set, and the remaining 15 regions are used as the training set. "COP.", "FAB.", and "Fat." represent BaseCOP30, BaseFABDEM, and BaseFathomDEM, respectively. Δ% represents the metric change percentage compared to baselines. The ↑ or ↓ indicates an increase or a decrease. The value after ↑ or ↓ is the change percentage compared to baselines. The red values highlight the most improvement, while the blue values highlight the lowest.

Region	Pixel %	Slope°		RMSE				Δ%COP.	Δ%FAB.	Δ%Fat.
		Avg.	Std.	COP.	FAB.	Fat.	JSPSR			
Angers	6.18	2.25	3.47	3.8748	2.0467	1.3129	1.0421	↓ 73.11	↓ 49.08	↓ 20.63
Brest	4.32	3.43	5.05	2.9449	2.0794	1.4164	1.0825	↓ 63.24	↓ 47.94	↓ 23.57
Caen	6.30	3.14	4.23	3.5006	2.0156	1.2933	0.9893	↓ 71.74	↓ 50.92	↓ 23.51
Calais Dunkerque	6.43	2.83	4.17	2.9356	1.6401	1.1805	1.2083	↓ 58.84	↓ 26.33	↑ 2.35
Cherbourg	2.84	3.63	4.50	2.8535	1.6931	1.5612	0.9416	↓ 67	↓ 44.39	↓ 39.69
Clermont–Ferrand	7.54	7.53	7.52	6.0747	3.1155	1.9411	2.2093	↓ 63.63	↓ 29.09	↑ 13.81
LeMans	5.38	2.64	3.48	5.7566	2.5362	1.2973	1.4077	↓ 75.55	↓ 44.5	↑ 8.51
Lille Arras Lens Douai Henin	10.22	2.00	3.12	3.4944	1.6858	1.2455	1.1283	↓ 67.71	↓ 33.07	↓ 9.41
Lorient	3.01	4.55	5.73	4.9893	2.8006	2.2847	2.1124	↓ 57.66	↓ 24.57	↓ 7.54
Marseille Martigues	7.76	8.66	10.48	3.0760	2.8171	2.2974	2.2606	↓ 26.51	↓ 19.75	↓ 1.6
Nantes Saint-Nazaire	10.88	2.06	3.01	2.7932	1.3676	1.1422	0.7918	↓ 71.65	↓ 42.1	↓ 30.68
Nice	8.36	23.52	13.10	7.0960	5.8516	4.9287	5.6147	↓ 20.88	↓ 4.05	↑ 13.92
Quimper	3.87	3.89	4.54	3.1250	1.8856	1.3329	0.9765	↓ 68.75	↓ 48.21	↓ 26.74
Rennes	9.82	2.82	3.34	3.7086	1.8336	1.4373	1.1217	↓ 69.75	↓ 38.83	↓ 21.96
Saint-Brieuc	3.42	3.73	4.84	4.3080	2.3262	1.2925	1.2245	↓ 71.57	↓ 47.36	↓ 5.26
Vannes	3.67	3.08	4.03	4.1938	1.9065	1.3968	1.1261	↓ 73.15	↓ 40.93	↓ 19.38

Metric [Unit]: RMSE [m].

4.4. *Assessment of JSPSR Predictions by Topographic Context*

The experimental results above validated the performance of the proposed method under various conditions. However, it does not take into account topographic attributes. In this section, we analyse the prediction of the proposed method in the topographic context.

4.4.1. Vertical Accuracy by Slope

Topographic slope is strongly influenced by DEM resolution due to the scale difference of a point under different resolutions [81]. Generally, lower elevation accuracy will be measured where an SR output has a higher slope. Thus, we assessed the RMSE based on different slope ranges (<5°, 5−10°, 10−25°, and >25°), as shown in Table 11, which indicated that accuracy decreased as the slope increased. However, JSPSR achieved superior accuracy across all slope ranges (except when the slope exceeded 25° on the 30 m to 8 m SR task), outperforming BaseCOP30 (an improvement of up to 73.2%), BaseFABDEM (an improvement of up to 43.65%), and BaseFathomDEM (an improvement of up to 17.72%), particularly in low-relief areas.

Table 11. RMSE comparison under different slope ranges on 30 m to 8 m and 30 m to 3 m SR tasks. Δ% represents prediction RMSE change percentage compared to BaseCOP30, BaseFABDEM, and BaseFathomDEM, respectively. The ↓ or ↑ indicates an increase or decrease compared to the corresponding baseline.

Task	Method	Guidance Data		Overall		Slope 0–5°		Slope 5–10°		Slope 10–25°		Slope > 25°	
		Image	Mask	RMSE	Δ%	RMSE	Δ%	RMSE	Δ%	RMSE	Δ%	RMSE	Δ%
30 m to 8 m	BaseCOP30			3.7492		3.5789		5.1544		6.611		7.1176	
	BaseFABDEM			1.8443		1.7021		2.7953		4.017		6.0347	
	BaseFathomDEM			1.2952		1.1656		2.0447		3.1646		5.5909	
	JSPSR	✓		1.0983	↓ 70.71 ↓ 40.45 ↓ 15.2	0.9591	↓ 73.2 ↓ 43.65 ↓ 17.72	1.8072	↓ 64.94 ↓ 35.35 ↓ 11.62	3.0084	↓ 54.49 ↓ 25.11 ↓ 4.94	5.566	↓ 21.8 ↓ 7.77 ↓ 0.45
	JSPSR	✓	✓	1.0596	↓ 71.74 ↓ 42.55 ↓ 18.19	0.9174	↓ 74.37 ↓ 46.1 ↓ 21.29	1.7888	↓ 65.3 ↓ 36 ↓ 12.52	2.8803	↓ 56.43 ↓ 28.3 ↓ 8.98	5.9622	↓ 16.23 ↓ 1.2 ↑ 6.64
30 m to 3 m	BaseCOP30			3.7547		3.569		5.077		6.067		5.81	
	BaseFABDEM			1.8487		1.7077		2.6284		3.5545		4.6316	
	BaseFathomDEM			1.2976		1.17		1.9		2.765		4.1696	
	JSPSR	✓		1.1314	↓ 69.87 ↓ 38.8 ↓ 12.81	1.0079	↓ 71.76 ↓ 40.98 ↓ 13.85	1.6968	↓ 66.58 ↓ 35.44 ↓ 10.69	2.5133	↓ 58.57 ↓ 29.29 ↓ 9.1	3.8077	↓ 34.46 ↓ 17.79 ↓ 8.68
	JSPSR	✓	✓	1.0851	↓ 71.1 ↓ 41.3 ↓ 16.38	0.9648	↓ 72.97 ↓ 43.5 ↓ 17.54	1.6396	↓ 67.71 ↓ 37.62 ↓ 13.71	2.424	↓ 60.05 ↓ 31.8 ↓ 12.33	3.625	↓ 37.61 ↓ 21.73 ↓ 13.06

Metric [Unit]: RMSE [m].

One of the reasons for lower performance in the higher slope range is that the slope distribution of the DEM30 dataset is highly skewed. The pixel percentage of each slope range is approximately 93% (<5°), 5% (5–10°), 1.6% (10–25°), and 0.1% (>25°), leading to potential under-fitting when pixel slopes become higher.

4.4.2. Vertical Accuracy by Land Use Mask Categories

Land use masks present the various land use or land cover categories, including water, urban fabric, pastures, forests, and others. They affect prediction accuracy due to the inclusion of semantic information from classification and segmentation. This semantic information may facilitate feature extraction and fusion when different data (e.g., images, DEMs, and land use masks) are pixel-wise matched. However, it may introduce noise if they are widely mismatched, which can impair prediction performance. Since the land mask classes are highly unbalanced, as shown in Table 12 (pixel percentage column), the RMSE of each category does not reveal the correlations between JSPSR and land use mask categories. However, by comparing the results with and without the land use mask guidance, we determined which category benefits the most (or least) from the land use mask guidance. Additionally, comparing predictions and baselines by land use mask classes helped to evaluate the network's performance and limitations. Figure 11 demonstrates elevation profiles from several samples to show the detailed elevation compared with baselines. Although several elevation profiles do not have a statistical meaning, it is a straightforward way to reveal whether a method is effective.

Table 12. RMSE comparison by land use mask classes on 30 m to 8 m SR task. "COP.", "FAB.", and "Fat." represent BaseCOP30, BaseFABDEM, and BaseFathomDEM, respectively. "W/O." and "W." mean without the land use mask guidance and with the land use mask guidance. The Δ% represents RMSE change percentage compared to baselines and W/O. The ↓ or ↑ indicates an increase or decrease. The red values highlight the most improvement, while the blue values highlight the lowest.

Class	Pixel %	Slope°		RMSE					Δ% W/O.			Δ% W.			
		Avg.	Std.	COP.	FAB.	Fat.	W/O.	W.	COP.	FAB.	Fat.	COP.	FAB.	Fat.	W/O.
0	24.42	1.92	2.52	4.15	1.8994	1.4645	1.3983	1.3318	↓66.3	↓26.38	↓4.52	↓67.91	↓29.88	↓9.06	↓4.76
1	8.93	1.92	2.07	1.8552	1.274	1.1689	0.67	0.66	↓63.89	↓47.41	↓42.68	↓64.42	↓48.19	↓43.54	↓1.49
2	7.27	2.22	2.89	2.1557	1.4947	1.3074	0.9651	0.9234	↓55.23	↓35.43	↓26.18	↓57.16	↓38.22	↓29.37	↓4.32
3	0.53	4.94	8.29	3.2909	3.2024	2.998	2.8292	3.0121	↓14.03	↓11.65	↓5.63	↓8.47	↓5.94	↑0.47	↑6.46
4	1.31	2.63	3.95	4.7996	2.9084	1.5242	1.5493	1.578	↓67.72	↓46.73	↑1.65	↓67.12	↓45.74	↑3.53	↑1.85
5	35.19	1.64	1.78	1.4872	1.2024	0.9892	0.5649	0.5396	↓62.02	↓53.02	↓42.89	↓63.72	↓55.12	↓45.45	↓4.48
6	0.86	2.93	2.3	0.9703	0.9784	0.9569	0.5286	0.5856	↓45.52	↓45.97	↓44.76	↓39.65	↓40.15	↓38.8	↑10.78
7	18.94	2.07	2.36	2.0208	1.3587	1.1338	0.6276	0.6287	↓68.94	↓53.81	↓44.65	↓68.89	↓53.73	↓44.55	↑0.17
10	7.81	3.05	4.12	9.8595	4.0118	1.7801	2.1412	2.0479	↓78.28	↓46.63	↑20.29	↓79.23	↓48.95	↑15.04	↓4.36
11	0.1	3.88	5.4	2.8077	1.7666	1.7443	1.3312	1.1125	↓52.59	↓24.65	↓23.68	↓60.38	↓37.03	↓36.22	↓16.43
12	0.07	1.77	3.1	3.0564	3.1069	2.8956	2.2358	1.958	↓26.85	↓28.04	↓22.79	↓35.94	↓36.98	↓32.38	↓12.43
13	0.39	1.3	2.55	1.5092	1.0942	1.1734	0.5971	0.5517	↓60.44	↓45.43	↓49.11	↓63.44	↓49.58	↓52.98	↓7.6
14	1.38	1.44	3.1	2.7732	2.6266	2.5293	1.8475	1.8838	↓33.38	↓29.66	↓26.96	↓32.07	↓28.28	↓25.52	↑1.96

Class Name					
1	Urban fabric	2	Industrial, commercial, public, military, private and transport units		
3	Mine, dump and construction sites	4	Artifical non-agricultural vegetated areas	5	Arable land (annual crops)
6	Permanent crops	7	Pastures	10	Forests
11	Herbaceous vegetation associations	12	Open spaces with little or no vegetation	13	Wetlands
14	Water	0	No information		

Metric [Unit]: RMSE [m].

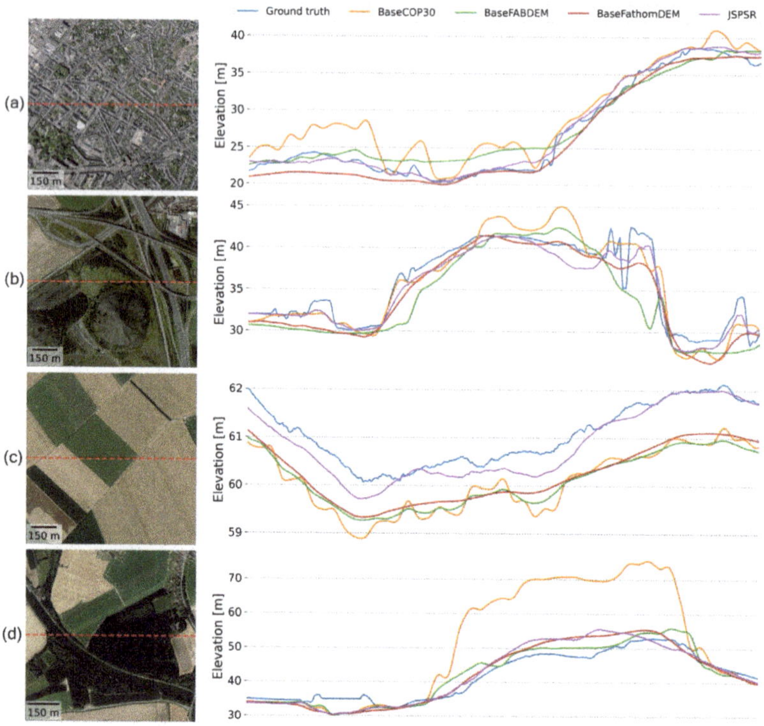

Figure 11. Elevation profiles by land use mask classes. The red-dashed lines are elevation cross-section projections on the remote sensing images. (**a**) Class 1 (urban fabric). (**b**) Class 2 (industrial, commercial, public, military, private, and transport units). (**c**) Class 5 (arable land (annual crops)). (**d**) Class 10 (forests) and 14 (water). (30 m to 3 m SR task, image + land use mask guidance).

All samples were resampled to the target resolutions (8 m and 3 m resolution) using bicubic interpolation to either upsample the low-resolution DTMs and DSMs from ~30 m resolution, or downsample the high-resolution DTMs, images, CHM, and land use masks from high resolutions, to the target resolutions. After this preprocessing, we generated an 8 m resolution dataset on pixels of 128 × 128 (including paddings) per sample (process 4 in Figure A1), with a total of ~65.2 million pixels, denoted as DFC30-8m, and a 3 m resolution dataset on pixels of 334 × 334 per sample (process 5 in Figure A1), with a total of ~444.1 million pixels, denoted as DFC30-3m. In brief, each of the DFC30-8m and DFC30-3m datasets contained 3981 samples with resolutions of 8 m and 3 m, respectively. Each sample included a low-resolution derived DSM, two low-resolution derived DTMs, a high-resolution derived DTM, a high-resolution derived RGB image, a high-resolution derived CHM and a high-resolution derived land use mask within each sample.

Appendix A.2. Metric Calculation Details

We calculated metrics iteratively on each batch, namely online mode, and once after an epoch, namely offline mode. Some metrics, such as RMSE and PSNR, differed between the online and offline calculation modes. Taking RMSE as an example, the online mode calculates and stores each batch's RMSE during an evaluation procedure and then averages all the stored batch RMSEs as follows:

$$\text{RMSE}_{\text{online}} = \frac{1}{M}\sum_{i=1}^{M}\sqrt{\sum_{i=1}^{B}(\hat{\mathcal{H}}^i - \mathcal{H}^i_{gt})^2/B}, \tag{A1}$$

where M denotes the iteration number of each epoch, B denotes the batch size. Specifically, this work defines the evaluation batch size as 1. Thus, the online mode RMSE is the average of the RMSE for each prediction in this case.

The benefits of the online mode are that it reveals trends during an epoch's training and has low memory consumption. In contrast, the offline mode calculates the RMSE for all predictions as described in Equation (9), which requires more memory space. However, online mode calculations can be unreliable for specific metrics under certain scenarios. For instance, if a batch sample is located entirely on the water, such as a lake or sea, the prediction could be identical or close to its corresponding ground truth. Under these circumstances, referring to Equation (13), the batch PSNR will be large due to the denominator (i.e., RMSE) being close to zero, resulting in an abnormally high online mode PSNR compared to the offline mode PSNR.

Since our DEM dataset contained samples from within a lake or sea, we adopted an offline mode as the calculation mode to provide a comprehensive description of the results. The metrics in this paper are offline mode values by default unless explicitly labelled as the online mode.

Appendix A.3. Training Set and Test Set Splitting

To maximise the use of data, we split the dataset into a training set (13 regions) and a test set (3 regions). The division was based on sample size, where the training set contains four times the number of samples in the test set (approximating an 80%/20% ratio). Figure A2 summarises the elevation, slope and land use class distributions for both sets. Specifically, the training set and test set sizes are 3182 and 799 for DFC30-8m, and 28,638 and 7191 for DFC30-3m. We maintained a fixed train/test split using a predefined list, while shuffling sample order in the dataloader during training.

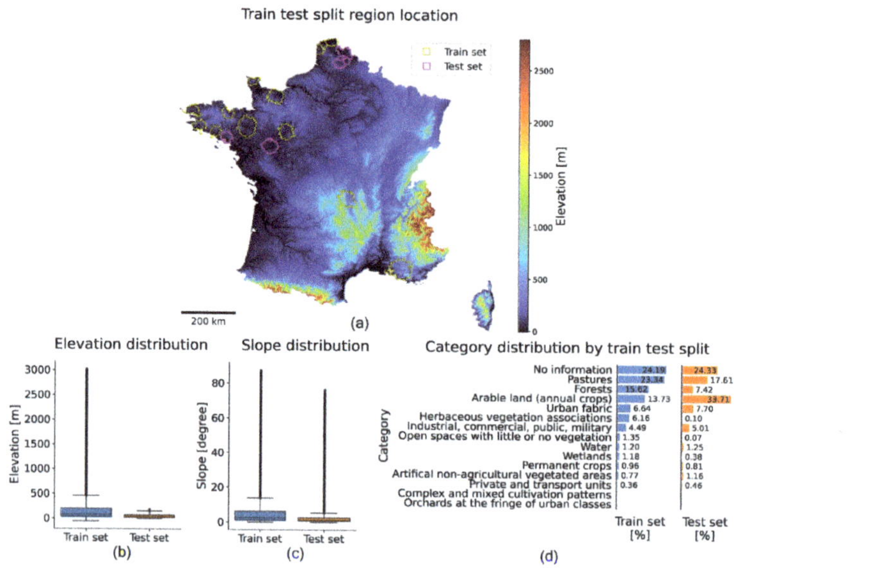

Figure A2. The training/test split details. (**a**) The region location of the training/test split; (**b**) the elevation distribution by boxplot for pixels in the train set and test set; (**c**) the slope distribution by boxplot for pixels in the train set and test set; (**d**) the category distribution by percentage of pixels in the train set and test set.

References

1. Rocha, J.; Duarte, A.; Silva, M.; Fabres, S.; Vasques, J.; Revilla-Romero, B.; Quintela, A. The importance of high resolution digital elevation models for improved hydrological simulations of a mediterranean forested catchment. *Remote Sens.* **2020**, *12*, 3287. [CrossRef]
2. Wechsler, S. Uncertainties associated with digital elevation models for hydrologic applications: A review. *Hydrol. Earth Syst. Sci.* **2007**, *11*, 1481–1500. [CrossRef]
3. McClean, F.; Dawson, R.; Kilsby, C. Implications of using global digital elevation models for flood risk analysis in cities. *Water Resour. Res.* **2020**, *56*, e2020WR028241. [CrossRef]
4. Nandam, V.; Patel, P. A framework to assess suitability of global digital elevation models for hydrodynamic modelling in data scarce regions. *J. Hydrol.* **2024**, *630*, 130654. [CrossRef]
5. Zandsalimi, Z.; Feizabadi, S.; Yazdi, J.; Salehi Neyshabouri, S.A.A. Evaluating the Impact of Digital Elevation Models on Urban Flood Modeling: A Comprehensive Analysis of Flood Inundation, Hazard Mapping, and Damage Estimation. *Water Resour. Manag.* **2024**, *38*, 4243–4268. [CrossRef]
6. Meadows, M.; Jones, S.; Reinke, K. Vertical accuracy assessment of freely available global DEMs (FABDEM, Copernicus DEM, NASADEM, AW3D30 and SRTM) in flood-prone environments. *Int. J. Digit. Earth* **2024**, *17*, 2308734. [CrossRef]
7. Guth, P.L.; Van Niekerk, A.; Grohmann, C.H.; Muller, J.P.; Hawker, L.; Florinsky, I.V.; Gesch, D.; Reuter, H.I.; Herrera-Cruz, V.; Riazanoff, S.; et al. Digital elevation models: Terminology and definitions. *Remote Sens.* **2021**, *13*, 3581. [CrossRef]
8. Dolloff, J.; Theiss, H.; Bollin, B. Assessment, specification, and validation of a geolocation system's accuracy and predicted accuracy. *Photogramm. Eng. Remote Sens.* **2024**, *90*, 157–168. [CrossRef]
9. Elaksher, A.; Ali, T.; Alharthy, A. A quantitative assessment of LiDAR data accuracy. *Remote Sens.* **2023**, *15*, 442. [CrossRef]
10. Ho, Y.F.; Grohmann, C.H.; Lindsay, J.; Reuter, H.I.; Parente, L.; Witjes, M.; Hengl, T. GEDTM30: Global ensemble digital terrain model at 30 m and derived multiscale terrain variables. *PeerJ* **2025**, *13*, e19673. [CrossRef]
11. Bielski, C.; López-Vázquez, C.; Grohmann, C.H.; Guth, P.L.; Hawker, L.; Gesch, D.; Trevisani, S.; Herrera-Cruz, V.; Riazanoff, S.; Corseaux, A.; et al. Novel approach for ranking dems: Copernicus DEM improves one arc second open global topography. *IEEE Trans. Geosci. Remote Sens.* **2024**, *62*, 4503922. [CrossRef]
12. European Space Agency. *Copernicus DEM—Global and European Digital Elevation Model*; Copernicus Data Space Ecosystem: Zaventem, Belgium, 2022. [CrossRef]
13. Hawker, L.; Uhe, P.; Paulo, L.; Sosa, J.; Savage, J.; Sampson, C.; Neal, J. A 30 m global map of elevation with forests and buildings removed. *Environ. Res. Lett.* **2022**, *17*, 024016. [CrossRef]

14. Uhe, P.; Lucas, C.; Hawker, L.; Brine, M.; Wilkinson, H.; Cooper, A.; Saoulis, A.A.; Savage, J.; Sampson, C. FathomDEM: An improved global terrain map using a hybrid vision transformer model. *Environ. Res. Lett.* **2025**, *20*, 034002. [CrossRef]
15. Dosovitskiy, A.; Beyer, L.; Kolesnikov, A.; Weissenborn, D.; Zhai, X.; Unterthiner, T.; Dehghani, M.; Minderer, M.; Heigold, G.; Gelly, S.; et al. An image is worth 16x16 words: Transformers for image recognition at scale. *arXiv* **2020**, arXiv:2010.11929.
16. Wing, O.E.J.; Bates, P.D.; Quinn, N.D.; Savage, J.T.S.; Uhe, P.F.; Cooper, A.; Collings, T.P.; Addor, N.; Lord, N.S.; Hatchard, S.; et al. A 30 m global flood inundation model for any climate scenario. *Water Resour. Res.* **2024**, *60*, e2023WR036460. [CrossRef]
17. Schumann, G.J.P.; Bates, P.D. The Need for a High-Accuracy, Open-Access Global DEM. *Front. Earth Sci.* **2018**, *6*, 225. [CrossRef]
18. Fisher, P.F.; Tate, N.J. Causes and consequences of error in digital elevation models. *Prog. Phys. Geogr.* **2006**, *30*, 467–489. [CrossRef]
19. Dong, C.; Loy, C.C.; He, K.; Tang, X. Learning a deep convolutional network for image super-resolution. In Proceedings of the Computer Vision–ECCV 2014: 13th European Conference, Zurich, Switzerland, 6–12 September 2014; Springer: Berlin/Heidelberg, Germany, 2014; pp. 184–199.
20. Zhang, Y.; Yu, W.; Zhu, D. Terrain feature-aware deep learning network for digital elevation model superresolution. *ISPRS J. Photogramm. Remote Sens.* **2022**, *189*, 143–162. [CrossRef]
21. Jiang, Y.; Xiong, L.; Huang, X.; Li, S.; Shen, W. Super-resolution for terrain modeling using deep learning in high mountain Asia. *Int. J. Appl. Earth Obs. Geoinf.* **2023**, *118*, 103296. [CrossRef]
22. Han, X.; Zhou, C.; Sun, S.; Lyu, C.; Gao, M.; He, X. An ensemble learning framework for generating high-resolution regional DEMs considering geographical zoning. *ISPRS J. Photogramm. Remote Sens.* **2025**, *221*, 363–383. [CrossRef]
23. Wu, Z.; Zhao, Z.; Ma, P.; Huang, B. Real-world DEM super-resolution based on generative adversarial networks for improving InSAR topographic phase simulation. *IEEE J. Sel. Top. Appl. Earth Obs. Remote Sens.* **2021**, *14*, 8373–8385. [CrossRef]
24. Zhang, Y.; Funkhouser, T. Deep Depth Completion of a Single RGB-D Image. In Proceedings of the IEEE Conference on Computer Vision and Pattern Recognition (CVPR), Salt Lake City, UT, USA, 18–22 June 2018.
25. Habib, M. Evaluation of DEM interpolation techniques for characterizing terrain roughness. *Catena* **2021**, *198*, 105072. [CrossRef]
26. Tsai, R.Y.; Huang, T.S. Multiframe image restoration and registration. *Multiframe Image Restor. Regist.* **1984**, *1*, 317–339.
27. Hu, J.; Bao, C.; Ozay, M.; Fan, C.; Gao, Q.; Liu, H.; Lam, T.L. Deep depth completion from extremely sparse data: A survey. *IEEE Trans. Pattern Anal. Mach. Intell.* **2023**, *45*, 8244–8264. [CrossRef]
28. Rajan, D.; Chaudhuri, S. Generalized interpolation and its application in super-resolution imaging. *Image Vis. Comput.* **2001**, *19*, 957–969. [CrossRef]
29. Zhao, X.; Su, Y.; Dong, Y.; Wang, J.; Zhai, L. Kind of super-resolution method of CCD image based on wavelet and bicubic interpolation. *Appl. Res. Comput.* **2009**, *26*, 2365–2367.
30. Lim, B.; Son, S.; Kim, H.; Nah, S.; Mu Lee, K. Enhanced deep residual networks for single image super-resolution. In Proceedings of the IEEE Conference on Computer Vision and Pattern Recognition Workshops, Honolulu, HI, USA, 21–26 July 2017; pp. 136–144.
31. Kim, J.; Lee, J.K.; Lee, K.M. Deeply-recursive convolutional network for image super-resolution. In Proceedings of the IEEE Conference on Computer Vision And Pattern Recognition, Las Vegas, NV, USA, 27–30 June 2016; pp. 1637–1645.
32. Zhang, Y.; Li, K.; Li, K.; Wang, L.; Zhong, B.; Fu, Y. Image super-resolution using very deep residual channel attention networks. In Proceedings of the European Conference on Computer Vision (ECCV), Munich, Germany, 8–14 September 2018; pp. 286–301.
33. Ledig, C.; Theis, L.; Huszár, F.; Caballero, J.; Cunningham, A.; Acosta, A.; Aitken, A.; Tejani, A.; Totz, J.; Wang, Z.; et al. Photo-realistic single image super-resolution using a generative adversarial network. In Proceedings of the IEEE Conference on Computer Vision and Pattern Recognition, Honolulu, HI, USA, 21–26 July 2017; pp. 4681–4690.
34. Chen, Z.; Wang, X.; Xu, Z.; Hou, W. Convolutional neural network based dem super resolution. *Int. Arch. Photogramm. Remote Sens. Spat. Inf. Sci.* **2016**, *41*, 247–250. [CrossRef]
35. Zhang, R.; Bian, S.; Li, H. RSPCN: Super-resolution of digital elevation model based on recursive sub-pixel convolutional neural networks. *ISPRS Int. J. Geo-Inf.* **2021**, *10*, 501. [CrossRef]
36. Zhou, A.; Chen, Y.; Wilson, J.P.; Su, H.; Xiong, Z.; Cheng, Q. An enhanced double-filter deep residual neural network for generating super resolution DEMs. *Remote Sens.* **2021**, *13*, 3089. [CrossRef]
37. Zhang, Y.; Yu, W. Comparison of DEM super-resolution methods based on interpolation and neural networks. *Sensors* **2022**, *22*, 745. [CrossRef] [PubMed]
38. Demiray, B.Z.; Sit, M.; Demir, I. D-SRGAN: DEM super-resolution with generative adversarial networks. *SN Comput. Sci.* **2021**, *2*, 48. [CrossRef]
39. Argudo, O.; Chica, A.; Andujar, C. Terrain super-resolution through aerial imagery and fully convolutional networks. *Comput. Graph. Forum* **2018**, *37*, 101–110. [CrossRef]
40. Xu, Z.; Chen, Z.; Yi, W.; Gui, Q.; Hou, W.; Ding, M. Deep gradient prior network for DEM super-resolution: Transfer learning from image to DEM. *ISPRS J. Photogramm. Remote Sens.* **2019**, *150*, 80–90. [CrossRef]

41. Sun, G.; Chen, Y.; Huang, J.; Ma, Q.; Ge, Y. Digital Surface Model Super-Resolution by Integrating High-Resolution Remote Sensing Imagery Using Generative Adversarial Networks. *IEEE J. Sel. Top. Appl. Earth Obs. Remote Sens.* **2024**, *17*, 10636–10647. [CrossRef]
42. Zhou, A.; Chen, Y.; Wilson, J.P.; Chen, G.; Min, W.; Xu, R. A multi-terrain feature-based deep convolutional neural network for constructing super-resolution DEMs. *Int. J. Appl. Earth Obs. Geoinf.* **2023**, *120*, 103338. [CrossRef]
43. Tang, J.; Tian, F.P.; Feng, W.; Li, J.; Tan, P. Learning guided convolutional network for depth completion. *IEEE Trans. Image Process.* **2020**, *30*, 1116–1129. [CrossRef]
44. Wang, Y.; Li, B.; Zhang, G.; Liu, Q.; Gao, T.; Dai, Y. Lrru: Long-short range recurrent updating networks for depth completion. In Proceedings of the IEEE/CVF International Conference on Computer Vision, Paris, France, 1–6 October 2023; pp. 9422–9432.
45. He, K.; Sun, J.; Tang, X. Guided image filtering. *IEEE Trans. Pattern Anal. Mach. Intell.* **2012**, *35*, 1397–1409. [CrossRef]
46. Li, Y.; Huang, J.B.; Ahuja, N.; Yang, M.H. Deep joint image filtering. In Proceedings of the Computer Vision–ECCV 2016: 14th European Conference, Amsterdam, The Netherlands, 11–14 October 2016; Springer: Berlin/Heidelberg, Germany, 2016; pp. 154–169.
47. Hu, M.; Wang, S.; Li, B.; Ning, S.; Fan, L.; Gong, X. PENet: Towards Precise and Efficient Image Guided Depth Completion. *arXiv* **2021**, arXiv:2103.00783. [CrossRef]
48. Lin, Y.; Cheng, T.; Zhong, Q.; Zhou, W.; Yang, H. Dynamic spatial propagation network for depth completion. In Proceedings of the AAAI Conference on Artificial Intelligence, Online, 22 February–1 March 2022; Volume 36, pp. 1638–1646.
49. Zhang, Y.; Guo, X.; Poggi, M.; Zhu, Z.; Huang, G.; Mattoccia, S. Completionformer: Depth completion with convolutions and vision transformers. In Proceedings of the IEEE/CVF Conference on Computer Vision and Pattern Recognition, Vancouver, BC, Canada, 17–24 June 2023; pp. 18527–18536.
50. Liu, S.; De Mello, S.; Gu, J.; Zhong, G.; Yang, M.H.; Kautz, J. Learning affinity via spatial propagation networks. *Adv. Neural Inf. Process. Syst.* **2017**, *30*, 1519–1529.
51. Cheng, X.; Wang, P.; Guan, C.; Yang, R.C. Learning Context and Resource Aware Convolutional Spatial Propagation Networks for Depth Completion. *arXiv* **2019**, arXiv:1911.05377. [CrossRef]
52. Liu, X.; Shao, X.; Wang, B.; Li, Y.; Wang, S. Graphcspn: Geometry-aware depth completion via dynamic gcns. In Proceedings of the European Conference on Computer Vision, Tel Aviv, Israel, 23–27 October 2022; Springer: Berlin/Heidelberg, Germany, 2022; pp. 90–107.
53. Park, J.; Joo, K.; Hu, Z.; Liu, C.K.; So Kweon, I. Non-local spatial propagation network for depth completion. In Proceedings of the Computer Vision–ECCV 2020: 16th European Conference, Glasgow, UK, 23–28 August 2020; Springer: Berlin/Heidelberg, Germany, 2020; pp. 120–136.
54. Xu, Z.; Yin, H.; Yao, J. Deformable spatial propagation networks for depth completion. In Proceedings of the 2020 IEEE International Conference on Image, Processing (ICIP), Online, 25–28 October 2020; IEEE: New York, NY, USA, 2020; pp. 913–917.
55. Cheng, X.; Wang, P.; Yang, R. Learning depth with convolutional spatial propagation network. *IEEE Trans. Pattern Anal. Mach. Intell.* **2019**, *42*, 2361–2379. [CrossRef]
56. Cheng, X.; Wang, P.; Guan, C.; Yang, R. Cspn++: Learning context and resource aware convolutional spatial propagation networks for depth completion. In Proceedings of the AAAI Conference on Artificial Intelligence, New York, NY, USA, 7–12 February 2020; Volume 34, pp. 10615–10622.
57. Kim, B.; Ponce, J.; Ham, B. Deformable kernel networks for joint image filtering. *Int. J. Comput. Vis.* **2021**, *129*, 579–600. [CrossRef]
58. Tolan, J.; Yang, H.I.; Nosarzewski, B.; Couairon, G.; Vo, H.V.; Brandt, J.; Spore, J.; Majumdar, S.; Haziza, D.; Vamaraju, J.; et al. Very high resolution canopy height maps from RGB imagery using self-supervised vision transformer and convolutional decoder trained on aerial lidar. *Remote Sens. Environ.* **2024**, *300*, 113888. [CrossRef]
59. Hänsch, R.; Persello, C.; Vivone, G.; Navarro, J.C.; Boulch, A.; Lefevre, S.; Saux, B.L. *Data Fusion Contest 2022 (DFC2022)*; IEEE DataPrt: New York, NY, USA, 2022. [CrossRef]
60. Huber, M.; Osterkamp, N.; Marschalk, U.; Tubbesing, R.; Wendleder, A.; Wessel, B.; Roth, A. Shaping the global high-resolution TanDEM-X digital elevation model. *IEEE J. Sel. Top. Appl. Earth Obs. Remote Sens.* **2021**, *14*, 7198–7212. [CrossRef]
61. Castillo-Navarro, J.; Le Saux, B.; Boulch, A.; Audebert, N.; Lefèvre, S. Semi-Supervised Semantic Segmentation in Earth Observation: The MiniFrance suite, dataset analysis and multi-task network study. *Mach. Learn.* **2022**, *111*, 3125–3160. [CrossRef]
62. French National Institute of Geographical and Forest Information (IGN). BD ORTHO Database. 2019. Available online: https://geoservices.ign.fr/bdortho (accessed on 10 August 2024).
63. Agency, E.E.; Agency, E.E. *Urban Atlas Land Cover/Land Use 2012 (Vector), Europe, 6-Yearly, Jan. 2021*; European Environment Agency (EEA): Copenhagen, Denmark, 2016. [CrossRef]
64. French National Institute of Geographical and Forest Information (IGN). RGE ALTI Database. 2012. Available online: https://geoservices.ign.fr/rgealti (accessed on 10 August 2024).
65. Zhang, C.; Bengio, S.; Hardt, M.; Recht, B.; Vinyals, O. Understanding deep learning requires rethinking generalization. *arXiv* **2016**, arXiv:1611.03530. [CrossRef]

66. Lahat, D.; Adali, T.; Jutten, C. Multimodal data fusion: An overview of methods, challenges, and prospects. *Proc. IEEE* **2015**, *103*, 1449–1477. [CrossRef]
67. Agustsson, E.; Timofte, R. NTIRE 2017 Challenge on Single Image Super-Resolution: Dataset and Study. In Proceedings of the IEEE Conference on Computer Vision and Pattern Recognition (CVPR) Workshops, Honolulu, HI, USA, 21–26 July 2017; pp. 1122–1131.
68. Geiger, A.; Lenz, P.; Stiller, C.; Urtasun, R. Vision meets Robotics: The KITTI Dataset. *Int. J. Robot. Res. IJRR* **2013**, *32*, 231–1237. [CrossRef]
69. Ronneberger, O.; Fischer, P.; Brox, T. U-net: Convolutional networks for biomedical image segmentation. In Proceedings of the Medical Image Computing and Computer-Assisted Intervention–MICCAI 2015: 18th International Conference, Munich, Germany, 5–9 October 2015; Springer: Berlin/Heidelberg, Germany, 2015; pp. 234–241.
70. Dai, J.; Qi, H.; Xiong, Y.; Li, Y.; Zhang, G.; Hu, H.; Wei, Y. Deformable convolutional networks. In Proceedings of the IEEE International Conference on Computer Vision, Venice, Italy, 22–29 October 2017; pp. 764–773.
71. Paszke, A.; Gross, S.; Massa, F.; Lerer, A.; Bradbury, J.; Chanan, G.; Killeen, T.; Lin, Z.; Gimelshein, N.; Antiga, L.; et al. Pytorch: An imperative style, high-performance deep learning library. *Adv. Neural Inf. Process. Syst.* **2019**, *32*, 721.
72. He, K.; Zhang, X.; Ren, S.; Sun, J. Deep residual learning for image recognition. In Proceedings of the IEEE Conference on Computer Vision and Pattern Recognition, Las Vegas, NV, USA, 27–30 June 2016; pp. 770–778.
73. Woo, S.; Park, J.; Lee, J.Y.; Kweon, I.S. CBAM: Convolutional Block Attention Module. In Proceedings of the European Conference on Computer Vision (ECCV), Munich, Germany, 8–14 September 2018.
74. Gesch, D.B. Best practices for elevation-based assessments of sea-level rise and coastal flooding exposure. *Front. Earth Sci.* **2018**, *6*, 230. [CrossRef]
75. Höhle, J.; Höhle, M. Accuracy assessment of digital elevation models by means of robust statistical methods. *ISPRS J. Photogramm. Remote Sens.* **2009**, *64*, 398–406. [CrossRef]
76. Hawker, L.; Neal, J.; Bates, P. Accuracy assessment of the TanDEM-X 90 Digital Elevation Model for selected floodplain sites. *Remote Sens. Environ.* **2019**, *232*, 111319. [CrossRef]
77. Loshchilov, I. Decoupled weight decay regularization. *arXiv* **2017**, arXiv:1711.05101.
78. Yan, Z.; Wang, K.; Li, X.; Zhang, Z.; Li, J.; Yang, J. RigNet: Repetitive image guided network for depth completion. In Proceedings of the European Conference on Computer Vision, Tel Aviv, Israel, 23–27 October 2022; Springer: Berlin/Heidelberg, Germany, 2022; pp. 214–230.
79. GDAL/OGR Contributors. *GDAL/OGR Geospatial Data Abstraction Software Library*; Open Source Geospatial Foundation: Beaverton, OR, USA, 2024. [CrossRef]
80. Bernardi, G.; Brisebarre, G.; Roman, S.; Ardabilian, M.; Dellandrea, E. A comprehensive survey on image fusion: Which approach fits which need. *Inf. Fusion* **2025**, *126*, 103594. [CrossRef]
81. Deng, Y.; Wilson, J.P.; Bauer, B. DEM resolution dependencies of terrain attributes across a landscape. *Int. J. Geogr. Inf. Sci.* **2007**, *21*, 187–213. [CrossRef]
82. Winsemius, H.C.; Ward, P.J.; Gayton, I.; ten Veldhuis, M.C.; Meijer, D.H.; Iliffe, M. Commentary: The Need for a High-Accuracy, Open-Access Global DEM. *Front. Earth Sci.* **2019**, *7*, 33. [CrossRef]
83. Winsemius, H.C.; Jongman, B.; Veldkamp, T.I.; Hallegatte, S.; Bangalore, M.; Ward, P.J. Disaster risk, climate change, and poverty: Assessing the global exposure of poor people to floods and droughts. *Environ. Dev. Econ.* **2018**, *23*, 328–348. [CrossRef]

remote sensing

MDPI

Article

Cross-View Geo-Localization via 3D Gaussian Splatting-Based Novel View Synthesis

Xiaokun Ding [1,2], Xuanyu Zhang [1], Shangzhen Song [2], Bo Li [1], Le Hui [1] and Yuchao Dai [1,*]

[1] School of Electronics and Information & Shaanxi Key Laboratory of Information Acquisition and Processing, Northwestern Polytechnical University, Xi'an 710072, China; xuanyuzhang@mail.nwpu.edu.cn (X.Z.)
[2] Xi'an Flight Automatic Control Research Institute, Xi'an 710076, China
* Correspondence: daiyuchao@nwpu.edu.cn

Highlights

What are the main findings?

- We propose a pipeline designed to enhance cross-view geo-localization (CVGL) by integrating novel view synthesis. The core of our framework reduces the cross-view feature discrepancy through the generation of perspective-aware overhead images, leading to superior geo-localization accuracy.
- A novel camera pose generation method is specifically designed for autonomous driving scenarios to address the challenge of missing vertical view pose.

What are the implications of the main findings?

- The proposed method establishes a continuous feature transition between street-level and satellite imagery, thereby enhancing the model's capability in cross-view geo-localization tasks.
- By integrating 3D Gaussian Splatting (3DGS)-based novel view synthesis into deep learning frameworks for CVGL, our approach enables the autonomous generation of corresponding bird's-eye-view images directly from street-view inputs.

Abstract

Cross-view geo-localization allows an agent to determine its own position by retrieving the same scene from images taken from dramatically different perspectives. However, image matching and retrieval face significant challenges due to substantial viewpoint differences, unknown orientations, and considerable geometric distribution disparities between cross-view images. To this end, we propose a cross-view geo-localization framework based on novel view synthesis that generates pseudo aerial-view images from given street-view scenes to reduce the view discrepancies, thereby improving the performance of cross-view geo-localization. Specifically, we first employ 3D Gaussian splatting to generate new aerial images from the street-view image sequence, where COLMAP is used to obtain initial camera poses and sparse point clouds. To identify optimal matching viewpoints from reconstructed 3D scenes, we design an effective camera pose estimation strategy. By increasing the tilt angle between the photographic axis and the horizontal plane, the geometric consistency between the newly generated aerial images and the real ones can be improved. After that, the DINOv2 is employed to design a simple yet efficient mixed feature enhancement module, followed by the InfoNCE loss for cross-view geo-localization. Experimental results on the KITTI dataset demonstrate that our approach can significantly improve cross-view matching accuracy under large viewpoint disparities and achieve state-of-the-art localization performance.

Keywords: cross-view geo-localization; novel view synthesis; 3D gaussian splatting; contrastive learning

1. Introduction

Vision-based localization is a fundamental technology in many intelligent systems, including autonomous driving [1], augmented reality [2], and mobile robotics [3]. However, traditional localization approaches that rely on ground-level image databases suffer from several inherent limitations. Firstly, ground images often provide limited coverage, making it difficult to meet the requirements of large-scale environments. Secondly, such datasets depend heavily on costly manual GPS annotation [4,5], which struggle to handle cross-view or multi-scale variations. In addition, ground-level images are sensitive to environmental change, including illumination, weather, and season, resulting in poor robustness. More critically, these methods are effective only when operating within similar view points, whose imaging perspectives are not significantly different. In some extreme matching applications between ground-level (street) views and aerial-level (satellite or UAV) views, conventional approaches struggle to establish reliable correspondences. To overcome this problem, cross-view geo-localization has recently become a promising research direction [6]. This task leverages satellite images as reference, which inherently provides wide spatial coverage with precise GPS labels. By establishing correspondences between ground-level and aerial-level images, it becomes possible to overcome the challenges of viewpoint variations, thereby enabling a robust localization even in GPS-denied environments. Nevertheless, cross-view geo-localization remains highly challenging due to the significant domain gap between aerial and ground perspectives. Early studies primarily relied on handcrafted features such as SIFT [7], SURF [8], and ORB [9] descriptors. These approaches attempted to exploit invariances in local gradients or texture patterns to build correspondences between images. Such handcrafted features are simple but inherently limited, as they are unable to capture semantic-level similarities under large viewpoint and scale variations, leading to significant performance degradation.

With the rapid development of deep learning, researchers have shifted their focus to learning deep feature representations [10–12]. CNN-based methods became dominant owing to their ability to provide robust representations invariant to photometric distortions. Workman et al. [6] first explored CNN-based features for cross-view matching based on the assumption that high-level semantic features from pre-trained networks encode geographical information. Subsequent studies incorporated more advanced backbones such as VGG [13], ResNet [14], and DenseNet [15–17], significantly improving retrieval performance. In addition to architectural improvements, metric learning played a pivotal role in forming discriminative embeddings through losses such as soft-margin triplet loss [18] and global descriptor networks like NetVLAD. Orientation-aware strategies were also developed, including coordinate embedding [19] and geometric transformation techniques [20] to reduce perspective distortions. More recently, Transformer-based architectures have gained attention for their ability to model long-range dependencies and global context, with several studies demonstrating their strong potential in capturing complex cross-view relationships. These approaches have shown particular effectiveness in handling large perspective changes and complex urban scenarios through self-attention mechanisms and adaptive feature learning.

Despite considerable progress, significant challenges also persist. The most critical issue stems from the severe perspective discrepancy between ground and aerial images: ground-level photos typically offer horizontal, often occluded views, while aerial images provide vertical, unobstructed overviews. This discrepancy is further exacerbated when using standard non-panoramic cameras in practical settings, where limited field of view results in substantial information loss, making consistent geometric correspondence difficult to establish. Another major challenge arises from the pronounced domain shift in imaging conditions, including variations in illumination, scale, and resolution. Ground images are often affected by dynamic lighting changes, while aerial views are generally captured under uniform natural light but at drastically different scales and typically with coarser spatial resolution. These intrinsic differences hinder the learning of invariant feature. Furthermore, semantic ambiguity poses a significant obstacle, particularly in areas with high visual self-similarity such as highways, farmlands, or repetitive urban structures. While such regions appear homogeneous from an aerial perspective, they exhibit distinct characteristics at ground level, leading to mismatches in feature space. These challenges highlight the need for innovative frameworks capable of bridging the large domain gap through both geometric reasoning and discriminative representation learning.

In recent years, generative models such as Generative Adversarial Networks (GANs) [21] and Neural Radiance Fields (NeRFs) [22] have opened new pathways for 3D scene reconstruction and localization through view synthesis. These methods aim to reconstruct realistic 3D scenes from multiple 2D images captured from different viewpoints, offering promising strategies for mitigating the domain gap in cross-view matching tasks. By learning implicit representations of geometry and appearance, they enhance feature consistency across highly divergent perspectives. Recent advances in 3D Gaussian Splatting (3DGS) [23] have demonstrated remarkable efficiency in high-fidelity novel view synthesis, achieving real-time rendering performance(often exceeding 100 frames per second) while preserving geometric detail. In contrast to NeRF's implicit volumetric representation, 3DGS explicitly models a scene using millions of Gaussian ellipsoids, which enables direct manipulation (e.g., moving, deleting, or modifying elements), greatly improving editability. Although 3DGS typically requires more storage due to a larger number of parameters, its computational efficiency during rendering leads to better overall memory utility compared to NeRF-based methods. Furthermore, 3DGS shows superior adaptability to dynamic scenes. While native NeRF is generally confined to static settings and requires non-trivial extensions to model motion, 3DGS can natively handle dynamics through mechanisms such as deformation fields. In terms of initialization, NeRF usually demands hundreds of input views for stable convergence, whereas 3DGS can start from a sparse point cloud generated via Structure-from-Motion (SfM), reducing data requirements and broadening applicability. These properties make 3DGS particularly suitable for applications requiring real-time interaction and high render efficiency, such as virtual reality, augmented reality, and interactive scene editing.

In this paper, we propose a novel cross-view geo-localization framework based on 3D Gaussian splatting, which synthesizes novel images of large tilt angles from street-view inputs to effectively bridge the domain gap between ground and aerial views. Specifically, for initializing the 3D Gaussians, we employ COLMAP [24] to estimate accurate camera poses and sparse point clouds from street-level imagery. Furthermore, we design a dedicated camera pose estimation strategy that determines optimal aerial viewpoints by progressively increasing the tilt angle of the photographic axis relative to the horizontal plane. This approach enhances the geometric consistency and realism of the synthesized aerial images. After synthesizing the novel aerial views, we process them through a mixed feature enhancement module that leverages both DINOv2 [25] and a feature-mixer network to extract discriminative and robust representations. These features are then used to perform cross-view matching. The entire framework is trained end-to-end using the InfoNCE loss, which facilitates effective learning of viewpoint-invariant features. Experimental

where W is the view transformation matrix and J is the Jacobian matrix representing the local linear approximation of the projection. This formulation ensures that the projected 3D Gaussians remain as 2D ellipses, which can be efficiently rasterized.

The final rendering process is performed using a tile-based rasterization pipeline. The 2D screen space is partitioned into pixel tiles to manage computational complexity. A filtering step, including frustum culling and bounding box tests, is first applied to retain only the Gaussians that fall within the current view frustum and can influence a given tile. Within each tile, the Gaussians are depth-sorted from front-to-back and blended using an alpha compositing formula to compute the final pixel color:

$$C = \sum_i \boldsymbol{c}_i \boldsymbol{\alpha}_i \prod_{j=1}^{i-1} (1 - \boldsymbol{\alpha}_j). \tag{4}$$

where $\boldsymbol{c}_i$ and $\boldsymbol{\alpha}_i$ represent the color and opacity of the i-th Gaussian, respectively. This rasterization-based approach bypasses the need for repeated, per-ray MLP inferences characteristic of NeRF, which significantly accelerates the rendering process and enables real-time frame rates.

3.2. Pseudo Aerial-View Image Synthesis

To effectively mitigate the perspective gap between street-view and aerial-view images, we design a synthesis strategy of pseudo aerial-view images directly from ground-level inputs. 3DGS combines explicit 3D representation with differentiable rendering. Its principle involves optimizing millions of parameterized 3D Gaussian ellipsoids to achieve high-quality real-time view synthesis. Capitalizing on these capabilities, we introduce an aerial-view synthesis module based on 3DGS to generate highly realistic pseudo-aerial images from street-view sequences. To the best of our knowledge, this work pioneers the use of 3D Gaussian Splatting (3DGS) to synthesize a pseudo aerial image from a given street-view image, effectively bridging the disparity between these two perspectives. The overall architecture of the proposed system is depicted in Figure 1.

Specifically, our approach utilizes a pre-trained 3DGS model to synthesizes multi-perspective images with larger tilt angles using a trained model. By processing sequences of street-view images, the model produces a variety of synthetic aerial perspectives that collectively form a enriched cross-view dataset, thereby enhancing feature alignment and improving match accuracy. We first employ COLMAP to estimate corresponding camera poses and reconstruct a sparse point cloud. This point cloud subsequently serves as the initial set of 3D Gaussian primitives, each defined by properties such as position, anisotropic covariance, opacity, and view-dependent color represented via spherical harmonics. These primitives undergo iterative optimization alongside the input images using gradient descent, minimizing a reconstruction loss that compares rendered against actual views. For novel view rendering, each Gaussian is projected into 2D screen space through a differentiable splatting process, followed by alpha-blending of overlapping points based on depth ordering. The entire pipeline supports rendering from arbitrary viewpoints, allowing flexible generation of pseudo-aerial images that exhibit high geometric and photometric consistency with the original street-level scene.

However, in practice, acquiring ideal 360° video streams to extract sufficient continuous images for training is often infeasible. This limitation makes it difficult for 3DGS to directly synthesize the required images. To overcome this problem, we introduce a two-step method to compute an optimal camera pose for a given tilt angle: (1) determining the 3D coordinates of the camera's optical center and (2) computing the corresponding rotation matrix.

The process of estimating the camera's optical center position involves finding both the average point cloud center and the average plane normal vector. The strategy for finding the average point cloud center leverages the prior knowledge that the captured altitude of street-view images remains relatively consistent. We hypothesize that the optimal camera viewpoint should position its optical center collinear with the centroid of the average point cloud, thereby maximizing scene coverage and information acquisition. The average point cloud center is calculated as follows:

$$\bar{t} = \frac{1}{n}\sum_{i=1}^{n} t_i, \tag{5}$$

where $t_i = (x, y, z)^\top$ refers to the 3D coordinates of the i-th point of all n points.

After computing the point cloud's average center, we proceed to estimate the camera pose. The normal vector of a plane is determined using three key points: the average center of the point cloud together with the optical centers from any two images. By iterating this procedure across multiple image pairs, we obtain a set of candidate normal vectors. Principal Component Analysis (PCA) is then applied to filter these candidates, yielding a robust average normal vector that guides the orientation adjustment of the camera's optical center. The process is illustrated in Figure 2, and corresponding formulation is written as

$$\mathcal{N} = \frac{1}{n-1}\sum_{i=2}^{n}[(\boldsymbol{P}_i - \bar{t}) \times (\boldsymbol{P}_{i-1} - \bar{t})], \tag{6}$$

where $\boldsymbol{P}_i$ denotes the optical center coordinates of the i-th image, n is the total number of images captured by the platform, and $\times$ indicates the cross product of two vectors. It is important to note that reversing the order of the vectors in the cross product yields a normal vector in the opposite direction. To ensure consistency, our method computes each pairwise product only once while retaining a consistent vector order throughout the process. The computed average plane normal vector $\mathcal{N}$ plays a critical role in aligning the camera's optical axis. By incorporating this geometric prior, we optimally adjust the orientation of the camera's optical center for subsequent rendering steps. This adjusted pose, combined with the 3D Gaussian representations and original camera pose data, enables the synthesis of high-quality 2D images from strategically chosen aerial viewpoints. Ultimately, this pipeline allows us to generate highly realistic pseudo aerial-view images directly from the input street-view sequences, effectively bridging the perspective gap between ground and aerial imagery.

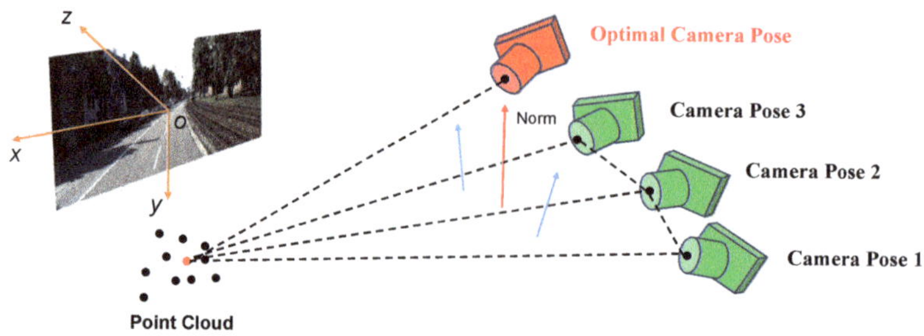

Figure 2. The process of solving the average plane normal vector and the optimal camera pose.

3.3. Mixed Features Enhancement

In recent years, foundational vision models have significantly advanced the field of computer vision by employing deep architectures such as CNNs and Transformers, scaled to hundreds of millions of parameters. Trained on large and diverse datasets, these models exhibit superior representational power and generalization capability. Among these, DINOv2 [25] a self-supervised visual model, learns general-purpose visual representations directly from unlabeled images, overcoming limitations of supervised pre-training. According to its advantages, we leverage DINOv2 as a feature extraction backbone to construct a Mixed Feature Enhancement module for learning discriminative representations for cross-view retrieval. Note that consistent with many other studies, we employed the pre-trained weights of DINOv2 without further fine-tuning. As illustrated in Figure 1, the module first processes both query (street-view or pseudo aerial-view) and reference (aerial) images using DINOv2 to extract visual features. A feature-mixing mechanism is then applied to capture global contextual relationships through cascaded transformations.

Specifically, we combine original street-view and generated pseudo aerial-images into a unified query set, with original aerial imagery serving as the reference. The goal is to identify optimal matches where the query and reference images are accurately aligned. The process begins by dividing an input image into patches and projecting them into patch-level embeddings. These are fed into DINOv2 to produce pre-trained features, taken from the last ViT block while excluding the classification head.

Let the pretrained feature map be donated as $\boldsymbol{F} \in \mathbb{R}^{N \times C}$, where N is the number of channels and C is the feature dimension. This can be interpreted as a set of one-dimensional representations, denoted as

$$\boldsymbol{F} = \{\boldsymbol{X}^i\}, i = \{1, \cdots, N\}. \tag{7}$$

The feature-mixer consists of L successive MLP blocks, which is illustrated in Figure 3. Each block refines the features by incorporating global interactions through a residual transformation:

$$\boldsymbol{X}^i \leftarrow \boldsymbol{W}_2\left(\sigma\left(\boldsymbol{W}_1\boldsymbol{X}^i\right)\right) + \boldsymbol{X}^i, i = \{1, \cdots, N\}, \tag{8}$$

where $\boldsymbol{W}_1$ and $\boldsymbol{W}_2$ are learnable weights of fully connected layer. σ denotes the ReLU activation function. It is desired that the feature-mixer can leverage the capacity of fully connected layers for holistic feature aggregation. After processing through all L feature-mixer layers, the final output feature $\boldsymbol{G}$ is given by

$$\boldsymbol{G} = FM_L(FM_{L-1}(\ldots FM_1(\boldsymbol{F}))). \tag{9}$$

Note that $\boldsymbol{G}$ has the same size $N \times C$ as $\boldsymbol{F}$. To further reduce the dimension, we adopt a depth-wise projection that maps G from $\mathbb{R}^{N \times C}$ to $\mathbb{R}^{N \times D}$ such as

$$\hat{\boldsymbol{G}} = \boldsymbol{W}_D(Transpose(\boldsymbol{G})), \tag{10}$$

where $\boldsymbol{W}_D$ is the weight of the fully connected layer. Similarly, a row-wise projection that maps $\hat{\boldsymbol{G}}$ from $\mathbb{R}^{N \times D}$ to $\mathbb{R}^{n \times D}$ is applied, such as

$$\bar{\boldsymbol{G}} = \boldsymbol{W}_n\left(Transpose\left(\hat{\boldsymbol{G}}\right)\right). \tag{11}$$

Finally, the feature is L_2-normalized to produce the global descriptor for retrieval.

To optimize our model, we adopt the InfoNCE [52] losswe, following the practice [53]. The loss function is defined as

$$\mathcal{L}_{InfoNCE} = -\log \frac{exp(q \cdot r_+/\tau)}{\sum_{i=0}^{N_R} exp(q \cdot r_i/\tau)}, \tag{12}$$

where q denotes the query image, which is the street-view image in the method. r_+ and $\{r_i\}_{i=1}^{N_R}$ indicate the reference images. r_+ is the positive sample, while r_i is the negative sample. Note that for each query q, there is exactly on positive sample r_+. The InfoNCE loss measures similarity via dot products in the latent space, causing the objective to decrease when the query closely aligns with its positive counterpart and increase when it is similar to negative samples.

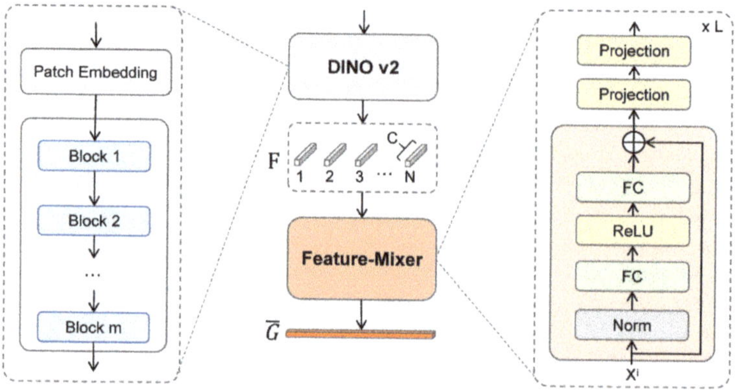

Figure 3. The detailed architecture of the mixed feature enhancement module.

4. Results

4.1. Dataset and Setting

Dataset. The proposed framework is rigorously evaluated using the KITTI dataset [26] and the Oxford Robot Car dataset [54] KITTI is a benchmark widely recognized in the field of autonomous driving and computer vision. The dataset comprises a diverse collection of image sequences captured by a moving vehicle, encompassing a variety of urban and suburban environments under different lighting and weather conditions. For the purpose of our study, the dataset is partitioned into distinct training and testing subsets to ensure a robust and unbiased evaluation. Specifically, the training set is meticulously curated by selecting specific trajectories from KITTI, adhering to the inherent serialization of the data and the requirements of feature-based localization methods like COLMAP [24]. To further enhance the complexity and generalizability of the evaluation, we adopt the extended KITTI dataset constructed by Shi [55]. This augmented dataset incorporates corresponding satellite imagery, thereby enabling a comprehensive cross-view analysis. The dataset is organized into two distinct test sets, namely Test-1 and Test-2. Notably, Test-2 is specifically designed to assess the model's robustness to domain shift, as its image sequences are deliberately chosen from scenes with significantly different visual characteristics compared to the training set.

Except for the KITTI dataset, we additionally conducted experiments on other datasets. Because the sparse nature of the panoramic image sequences in CVUSA, VIGOR, and TorontoCity dataset fails to provide a good initialization for 3DGS in large-scale scenes, which leads to degraded reconstruction quality. The Oxford Robot Car dataset is originally designed for autonomous driving research, which shares a similar data format with KITTI. It contains a total of 23,854 valid ground-to-satellite image pairs, divided into 17,067 pairs for training, 1698 for validation, and 5089 for testing. The street-view images cover a variety of illumination and weather conditions—including sunny, overcast, and cloudy scenes—across both summer and winter seasons.From this perspective, we apply the dataset to further verify our method.

The satellite images are sourced from Google Maps [56], providing a per-pixel ground resolution of 0.20 m. To facilitate effective training and inference, a large geographical area covering the vehicle trajectories is first identified. This region is then uniformly subdivided into a grid of overlapping satellite image blocks, each with a spatial resolution of 1280 × 1280 pixels. This block-based approach ensures that the model can handle large-scale geographical areas efficiently while maintaining sufficient contextual information for effective localization.

Evaluation Metrics. The performance of our proposed method is quantitatively assessed using the widely adopted recall at top k (Rk) metric, a standard practice in the cross-view geo-localization literature [57]. This metric quantifies the retrieval accuracy by measuring the proportion of query images for which the correct corresponding reference image is found within the top k retrieved candidates. Specifically, for each query image, we compute its cosine similarity with all reference images in the embedded feature space. The top k nearest neighbors are then retrieved. A retrieval is considered successful if the ground truth reference image is present within this set of top k candidates. This metric provides a clear and intuitive measure of the model's ability to localize a street-view image within a large-scale satellite map.

Experimental Settings. All experiments were conducted on a high-performance computing platform equipped with an NVIDIA GeForce RTX 3080 Ti GPU and an Intel Xeon CPU operating at 2.40 GHz. Our framework is implemented in PyTorch 1.12, a widely used deep learning framework, enabling efficient training and deployment. The input resolutions for the satellite and street-view images were resized to 640 × 640 and 512 × 128 pixels, respectively, balancing computational efficiency with information preservation. The training process was configured with a batch size of 16, an initial learning rate of 1e-4, and a total of 100 epochs. The AdamW optimizer [58] was employed for its superior performance in weight decay regularization. The majority of the hyperparameters were set to align with established practices in the field to ensure a fair comparison with prior works. The final embedding dimension for both views was set to 1000. This is a deliberate choice, as it results in a significantly more compact and efficient representation compared to many conventional CNN-based methods, which often rely on high-dimensional feature vectors. For 3D Gaussian initialization, regarding the choice of initial scale based on the local density of the SfM point cloud, this strategy was adopted to adaptively determine the initial size of each Gaussian primitive according to the spatial distribution of the reconstructed 3D points. In dense regions, a smaller initial scale helps preserve finer details, while in sparser areas, a larger scale offers better coverage and stability in optimization. This density-aware initialization leads to more stable training and higher-quality reconstruction compared to using a uniform initial scale. For the COLMAP settings, we follow prior works on large-scale outdoor reconstruction. Specifically, the maximum number of features is set to 8192, "Sequential" is used as the matching strategy, and the minimum number of matches is set to 15.

In the experiment, we also tested the retrieval results with varying quantities of synthesized viewpoint images used as training data, specifically 50, 100, 150, and 200 novel images. The results indicated that using 100 synthesized images yielded better retrieval performance compared to 50. When the quantity was increased to 150 and 200, no further significant improvement in retrieval results was observed. Instead, the computational cost increased. Therefore, considering computational efficiency, 100 images were selected as the optimal quantity.

4.2. Performance Comparison

To rigorously validate the efficacy of our proposed framework, we conducted a comprehensive performance evaluation against several mainstream methods on our designated test datasets. The quantitative results, summarized in Table 1, unequivocally demonstrate the superior performance of our approach.

Table 1. Comparison with different methods on single image based localization. The best results are highlighted in bold.

Method	Test-1				Test-2			
	R@1	R@5	R@10	R@1%	R@1	R@5	R@10	R@1%
CVM-NET [38]	6.43	20.74	32.47	84.07	1.01	4.33	7.52	32.88
CVFT [20]	1.78	7.20	14.40	73.55	0.20	1.29	3.03	16.86
SAFA [59]	4.89	15.77	23.29	87.75	1.62	4.73	7.40	30.13
DSM [60]	13.18	41.16	58.67	97.17	5.38	18.12	28.63	75.70
Zhu et al. [15]	5.26	17.79	28.22	88.44	0.73	3.28	5.66	27.86
Toker et al. [61]	2.79	7.72	11.69	58.92	2.39	5.50	8.90	27.05
CVLNet [55]	17.71	44.56	62.15	98.38	9.38	24.06	34.45	85.00
TransGeo [41]	80.65	97.24	97.31	95.48	17.82	34.08	45.50	90.10
Ours	**82.90**	**98.38**	**98.43**	**98.46**	**19.20**	**38.04**	**48.90**	**91.38**

Quantitative Analysis. The results in Table 1 highlight the critical role of our proposed methodology in enhancing cross-view geo-localization performance. The performance improvement observed across all metrics is directly attributable to the introduction of synthesized high-tilt images generated via 3DGS. This novel approach effectively bridges the inherent domain gap between the query street-view images and the reference satellite-view images. The results on the Oxford Robot Car dataset are shown in Table 2. It is shown that on the second dataset, compared to the best-performing method TransGeo among the comparison methods, our approach still demonstrates superior performance. In addition, our work introduces a paradigm-shifting insight: leveraging generative models to synthesize cross-view imagery. This approach illuminates a versatile pathway for a broader spectrum of cross-view geo-localization challenges. The core methodology, which translates one data modality into the view of another, can be directly adapted to bridge other modality gaps. Therefore, it offers a foundational insight for the broader cross-view geo-localization field.

Table 2. Performance of the proposed method on the Oxford Robot Car dataset. The best results are highlighted in bold.

Method	R@1	R@5	R@10	R@1%
TransGeo [41]	70.14	87.63	92.91	94.33
Ours	**71.62**	**89.03**	**95.41**	**96.10**

By generating these intermediate, geometrically consistent views, our method transforms the complex retrieval task into a more manageable feature matching problem. The synthesized images provide a richer, multi-perspective representation of the scene, which significantly improves the similarity measurement between the query and reference domains. This strategic geometric alignment simplifies the feature learning process, leading to a substantial boost in retrieval accuracy and overall localization performance. The proposed method consistently surpasses all baseline algorithms, achieving the highest recall rates and demonstrating its superior robustness and effectiveness. While a Transformer-based architecture is employed for robust feature extraction, the primary driver for the observed performance gains is the innovative use of 3DGS to create a more favorable feature space for cross-view matching.

The synergistic interplay between 3DGS-driven augmentation, DINOv2 features, and contrastive learning forms the cornerstone of our approach, and its interpretation is key to understanding the observed performance gains. The synergy is multiplicative: 3DGS creates the geometric bridge, DINOv2 provides the semantic stability to cross it, and contrastive learning trains the model to traverse it effectively. This integrated approach moves beyond mere data augmentation, providing an end-to-end strategy for closing the cross-view domain gap.

Qualitative Visualization. To further investigate the efficacy of our proposed query synthesis method, we present a qualitative analysis of the visual results under two typical yet challenging scenarios: a suburban scene with dense foliage and an urban environment with complex building structures. These examples are intended to provide an intuitive understanding of how our approach successfully bridges the significant domain gap between ground and aerial views.

Robustness to Foliage Occlusion. Figure 4 illustrates a representative case from a suburban area, where the street-level view is heavily occluded by trees. In such scenarios, traditional feature matching methods often fail because the discriminative ground-level features (e.g., building facades, road markings) are largely invisible in the corresponding top-down aerial image. As shown in the figure, our model synthesizes a set of pseudo aerial-views from novel pitch angles. These synthesized images effectively learn to "see through" the foliage, hallucinating the underlying geometric layout of the road and the approximate footprint of the building. The synthesized views at 45° and 60° are particularly crucial, as they create an intermediate representation that shares contextual information with both the ground-level perspective (building sides) and the aerial perspective (rooftops and layout). This ability to infer and render the essential spatial structure despite significant natural occlusion demonstrates the robustness and generalization capability of our method in cluttered real-world environments.

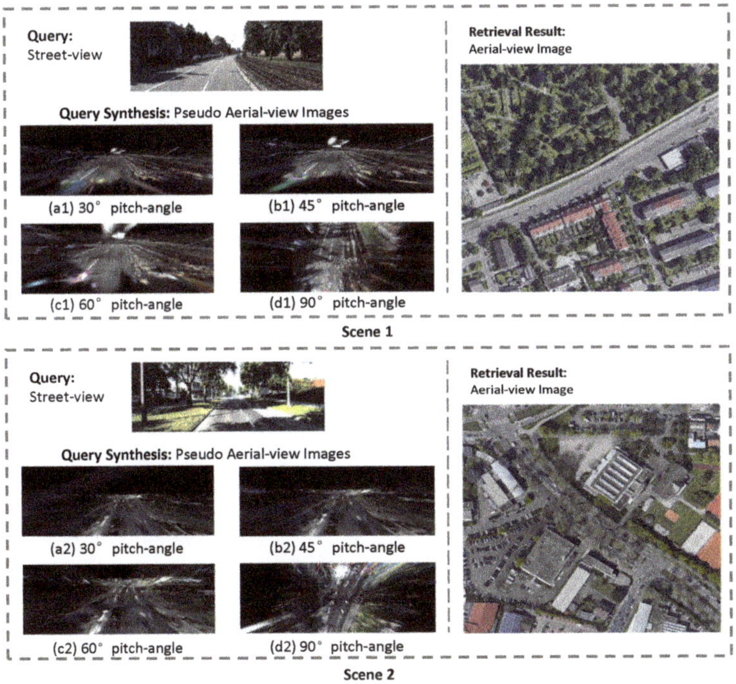

Figure 4. Visualization results for cross-view localization in challenging suburban scenes characterized by dense foliage. For a given street-view query, our method synthesizes pseudo aerial-views at varying pitch angles for matching. The images presented showcase: the input street-view query, the synthesized views at pitch angles of (**a1**,**a2**) 30°, (**b1**,**b2**) 45°, (**c1**,**c2**) 60°, and (**d1**,**d2**) 90°, and the corresponding top-retrieved true aerial image from the database.

Handling of Extreme Viewpoint Disparity. Figure 5 showcases a dense urban scene, which presents a different challenge: severe perspective distortion and complex geometric relationships between buildings. The direct matching between a ground-level image capturing vertical building facades and a nadir (90°) aerial image capturing horizontal rooftops is inherently ill-posed. Our approach mitigates this by progressively generating views that bridge this geometric transformation. The sequence of synthesized images from (a) to (d) clearly shows a smooth transition from an oblique perspective to a top-down view. This process correctly models the spatial arrangement and relative positioning of the surrounding buildings, transforming the street-view perspective into an aerial-view representation that is structurally consistent with the ground truth. The success in this complex urban setting highlights that our method does not merely rely on appearance cues but effectively learns and reasons about the underlying 3D geometry of the scene to perform accurate localization.

In summary, these qualitative results validate that our query synthesis module is the key to overcoming the challenges of cross-view localization. By generating geometrically plausible intermediate views, our method significantly enhances matching accuracy in diverse and complex real-world scenarios.

Computational costs. We report the computational cost of the proposed method on the KITTI dataset. During training, the model consumes 11.8GB of memory and takes about 4 days to complete. During testing, the model consumes 2.18GB of memory and takes about 5 days.

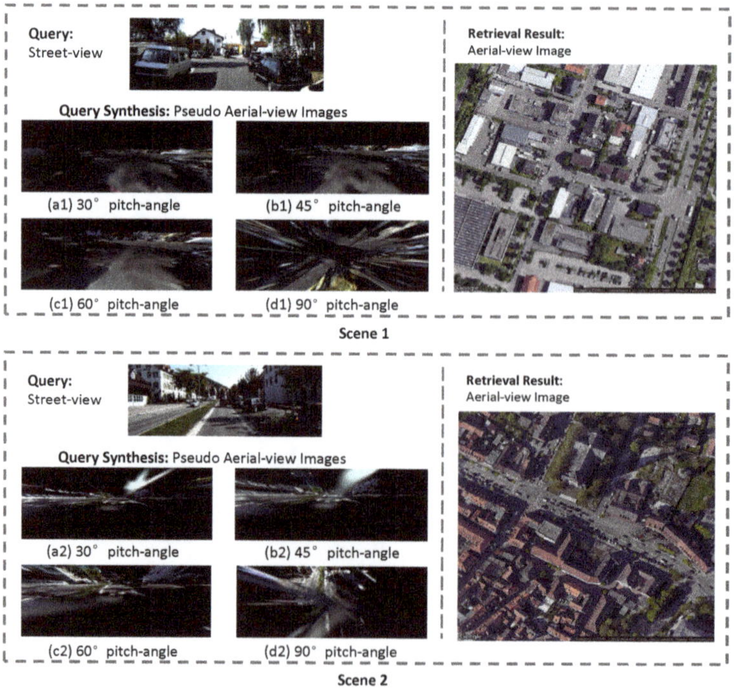

Figure 5. Visualization results for cross-view localization in challenging urban environments with dense building structures. For a given street-view query, our method synthesizes pseudo aerial-views at varying pitch angles for matching. The figure illustrates: the input street-view query, the synthesized views at pitch angles of (**a1**,**a2**) 30°, (**b1**,**b2**) 45°, (**c1**,**c2**) 60°, and (**d1**,**d2**) 90°, and the corresponding top-retrieved true aerial image from the database.

4.3. Ablation Study

To systematically validate the contribution of each key component within our proposed framework, we conducted a series of comprehensive ablation experiments. These studies were designed to quantify the performance impact and confirm the generalization capability of our method over a strong baseline. The results are meticulously analyzed below.

Impact of pseudo aerial-view image. A core component of our approach is the synthesis of pseudo-aerial-view images to enrich the training data. To assess its efficacy, we performed an ablation study on the Test-1 and Test-2 dataset. The results, as detailed in Table 3, clearly demonstrate that incorporating the pseudo-aerial-view synthesis module significantly improves the performance of our baseline model. While the generated pseudo-views may not possess the photorealistic quality of genuine aerial imagery, their primary value lies in their ability to effectively mitigate the substantial domain gap between street-view and satellite-view images. By providing geometrically aligned, albeit non-photorealistic, representations, the network is empowered to learn a richer, more robust cross-view scene representation. This data-level augmentation inherently reduces the difficulty of the cross-view localization task and simultaneously enhances the model's generalization capability to unseen scenes. The experimental evidence confirms that this module is a crucial contributor to the overall performance gains.

Table 3. Ablation study of the proposed components. The best results are highlighted in bold.

Method	R@1	R@5	R@10	R@1%
	Test-1			
Baseline	80.80	96.51	97.40	95.83
Baseline + Pseudo Aerial-view	81.80	97.50	97.01	97.98
Baseline + Pseudo Aerial-view + Mixed feature	**82.90**	**98.38**	**98.43**	**98.46**
	Test-2			
Baseline	17.80	34.11	45.37	89.98
Baseline + Pseudo Aerial-view	18.73	36.92	47.14	90.77
Baseline + Pseudo Aerial-view + Mixed feature	**19.20**	**38.04**	**48.90**	**91.38**

Effect of mixed feature enhancement. We further investigated the effectiveness of our proposed Mixed Feature Enhancement (MFE) module. The ablation results, also presented in Table 3, illustrate a notable performance boost when this module is integrated. The underlying rationale for the MFE module is to refine the generic features learned from a pre-trained model like DINOv2. While DINOv2 features are powerful and generalize well to a variety of tasks due to their training on diverse datasets, they are not inherently optimized for the specific nuances of cross-view geo-localization. Our feature-mixer operation is specifically designed to fine-tune these generic features, allowing them to capture the subtle but critical details required for accurate cross-view matching. The experimental findings validate that this operation effectively enhances the discriminative power of the feature embeddings, thereby leading to improved performance in the retrieval task. The consistent performance uplift across the board confirms the MFE module's role as a vital component for maximizing localization accuracy.

Effect of synthesized tilted views. In our process of synthesizing novel viewpoint images based on 3DGS, we indeed synthesized new images with tilt angles of 30°, 45°, 60°, and 90°, respectively. The results of ablation studies are listed in Table 4. It can be observed that the tilt angles of 60° and 90° achieve comparable results. The selection of specific tilt angles such as 60°/90° is primarily motivated by their role in establishing a smoother transitional path in the feature space between street-level and aerial perspectives.

These intermediate viewpoints facilitate better feature alignment, effectively reducing the domain gap and enhancing the model's cross-view geo-localization accuracy. Moreover, by intentionally constraining the number of synthesized transitional views, we are able to not only validate the robustness of this smooth-interpolation strategy but also maintain high efficiency and low computational overhead throughout the novel view synthesis process.

Table 4. Ablation study of different tilt angles on the KITTI Test-1 subset. The best results are highlighted in bold.

Method	R@1	R@5	R@10	R@1%
Baseline + Pseudo Aerial-view (tilt angle 30°)	81.05	96.50	96.56	97.11
Baseline + Pseudo Aerial-view (tilt angle 45°)	81.65	97.44	97.03	97.82
Baseline + Pseudo Aerial-view (tilt angle 60°)	81.61	97.00	**97.10**	97.53
Baseline + Pseudo Aerial-view (default tilt angle 90°)	**81.80**	**97.50**	97.01	**97.98**

5. Discussion

Although our method produces good results in some complex scenarios, it still struggles with certain challenges such as occlusion, illumination variation, and high urban density. As illustrated in the Figure 6, our method currently struggles with challenging street scenes characterized by significant lighting variations and complex clutter, which can lead to retrieval failures. Regarding occlusion, we acknowledge that severe occlusion can pose challenges for 3D reconstruction and novel view synthesis based on 3DGS. We have considered some factors in our method to alleviate these issues. Specifically, by incorporating DINOv2, which provides powerful and robust visual features, and combining it with 3DGS, our approach is engineered to mitigate the adverse effects posed by such challenging conditions.

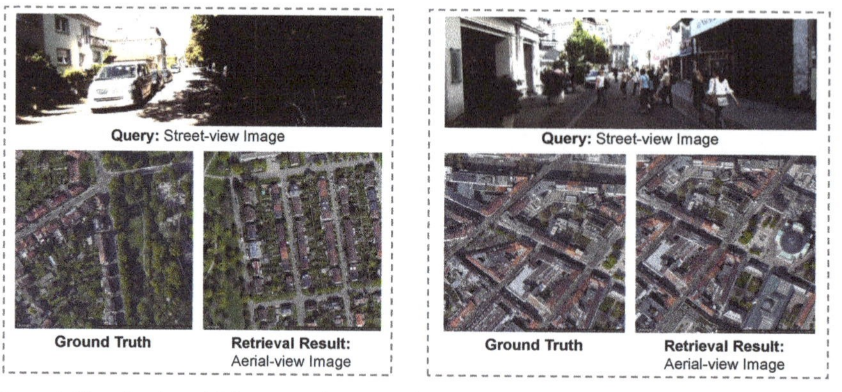

Figure 6. Visualization of failure cases in our method.

6. Future Work

Our current approach has limitations in generalizing to diverse cross-view scenarios, particularly for panoramic-to-perspective benchmarks like CVUSA and VIGOR. Indeed, the dense, sequential nature of perspective images in datasets such as KITTI and Oxford RobotCar enables high-quality 3D reconstruction with 3DGS. In contrast, panoramic benchmarks like CVUSA and VIGOR are composed of sparsely captured images with limited overlap, which challenges the current 3DGS-based pipeline that relies on dense views for robust geometry modeling. This structural difference currently restricts the direct applicability of our method to such panoramic-to-perspective settings. we regard overcoming this domain gap as a vital research direction. In the future, we plan to explore techniques tailored to sparse or non-sequential imagery, such as cross-view generative models that bypass explicit 3D reconstruction, or geometry-aware methods capable of learning from limited overlapping views.

7. Conclusions

In this paper, we proposed a novel 3D Gaussian splatting-based cross-view geo-localization framework to resolve the difficulty of geo-localization caused by low feature similarity between street-view and aerial image. We first synthesized novel aerial perspectives from street-view sequences via 3D Gaussian splatting, utilizing COLMAP-derived initial poses and sparse point clouds. A key contribution is our camera pose estimation strategy, which optimizes matching viewpoints by increasing the tilt angle relative to the horizontal plane, thereby improving geometric consistency between the synthesized and real aerial imagery. Following this, we employed DINOv2 in a straightforward yet efficient mixed feature enhancement module, optimized using InfoNCE loss. Experiments on the KITTI dataset demonstrate that our method delivers substantial improvements in matching accuracy despite significant viewpoint differences and achieves advanced retrieval results.

Author Contributions: Conceptualization, X.D.; Methodology, X.D.; Software, X.D. and X.Z.; Validation, X.D., X.Z., S.S. and L.H.; Formal analysis, X.D. and S.S.; Investigation, S.S. and L.H.; Resources, Y.D.; Data curation, Y.D.; Writing—original draft, X.D.; Writing—review & editing, B.L., L.H. and Y.D.; Supervision, B.L. and Y.D.; Project administration, Y.D. All authors have read and agreed to the published version of the manuscript.

Funding: This research received no external funding.

Data Availability Statement: The raw data supporting the conclusions of this article will be made available by the authors on request.

Conflicts of Interest: Author Shangzhen Song was employed by the company Xi'an Flight Automatic Control Research Institute. The remaining authors declare that the research was conducted in the absence of any commercial or financial relationships that could be construed as a potential conflict of interest.

References

1. Caesar, H.; Bankiti, V.; Lang, A.H.; Vora, S.; Liong, V.E.; Xu, Q.; Krishnan, A.; Pan, Y.; Baldan, G.; Beijbom, O. nuScenes: A multimodal dataset for autonomous driving. In Proceedings of the IEEE Conference on Computer Vision and Pattern Recognition (CVPR), Seattle, WA, USA, 13–19 June 2020; pp. 11621–11631.
2. Chen, H.; Hou, L.; Wu, S.; Zhang, G.; Zou, Y.; Moon, S.; Bhuiyan, M. Augmented reality, deep learning and vision-language query system for construction worker safety. *Autom. Constr.* **2024**, *157*, 105158. [CrossRef]
3. Rubio, F.; Valero, F.; Llopis-Albert, C. A review of mobile robots: Concepts, methods, theoretical framework, and applications. *Int. J. Adv. Robot. Syst.* **2019**, *16*, 1729881419839596. [CrossRef]
4. Lin, T.Y.; Belongie, S.; Hays, J. Cross-view image geolocalization. In Proceedings of the IEEE Conference on Computer Vision and Pattern Recognition (CVPR), Portland, OR, USA, 23–28 June 2013; pp. 891–898.
5. Tian, Y.; Chen, C.; Shah, M. Cross-view image matching for geo-localization in urban environments. In Proceedings of the IEEE Conference on Computer Vision and Pattern Recognition (CVPR), Honolulu, HI, USA, 21–26 July 2017; pp. 3608–3616.
6. Workman, S.; Jacobs, N. On the location dependence of convolutional neural network features. In Proceedings of the IEEE Conference on Computer Vision and Pattern Recognition Workshops (CVPRW), Boston, MA, USA, 7–12 June 2015; pp. 70–78.
7. Lowe, D.G. Distinctive image features from scale-invariant keypoints. *Int. J. Comput. Vis.* **2004**, *60*, 91–110. [CrossRef]
8. Bay, H.; Tuytelaars, T.; Van Gool, L. SURF: Speeded up robust features. In Proceedings of the European Conference on Computer Vision (ECCV), Graz, Austria, 7–13 May 2006; pp. 404–417.
9. Rublee, E.; Rabaud, V.; Konolige, K.; Bradski, G. ORB: An efficient alternative to SIFT or SURF. In Proceedings of the International Conference on Computer Vision (ICCV), Barcelona, Spain, 6–13 November 2011; pp. 2564–2571.

10. Krizhevsky, A.; Sutskever, I.; Hinton, G.E. ImageNet classification with deep convolutional neural networks. In Proceedings of the Advances in Neural Information Processing Systems (NeurIPS), Lake Tahoe, CA, USA, 3–6 December 2012; Volume 25.
11. Vaswani, A.; Shazeer, N.; Parmar, N.; Uszkoreit, J.; Jones, L.; Gomez, A.N.; Kaiser, Ł.; Polosukhin, I. Attention is all you need. In Proceedings of the Advances in Neural Information Processing Systems (NeurIPS), Long Beach, CA, USA, 4–9 December 2017; Volume 30.
12. Zhai, X.; Kolesnikov, A.; Houlsby, N.; Beyer, L. Scaling vision Transformers. In Proceedings of the IEEE Conference on Computer Vision and Pattern Recognition (CVPR), New Orleans, LA, USA, 18–24 June 2022; pp. 12104–12113.
13. Simonyan, K.; Zisserman, A. Very deep convolutional networks for large-scale image recognition. *arXiv* **2014**, arXiv:1409.1556.
14. He, K.; Zhang, X.; Ren, S.; Sun, J. Deep residual learning for image recognition. In Proceedings of the IEEE Conference on Computer Vision and Pattern Recognition (CVPR), Las Vegas, NV, USA, 27–30 June 2016; pp. 770–778.
15. Zhu, S.; Yang, T.; Chen, C. VIGOR: Cross-view image geo-localization beyond one-to-one retrieval. In Proceedings of the IEEE Conference on Computer Vision and Pattern Recognition (CVPR), Nashville, TN, USA, 20–25 June 2021; pp. 3640–3649.
16. Cai, S.; Guo, Y.; Khan, S.; Hu, J.; Wen, G. Ground-to-aerial image geo-localization with a hard exemplar reweighting triplet loss. In Proceedings of the IEEE International Conference on Computer Vision (ICCV), Seoul, Republic of Korea, 27 October–2 November 2019; pp. 8391–8400.
17. Regmi, K.; Borji, A. Cross-view image synthesis using conditional GANs. In Proceedings of the IEEE Conference on Computer Vision and Pattern Recognition (CVPR), Salt Lake City, UT, USA, 18–22 June 2018; pp. 3501–3510.
18. Vo, N.N.; Hays, J. Localizing and orienting street views using overhead imagery. In Proceedings of the European Conference on Computer Vision (ECCV), Amsterdam, The Netherlands, 11–14 October 2016; pp. 494–509.
19. Liu, L.; Li, H. Lending orientation to neural networks for cross-view geo-localization. In Proceedings of the IEEE Conference on Computer Vision and Pattern Recognition (CVPR), Long Beach, CA, USA, 15–20 June 2019; pp. 5624–5633.
20. Shi, Y.; Yu, X.; Liu, L.; Zhang, T.; Li, H. Optimal feature transport for cross-view image geo-localization. In Proceedings of the AAAI Conference on Artificial Intelligence (AAAI), New York, NY, USA, 7–12 February 2020; pp. 11990–11997.
21. Goodfellow, I.J.; Pouget-Abadie, J.; Mirza, M.; Xu, B.; Warde-Farley, D.; Ozair, S.; Courville, A.; Bengio, Y. Generative adversarial nets. In Proceedings of the Advances in Neural Information Processing Systems (NeurIPS), Montreal, QC, Canada, 8–13 December 2014.
22. Mildenhall, B.; Srinivasan, P.P.; Tancik, M.; Barron, J.T.; Ramamoorthi, R.; Ng, R. NeRF: Representing scenes as neural radiance fields for view synthesis. In Proceedings of the European Conference on Computer Vision (ECCV), Glasgow, UK, 23–28 August 2020; Springer: Virtual, 2020; pp. 405–421.
23. Kerbl, B.; Kopanas, G.; Leimkühler, T.; Drettakis, G. 3D Gaussian splatting for real-time radiance field rendering. *ACM Trans. Graph.* **2023**, *42*, 139–152 . [CrossRef]
24. Schönberger, J.L.; Frahm, J.M. Structure-from-Motion Revisited. In Proceedings of the IEEE Conference on Computer Vision and Pattern Recognition (CVPR), Las Vegas, NV, USA, 27–30 June 2016.
25. Oquab, M.; Darcet, T.; Moutakanni, T.; Vo, H.; Szafraniec, M.; Khalidov, V.; Fernandez, P.; Haziza, D.; Massa, F.; El-Nouby, A.; et al. DINOv2: Learning robust visual features without supervision. *arXiv* **2023**, arXiv:2304.07193.
26. Geiger, A.; Lenz, P.; Stiller, C.; Urtasun, R. Vision meets robotics: The KITTI dataset. *Int. J. Robot. Res.* **2013**, *32*, 1231–1237. [CrossRef]
27. Castaldo, F.; Zamir, A.; Angst, R.; Palmieri, F.; Savarese, S. Semantic cross-view matching. In Proceedings of the IEEE International Conference on Computer Vision Workshops (ICCVW), Santiago, Chile, 7–13 December 2015; pp. 9–17.
28. Senlet, T.; Elgammal, A. A framework for global vehicle localization using stereo images and satellite and road maps. In Proceedings of the IEEE International Conference on Computer Vision Workshops (ICCVW), Barcelona, Spain, 6–13 November 2011; IEEE: New York, NY, USA, 2011; pp. 2034–2041.
29. Bansal, M.; Sawhney, H.S.; Cheng, H.; Daniilidis, K. Geo-localization of street views with aerial image databases. In Proceedings of the ACM International Conference on Multimedia (ACM MM), Scottsdale, Arizona, 28 November–1 December 2011; pp. 1125–1128.
30. Workman, S.; Souvenir, R.; Jacobs, N. Wide-area image geolocalization with aerial reference imagery. In Proceedings of the IEEE International Conference on Computer Vision (ICCV), Santiago, Chile, 7–13 December 2015; pp. 3961–3969.
31. Lin, T.Y.; Cui, Y.; Belongie, S.; Hays, J. Learning deep representations for ground-to-aerial geolocalization. In Proceedings of the IEEE Conference on Computer Vision and Pattern Recognition (CVPR), Boston, MA, USA, 7–12 June 2015; pp. 5007–5015.
32. Hadsell, R.; Chopra, S.; LeCun, Y. Dimensionality reduction by learning an invariant mapping. In Proceedings of the IEEE Computer Society Conference on Computer Vision and Pattern Recognition (CVPR), New York, NY, USA, 17–22 June 2006; pp. 1735–1742.
33. Deng, W.; Zheng, L.; Ye, Q.; Kang, G.; Yang, Y.; Jiao, J. Image-image domain adaptation with preserved self-similarity and domain-dissimilarity for person re-identification. In Proceedings of the IEEE Conference on Computer Vision and Pattern Recognition (CVPR), Salt Lake City, UT, USA, 18–23 June 2018; pp. 994–1003.

34. He, K.; Fan, H.; Wu, Y.; Xie, S.; Girshick, R. Momentum contrast for unsupervised visual representation learning. In Proceedings of the IEEE Conference on Computer Vision and Pattern Recognition (CVPR), Seattle, WA, USA, 13–19 June 2020; pp. 9729–9738.
35. Xu, C.; Hui, L.; Xie, J.; Yang, J. Weakly Supervised Object Localization with Progressive Activation Diffusion. *IEEE Trans. Neural Netw. Learn. Syst.* **2025**, *36*, 15194–15206. [CrossRef] [PubMed]
36. Zhai, M.; Bessinger, Z.; Workman, S.; Jacobs, N. Predicting ground-level scene layout from aerial imagery. In Proceedings of the IEEE Conference on Computer Vision and Pattern Recognition (CVPR), Honolulu, HI, USA, 21–26 July 2017; pp. 867–875.
37. Arandjelovic, R.; Gronat, P.; Torii, A.; Pajdla, T.; Sivic, J. NetVLAD: CNN architecture for weakly supervised place recognition. In Proceedings of the IEEE Conference on Computer Vision and Pattern Recognition (CVPR), Las Vegas, NV, USA, 27–30 June 2016; pp. 5297–5307.
38. Hu, S.; Feng, M.; Nguyen, R.M.; Lee, G.H. CVM-NET: Cross-view matching network for image-based ground-to-aerial geo-localization. In Proceedings of the IEEE Conference on Computer Vision and Pattern Recognition (CVPR), Salt Lake City, UT, USA, 18–23 June 2018; pp. 7258–7267.
39. He, Q.; Xu, A.; Zhang, Y.; Ye, Z.; Zhou, W.; Xi, R.; Lin, Q. A contrastive learning based multiview scene matching method for UAV view geo-localization. *Remote Sens.* **2024**, *16*, 3039. [CrossRef]
40. Pillai, M.S.; Rizve, M.N.; Shah, M. GAReT: Cross-view video geolocalization with adapters and auto-regressive transformers. In Proceedings of the European Conference on Computer Vision (ECCV), Milan, Italy, 29 September–4 October 2024; pp. 466–483.
41. Zhu, S.; Shah, M.; Chen, C. TransGeo: Transformer is all you need for cross-view image geo-localization. In Proceedings of the IEEE Conference on Computer Vision and Pattern Recognition (CVPR), New Orleans, LA, USA, 18–24 June 2022; pp. 1162–1171.
42. Kwon, J.; Kim, J.; Park, H.; Choi, I.K. ASAM: Adaptive sharpness-aware minimization for scale-invariant learning of deep neural networks. In Proceedings of the International Conference on Machine Learning (ICML), Virtual, 18–24 July 2021; pp. 5905–5914.
43. Cui, Z.; Zhou, P.; Wang, X.; Zhang, Z.; Li, Y.; Li, H.; Zhang, Y. A novel geo-localization method for UAV and satellite images using cross-view consistent attention. *Remote Sens.* **2023**, *15*, 4667. [CrossRef]
44. Ding, L.; Zhou, J.; Meng, L.; Long, Z. A practical cross-view image matching method between UAV and satellite for UAV-based geo-localization. *Remote Sens.* **2020**, *13*, 47. [CrossRef]
45. Chen, G.; Wang, W. A survey on 3D gaussian splatting. *arXiv* **2024**, arXiv:2401.03890. [CrossRef]
46. Barron, J.T.; Mildenhall, B.; Tancik, M.; Hedman, P.; Martin-Brualla, R.; Srinivasan, P.P. Mip-NeRF: A multiscale representation for anti-aliasing neural radiance fields. In Proceedings of the IEEE/CVF International Conference on Computer Vision (ICCV), Montreal, QC, Canada, 11–17 October 2021; pp. 5855–5864.
47. Fridovich-Keil, S.; Yu, A.; Tancik, M.; Chen, Q.; Recht, B.; Kanazawa, A. Plenoxels: Radiance fields without neural networks. In Proceedings of the IEEE/CVF Conference on Computer Vision and Pattern Recognition, New Orleans, LA, USA, 18–24 June 2022; pp. 5501–5510.
48. Müller, T.; Evans, A.; Schied, C.; Keller, A. Instant neural graphics primitives with a multiresolution hash encoding. *ACM Trans. Graph.* **2022**, *41*, 1–15. [CrossRef]
49. Pumarola, A.; Corona, E.; Pons-Moll, G.; Moreno-Noguer, F. D-NeRF: Neural radiance fields for dynamic scenes. In Proceedings of the IEEE/CVF Conference on Computer Vision and Pattern Recognition (CVPR), Montreal, QC, Canada, 11–17 October 2021; pp. 10318–10327.
50. Wu, G.; Yi, T.; Fang, J.; Wang, L.; Zhang, X.; Wang, W.; Wang, Q.; Zha, C.; Tai, Y.L.; Tang, C.Z. 4D Gaussian splatting for real-time dynamic scene rendering. *arXiv* **2023**, arXiv:2310.08528. [CrossRef]
51. Zollmann, S.; Zafeiridis, P.; Agapito, L.; Pont-Tuset, J.; Ranftl, R. Relightable 3D Gaussians: Real-time Point Cloud Relighting with BRDF Decomposition and Ray Tracing. *arXiv* **2024**, arXiv:2311.17922.
52. Oord, A.v.d.; Li, Y.; Vinyals, O. Representation learning with contrastive predictive coding. *arXiv* **2018**, arXiv:1807.03748.
53. Deuser, F.; Habel, K.; Oswald, N. Sample4Geo: Hard negative sampling for cross-view geo-localisation. In Proceedings of the IEEE International Conference on Computer Vision (ICCV), Paris, France, 2–6 October 2023; pp. 16847–16856.
54. Maddern, W.; Pascoe, G.; Linegar, C.; Newman, P. 1000 km: The Oxford RobotCar dataset. *Int. J. Robot. Res.* **2017**, *36*, 3–15. [CrossRef]
55. Shi, Y.; Yu, X.; Wang, S.; Li, H. CVLNet: Cross-view semantic correspondence learning for video-based camera localization. In Proceedings of the Asian Conference on Computer Vision (ACCV), Macao, China, 4–8 December 2022; pp. 123–141.
56. Mehta, H.; Kanani, P.; Lande, P. Google maps. *Int. J. Comput. Appl.* **2019**, *178*, 41–46. [CrossRef]
57. Shi, Y.; Yu, X.; Liu, L.; Campbell, D.; Koniusz, P.; Li, H. Accurate 3-DoF camera geo-localization via ground-to-satellite image matching. *IEEE Trans. Pattern Anal. Mach. Intell.* **2022**, *45*, 2682–2697. [CrossRef] [PubMed]
58. Loshchilov, I.; Hutter, F. Decoupled weight decay regularization. *arXiv* **2017**, arXiv:1711.05101.
59. Shi, Y.; Liu, L.; Yu, X.; Li, H. Spatial-aware feature aggregation for image based cross-view geo-localization. In Proceedings of the Advances in Neural Information Processing Systems (NeurIPS), Vancouver, BC, Canada, 8–14 December 2019; Volume 32.

60. Shi, Y.; Yu, X.; Campbell, D.; Li, H. Where am i looking at? Joint location and orientation estimation by cross-view matching. In Proceedings of the IEEE Conference on Computer Vision and Pattern Recognition (CVPR), Seattle, WA, USA, 13–19 June 2020; pp. 4064–4072.
61. Toker, A.; Zhou, Q.; Maximov, M.; Leal-Taixé, L. Coming down to earth: Satellite-to-street view synthesis for geo-localization. In Proceedings of the IEEE Conference on Computer Vision and Pattern Recognition (CVPR), Virtual, 19–25 June 2021; pp. 6488–6497.

remote sensing

MDPI

Article

SAR-Conditioned Consistency Model for Effective Cloud Removal in Remote Sensing Images

Qizhuo Han [1,†], Bo Huang [2,†] and Ying Li [1,*]

[1] School of Computer Science, Northwestern Polytechnical University, Xi'an 710129, China; hqz@mail.nwpu.edu.cn
[2] School of Software, Northwestern Polytechnical University, Xi'an 710129, China; bohuang@mail.nwpu.edu.cn
* Correspondence: lybyp@nwpu.edu.cn
† These authors contributed equally to this work.

Highlights

What are the main findings?

- We propose CM-CR, a SAR-conditioned cloud-removal framework that distills a SAR-Conditioned Score-Based Diffusion (teacher) into a SAR-conditioned consistency model (student) and refines outputs via multistep resampling.
- CM-CR achieves state-of-the-art PSNR/SSIM/SAM/MAE on SEN12MS-CR while requiring substantially fewer sampling steps than standard diffusion models.

What is the implications of the main findings?

- The method improves the usability of optical remote sensing data under thick-cloud conditions across diverse scenes.
- It preserves the reconstruction fidelity of diffusion models with markedly reduced inference complexity, making it suitable for large-scale and operational remote sensing tasks.

Abstract

Cloud contamination, especially thick cloud cover, severely limits the usability of optical remote sensing imagery by obscuring surface information. Due to the strong penetrability of microwave signals, Synthetic Aperture Radar (SAR) has emerged as an effective source for thick cloud removal. While SAR-assisted deep learning methods, such as CNNs and GANs, have made notable progress, the quality of generated imagery still requires improvement. Diffusion models, which offer strong potential for enhancing generation fidelity, could address this limitation but suffer from slow sampling speeds that constrain practical use and underscore the need for greater efficiency. To simultaneously enhance both reconstruction quality and sampling efficiency, this paper proposes a fast-sampling SAR-conditioned consistency model based on consistency distillation, named CM-CR, which adopts a teacher–student architecture to divide the reconstruction process into a rapid coarse prediction stage and a detailed refinement stage, significantly reducing per-scene processing time while maintaining high reconstruction fidelity. Specifically, a SAR-Conditioned Score-Based Diffusion Model (SCSBD) is first developed as the teacher network for learning a SAR-conditioned optical image generation model. Consistency distillation is then used to derive the student network SAR-conditioned consistency model (SCCM), which enables a rapid coarse prediction through single-step sampling. Finally, a Progressive Denoising via Multistep Resampling (PDMSR) strategy is introduced to iteratively refine the single-step output, producing fine-grained reconstructions. Comparative experiments conducted on the widely used cloud removal benchmark dataset SEN12MS-CR demonstrate that the proposed CM-CR method achieves state-of-the-art

(SOTA) performance across all image quality metrics. Notably, although its design uses approximately 80 times more parameters compared with a standard Denoising Diffusion Probabilistic Model (DDPM), it delivers up to a 40-fold acceleration at inference.

Keywords: cloud removal; SAR; optical remote sensing images; consistency model

1. Introduction

With the rapid advancement of remote sensing technology, optical remote sensing imagery has become indispensable for a wide range of applications, including meteorological monitoring [1], agricultural assessment [2], urban planning [3], and disaster management [4]. High-resolution and wide-coverage optical images offer crucial support for obtaining surface information on Earth. However, these images are frequently compromised by atmospheric interference such as clouds and haze, which significantly degrade image quality and usability. Among these factors, cloud contamination is the most prominent, as it not only obscures surface features and causes information loss, but also introduces artifacts and blurring, thereby hindering subsequent analysis and interpretation [5]. Effectively removing cloud interference from optical remote sensing images has thus emerged as a critical challenge in the field.

Cloud cover can be categorized into thin and thick clouds based on their optical thickness and impact on surface visibility. Thin clouds partially obscure ground features, whereas thick clouds block surface information entirely, often causing severe spectral distortion and shadow effects [6]. The task of thick cloud removal aims to recover ground information from regions severely occluded by dense clouds. Existing methods for thick cloud removal can be broadly grouped into three categories: inpainting-based, multi-temporal, and multi-modal approaches [7].

Inpainting-based methods assume spatial and semantic correlations between cloud-covered and cloud-free regions within the same image [8–13]. These methods use the surrounding cloud-free areas to infer and reconstruct the missing content. While they can produce visually plausible results when the scene is simple and cloud coverage is limited, their reliance on single-modal information and lack of prior knowledge limits their ability to recover complex surface features accurately.

Multi-temporal methods [14–20] leverage multiple images of the same region acquired at different times, using cloud-free references to reconstruct cloud-obscured regions. However, these approaches often suffer from difficulties in acquiring temporally aligned and high-quality references, and inconsistencies caused by temporal differences may degrade reconstruction performance.

Multi-modal approaches [21–27] address these limitations by incorporating complementary data from different sensors. In particular, Synthetic Aperture Radar (SAR), with its all-weather and day-and-night imaging capabilities, can provide reliable structural and textural information for cloud-covered areas. By circumventing the temporal inconsistencies associated with multi-temporal methods, SAR data offer a promising modality for the accurate reconstruction of heavily clouded regions. Accordingly, this work adopts SAR imagery as a conditioning input to guide the cloud removal process.

Generative Adversarial Networks (GANs) have been widely applied in deep learning-based cloud removal frameworks [28–30]. While effective, GANs often suffer from inherent instability during training, difficulties in convergence, and vulnerability to mode collapse. Moreover, the limited generative capacity and poor generalization of GAN-based methods frequently result in blurred textures and loss of fine details, which restrict their ability to meet the precision requirements for high-quality cloud removal.

Recently, diffusion models [31] have emerged as state-of-the-art generative models, outperforming GANs in various vision tasks [32]. Built upon a Markovian denoising process, diffusion models offer more stable and reliable training along with superior generative fidelity. They have been successfully applied to a wide range of image generation tasks such as inpainting [33], super-resolution [34], and style transfer [35]. These advancements have inspired the use of diffusion models in cloud removal, with several works reporting promising results [36–41]. However, vanilla diffusion-based approaches still suffer from slow inference, as the iterative denoising process required for high-quality synthesis incurs high computational costs. This inefficiency remains a major bottleneck for the practical deployment of diffusion-based cloud removal techniques.

To address the inefficiency of diffusion models, recent advances have introduced consistency models [42], which preserve high generative fidelity and accelerate inference, providing an efficient solution for cloud removal tasks. Inspired by this line of work, we propose CM-CR, a novel and efficient cloud removal framework based on SAR-conditioned consistency models. It is designed to simultaneously achieve high-quality reconstruction and fast inference, enabling practical cloud removal for optical remote sensing images. The main contributions of this work are as follows:

1. We develop a SAR-Conditioned Score-Based Diffusion (SCSBD) model as a teacher network, where SAR data are utilized as conditional input to guide the generation of structural features and spatial layouts under SAR constraints, establishing a solid foundation for the subsequent distillation process.
2. We introduce a consistency distillation strategy that distills the SCCM (SAR-Conditioned Consistency Model) student model from the trained SCSBD, enabling efficient single-step cloud removal with coarse predictions.
3. To further refine the initial output, we propose a Progressive Denoising via Multi-step Resampling (PDMSR) strategy. By injecting noise into the coarse results and resampling, this strategy recovers fine-grained spectral details, effectively balancing inference efficiency and reconstruction quality.

2. Preliminaries

2.1. Diffusion Models

Diffusion models are a family of generative models that formulate data synthesis as a two-stage process. The forward process gradually perturbs data with Gaussian noise, while the reverse process, parameterized by a neural network, iteratively reconstructs the original distribution. The seminal denoising diffusion probabilistic model (DDPM) [32] first established this formulation, and Song et al. [43] further extended it through a stochastic differential equation (SDE) framework, leading to score-based generative models capable of accurately approximating complex data distributions. Our method builds upon the score-based diffusion models, and the following section provides a concise theoretical overview.

In the SDE-based formulation of diffusion models, data $\mathbf{x}_0 \sim p_{\text{data}}(\mathbf{x})$ are progressively perturbed along a continuous time variable $t \in [0, T]$. The forward process is defined by the following equation:

$$d\mathbf{x}_t = \mu(\mathbf{x}_t, t)\,dt + \sigma(t)\,d\mathbf{w}_t, \tag{1}$$

where $\mu(\mathbf{x}_t, t)$ is the drift term, $\sigma(t)$ controls the noise intensity, and $\mathbf{w}_t$ denotes a standard Wiener process. Solving this SDE transforms the data distribution p_{data} into a simple prior, typically a standard Gaussian $p_T(\mathbf{x})$, which serves as the starting point for the generative reverse process. To generate new data, sampling begins by drawing noise from the prior $\hat{\mathbf{x}}_T \sim \mathcal{N}(0, T^2\mathbf{I})$ and reversing the diffusion process. The reverse-time SDE can be defined as:

$$d\mathbf{x} = \left[\mu(\mathbf{x}, t) - \sigma(t)^2 \nabla_{\mathbf{x}} \log p_t(\mathbf{x})\right] dt + \sigma(t)\, d\bar{\mathbf{w}}, \tag{2}$$

where $\nabla_{\mathbf{x}} \log p_t(\mathbf{x})$ is the score function and $\bar{\mathbf{w}}$ denotes a Wiener process with time flowing backward from T to 0. By integrating this reverse SDE, samples $\hat{\mathbf{x}}_0$ can be obtained, which approximate the target distribution $p_{\text{data}}(\mathbf{x})$.

Song et al. [43] demonstrated that the reverse SDE has an equivalent deterministic formulation, termed the probability flow ODE (PF-ODE), which preserves the same marginal distributions:

$$d\mathbf{x} = \left[\mu(\mathbf{x}, t) - \tfrac{1}{2}\sigma(t)^2 \nabla_{\mathbf{x}} \log p_t(\mathbf{x})\right] dt. \tag{3}$$

In practice, a score network $\mathbf{s}_\phi(\mathbf{x}, t) \approx \nabla_{\mathbf{x}} \log p_t(\mathbf{x})$ is trained via score matching. Under the setting of Karras et al. [44], where $\mu(\mathbf{x}, t) = 0$ and $\sigma(t) = \sqrt{2t}$, Equation (3) reduces to

$$\frac{d\mathbf{x}_t}{dt} = -t\, \mathbf{s}_\phi(\mathbf{x}_t, t). \tag{4}$$

2.2. Consistency Models

Consistency models [42] have recently been proposed to support efficient single-step sampling while still permitting iterative generation for improved trade-offs between sample quality and computational cost. Unlike conventional diffusion models that rely on lengthy sampling trajectories, consistency models directly learn a consistency function $f : (\mathbf{x}_t, t) \mapsto \mathbf{x}_\epsilon$ that enforces self-consistency across different time steps along the PF-ODE trajectory, $f(\mathbf{x}_t, t) = f(\mathbf{x}_{t'}, t')$ for all $t, t' \in [\epsilon, T]$, where ϵ is a fixed small positive number. This property enables them to achieve one-step generation.

To ensure reliable training, a boundary condition $f(\mathbf{x}_\epsilon, \epsilon) = \mathbf{x}_\epsilon$ is imposed, guaranteeing identity mapping at the start of the trajectory. In practice, the consistency model $f_\theta(\mathbf{x}, t)$ is parameterized by a neural network subject to this constraint:

$$f_\theta(\mathbf{x}, t) = c_{\text{skip}}(t)\mathbf{x} + c_{\text{out}}(t) F_\theta(\mathbf{x}, t) \tag{5}$$

where $c_{\text{skip}}(t)$ and $c_{\text{out}}(t)$ are differentiable functions with the $c_{\text{skip}}(\epsilon) = 1$ and $c_{\text{out}}(\epsilon) = 0$. $F_\theta(\mathbf{x}, t)$ denotes the output of the deep neural network. Sampling with a trained consistency model is highly efficient: starting from Gaussian noise $\hat{\mathbf{x}}_T \sim \mathcal{N}(0, T^2 I)$, a single forward evaluation $\hat{\mathbf{x}}_\epsilon = f_\theta(\hat{\mathbf{x}}_T, T)$ suffices to produce high-quality samples. These properties distinguish consistency models as an independent family of generative models, complementing and extending diffusion-based approaches.

3. Methodology

We propose CM-CR, a cloud removal framework built upon SAR-conditioned consistency modeling. As illustrated in Figure 1, CM-CR comprises three main components.

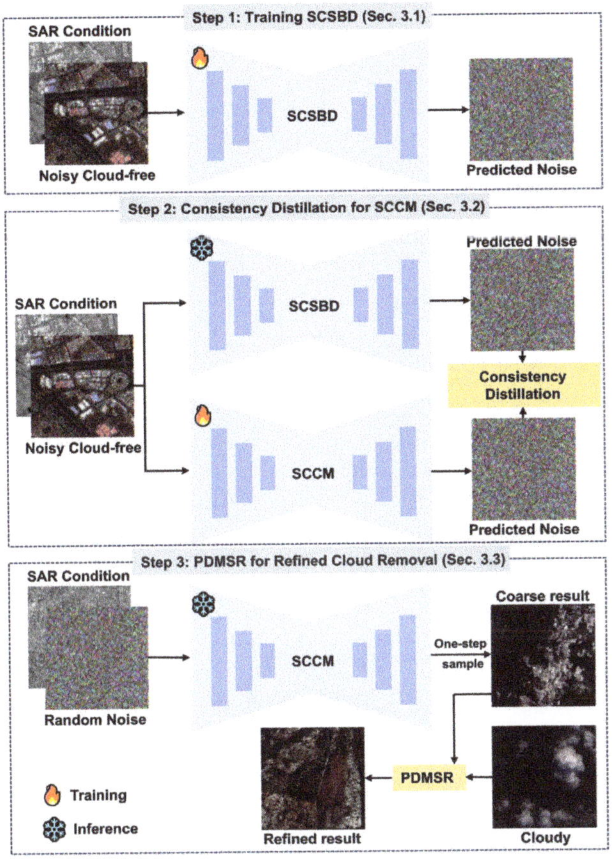

Figure 1. Overall architecture of the proposed CM-CR framework. It consists of three main components: (1) training the SCSBD model as the teacher; (2) consistency distillation for student model SCCM; and (3) refining the coarse output via the PDMSR strategy to obtain high-quality cloud-free images. Step 1 trains the SCSBD as the teacher model, as elaborated in Section 3.1. Step 2 employs consistency distillation to transfer knowledge from SCSBD to the student model SCCM, enabling single-step sampling for coarse cloud removal, detailed in Section 3.2. Step 3 further refines these coarse results via the proposed PDMSR strategy, yielding high-quality, cloud-free reconstructions, as described in Section 3.3.

3.1. SAR-Conditioned Score-Based Diffusion (SCSBD) Model

As mentioned in Section 2.2, we need to train a teacher network to estimate the score, which will be used for subsequent sampling and cloud removal processes. Figure 2 illustrates the training procedure of our SCSBD network. We utilize U-Net [45] as the backbone network to construct the SCSBD network. The U-Net architecture, with its symmetrical encoder–decoder structure, iteratively compresses and reconstructs the spatial features of the image, while employing skip connections to retain high-resolution spatial information. Owing to its all-weather and all-day imaging capability, SAR imagery provides stable ground information even under cloud coverage. This feature enables SAR data to effectively compensate for the missing information in optical images caused by cloud occlusion, significantly enhancing the model's ability to reconstruct realistic scenes.

To further improve the accuracy of cloud removal, we integrate SAR imagery as auxiliary conditional information, which is concatenated with noisy cloud-free optical images to serve as input to train the SCSBD. Specifically, the SAR image $\mathbf{c}_{sar}$ is merged with the noisy optical image $\mathbf{x}_t$ at time step t and jointly processed as input to the model. This fusion approach ensures effective integration of SAR and optical features at the input stage, allowing the model to effectively capture their relationships during encoding, thereby leveraging SAR data as prior knowledge to enhance scene understanding and reconstruction.

Within the U-Net architecture, SAR data is not only combined with cloud-free optical images at the initial input stage but also further incorporated via skip connections during the decoder phase to facilitate better learning and utilization of SAR conditional information. Ultimately, the model produces a predicted score $\mathbf{s}_\phi(\mathbf{x}, \sigma, \mathbf{c}_{sar})$ under the SAR condition, which guides the reconstruction process. This approach allows the model to manage complex weather conditions and occlusions more effectively, generating clearer and more accurate cloud-free images.

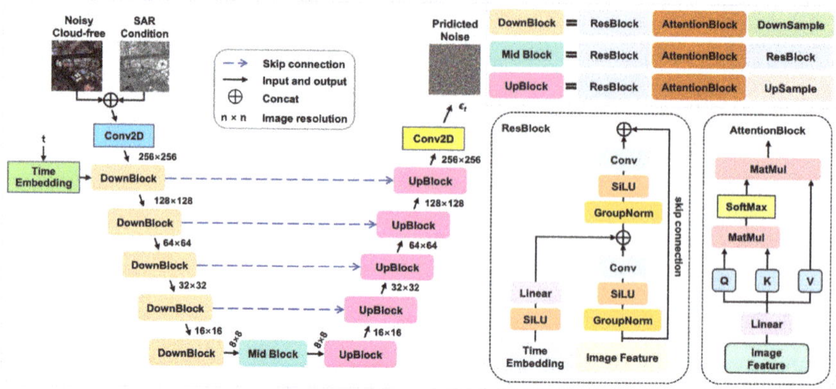

Figure 2. Architecture of the proposed SCSBD and SCCM. The network adopts a U-Net-like encoder–decoder structure to iteratively downsample and upsample the noisy optical image, conditioned on the corresponding SAR image and time embedding. The final predicted noise is estimated to guide the sampling process for effective cloud removal.

In the following sections, we will elaborate on the modeling details of the SCSBD from a theoretical perspective. We define $p_\sigma(\tilde{\mathbf{x}}) = \int p_{\text{data}}(\mathbf{x})\mathcal{N}(\tilde{\mathbf{x}}; \mathbf{x}, \sigma^2 I)dt$ as the perturbed data distribution. We denote $\left\{\sigma_i\right\}_{i=1}^{L}$ to be a positive noise levels sequence that satisfies $\sigma_{min} = \sigma_1 < \sigma_2 < \cdots < \sigma_L = \sigma_{\max}$. The noise levels are selected such that σ_1 is small enough to minimize its impact on the data $p_{\sigma_{\min}}(\mathbf{x}) \approx p_{\text{data}}(\mathbf{x})$, while σ_L is large enough such that $p_{\sigma_{\max}}(\mathbf{x}) \approx \mathcal{N}(\mathbf{x}; \mathbf{0}, \sigma_{\max}^2 \mathbf{I})$. Our goal is to train an SAR-conditioned score network that can estimate the scores of all perturbed data distributions simultaneously. Specifically, for each $\sigma \in \left\{\sigma_i\right\}_{i=1}^{L}$, the relationship $\mathbf{s}_\phi(\tilde{\mathbf{x}}, \sigma, \mathbf{c}_{sar}) \approx \nabla_{\tilde{\mathbf{x}}} \log p_\sigma(\tilde{\mathbf{x}}|\mathbf{c}_{sar})$ should hold. Note that $\mathbf{s}_\phi(\mathbf{x}, \sigma, \mathbf{c}_{sar}) \in \mathbb{R}^D$ when $\mathbf{x} \in \mathbb{R}^D$. We refer to $\mathbf{s}_\phi(\mathbf{x}, \sigma, \mathbf{c}_{sar})$ as the SCSBD.

The denoising score matching method was employed to train the SCSBD. As shown in Algorithm 1, let the noise distribution be $p_\sigma(\tilde{\mathbf{x}} \mid \mathbf{x}) = \mathcal{N}(\tilde{\mathbf{x}} \mid \mathbf{x}, \sigma^2 I)$. Consequently, the gradient of the log-probability is given by $\nabla_{\tilde{\mathbf{x}}} \log p_\sigma(\tilde{\mathbf{x}} \mid \mathbf{x}) = -\frac{\tilde{\mathbf{x}}-\mathbf{x}}{\sigma^2}$. For a specific value of σ, the objective function for denoising score matching is:

$$\ell(\phi; \sigma_i) = \frac{1}{2}\mathbb{E}_{p_{\text{data}}(\mathbf{x})}\mathbb{E}_{\tilde{\mathbf{x}}_i \sim \mathcal{N}(\mathbf{x}_i, \sigma_i^2 I)}\left[\left\| s_\phi(\tilde{\mathbf{x}}_i, \sigma_i, \mathbf{c}_{sar}) + \frac{\tilde{\mathbf{x}}_i - \mathbf{x}_i}{\sigma_i^2} \right\|_2^2\right] \tag{6}$$

By performing a weighted summation of all $\sigma \in \{\sigma_i\}_{i=1}^{L}$ objectives, we obtain a final objective:

$$\mathcal{L}(\phi; \{\sigma_i\}_{i=1}^{L}) = \frac{1}{L}\sum_{i=1}^{L} \lambda(\sigma_i)\ell(\phi; \sigma_i) \tag{7}$$

where $\lambda(\sigma_i) > 0$ be a coefficient function dependent on σ_i. Provided that $\mathbf{s}_\phi(\mathbf{x}, \sigma, \mathbf{c}_{sar})$ is well trained, the function $\mathbf{s}_{\phi^*}(\mathbf{x}, \sigma, \mathbf{c}_{sar})$ will minimize Equation (7) for almost all $i \in \{1, 2, \cdots, L\}$.

Algorithm 1 Training SCSBD via Denoising Score Matching

Require: Training dataset $D = \{\mathbf{x}_i\}_{i=1}^{N}$, noise levels $\{\sigma_i\}_{i=1}^{L}$, coefficients $\lambda(\sigma)$, Model $\mathbf{s}_\phi(\mathbf{x}, \sigma, \mathbf{c}_{sar})$, learning rate η, number of epochs E, batch size B
Ensure: Trained model parameters ϕ

```
for epoch = 1 to E do
    for each data point x_i in D do
        for each noise level σ_i do
            Sample noise ε ~ N(0, I)
            Perturb data x̃_i ← x_i + σ_i ε
            Noise distribution p_{σ_i}(x̃_i | x_i) = N(x̃_i | x_i, σ_i^2 I)
            Compute the score of the perturbed data ∇_{x̃_i} log p_{σi}(x̃_i | x_i) = −(x̃_i − x_i)/σ_i^2
            Estimate the score by model s_φ(x̃_i, σ_i, c_sar)
            ℓ(φ; σ_i) ← (1/2) E_{p_data(x)} E_{x̃_i ~ N(x_i, σ_i^2 I)} [ || s_φ(x̃_i, σ_i, c_sar) + (x̃_i − x_i)/σ_i^2 ||_2^2 ]
        end for
        L(φ; {σ_i}_{i=1}^L) ← (1/L) Σ_{i=1}^L λ(σ_i) ℓ(φ; σ_i)
        φ ← φ − η ∇_φ L(φ; {σ_i}_{i=1}^L)
    end for
end for
```

Once the SAR-Conditioned Score Network $\mathbf{s}_{\phi^*}(\mathbf{x}, \sigma, \mathbf{c}_{sar})$ is trained, the cloud-free image sampling process can be conducted by plugging the score model into the empirical PF-ODE described in Equation (4). As illustrated by Equation (8), the sampling process starts from the prior Gaussian distribution $\hat{\mathbf{x}}_T \sim \mathcal{N}(0, T^2\mathbf{I})$. An accurate estimate of $\hat{\mathbf{x}}_{t_{n-1}}^{\boldsymbol{\phi}}$ can be derived from $\mathbf{x}_{t_n}$ by executing a single discretization step with a numerical ODE solver.

$$\hat{\mathbf{x}}_{t_{n-1}}^{\boldsymbol{\phi}} := \mathbf{x}_{t_n} + (t_{n-1} - t_n)\Phi(\mathbf{x}_{t_n}, t_n, \mathbf{c}_{sar}; \phi) \tag{8}$$

Here, Φ represents the numerical solver for the PF-ODE; we employ the Euler solver $\Phi(\mathbf{x}, t, \mathbf{c}_{sar}; \boldsymbol{\phi}) = -t\mathbf{s}_\phi(\mathbf{x}, t, \mathbf{c}_{sar})$ to solve the aforementioned equation. The variable t_i denotes a specific time point, and we follow the time setting approach proposed by Karras for t_i. Specifically, the time interval $[\epsilon, T]$ is divided into $N-1$ segments, with boundaries defined by $t_1 = \epsilon < t_2 < \cdots < t_N = T$. In practice, t_i can be calculated using the following formula:

$$t_i = \left(\epsilon^{1/\rho} + \frac{i-1}{N-1}\left(T^{1/\rho} - \epsilon^{1/\rho}\right)\right)^{\rho} \tag{9}$$

For numerical stability, ϵ is set to a very small positive value, and ρ is assigned a value of 7 in this work.

The noise $\mathbf{x}_T$, sampled from the prior Gaussian distribution, along with the SAR image corresponding to the cloud-covered image, serves as input for the model. Using an ODE solver, Equation (8) is iteratively solved to produce the cloud-free image $\hat{\mathbf{x}}_0$. Analogous to image editing approaches based on diffusion models, the blending technique is employed on the cloud-covered image and the generated cloud-free image $\hat{\mathbf{x}}_0$ to derive the final de-clouded result:

$$\mathbf{x} = m \odot \hat{\mathbf{x}}_0 + (1 - m) \odot \mathbf{x}_{cloudy} \tag{10}$$

where m represents a binary mask denoting cloud-covered regions, with the value set to 1 for cloud-covered areas and 0 for cloud-free areas. $\mathbf{x}_{cloudy}$ denotes the cloud-covered image.

3.2. SAR-Conditioned Consistency Model (SCCM) via Consistency Distillation

The slow sampling speed of diffusion models represents a significant bottleneck, limiting their application in cloud removal tasks. Compared to other cloud removal methods based on DDPM models, our proposed approach, based on the score-based diffusion model, demonstrates significant improvements in sampling efficiency under the ODE framework. However, iteratively solving the ODE with a numerical solver requires multiple evaluations of the score model $\mathbf{s}_\phi(\mathbf{x}, \sigma, \mathbf{c}_{sar})$, which renders the process computationally intensive. Therefore, enhancing the speed and efficiency of cloud removal remains a crucial challenge that we aim to address.

Song et al. [42] proposed a novel addition to the family of diffusion models: consistency models, which enable single-step generation and additionally support iterative generation, balancing sample quality with computational efficiency. Inspired by the Consistency Model, we employed a consistency distillation strategy based on our pre-trained Score Model, ultimately developing a framework capable of rapid cloud removal. This approach allows for efficient inference by distilling the capabilities of the Score Model into a more streamlined process, significantly enhancing the speed of cloud removal while maintaining high-quality output. The resulting framework effectively addresses the challenges of slow sampling typically associated with diffusion models, offering a promising solution for real-time applications.

In the following section, we will introduce the consistency distillation training strategy, which builds upon the SCSBD model $\mathbf{s}_\phi(\mathbf{x}, \sigma, \mathbf{c}_{sar})$.

Figure 3 presents the consistency distillation strategy utilized in this study. The objective of the consistency distillation strategy is to establish a SAR-conditioned consistency function, denoted as $\mathcal{G}_\theta$. For the sequence of solution trajectories obtained from Equation (4), $\{\hat{\mathbf{x}}_t\}_{t\in[0,T]}$, the consistency function should satisfy the following property: for any pair $(\mathbf{x}, \mathbf{t}, \mathbf{c}_{sar})$ associated with the same PF-ODE, the consistency function should map them consistently to the identical point $\hat{x}_0$, i.e., $\mathcal{G}(\mathbf{x}_t, t, \mathbf{c}_{sar}) = \mathcal{G}(\mathbf{x}_{t'}, t', \mathbf{c}_{sar}) = \hat{x}_0$ for all $t, t' \in [0, T]$. Consequently, the distilled model allows for single-step generation, eliminating the requirement for multiple iterations typically performed by an ODE solver.

The consistency distillation training process is presented in Algorithm 2. In this process, a pair of adjacent points is sampled from the ODE trajectory, and a consistency loss is utilized to supervise their mapping back to the same origin, thereby facilitating the distillation training. Specifically, a data point $\mathbf{x} \sim p_{\text{data}}$ is initially sampled from the dataset $\mathcal{D}$, and Gaussian noise is subsequently added to it. From the SDE transition density $\mathcal{N}(\mathbf{x}, t_{n+1}^2 \boldsymbol{I})$, $\mathbf{x}_{t_{n+1}}$ is sampled. A single discretization step using an ODE numerical solver is then performed according to Equation (8) to obtain $\hat{\mathbf{x}}_{t_n}^{\phi}$, yielding a pair of adjacent points $(\hat{\mathbf{x}}_{t_n}^{\boldsymbol{\phi}}, \mathbf{x}_{t_{n+1}})$. These two points, belonging to the same ODE trajectory, should satisfy the properties of the SAR-conditioned consistency function $\mathcal{G}_\theta$. The following loss function is used to perform the distillation training of the model:

$$\mathcal{L}_{CD}^N(\boldsymbol{\theta}, \boldsymbol{\theta}'; \boldsymbol{\phi}) = \mathbb{E}[\lambda(t_n) d(\mathcal{G}_\theta(\mathbf{x}_{t_{n+1}}, t_{n+1}, \mathbf{c}_{sar}), \mathcal{G}_{\theta'}(\hat{\mathbf{x}}_{t_n}^{\boldsymbol{\phi}}, t_n, \mathbf{c}_{sar}))] \tag{11}$$

where $n \sim \mathcal{U}[[1, N-1]]$, $\mathbf{x} \sim p_{data}$ and $\mathbf{x}_{t_{n+1}} \sim \mathcal{N}(\mathbf{x}; t_{n+1}^2 \boldsymbol{I})$. $\lambda(\cdot)$ is the positive weighting function. Furthermore, θ' refers to the running average of the parameter θ throughout the optimization process. The function $d(\cdot, \cdot)$ serves as a metric for measuring the discrepancy in outputs between two adjacent points under the SAR-conditioned consistency function. In this paper, the mean squared error (MSE) is employed as the metric.

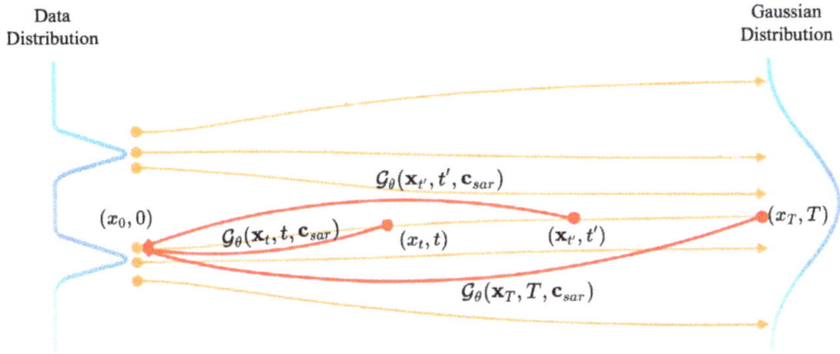

Figure 3. The SCCM is trained to map points on any trajectory of the PF ODE to the trajectory's origin.

Algorithm 2 Training SCCM via Consistency Distillation

Require: Training dataset D, initial model parameter θ, learning rate η, ODE solver $\Phi(\cdot,\cdot,\cdot;\phi)$, metric function $d(\cdot,\cdot)$, weighting function $\lambda(\cdot)$, and EMA decay rate μ
Ensure: Trained model parameter θ
Initialize target network parameter $\theta' \leftarrow \theta$
repeat
  Sample $\mathbf{x} \sim D$ and $n \sim \mathcal{U}[[1, N-1]]$
  Sample $\mathbf{x}_{t_{n+1}} \sim \mathcal{N}(\mathbf{x}; t_{n+1}^2 I)$
  Compute $\hat{\mathbf{x}}_{t_n}^{\phi} \leftarrow \mathbf{x}_{t_{n+1}} + (t_n - t_{n+1})\Phi(\mathbf{x}_{t_{n+1}}, t_{n+1}, \mathbf{c}_{sar}; \phi)$
  Compute loss: $\mathcal{L}(\theta, \theta'; \phi) \leftarrow \lambda(t_n) d(\mathcal{G}_\theta(\mathbf{x}_{t_{n+1}}, t_{n+1}; \mathbf{c}_{sar}), \mathcal{G}_{\theta'}(\hat{\mathbf{x}}_{t_n}^{\phi}, t_n; \mathbf{c}_{sar}))$
  Update model parameter: $\theta \leftarrow \theta - \eta \nabla_\theta \mathcal{L}(\theta, \theta'; \phi)$
  Update target network parameter: $\theta' \leftarrow \text{stop grad}(\mu\theta' + (1-\mu)\theta)$
until convergence

3.3. *Progressive Denoising via Multistep Resampling for Refined Cloud Removal*

Building upon SCSBD and the distillation consistency model (SCCM) described in Sections 3.1 and 3.2, this section introduces the Progressive Denoising via Multistep Resampling (PDMSR) strategy, which serves as the core inference mechanism in the CM-CR framework. PDMSR is specifically designed to enhance cloud removal fidelity while preserving high inference efficiency.

As shown in Figure 4, the PDMSR strategy begins by sampling a noise image $\mathbf{x}_T \sim \mathcal{N}(0, \mathbf{I})$ and feeding it, along with the conditional SAR image $\mathbf{c}_{sar}$, into the consistency function $\mathcal{G}_\theta$ to generate an initial cloud-removed result $\hat{\mathbf{x}}_0$. This result is fused with the cloud-free regions of the original image $\mathbf{x}_{cloudy}$ using a binary cloud mask to obtain a hybrid image. However, directly using this one-step prediction often leads to artifacts or inconsistencies in reconstructed regions due to limited spectral guidance.

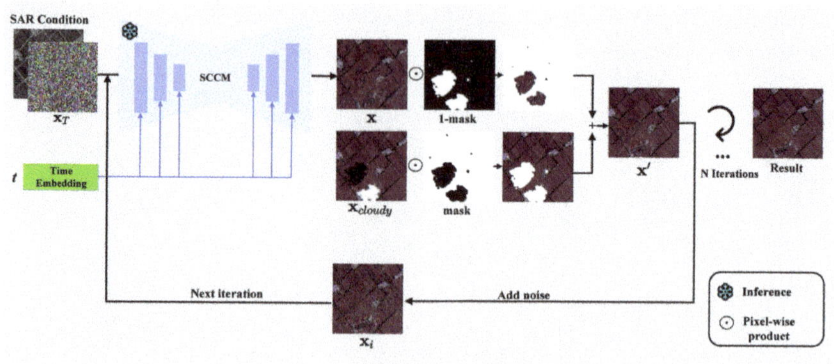

Figure 4. Illustration of the proposed PDMSR inference strategy, which progressively refines the cloud removal results by leveraging multistep denoising and re-noising guided by cloud-free regions. $\mathbf{x}_T$ denotes the initial noisy image, $\mathbf{x}_{\text{cloudy}}$ is the cloudy input, $\mathbf{x}_i$ is the intermediate noisy sample at iteration i, and $\mathbf{x}'$ is the progressively refined output.

To overcome this limitation, PDMSR introduces a multistep inference scheme that progressively reintroduces noise and refines the prediction in each step as detailed in Algorithm 3. Specifically, at each iteration, the intermediate result is perturbed with decreasing levels of Gaussian noise and then passed back through the consistency function. Moreover, cloud-free regions from the original image are preserved and fused back into the estimate after each step. This process allows the model to incorporate rich contextual and spectral priors from unoccluded areas, guiding the reconstruction of cloud-covered regions toward more semantically consistent and visually plausible outputs.

Algorithm 3 Progressive Denoising via Multistep Resampling (PDMSR)

Input: Consistency function $\mathcal{G}_\theta(\cdot,\cdot,\cdot)$, time steps $t_1 > t_2 > \cdots > t_N$, cloudy image $\mathbf{x}_{cloudy}$, binary mask m, SAR condition $\mathbf{c}_{sar}$, initial noise $\mathbf{x}_T$
$\mathbf{x} \leftarrow \mathcal{G}_\theta(\mathbf{x}_T, T, \mathbf{c}_{sar})$
$\mathbf{x}' \leftarrow \mathbf{x}_{cloudy} \odot m + \mathbf{x} \odot (1-m)$
for $i = 2$ to N **do**
    Sample $\mathbf{x}_i \sim \mathcal{N}(\mathbf{x}', (t_i^2 - \epsilon^2)\boldsymbol{I})$
    $\mathbf{x} \leftarrow \mathcal{G}_\theta(\mathbf{x}_i, t_i, \mathbf{c}_{sar})$
    $\mathbf{x}' \leftarrow \mathbf{x}_{cloudy} \odot m + \mathbf{x} \odot (1-m)$
end for
Output: $\mathbf{x}'$

Although PDMSR involves N iterative steps, each step is computationally efficient due to the single-pass property of the distilled model $\mathcal{G}_\theta$. Consequently, the overall inference speed remains significantly faster than traditional diffusion-based methods, which typically require hundreds of ODE solver steps. Our ablation studies further confirm that PDMSR substantially improves the structural consistency and visual fidelity of cloud-removed images.

4. Experimental Results

4.1. Data

The dataset utilized in this study is the publicly available SEN12MS-CR [46], comprising 169 non-overlapping regions of interest (ROIs) sampled across all inhabited continents and across various meteorological seasons. Each ROI contains a triplet of orthorectified and geo-referenced images: a cloudy Sentinel-2 optical observation, its corresponding cloud-free counterpart, and a co-registered Sentinel-1 SAR image that integrates both VV and VH polarization channels as a dual-channel input. All three images were acquired within the same season to minimize surface variability. As illustrated in Figure 5, each ROI was further partitioned into overlapping triplet patches of 256 × 256 pixels using a stride of 128 pixels. Note that the cloudy and cloud-free Sentinel-2 images in SEN12MS-CR are not always captured on the same day. They are selected as the closest-available temporal pair within the same season to minimize surface changes, as defined by the dataset protocol. Likewise, Sentinel-1 SAR images are temporally aligned within the same seasonal window. We follow the official pairing to avoid manual alignment bias, which is a standard practice in cloud-removal studies.

The Sentinel-2 data are sourced from the Level-1C top-of-atmosphere (TOP) reflectance product, with pixel values ranging from 0 to 10,000 and including all 13 spectral bands. In contrast, Sentinel-1 images are derived from the Level-1 GRD product, acquired in Interferometric Wide (IW) swath mode with dual-polarization channels (VV and VH), and represented as backscatter coefficients in the decibel (dB) scale.

For model training, 20,000 triplet patches were selected, where only the red, green, and blue (RGB) bands from the Sentinel-2 imagery were preserved and used as input. To evaluate performance, an additional 400 representative test samples were curated according to cloud fraction and type of land cover. Specifically, 80 samples were drawn from each cloud coverage interval: 0–20%, 20–40%, 40–60%, 60–80%, and 80–100%.

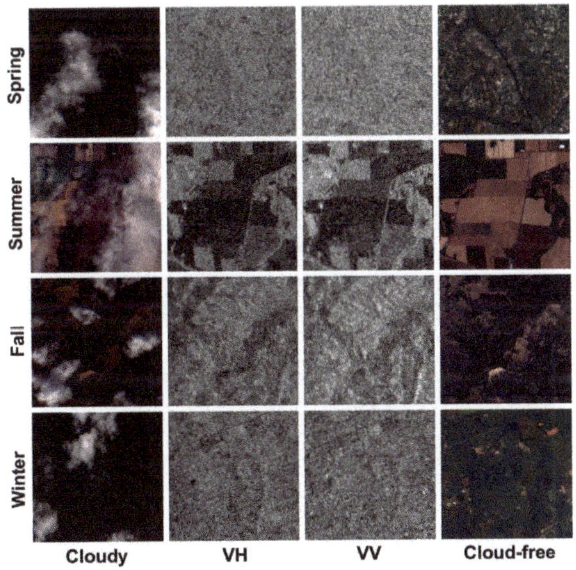

Figure 5. Representative samples from the SEN12MS-CR dataset. Rows correspond to the four meteorological seasons (spring, summer, fall, and winter), while columns represent the geo-referenced cloudy Sentinel-2 image, the Sentinel-1 SAR image with VH polarization, the SAR image with VV polarization, and a temporally matched cloud-free Sentinel-2 image.

4.2. Implementation Details

To ensure experimental reproducibility, this section presents the detailed training hyperparameter settings for SCSBD and SCCM and the evaluation metrics adopted to assess model performance.

4.2.1. Training Setting

All experiments were conducted on a high-performance computing server equipped with an AMD EPYC 7763 64-core CPU and an NVIDIA A100-SXM4-80GB GPU, running the Ubuntu operating system. The implementation was built on Python 3.10 using the PyTorch framework.

For training the SCSBD, we adopted an input image resolution of 256 × 256 pixels with a batch size of 4. The model was trained for 700,000 steps (approximately 7 days) across one A100 GPU using mixed-precision arithmetic to enhance computational efficiency. The initial learning rate was set to 0.0001, with a three-tiered exponential moving average (EMA) strategy employing decay rates of 0.999, 0.9999, and 0.9999432189950708 respectively.

During the SCCM distillation phase, we maintained identical configurations for batch size, input resolution, and computational resources while modifying specific hyperparameters: the learning rate was reduced to 0.00001, and a dropout rate of 0.1 was introduced in the teacher model. This phase utilized Heun's method as the ODE solver and incorporated LPIPS as the weighting function to quantify the differences between generated and ground-truth images.

4.2.2. Evaluation Metrics

In all experiments, we report the Peak Signal-to-Noise Ratio (PSNR), Structural Similarity Index Measure (SSIM), Spectral Angle Mapper (SAM), and Mean Absolute Error (MAE) on the test set to assess the quality of the cloud removal results.

PSNR is a widely used metric in Image Quality Assessment(IQA) , where higher values generally correspond to better image quality. Its formulation is provided in Equation (12):

$$\text{PSNR} = 10 \times log_{10}\left(\frac{MAX^2}{MSE}\right) \tag{12}$$

$$MSE = \frac{\sum_{i=1}^{N}(y_i - \hat{y}_i)^2}{N} \tag{13}$$

where y_i and $\hat{y}_i$ are the ground truth and predicted intensity values at the $i-$th pixel, respectively, and N is the number of pixels. MAX represents the maximum pixel intensity, set to 10,000 in this study to match the TOP reflectance scale. The Mean Squared Error (MSE), defined in Equation (13), quantifies the average squared difference between corresponding pixels.

The Structural Similarity Index Measure (SSIM) evaluates image similarity by comparing luminance, contrast, and structural information between the predicted and reference images. It is computed as:

$$\text{SSIM}(x,y) = \frac{(2\mu_x\mu_y + C_1)(2\sigma_{xy} + C_2)}{(\mu_x^2 + \mu_y^2 + C_1)(\sigma_x^2 + \sigma_y^2 + C_2)} \tag{14}$$

where μ_x and μ_y denote the local means of images x and y, σ_x^2 and σ_y^2 are the corresponding variances, and σ_{xy} is the covariance between them. Constants C_1 and C_2 are used to stabilize the division and are derived from the dynamic range of the pixel values. The SSIM value ranges from 0 to 1, with higher values indicating greater structural similarity.

Spectral Angle Mapper (SAM) measures the spectral consistency between the predicted and reference images by calculating the angle between their spectral vectors. It is computed as:

$$\text{SAM}(x,y) = \arccos\left(\frac{\langle x,y\rangle}{\|x\|_2 \cdot \|y\|_2}\right) \tag{15}$$

where x and y denote the spectral vectors of the reference and predicted images at a given pixel location, respectively. $\langle x,y\rangle$ represents the dot product of the two vectors, and

$\|x\|_2$ and $\|y\|_2$ are their Euclidean norms. A smaller SAM value indicates higher spectral consistency, with 0 representing perfect spectral alignment.

The Mean Absolute Error (MAE) quantifies the average magnitude of pixel-wise differences between the predicted and reference images. It is insensitive to the direction of the error and directly reflects overall reconstruction accuracy. The MAE is defined as:

$$\text{MAE} = \frac{1}{N}\sum_{i=1}^{N}|y_i - \hat{y}_i| \tag{16}$$

where y_i and $\hat{y}_i$ represent the ground truth and predicted values at the i-th pixel, and N is the total number of pixels. A lower MAE value indicates better performance, with 0 corresponding to a perfect reconstruction.

4.3. Cloud Removal Results

In this section, four representative terrain types—grassland, farmland, mountainous terrain, and urban areas—were selected to assess the performance of CM-CR under diverse geomorphological conditions. All data were derived from Sentinel-2 imagery within the SEN12MS-CR dataset, and true-color composites were generated using the red, green, and blue spectral bands. Despite considerable local variability in spectral and radiometric properties, as well as complex topography and significant elevation differences, the proposed CM-CR exhibited strong performance, effectively recovering most of the information obscured by cloud cover.

As shown in Figure 6, CM-CR effectively removes thick cloud cover in grassland scenes and demonstrates strong capability in reconstructing homogeneous surface areas. In particular, the red box in Figure 6a highlights that under extensive cloud coverage, the method may still introduce noticeable artifacts. Nevertheless, as illustrated in Figure 6b, even in visually complex regions, CM-CR can reliably recover uniform structures. It is worth noting that the reconstruction fidelity is influenced by the quality and structural details present in the SAR input.

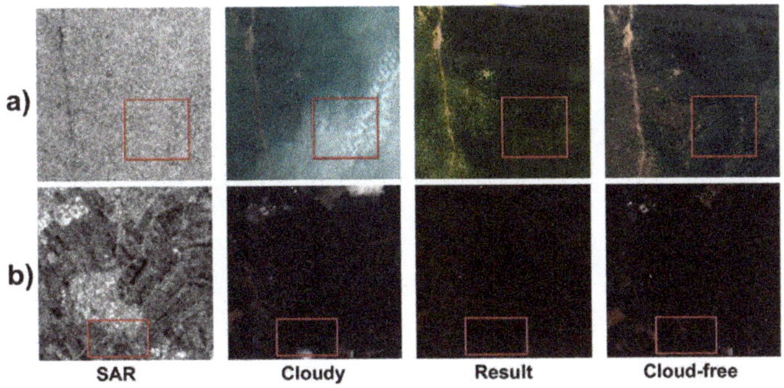

Figure 6. Cloud removal results in grassland scenes: (**a**) under extensive cloud coverage; (**b**) under complex scene conditions. Red bounding boxes indicate key regions of reconstruction.

As shown in Figure 7, CM-CR achieves notable performance in removing thick cloud cover over farmland areas. Leveraging SAR guidance, the method effectively reconstructs both structural and textural details. In the region highlighted by the red box in Figure 7a, CM-CR successfully distinguishes multiple land cover types and restores them with high fidelity. However, due to the limited accuracy of existing cloud detection algorithms, some residual cloud artifacts remain in the reconstructed output. Figure 7b further demonstrates that, even in scenes characterized by complex layouts, the model can generate content consistent with the surrounding semantic context. Nevertheless, in regions with dense cloud coverage, the SAR input may lack sufficient structural cues, which in turn affects reconstruction accuracy and leads to noticeable deviations.

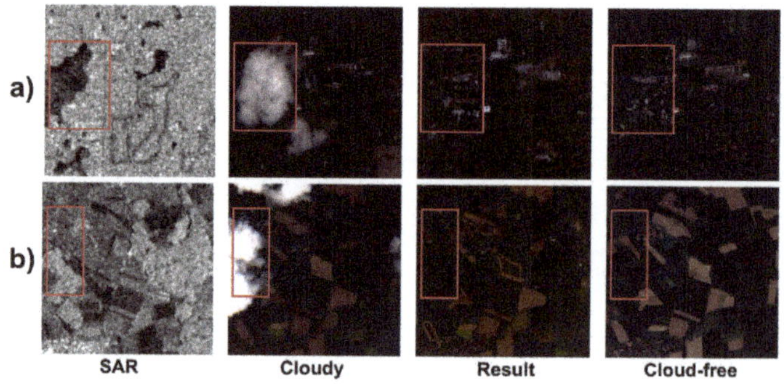

Figure 7. Cloud removal results in farmland scenes: (**a**) with multiple land cover types; (**b**) under complex layout conditions. Red bounding boxes indicate key regions of reconstruction. Red bounding boxes indicate key regions of reconstruction.

As illustrated in Figure 8, CM-CR exhibits strong reconstruction performance even in mountainous terrains with complex textures and elevation variations. In the region marked by the red box in Figure 8a, the model accurately recovers structural features present in the SAR image. However, due to the limitations of SAR in capturing fine topographic details—particularly over the central hill—noticeable discrepancies remain between the result and the reference cloud-free image. Figure 8b further illustrates the model's ability to restore mountainous structures in challenging scenarios. Nonetheless, in some areas, inconsistencies arise due to differences in acquisition time between the SAR and cloudy optical image. For example, water accumulation observed in the SAR image within valley regions is not reflected in the cloudy image, resulting in differences between the preserved cloud-free regions and reference cloud-free image.

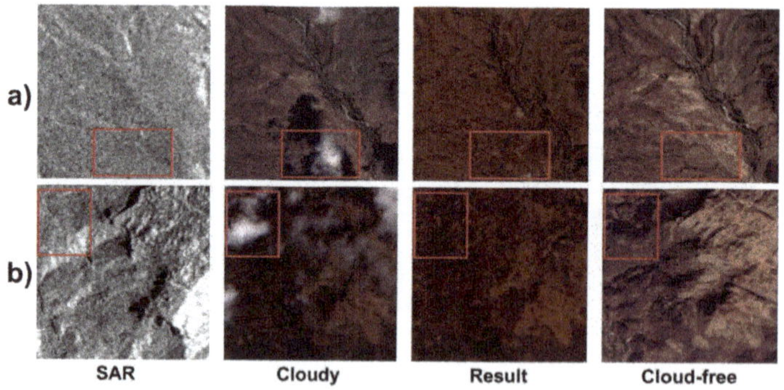

Figure 8. Cloud removal results in mountainous scenes: (**a**) with complex textures and elevation changes; (**b**) under temporal inconsistency between SAR and optical data. Red bounding boxes indicate key regions of reconstruction.

As shown in Figure 9, CM-CR demonstrates strong reconstruction performance in urban environments characterized by complex layouts and high-frequency textures. In Figure 9a, the model attempts to recover dense road networks and their local branching structures from a heavily cloud-obscured input. While it successfully reconstructs portions that are clearly reflected in the SAR image, a downward-branching segment is missing due to its poor visibility and ambiguity in the SAR signal. In contrast, Figure 9b illustrates a more favorable outcome. Despite thick cloud cover in the optical observation, CM-CR effectively restores primary roadways and building layouts with notable consistency. The clearer structural cues in the SAR image significantly enhance reconstruction quality in occluded regions. Nevertheless, minor discrepancies persist in areas with highly textured content, underscoring the inherent challenges of urban reconstruction under severely degraded observations.

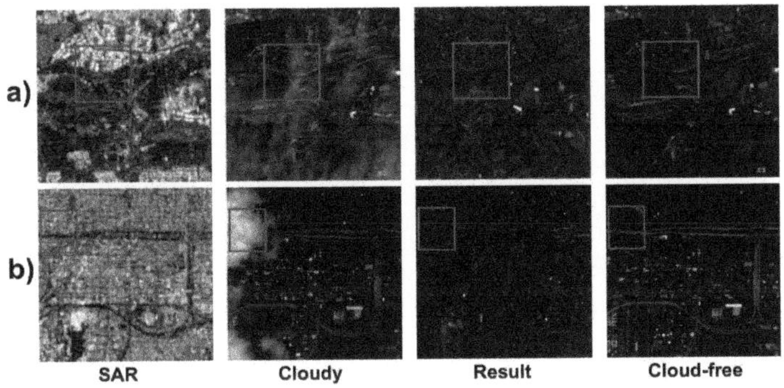

Figure 9. Cloud removal results in urban scenes: (**a**) with dense road networks; (**b**) under heavy cloud occlusion with clear structural guidance. Red bounding boxes indicate key regions of reconstruction.

4.4. Comparisons with State-of-the-Art Methods

We conducted a comparative analysis of the proposed model against existing methods—including the discriminative baselines Dsen2-CR [46], GLF-CR [47], and UnCR [48], as well as diffusion-based approaches DiffCR [36] and Repaint [49]—evaluating both cloud removal performance and computational efficiency. All models were trained on the same set of 20,000 triplet samples and tested on the same evaluation dataset. For DiffCR and Repaint, the number of sampling steps was kept consistent with their original implementations, both using 200 steps. Since our CM-CR model achieves the reconstruction results shown in Table 1 with only 13 PDMSR steps, we further included a qualitative comparison where Repaint's sampling steps were artificially reduced to 13—denoted as Repaint-13—to enable a more direct comparison with our approach. Since the GLF-CR method uses 128 × 128 inputs while all other methods use 256 × 256 images, we combined four non-overlapping 128 × 128 patches to form a single 256 × 256 image, ensuring fairness when calculating reconstruction quality metrics. Additionally, the "Time" reported for GLF-CR reflects the total time needed to process these four 128 × 128 patches.

Table 1. Quantitative comparison of cloud removal methods. Bold indicates the best, and underlined indicates the second-best results.

Method	PSNR (dB) ↑	SSIM ↑	SAM ↓	MAE (TOP) ↓	Params (M)	Time (s/img) ↓
Dsen2-CR [46]	32.214	0.906	0.048	244.03	75.9	**0.062**
GLF-CR [47]	<u>33.159</u>	<u>0.922</u>	<u>0.043</u>	<u>221.08</u>	73.1	0.095
UnCR [48]	30.686	0.897	0.062	290.53	97.1	<u>0.088</u>
DiffCR [36]	29.317	0.861	0.105	364.85	87.5	2.218
Repaint [49]	32.508	0.907	0.054	246.05	34.62	83.062
CM-CR (Ours)	**34.191**	**0.935**	**0.042**	**202.69**	2730.71	2.023

We first conducted quantitative comparative experiments with current state-of-the-art cloud removal methods. Table 1 summarizes the detailed image reconstruction quality metrics, including the average PSNR, SSIM, SAM, and MAE. In addition, it reports model performance metrics, specifically the number of parameters (Params) and the time required to reconstruct a single image (Time). The experimental results show that our method consistently outperforms all other approaches in evaluation metrics, fully demonstrating its effectiveness for the cloud removal task. Specifically, compared to the second-best method, our approach achieves notable improvements: the PSNR increases by 3.1%, the SSIM improves by 1.4%, while the SAM and MAE decrease by 2.3% and 8.3%, respectively. Although the inference time of CM-CR is still slightly longer than that of discriminative models, its parameter count is approximately 28 times greater than that of UnCR, the largest among the discriminative baselines. This larger parameter scale provides CM-CR with stronger feature extraction capacity, enabling it to learn more robust representations and achieve superior reconstruction performance. Notably, compared to the Repaint method, which adopts a standard DDPM sampling strategy, CM-CR achieves an impressive 40× reduction in per-image processing time while using about 80 times more parameters. Even when compared with the efficient diffusion-based model DiffCR, CM-CR still improves per-image processing speed by approximately 8.8% despite having about 30 times more parameters. These results demonstrate the high sampling efficiency of CM-CR.

We next conducted qualitative comparative experiments with current state-of-the-art cloud removal methods. Figures 10–13 present qualitative comparison results of different methods across various scenes. As shown in Figure 10, the comparison illustrates how each method, assisted by SAR, performs in reconstructing scene structures. Figure 10a depicts a scene with simple structural layouts, whereas Figure 10b shows a more complex structural scenario. The discriminative models Dsen2-CR, GLF-CR, and UnCR can partially recover missing structures; however, due to their limited capacity to restore fine details, the reconstructed regions appear overly smoothed. DiffCR fails to preserve structural consistency, leading to incomplete or distorted reconstructions. Repaint-13, which reduces the sampling steps from 200 to 13, results in insufficient denoising and noticeable residual noise. In contrast, both Repaint and CM-CR successfully reconstruct clear and well-defined structural elements, with the restored regions exhibiting abundant fine-grained details.

Figure 11 presents a scene containing both textural and structural features, where Figure 11a depicts a simple texture–structure scenario and Figure 11b illustrates a more complex one. Taking the red-marked region in Figure 11a as an example, in the simple setting, the discriminative models can accurately distinguish edges and texture structures, producing recognizable shapes with coherent and naturally smooth textures. However, the reconstruction by UnCR shows noticeable blurring in the restored areas. In addition, both DiffCR and Repaint-13 fail to preserve structural consistency. While Repaint and CM-CR can both recover accurate structural information, Repaint exhibits color deviations in the restored textures. By contrast, the reconstruction by CM-CR yields smoother textures with better structural fidelity. In Figure 11b, the red-marked area highlights a region with complex textures and structural content. In this more challenging scenario, Dsen2-CR, GLF-CR, UnCR, DiffCR, and Repaint-13 are unable to faithfully reconstruct either the structures or the detailed textures. Although Repaint partially recovers complex structures and textures, its accuracy remains limited. In comparison, our method, CM-CR, can more precisely reconstruct both complex structural elements and multi-scale texture details.

Figure 12 shows reconstruction results for scenes containing complex high-frequency details. Specifically, Figure 12a presents a scene with a small amount of such information, while Figure 12b illustrates a scene rich in complex high-frequency features. As shown in the red-marked area of Figure 12a, in a scene with limited complex high-frequency information, the Dsen2-CR, GLF-CR, and UnCR methods can only recover coarse structural outlines and fail to capture fine details. DiffCR and Repaint-13 fail to produce meaningful reconstructions altogether. The Repaint method achieves relatively better results but still loses typical high-frequency elements such as buildings. In contrast, our method not only restores the structural content but also fully preserves high-frequency features like buildings. This advantage arises because the standard DDPM sampling mechanism used by Repaint tends to generate content that aligns with surrounding semantic context, making it prone to missing localized high-frequency details. By comparison, our CM-CR method requires only 13 sampling steps, significantly reducing the risk of neglecting such high-frequency information. In the red-marked area of Figure 12b, the cloud-covered region contains dense buildings and other complex high-frequency details. In this case, models such as Dsen2-CR, GLF-CR, UnCR, DiffCR, and Repaint-13 all fail to effectively reconstruct such regions rich in fine-grained structures. Among them, the Repaint model can only partially recover structural information, whereas our CM-CR model clearly reconstructs the dense and complex high-frequency content. This result demonstrates the superior generative capability and reconstruction effectiveness of CM-CR in challenging scenarios.

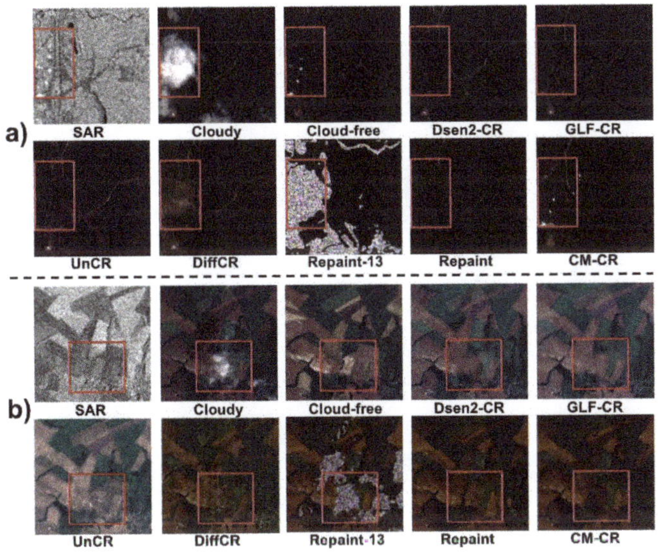

Figure 10. Qualitative comparison of scene structural reconstruction capabilities for cloud removal algorithms. (**a**) shows a test scene with simple geometric structures, while (**b**) depicts a scene with more complex topological patterns. Red-marked areas highlight key regions of reconstruction. For better visual inspection, zooming in is recommended to examine differences in structural reconstruction quality.

Figure 13 provides a qualitative comparison of various cloud removal algorithms applied to scenes with prominent high-frequency details and mixed-frequency characteristics. As shown in the red-marked area of Figure 13a, the scene features dominant high-frequency details, specifically bright building rooftops. Here, Dsen2-CR, GLF-CR, and UnCR recover only coarse structural outlines and miss fine rooftop details. DiffCR and Repaint-13 fail to preserve these features, leading to incomplete reconstructions with visible artifacts. While Repaint achieves better structural recovery, it still shows color inconsistencies and blurred rooftop edges. In contrast, our CM-CR model clearly restores the bright rooftops with sharp structures and fine-grained details, demonstrating strong localized high-frequency reconstruction. In Figure 13b, the scene combines low-frequency textures with high-frequency details. For this mixed region, Dsen2-CR, GLF-CR, UnCR, DiffCR, and Repaint-13 struggle to maintain texture continuity and structural sharpness, often producing blurred or inconsistent areas. Repaint partially recovers textures and boundaries but retains artifacts. By comparison, CM-CR generates coherent results that preserve both textures and embedded high-frequency details, showing its effectiveness in complex mixed-frequency scenarios.

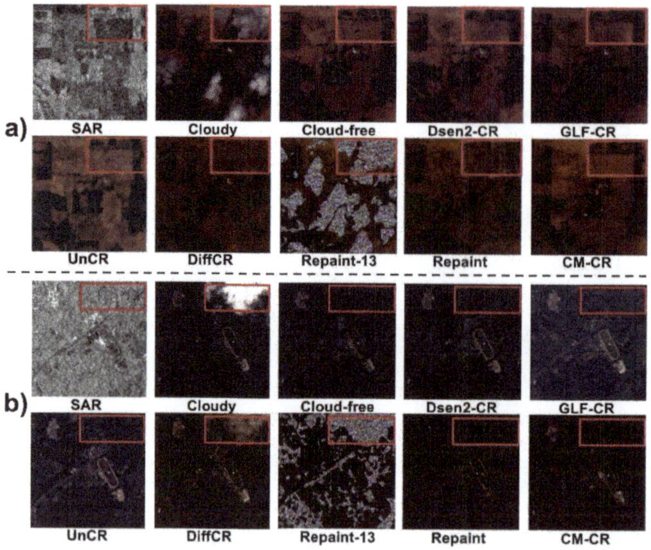

Figure 11. Qualitative comparison of the structural and textural co-reconstruction performance of cloud removal algorithms. (**a**) shows a test scene with simple geometric structures and uniform texture features, while (**b**) depicts a representative scene containing complex topological structures and multi-scale textural details. Red-marked areas highlight key regions of reconstruction. For better visual inspection, zooming in is recommended to examine differences in structural reconstruction quality.

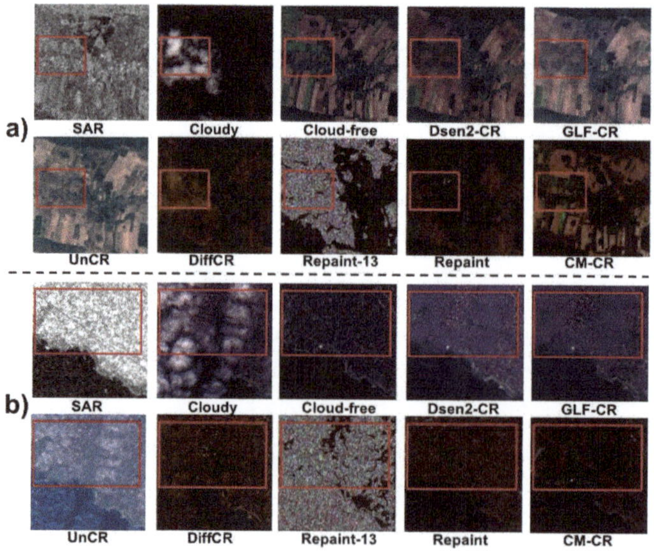

Figure 12. Qualitative comparison of the reconstruction performance of cloud removal algorithms in scenes with varying levels of high-frequency information. (**a**) shows a relatively simple scene with sparse high-frequency details, while (**b**) depicts a more complex scene rich in dense high-frequency content. Red-marked areas highlight key regions of reconstruction. For better visual inspection, zooming in is recommended to examine differences in structural reconstruction quality.

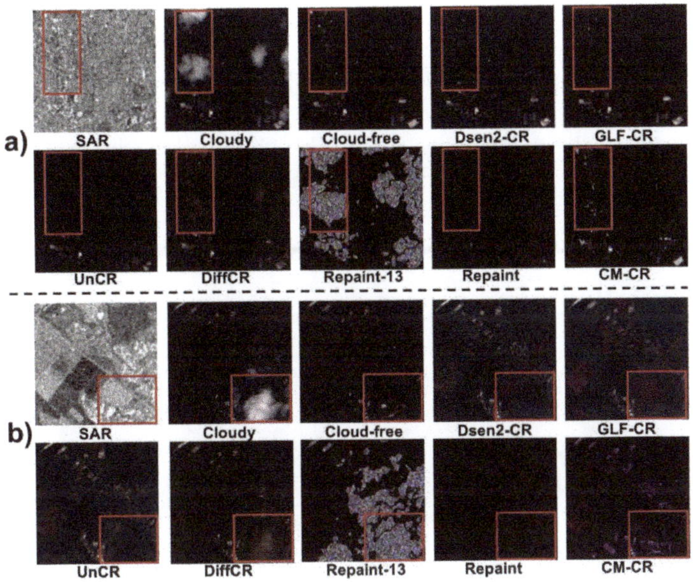

Figure 13. Qualitative comparison of the reconstruction performance of cloud removal algorithms in scenes featuring dominant high-frequency details and mixed-frequency characteristics. (**a**) shows a test scene where bright building rooftops serve as distinct high-frequency components. (**b**) presents a composite scene where low-frequency textures and high-frequency details coexist. Red-marked areas highlight key regions of reconstruction. For better visual inspection, zooming in is recommended to examine differences in structural reconstruction quality.

In summary, the qualitative results across diverse scenes confirm that all baseline methods struggle to simultaneously restore structural, textural, and spectral details under dense cloud cover. Discriminative models often oversmooth fine structures, while DiffCR and Repaint-13 fail to fully recover high-frequency elements due to limited sampling steps. The standard Repaint method with longer sampling partially improves structural quality but still shows color inconsistencies and high computational cost. Compared to these baselines, CM-CR consistently achieves clearer structures, richer textures, and better local detail preservation with a much faster sampling process, demonstrating its strong potential for robust cloud removal in complex scenarios.

4.5. Ablation Study

4.5.1. The Effectiveness of SAR Image

To verify the effectiveness of SAR condition in cloud removal, both quantitative and qualitative comparisons are conducted, as shown in Table 2 and Figure 14, respectively.

Quantitatively, the inclusion of SAR auxiliary information significantly enhances reconstruction quality across all evaluation metrics. Specifically, compared to the w/o SAR setting, the $w/$SAR configuration improves the PSNR from 28.431 to 34.191 and the SSIM from 0.794 to 0.9346. Meanwhile, the SAM and MAE values drop from 0.177 to 0.042 and from 379.04 to 202.69, respectively. These results clearly demonstrate that SAR conditioning improves not only the fidelity but also the structural and spectral consistency of the reconstructed images.

Qualitatively, as illustrated in Figure 14, reconstructions without SAR exhibit pronounced randomness in the generated textures and structures, especially in the heavily cloud-covered regions, leading to unrealistic or distorted outcomes. In contrast, with SAR assistance, the model effectively reconstructs terrain-aligned structures and fine-grained textures, guided by backscattering priors inherent in SAR data. This improvement can be attributed to the auxiliary structural and backscattering information provided by SAR imagery, which effectively compensates for the information lost due to cloud occlusion in the optical domain.

These results jointly confirm the substantial benefit of incorporating SAR data into the cloud removal framework, enabling more accurate, consistent, and reliable image reconstruction under challenging cloud conditions.

Table 2. Ablation study on the impact of SAR conditioning for cloud removal.

Method	PSNR (↑)	SSIM (↑)	SAM (↓)	MAE (↓)
w/o SAR	28.431	0.794	0.177	379.04
$w/$SAR	34.191	0.9346	0.042	202.69

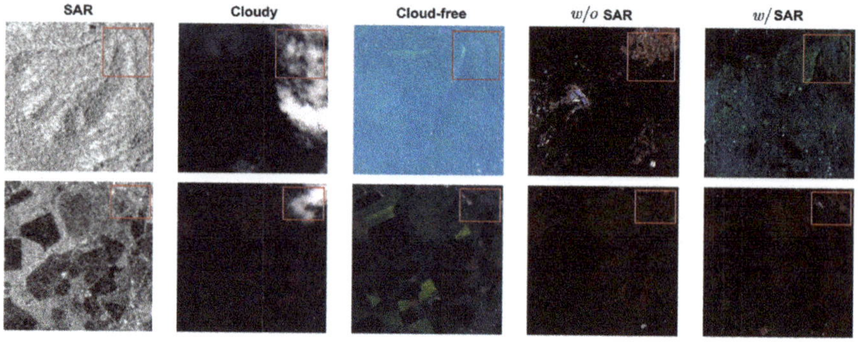

Figure 14. Qualitative comparison results illustrating the impact of SAR are shown. The label "w/o SAR" denotes cloud removal outcomes without incorporating SAR imagery, whereas "$w/$SAR" indicates results generated with SAR auxiliary.

4.5.2. Numbers of PDMSR

To investigate the impact of the number of resampling steps in the PDMSR strategy, we conduct a visual analysis of the reconstruction quality under different sampling iterations. The results are presented in Figure 15, which shows the cloud removal progression from the initial noise (index 1) and the one-step coarse prediction (index 2), followed by PDMSR refinement results corresponding to 1 to 18 PDMSR steps (indices 3–20).

It is observed that single-step sampling (index 2) struggles to produce satisfactory reconstruction results, often leading to incomplete or noisy reconstructions in heavily cloud-covered regions. As the number of PDMSR steps increases, the reconstructed regions gradually improve in visual quality, exhibiting enhanced structural continuity and reduced artifacts. Notably, by the 13th PDMSR step (index 15), CM-CR is already able to produce high-quality reconstructions that closely resemble the underlying terrain. Further increasing the number of steps beyond this point yields diminishing returns, with negligible improvements observed in visual fidelity or detail enhancement. As summarized in Table 3, reconstruction accuracy improves gradually with more PDMSR steps and stabilizes around 13 steps, while runtime grows nearly linearly with the number of steps. This supports our choice of roughly 13 PDMSR steps as a practical efficiency–quality trade-off.

These findings suggest that while increasing the number of PDMSR steps enhances reconstruction effectiveness, there exists an optimal threshold (around Step 13) beyond which the benefits plateau. This insight provides a practical guideline for balancing inference efficiency and reconstruction quality in real-world applications of the CM-CR method.

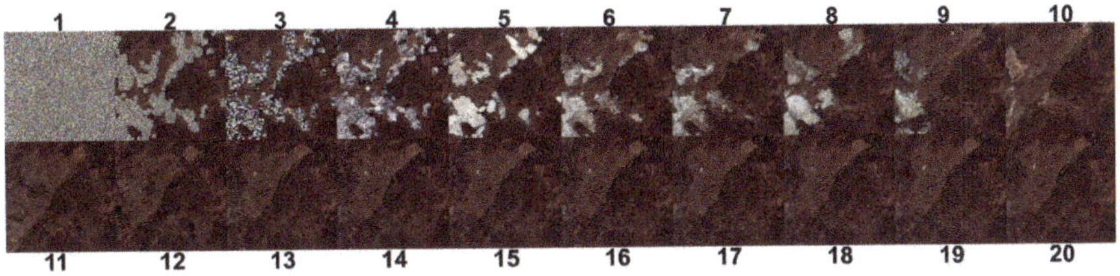

Figure 15. Cloud removal progression with PDMSR steps. Index 1 denotes the initial noise; index 2 denotes the coarse prediction (one-step student inference); indices 3–20 denote results after applying PDMSR with 1 to 18 refinement steps.

Table 3. Effect of PDMSR steps on reconstruction quality and runtime. Note that "Step = 1" corresponds to the first PDMSR refinement output in Figure 15 (i.e., index 3 in that figure), following the initial noise (index 1) and the one-step coarse prediction (index 2).

Steps	PSNR ↑	SSIM ↑	SAM ↓	MAE (TOP) ↓	Time (s/img) ↓
1	29.125	0.858	0.1080	372.0	0.311
5	31.642	0.905	0.0550	245.0	0.933
9	33.172	0.928	0.0465	210.0	1.555
13	34.191	0.935	0.0420	202.69	2.178
17	34.213	0.936	0.0418	201.8	2.801

5. Discussion

In this section, we focus on two key questions: (1) How does CM-CR perform under low-quality SAR input conditions? (2) How does its cloud removal performance compare to baseline models across different levels of cloud coverage? Figure 16 illustrates two representative failure cases of reconstruction due to poor SAR quality. Figure 17 provides a quantitative comparison of image quality trends across methods under cloud coverage ratios ranging from 0% to 100%.

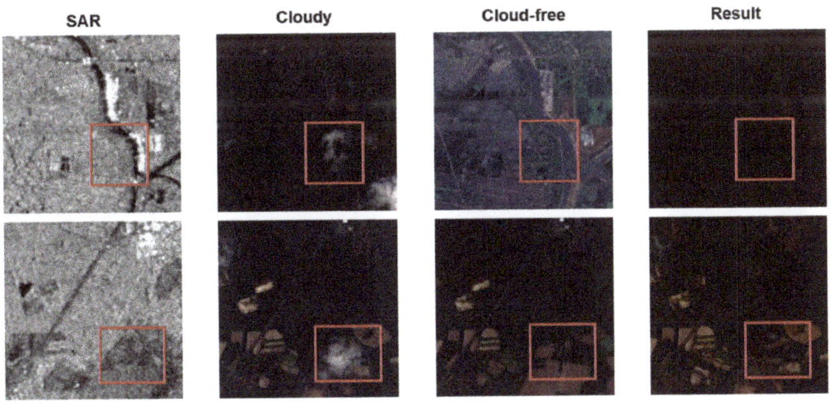

Figure 16. Qualitative performance analysis under low-quality SAR image conditions.

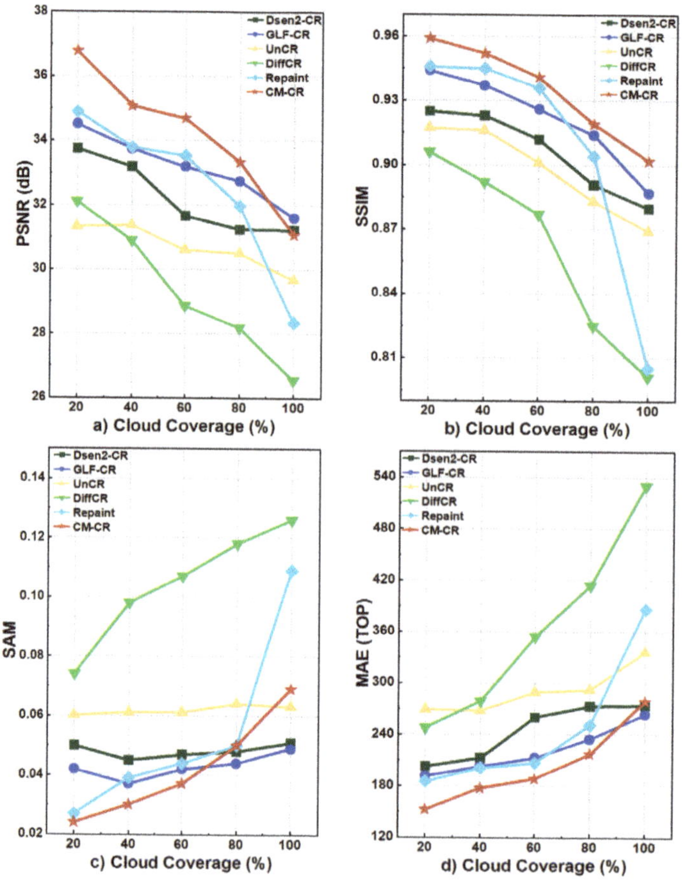

Figure 17. Image quality metrics for different methods vary with cloud coverage levels. Subfigures (**a–d**) show the PSNR, SSIM, SAM, and MAE variations across different cloud coverage ranges, respectively.

5.1. Performance Analysis Under Low-Quality SAR Image

The reconstruction process of CM-CR is highly dependent on the auxiliary information provided by SAR imagery, which places high demands on the quality of the SAR input. As discussed in Section 4.4, we found that when SAR images accurately provide both low-frequency and high-frequency information, CM-CR consistently achieves favorable reconstruction results. However, in real-world applications, the quality of SAR imagery often cannot be maintained at a consistently high level and may fail to deliver reliable low- and high-frequency information. For example, as shown in the red-marked area of the first row in Figure 16, the SAR image appears as a homogeneous region, whereas the cloud-free reference image from another time indicates that the same region contains complex structural details. This suggests that the SAR image has lost structural information in that area, resulting in CM-CR failing to recover the corresponding structural features. This demonstrates the limitation of CM-CR in its strong dependence on SAR image quality.

As shown in the second row of Figure 16, the reconstruction results produced by CM-CR exhibit some randomness; nevertheless, some details are still recovered, and the visual quality of the reconstructed region remains acceptable. This may be attributed to the fact that although the efficient sampling strategy adopted by CM-CR enhances the model's generalization capability to some extent, it is not universally applicable to all scenarios, particularly when the auxiliary information provided by SAR imagery is relatively limited.

In the SEN12MS-CR dataset, the SAR images have already undergone standard pre-processing, including radiometric calibration, speckle suppression, and terrain correction. Therefore, the "low-quality" SAR samples observed in this study mainly originate from intrinsic acquisition limitations rather than post-processing imperfections. Typical cases include geometric distortions (layover or shadowing) and weak backscatter from smooth or specular surfaces, where structural details are genuinely absent from the SAR signal and cannot be recovered by conventional enhancement. To address this limitation, incorporating complementary information from multi-temporal optical observations or auxiliary modalities such as Landsat-8, which provide reliable spectral reflectance and temporal consistency, could effectively compensate for the missing structural or textural cues. From the modeling perspective, designing modules that better capture the contextual and semantic information of optical imagery—such as cross-modal attention or spatial–semantic reasoning blocks—may further enhance reconstruction performance when SAR guidance is degraded. These strategies indicate a promising direction toward a unified, multi-source framework for robust cloud removal under challenging SAR conditions.

5.2. Analysis of Different Cloud Coverage

Figure 17 illustrates the quantitative trends of reconstruction quality for different cloud removal algorithms as cloud coverage varies.

Figure 17a shows that as cloud coverage increases, the PSNR of all algorithms steadily decreases, mainly because greater cloud coverage raises the complexity of recovering surface information. Among the discriminative models, GLF-CR performs better than Dsen2-CR and UnCR under light to moderate cloud coverage (coverage < 60%), consistently maintaining higher PSNR values. However, once the coverage exceeds this threshold, its performance deteriorates more rapidly. DiffCR consistently shows relatively low reconstruction quality across all cloud coverage levels, with PSNR values noticeably lower than those of other baselines. Repaint and CM-CR, which rely on explicit cloud region masks during reconstruction, are more affected under high-cloud-coverage conditions (coverage > 60%). Notably, when cloud coverage approaches 100%, the PSNR of CM-CR even falls below that of GLF-CR and Dsen2-CR. This indicates that explicit mask-based models may become less robust in extremely dense cloud scenarios where accurate mask estimation and guidance become more challenging.

In Figure 17b, a similar decreasing trend is observed for the SSIM. As cloud coverage increases, the structural similarity achieved by the discriminative methods (Dsen2-CR, GLF-CR, and UnCR) gradually declines. DiffCR and Repaint also exhibit a pronounced drop in SSIM under heavy-cloud conditions, indicating limitations in maintaining structural consistency. In contrast, the CM-CR method demonstrates a stronger capability to preserve structural information, with its SSIM values consistently leading the other methods. This result highlights that CM-CR can better leverage the auxiliary information provided by SAR imagery to maintain structural coherence even under dense cloud coverage.

Figure 17c shows the evaluation results for the SAM. For this metric, a lower SAM value indicates better spectral consistency. The discriminative models Dsen2-CR, GLF-CR, and UnCR demonstrate relatively stable SAM values, with only slight increases as cloud coverage increases. In contrast, the SAM value for the Repaint model rises significantly when cloud coverage exceeds 80%, reflecting poorer spectral consistency under dense clouds. However, although the CM-CR model exhibits clear advantages when cloud coverage is below 80%, its SAM value surpasses that of the UnCR model when cloud coverage exceeds this level. This indicates that our method may face limitations in maintaining spectral consistency under very high-cloud-coverage conditions.

Figure 17d shows the variation in MAE with increasing cloud coverage. Among the discriminative methods, UnCR generally produces higher MAE values under thick-cloud conditions. As cloud coverage increases, DiffCR shows a pronounced increase in error. While the Repaint method maintains moderate error levels, it does not match the lower MAE achieved by CM-CR. The CM-CR method consistently yields the lowest MAE values, with only slight increases over GLF-CR and Dsen2-CR when cloud coverage exceeds 80%. This highlights the advantage of CM-CR in minimizing per-pixel reconstruction errors across different cloud scenarios.

Overall, the results under different cloud coverage levels show that all methods degrade as cloud coverage increases, reflecting the increasing challenge of recovering structural and spectral details under dense clouds. Among the discriminative models, methods like GLF-CR and Dsen2-CR remain relatively stable at low to moderate coverage but decline more sharply beyond 60%. DiffCR consistently performs worse than the discriminative baselines across all metrics, while Repaint achieves better reconstruction quality than DiffCR and most discriminative models under moderate coverage but suffers under very high cloud amounts due to its dependence on accurate masks. CM-CR maintains clear advantages across most metrics and coverage levels, though its performance gap narrows when coverage exceeds 80%, highlighting that further improvements are needed to handle near-complete occlusion.

6. Conclusions

In this study, we proposed CM-CR, a novel consistency model-based architecture that effectively removes thick clouds from optical remote sensing imagery. By integrating SAR information and adopting a consistency distillation strategy, the model achieves high-quality reconstruction while significantly improving sampling efficiency compared to standard diffusion models. Extensive experiments conducted on the SEN12MS-CR benchmark demonstrate that CM-CR consistently outperforms mainstream discriminative and diffusion-based cloud removal methods in terms of PSNR, SSIM, SAM, and MAE metrics. The key contribution of this work lies in dividing the complex reconstruction process into a rapid coarse prediction and a progressive refinement stage, which balances reconstruction fidelity and inference speed. In the future, further research will focus on enhancing the model's generalization capability for different satellite data sources, exploring multi-modal data fusion, and reducing reliance on explicit cloud masks. This work provides a promising direction for improving the usability of optical remote sensing data under challenging cloud conditions.

Author Contributions: Conceptualization, Q.H.; methodology, Q.H., B.H. and Y.L.; software, Q.H. and B.H.; validation, Q.H. and B.H.; formal analysis, Q.H. and B.H.; investigation, Q.H.; resources, Q.H. and Y.L.; data curation, Q.H. and B.H.; writing—original draft, Q.H., B.H. and Y.L.; writing—review and editing, Q.H., B.H. and Y.L. All authors have read and agreed to the published version of the manuscript.

Funding: This research was funded by the National Natural Science Foundation of China (62271400).

Institutional Review Board Statement: Not applicable.

Informed Consent Statement: Not applicable.

Data Availability Statement: The SEN12MS-CR dataset is available online at https://patricktum.github.io/cloud_removal/sen12mscr/(accessed on 10 November 2025).

Conflicts of Interest: The authors declare no conflicts of interest.

References

1. He, J.; Wang, W.; Fu, M.; Wang, Y. Insights into global visibility patterns: Spatiotemporal distributions revealed by satellite remote sensing. *J. Clean. Prod.* **2024**, *468*, 143069. [CrossRef]
2. Victor, N.; Maddikunta, P.K.R.; Mary, D.R.K.; Murugan, R.; Chengoden, R.; Gadekallu, T.R.; Rakesh, N.; Zhu, Y.; Paek, J. Remote Sensing for Agriculture in the Era of Industry 5.0–A survey. *IEEE J. Sel. Top. Appl. Earth Obs. Remote Sens.* **2024**, *17*, 5920–5945. [CrossRef]
3. Jia, P.; Chen, C.; Zhang, D.; Sang, Y.; Zhang, L. Semantic segmentation of deep learning remote sensing images based on band combination principle: Application in urban planning and land use. *Comput. Commun.* **2024**, *217*, 97–106. [CrossRef]
4. Ahmad, R. Smart remote sensing network for disaster management: an overview. *Telecommun. Syst.* **2024**, *87*, 213–237. [CrossRef]
5. Gao, J.; Yuan, Q.; Li, J.; Zhang, H.; Su, X. Cloud Removal with Fusion of High Resolution Optical and SAR Images Using Generative Adversarial Networks. *Remote Sens.* **2020**, *12*, 191. [CrossRef]
6. Xu, M.; Jia, X.; Pickering, M.; Jia, S. Thin cloud removal from optical remote sensing images using the noise-adjusted principal components transform. *ISPRS J. Photogramm. Remote Sens.* **2019**, *149*, 215–225. [CrossRef]
7. Shen, H.; Li, X.; Cheng, Q.; Zeng, C.; Yang, G.; Li, H.; Zhang, L. Missing information reconstruction of remote sensing data: A technical review. *IEEE Geosci. Remote Sens. Mag.* **2015**, *3*, 61–85. [CrossRef]
8. Rossi, R.E.; Dungan, J.L.; Beck, L.R. Kriging in the shadows: geostatistical interpolation for remote sensing. *Remote Sens. Environ.* **1994**, *49*, 32–40. [CrossRef]
9. Shen, H.; Zhang, L. A MAP-based algorithm for destriping and inpainting of remotely sensed images. *IEEE Trans. Geosci. Remote Sens.* **2008**, *47*, 1492–1502. [CrossRef]
10. Maalouf, A.; Carré, P.; Augereau, B.; Fernandez-Maloigne, C. A bandelet-based inpainting technique for clouds removal from remotely sensed images. *IEEE Trans. Geosci. Remote Sens.* **2009**, *47*, 2363–2371. [CrossRef]
11. Lorenzi, L.; Melgani, F.; Mercier, G. Missing-area reconstruction in multispectral images under a compressive sensing perspective. *IEEE Trans. Geosci. Remote Sens.* **2013**, *51*, 3998–4008. [CrossRef]
12. Wang, L.; Wang, Q.; Tong, X.; Atkinson, P.M. Mst-net: A general deep learning model for thick cloud removal from optical images. *IEEE Trans. Geosci. Remote Sens.* **2025**, *63*, 5612518. [CrossRef]
13. Sekrecka, A.; Karwowska, K. Classical vs. Machine Learning-Based Inpainting for Enhanced Classification of Remote Sensing Image. *Remote Sens.* **2025**, *17*, 1305. [CrossRef]
14. Chen, Y.; Chen, M.; He, W.; Zeng, J.; Huang, M.; Zheng, Y.B. Thick cloud removal in multitemporal remote sensing images via low-rank regularized self-supervised network. *IEEE Trans. Geosci. Remote Sens.* **2024**, *62*, 5506613. [CrossRef]
15. Zhou, H.; Wang, Y.; Liu, W.; Tao, D.; Ma, W.; Liu, B. MSC-GAN: A Multi-Stream Complementary Generative Adversarial Network with Grouping Learning for Multitemporal Cloud Removal. *IEEE Trans. Geosci. Remote Sens.* **2024**, *63*, 5400117. [CrossRef]
16. Zou, X.; Li, K.; Xing, J.; Tao, P.; Cui, Y. PMAA: A progressive multi-scale attention autoencoder model for high-performance cloud removal from multi-temporal satellite imagery. *arXiv* **2023**, arXiv:2303.16565
17. Zhang, Q.; Yuan, Q.; Li, Z.; Sun, F.; Zhang, L. Combined deep prior with low-rank tensor SVD for thick cloud removal in multitemporal images. *ISPRS J. Photogramm. Remote Sens.* **2021**, *177*, 161–173. [CrossRef]
18. Peng, H.; Huang, T.Z.; Zhao, X.L.; Lin, J.; Wu, W.H.; Li, L.Y. Deep Domain Fidelity and Low-Rank Tensor Ring Regularization for Thick Cloud Removal of Multitemporal Remote Sensing Images. *IEEE Trans. Geosci. Remote Sens.* **2024**, *62*, 5409314. [CrossRef]
19. Li, J.; Wang, Y.; Sheng, Q.; Wu, Z.; Wang, B.; Ling, X.; Liu, X.; Du, Y.; Gao, F.; Camps-Valls, G.; et al. CloudRuler: Rule-based transformer for cloud removal in Landsat images. *Remote Sens. Environ.* **2025**, *328*, 114913. [CrossRef]
20. Wang, L.; Wang, Q.; Atkinson, P.M. Thick cloud removal of Landsat time-series using convolutional LSTM with embedded residual modules. *IEEE Trans. Geosci. Remote Sens.* **2025**, *63*, 5404816. [CrossRef]
21. Xia, Y.; He, W.; Huang, Q.; Yin, G.; Liu, W.; Zhang, H. CRformer: Multi-modal data fusion to reconstruct cloud-free optical imagery. *Int. J. Appl. Earth Obs. Geoinf.* **2024**, *128*, 103793. [CrossRef]
22. Duan, C.; Belgiu, M.; Stein, A. Efficient Cloud Removal Network for Satellite Images Using SAR-optical Image Fusion. *IEEE Geosci. Remote Sens. Lett.* **2024**, *21*, 6008605. [CrossRef]
23. Ebel, P.; Meraner, A.; Schmitt, M.; Zhu, X.X. Multisensor data fusion for cloud removal in global and all-season sentinel-2 imagery. *IEEE Trans. Geosci. Remote Sens.* **2020**, *59*, 5866–5878. [CrossRef]
24. Bermudez, J.D.; Happ, P.N.; Oliveira, D.A.B.; Feitosa, R.Q. SAR to optical image synthesis for cloud removal with generative adversarial networks. *ISPRS Ann. Photogramm. Remote Sens. Spat. Inf. Sci.* **2018**, *4*, 5–11. [CrossRef]
25. Bhambani, K.; Takalikar, M. DeCloud GAN: An Advanced Generative Adversarial Network for Removing Cloud Cover in Optical Remote Sensing Imagery. In Proceedings of the 2021 4th International Conference on Computational Intelligence and Intelligent Systems, Tokyo, Japan, 20–22 November 2021; pp. 25–30. [CrossRef]
26. Zhu, H.; Wang, Z.; Han, L.; Xu, M.; Li, W.; Liu, Q.; Liu, S.; Du, B. TSMCF: Transformer-Based SAR and Multi-Spectral Cross-Attention Fusion for Cloud Removal. *IEEE J. Sel. Top. Appl. Earth Obs. Remote Sens.* **2025**, *18*, 6710–6720. [CrossRef]

27. Zhang, W.; Mei, J.; Wang, Y. Dmdiff: A dual-branch multimodal conditional guided diffusion model for cloud removal through sar-optical data fusion. *Remote Sens.* **2025**, *17*, 965. [CrossRef]
28. Singh, P.; Komodakis, N. Cloud-gan: Cloud removal for sentinel-2 imagery using a cyclic consistent generative adversarial networks. In Proceedings of the IGARSS 2018-2018 IEEE International Geoscience and Remote Sensing Symposium, Valencia, Spain, 22–27 July 2018; pp. 1772–1775. [CrossRef]
29. Zhao, Y.; Shen, S.; Hu, J.; Li, Y.; Pan, J. Cloud removal using multimodal GAN with adversarial consistency loss. *IEEE Geosci. Remote Sens. Lett.* **2021**, *19*, 8015605. [CrossRef]
30. Darbaghshahi, F.N.; Mohammadi, M.R.; Soryani, M. Cloud removal in remote sensing images using generative adversarial networks and SAR-to-optical image translation. *IEEE Trans. Geosci. Remote Sens.* **2021**, *60*, 4105309. [CrossRef]
31. Ho, J.; Jain, A.; Abbeel, P. Denoising diffusion probabilistic models. *Adv. Neural Inf. Process. Syst.* **2020**, *33*, 6840–6851.
32. Dhariwal, P.; Nichol, A. Diffusion models beat gans on image synthesis. *Adv. Neural Inf. Process. Syst.* **2021**, *34*, 8780–8794.
33. Yang, S.; Chen, X.; Liao, J. Uni-paint: A unified framework for multimodal image inpainting with pretrained diffusion model. In Proceedings of the 31st ACM International Conference on Multimedia, Ottawa, ON, Canada, 29 October–3 November 2023; pp. 3190–3199. [CrossRef]
34. Li, H.; Yang, Y.; Chang, M.; Chen, S.; Feng, H.; Xu, Z.; Li, Q.; Chen, Y. Srdiff: Single image super-resolution with diffusion probabilistic models. *Neurocomputing* **2022**, *479*, 47–59. [CrossRef]
35. Chung, J.; Hyun, S.; Heo, J.P. Style injection in diffusion: A training-free approach for adapting large-scale diffusion models for style transfer. In Proceedings of the IEEE/CVF Conference on Computer Vision and Pattern Recognition, Seattle, WA, USA, 17–21 June 2024; pp. 8795–8805. [CrossRef]
36. Zou, X.; Li, K.; Xing, J.; Zhang, Y.; Wang, S.; Jin, L.; Tao, P. DiffCR: A Fast Conditional Diffusion Framework for Cloud Removal From Optical Satellite Images. *IEEE Trans. Geosci. Remote Sens.* **2024**, *62*, 5612014. [CrossRef]
37. Zhao, X.; Jia, K. Cloud removal in remote sensing using sequential-based diffusion models. *Remote Sens.* **2023**, *15*, 2861. [CrossRef]
38. Jing, R.; Duan, F.; Lu, F.; Zhang, M.; Zhao, W. Denoising diffusion probabilistic feature-based network for cloud removal in Sentinel-2 imagery. *Remote Sens.* **2023**, *15*, 2217. [CrossRef]
39. Wang, M.; Song, Y.; Wei, P.; Xian, X.; Shi, Y.; Lin, L. IDF-CR: Iterative Diffusion Process for Divide-and-Conquer Cloud Removal in Remote-sensing Images. *IEEE Trans. Geosci. Remote Sens.* **2024**, *62*, 5615014. [CrossRef]
40. Sui, J.; Ma, Y.; Yang, W.; Zhang, X.; Pun, M.O.; Liu, J. Diffusion Enhancement for Cloud Removal in Ultra-Resolution Remote Sensing Imagery. *IEEE Trans. Geosci. Remote Sens.* **2024**, *62*, 5615014. [CrossRef]
41. Liu, Y.; Li, W.; Guan, J.; Zhou, S.; Zhang, Y. Effective cloud removal for remote sensing images by an improved mean-reverting denoising model with elucidated design space. In Proceedings of the Computer Vision and Pattern Recognition Conference, Nashville, TN, USA, 11–15 June 2025; pp. 17851–17861. [CrossRef]
42. Song, Y.; Dhariwal, P.; Chen, M.; Sutskever, I. Consistency Models. In Proceedings of the 40th International Conference on Machine Learning. PMLR, Honolulu, HI, USA, 23–29 July 2023; Volume 202; pp. 32211–32252.
43. Song, Y.; Sohl-Dickstein, J.; Kingma, D.P.; Kumar, A.; Ermon, S.; Poole, B. Score-based generative modeling through stochastic differential equations. *arXiv* **2020**, arXiv:2011.13456.
44. Karras, T.; Aittala, M.; Aila, T.; Laine, S. Elucidating the design space of diffusion-based generative models. *Adv. Neural Inf. Process. Syst.* **2022**, *35*, 26565–26577.
45. Ronneberger, O.; Fischer, P.; Brox, T. U-net: Convolutional networks for biomedical image segmentation. In Proceedings of the International Conference on Medical image Computing and Computer-Assisted Intervention, Munich, Germany, 5–9 October 2015; Springer: Cham, Switzerland, 2015; pp. 234–241. [CrossRef]
46. Meraner, A.; Ebel, P.; Zhu, X.X.; Schmitt, M. Cloud removal in Sentinel-2 imagery using a deep residual neural network and SAR-optical data fusion. *ISPRS J. Photogramm. Remote Sens.* **2020**, *166*, 333–346. [CrossRef]
47. Xu, F.; Shi, Y.; Ebel, P.; Yu, L.; Xia, G.S.; Yang, W.; Zhu, X.X. GLF-CR: SAR-enhanced cloud removal with global–local fusion. *ISPRS J. Photogramm. Remote Sens.* **2022**, *192*, 268–278. [CrossRef]
48. Ebel, P.; Garnot, V.S.F.; Schmitt, M.; Wegner, J.D.; Zhu, X.X. UnCRtainTS: Uncertainty quantification for cloud removal in optical satellite time series. In Proceedings of the IEEE/CVF Conference on Computer Vision and Pattern Recognition, Vancouver, BC, Canada, 17–24 June 2023; pp. 2086–2096. [CrossRef]
49. Lugmayr, A.; Danelljan, M.; Romero, A.; Yu, F.; Timofte, R.; Van Gool, L. Repaint: Inpainting using denoising diffusion probabilistic models. In Proceedings of the IEEE/CVF Conference on Computer Vision and Pattern Recognition, New Orleans, LA, USA, 19–24 June 2022; pp. 11461–11471. [CrossRef]

MDPI AG
Grosspeteranlage 5
4052 Basel
Switzerland
Tel.: +41 61 683 77 34

Remote Sensing Editorial Office
E-mail: remotesensing@mdpi.com
www.mdpi.com/journal/remotesensing

www.ingramcontent.com/pod-product-compliance
Lightning Source LLC
Chambersburg PA
CBHW061621220926
51850CB00005B/570
9783725870165